AI-Powered HyFlex Learning for Student Engagement

Chee Leong Lim
https://orcid.org/0000-0001-6785-9280
Taylor's University, Malaysia

Kwok Shing Cheng
https://orcid.org/0000-0002-5614-3348
The Education University of Hong Kong, Hong Kong

IGI Global
Scientific Publishing
Publishing Tomorrow's Research Today

Vice President of Editorial Melissa Wagner
Director of Acquisitions Mikaela Felty
Director of Book Development Jocelynn Hessler
Production Manager Mike Brehm
Cover Design Jose Rosado

Published in the United States of America by
IGI Global Scientific Publishing
701 East Chocolate Avenue
Hershey, PA, 17033, USA
Tel: 717-533-8845 | Fax: 717-533-7115
Website: https://www.igi-global.com E-mail: cust@igi-global.com

Library of Congress Cataloging-in-Publication Data

Names: Lim, Chee Leong, 1976- editor | Cheng, Kwok Shing, 1973- editor
Title: AI-powered hyflex learning for student engagement / [edited by] Chee Leong Lim, Kwok Shing Cheng.
Description: Hershey, PA : IGI Global Scientific Publishing, [2026] | Includes bibliographical references and index. | Summary: "This book explores how artificial intelligence can transform HyFlex education into a personalized, inclusive, and engaging model. Through research, case studies, and practical frameworks, it examines AI tools like avatars, learning companions, and adaptive assessments to enhance accessibility, equity, and scalability in higher education"-- Provided by publisher.
Identifiers: LCCN 2025039346 (print) | LCCN 2025039347 (ebook) | ISBN 9798337361826 hardcover | ISBN 9798337361833 paperback | ISBN 9798337361840 ebook
Subjects: LCSH: Artificial intelligence--Educational applications | Open learning | Blended learning | Motivation in education
Classification: LCC LB1028.43 .A39744 2026 (print) | LCC LB1028.43 (ebook)
LC record available at https://lccn.loc.gov/2025039346
LC ebook record available at https://lccn.loc.gov/2025039347

British Cataloguing in Publication Data
A Cataloguing in Publication record for this book is available from the British Library.

Table of Contents

Detailed Table of Contents

As artificial intelligence (AI) technologies become increasingly integrated into HyFlex learning environments, the need for secure, scalable, and pedagogically aligned software systems has never been greater. This chapter examines how software engineering practices can support the development of AI-enhanced learning platforms that are both engaging for students and resilient against emerging cyber threats. Drawing on the Theories of Deskilling of Jobs, Job Characteristics, and Technology Threat Avoidance, the chapter explores secure coding methodologies, privacy-preserving AI features, and the role of DevSecOps in maintaining continuous trust within educational ecosystems. Through semi-structured interviews, document analysis, and interaction analytics, the chapter presents multiple case studies illustrating how secure, inclusive, and human-centered design enhances student trust, system usability, and learning outcomes.

Creative writing modules in universities taught in English can be a challenge for students who are non-native English speakers. They often struggle to express creative ideas fluently, focusing more on grammatical accuracy than on free expression. This research explores a combined methodology that integrates the traditional "Pantser" method of writing with Hyflex learning to support non-native English-speaking students in creative text composition. The Pantser method emphasizes spontaneity and authenticity in creative writing, while Hyflex learning allows students to review lectures in their mother tongue. Together, these approaches form a systematic method that guides students from finding a stimulus for a story through to preparing a final draft. The study examines the application of this combined approach in a monologue writing assignment within the Introduction to Creative Writing module and evaluates student work using the module's assessment rubrics. The findings suggest that this combined approach offers a promising pedagogy for teaching creative writing.

In the evolving landscape of HyFlex education, learning analytics has emerged as a key enabler of adaptive and personalized learning pathways that enhance student engagement and success. This conceptual chapter examines how AI-powered learning analytics can transform traditional educational practices into data-informed systems responsive to individual learner needs across digital and physical environments. By capturing and analyzing learner behavior, engagement patterns, and performance data, educators can design timely interventions and predictive supports to improve academic outcomes. The chapter is grounded in two foundational frameworks: the Learning Analytics Cycle (LAK), which guides data-driven instructional action, and Zimmerman's Self-Regulated Learning (SRL) model, which emphasizes learner autonomy through planning, monitoring, and reflection. Drawing on examples from higher education and professional learning contexts, the chapter also addresses ethical considerations, data privacy, and faculty readiness.

This chapter presents an exploration of AI-powered HyFlex learning environments to enhance student engagement and participation. The authors examine the integration of artificial intelligence tools in co-designing flexible learning experiences that accommodate both in-person and remote learners. Through qualitative analysis of student voices and experiences, the chapter highlights strategies for personalized and adaptive learning, the impact of AI on collaborative learning, and challenges in implementing HyFlex systems. Findings provide actionable insights for educators and institutions seeking to optimize hybrid learning models using AI technologies.

This chapter examines student perceptions of an AI-augmented HyFlex learning model at a private university in Malaysia, using mixed-methods data from 1,168 undergraduates across 28 countries. Guided by the Technology Acceptance Model, Self-Determination Theory, and cultural dimensions theory, the findings show generally positive sentiment (60.7%), with technology effectiveness as the dominant theme. However, acceptance is polarized: while features such as recorded sessions and interactive tools are well received, AI avatar lectures face strong resistance (67.5% negative) due to their perceived lack of human presence. Although overall sentiment does not differ significantly by nationality or academic level, qualitative insights reveal different emphases across groups. The study concludes that effective AI integration in HyFlex learning requires human–AI complementarity, supported by platform reliability and culturally responsive design.

This chapter examines how assessment can be reimagined in HyFlex environments in response to the growing influence of artificial intelligence (AI). It argues that AI should not be positioned primarily as a tool for automation or surveillance, but as a carefully governed support for authentic, equitable, and pedagogically meaningful assessment. Drawing on TPACK and PESTEL as complementary analytical lenses, the chapter explores the challenges of multimodal assessment, including equivalency, workload, access, governance, and institutional readiness. It further proposes that authentic AI-supported assessment in HyFlex depends on the alignment of human academic judgement, equity-conscious design, and institutional capacity. In doing so, the chapter offers a practice-informed conceptual contribution with illustrative South African insights for institutions seeking to move from automation-centred assessment toward more transparent, responsive, and sustainable assessment practices. .

Foreword

The question facing higher education today is no longer whether artificial intelligence (AI) will influence teaching and learning, but how institutions might respond in ways that are responsible, thoughtful, and ultimately beneficial for students. Across the sector, a range of approaches are emerging as educators seek to make learning more flexible, inclusive, and responsive. Among these, 'HyFlex' learning has shown promise in enabling academics to engage students across different contexts and circumstances. When supported by artificial intelligence, HyFlex can extend way beyond the constraints of time and place, while providing more personalised and responsive learning experiences. For many of us, this represents not simply a change in delivery, but an opportunity to reflect more deeply on how teaching and learning might continue to evolve.

At Taylor's University, we are exploring HyFlex learning as part of broader efforts to enhance the student learning experience. Our intent, shared by many colleagues across the sector, is to develop learning environments that are increasingly personalised, inclusive, and responsive to a rapidly changing world. We view HyFlex not as a replacement for in-person teaching, but as a framework for more thoughtfully integrated online and face-to-face learning across synchronous and asynchronous contexts. This perspective continues to inform our teaching and learning strategy as we engage with the opportunities and challenges presented by artificial intelligence.

This volume brings together a wide range of perspectives that reflect both the complexity and the global nature of AI-enhanced flexible learning. The sixteen chapters span multiple disciplines, institutional contexts, and cultural settings, drawing on research, conceptual work, and practical experience from Malaysia, Hong Kong, mainland China, South Africa, the United States, India, Indonesia, and Germany. Rather than presenting a single model or solution, these contributions offer insights, questions, and reflections that invite dialogue and shared learning, recognising that the future of teaching and learning will be shaped collectively through ongoing inquiry and exchange.

I would like to commend the academics and researchers who contributed to this publication, and to thank them for their generosity in sharing their ideas, experiences, and practices. It is my hope that this collection of work will serve as a platform for conversation across institutions and contexts, and that it will support educators and researchers as they explore HyFlex learning as a pathway towards more self-directed, adaptable, and innovative approaches to teaching and learning.

Darren Bagnall
Taylor's University, Malaysia

Preface

The rapid evolution of artificial intelligence and digital learning environments is transforming education, challenging traditional pedagogies while opening new pathways for inclusion, engagement, and innovation. *AI-Powered HyFlex Learning for Student Engagement* is situated at this intersection, offering a comprehensive exploration of how HyFlex models, enriched by AI technologies, are reshaping teaching and learning across diverse contexts.

This edited volume is designed to serve a broad and interdisciplinary audience. It speaks to researchers and scholars advancing the fields of educational technology, digital pedagogy, and instructional design, as well as faculty and academic leaders navigating the implementation of HyFlex learning environments. Educational technologists, instructional designers, and digital learning strategists will find practical insights, while graduate students and emerging scholars will discover a rich foundation for study and inquiry. Additionally, policymakers, institutional administrators, and educational technology developers will gain valuable perspectives on equity-driven transformation and the design of intelligent educational systems.

The chapters within this book collectively examine the foundational principles and emerging practices that define HyFlex pedagogy in the age of AI. Contributors explore innovative approaches such as AI avatar-supported instruction to enhance accessibility and engagement, and the integration of AI learning buddies and virtual companions to provide personalized student support. The use of learning analytics to create adaptive pathways is critically examined alongside real-world case studies that highlight implementation across diverse cultural and institutional settings.

Assessment practices are reimagined through the lens of AI, moving beyond automation toward authenticity and deeper learning. The volume also addresses the essential role of faculty readiness and professional development, recognizing that meaningful integration of AI requires both technical fluency and pedagogical transformation. Importantly, student voice is centered, emphasizing co-design approaches that position learners as active partners in shaping AI-enhanced HyFlex systems.

Looking ahead, the book engages with future-oriented themes, including extended reality (XR), AI avatars, and the evolving nature of human-AI pedagogical partnerships. It also critically evaluates the impact of these innovations on student outcomes, ensuring that technological advancement remains aligned with educational purpose and equity.

As editors, we believe this volume functions both as a reference work and as an instructional resource. It is well-suited for professional development initiatives, higher education teaching certification programmes, and graduate-level courses focused on innovation in education. Our aim is to bridge theory and practice, offering readers both conceptual frameworks and actionable strategies.

We extend our gratitude to the contributing authors, whose scholarship and dedication have made this collection possible. Their work reflects a shared commitment to advancing inclusive, adaptive, and student-centered learning in an increasingly complex digital landscape.

Finally, we recognize that this project originated as a call for contributions that brought together a global community of researchers and practitioners. Through a rigorous double-anonymized peer review process, each chapter has been carefully selected to ensure quality, relevance, and impact. We are confident that this volume will contribute to ongoing conversations about the future of education and inspire continued innovation in AI-powered HyFlex learning.

ORGANIZATION OF THE BOOK

In Chapter 1, the authors introduce a foundational reimagining of HyFlex learning through the integration of artificial intelligence as a driver of personalization, inclusivity, and data-informed pedagogy. Drawing on a large-scale mixed-method study, this chapter demonstrates how AI learning assistants, avatar-based instruction, and extended reality simulations can significantly enhance student engagement and autonomy. This chapter reports a positive response from diverse and international student populations, underscoring the role of AI in enabling multilingual access and culturally responsive learning. The chapter culminates in the proposal of an AI-powered HyFlex framework that repositions educators as facilitators of adaptive, student-centered learning while reinforcing core HyFlex principles.

Chapter 2 expands this vision by examining how AI and immersive technologies converge to bridge physical and virtual learning environments. The authors highlight how multi-platform ecosystems spanning mobile devices, virtual reality, and advanced immersive systems create dynamic, interactive, and flexible learning experiences. This chapter emphasizes the potential of these technologies to deepen engagement, improve knowledge retention, and foster collaboration, while also offering a practical framework for institutions seeking to adopt scalable and inclusive immersive learning strategies.

In Chapter 3, attention turns to the persistent challenge of equitable collaboration in HyFlex environments. The authors present Collaborative Generative AI (Co-GenAI) as an innovative pedagogical approach that leverages collective intelligence to support group-based learning across modalities. Grounded in social constructivist theory, this chapter demonstrates how AI-mediated collaboration enhances task quality, metacognitive awareness, and creative problem-solving. The inclusion of real-world implementations illustrates how generative AI can function as a sustained collaborative partner, enabling more equitable participation and deeper engagement among learners.

Chapter 4 explores the evolving relationship between educators and artificial intelligence, framing it as a continuum of assistive, augmentative, and transformative collaboration. The authors underscore the importance of a Teacher–AI synergy that integrates data-driven insights with pedagogical expertise. This chapter not only outlines a conceptual framework for such collaboration but also addresses the competencies educators must develop, including data literacy, ethical awareness, and adaptive teaching practices. Institutional readiness and governance are positioned as critical enablers of sustainable and responsible AI integration.

In Chapter 5, the focus shifts to educator readiness in leveraging learning analytics to support adaptive learning pathways. The authors emphasize that the success of analytics-driven education depends not only on technological infrastructure but also on faculty capacity to interpret and act on data insights. This chapter proposes a comprehensive framework for developing educator competencies in data literacy and ethical practice, while also addressing institutional challenges. It argues that empowering educators is essential to unlocking the full potential of learning analytics for student success.

Chapter 6 continues this theme by examining faculty readiness at the intersection of HyFlex pedagogy and generative AI. The authors highlight the complexities of designing and delivering instruction across multiple modalities while maintaining consistency and quality. This chapter underscores the need for targeted professional development that equips educators with digital fluency, ethical awareness, and flexible pedagogical strategies. It positions faculty preparedness as a central determinant of successful HyFlex implementation in an AI-enhanced educational landscape.

In Chapter 7, the authors present a diverse collection of global case studies that illustrate the diverse applications of AI-enhanced HyFlex learning. Organized through the Community of Inquiry framework, these cases span disciplines, institutions, and cultural contexts. The chapter showcases innovative uses of virtual reality, metaverse environments, and AI-supported tools to facilitate collaboration, assessment, and professional skills development. By synthesizing these examples, the chapter offers valuable insights into scalable and context-sensitive approaches to HyFlex implementation.

Chapter 8 provides an empirical examination of HyFlex learning within the context of undergraduate life sciences education. The authors highlight findings that suggest stable or improved academic performance following the adoption of AI-supported HyFlex models. While increased flexibility and personalized feedback are identified as key benefits, the chapter also addresses challenges related to student interaction, self-regulation, and community building. Educator perspectives further reveal tensions between efficiency gains and concerns about ethics and reduced human connection, pointing to the need for balanced and thoughtful implementation.

In Chapter 9, the authors address the unique challenges of adapting laboratory-based science education to HyFlex formats. This chapter explores how inclusive and equitable access to hands-on learning can be maintained in technology-mediated environments. It highlights the pedagogical and logistical complexities of translating tactile, collaborative experiences into flexible modalities, while also identifying emerging strategies to preserve experiential learning in STEM education.

Chapter 10 examines the transformative potential of artificial intelligence in rethinking assessment practices within HyFlex learning environments. The authors present a balanced perspective, exploring both the opportunities for automation and personalization as well as the limitations of AI in ensuring authentic assessment. With a particular focus on generative AI, the chapter critically evaluates current practices and outlines implications for research and implementation, emphasizing the need for thoughtful integration that aligns with pedagogical goals.

In Chapter 11, the focus shifts to the technological backbone of AI-powered HyFlex learning: secure and scalable software systems. The authors highlight the importance of integrating robust software engineering practices with pedagogical design to create trustworthy and engaging learning platforms. Drawing on theoretical frameworks and case studies, this chapter demonstrates how secure coding, privacy-preserving features, and DevSecOps practices contribute to student trust, system usability, and improved learning outcomes.

Chapter 12 offers a creative and pedagogical exploration of HyFlex learning in the context of teaching writing to non-native English speakers. The authors present an innovative integration of the "Pantser" writing approach with HyFlex delivery, enabling students to balance spontaneity with structured support. By allowing learners to engage with content in their preferred language while developing creative expression, this chapter highlights the potential of HyFlex models to support linguistic diversity and creative confidence.

In Chapter 13, the authors revisit the role of learning analytics as a catalyst for adaptive and personalized learning pathways. Grounded in established theoretical frameworks, this conceptual chapter illustrates how data-driven insights can inform timely interventions and support self-regulated learning. It also addresses critical considerations related to ethics, privacy, and faculty readiness, reinforcing the importance of aligning analytics practices with educational values.

Chapter 14 centers student voice as a critical component in the design of AI-powered HyFlex learning systems. The authors emphasize the importance of co-creation, presenting insights derived from student experiences and perceptions. This chapter highlights how AI can support personalized and collaborative learning while also identifying implementation challenges. It offers practical strategies for educators and institutions seeking to design more responsive and engaging learning environments.

In Chapter 15, the authors present a nuanced analysis of student perceptions of AI-augmented HyFlex learning. While overall sentiment is positive, the chapter reveals important tensions, particularly regarding AI avatar lectures and their perceived lack of human presence. Drawing on theoretical models and diverse student perspectives, the chapter underscores the importance of human–AI complementarity, platform reliability, and culturally responsive design in achieving meaningful student engagement.

Finally, Chapter 16 reexamines assessment in HyFlex environments through the lens of authenticity and equity. The authors argue for a shift away from automation-centered approaches toward more human-centered, pedagogically grounded assessment practices. By integrating theoretical frameworks with practical insights, the chapter highlights the importance of institutional readiness, governance, and alignment between technology and academic judgment. It offers a vision for sustainable and transparent assessment in the age of AI-enhanced education.

CONCLUSION

As this volume demonstrates, the convergence of artificial intelligence and HyFlex pedagogy represents not merely a technological shift, but a profound rethinking of how education can be designed, delivered, and experienced. Across the chapters, a unifying theme emerges: the potential of AI to enhance flexibility, personalization, and inclusivity must be guided by sound pedagogical principles, ethical awareness, and a sustained commitment to human-centered learning.

The contributions in this collection collectively affirm that AI-powered HyFlex learning is not a one-size-fits-all model, but rather a dynamic and evolving ecosystem. Its success depends on the thoughtful integration of technologies such as learning analytics, generative AI, immersive environments, and intelligent systems with the lived realities of students, educators, and institutions. While the promise of adaptive pathways, enhanced engagement, and scalable innovation is evident, so too are the challenges, ranging from faculty readiness and student perceptions to issues of equity, trust, governance, and authenticity in assessment.

Importantly, this volume underscores that the role of educators remains central. Far from being replaced, instructors are repositioned as designers of learning experiences, facilitators of inquiry, and critical mediators of AI-enhanced environments. Similarly, students are no longer passive recipients but active co-creators, whose voices and experiences shape the development of more responsive and inclusive systems.

Looking forward, the future of AI-powered HyFlex learning will be defined by our ability to balance innovation with intentionality. Emerging developments in extended reality, AI companions, and intelligent assessment systems will continue to expand the boundaries of what is possible. Yet, the enduring question remains not what technology can do, but what it should do in service of meaningful, equitable, and transformative education.

As editors, we hope this volume serves as both a foundation and a catalyst for research, practice, and ongoing dialogue. The ideas, frameworks, and case studies gathered here are an invitation to educators, researchers, and leaders to think boldly, engage critically, and act with purpose. The future of education will not emerge from technology alone, nor from human effort alone, but from the powerful convergence of both. It is this joint intelligence between human wisdom and machine capability that holds the greatest promise for transforming future education.

Chapter 1
Reimagining Learning Through Artificial Intelligence:
Enhanced HyFlex Learning as a Framework for Personalized and Inclusive Pedagogy

Mike Wai Keng Choong
http://orcid.org/0009-0008-2575-1149
Taylor's University, Malaysia

Chee Leong Lim
http://orcid.org/0000-0001-6785-9280
Taylor's University, Malaysia

ABSTRACT

This study looks at how Artificial Intelligence (AI) improves the Hybrid-Flexible (HyFlex) Learning model to create personalised, inclusive, and data-driven higher education. It uses a mixed-method design with 1,168 students across 60 modules. The study evaluates how AI Learning Assistants, AI Avatar videos, and Extended Reality (XR) simulations impact engagement and autonomy. The results show that 82.1% of students valued AI support, while international groups reported a satisfaction rate of 94.9% due to multilingual access and flexibility. AI-enhanced HyFlex strengthens Beatty's (2019) principles of Choice, Equivalency, Reusability, and Accessibility through adaptive feedback, analytics, and experiential tools. The

DOI: 10.4018/979-8-3373-6182-6.ch001

proposed AI-Powered HyFlex Framework positions educators as facilitators of self-directed, culturally responsive learning. It also demonstrates a sustainable, globally adaptive model for future-ready education.

INTRODUCTION

The interchanging technological disruption and pedagogical paradigm shift of the 21st century is transforming the educational scene. The transformation was accelerated by the COVID-19 pandemic, necessitating universities to reassess the teaching and learning approach to meet the needs of diverse students, learning modes and changing environments (Holmes & Miao, 2023). Passive traditional lecturing, which is the preferred mode of content disseminating classes; is deficient in preparing students for the self-regulating AI-interpolated societies where adaptability and digital competencies are needed (OECD, 2024).

Under these circumstances, the Hybrid-Flexible or HyFlex Learning model was introduced as an innovative pedagogical alternative that afford students the choice to choose either learning on-campus, online synchronously or asynchronously while attaining similar learning outcomes (Beatty, 2019). Regardless of the flexibility, challenges in sustaining student engagement, inclusivity and personalised learning at scale persists. The advent of Artificial Intelligence (AI) identifies new solutions to address these challenges in providing responsive, personalised learning assistance, environment and data analytics (Zawacki-Richter et al., 2024).

This study examines how AI can empower HyFlex Learning by transforming from "doing things better" (process automation) to "doing better things" (reinventing learning design). Explicitly, it investigates how AI-powered tools such as AI-Avatar Video Production, AI Learning Assistants or Tutors, and Extended Reality (XR) simulations; can enhance HyFlex Learning principles of student choice, equivalency, reusability and accessibility

With a campus-wide scale pilot implementation at Taylor's University, Malaysia; this study proposes and validates an AI-Powered HyFlex Learning Framework that demonstrates measurable improvements in learning satisfaction, engagement and inclusivity.

LITERATURE REVIEW

The Evolution of HyFlex Learning

HyFlex Learning is the combination of hybrid and flexible learning modes that provide students with the flexibility and autonomy to engage synchronously or asynchronously based on their personal preference and learning needs (Beatty, 2019). This study's HyFlex Learning model is built on four principles, namely student choice, equivalency, reusability and accessibility. This particular model assures consistency across modalities and ensures inclusivity for students with diverse learning needs (Finkel-Gates, 2024).

Current research findings promote HyFlex Learning's versatility in providing inclusive accessibility for students with diverse learning needs (Hidayati et al., 2025). Nonetheless, the challenge to sustain engagement and equivalency through various modalities persists; due to static learning content and the scarcity of feedback mechanisms. Hence, adaptive integration of AI technology into the HyFlex Learning experience offers a transformative route into a responsive and data-driven learning mode (Boehm & Boerboom, 2023).

Artificial Intelligence in Higher Education

Presently, AI in higher education had advanced beyond automation to involve personalisation of learning, teaching and learning analytics, and conversational tutoring. AI Learning Assistants or Tutors (2D or 3D chatbots) facilitates real-time feedback, formatively assess learning development and curate adaptive learning pathways (Deckker et al., 2025). In tandem, AI Avatars and Extended Reality (XR) learning environments encourage immersive and human-centric interactions that boosts authentic learning affordances (Gu et al., 2024; Alasgarova & Rzayev, 2025; Stracke et al., 2025).

Aspandi and Muttaqin (2025) affirms that AI in higher education empower educators to become designers of digital learning ecosystems instead of merely being content transmitters (Rigopouli et al., 2025). Educators could design and facilitate learning experiences that motivates personalised learning and fosters critical thinking rather than the mere presentation of content (Niemi, 2024). Furthermore, OECD (2024) emphasized the role of AI in achieving equity for students of diverse learning styles or preferences. Conjointly, these studies promote AI as the higher education transformer that enhances students' learning engagement, autonomy and inclusivity.

Personalising Learning with AI Learning Assistant

Personalization of learning is key to AI-supported HyFlex Learning environments. Traditional lecture-based or content-focused teaching methods often fall short in addressing the diverse pace, needs, and backgrounds of students. This limitation can affect engagement and the long-term retention of knowledge. The emergence and integration of the AI Learning Assistants into the individual student's learning journey, addresses this limitation by customizing and designing the learning pathways while maintaining academic integrity and scalable campus-wide adoption (Aspandi & Muttaqin, 2025; Gregorac et al., 2025; Rigopouli et al., 2025).

This study's AI-powered HyFlex Learning model employed the Noodle Factory solution which serves as the AI Learning Assistant platform, in personalising and scaling learning assistance similar to an AI tutor within a closed intelligent infrastructure. The Noodle Factory platform is an AI-driven conversational learning system that equips academics in converting and adapting their courses' teaching and learning material into interactive and guided learning experiences without the challenges of technical expertise and AI 'hallucination'.

Figure 1. Noodle factory AI learning assistant

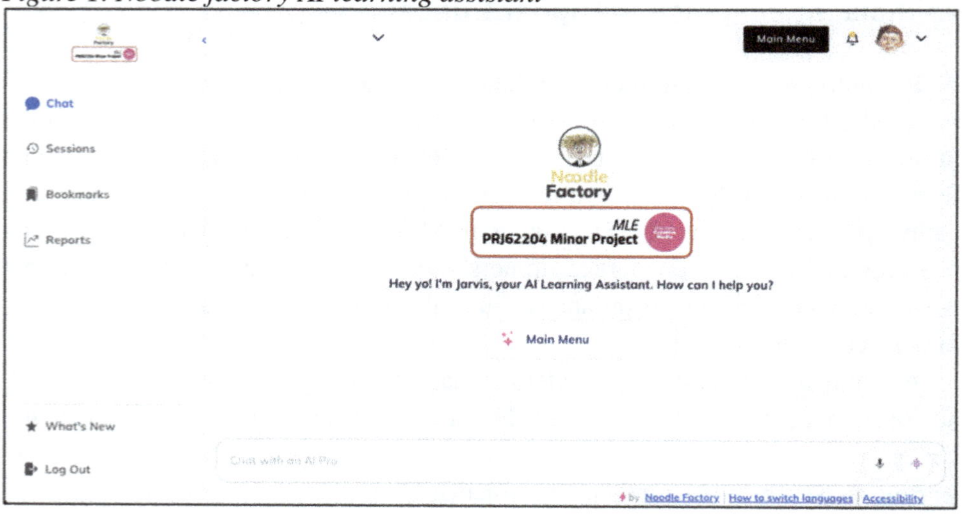

By providing real-time, contextual and 'just-in-time' learning support to guide students in tackling complex content, the Noodle Factory AI Learning Assistant or tutor (Figure 1) becomes the intelligent learning companion to every student all day long regardless of location via the internet. Noodle Factory is able to dynamically adapt learning resources that have been curated and uploaded by the academics, based on the students' learning performance and interactive behaviour. And because the platform provides the option to a closed-content environment, the platform's large language model (LLM) does not search and retrieve information from external sources other than what had been curated by the academics. This option ensures that Noodle Factory does not 'hallucinate' or generates information that is beyond the syllabus or learning requirement, hence removing inaccuracies and errors from the students. Students have access to the Noodle Factory learning assistant via the university's Moodle Learning Management System (LMS) called myTIMeS. Academics provide links to the AI learning assistant according to specific topics and lesson weeks. This helps create a smooth learning path to relevant activities, like multiple-choice questions or short-answer quizzes, role-playing and gamified elements (Figure 2). The interactive learning activities allow students to explore at their own pace while meeting the course learning outcomes.

Figure 2. Noodle factory AI learning assistant with role-play learning activity

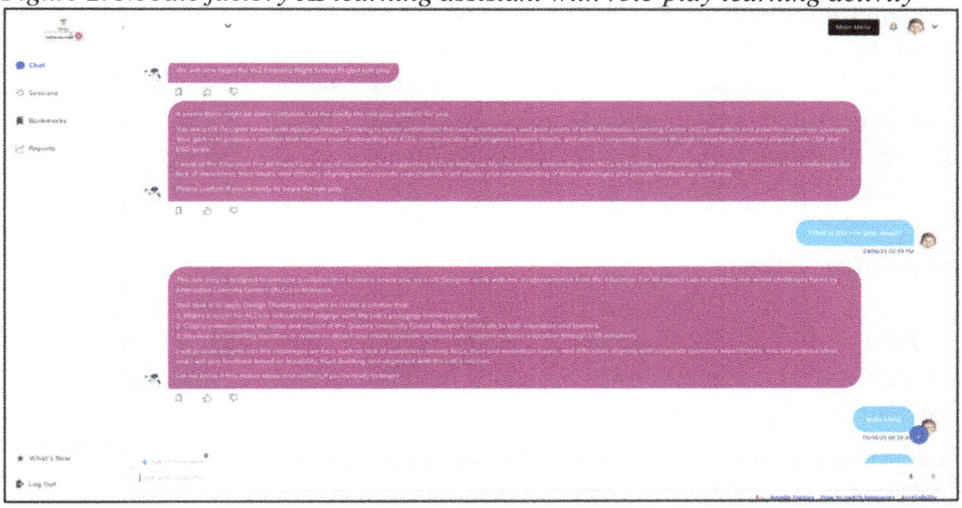

In comparison to static learning management systems, AI Learning Assistants such as Noodle Factory utilizes large language models (LLMs) and adaptive algorithms to suggest personalised learning pathways and conversationally responding to students by identifying the students' learning intent. The Noodle Factory platform can support micro-adaptive scaffolding. It makes real-time adjustments to prompts, examples, or challenges based on each student's skill level and learning goals. This process creates individualized learning experiences that cultivates autonomy, cognitive engagement and motivation; all of which are key characteristics for inculcating future-ready students (Holmes & Miao, 2023).

The personalisation of learning with AI Learning Assistant such as Noodle Factory, underlines the university's strategic goals of providing equitable, inclusive and digital transformative education (Zawacki-Richter et al., 2024). This AI-powered personalisation solution aligns closely with Self-Regulated Learning (SRL) theory (Zimmerman, 2002; Pintrich, 2004), which highlight learners' active role in planning, monitoring, and reflecting on their learning processes. These phases are facilitated by the AI with structured quizzes (monitoring), adaptive feedback (reflection), and scaffolded prompts (strategic planning). The AI-powered framework operationalises SRL principles in a digitally mediated environment, via embedding metacognitive feedback loops within HyFlex modalities extending traditional HyFlex flexibility into a cognitively responsive learning ecosystem.

The AI Learning Assistant extend learning access to mobile or 'on-the-go' students without time constraints, reducing the reliance on time-bound faculty access and providing a more equitable academic ecosystem. Added, the modularity integration with the LMS platform affords scalable deployment regardless of disciplines in supporting lifelong-learning and industry upskilling, and reskilling initiatives. In summary, the AI Learning Assistant personalised learning does not solely supports the HyFlex Learning implementation but reformulate it as a transformative, student-centric ecosystem with the potential to transform with the evolving demands of higher learning in the AI era (Zawacki-Richter et al., 2024; Deckker et al., 2025; Gregorac et al., 2025).

AI Avatar Videos

The AI Avatar Videos serves as the core synchronous lecture or instructional component within the AI-powered HyFlex model, enabling scalable, multilingual, and consistent lecture delivery. With the AI video generation technology, lecturers transform their lecture into video scripts that creates the avatar-based instructional content. It is reusable and adaptable across cohorts, enhancing accessibility, ensuring alignment with module learning outcomes, and supports equivalency across on campus in-person, interactive synchronous live, and flexible asynchronous participation modes (Figure 3).

Figure 3. AI avatar videos with multilanguage voice, acting and subtitle translations

The AI Avatar videos are embedded within the 'myTIMeS' LMS complemented with interactive quizzes and scaffolded learning materials. These functions as structured learning experiences that inculcate active recall, self-paced reinforcement, and concept consolidation. The combination with formative assessments and adaptive prompts, provide students with flexible access to rewatch content, track their understanding and support their preparation for on campus in-person sessions (Lee & Chang, 2025).

Analytics generated from the myTIMeS LMS provide lecturers with insights into their individual student's video viewing behaviour such as frequency, time spent and repetitions; together with the interactive learning data from the quizzes. These insights provide lecturers the required information to make informed decisions for learning improvements and development. This model lessens repetitive content delivery and frees up lecture time for personal mentoring and the implementation of higher-order learning activities. Even during class time, the AI Avatar videos could be used for revision and recall, thus freeing up lecturers to spend more time on weaker students, group collaboration facilitations and develop higher-order thinking skills. The AI Avatar video solution truly provides scalable, sustainable, adaptive, accessible and inclusive learning content that supports the HyFlex Learning aim of "anywhere, anytime, any-mode learning" while making certain that the delivery quality, learning engagement and personalisation remain consistent across modalities.

Extended Reality (XR) Simulations

In extending the learning beyond theoretical understanding and complementing the AI-powered learning experience; the HyFlex Learning model utilizes Extended Reality (XR) Simulations as an enhanced experiential learning component that promotes authentic learning principles of knowledge and practice.

Figure 4. The virtuality continuum

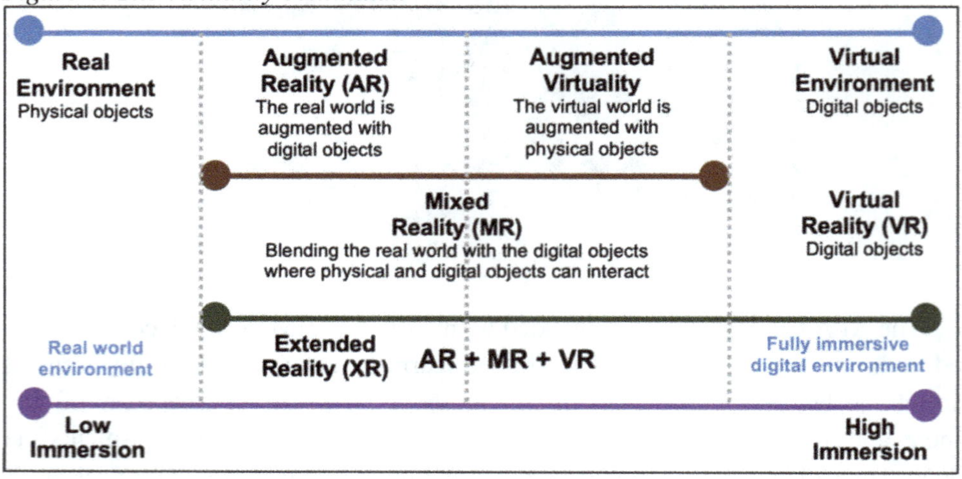

Extended Reality or XR, encompasses Virtual Reality (VR), Augmented Reality (AR) and Mixed Reality (MR) (Figure 4), enabling students to interact with simulated discipline-specific practices and environments that replicate real-world professional contexts. The XR simulations motivate students to apply theoretical concepts, practice contextual decisions and implement complex skills in a safe, replicable and controlled learning environment (Merchant et al., 2024; Samala et al., 2024).

The XR Simulations facilitate the AI-powered HyFlex Learning ecosystem in complementing the AI Avatar videos and AI Learning Assistant during the application phase of the students' learning journey. Students could engage with the AI Avatar videos as pre-class learning and access personalized tutoring with the AI Learning Assistant. After that, they would move on to the immersive XR scenarios, where they need to apply the knowledge they gained from the pre-class session. For example, psychology degree students study and prepare for the week's lesson on counselling practice virtually via the LMS before their on-campus class session. And when they attend their on-campus class, they could practice their counselling skills in a safe and controlled environment with a realistic, lifelike 3D avatar patient (Figure 5).

Figure 5. A 3D lifelike virtual patient avatar

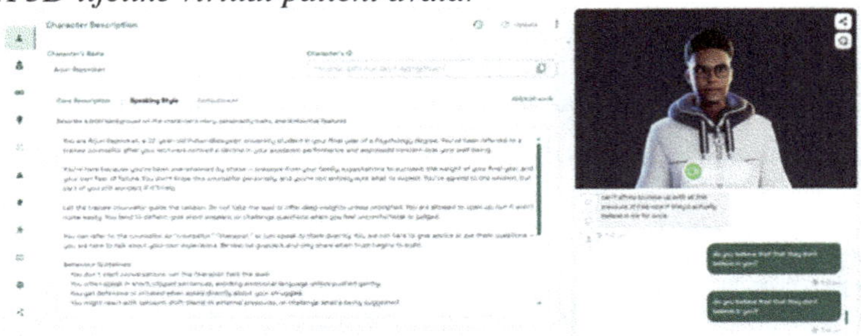

Figure 6. An XR practice counselling session during on-campus class session

Other examples could involve engineering students creating and manipulating 3D prototypes in virtual labs and testing mechanical systems; healthcare students can conduct digital patient assessments as clinical studies. The XR platform's AI analytics provide tracking on each student's performance data, such as decision attempts, response time and error patterns. The platform's real-time adaptive feedback strengthen students' critical thinking and the simulated precision develop skills mastery (Stracke et al., 2025). These XR simulated learning builds upon the experiential and situated learning principles where students construct meaning through interaction and reflection (Kolb, 2015; Hmoud & Ayyoub, 2025). The immersive learning experience creates a sense of presence which removes the gap between theory and application in meeting workplace demands and expectations. As for the academicians or lecturers, the role transforms from mere content delivery to facilitative coaching in guiding collaborative learning and individual student development from the synthesized insights gathered from the XR platform's data analytics.

AI-Powered HyFlex Learning Model Framework

The AI-Powered HyFlex Learning Model Framework integrates AI technology with HyFlex Learning principles to enable personalised, inclusive and data-driven learning experiences (Figure 7).

Figure 7. AI-powered HyFlex learning model framework

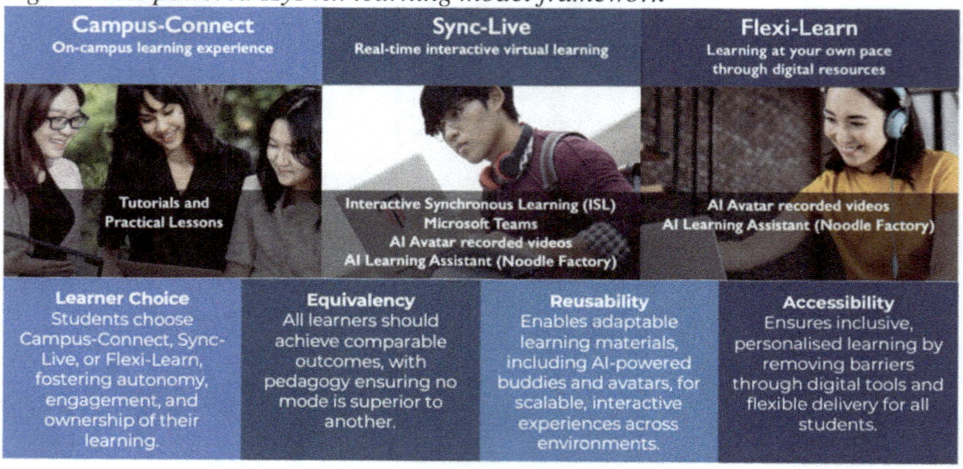

The university's HyFlex Learning model is based on four principles: Student Choice, Equivalency, Reusability, and Accessibility (Beatty, 2019). Students can choose where to learn: on campus, in cafés, or libraries when they join Interactive Synchronous Learning (ISL) or 'Sync-Live' sessions. They can also access recorded ISL sessions and interactive activities anytime, anywhere through the asynchronous 'Flexi-Learn' mode. In the 'Campus-Connect' mode, students meet their course mates and lecturers in person for ongoing engagement. All three modes are supported by the AI Learning Assistant, which gives consistent, personalized guidance. The model ensures equivalent learning outcomes through AI-curated adaptive and formative assessments that include real-time feedback and personalized tutoring. The adaptive assessments transform HyFlex learning into a self-regulated learning ecosystem where structured metacognitive scaffolds support student choices. Learning materials, AI-driven discussions, feedback, and XR simulations are saved for reusability. These resources are made for scalability and diverse learner needs. The multilingual AI Assistant and AI Avatar Videos, which come with captions and adaptive solutions, help address accessibility issues for international students.

The HyFlex Learning model's four integrated principles:

1. Student Choice: Students select their mode of participation ('Campus-Connect' in-person, 'Sync-Live' online synchronous ISL, or 'Flexi-Learn' asynchronous) with AI Learning Assistant and the AI Avatar Videos' providing consistent, personalised guidance across all modes.
2. Equivalency: AI Learning Assistant and the AI Avatar Videos' ensures uniformity of learning outcomes by curating adaptive, formative assessments and real-time feedback mechanisms. Beatty (2019) defines 'Equivalency' as ensuring students achieve comparable learning outcomes across participation modes, and should not be confused with equity, which concerns fairness of access and support.
3. Reusability: Learning artefacts, AI-driven discussions and feedbacks, and XR simulations archived as reusable content assets that extend beyond individual cohorts.
4. Accessibility: AI Learning Assistant and AI Avatar Videos' mitigate learning challenges by offering multilingual support, closed captions and adaptive resources for international students.

METHODOLOGY

The empirical investigation of the AI-powered HyFlex Learning model is guided by three primary research questions (RQ), which are aligned with the theoretical framing of HyFlex principles and AI-powered self-regulated learning:

RQ1: How do students perceive the AI-powered HyFlex Learning model in terms of engagement, satisfaction, and academic support?

RQ2: Are there statistically significant differences in acceptance and engagement across demographic variables such as nationality, faculty, and semester level?

RQ3: In what ways do AI tools, including the AI Learning Assistant, AI Avatar Videos, and XR simulations influence learner autonomy, inclusivity, and patterns of interaction within HyFlex modalities?

The quantitative survey design and the qualitative thematic analysis are based on these research questions. The mixed-methods approach facilitated the empirical investigation on not only the overall acceptance patterns, but also variations across learner groups and deeper experiential insights.

Research Design

This study employed a mixed-methods design, combining quantitative and qualitative data to evaluate students' perception of the learning engagement and satisfaction with the AI-powered HyFlex Learning pedagogy and the lecturers' perception of the workload, sustainability and benefits of the HyFlex Learning pedagogy. The quantitative phase used structured online surveys, while the qualitative phase involved open-ended reflections.

Participants and Context

Data was collected from 1,168 undergraduate students across 60 HyFlex modules at Taylor's University, Malaysia. The 60 modules were selected from diverse disciplines such as Design, Business, Computing, and Education from four faculties namely the Faculty of Social Sciences and Leisure Management (FSLM), Faculty of Innovation and Technology (FIT), Faculty of Business and Law (FBL) and Faculty of Health and Medical Sciences (FHMS). The study period was for one academic semester of 14-16 weeks, with international students comprising approximately 45% of the participants.

Table 1. Undergraduate student numbers and percentages

Nationality	Number of students and percentages
Malaysian	**516 (44.18%)**
International:	**652 (55.82%)**
Chinese	429 (36.73%)
Indonesian	74 (6.34%)
Others	138 (12.75%)

Figure 8. Survey participants according to faculties

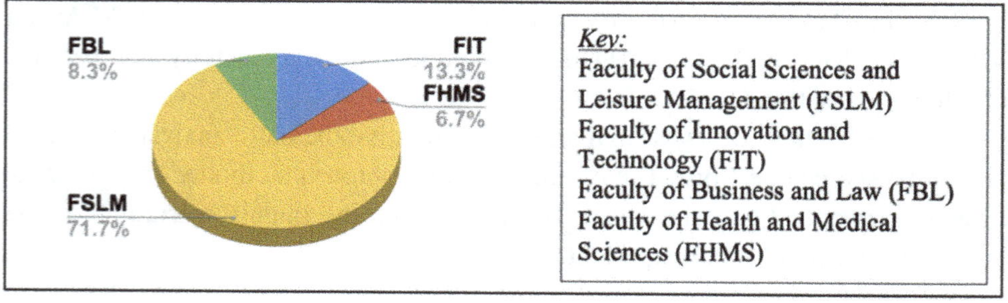

Instruments

Structured online surveys was utilized to gather student perceptions of AI usefulness, acceptance and satisfaction. Open-ended questions solicited qualitative reflections on learning experiences, perceived academic outcomes and lecturers' influence with AI tools. The online surveys were conducted with Survey Monkey over a five weeks duration, where students were to complete the survey during their class time. The online survey for the lecturers were also conducted parallel to the students' survey, with the exception that it could be completed at their own preferred time.

Data Analysis

The data was collected from 1,168 students across 60 university modules, including Malaysian (44.18%) and international (55.82%) groups. The analysis used a mix of descriptive and inferential statistical methods to evaluate students' acceptance of AI Learning Assistants, AI Avatar videos, and XR-based activities. Descriptive statistics, such as frequencies, percentages, and means, summarized trends. Independent-samples t-tests and ANOVA examined variations based on demographic factors like nationality, faculty, and semester. A significance level of $p < 0.05$ established statistical relevance. This highlighted key differences, such as higher acceptance of AI assistants among international students and varying preferences for AI Avatar videos across faculties. Comparative and longitudinal analyses ensured that findings reflected both the diversity at a single point in time and consistency across semesters, which strengthened the reliability of the results.

The researchers analysed qualitative data through Thematic Analysis of 487 open-ended student responses and 15 responses from lecturers. They identified four main themes: Engagement in Learning, Academic Outcomes, Lecturer Influence, and Access Issues. Each theme highlights different aspects of the HyFlex Learning experience. Within these themes, responses were categorized as positive or negative. They used direct quotes to show common opinions. To determine prevalence, how often each theme appeared was counted. For example, Positive Engagement accounted for 89.1% and Negative for 10.9%. This allowed for comparison of findings with quantitative results. This organized coding and comparison method provided a well-rounded view of both statistical and narrative data, offering deep insights into how students experienced and reacted to AI-based HyFlex Learning.

FINDINGS

Quantitative Results

Overview of Quantitative Findings

Overall acceptance of the AI-powered HyFlex Learning model was high across the 1,168 students. The AI Learning Assistant received a positive response across faculties and semesters, especially from international students. AI AV showed moderate to high acceptance and varied between fields. Usage trends reveal that students rely mainly on AI tools for problem solving and clarification and iterative refinement to the output, rather than for generation of output at once. Taken together, these findings indicate that AI serves as a cognitive tool in HyFlex modalities with differences in context across learner populations.

1. Overview of Respondents

The HyFlex Learning study involved a diverse group of 1,168 students across 60 university modules. This provided a solid data set to analyse how learners perceive an AI-enhanced educational environment. The demographic makeup included a fairly even mix of Malaysian students (44.18%) and international students (55.82%), with the latter forming a slight majority. Among the international students, those from China made up the largest subgroup (36.73%), followed by Indonesia (6.34%) and students from various other countries (12.75%). This demographic setup allowed for observing how learners from different cultural and educational backgrounds engaged with AI-driven HyFlex Learning features.

Figure 9. Survey participants according to nationalities

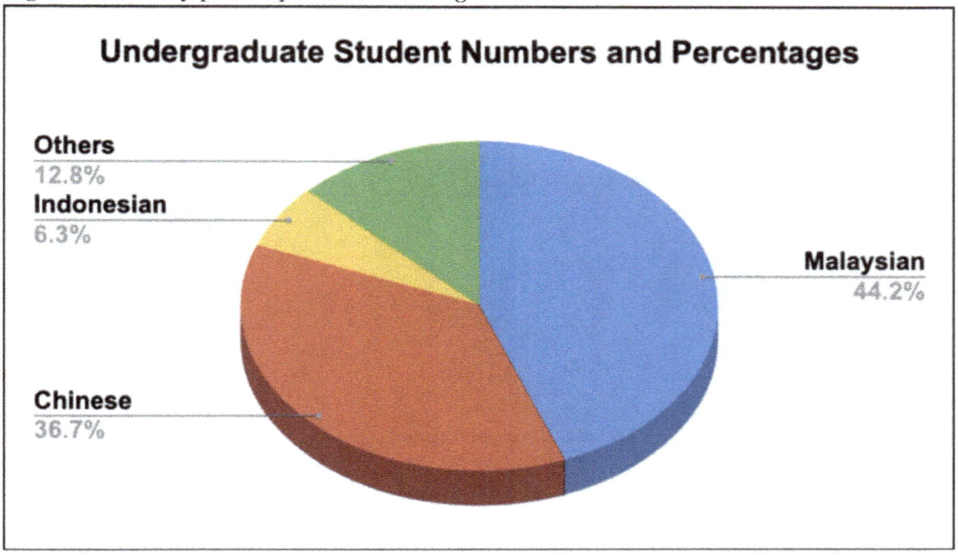

Early trends from the quantitative data show that international learners consistently demonstrated higher levels of acceptance and satisfaction with both the AI Learning Assistants and AI Avatar Videos. International students were significantly more accepting than Malaysian students ($p < 0.001$) and among the latter, Chinese were the most receptive sub-group. This result was the same between both AI Learning Assistant and AI Avatar Video.

In contrast, some Malaysian students voiced concerns about a lack of human interaction, the repetitiveness of AI Avatar Videos, or a preference for traditional lecturer-led instruction. This shows that cultural expectations regarding teaching presence, interaction style, and the value of face-to-face engagement can affect acceptance levels. Overall, the demographic distribution and related insights indicate that the AI-powered HyFlex Learning model is particularly beneficial for international and multilingual learners. They gain from structured, repeatable, and linguistically adaptable learning paths. At the same time, the findings underline the need to balance AI with human teaching presence, especially for learners who value interpersonal interaction and contextualized explanations.

2. Overall Acceptance of AI-Learning Assistant

The results show strong support for the AI-powered HyFlex Learning model, especially the Noodle Factory AI Learning Assistant (Figure 10). Out of 1,168 students surveyed, 82.1% said the AI Assistant helped them learn. This confirms its role as a valuable aid for both live and online learning. This high approval rate means most students recognized the AI Learning Assistant's worth in improving understanding, explaining content, and offering convenient, on-demand help that traditional lectures might not always provide.

Figure 10. Noodle factory AI learning assistant

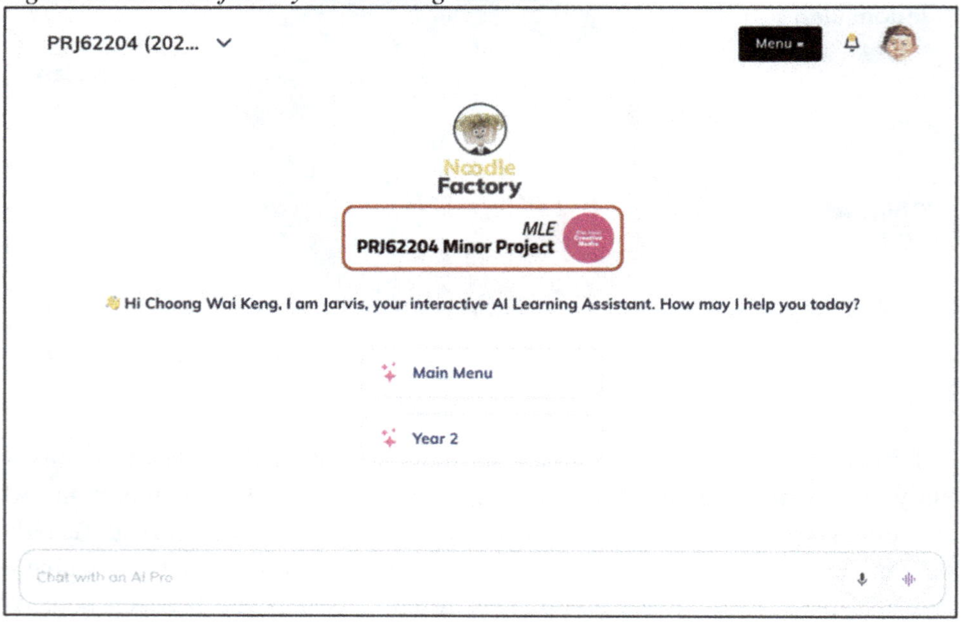

The acceptance rates across different academic faculties further support the model's wide relevance. Levels of acceptance were uniformly high between the teaching bodies and no significant differences were found ($p = 0.066$). It seems that the perceived value of the AI Learning Assistant was relatively consistent across discipline contexts. This suggests that the AI system can effectively support learning in various types of programmes, whether they are content-heavy, practice-based, or theory-focused.

Figure 11. AI learning assistant acceptance rates by faculties

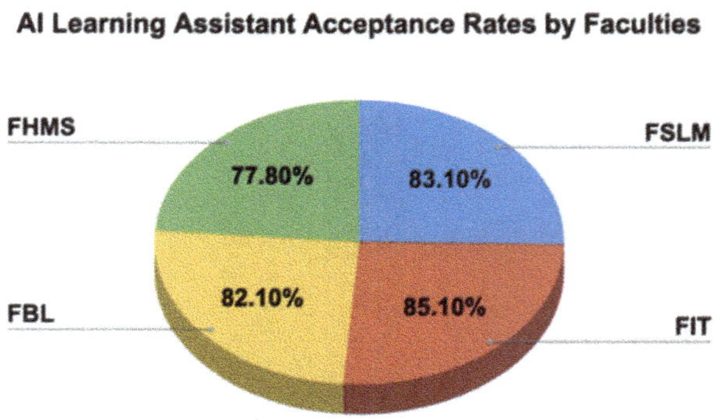

Key:
Faculty of Social Sciences and Leisure Management (FSLM)
Faculty of Innovation and Technology (FIT)
Faculty of Business and Law (FBL)
Faculty of Health and Medical Sciences (FHMS)

This broad acceptance indicates that students are becoming more willing to use AI for immediate feedback, reinforcing concepts, and personalized micro-tutoring. It allows them to revisit challenging topics without the stress of time limits in class. From the institution's perspective, the consistent feedback across faculties strengthens the argument for expanding the AI-powered HyFlex Learning model. It shows that the approach works well regardless of differences in curriculum, workload, or assessment methods. Overall, these findings confirm that adding AI Learning Assistants enhances student learning across disciplines. They support better accessibility, flexibility, and responsiveness within the HyFlex Learning model and significantly contribute to the institution's goals for digital transformation.

3. AI-Learning Assistant Acceptance Differences by Nationality

The analysis showed clear differences in acceptance of the AI-powered HyFlex Learning model among different nationality groups. This suggests that cultural and educational backgrounds significantly shape how students view AI-driven learning tools. International students demonstrated significantly higher acceptance than Malaysian students ($p < 0.001$), with Chinese students representing the highest-acceptance subgroup. This reflects very positive engagement with the Noodle Factory AI Learning Assistant.

Figure 12. AI learning assistant multilingual support

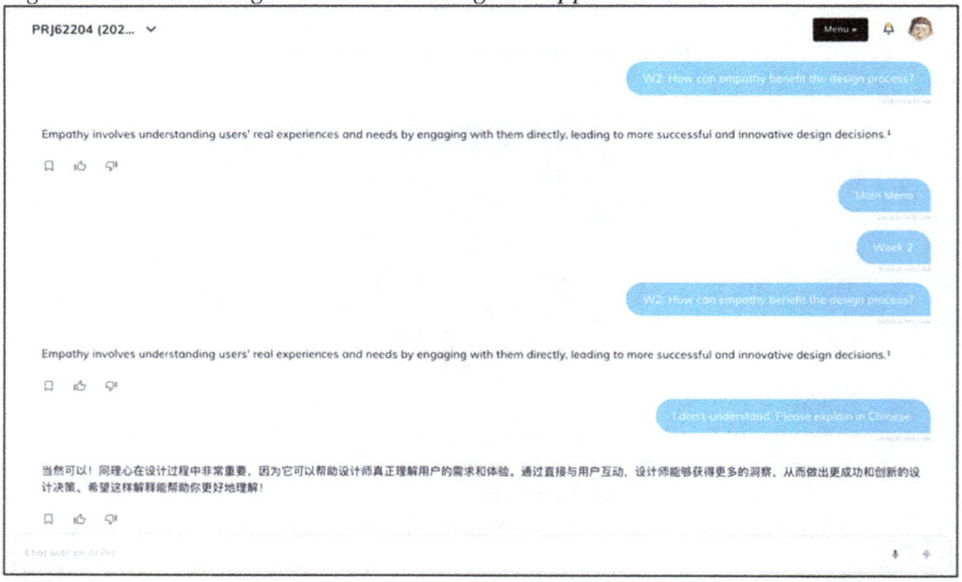

In contrast, the lower acceptance rate among Malaysian students might reflect a stronger preference for human-led instruction, face-to-face interaction, and familiar teaching practices. Several Malaysian respondents expressed concerns about less lecturer presence or a perceived lack of depth in AI-generated videos. These feelings suggest that the shift to AI-generated content may need extra support, communication, or blended teaching strategies to better meet local learning expectations. Overall, the differences based on nationality show that the AI-powered HyFlex Learning model is especially beneficial for international and multilingual learners. They gain from the clarity, accessibility, and independence that AI-enabled systems offer. At the same time, the findings underscore the need for context-sensitive implementation, ensuring that digital innovation responds to diverse cultural expectations and teaching preferences within the student population.

4. AI-Learning Assistant Acceptance Trends Across Semesters

Acceptance of the AI Learning Assistant remained positive across all semesters, showing that the AI-powered HyFlex Learning model was stable and reliable throughout students' academic journeys. Reported acceptance remained consistently high across semesters, with no statistically significant variation observed ($p = 0.126$). This consistency suggests that the AI Learning Assistant meets students' needs, regardless of their familiarity with university learning. For Semester 1 students, the AI

Learning Assistant serves as an important support system, helping them transition into self-paced and technology-based learning. In contrast, the higher acceptance in Semester 5 may indicate greater student maturity, improved digital skills, and a better match between AI-driven feedback and their advanced learning needs.

The steady satisfaction levels show that the AI Learning Assistant not only encourages short-term engagement but also remains relevant as students advance academically. This suggests its potential as a long-term teaching partner, fostering continuity in learning, encouraging independent study habits, and helping students gain confidence over multiple semesters. The lack of significant variation across academic levels supports the idea of expanding the AI-powered HyFlex Learning model across the entire institution, proving it is effective for diverse learners.

5. Reasons for AI-Learning Assistant Student Satisfaction

The quantitative data show clear patterns in why students valued the AI Learning Assistant. The findings align with principles of personalized and student-centred learning. The most common reason for satisfaction was the availability of quizzes to confirm understanding at 81.8%. This highlights the importance of ongoing formative assessment in supporting students' comprehension and confidence. These automated quizzes provided immediate feedback, allowing learners to check their understanding and revisit areas of uncertainty at their own pace. This feature is crucial for both early-year students building foundational knowledge and advanced students tackling more complex concepts.

Figure 13. AI learning assistant quizzes

A significant number of students also valued the tutoring support from the AI Learning Assistant at 74.2%. This reflects the benefit of having a learning companion that is always available to answer questions, explain concepts, and clarify misunderstandings. This on-demand tutoring reduces reliance on lecture time and eases the hesitation some students may feel when asking questions in live settings. International learners particularly noted that the AI tutor created a supportive and pressure-free environment to practice understanding course material.

Figure 14. AI learning assistant tutoring support

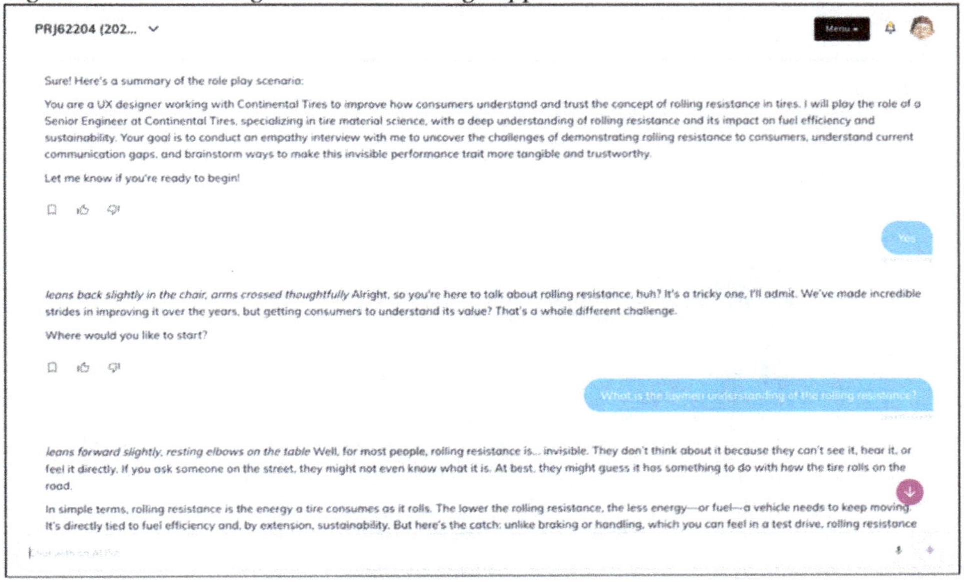

In addition, personalized feedback at 74.0% was a major factor in positive student experiences. Unlike traditional one-size-fits-all feedback, the AI assistant adjusted its responses based on the learner's input. It offered targeted explanations, additional examples, and suggestions for improvement. This level of individual guidance is especially valuable in large classes where feedback from lecturers may be limited by time. Overall, these findings show that the AI Learning Assistant effectively tackles important aspects of assessment, personalization, and formative feedback, all of which are key to modern teaching methods. By promoting self-paced learning and offering tailored support, the AI assistant improves students' sense of autonomy and readiness, strengthening their engagement with the HyFlex Learning model.

6. AI Avatar Video Acceptance

The findings indicate that AI Avatar Videos received moderate overall acceptance across the sample (72.3%). However, significant differences emerged across nationality groups ($p < 0.001$), suggesting that perceptions of AI-generated instruction are influenced by cultural expectations and prior learning experiences. International students demonstrated substantially higher approval than Malaysian students, with Chinese students representing the most receptive subgroup. In contrast, Malaysian students expressed comparatively lower acceptance, indicating more cautious attitudes toward avatar-based instruction. These differences suggest that AI Avatar

Videos may serve distinct pedagogical roles across learner groups. For international students, the structured and reviewable nature of avatar-based lectures appears to support comprehension and linguistic accessibility, particularly in second-language learning contexts.

Figure 15. AI avatar videos

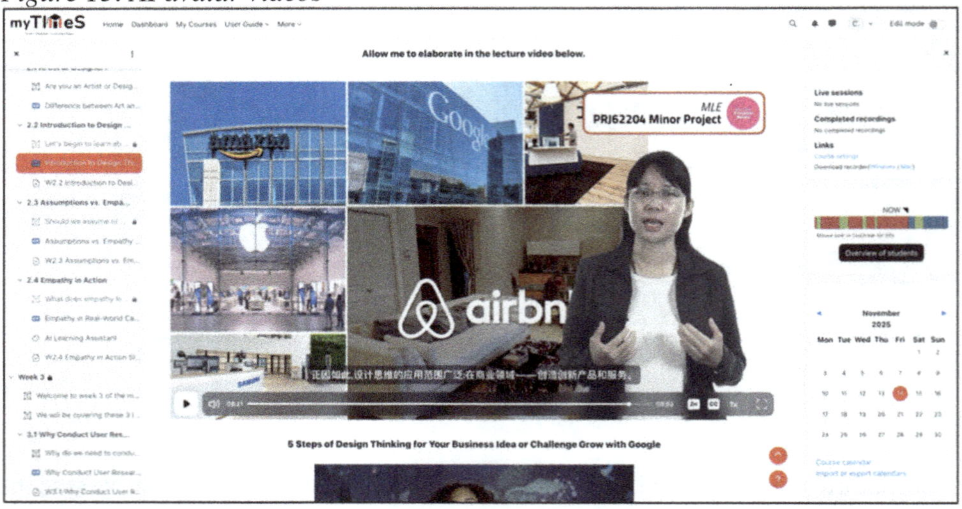

For local students, whose learning norms often stress the importance of lecturer presence, relational interaction, and contextual examples, AI-generated videos may seem less engaging. These differences emphasize the need for context-sensitive strategies. This might include blending AI Avatar Videos with interactive live sessions, providing culturally familiar examples, or adding lecturer voiceovers to ensure that avatar-based content stays meaningful for all student groups. The findings show that while AI Avatar Videos have considerable value, particularly for multilingual and international learners, their effectiveness is enhanced when paired with thoughtful human support and instructional design.

7. AI Avatar Video Acceptance by School Comparisons

Analysis of acceptance levels across faculties and schools shows clear differences in how students value AI Avatar Videos depending on their discipline. Acceptance of AI Avatar Videos varied significantly across faculties ($p = 0.046$), with visually oriented programmes demonstrating higher acceptance compared to clinically intensive disciplines. Looking closer at the school-level data confirms this trend. Students in visually focused and practice-oriented schools showed the highest acceptance. The School of Education (SoEd) had an acceptance rate of 82.0%, the School of Architecture, Built Environment and Design (SABD) had 80.6%, the School of Hospitality, Tourism and Events (SHTE) had 77.7%, and the School of Accounting and Finance (SoAF) had 75.7%. These programmes typically focus on multimedia learning, structured instruction, and visual examples, likely explaining their preference for avatar-based video content that offers clarity, repeatability, and concise explanations that fit their coursework.

Figure 16. AI avatar videos acceptance rates by faculties

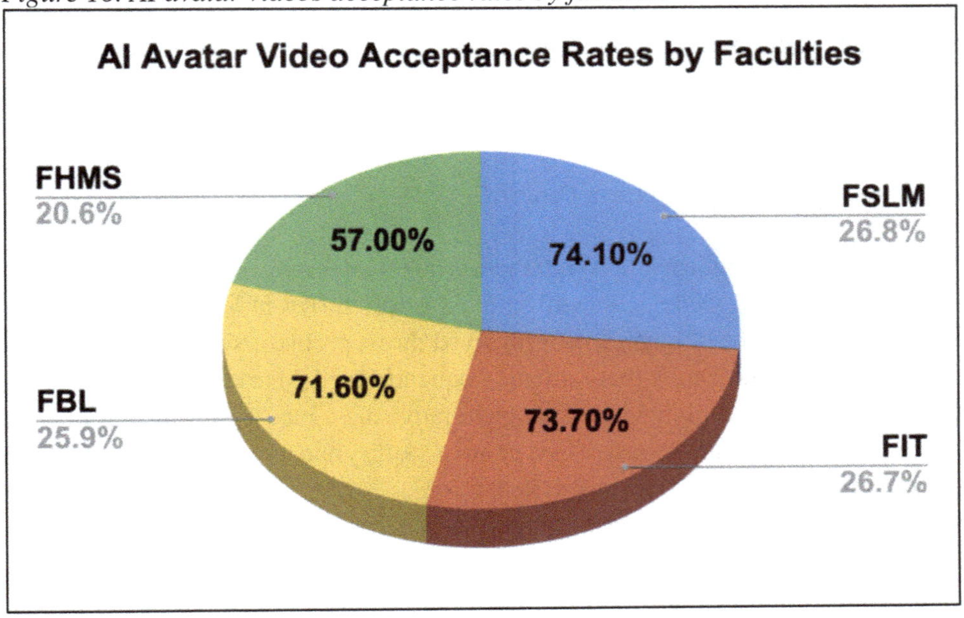

Table 2. Undergraduate student numbers and percentages

Schools	AI Avatar Video Acceptance Rate in Percentages
School of Education (SoEd)	82.0%
School of Architecture, Built Environment and Design (SABD)	80.6%
School of Hospitality, Tourism and Events (SHTE)	77.7%
School of Accounting and Finance (SoAF)	75.7%
School of Pharmacy (SoP)	39.3%

On the other hand, the School of Pharmacy (SoP) had the lowest acceptance rate at only 39.3%, indicating a significant difference. Pharmacy students often deal with complex scientific concepts, lab work, and clinical explanations, where they may expect more human interaction, detailed clarification, and practical examples. Student feedback supports this, with many describing avatar videos as lacking the depth, natural expression, or immediacy that deeply technical or health-related subjects require. Overall, the significant differences suggest that AI Avatar Videos are more effective in fields that prioritize visual content, structured delivery, and flexible review. In contrast, disciplines that rely on hands-on, relational, or clinical learning may need additional teaching support for successful use. These results point to the need for strategies that consider each discipline's unique requirements, such as combining avatar videos with lab demonstrations, including case studies, or offering a mix of human and AI explanations to better address specialized learning needs.

8. Student and AI Engagement Patterns

The analysis of student and AI interaction behaviours reveal distinct engagement patterns that reflect strategic use of AI tools across different learning stages. The most common forms of engagement involved direct problem-solving and collaborative reasoning, indicating that students frequently used AI to clarify concepts, test understanding, and explore ideas through iterative dialogue. These patterns suggest that AI functioned as a responsive first point of inquiry and a conversational thinking partner rather than merely a content generator.

In contrast, direct output generation was comparatively less common, suggesting that students were less likely to rely on AI to produce complete assignments. This pattern reflects a constructive use of AI as a cognitive support tool that aids analysis, refinement, and reflection instead of replacing independent reasoning.

These findings have important implications for assessment design. Since students predominantly engage AI to enhance reasoning and iterative improvement, instructional strategies should emphasize process-oriented tasks, reflective components, and staged drafting. Embedding checkpoints, reasoning logs, or reflective commentaries can ensure that AI-supported learning remains transparent, ethical, and intellectually rigorous.

9. Summary Insight

The quantitative analysis shows that the AI-powered HyFlex Learning model provides strong value across different student groups. Overall acceptance is 82.1% for the AI Learning Assistant and 72.3% for AI Avatar Videos. International and multilingual learners, especially students from China, showed the highest satisfaction.

They benefited most from structured, repeatable, and adaptable content. Malaysian students also had a positive view but preferred more human interaction and contextual explanations, which suggests a need for blended approaches. Acceptance remained steady throughout the semesters and was mostly consistent across faculties. This confirms the AI Assistant's broad relevance and reliability as a feedback and micro-tutoring tool. Students appreciated quizzes, personalized feedback, and on-demand explanations. They mainly used AI for problem solving, clarifying concepts, and refining ideas rather than for generating direct output. This is a positive indicator for academic integrity and genuine learning engagement. Acceptance of AI Avatar Videos varied by discipline, being higher in visually oriented programmes and lower in clinically intensive fields. This highlights the need for instructional design that considers different disciplines. Overall, the findings show that AI significantly improves accessibility, autonomy, and learning continuity. They also stress the importance of maintaining strong human teaching presence to support learners from diverse backgrounds.

Qualitative Themes

1. Overview of Analysis

The qualitative part of the study looked closely at 487 open-ended student responses. Researchers used a systematic Thematic Analysis to find recurring feelings and patterns related to HyFlex Learning, the Noodle Factory AI Learning Assistant, and AI Avatar Videos. Through coding, four main themes came up: Engagement in Learning, Academic Outcomes, Lecturer Influence, and Access Issues. Each theme captured a different aspect of how students interact with AI-mediated learning. Each theme was also divided into positive and negative sentiment subthemes. This breakdown allowed for a better understanding of both the strengths and challenges that students identified. The analysis included frequency counts to show how prominent each theme was. For example, 89.1% of engagement was positive, while 10.9% was negative. This data highlighted the overall tone of student experiences and pointed out areas for improvement.

To enhance interpretation, the analysis included direct quotes from students. This provided real insights into their attitudes, ranging from excitement about flexibility and personalized learning to worries about boredom, less human interaction, or tech issues. This method ensured that the qualitative findings supported the quantitative trends. It also revealed the human experiences behind the numbers, giving a rich understanding of how different learner groups view AI-powered HyFlex Learning.

2. Engagement in Learning

The theme of Engagement in Learning was one of the strongest signs of student satisfaction in the AI-powered HyFlex Learning environment. An overwhelming 89.1% of responses indicated positive engagement. This shows that most students found the learning experience flexible, intuitive, and supportive of their study habits. Students often praised the ability to review content at their own pace, go back to explanations, and use short AI-generated video lectures to improve their understanding. Comments like "short and straight to the point" and "I could review and consolidate what I learned anytime" highlight how the combination of the AI Learning Assistant and AI Avatar Videos helped deepen comprehension and encouraged students to take more control over their learning. Many students mentioned that quizzes, translation features, and immediate feedback helped keep them motivated and reduced learning anxiety. The chance to engage with content on their own schedule, while facing the stress of keeping up with real-time classes, was especially appreciated by international students and those managing busy schedules.

Despite these positive trends, 10.9% of students reported feeling disengaged or dissatisfied. Negative feedback often focused on the perceived dullness of AI Avatar Videos, the absence of emotional presence, and concerns that AI-generated content felt less "authentic" than traditional lectures. Comments like "I paid for real lectures, not videos" indicate a desire for human connection and relational teaching, which are still important for some learners. Some students also noted that content led by AI was not enough without chances for discussion, interaction, and guidance from instructors. These differing viewpoints highlight the need to balance AI efficiency with human teaching presence. While AI-driven resources improve flexibility and personalization, keeping meaningful lecturer-student interaction, opportunities for discussion, and emotionally engaging learning experiences is vital for keeping all students engaged. The findings suggest that the best HyFlex Learning experiences combine AI to enhance, rather than replace, human teaching elements.

3. Academic Outcomes

The theme of Academic Outcomes showed strong support from students for the AI-powered HyFlex Learning model. About 88.4% of qualitative responses indicated better understanding, preparedness, and knowledge retention. Students often pointed out how the mix of automated quizzes, AI explanations, and multilingual translation tools helped them grasp course content. These features were particularly helpful for international learners, who frequently mentioned that translation support was essential in overcoming language challenges. Comments like "Noodle Factory can translate the language to help me understand better" and "It helped me understand abstract knowledge" show how AI tools acted as supports, allowing learners to access and understand complex material more effectively. Students also found that being able to review lectures and AI responses multiple times improved their readiness for class discussions, assessments, and synchronous on-campus activities. This fits with the principles of spaced repetition and self-paced reinforcement. It suggests that AI-generated micro-learning content significantly aids deeper processing and long-term retention. The flexibility of the HyFlex Learning model, which lets students switch between in-person, synchronous online, and asynchronous formats, also boosted ongoing academic engagement. Learners could revisit materials whenever they needed clarity.

However, 11.6% of responses revealed frustration, indicating that AI-mediated learning does not work equally well for all students. Some comments mentioned limited engagement or inadequate depth in AI-generated explanations, especially when these tools were used without strong support from instructors. Responses like "Noodle Factory was not helpful for clearing doubts" and "It's ineffective if students are expected to rely solely on HyFlex without proper guidance" highlight that AI alone cannot replace the teaching value of timely human involvement. These insights suggest that while AI greatly improves comprehension, its benefits are maximized when it is part of a guided instructional framework. In this framework, instructors interpret data, provide clarifications, lead discussions, and relate content to real-world or disciplinary contexts. In other words, the combination of AI-driven personalization and human-led support creates the best foundation for improved academic outcomes within the HyFlex Learning model.

4. Lecturer Influence

The theme of Lecturer Influence stood out as a key factor shaping students' views on AI-enabled HyFlex Learning. An impressive 74.4% of comments showed positive sentiment, highlighting the importance of lecturer presence, guidance, and facilitation for creating a meaningful learning experience, even in an AI-rich environment. Students often pointed out how skilled lecturers integrated AI tools into the learning process. They used these tools to improve clarity, organize discussions, and support learning tasks. Comments like "My lecturer engages and opens the floor for Q&A" and "HyFlex gave me flexibility when combined with lecturer input" suggest a model where AI provides essential support, while lecturers offer the human connection, context, and academic reassurance that students highly value. These responses indicate that students see the most benefits when AI and educators work well together, rather than one replacing the other. AI tools like Noodle Factory help with understanding, immediate feedback, and flexible access. Meanwhile, lecturers bring interpretive skills, emotional connection, and real-time responsiveness; qualities that technology cannot match. This combination seems especially effective in boosting student confidence, engagement, and a sense of belonging in their academic journey.

However, 25.6% of comments raised concerns about the risks of having too little lecturer presence, particularly in online or asynchronous formats. Students who felt disconnected often linked this to a lack of human interaction, noting remarks like, "I feel as though important human interaction was lost with HyFlex." Others commented that AI-generated content alone did not offer the nuances, spontaneity, or relational depth they associated with traditional teaching. These concerns highlight that learning is not just a mental exercise; it is also a relational and social activity. While AI tools can be useful, they cannot fully replace personal connections. Overall, these insights stress the need for thoughtful instructional design. Educators should actively engage and interact in all HyFlex Learning formats. Approaches like live Q&A sessions, personalized feedback, visible presence cues, and cooperative activities can help maintain the relational aspect of learning. This way, students can benefit from the efficiency of AI alongside the empathy of human mentorship. In summary, lecturer influence is crucial for successful HyFlex Learning implementation, acting as the link between technology and meaningful human learning experiences.

5. Access Issues

Access-related concerns emerged as an important theme in the qualitative analysis. While HyFlex Learning offers significant benefits in flexibility and accessibility, digital equity remains a major challenge. A substantial 68% of responses pointed out barriers that limited students' ability to fully benefit from AI-enabled HyFlex Learning resources. The most common issues included unstable internet connections, which disrupted live participation and caused delays in following lecture content. Other issues were the lack of subtitles or translation options in certain AI Avatar Videos and device limitations, especially among students who relied on mobile phones or older laptops for their coursework. Several students also had difficulties with understanding non-native English, particularly when AI-generated speech lacked natural intonation or when technical terms were not simplified. One student noted, "Sometimes internet issues made it hard to follow the class clearly." This highlights how gaps in infrastructure can have a significant impact on learning quality.

Despite these challenges, 32% of responses reflected positive experiences with accessibility. These responses highlighted the strengths of AI-supported HyFlex Learning systems in overcoming traditional barriers. Students appreciated the ability to access learning materials anytime and anywhere, especially those balancing part-time work, long commutes, or irregular schedules. For many international learners, multilingual features, like translation tools in Noodle Factory and AI Avatars speaking in multiple languages; played a key role in allowing equitable participation and understanding. Comments mentioned how AI tools helped them "understand better" and "review content even with a bad connection," showing the potential of AI to support learners in low-bandwidth or linguistically diverse situations. Overall, these findings suggest that while technical constraints still present significant obstacles, AI-powered HyFlex Learning systems can help reduce access disparities when combined with inclusive design features, such as subtitles, language options, compressed media formats, and mobile-friendly interfaces. They also point to the ongoing need for institutions to invest in digital infrastructure, student support resources, and localized content adaptations to ensure that the benefits of AI-enhanced learning are distributed fairly to all student groups.

6. Overall Qualitative Themes Insight

The qualitative findings show that students generally see AI-powered HyFlex Learning as flexible, supportive, and helpful for their studies. Positive feelings are strong in areas like Engagement (89.1%), Academic Outcomes (88.4%), and Lecturer Influence (74.4%). Learners valued the chance to review content at their own pace, get instant AI feedback, access multilingual support, and strengthen their understanding through quizzes and repeatable micro-learning. These features boosted their confidence and comprehension, especially for international students. However, students stressed that meaningful human teaching is still important. Some described AI Avatar videos as dull or lacking emotional presence. Others pointed out that learning suffers when lecturer guidance is limited. Access issues, like unstable internet, device limitations, and few subtitles or translations, highlighted the need for inclusive design and better digital infrastructure. Overall, the qualitative data indicate that the best HyFlex Learning experiences happen when AI efficiency is combined with active lecturer engagement and fair access supports. This ensures that technology improves rather than replaces the personal, contextual, and human aspects of learning.

DISCUSSION

The findings of this study show that AI significantly improves the HyFlex Learning environment by adding flexibility, personalization, and multimodal engagement into a clear teaching system. Students consistently reported that the AI Learning Assistant offered valuable real-time support, helping them clarify doubts, practice concepts, and get immediate feedback. These functions encouraged greater self-directed learning, allowing students to track their understanding, spot gaps, and engage in ongoing self-assessment. This matches what Yin et al. (2024) discovered, which is that AI-powered chatbots strengthen metacognitive processes by prompting learners to reflect, ask questions, and evaluate their own thinking.

This study's results can also be interpreted through the lens of Self-Regulated Learning theory (Zimmerman, 2002; Pintrich, 2004); where the persistent engagement of AI-assisted quizzes, iterative dialogue and adaptive feedback affords metacognition monitoring for strategic adjustments. Students demonstrated competent use of AI tools to clarify their understanding, check their reasoning and scaffold independent problem-solving. This emphasises the AI as a cognitive partner promoting self-regulation rather than replacing instructional guidance.

In the HyFlex model, the AI assistant acts as a constant learning partner, promoting independence and cognitive engagement across online, in-person, and asynchronous pathways. The cross-cultural data also show that AI-supported HyFlex Learning can improve inclusivity in international education. International students, especially those from China, expressed high satisfaction with both AI Learning Assistants and AI Avatar Videos. They praised features like translation, clarity, and flexible content review. These results support Finkel-Gates (2024), who argues that AI can help reduce cultural and language barriers by providing multilingual support, consistent explanations, and tailored learning pathways. The strong preference among international groups suggests that AI tools may be particularly effective in transnational university settings, helping learners adapt to unfamiliar academic environments while giving them personalized support that bridges language and context gaps.

From a teaching perspective, the findings show a significant change in the identity and role of educators. Instead of just delivering content, educators are increasingly acting as learning experience designers, using AI tools to enhance student engagement and understanding. By utilizing data from AI Learning Assistants, Avatar Videos, and XR platforms, teachers gain better insights into student performance trends, misconceptions, and engagement patterns. This allows for more targeted interventions, timely facilitation, and adaptive teaching strategies. Such a model reflects the "human-in-the-loop" approach promoted by Holmes and Miao (2023), which highlights that AI should support, not replace human teaching. In this approach, technology offers scalable support and personalization, while educators provide interpretation, empathy, and contextual expertise that AI cannot replicate.

While this study's findings showed strong evidence of student engagement and perceived academic value, the focus is primarily on learner perceptions rather than academic achievement indicators. Therefore, the reported results showed acceptance, interaction patterns, and self-reported learning support rather than longitudinal learning performance. Future research should further evaluate the sustained academic impact of AI-powered HyFlex Learning across semesters and disciplines by triangulating engagement data with learning analytics, academic grades, and longitudinal learning retention.

Ethical, Governance, and Risk Considerations

Despite the strong student acceptance and engagement demonstration, the integration of AI within HyFlex Learning environments raises important ethical, governance, and pedagogical considerations. Firstly, data privacy and informed consent are central concerns in AI-integrated education. The use of AI Learning Assistants with analytic platforms demands transparent communication about data collection, storage, and usage. Universities must inform and clarify with students about how the interaction data which drives learning analytics and system improvement are following relevant data protection regulations.

Second, to maintain academic trust AI transparency and explainability are critical factors. Students and lecturers too must understand the scope and limitations of AI-generated responses, even with the use of closed-content language models. There must be clear definition of what AI can and cannot do, framing these boundaries help prevent over-reliance and emphasises the role of human facilitation.

Third, discreet learning design produces assessment integrity. Although this study's engagement results suggest that students primarily used AI as a cognitive support tool rather than an output generation accelerator, the threat of generative AI misuse remains a systemic risk in universities. Therefore process-oriented assessments, reflective components, and transparent AI-use declarations needs to be introduced to protect academic integrity while supporting constructive AI-powered learning.

Finally, without intentional design in AI tools integration there is a pedagogical risk of diminishing human presence. The qualitative findings demonstrate that lecturer facilitation remains essential in maintaining relational, contextual, and emotional dimensions of learning. The "Human-in-the-loop" framework should therefore drive the AI-powered HyFlex Learning, where technology enhances but does not replace lecturers' judgment, mentorship, and ethical oversight.

In summary, the results reinforce that AI-powered HyFlex Learning represents a strong, culturally aware, and increasingly essential method in modern higher education. By combining human teaching expertise with adaptable AI tools, institutions can create learning environments that are more equitable, flexible, and responsive to the diverse needs of global learners.

IMPLICATIONS

Pedagogical Implications

1. Design for Autonomy

The findings clearly demonstrate that both the AI Learning Assistant and AI Avatar Videos play a central role in supporting students' ability to manage their own learning processes. These AI tools enable learners to work at their own pace by providing automated quizzes, personalised feedback, and repeatable micro-lectures that can be revisited as needed. The high acceptance rates of 82.1% overall, with an exceptional 94.9% among Chinese students-underscore students' readiness to engage in self-directed learning when supported by adaptive technologies. These results highlight the importance of designing HyFlex Learning environments that prioritise learner agency, offering students meaningful choices about when, how, and where they engage with course content.

The shift toward autonomy also requires educators to embrace a new role as facilitators of self-regulated learning, rather than traditional content transmitters. In this model, instructors guide students in developing reflective habits, monitoring their progress, and understanding their cognitive processes. Integrating structured prompts and reflective activities within AI-assisted modules can help learners assess their understanding and identify areas requiring further exploration. Similarly, embedding micro-assessments that offer immediate AI-driven feedback supports continuous self-reflection and goal-setting-key components of metacognitive development highlighted in Yin et al. (2024), who found that AI Learning Assistants significantly enhance self-regulation and metacognitive engagement.

To operationalise autonomy within the HyFlex Learning environment, learning design should incorporate:

- Reflection prompts embedded within AI modules to promote awareness of learning progress.
- Micro-assessments that provide personalised, real-time feedback, enabling iterative refinement of understanding.
- Choice-driven learning pathways within the LMS, allowing learners to determine content sequence, depth, and modality based on their needs.

When implemented effectively, these strategies create a learning ecosystem where students become independent, confident, and self-motivated learners. Importantly, autonomy does not imply isolation; rather, students remain meaningfully connected through guided AI interactions and educator-facilitated checkpoints. This hybrid model ensures the benefits of personalised learning while maintaining the relational and academic support essential for student success.

2. Inclusive Design

The clear differences in acceptance between Malaysian and international students show the need for inclusivity in AI-supported HyFlex Learning environments. International students, especially those from China, appreciated features like translation tools, flexible content review, and clear AI voice narration. These help to lessen language and cultural barriers. In contrast, local students showed a greater preference for human connection and emotional expressiveness. This highlights the varied cultural expectations of what constitutes "good teaching."

Pedagogically, this means that inclusive HyFlex Learning design should do more than just focus on accessibility. It must also consider cultural sensitivity, language flexibility, and engagement through multiple formats. Important strategies include:

- AI-driven multilingual subtitles and translation options to improve cross-cultural inclusivity.
- Dual-mode video delivery, combining AI Avatar narration with short clips or commentary from human lecturers to maintain emotional connection.
- Universal Design for Learning (UDL) principles, offering multiple ways to engage (interactive polls, adaptive quizzes) and represent (AI text summaries, visual cues, transcriptions).

Finkel-Gates (2024) supports the idea that AI-enabled hybrid education helps promote inclusivity across borders by closing linguistic gaps. Therefore, inclusive design should combine technological features with empathetic human design. This way, every student, no matter their background, feels recognized, supported, and empowered.

3. Curriculum Integration

The study shows a steady positive acceptance rate of 82 to 90% across semesters and strong engagement data of 62.5% for problem-solving and 59.2% for collaboration. This suggests that AI tools work best when they are built into the curriculum instead of being offered as optional aids. When these tools connect with course goals, AI assistants and avatars can help maintain learning across different formats. This approach ensures that both HyFlex Learning and traditional students gain a similar level of understanding.

Pedagogically, this requires a redesign of the curriculum that incorporates AI and HyFlex Learning tools into the learning structure. They should not be added on separately but should serve as essential teaching aids. Integration should:

- Map AI tools to specific learning outcomes: Ensure a strong connection between assessment, feedback, and the benefits of AI.

- Include reflective and collaborative tasks in AI-enabled environments: This will promote deeper learning and social involvement.
- Train educators as "learning experience designers" who understand AI analytics for personalised support: This aligns with Holmes and Miao's (2023) "human-in-the-loop" model that highlights ethical, teacher-led AI use.

Curriculum integration also offers a way to improve innovation and helps institutions keep quality across different fields. However, the differences between faculties, show that adapting to each discipline is important. Design-focused and hospitality programmemes may focus on visual and hands-on AI delivery. In contrast, health sciences might need more structured, empathy-driven support.

Institutional Implications

The strong and consistent acceptance of AI-powered HyFlex Learning across faculties shows that it is ready to be included in institutional strategies and teaching policies. Universities should start recognizing AI-powered HyFlex Learning as an official delivery mode. This recognition must come with clear ethical and data governance guidelines. Policies should also ensure that lecturers who integrate AI and HyFlex Learning tools into their courses receive adequate time, recognition, and support. This approach helps sustain innovation without overwhelming academic staff. It aligns with the broader "human-in-the-loop" approach highlighted by Holmes and Miao (2023). Access and infrastructure remain critical factors as well. Many students still experience unstable internet connections. Institutions need to improve their technological infrastructure. They must ensure reliable Wi-Fi with a responsive IT support system to quickly resolve technical issues. This way, technology boosts learning instead of hindering it.

Faculty Readiness and Institutional Support

While technological infrastructure is needed, but it is the faculty readiness and institutional support system that determines the successful implementation of AI-powered HyFlex Learning. Structured professional development that empowers lecturers with both technical proficiency and pedagogical competency, is what sustains AI-enhanced teaching. Targeted training workshops on integrating AI tools, ethical use of AI, and data-informed learning design should be provided by the learning institutions. The creation of Communities of Practice (COP) is vital to facilitate the sharing of best practices, experiences, challenges, and effective strategies for blending human facilitation with AI. To reduce 'change' resistance and promote gradual pedagogical transformation, peer mentoring and multi-disciplinary collaboration should be introduced. And to prevent transformation fatigue, the lecturers' workload and AI-powered module or course redesign efforts need to be acknowledged formally. These initiatives ensures that the universities evolve their AI-powered HyFlex Learning as a sustainable ecosystem rather than a short-term technological implementation.

Lecturers are crucial in shaping students' experiences with AI-HyFlex mediated learning. Institutions should focus on professional development through short, practical training on AI-powered HyFlex Learning design, peer learning sessions, community of practice and recognition of innovative teaching practices. Building faculty confidence and skills is key for long-term success. The study's large dataset emphasizes the importance of using student feedback and analytics for improvement. Institutions can collect data on engagement, satisfaction and learning performance to refine AI-powered HyFlex Learning design and monitor learning quality each semester. This data-driven approach supports ongoing improvement and accountability in teaching methods. Finally, the notably higher satisfaction among international students, especially those from China, suggests that AI-powered HyFlex Learning promotes inclusivity and global readiness. Institutions can enhance this by maintaining multilingual, culturally adaptive content and positioning AI-powered HyFlex Learning as a central part of their transnational education initiatives.

In summary, institutions should focus on policy support, better infrastructure, staff readiness, data-informed decision-making, and inclusive internationalization. These practical measures offer a realistic way for universities to effectively and fairly sustain and expand AI-powered HyFlex Learning.

Theoretical Implications

The findings of this study improve the understanding of HyFlex Learning by confirming Beatty's (2019) four foundational principles: Student Choice, Equivalency, Reusability, and Accessibility, within an AI-augmented environment. Quantitative data show consistent acceptance across disciplines and sustained satisfaction over semesters. This evidence confirms that the AI-powered HyFlex Learning model can maintain equivalency (achieving comparable learning outcomes across participation modes) and accessibility across different learning formats. Student autonomy and flexibility increased thanks to AI-driven features such as personalised quizzes, feedback loops, and adaptive tutoring. This shows how technology can support student choice and promote ongoing engagement. These results expand HyFlex Learning theory beyond flexibility in formats to intelligent flexibility, where adaptive AI systems adjust learning paths to meet individual needs.

In connection with the growing research on AI in higher education, this study reinforces the idea that AI serves not only as a tool for automation but also as a teaching aid that personalises learning experiences (Aspandi & Muttaqin, 2025; Deckker et al., 2025; Rigopouli et al., 2025). The Noodle Factory AI Learning Assistant demonstrates how large language models (LLMs) can support learning in real-time by contextualizing instructional content and guiding students through adaptive micro-interactions. This fits with Holmes and Miao's (2023) 'human-in-the-loop' framework, where AI aids metacognitive growth and self-regulation rather than replacing educator support. The use of AI Learning Assistants and AI Avatar videos together advances theories of constructivist and self-regulated learning, showing that student autonomy and reflection work best with a balance of human presence and AI support.

Lastly, by linking HyFlex Learning design with AI Avatar videos and XR simulations, the study contributes to experiential and situated learning theories (Kolb, 2015; Samala et al., 2024). XR-based extensions show how AI-powered HyFlex Learning ecosystems can close the gap between theory and practice, shifting learning from being content-focused to experience-focused. In summary, this study refines existing theories of HyFlex and AI-mediated learning by positioning AI as an essential cognitive partner that enhances student autonomy, inclusivity, and engagement across different contexts.

CONCLUSION

This study shows that using AI in the HyFlex Learning model significantly improves student independence, inclusiveness, and engagement. It highlights the teaching potential of AI-powered environments in today's higher education. Based on Beatty's (2019) four key principles namely, Student Choice, Equivalency, Reusability, and Accessibility, the AI-powered HyFlex Learning model shows how technology can enhance flexible learning methods in in-person, synchronous online, and asynchronous settings. Tools like the AI Learning Assistant and AI Avatar Videos help students learn at their own pace, provide more chances for reflection, and increase metacognitive engagement. International students, in particular, reported very high levels of satisfaction, highlighting the model's effectiveness in supporting multilingual learners and easing cultural and language challenges.

From a pedagogical standpoint, the findings underline the need for thoughtfully designed HyFlex Learning environments that incorporate AI tools. These tools promote self-directed learning, offer adaptive support, and enable culturally responsive instruction. The results indicate that AI should be viewed as an essential part of the learning system, providing real-time feedback, personalized guidance, and flexible content review. This shifts the role of educators to learning experience designers who use AI insights to customize interventions, promote deeper learning, and maintain meaningful interaction with students.

On an institutional level, the study shows strong support for the broader use of AI-powered HyFlex Learning. The widespread acceptance across faculties, especially high engagement from international groups, suggests that universities can effectively scale this model by developing clear policy frameworks, strong infrastructure, and solid faculty development programmes. These structural supports are crucial for ensuring equitable access and maximizing the teaching benefits of AI-enhanced learning tools.

Theoretically, the study expands the idea of HyFlex Learning to include a model of intelligent flexibility. In this model, AI adapts to student needs while partnering with human facilitators. This adds a new aspect to existing frameworks by including AI presence alongside established elements like teaching presence and cognitive presence. AI presence reflects the system's ability to deliver personalized guidance, automated feedback, and tailored learning paths, greatly improving the HyFlex Learning experience.

Overall, the AI-powered HyFlex Learning model provides a sustainable and forward-looking approach to higher education. By combining the strengths of technology with the unique value of human guidance, it creates learning environments that are accessible, adaptive, fair, and globally relevant. This positions institutions to meet the changing demands of a digitally driven academic landscape. While implemented at Taylor's University, the proposed framework is tool-agnostic and adaptable to institutions operating with different learning management systems, AI assistants, or immersive learning platforms. The model emphasizes pedagogical design principles rather than reliance on specific technologies, enabling contextual adaptation across diverse institutional environments.

REFERENCES

Alasgarova, R., & Rzayev, J. (2024). The changing role of educators in the age of artificial intelligence: Molding minds at the digital dawn. *Ubiquity Proceedings*, *4*(1), 6. Advance online publication. DOI: 10.5334/uproc.128

Aspandi, A., & Muttaqin, M. A. (2025). Transforming Teacher Roles in Indonesia's Digital Era: Enhancing Learning Effectiveness and Student Engagement. *Journal of General Education and Humanities*, *4*(4), 1495–1510. DOI: 10.58421/gehu.v4i4.616

Beatty, B. J. (2019). *Hybrid-Flexible Course Design: Implementing student-directed hybrid classes*. EdTech Books., DOI: 10.59668/33

Boehm, M., & Boerboom, S. (2023). Faculty Experiences of HyFlex: An Exploratory Study. *Educational Research: Theory and Practice*, *34*(2), 43–47. DOI: 10.46799/ijssr.v3i11.605

Deckker, D., Sumanasekara, S., & Fakhrou, A. (2025). AI-Powered Personalised Learning: Promise and Pitfalls. DOI: 10.30574/wjarr.2025.26.3.2425

Finkel-Gates, A. (2024). *Embracing inclusivity and flexibility in higher education: A study of HyFlex delivery and its impact on diverse undergraduates in the post-pandemic era*. Open Scholarship of Teaching and Learning., DOI: 10.56230/osotl.113

Gregorac, A., Brünner, B., & Ebner, M. (2025, March). Chatbots in Education: A Systematic Rapid Literature Review. In Society for Information Technology & Teacher Education International Conference (pp. 652-657). Association for the Advancement of Computing in Education (AACE). DOI: 10.3217/0NQA4-6XH12

Gu, Y., Feijoo-Garcia, M. A., Zhang, Y., Magana, A. J., Benes, B., & Popescu, V. (2024, March). An xr environment for ai education: Design and first implementation. In 2024 IEEE Conference on Virtual Reality and 3D User Interfaces Abstracts and Workshops (VRW) (pp. 157-162). IEEE. DOI: 10.1109/VRW62533.2024.00032

Hidayati, N., Sindangsari, L. P., & Mustika, N. (2025). Optimizing HyFlex Learning: Pedagogical, Technological, and Policy Perspectives. *Sinergi International Journal of Education*, *3*(1), 13–25. DOI: 10.61194/education.v3i1.700

Hmoud, M., Daher, W., & Ayyoub, A. (2025). *The Impact of AI, XR, and Combined AI-XR on Student Satisfaction: A Moderated Mediation Analysis of Engagement and Student Characteristics*. IEEE., DOI: 10.1109/ACCESS.2025.3597239

Holmes, W., & Miao, F. (2023). *Guidance for generative AI in education and research*. Unesco Publishing., DOI: 10.54675/EWZM9535

Kolb, D. A. (2015). *Experiential learning: Experience as the source of learning and development.* Pearson Education.

Lee, D. C., & Chang, C. Y. (2025). Evaluating self-directed learning competencies in digital learning environments: A meta-analysis. *Education and Information Technologies, 30*(6), 6847–6868. DOI: 10.1007/s10639-024-13083-2

Merchant, Z.. (2024). Virtual reality-based versus conventional instruction: A systematic review. *Computers & Education, 212*, 104678. DOI: 10.1016/j.compedu.2023.104678

Niemi, H. (2024). AI in education and learning: Perspectives on the education ecosystem. In *New Frontiers in Science in the Era of AI* (pp. 169–194). Springer Nature Switzerland., DOI: 10.1007/978-3-031-61187-2_11

OECD. (2024). *The potential impact of artificial intelligence on equity and inclusion in education.* OECD Publishing., DOI: 10.1787/6b6db410-

Pintrich, P. R. (2004). A conceptual framework for assessing motivation and self-regulated learning in college students. *Educational Psychology Review, 16*(4), 385–407. DOI: 10.1007/s10648-004-0006-x

Rigopouli, K., Kotsifakos, D., & Psaromiligkos, Y. (2025). Vygotsky's creativity options and ideas in 21st-century technology-enhanced learning design. *Education Sciences, 15*(2), 257. DOI: 10.3390/educsci15020257

Samala, A. D., Bojic, L., Soha, R., Miftachul Arif, Y., Tsoy, D., & Pereira Coelho, D. (2024). Extended reality for education: Mapping current trends, challenges, and applications. *Jurnal Pendidikan Teknologi Kejuruan, 7*(3), 140–169. DOI: 10.24036/jptk.v7i3.37623

Stracke, C. M., Bothe, P., Adler, S., Heller, E. S., Deuchler, J., Pomino, J., & Wölfel, M. (2025). Immersive virtual reality in higher education: A systematic review of the scientific literature. *Virtual Reality (Waltham Cross), 29*(2), 1–21. DOI: 10.1007/s10055-025-01136-x

Yin, J., Zhu, Y., Goh, T. T., Wu, W., & Hu, Y. (2024). Using Educational Chatbots with Metacognitive Feedback to Improve Science Learning. *Applied Sciences (Basel, Switzerland), 14*(20), 9345. DOI: 10.3390/app14209345

Zawacki-Richter, O., Bai, J. Y., Lee, K., Slagter van Tryon, P. J., & Prinsloo, P. (2024). New advances in artificial intelligence applications in higher education? *International Journal of Educational Technology in Higher Education, 21*(1), 32. DOI: 10.1186/s41239-024-00464-3

Zimmerman, B. J. (2002). Becoming a self-regulated learner: An overview. *Theory into Practice*, *41*(2), 64–70. DOI: 10.1207/s15430421tip4102_2

Chapter 2

Bridging Physical and Virtual Realms:

The Role of AI and Immersive Technologies in Next-Generation Learning

Jiaoyang Ding
http://orcid.org/0009-0004-6760-3102
The Education University of Hong Kong, Hong Kong

Tsz Cheung Chan
http://orcid.org/0009-0006-8072-0244
The Education University of Hong Kong, Hong Kong

Winnie Wong
http://orcid.org/0009-0009-4030-562X
The Education University of Hong Kong, Hong Kong

Hong Fu
http://orcid.org/0000-0003-2246-7552
The Education University of Hong Kong, Hong Kong

ABSTRACT

The integration of artificial intelligence (AI) and immersive technologies in education has created a dynamic shift in how learning is delivered and experienced. This chapter examines the potential of AI-driven immersive technologies to bridge physical and virtual realms, enabling next-generation learning experiences that are more engaging, inclusive, and personalized. By utilizing a diverse range of platforms, including web interfaces, mobile devices, personal computers, VR headsets,

DOI: 10.4018/979-8-3373-6182-6.ch002

and Cave Automatic Virtual Environment (CAVE) systems, educators can create flexible, interactive learning ecosystems that cater to the diverse needs of students. It explores how these technologies enhance student engagement, to improve knowledge retention, and foster collaboration, offering a framework for institutions to adopt multi-device and immersive approaches in education.

1. INTRODUCTION

Technological advancements have often shaped education, offering new opportunities for students and educators alike with each innovation. In recent years, the rise of artificial intelligence (AI) and immersive technologies has presented the potential to transform learning environments (Selvakumar & Sivakumar, 2023). These technologies enable the creation of dynamic, interactive and adaptive educational experiences that transcend the limitations of traditional classrooms (Selvakumar & Sivakumar, 2023). Unlike conventional approaches, where physical and digital learning are separate, AI-powered immersive technologies uniquely bridge these realms. They provide students with a holistic and engaging learning experience, preparing them for the complexities of the modern world. Integrating virtual reality (VR) and augmented reality (AR) enables educators to transform traditional paradigms and enhance student engagement through immersive learning experiences (Pramanik & Kayyali, 2024; Alhazzaa & Yan, 2025). This integration promotes active participation and fosters a deeper understanding of complex concepts, reshaping educational paradigms for future learners (Seenathmol, 2024). This chapter will discuss the implications of these technologies for educators, including the need for specialised training to implement immersive learning strategies effectively. It will also explore the role of AI and immersive technologies in reshaping the landscape of higher education, with a focus on multi-device accessibility and on creating diverse learning environments. The ability to deliver content across diverse devices, such as web platforms, mobile applications, PCs, VR headsets, and CAVE systems, ensures that students can engage with learning materials regardless of their technological resources. This flexibility supports hybrid learning environments and fosters accessibility (Jacka & Lindsay, 2022). The chapter emphasises that these technologies, when integrated into education, can enhance student engagement, motivation, and practical skill development. Moreover, the chapter delves into the role of AI in personalising and adapting learning experiences. AI's ability to identify student behaviour (Dai & Ke, 2022) provides real-time feedback and adjusts content delivery based on individual needs (Kataria, 2023), ensuring that every learner receives a tailored educational journey. Coupled with immersive technologies, AI creates a powerful synergy that transforms passive learning into an active, participatory process (Alhazzaa & Yan, 2025). The chapter also examines the challenges associated with implementing these technologies, including accessibility, inclusivity, and the digital divide, and offers strategies to overcome these barriers.

Building on these foundations, the chapter presents cases where AI-driven immersive environments improve knowledge retention and foster collaboration among students. For instance, AI-powered simulations enable learners to experiment with real-world scenarios in safe, controlled settings, thereby increasing retention through experiential learning (Dai & Ke, 2022). Studies show that immersive VR experiences can increase student engagement by enabling collaborative problem-solving in shared virtual spaces, breaking down geographical barriers, and encouraging diverse perspectives (Conrad et al., 2024). This is particularly evident in STEM fields, where AI algorithms adapt content difficulty in real time, thereby promoting deeper comprehension and teamwork (Avci et al., 2025).

To facilitate widespread adoption, the chapter outlines practical approaches for educational institutions to integrate these technologies. This includes phased implementation strategies, starting with pilot programs on accessible devices, such as mobile apps and web interfaces, before scaling to advanced setups such as VR/AR environments. Institutions are encouraged to leverage AI for data-driven decision-making, such as predicting student needs and optimising resource allocation, while partnering with tech providers to ensure compatibility across platforms (Khan et al., 2025). Additionally, the approaches emphasise developing students' skills, including workshops on AI ethics and immersive content creation, to empower them to design hybrid learning ecosystems (Tan et al., 2025).

Addressing the persistent challenges, the chapter proposes targeted strategies to promote equity. To address the digital divide, recommendations include subsidised device programs and cloud-based access to immersive content, with low-bandwidth options for underserved regions (Zhao et al., 2021). Inclusivity efforts focus on AI features such as adaptive interfaces for students with disabilities, including voice-guided VR navigation, while accessibility standards are integrated into technology design from the outset (Chalkiadakis et al., 2024). By mitigating these barriers, institutions can create truly equitable learning opportunities. This chapter also serves as a comprehensive roadmap for harnessing AI and immersive technologies in higher education. It equips stakeholders with insights to navigate the transition to next-generation learning, preparing students for academic success and thriving in a technology-driven future in which the physical and virtual realms converge (Kamalov et al., 2023; Song et al., 2024).

2. AI AND IMMERSIVE TECHNOLOGIES IN FUTURE LEARNING

The adoption of AI-integrated immersive technologies in education is shifting from experimental tools to integral components of hybrid learning models. Kamalov et al. (2023) utilised bibliometric analysis to map thematic clusters around AI and VR/AR in education, emphasising the potential for sustainable revolutions in skill development. Stracke et al. (2025) identified a lack of standardised frameworks but growing integration in extracurricular labs, with single-player setups prevalent and minimal collaborative features. Zekeik et al. (2025) synthesised studies from 2014 to 2024, aligning AR and VR with constructivist theories and noting an increase in their adoption in distance learning for virtual collaboration. Adoption is most prominent in STEM and health sciences, where AI facilitates real-time adaptations, but remains underexplored in the humanities due to content challenges (Avci et al., 2025; Sümer & Vaněček, 2025).

Empirical evidence demonstrates substantial benefits in engagement, retention, and skill acquisition when AI augments immersive technologies. Dai and Ke (2022) mapped AI applications in simulation-based learning, revealing that techniques such as machine learning and NLP improve VR/AR feedback mechanisms, yielding retention rates 20-40% higher than those of traditional approaches. In higher education, Stracke et al. (2025) found mixed but generally positive effects on motivation and knowledge retention, including enhanced spatial awareness in medical simulations, although these effects were sometimes offset by cognitive overload. Llanos-Ruiz et al. (2025) analysed data from 2020 to 2025, highlighting VR's role in enhancing digital competencies, reducing anxiety in language learning, and managing cognitive load among learners with low spatial ability. Zekeik et al. (2025) reported improved academic performance in mathematics and science through interactive visuals, as well as non-cognitive gains in critical thinking and collaboration through game-based activities. S. Park et al. (2024) conducted a meta-analysis in nursing education, showing moderate-to-high effects on knowledge and self-efficacy in AI-augmented VR scenarios. Khan et al. (2025) underscored AI's predictive analytics for identifying learning gaps and enhancing achievement through personalised, immersive pathways. AI-enhanced immersive technologies have diverse applications, particularly in fields that require experiential learning. In STEM, Avci et al. (2025) surveyed educators and found that AI-enabled VR/AR systems promote collaborative problem-solving and the comprehension of complex concepts, such as those in engineering simulations. Sümer and Vaněček (2025) note the predominant use of scenario-based simulations in medical and engineering courses, though their effectiveness is mixed due to limited interactivity. In health sciences, Conrad et al. (2024) examined the efficacy of VR for training and enabling safe practice in high-stakes environments. Chalkiadakis et al. (2024) focused on inclusivity, reviewing 28 articles in which AI/VR tools support students with disabilities by improving autonomy and social skills through adaptive interfaces. In the context of teacher professional development, Tan et al. (2025) emphasised AI's role in creating hybrid ecosystems for designing immersive content. Zekeik et al. (2025) highlighted applications in special education for autism, including autism-specific simulations that foster inclusion. Non-STEM areas, such as language and arts, show potential but limited adoption, often restricted to AR overlays (Song et al., 2024; Llanos-Ruiz et al., 2025).

Despite advantages, significant barriers may reduce widespread implementation. Zhao et al. (2021) analysed data, identifying infrastructure and literacy gaps that widen the digital divide, particularly for rural learners. Ethical issues, including algorithmic bias and privacy, are prominent; Kamalov et al. (2023) warned that over-reliance on AI may diminish critical thinking. Stracke et al. (2025) noted technical limitations, including cybersickness and small-sample bias, while Zekeik et al. (2025) cited high costs, usability issues, health risks (e.g., motion sickness), and a lack of teacher training. Sümer and Vaněček (2025) highlighted pedagogical challenges, such as inadequate guidelines, which lead to reduced effectiveness. Llanos-Ruiz et al. (2025) raised concerns about data misuse in VR environments and the need for governance in AI-VR convergence. Institutional resistance and methodological shortcomings, like short-term designs, further limit generalizability (Dai & Ke, 2022; Conrad et al., 2024). Drawing upon the transformative potential, benefits, and persistent challenges of AI-integrated immersive technologies in higher education, this chapter proposes a series of practical case studies and technology solutions to address implementation gaps and cultivate essential future-ready skills among learners. These cases demonstrate innovative applications that leverage metaverse environments, digital gamification, and AI-powered immersive systems to bridge physical and virtual realms, fostering competencies in data security, ethical AI use, and creative problem-solving. By presenting actionable strategies grounded in multi-device accessibility and inclusivity, we provide a framework for educators and institutions to adopt these technologies, ensuring access and preparing students for a technology-driven future through experiential, personalised learning pathways.

Synthesising the literature above, four interconnected thematic strands emerge that frame the subsequent case studies. First, AI-driven personalisation acts as a key enabler, with research consistently showing that adaptive algorithms and predictive analytics can customise immersive content to meet individual learners' needs, leading to higher retention and engagement (Dai & Ke, 2022; Khan et al., 2025). Second, immersive experiential learning via VR/AR, metaverse, and CAVE environments offers a pedagogical approach that makes abstract concepts concrete, supporting constructivist learning and embodied cognition across various fields (Zekeik et al., 2025; Stracke et al., 2025). Third, ethical and inclusive design is a critical, cross-cutting concern: the literature highlights the importance of bias mitigation, data privacy protections, and adaptable interfaces to provide equitable access for all learners, including those with disabilities (Chalkiadakis et al., 2024; Holmes et al., 2022; Zhao et al., 2021). Fourth, ongoing barriers, such as infrastructure deficiencies, potential cognitive overload, and a lack of teacher training, emphasise the need for phased, evidence-based implementation strategies (Stracke et al., 2025; Zekeik et al., 2025).

3. CASE 1: LEVERAGING AI-EMPOWERED METAVERSE FOR PROMOTING DATA SECURITY AND ETHICAL USE OF AI

3.1. Designing Virtual Environments in the Gamified Metaverse

Generative AI empowers the metaverse by autonomously creating new content, such as text, images, audio, and video, tailoring virtual worlds to individual users and enhancing their educational experiences through personalised storytelling, adaptive learning paths, and dynamic interactions (Hart & Shakir, 2024). In this context, gamification, the application of game design elements and principles in non-game contexts, has proven effective for enhancing student engagement and motivation in higher education (Hamari et al., 2016; Hong et al., 2024; Alhazzaa & Yan, 2025). By leveraging the inherent appeal of games, gamification transforms traditional learning environments into dynamic, interactive spaces that foster active participation and deeper understanding. When combined with AI, gamification can further amplify its potential, creating adaptive and personalised learning experiences that cater to diverse student needs.

The affordance of metaverse technology in education lies in its ability to provide users with an "immersive" experience (J. Park et al., 2024). When applied to educational settings, the metaverse mainly takes the form of games and is based on constructivism and embodied cognition theory to conduct teaching activities (Ye et al., 2024), which helps enhance collaboration and interactive learning among students, greatly enhancing the learning experience (Luo et al., 2024; Kang et al., 2024). The integration of generative AI (e.g., LLMs, VLMs) into the metaverse can enhance the authenticity and immersion of the game experience. Generative AI can apply the knowledge-rich and contextually relevant content it generates within the metaverse to enable intelligent reasoning in teaching, rapid content generation, and intelligent collaboration (An et al., 2025), thereby supporting personalised, gamified self-regulated learning, achieving precise instruction, and enhancing learning efficiency. In terms of learning outcomes, J. Park et al. (2024) developed an English practice platform based on Unity3D that emphasises interactive dialogue with AI avatars in specific scenarios, thereby enhancing learners' second language learning outcomes; NivTA (Ye et al., 2024), a virtual teaching assistant, integrates LLM, CAVE, and virtual avatars to achieve simulated interaction in teaching, thereby enhancing students' collaborative learning levels. On the emotional front, using generative AI-supported tasks in the metaverse significantly increased pre-service English teachers' confidence and intention to learn English (Lee et al., 2025). Due to the authentic communication opportunities, interactive environment, and emotional support it provided, while learning and interaction in metaverse platforms may not satisfy all students, most students found them enjoyable (Rojas et al., 2023), as well as enhancing students' sense of interaction and belonging (Ng et al., 2023).

It is essential in developing a cohesive system that ensures compatibility between gamified generative AI and the metaverse while addressing data security and ethical imperatives. Existing studies focus on individual components, such as AI personalisation or gamification strategies (Hamari et al., 2016; Abbas et al., 2023), but lack an integrated approach that optimises their synergy in educational settings (Velazquez-Garcia et al., 2024). Moreover, fostering university students' awareness of data security and AI ethics is essential for responsible engagement in these environments. Students, as digital natives, frequently interact with technology but often lack the knowledge to navigate privacy risks or recognise ethical issues in AI applications (Holmes et al., 2022). This case proposes that the educational potential of the metaverse be optimised by integrating generative AI practices with data security and ethical AI in higher education, thereby creating gamified content to deliver immersive and compatible learning experiences. Additionally, it emphasises embedding data literacy and AI ethics education within the curriculum to empower students to be responsible, independent learners throughout their university education.

While virtual learning environments have been increasingly adopted in higher education, including applications in language learning (J. Park et al., 2024), collaborative knowledge building (Ng et al., 2023), and professional training (Conrad et al., 2024), the distinctiveness of this case lies in its integrated approach that simultaneously addresses three critical dimensions: (a) the synergy of generative AI with gamified metaverse design, (b) the embedding of data security and AI ethics education within immersive experiences, and (c) the compatibility across multiple devices to ensure broad accessibility. Conceptually, this case follows an Input–Process–Output framework: the input comprises students' prior knowledge, the metaverse platform infrastructure, and AI-driven NPC capabilities; the process involves guided exploration, gamified scenario-based learning, and AI-personalised interactions within themed zones; and the output encompasses enhanced knowledge of data security and AI ethics, demonstrated through achievement scores, qualitative feedback, and observed behavioural changes.

We developed a metaverse environment that integrates gamified elements to address the complex challenges of data security and the ethical use of AI in higher education. This system creates a comprehensive virtual learning ecosystem that reinforces principles of academic integrity in AI and essential cybersecurity competencies through immersive, interactive experiences. First, the environment is structured around a central space that serves as an orientation hub and social gathering area. Upon entry, students encounter interactive displays presenting foundational concepts in data security, privacy protection, and academic integrity. From this central hub, learners navigate to specialised learning zones using personalised avatars controlled via a keyboard-and-mouse interface, with additional gesture-based controls available for VR users. Second, our environment comprises 10 primary thematic zones, each with a distinct visual identity and contextual elements that reflect its respective focus area (see Table 1). Within each thematic zone, students engage with gamified scenarios that embody fundamental values identified in contemporary academic integrity frameworks. These scenarios present contextually appropriate challenges mirroring real-world academic and professional settings. For instance, in certain data protection domains, students participate in data classification exercises that require them to identify categories of sensitive information and implement appropriate security controls. The system employs progressive difficulty scaling to maintain an optimal challenge level corresponding to each student's demonstrated competence (Csikszentmihalyi & Larson, 2014; Hamari et al., 2016).

Additionally, non-Player Characters (NPCs) were designed as specialised domain experts who provide targeted assistance across distinct areas of expertise (e.g., regulatory compliance, technical security, ethics). The primary AI NPC appears as a human-like avatar capable of contextually relevant dialogue. This NPC was developed through a customisation process with the latest LLM, which is named 'DeepSeek v3', involving pre-defined prompts, structured knowledge bases for efficient information retrieval, and an interpreter defining personality parameters and behavioural constraints. The NPC employs context-aware dialogue capabilities that maintain a memory of personal character interactions across learning sessions and adapt guidance approaches accordingly (Luckin & Cukurova, 2019). The games in each thematic zone reinforce domain-specific concepts through interactive challenges requiring theoretical knowledge. In the Data Handling and Protection zone, for instance, students need to classify different types of information and implement appropriate security measures, such as encryption or access controls. Figure 1 shows the designed environment, gamified elements, and AI-driven NPCs in this system.

Figure 1. Environment and gamified element design. (a) badges. (b) learning materials. (c) AI-driven NPC dialogue. (d) a game level-maze

(a)

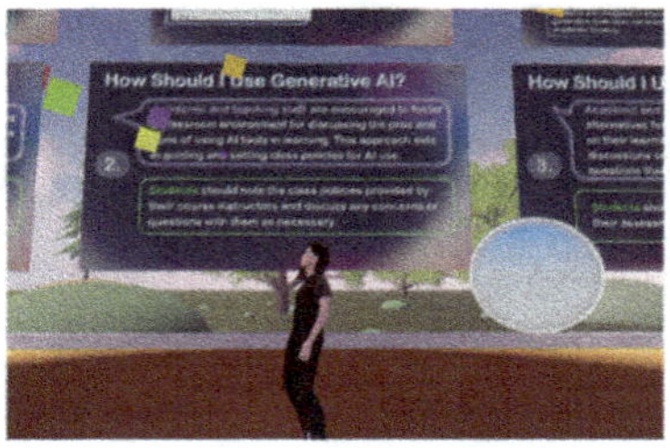

(b)

(c)

(d)

With respect to the design principle, the learning environment employs multiple layers of gamification mechanisms aligned with self-determination theory (Ryan & Deci, 2000) to enhance engagement and motivation for students' competence and activate their autonomy. Beyond basic achievement badges, the skill development pathways were designed to evaluate security clearance levels in some restricted areas of space. For example, a hidden exam for in-depth exploration, and a reward system in which students earn "tokens" by consistently demonstrating ethical behaviour and security awareness in scenarios. Collaborative mechanics include team-based ethical challenges that require specialised roles and decision-making scenarios involving human-machine collaboration. These gamified elements foster both autonomy and relatedness, thereby sustaining engagement in educational contexts (Dicheva et al., 2015).

Table 1. Design of thematic zones of the system

Theme	Design of thematic zones	Game elements
Main Lobbies	• The comprehensive spaces based on the university model, featuring AI-driven NPCs, task introduction videos, learning materials, and sub-space portals.	NPC instant responses; Levels.
Data security and personal awareness with AI (five zones)	• Answer 6 questions about personal data protection and escape from the locked room. • Find the correct path of knowledge to get out of the maze. • Survival game: Find the exit of the maze. One wrong answer and the player fall into the abyss. • Identify parts of messages, websites, AI, or phone calls that contain phishing. • Identify five common mistakes in learning environments that could lead to information leaks.	Badges; Quests; Challenges.
Academic integrity and ethical use of AI	• Discuss with NPC for responsibly teamworking and assign tasks to them. • Make decisions when faced with ambiguous data sources in assignments and the dilemma of whether to declare the use of AI. • Make decisions among the honestly of writing a paper with AI declaration. • Identify that some behaviours could be considered unethical. • Identify that some behaviours could be considered respectful.	Badges; Levels; Quests; Narratives; Scores.

3.2. Developing the Compatible Virtual Environments with Generative AI

The design and development of our integrated metaverse learning platform represented an advancement in integrating the metaverse with educational objectives, emphasising broad access, effective teaching strategies, and careful integration of artificial intelligence. We structured the system as interconnected modules, each addressing a core aspect of the user experience. This section outlines the primary technical decisions and methods we adopted, with particular emphasis on how they enhance educational outcomes in higher education. By prioritising simplicity for users, reliable performance, and ethical standards, we crafted a digital space that promotes group learning and practical insights into topics such as maintaining academic honesty and navigating cybersecurity risks.

From the outset, the access layer aimed to ensure seamless entry into the virtual environment across everyday devices such as phones, laptops, and VR gear. Our goal was inclusivity, so we incorporated adaptive features that automatically adjust to device capabilities, avoiding any need for special setups. On mobile phones, this meant streamlined loading to conserve data and battery life, enabling quick joins via web-based apps. For computers, we enabled sharper images and faster interactions, while VR headsets introduced depth through 3D immersion and gesture controls. A built-in system facilitates customisation of the experience, ensuring smooth operation. Our evaluations confirmed high compatibility rates, making the platform truly welcoming for diverse learners and reducing tech-related barriers in education.

In the front-end user interface and services layer, we focused on creating an intuitive, engaging navigation and collaboration experience. We selected a proven virtual world builder for its robust support for multi-user spaces, device flexibility, and straightforward integration with educational tools such as course management systems. Avatar customisation became a key feature, allowing users to design representations that reflect their identities, a feature that research shows boosts engagement in online learning. We also integrated real-time group tools, such as virtual meeting spaces within themed zones, to enable students to brainstorm or share ideas. To enhance interactivity, we employed a versatile engine, such as Unity, that renders dynamic scenes across platforms. This enabled natural movements, conversations, and responses within the environment, fostering a sense of presence. In terms of environment settings in Unity, we carefully designed virtual spaces to mimic real-world learning areas, using modular building blocks (prefabs) to efficiently construct themed zones. For instance, cybersecurity areas featured fortified digital landscapes with interactive elements such as virtual firewalls, whereas academic integrity zones resembled libraries with searchable bookshelves. These settings were optimised for educational flow, with pathways that guide users through progressively challenging tasks, encouraging exploration and discovery. Progress tracking was integrated to monitor student achievement, including quiz and discussion completions, and to link to external learning platforms for grading and feedback. Data on user behaviour helped personalise paths, suggesting resources tailored to individual needs. In practice, this meant that themed areas could adapt visually and interactively, maintaining consistent performance even during group sessions.

Lighting design in the virtual classroom spaces served both functional and pedagogical purposes. Realistic lighting simulations, using both baked and real-time global illumination techniques, created inviting, focused environments that enhance concentration while maintaining consistent performance. The symbolic use of lighting reinforced educational themes: in cybersecurity modules, dimmer, shadowy areas evoked hidden threats, while brighter, open spaces in integrity zones conveyed transparency.

From a pedagogical perspective, these technical design decisions directly support student engagement and HyFlex learning goals. The adaptive multi-device architecture ensures that all students can participate meaningfully regardless of their technological resources. The symbolic use of lighting and spatial design reinforces conceptual understanding through environmental cues, a strategy grounded in situated cognition theory, wherein the learning context itself becomes part of the instructional message. Moreover, the modular construction of thematic zones enables educators to reconfigure learning pathways for different cohorts.

For the AI services layer, we developed a sophisticated AI agent embedded within a non-player character (NPC) avatar to serve as an interactive guide. This AI agent was crafted to align closely with educational aims, providing tailored support while upholding principles of accuracy and fairness. The development process emphasised creating an agent that is approachable yet knowledgeable, akin to a virtual mentor. We began by outlining core behaviours through guided instruction, ensuring that the agent focused on key domains, such as explaining proper citation to avoid plagiarism and identifying phishing tactics in cybersecurity scenarios.

A key step in developing this AI agent was building a robust knowledge base. We organised information into accessible categories, drawing from trusted educational sources on ethics and digital safety. This setup enabled the agent to quickly retrieve relevant facts during interactions, making responses contextually rich and reliable. For instance, if a student asks about data privacy, the agent could draw on real-world examples and adapt explanations to the learner's level. We refined the agent's personality to be encouraging and patient, using techniques to simulate empathy, such as rephrasing questions to confirm understanding or offering follow-ups to deepen discussions. This personalisation helped transform passive learning into active dialogue, in which the agent might pose scenarios such as "What would you do if you found uncredited content?" to stimulate critical thinking.

To further enhance the AI agent's role within the NPC, we incorporated adaptive learning mechanisms. The agent subtly tracks user progress, adjusting difficulty based on responses—for beginners, it provides simple breakdowns; for advanced users, it introduces complex challenges such as ethical dilemmas in AI use. Ethical safeguards were integral: we embedded filters to detect and correct potential biases, ensured diverse perspectives in the advice, and limited the agent's access to verified information to prevent the spread of misinformation. Testing showed that this approach increased students' concept retention by encouraging repeated interactions. Powered by scalable cloud resources, the agent can handle multiple conversations simultaneously and respond within seconds to maintain a natural, immersive flow.

Supporting all this, the back-end services layer managed the underlying connections and operations. We implemented reliable syncing for shared actions, ensuring that when one user interacts with an object, others see it instantly. Cloud-based scaling handled varying class sizes, from small groups to larger lectures. Open standards facilitated the addition of new content, such as 3D models of security tools, and educator-friendly tools enabled instructors to customise zones without deep technical knowledge. Visually, we prioritised realistic elements, such as lifelike textures and animations, to make the space inviting. User controls were designed for ease and to adapt to different devices, ensuring a consistent experience.

Figure 2. Technological stack and system architecture

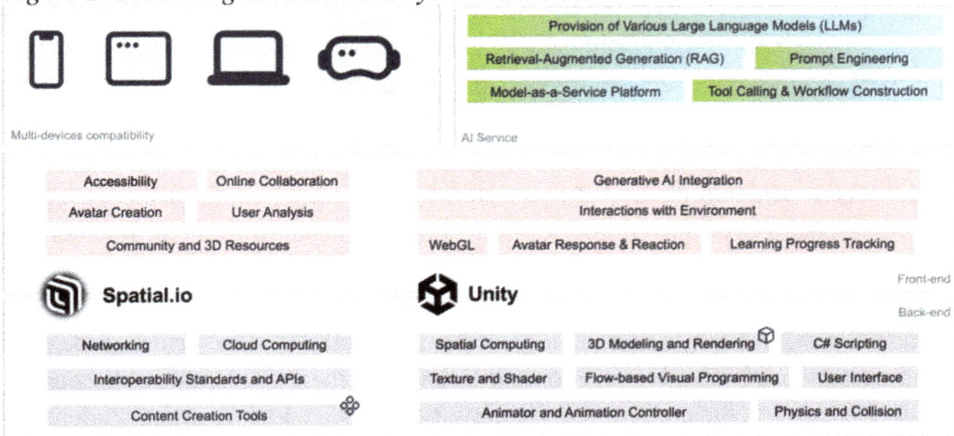

3.3 Implementation and Evaluation for the virtual learning environment

The workshops were attended by 62 university students from diverse academic backgrounds (see Figure 3). The implementation was a resounding success, demonstrating strong learner engagement and satisfaction. The assessment revealed near-universal approval among participants. The core educational objective, enhancement of knowledge in AI ethics and data security, garnered strong endorsement, with students affirming that this immersive, contextualised learning model effectively conveyed complex concepts and "enhanced their knowledge." Furthermore, the perceived value and motivational impact of the learning experience were robustly validated. The workshop inspired students to protect their data and use AI responsibly, actively, and participants overwhelmingly agreed that the session was "worth attending." This high satisfaction was grounded in the workshop's structure, with students praising the workshop's organisation, reflecting the efficacy of the structured four-phase flow, straightforward navigation, and seamless alignment between content and student expectations. This foundational structure proved essential for facilitating a highly engaging immersive experience. Observational evidence from system logs and in-depth focus group interviews provided rich, narrative substantiation that the system achieved its pedagogical objectives. Logs indicated a pronounced level of engagement with the AI-driven components; the AI NPC was recurrently consulted, evolving from a mere functional tool into an indispensable element of the immersive narrative, esteemed for its contextual acuity and personalised, anthropomorphic responses.

To ensure the effectiveness of the system implementation, the workshop was designed around a four-phased structured learning process, aimed at maximising student engagement and deepening their understanding of complex ethical concepts. The workshop was student-centred, using an AI-driven metaverse environment as the primary teaching platform for approximately 90–120 minutes. The workshop followed a four-stage process. It began with the onboarding and orientation phase, where students entered the metaverse platform, customised their avatars, and completed a brief navigation tutorial to master basic movement, interaction, and communication with the AI NPC. This progressed to the guided exploration phase, in which the AI virtual assistant guided students to the main learning space to grasp the workshop's theme (data security and AI ethics). The virtual guide provided personalised introductory content tailored to their academic backgrounds. Following this was the core immersive activities phase, which required students to enter distinct thematic sub-spaces. In these spaces, they engaged deeply with the material by completing interactive, gamified tasks, such as scenario simulations and ethical dilemma decision-making, to earn scores and achievements. The process concluded with the conclusion and reflection phase, where students returned to the main space, the system displayed their task completion and achievement scores, and they were guided through a review session before proceeding to the post-workshop evaluations. The experience design focused on three core pillars to transform abstract theoretical knowledge into tangible, relatable experiences. Foremost were spatial storytelling and contextualization, in which abstract concepts such as "data security" and "AI ethics" were translated into concrete virtual spaces and interactive scenarios. For instance, students directly experienced the urgency of data protection by solving encryption challenges. Secondly, AI-driven personalised guidance was central: the AI NPC in the environment served as a faithful learning companion, with contextual awareness that enabled it to offer customised hints and answers based on the student's real-time progress, ensuring personalised support. Finally, the design incorporated gamification mechanics and community elements. A clear achievement system and score ranking was implemented to transform learning into an engaging digital adventure. At the same time, participation via customised avatars encouraged peer-to-peer communication and collaborative problem-solving to address virtual ethical dilemmas.

To systematically evaluate the effectiveness of the AI agent-empowered gamified metaverse system, a mixed-methods study with a quasi-experimental design was conducted. A total of 62 university students who participated in the workshop were assigned to an experimental group (N = 32) using the AI agent-empowered gamification system and a control group (N = 30) using conventional digital gamification without the AI agent. Both groups underwent pre- and post-surveys, knowledge tests, in-process interim assessments, and semi-structured focus group interviews to measure their engagement, learning outcomes, and perceptions of technology use. The perception questionnaire was based on the Technology Acceptance Model (TAM), adapted from Al-Adwan et al. (2023), comprising 14 items across six dimensions: Perceived Usefulness (PU), Perceived Ease of Use (PEU), Perceived Classroom Relevance (PCR), Perceived Enjoyment (PE), Self-Efficacy (SE), and Perceived Intention to Use (PI). The questionnaire employed a 5-point Likert scale (1 = strongly disagree; 5 = strongly agree), with an overall Cronbach's alpha of 0.93, indicating excellent internal consistency.

The analysis of students' perceptions revealed significantly more positive overall ratings in the experimental group (M = 4.62, SD = 0.47) compared to the control group (M = 3.96, SD = 0.83), U = 229, $p < 0.001$. This pattern of significantly higher ratings was consistent across all six TAM dimensions. Specifically, perceived usefulness was significantly higher in the experimental group (M = 4.67, SD = 0.43) than in the control group (M = 3.91, SD = 1.03; U = 278, p = 0.003), suggesting that students recognised the AI agent as a valuable learning tool. Perceived ease of use was also significantly higher (experimental: M = 4.48, SD = 0.72; control: M = 3.68, SD = 1.12; U = 261, p = 0.001), indicating that the AI-driven interface facilitated intuitive interaction. Perceived classroom relevance (experimental: M = 4.62, SD = 0.55; control: M = 4.11, SD = 0.85; U = 311, p = 0.011) and perceived enjoyment (experimental: M = 4.71, SD = 0.47; control: M = 4.10, SD = 0.94; U = 289, p = 0.003) were both significantly higher, demonstrating that the AI agent enhanced both the practical relevance and the affective quality of the learning experience. Furthermore, self-efficacy (experimental: M = 4.45, SD = 0.79; control: M = 3.76, SD = 1.04; U = 261, p = 0.001) and intention to use (experimental: M = 4.70, SD = 0.43; control: M = 4.20, SD = 0.89; U = 311, p = 0.011) were significantly higher in the experimental group, indicating that the AI agent not only boosted students' confidence in navigating ethical content but also fostered a strong willingness to engage with such systems in future learning. Table 2 presents the detailed results.

Table 2. Results of Mann-Whitney U-tests for students' perceptions

Variables	Groups	N	Mean	SD	U	Sig.
Overall Perceptions	Experimental	32	4.62	0.47	229	<0.001***
	Control	30	3.96	0.83		
PU	Experimental	32	4.67	0.43	278	0.003**
	Control	30	3.91	1.03		
PEU	Experimental	32	4.48	0.72	261	0.001**
	Control	30	3.68	1.12		
PCR	Experimental	32	4.62	0.55	311	0.011*
	Control	30	4.11	0.85		
PE	Experimental	32	4.71	0.47	289	0.003**
	Control	30	4.10	0.94		
SE	Experimental	32	4.45	0.79	261	0.001**
	Control	30	3.76	1.04		
PI	Experimental	32	4.70	0.43	311	0.011*
	Control	30	4.20	0.89		

Note: PU = Perceived Usefulness; PEU = Perceived Ease of Use; PCR = Perceived Classroom Relevance; PE = Perceived Enjoyment; SE = Self-Efficacy; PI = Perceived Intention to Use. ***$p < .001$, **$p < .01$, *$p < .05$.

In the subsequent focus group interviews, participants provided detailed accounts of their learning experience, elucidating several pivotal factors. First, students consistently highlighted the spatial immersion of the metaverse as key to making abstract ethical concepts feel tangible and applicable. Second, the AI NPC was praised for its contextually relevant, personalised responses, with many participants describing it as a 'virtual mentor' rather than a simple chatbot. Third, the gamification mechanics — particularly the achievement and token reward system — were identified as primary drivers of sustained motivation across the session. Fourth, participants noted that the multi-device accessibility of the platform reduced anxiety around participation, enabling students who were less technically confident to engage fully.

These quantitative findings provide robust empirical evidence that the AI agent-empowered gamification system was perceived significantly more favourably than conventional digital gamification across all dimensions of technology acceptance. The following qualitative evidence from focus group interviews further contextualises and enriches these statistical patterns, revealing the experiential mechanisms underlying students' positive perceptions. Participants emphasised that the spatial layout of content within themed metaverse zones fundamentally reshaped their understanding of abstract ethical principles. One respondent noted: "Observing security principles enacted within a virtual environment resembling an authentic environment made them more accessible for understanding and retention." This suggests that the metaverse converts abstract concepts into dynamic, practical scenarios.

In summary, Case 1 demonstrates that integrating generative AI with a gamified metaverse environment can effectively promote university students' awareness of data security and ethical AI use. Key takeaways include: (a) spatial storytelling and contextualised virtual scenarios transform abstract ethical principles into concrete, relatable experiences; (b) AI-driven NPCs serve as responsive, personalised learning companions that provide scaffolded guidance adapted to individual learner progress; (c) gamification mechanics, including achievement systems, progressive challenges, and collaborative tasks, sustain engagement and motivation in technically complex subject matter; and (d) multi-device compatibility ensures broad accessibility, supporting diverse learner populations. These findings reinforce the pedagogical value of combining immersive technologies with AI-driven personalisation to enhance both cognitive outcomes and ethical awareness in higher education settings.

Figure 3. Highlights of workshops with the system. (a) Group discussion in the immersive environment. (b) Students are listening to the workshop. (c) VR experience of the system. (d) Tablet experience of the system

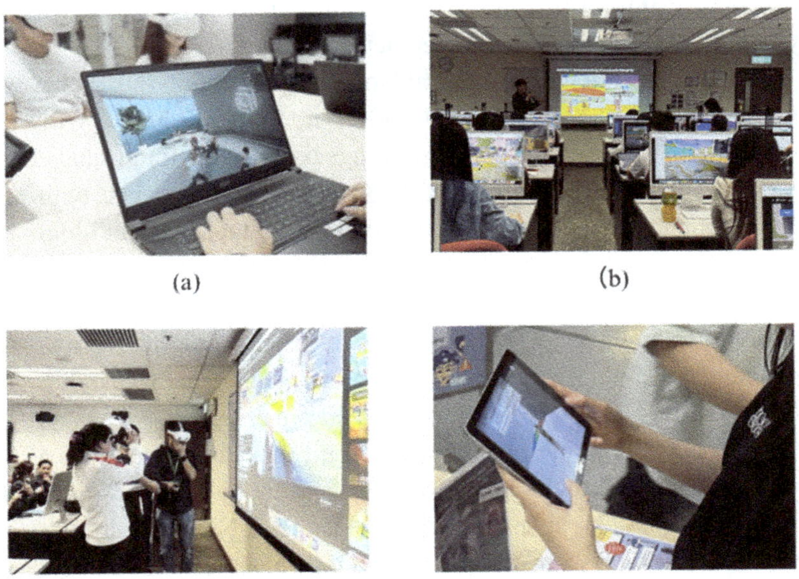

(a) (b) (c) (d)

4. CASE 2: AI-POWERED IMMERSIVE CAVE FOR CREATIVE LEARNING

4.1. Designing Agentic AI in the Cave Automatic Virtual Environment (CAVE)

In the increasingly dynamic and complex intersection of higher education paradigms and rapid advancements in emerging technologies, the physical classroom and virtual immersion are no longer disparate entities. Within this context, fostering AI literacy and comprehensive digital competence has emerged as a critical pedagogical imperative, essential for equipping diverse learners with the future-ready skills demanded by a technology-driven society. The Cave Automatic Virtual Environment (CAVE), defined as a sophisticated multi-projection immersive system, serves as a powerful and transformative bridge between these physical and virtual realms. By enabling users to step into fully enveloping, room-scale 3D simulations that respond dynamically to their creative inputs, the CAVE transcends the limitations of traditional desktop computing. This case study comprehensively examines a pioneering CAVE-based generative AI storytelling system. The system strategically leverages voice-activated generative AI to instantaneously transform verbal narratives into deeply interactive 3D worlds, thereby significantly enhancing user creativity, digital literacy, and sustained cognitive engagement.

By systematically integrating natural language processing (NLP) and advanced large language models (LLMs) with state-of-the-art CAVE technology, this initiative directly addresses several critical shortcomings prevalent in traditional educational settings. These include a pervasive lack of hands-on experience with emerging AI tools, a tendency towards passive learning of digital skills, and high technical barriers that exclude non-expert users. Instead of requiring extensive coding or 3D modelling expertise, this platform democratises the content creation process. Its core mission is to empower a broad spectrum of users—ranging from primary and university students to educators and community members—to express their creativity through an intuitive, accessible, voice-activated pipeline.

At the very core of this system operates a highly specialised generative AI agent, built upon robust LLM architectures and subject to rigorous human-in-the-loop refinement protocols. This agent employs sophisticated NLP algorithms to interpret nuanced spoken stories, seamlessly and instantaneously generating corresponding 3D models, dynamic environments, and high-fidelity skyboxes in real time. Unlike existing immersive applications that predominantly focus on single-modality interactions or the passive delivery of pre-rendered content, this system distinguishes itself through its interactive voice-to-visual pipeline. The real-time nature of this generation process enables immediate and continuous feedback loops. Users can observe the direct, tangible visual impact of their verbal inputs, reinforcing the cognitive connection between linguistic expression and digital output.

Furthermore, the system's architecture is designed for seamless metaverse integration, facilitating a smooth transition from individual narrative crafting to collaborative exploration and the sharing of generated worlds across interconnected digital platforms. The foundational design principles of this system are deeply rooted in constructivism, embodied cognition, and self-regulated learning theory (Stracke et al., 2025; Zekeik et al., 2025). Adaptive AI algorithms continuously analyse user interactions and prompting behaviours to suggest contextual improvements, thereby actively building learners' metacognitive skills. Meanwhile, carefully integrated gamified elements and immersive sensory feedback draw upon established motivational theories to sustain long-term user engagement.

Through this experiential approach to storytelling, highly abstract computational concepts become tangible and malleable. For example, a student might verbally prompt, "A brave knight in an enchanted forest battling a dragon." This simple input triggers the AI to rapidly compile and render dynamic assets, including animated character models and panoramic, interactive skyboxes. The system relies on a human-in-the-loop mechanism. Users are encouraged to iteratively refine these outputs, including adjusting the style, modifying the forest's lighting to reflect a specific time of day, or altering the dragon's behaviour. Through this iterative process of negotiation with the AI, users organically develop critical evaluation skills and gain a practical, nuanced understanding of AI's interpretive capabilities, inherent biases, and systemic limitations (Dai & Ke, 2022; Llanos-Ruiz et al., 2025). Pilot implementations conducted across diverse settings, ranging from formal academic classrooms to community cultural workshops, have yielded highly promising results. Participants consistently report feeling "empowered" by the ability to instantly visualise their imagination, demonstrating greater confidence when interacting with complex AI systems. Nevertheless, ongoing research and iterative refinements are still required to address specific technical challenges, such as improving voice-recognition accuracy across highly diverse linguistic accents and ensuring robust accessibility features for neurodiverse learners and individuals without prior virtual reality experience (Zhao et al., 2021; Chalkiadakis et al., 2024; Sümer & Vaněček, 2025).

4.2. Developing Extended Reality (XR) Environments in the Cave Automatic Virtual Environment (CAVE)

The successful integration of Extended Reality (XR) environments within the physical confines of the Cave Automatic Virtual Environment (CAVE) space necessitates a highly deliberate and sophisticated synthesis of advanced hardware apparatus and robust software ecosystems. This synthesis must be meticulously calibrated to meet stringent educational standards and pedagogical requirements. This section explores the precise specifications and implementation strategies critical for establishing such a hybrid, immersive setup. Configured as a high-fidelity, LED-based immersive room, the system establishes a new benchmark for educational XR platforms. It seamlessly fuses the physical architectural elements of the room with dynamic XR simulations, rendering it highly suitable for both rigorous curriculum-based instruction and specialised applications for diverse educational needs.

The software architecture is anchored by the Unity game engine, deliberately selected for its unparalleled capacity to construct and render complex, high-fidelity 3D models, intricate animations, and physics-based interactive simulations. Unity's robust toolset allows for direct, low-latency communication with the CAVE's overarching hardware ecosystem (Ye et al., 2024; Stracke et al., 2025). To achieve a truly seamless fusion of physical and virtual spatial paradigms, the system leverages an advanced optical motion tracking infrastructure. This network of high-speed cameras meticulously captures users' physical movements and spatial positioning, outputting highly stable data signals at 60 to 120Hz. This high refresh rate is critical; it enables the system to render perspective-correct XR content across up to six projection surfaces (walls, floor, and ceiling) with near-zero noticeable latency. Consequently, the environment supports a multi-user dynamic where participants can engage in unencumbered, free walking within the physical boundaries of the CAVE, experiencing a shared, stable virtual world that reacts instantly to their presence (Dai & Ke, 2022; Llanos-Ruiz et al., 2025).

The selection of these technological features is not driven merely by a desire for technical novelty but is strictly dictated by fundamental pedagogical goals. Most notably, the deliberate omission of cumbersome head-mounted displays (HMDs) is a strategic design choice. By eschewing HMDs, the system ensures that users can maintain sustained, natural eye contact and read interpersonal body language—elements that are absolutely vital for facilitating effective collaborative learning and group problem-solving. To deeply support the principles of embodied cognition—the theory that active physical and bodily engagement profoundly reinforces memory encoding and conceptual comprehension—the environment is outfitted with a comprehensive multisensory suite. This suite includes interactive multi-touch wall sensors that enable highly intuitive gestural interactions, allowing users to physically "touch," scale, and manipulate digital objects projected onto the screens. Furthermore, floor-based spatial tracking systems monitor foot traffic and positioning, allowing the virtual environment to respond to where students stand or walk. To enhance depth perception during complex 3D modelling tasks, participants utilise lightweight, wireless 3D stereo glasses that permit extended collaborative sessions without the physical fatigue commonly associated with heavy VR headsets (Chalkiadakis et al., 2024; Avci et al., 2025). By integrating visual, auditory, tactile, and potentially even olfactory stimuli, the system promotes deeply engaging multisensory learning experiences. Ultimately, these intentional hardware and software design decisions elevate the CAVE from being merely a sophisticated display technology into a highly interactive, kinesthetic, and pedagogically valuable learning space.

4.3 Implementation for Enhancing Student AI Literacy in CAVE

The implementation of our AI literacy enhancement program in CAVE utilises generative AI tools to cultivate creative, collaborative, and metacognitive skills among students. To design the agentic AI tools that support the constructive process of immersive environment, the process includes five interconnected stages: (1) Perception, where AI gathered ideas from diverse sources from students; (2) Reasoning, involving analysis of these ideas to build contextual understanding for students preview; (3) Planning, focused on developing and refining goals with step-by-step strategies for the immersive environment; (4) Action, executing plans through AI-driven tools for world-building; and (5) Reflection, AI evaluating outcomes and iterating on realistic adjustments and seek comments from student. This framework highlighted a dynamic progression from abstract imagination to tangible realisation, incorporating abstract concepts to represent adaptive growth and environmental interaction. The typical flow of the students interacting with AI in the CAVE is as follows:

- Voice command & prompting: Using natural language minimised barriers to creative expression. For example, a student might say, “Hi, everyone! Where do you guys want to go today? I want to explore a forest full of animals! Sure thing! Let's go!” prompting the AI to generate a vibrant woodland scene complete with deer, trees, and interactive elements.
- Showcase creativity: The instant visualisation of ideas in the CAVE validated concepts, fostering a sense of accomplishment and encouraging bolder storytelling. Scenes materialised on large projections, allowing students to see their narratives come alive, such as a forest teeming with wildlife where they could virtually touch trees or observe animal behaviours.
- Peer-to-peer exploration: Multiplayer capabilities transformed individual ideas into group adventures, promoting shared storytelling and collaborative problem-solving. In the CAVE, students physically moved through projected worlds, waving their hands to interact with elements like giraffes or rivers, enhancing social bonds and adaptive learning.

To effectively build both AI and digital competency, the platform serves as a highly sophisticated sandbox for self-regulated learning (Zimmerman, 2002). Students were challenged to delve into a wide array of highly complex thematic domains, encompassing cultural, scientific, and futuristic concepts. These included exploring Hong Kong Culture & History, visualizing the Quantum World, designing simulations for Sports & Health, conceptualizing Alien ecologies, rendering intricate Natural Landscapes, visualizing the Double-Slit Experiment, mapping Planetary systems, crafting Life Narratives, building Steampunk architectural cities, and even visualizing abstract concepts like the Spatial Relationships of the English language.

Navigating these diverse topics required students to engage deeply in a metacognitive cycle: (1) Planning: Defining precise conceptual goals, such as articulating the prompt to recreate a steampunk city intricately infused with traditional Chinese cultural elements, or designing a simulated planetary ecosystem to study the cascading effects of species extinction. (2) Monitoring: Actively observing the AI-generated environments in real time, critically assessing how accurately the AI outputs aligned with their intended narratives (e.g., rigorously evaluating the visual accuracy and scientific validity of an AI-generated quantum mechanics simulation). (3) Reflecting: Collaborating intimately with the AI to continuously modify the worlds. For instance, if an alien landscape lacked proper spatial dynamics, students would reflect on the deficiency, adjust their verbal parameters, and command the AI to iterate, thereby deepening their comprehension of the AI as an active, malleable creative partner.

The agentic nature of the AI system was the cornerstone of this programmatic success. The AI did not merely act as a passive rendering tool; it functioned as a proactive, intelligent collaborator that democratized access to professional-grade 3D scene creation. It autonomously managed highly complex backend workflows—such as intricate 3D mesh modeling, rendering optimization for the CAVE's multi-screen layout, and behavioral scripting—tasks that typically demand years of specialized training in software like Blender, Unity, or Python. For students completely lacking these technical skills, the AI bridged the gap by independently breaking down high-level creative prompts into actionable computational sub-tasks.

For example, a complex student request such as "Simulate a quantum world incorporating elements of the double-slit experiment" would be autonomously parsed by the AI. The agentic system would independently source relevant physics data, generate the appropriate geometric mesh structures, optimize the lighting and rendering for full CAVE immersion, and ensure interactive physics were applied—all without requiring a single line of code from the user. Collaboration unfolded through highly iterative, conversational exchanges. Students issued high-level commands (e.g., "Add realistic wave interference patterns to the light source"), and the AI responded not only by generating the visual update but also by explicitly explaining its reasoning process (e.g., "I have calculated and planned the interference patterns based on Young's equation, adjusting the visible wavelengths to ensure maximum visual clarity in the CAVE projection—previewing the scene now").

When technical or conceptual issues arose, students could directly ask the AI for solutions (e.g., "Resolve the animation lag on the steampunk gears"), prompting the system to independently troubleshoot the rendering pipeline and suggest optimized alternatives. This dynamic partnership effectively positioned the students as creative directors supervising an autonomous digital crew. Through this process, they progressively learned to refine their prompt engineering, crucially learning to inject ethical and cultural qualifiers into their commands, such as stipulating, "Ensure there is absolutely no cultural appropriation or stereotyping in the rendering of these historical Hong Kong elements." By successfully automating the exclusionary technical workflows, the agentic AI empowered all participants, regardless of their prior academic backgrounds, to construct professional-grade immersive scenes.

4.4 Evaluation of CAVE and Creative Learning from Student Feedback

The comprehensive evaluation of the CAVE-based program intentionally prioritized profound qualitative insights to accurately assess the intervention's multifaceted impact on students' AI literacy. This evaluation meticulously triangulated data drawn from in-depth participant reflections, rigorous observational data recorded during the sessions, and the final digital artefacts (the 3D worlds) created by the users. This multifaceted approach allowed researchers to deeply examine the participants' metacognitive development, their capacity for creative expression, and the evolving dynamics of their collaborative interactions within the immersive space.

Overall, the student feedback confirmed a highly significant paradigm shift regarding their perception of artificial intelligence. Participants across diverse age groups articulated a clear transition from viewing AI as an opaque, autonomous, and somewhat "magical" entity to fundamentally understanding it as a highly malleable, controllable, and collaborative tool requiring human guidance. University students, in their detailed written reflections, consistently emphasized how the physical, 360-degree immersion of the CAVE dramatically amplified their cognitive engagement with complex ideation and systemic design.

Rather than merely listing the prompts they used, participants provided deep reflections on the iterative process itself. One participant vividly described the process of refining a complex scientific scene: "Starting with a very basic prompt for a double-slit experiment, I carefully monitored how the AI attempted to render the complex concept of wave-particle duality. I then reflected on the visual inaccuracies—specifically noting mismatched light interference patterns—and had to actively collaborate with the system, feeding it more precise physics terminology to adjust the simulation for true scientific realism." This iterative friction cultivated a much deeper, more nuanced appreciation of both the AI's remarkable generative strengths and its critical interpretive limitations. Consequently, students reported significant improvements in digital competency, specifically in advanced prompt engineering techniques and their capacity for ethical world-building (e.g., heightened awareness of how to instruct the AI to avoid perpetuating cultural stereotypes when generating historical Chinese simulations).

Group discussions held within the CAVE environments consistently revealed strong themes of academic and creative empowerment. Students enthusiastically shared how physically navigating and reflecting upon vastly different generated environments—such as intricately detailed steampunk metropolises or highly speculative alien ecologies—sparked unexpected interdisciplinary connections. For instance, students excitedly discussed linking the spatial prepositions and relationships taught in their English linguistics courses to the practical challenges of navigating an AI-generated planetary surface. Observational data systematically gathered from the workshop sessions further underscored the pedagogical framework's profound effectiveness in promoting thoughtful realism and critical inquiry. Video analyses highlighted numerous instances of deep, physically embodied reflective engagement. Researchers noted moments when students would sit and meditate near a culturally significant, AI-projected Buddha statue, or walk around the CAVE to inspect the underside of a simulated hot air balloon floating over a generated desert sky. In these moments, participants frequently paused the simulation entirely to engage in rigorous peer debates regarding the scientific accuracy of the generated physics or the cultural sensitivity and historical authenticity of a projected heritage site.

Technical challenges, such as occasional voice-recognition glitches or processing lag in lively, noisy group settings, did not lead to user frustration or disengagement. Instead, these technical hurdles acted as catalysts for resilience. Students demonstrated impressive adaptability, seamlessly switching from voice commands to gesture-based communication or dynamically restructuring their collaborative workflows on the spot to bypass the technical bottleneck, thereby further strengthening their real-world digital problem-solving skills. Educators observing the program offered glowing praise for the system's remarkable inclusivity. They specifically noted the platform's unparalleled ability to accommodate a wide spectrum of diverse learning styles and cognitive processes within a single session. The system seamlessly supported highly verbal students who preferred to narrate elaborate stories, while equally accommodating analytical, detail-oriented thinkers who thrived on the iterative, parameter-tweaking process of prompt refinement. The CAVE environment successfully achieved a rare pedagogical balance, blending highly imaginative, open-ended storytelling with the requirement for rigorous, continuous self-assessment and logical planning.

By actively instilling these critical metacognitive habits: prompting, monitoring, evaluating, and refining the immersive program provided students with a robust, highly adaptable foundation for lifelong engagement with emerging AI technologies. Looking forward, future iterations of the project will focus on expanding the diversity and inclusivity of the cultural training data utilised by the underlying LLMs to further reduce inherent biases. Additionally, researchers plan to incorporate comprehensive digital portfolios, allowing students to systematically capture, document, and reflect upon their prompt histories and generated artefacts, thereby facilitating the rigorous tracking of their long-term, longitudinal development in AI literacy and digital competence.

Figure 4. Students are viewing, monitoring, and modifying CAVE scenes created collaboratively with AI

5. CONCLUSION

The integration of AI and immersive technologies into education marks a significant shift, demonstrated by their ability to tailor learning, improve engagement through VR/AR, and promote collaborative knowledge across various fields (Wang & Huang, 2025). The case studies in this chapter—the AI-powered metaverse for gamified ethical training and the CAVE-based storytelling system—show real-world applications that develop essential future skills such as digital literacy, creativity, and ethical awareness, while also tackling issues such as data security and academic honesty. The development and implementation sections focus on the technical basics needed for wide adoption, emphasizing multi-device access so learning can span from mobile and web to immersive CAVE environments, helping close the digital gap. By using AI agents that give context-sensitive support, adaptable designs, and ethical safeguards—like bias reduction and privacy protection—these systems foster inclusive learning environments grounded in fairness and responsibility.

For practical use, institutions should invest in infrastructure supporting HyFlex blended learning models and train educators in AI literacy and immersive teaching. Ethical design, prioritising equity, accessibility, and privacy, is essential for implementation. Future research should include long-term studies to evaluate impacts on lifelong learning and career flexibility, as well as strategies to manage issues like cognitive overload and cybersickness. By focusing on inclusivity, ethical practices, and ongoing assessment, we can leverage AI and immersive tech to build holistic educational ecosystems where curiosity grows, collaboration thrives, and the line between physical and virtual learning fades.

REFERENCES

Abbas, N., Ali, I., Manzoor, R., Hussain, T., & Hussain, M. H. A. I. (2023). Role of artificial intelligence tools in enhancing students' educational performance at higher levels. *Journal of Artificial Intelligence. Machine Learning and Neural Network, 3*(5), 36–49. DOI: 10.55529/jaimlnn.35.36.49

Al-Adwan, A. S., Li, N., Al-Adwan, A., Abbasi, G. A., Albelbisi, N. A., & Habibi, A. (2023). Extending the technology acceptance model (TAM) to Predict University Students' intentions to use metaverse-based learning platforms. *Education and Information Technologies, 28*(11), 15381–15413. DOI: 10.1007/s10639-023-11816-3 PMID: 37361794

Alhazzaa, K., & Yan, W. (2025). Immersive technologies in Education: Exploring user experience and engagement in building energy simulations through AR and VR. *Computers & Education: X Reality, 6*, 100097. https://doi.org/DOI: 10.1016/j.cexr.2025.100097

An, S., Zhang, S., Guo, T., Lu, S., Zhang, W., & Cai, Z. (2025). Impacts of generative AI on student teachers' task performance and collaborative knowledge construction process in mind mapping-based collaborative environment. *Computers & Education, 227*, 105227. DOI: 10.1016/j.compedu.2024.105227

Avci, H., Lunn, S. J., & Hazari, Z. (2025). Exploring STEM educators' perspectives on the integration of AI-enabled technologies in teaching and learning. *Computers and Education Open, 9*, 100304. Advance online publication. DOI: 10.1016/j.caeo.2025.100304

Chalkiadakis, A., Seremetaki, A., Kanellou, A., Kallishi, M., Morfopoulou, A., Moraitaki, M., & Mastrokoukou, S. (2024). Impact of artificial intelligence and virtual reality on educational inclusion: A systematic review of technologies supporting students with disabilities. *Education Sciences, 14*(11), 1223. Advance online publication. DOI: 10.3390/educsci14111223

Conrad, M., Kablitz, D., & Schumann, S. (2024). Learning effectiveness of immersive virtual reality in education and training: A systematic review of findings. *Computers & Education: X Reality, 4*, Article 100053. https://doi.org/DOI: 10.1016/j.cexr.2024.100053

Csikszentmihalyi, M., & Larson, R. (2014). *Flow and the foundations of positive psychology*. Springer. DOI: 10.1007/978-94-017-9088-8

Dai, C.-P., & Ke, F. (2022). Educational applications of artificial intelligence in simulation-based learning: A systematic mapping review. *Computers and Education: Artificial Intelligence, 3*, 100087. Advance online publication. DOI: 10.1016/j.caeai.2022.100087

Dicheva, D., Dichev, C., Agre, G., & Angelova, G. (2015). Gamification in education: A systematic mapping study. *Journal of Educational Technology & Society, 18*(3), 75–88. https://www.jstor.org/stable/jeductechsoci.18.3.75

Hamari, J., Shernoff, D. J., Rowe, E., Coller, B., Asbell-Clarke, J., & Edwards, T. (2016). Challenging games help students learn: An empirical study on engagement, flow and immersion in game-based learning. *Computers in Human Behavior, 54*, 170–179. DOI: 10.1016/j.chb.2015.07.045

Hart, A., & Shakir, M. (2024). Realtime AI driven environment development for virtual metaverse. In *2024 IEEE International Conference on Metaverse Computing, Networking and Applications (MetroXRAINE)* (pp. 313–318). IEEE. https://doi.org/ DOI: 10.1109/MetroXRAINE62247.2024.10796022

Holmes, W., Porayska-Pomsta, K., Holstein, K., Sutherland, E., Baker, T., Shum, S. B., & Koedinger, K. R. (2022). Ethics of AI in education: Towards a community-wide framework. *International Journal of Artificial Intelligence in Education, 32*(3), 504–526. Advance online publication. DOI: 10.1007/s40593-021-00239-1

Hong, Y., Saab, N., & Admiraal, W. (2024). Approaches and game elements used to tailor digital gamification for learning: A systematic literature review. *Computers & Education, 212*, 105000. Advance online publication. DOI: 10.1016/j.compedu.2024.105000

Jacka, L., & Lindsay, J. (2022). Flexible learning and the virtual campus. In *Proceedings of the 39th International Conference on Innovation, Practice and Research in the Use of Educational Technologies in Tertiary Education (ASCILITE 2022)* (p. e22154). https://doi.org/DOI: 10.14742/apubs.2022.154

Kamalov, F., Santandreu Calonge, D., & Gurrib, I. (2023). New era of artificial intelligence in education: Towards a sustainable multifaceted revolution. *Sustainability (Basel), 15*(16), 12451. Advance online publication. DOI: 10.3390/su151612451

Kang, J., Zhou, Y., Rajarathinam, R. J., Tan, Y., & Shaffer, D. W. (2024). Unveiling joint attention dynamics: Examining multimodal engagement in an immersive collaborative astronomy simulation. *Computers & Education, 213*, 105002. DOI: 10.1016/j.compedu.2024.105002

Kataria, K. (2023). AI-powered learning: The future of education. *International Journal of Advanced Research, 11*(08), 384–388. DOI: 10.21474/IJAR01/17520

Khan, S., Mazhar, T., Shahzad, T., Khan, M. A., Waheed, W., Waheed, A., & Hamam, H. (2025). Predictive analytics in education—Enhancing student achievement through machine learning. *Social Sciences & Humanities Open, 12*, 101824. Advance online publication. DOI: 10.1016/j.ssaho.2025.101824

Lee, S., Jeon, J., & Choe, H. (2025). Enhancing Pre-Service Teachers' Global Englishes Awareness with Technology: A Focus on AI Chatbots in 3D Metaverse Environments. *TESOL Quarterly, 59*(1), 49–74. DOI: 10.1002/tesq.3300

Llanos-Ruiz, D., Abella-García, V., & Ausín-Villaverde, V. (2025). Virtual Reality in Higher Education: A Systematic Review Aligned with the Sustainable Development Goals. *Societies (Basel, Switzerland), 15*(9), 251. DOI: 10.3390/soc15090251

Luckin, R., & Cukurova, M. (2019). Designing educational technologies in the age of AI: A learning sciences-driven approach. *British Journal of Educational Technology, 50*(6), 2824–2838. DOI: 10.1111/bjet.12861

Luo, H., Li, X., Zhang, J., Zhang, F., Liang, J., & Yin, X. (2024). Metaverse improves the learning experiences rather than learning outcomes: Evidence from an experimental study in higher education. In *2024 9th International STEM Education Conference (iSTEM-Ed)* (pp. 217–222). IEEE. https://doi.org/DOI: 10.1109/ISET61814.2024.00050

Ng, P. H. F., Xie, H., Lai, C. L., Chen, W., Xu, G., & Popescu, E. (2023). From classroom to metaverse: A study on gamified constructivist teaching in higher education. In Xie, H., Lai, C. L., Chen, W., Xu, G., & Popescu, E. (Eds.), Lecture Notes in Computer Science: Vol. 14409. *Advances in web-based learning – ICWL 2023* (pp. 96–108). Springer., DOI: 10.1007/978-981-99-8385-8_8

Park, J., Yang, S., Yoon, C., Si, J., Jung, Y., & Kim, S. (2024). AI English conversation coaching platform in the metaverse: Focused on Korean users. In *2024 IEEE 3rd International Conference on AI in Cybersecurity (AIC)* (pp. 1–6). IEEE. https://doi.org/DOI: 10.1109/AICT61888.2024.10740456

Park, S., Shin, H. J., Kwak, H., & Lee, H. J. (2024). Effects of immersive technology–based education for undergraduate nursing students: Systematic review and meta-analysis using the Grading of Recommendations, Assessment, Development, and Evaluation (GRADE) approach. *Journal of Medical Internet Research, 26*, e57566. Advance online publication. DOI: 10.2196/57566 PMID: 38978483

Pramanik, S., & Kayyali, M. (2024). Immersive innovations: Exploring the use of virtual and augmented reality in educational institutions. In *Augmented Reality and the Future of Education Technology* (pp. 66–85). IGI Global., DOI: 10.4018/979-8-3693-3015-9.ch006

Rojas, E., Hülsmann, X., Estriegana, R., Rückert, F., & Garcia-Esteban, S. (2023). Students' perception of metaverses for online learning in higher education: Hype or hope? *Electronics (Basel)*, *12*(8), 1867. Advance online publication. DOI: 10.3390/electronics12081867

Ryan, R. M., & Deci, E. L. (2000). Self-determination theory and the facilitation of intrinsic motivation, social development, and well-being. *The American Psychologist*, *55*(1), 68–78. DOI: 10.1037/0003-066X.55.1.68 PMID: 11392867

Seenathmol, S. (2024). Implementation of augmented reality media through the metaverse approach in social science learning. [RaDEn]. *Research and Development in Education*, *4*(2), 736–745. DOI: 10.22219/raden.v4i2.35675

Selvakumar, S., & Sivakumar, S. (2023). Immersive learning: Unlocking the future of education. *Thiagarajar College of Preceptors Edu Spectra*, *5*(S1), 12–20. DOI: 10.34293/eduspectra.v5is1-may23.003

Song, Y., Wu, K., & Ding, J. (2024). Developing an immersive game-based learning platform with generative artificial intelligence and virtual reality technologies–"LearningverseVR". Computers & Education: X Reality, 4, 100069. DOI: 10.1016/j.cexr.2024.100069

Stracke, C. M., Bothe, P., Adler, S., Heller, E. S., Deuchler, J., Pomino, J., & Wölfel, M. (2025). Immersive virtual reality in higher education: A systematic review of the scientific literature. *Virtual Reality (Waltham Cross)*, *29*(2), 1–21. DOI: 10.1007/s10055-025-01136-x

Sümer, M., & Vaněček, D. (2025). A systematic review of virtual and augmented realities in higher education: Trends and issues. *Innovations in Education and Teaching International*, *62*(3), 811–822. DOI: 10.1080/14703297.2024.2382854

Tan, X., Cheng, G., & Ling, M. H. (2025). Artificial intelligence in teaching and teacher professional development: A systematic review. *Computers and Education: Artificial Intelligence*, *8*, 100355. Advance online publication. DOI: 10.1016/j.caeai.2024.100355

Velazquez-Garcia, L., Cedillo-Hernandez, A., Longar-Blanco, M. D. P., & Bustos-Farias, E. (2024). Enhancing educational gamification through AI in higher education. In *Proceedings of the 2024 16th International Conference on Education Technology and Computers (ICETC)* (pp. 213–218). ACM. DOI: 10.1145/3702163.3702416

Wang, D., & Huang, X. (2025). Transforming education through artificial intelligence and immersive technologies: Enhancing learning experiences. *Interactive Learning Environments*, *33*(7), 1–20. DOI: 10.1080/10494820.2025.2465451

Ye, J., Sin, Z. P. T., Wang, X. E., Li, C., Ng, P. H. F., Huang, X., Dong, J., Wang, Y., Baciu, G., Cao, J., & Li, Q. (2024). NivTA: Towards a naturally interactable edu-metaverse teaching assistant for CAVE. In *2024 IEEE International Conference on Metaverse Computing, Networking, and Applications (MetaCom)* (pp. 57–64). IEEE. https://doi.org/DOI: 10.1109/MetaCom62920.2024.00023

Zekeik, H., Chahbi, M., Lamarti Sefian, M., & Bakkali, I. (2025). Augmented reality and virtual reality in education: A systematic narrative review on benefits, challenges, and applications. *Eurasia Journal of Mathematics, Science and Technology Education*, *21*(9), em2699. Advance online publication. DOI: 10.29333/ejmste/16830

Zhao, L., Cao, C., Li, Y., & Li, Y. (2021). Determinants of the digital outcome divide in E-learning between rural and urban students: Empirical evidence from the COVID-19 pandemic based on capital theory. *Computers in Human Behavior*, *130*, 107177. Advance online publication. DOI: 10.1016/j.chb.2021.107177 PMID: 36568533

Zimmerman, B. J. (2002). Becoming a self-regulated learner: An overview. *Theory into Practice*, *41*(2), 64–70. DOI: 10.1207/s15430421tip4102_2

Chapter 3
Collaborative Generative AI in HyFlex Learning:
Designing AI-Mediated Group Learning Activities

Fridolin Sze Thou Ting
http://orcid.org/0000-0001-7432-0187
The Education University of Hong Kong, Hong Kong

ABSTRACT

HyFlex learning models promise flexibility but struggle with collaboration equity across synchronous in-person, synchronous online, and asynchronous modalities. This chapter introduces Collaborative Generative AI (CoGenAI) as a transformative approach for facilitating group-based learning across all HyFlex modalities. Through theoretical frameworks grounding CoGenAI in social constructivism, collective intelligence, and TPACK, the authors present the CoGenAI Prompt Template, a discipline-flexible scaffold for designing AI-mediated collaborative activities. Three cross-disciplinary case studies demonstrate implementation using YoChatGPT, a multi-user platform serving as a persistent collaborative partner accessible regardless of attendance mode. Evidence shows increased engagement, equitable participation, and enhanced critical thinking when students engage collectively with generative AI

INTRODUCTION

The COVID-19 pandemic accelerated adoption of HyFlex learning models that allow students to choose between attending synchronously in-person, synchronously online, or asynchronously at their own pace (Beatty, 2019). While offering unprecedented flexibility, HyFlex instruction creates significant pedagogical challenges,

DOI: 10.4018/979-8-3373-6182-6.ch003

particularly regarding the "equivalency principle", ensuring comparable learning experiences across all modalities (Abdelmalak & Parra, 2016). This challenge intensifies when collaborative learning activities are introduced in a blended synchronous courses, e.g., when in-person groups engage with synchronous online participants navigate, whose technical barriers in breakout rooms often make them feel like "second-class" students, while asynchronous learners frequently receive isolated individual assignments that exclude them from collaborative benefits entirely (Lakhal et al., 2020).

Recent meta-analyses demonstrate that generative AI tools like ChatGPT significantly impact student engagement when designed thoughtfully (Heung & Chiu, 2025; Zhang et al., 2025). However, current AI educational applications overwhelmingly focus on individual learner support through one-on-one AI tutors, personalized feedback systems, and chatbots (Bond et al., 2024). There remains limited research and practical guidance on how generative AI can facilitate collaborative learning across the diverse modalities defining HyFlex instruction.

This chapter addresses this critical gap by introducing Collaborative Generative AI (CoGenAI), a pedagogical approaches that harness multi-user generative AI platforms as collaborative partners accessible across multiple HyFlex modalities. Rather than replacing human interaction or automating existing processes for efficiency gains, CoGenAI reimagines collaboration itself as AI-mediated collective intelligence where technology serves as a thinking partner that provokes questioning, synthesizes disparate ideas, and scaffolds and promotes deeper inquiry (Malone, 2018).

The chapter demonstrates how CoGenAI activities designed through theoretically-grounded frameworks and evaluated using TPACK principles can transform HyFlex learning from a logistics challenge into a pedagogical opportunity for inclusive, scalable, and equitable collaboration. Through case studies across STEM, social sciences, and business education, readers will discover actionable strategies for implementing CoGenAI in diverse disciplinary contexts, critically examine when and why these approaches succeed or fail, and understand the ethical considerations and faculty competencies required for effective practice.

SECTION 1: THE HYFLEX COLLABORATION CHALLENGE

Evolution from Emergency Remote Teaching to Intentional HyFlex Design

The rapid shift to emergency remote teaching in 2020 forced educators worldwide to accommodate students and teachers synchronously in different physical locations (office, classroom or home) on video conferencing tools (like Zoom, Microsoft

Teams and Google Meet) and accessing recordings asynchronously. While initially conceived as a temporary response to the COVID-19 pandemic, many institutions discovered student demand for continued flexibility post-pandemic, leading to intentional HyFlex course design (Raes et al., 2020). Unlike fully online or traditional face-to-face instruction, HyFlex models require simultaneously serving three distinct student populations within a single course section, each with different technological affordances, social dynamics, and temporal constraints.

Beatty's (2019) seminal framework identifies four core HyFlex principles: learner choice (students select their preferred mode of participation), equivalency (comparable learning experiences across different modes), reusability (recorded materials accessible asynchronously), and accessibility (removing barriers to participation). While these principles provide valuable guidance for course structure, they offer limited insight into designing active learning strategies (Bonwell & Eison, 1991), particularly collaborative activities that increase students' cognitive engagement across disciplines (Chi & Wylie, 2014).

Current State of AI in HyFlex Environments: Identifying the Collaboration Gap

Recent systematic reviews reveal explosive growth in AI educational applications, with meta-analyses documenting positive effects on engagement and learning outcomes (Heung & Chiu, 2025; Zhang et al., 2025). However, these studies predominantly examine individual student-AI interactions: intelligent tutoring systems providing personalized feedback, chatbots answering administrative questions, AI writing assistants supporting composition tasks, and automated assessment tools grading assignments (Bond et al., 2024).

Emerging research on AI in HyFlex contexts similarly focuses on individual support mechanisms. For instance, AI avatars facilitate multilingual accessibility by providing real-time translation for international students attending synchronously online (Wang et al., 2023), while AI-powered analytics dashboards help instructors monitor individual student engagement across different modes (Cabral, 2024). These applications address important challenges but leave the collaborative learning gap unaddressed.

Standard Zoom breakout rooms and equivalent video-conferencing tools suffer from familiar technical barriers: audio delays and frozen video feeds, awkwardness when participants talk over one another, and the inability for asynchronous learners to join the same conversation later. These limitations create inferior experiences for online and asynchronous students. In contrast, online multi-user generative AI platforms eliminate these barriers through persistent conversation history, simultaneous multi-user participation, and AI-moderated continuity that keeps every group member, regardless of attendance mode, fully included in the same collaborative space.

This gap proves particularly significant given robust evidence that collaborative learning enhances critical thinking, problem-solving abilities, and long-term retention compared to individual study (Johnson & Johnson, 2009). Social constructivist learning theories emphasize that knowledge construction occurs through social interaction, with dialogue and collaborative inquiry serving as primary mechanisms for cognitive development (Vygotsky, 1978). When asynchronous students are systematically excluded from collaborative experiences due to temporal differences, they receive fundamentally unequal learning opportunities despite superficial compliance with HyFlex equivalency principles.

The Collaboration Equity Problem: How Different Modalities Create Inequitable Experiences

Consider a typical collaborative learning scenario in a HyFlex course: The instructor assigns small group projects requiring students to analyze case studies and develop solutions. In-person students naturally cluster into groups, engage in spontaneous discussion, sketch diagrams on whiteboards, and read each other's body language to negotiate roles and responsibilities. Synchronous online students are sorted into Zoom breakout rooms where they struggle with audio delays, frozen video feeds, and awkward silences punctuated by people talking over each other. Asynchronous students watch the lecture recording alone at 11 PM, complete an individual written assignment as substitute for group work, and never experience the cognitive benefits of collaborative sense-making.

This modality-based inequity manifests across multiple dimensions:

Temporal synchronization: In-person and synchronous online students share real-time interaction enabling immediate clarification, spontaneous idea generation, and dynamic turn-taking. Asynchronous students lack these affordances entirely, relegated to time-delayed discussion forums where conversations unfold over days rather than minutes (Lakhal et al., 2020).

Social presence: Learners being physically side-by-side by each other enables rich multimodal communication through gesture, tone and facial expression that establish interpersonal connection and group cohesion. Synchronous online students experience diminished social presence through video-mediated interaction, while asynchronous students often feel completely isolated (Richardson et al., 2017).

Cognitive load distribution: Effective group work distributes cognitive processing across members through transactive memory systems where individuals specialize in different knowledge domains and rely on each other's expertise (Wegner, 1987). This cognitive distribution cannot emerge when asynchronous students work alone, forcing them to individually master all content rather than benefit from collaborative specialization.

Participation equity: In-person discussions privilege extroverted students comfortable with spontaneous verbal contribution, potentially marginalizing quieter participants. While synchronous online formats partially mitigate this through chat functions allowing text-based contribution, asynchronous students entirely miss these negotiated interactions (Beatty, 2019).

Traditional approaches to addressing HyFlex collaboration challenges include rotating required in-person attendance, creating mode specific assignments, or abandoning collaborative work entirely in favor of individual tasks. Each solution proves problematic: mandatory attendance undermines the flexibility HyFlex promises, separate assignments violate equivalency principles, and eliminating collaboration sacrifices pedagogical benefits.

CoGenAI offers a fourth option: leveraging multi-user generative AI platforms as persistent collaborative spaces accessible synchronously and asynchronously, where AI serves as both conversational partner and knowledge resource that maintains group continuity across time and space. The next section elaborates the theoretical foundations and practical framework for this approach.

SECTION 2: COLLABORATIVE GENERATIVE AI FRAMEWORK

Defining CoGenAI Pedagogies: Distinguishing from AI Tutors and Graders

Active learning is, essentially, anything other than traditional passive lecturing, which involves reflection and engagement in meaningful learning experiences (Prince, 2004). It has been shown extensively in literature that active learning benefits student learning outcomes, including increased conceptual understanding, motivation, and academic performance (Freeman et al., 2014). Examples of active learning pedagogies include problem-based learning (PBL), case-based learning, experiential learning, flipped classroom, peer instruction, think-pair-share, debates, and basic question-and-answer pedagogy.

We define collaborative generative AI (CoGenAI) pedagogies as an active teaching pedagogy augmented with a generative AI component involving at least one of the following two categories of groupings, each containing at least 3 or more entities in each grouping: (i) teacher(s)-AI-student(s) or (ii) at least two students working with AI. Note that CoGenAI pedagogies can be implemented in any environment: face-to-face, hybrid, or purely online, i.e., in hyflex environments.

Collaborative generative AI represents a pedagogical paradigm distinct from dominant AI educational applications. Rather than one-to-one student-AI interaction (intelligent tutoring systems), automated evaluation (AI grading tools), or administrative support (chatbots answering FAQs), CoGenAI facilitates **many-to-one group-AI interaction** where the AI serves as shared collaborative partner for student teams working together.

This distinction proves crucial: AI tutors optimize individual learning paths through adaptive sequencing and personalized feedback (VanLehn, 2011), while CoGenAI optimizes collective intelligence—the enhanced problem-solving capacity emerging when groups think together (Woolley et al., 2010). The pedagogical goals differ fundamentally. Individual AI tutors aim to move each student toward expert performance through scaffolded practice; CoGenAI aims to create knowledge synthesis exceeding what any individual (human or AI) could generate alone.

Platform architecture reflects these different purposes. Individual AI applications require user authentication, learning analytics tracking individual progress, and algorithms personalizing content based on student performance history. CoGenAI platforms require **multi-user rooms** enabling simultaneous participation, persistent conversation history maintaining continuity across sessions, and instructor observation functionality monitoring group dynamics rather than individual metrics.

Theoretical Foundations: Grounding CoGenAI in Established Learning Theories

Social Constructivism: AI as "More Knowledgeable Other"

Vygotsky's (1978) social constructivist theory postulates that cognitive development occurs through social interaction, particularly when learners engage with "more knowledgeable others" who scaffold understanding within the Zone of Proximal Development (ZPD), which is the gap between what learners can accomplish independently versus with assistance. Traditionally, teachers and more advanced peers serve this scaffolding role.

Large language models like GPT-4 possess unprecedented breadth of knowledge across disciplines combined with ability to generate explanations modified to different expertise levels (Brown et al., 2020). Dialogic education emphasizes learning through questioning, multiple perspectives, and collaborative meaning-making (Wegerif, 2013). When applied to AI-enhanced pedagogy, this suggests positioning AI as collaborative partner rather than authoritative answer key; AI can scaffold group ZPD through dialogic learning that provokes questions, challenges assumptions, and synthesizes multiple perspectives (Wei et al., 2025).

However, critical differences distinguish AI from human collaborative partners. AI lacks genuine understanding, possesses no intentionality, and cannot assess context through embodied social cues (Bender et al., 2021). These limitations prove pedagogically significant: while AI can surface information and generate text, it cannot evaluate which ideas matter most for a specific group's learning goals or recognize when students need encouragement versus challenge. Effective CoGenAI pedagogy therefore positions AI as collaborative **resource** requiring human facilitation, not autonomous collaborative **agent** replacing human interaction.

Active Learning and Cognitive Engagement: The ICAP Framework

Chi and Wylie's (2014) ICAP framework provides a systematic lens for understanding how different modes of student engagement predict learning outcomes. The framework categorizes active learning activities into four hierarchical levels: Passive (receiving information without overt cognitive processing), Active (manipulating information through activities like note-taking), Constructive (generating new ideas beyond presented material), and Interactive (dialogically co-constructing knowledge with peers). Meta-analytic evidence demonstrates that active learning strategies produce moderately large effect sizes (ES = 0.66) on STEM academic performance compared to traditional lecture-based instruction (Freeman et al., 2014). CoGenAI pedagogies directly target the highest ICAP levels by positioning AI as a dialogic partner that provokes **Interactive** engagement—students must negotiate meaning with both human peers and AI, defend interpretations, and synthesize conflicting perspectives—while simultaneously scaffolding Constructive processes through structured prompts requiring students to generate explanations, create analogies, and extend concepts beyond the training data the AI provides. This theoretical grounding positions CoGenAI as an intentional pedagogical design for maximizing cognitive engagement rather than merely adding technology to existing instructional approaches.

Collective Intelligence: Humans and Machines Thinking Together

Research on collective intelligence demonstrates that groups exhibit measurable intelligence distinct from individual member capabilities (Woolley et al., 2010). Groups with higher collective intelligence outperform lower-CI groups on complex problem-solving tasks even when individual member IQs are equivalent. Factors contributing to collective intelligence include equal turn-taking, social perceptiveness, and gender diversity—not the intelligence of the smartest member.

Malone's (2018) “Superminds” framework extends collective intelligence to human-AI collaboration. When humans and AI think together effectively, they create “superminds” capable of innovations exceeding either human or machine capability alone. Examples include AI-assisted drug discovery identifying pharmaceutical compounds human researchers would never conceive, and human-AI chess teams outperforming both grandmasters and chess engines competing independently.

The Superminds framework identifies six specific cognitive moves enhancing collective intelligence: Zoom In (examining details), Zoom Out (considering systems/context), Analogize (finding parallel cases), Groupify (categorizing information), Cognify (explaining reasoning), and Technify (identifying implementation tools). These moves provide actionable scaffolding for CoGenAI activity design, as Section 3 demonstrates through case studies.

TPACK Framework: Integrating Technology, Pedagogy, and Content

Effective educational technology integration requires balancing three knowledge domains: Technology (understanding platform affordances and constraints), Pedagogy (active learning strategies promoting engagement and understanding), and Content (disciplinary knowledge construction) (Mishra & Koehler, 2006). CoGenAI activities must thoughtfully align all three TPACK domains.

Technology considerations include which AI model capabilities (text generation, code execution, image analysis) support the learning objectives? How do platform features (multi-user rooms, conversation persistence, instructor dashboards) enable or constrain collaboration? What technical barriers (internet access, device compatibility, AI literacy) might exclude students?

Pedagogical considerations include which active learning strategies (inquiry-based learning, problem-based learning, design thinking) best leverage AI capabilities? How should group size and composition be determined? What instructor facilitation proves necessary versus counterproductive?

Content considerations include how does disciplinary epistemology shape appropriate AI use? What domain-specific knowledge must students construct versus AI-generated information they can reference? How might AI limitations (hallucinations, training data biases) create content-specific challenges?

Section 3's case studies demonstrate TPACK-aligned CoGenAI design across disciplines with different technology affordances, pedagogical approaches, and content requirements.

The CoGenAI Prompt Template: A Discipline-Flexible Scaffold

Based on theoretical foundations above and iterative refinement across pilot implementations, we developed a **CoGenAI Prompt Template** providing structured guidance for designing AI-mediated collaborative activities. The template proves discipline-flexible, working across STEM, humanities, social sciences, and professional education with contextual adaptation.

CoGenAI Prompt Template Structure:

"I am an instructor teaching a course called [Course Name]. Please help me design an active learning in-class activity based on [active teaching pedagogy name] pedagogy (and the [model/framework (if any)] using [educational technology goes here] technology on the topic of [topic] in the subject of [subject] for students in grade/year [grade/year] in [K12/College/University/Adult Learning] (K12/University".

This template proves adaptable to different disciplines by modifying specific active learning pedagogies emphasized, adjusting to possible frameworks developed for active learning strategy and adopted towards the choice of technology enhancement, if any. The topic, subject, grade and learning level are also included. An explicit example of the CoGenAI prompt would be:

"I am an instructor teaching a course called [MTH6134: Technology in Mathematics Education].Please help me design an active learning in-class activity based on [Inquiry Based Learning (IBL)] pedagogy and the [5E-model] for [IBL] pedagogy using [YoChatGPT!] technology on the topic of[fractions] in the subject of [Mathematics] for students in [Grade 8] in [Secondary School]".

As suggested in (Moore et al., 2025), generative AI guided instructional design yield best results on well-established pedagogies, i.e., those that are structured and well documented. Structured pedagogies include those that follow established frameworks: e.g., 5E model, universal design for learning (UDL) (Meyer et al., 2014) and design thinking; while well documented pedagogies appear in many publicly discussed internet sites with clear steps. For those pedagogies that are novel or niche, i.e., those that are cutting-edge research or only appear in locally specific contexts, generative AI may not be as capable in suggesting a feasible instructional design (Moore et al., 2025). Therefore, for more pedagogies, and even technologies which are new, more context needs to be given to the large language model for it to produce a more reasonable instructional design, i.e., we may add the following extra context to the CoGenAI prompt above:

"YoChatGPT is a platform that is an online chatroom integrated with multiple Generative AI (including text to image model), text to scientific diagram, a drawboard and math handwriting recognition; teachers and students can either send a question or comment to the chatroom, or to a generative AI."

Instructor Orchestration in CoGenAI

The human instructor remains the essential orchestrator of CoGenAI activities. Effective practice emerges only through cycles of design, implementation, critical evaluation, and evidence-based revision informed by learning analytics and student feedback.

This iterative refinement approach positions initial implementations as prototypes requiring adjustment rather than expecting immediate pedagogical success. Instructors must adopt a design-thinking mindset, treating pilot failures not as pedagogical inadequacies but as valuable diagnostic information guiding subsequent modifications, e.g., clarifying activity instructions, adjusting group sizes, modifying prompt scaffolds, or extending allocated time for complex tasks.

Beyond design iteration, real-time facilitation during CoGenAI activities demands substantial human resources. Effective orchestration typically requires at one teaching assistant (TAs) circulating among groups to ensure students follow intended procedures, use scaffolding tools appropriately, and engage critically with AI outputs rather than passively accepting generated content. These facilitators perform essential functions: redirecting groups that have gone off-task, clarifying misunderstood instructions before confusion compounds, modelling effective prompt refinement techniques, and identifying struggling groups requiring instructor intervention.

Key facilitation practices enabled by collaborative AI platforms include:

- **Real-time monitoring via instructor dashboards** that display all group conversations simultaneously, allowing rapid identification of groups showing low participation, off-task discussion, or pedagogical stagnation;
- **Strategic prompting of the AI** to ensure equitable turn-taking and prevent dominant voices from monopolizing interaction;
- **Explicit human-AI handoff moments** where instructors deliberately transition between AI-mediated exploration and human-led synthesis, clarifying what AI can support versus what requires human judgment; and
- **Structured debriefs** where groups systematically critique AI contributions, identify instances of hallucination or bias, and articulate what collective intelligence emerged that neither humans nor AI alone could produce.

These orchestration moves, spanning iterative design refinement, multi-facilitator classroom support, and strategic real-time intervention, transform collaborative AI platforms from passive tools into powerful scaffolds for collective intelligence.

YoChatGPT Platform: Design Rationale and Technical Affordances

Implementing CoGenAI pedagogy requires platforms architected specifically for multi-user collaborative interaction rather than individual tutoring. A collaborative online chatroom integrated with multiple multimodal large language models,

YoChatGPT (https://www.yochatgpt.io/), represents one such platform, designed through iterative refinement based on educator and student feedback across pilot implementations (Ting et al., 2025). While YoChatGPT! currently offers the most mature implementation of these features, the CoGenAI framework is platform-agnostic. Any multi-user generative AI environment providing persistent conversation history, simultaneous participation, instructor observation dashboards, and curriculum-aligned context (RAG) can achieve equivalent results. Comparable alternatives include ChatGPT Plus Team workspaces, Microsoft Copilot shared channels with persistent threads, and emerging tools such as BoodleBox or Breakout Learning. The essential requirement remains the same: technology that treats the AI as a shared thinking partner rather than an individual tutor.

Key technical affordances supporting Hyflex implementation are:

1. *Multi-user rooms*: Unlike standard ChatGPT individual accounts, YoChatGPT creates persistent "rooms" where multiple students simultaneously interact with a shared AI instance. All participants see the complete conversation history, enabling collective knowledge construction where each contribution builds on previous exchanges.
2. *Cross-session continuity*: Conversation histories persist across multiple sessions, allowing asynchronous students to join ongoing discussions, review previous exchanges, and contribute at their own pace. This proves crucial for HyFlex equivalency: synchronous students might complete an activity during class time, while asynchronous students engage with the same collaborative AI space over several days.
3. *Instructor observation dashboards*: Teachers access real-time views of all group rooms simultaneously, monitoring participation patterns, identifying groups needing support, and reviewing conversation quality without directly interrupting student work. This "fly on the wall" capability enables facilitation responsive to actual group dynamics.
4. *Contexted rooms:* Instructors may switch on "Contexted Room" to give each large language model all the conversation history in the room, as part of the context of any question submitted to a large language model on YoChatGPT. This allows for teachers and students to summarize any discussions during class time and allows for the generative AI to support collaborative problem solving know the learning objectives and any activity scaffolding before students enter rooms.
5. *Anonymous participation options:* Students can choose usernames rather than real names, partially addressing equity concerns around participation anxiety and status hierarchies based on perceived academic standing.

Pilot implementations across Hong Kong institutions documented educator and student perspectives on YoChatGPT affordances (Ting & Chan, 2025). Teacher feedback highlighted three primary benefits: (1) ability to simultaneously monitor multiple group discussions impossible in physical classroom environments, (2) persistent records enabling assessment of collaborative process not just final products, and (3) reduced setup friction compared to coordinating Zoom breakout rooms or separate ChatGPT accounts.

Student feedback revealed more mixed perspectives. Positive themes included appreciation for asynchronous access enabling participation despite scheduling conflicts, comfort asking "basic" questions without peer judgment, and AI's "patience" providing multiple explanations without frustration. Concerns centered on uncertainty about appropriate AI reliance (when using AI constitutes "cheating"), technical learning curves navigating the platform interface, and occasional technical limitation of the platform, like a lag time in the AI responding to their questions. These mixed perspectives prove pedagogically significant: CoGenAI should be positioned as one pedagogical approach among many, not universal replacement for all collaborative learning.

Assessment & Academic Integrity in CoGenAI

Effective assessment in CoGenAI environments shifts focus from final products to collaborative processes. YoChatGPT! persistent conversation histories and audit trails enable instructors to evaluate contribution quality, idea evolution, and critical evaluation of AI outputs rather than only final answers. Recommended practices include: (1) process-based rubrics weighting prompt quality, peer negotiation, and AI critique (30% each) alongside final output (10%); (2) requiring students to submit "prompt logs" with reflections on how they verified or challenged AI responses; (3) incorporating oral defences or peer presentations of group reasoning; and (4) using the platform's teacher-verified icon feature to flag instructor-checked outputs. These approaches maintain academic integrity while rewarding the higher-order thinking CoGenAI is designed to cultivate.

SECTION 3: CROSS-DISCIPLINARY IMPLEMENTATION

This section presents three detailed case studies demonstrating CoGenAI across disciplines: mathematics (STEM), psychology (social sciences), and business innovation. Each case study includes the specific CoGenAI activity design with adapted prompt template, evidence of impact, HyFlex modality implementations, TPACK analysis and iterative refinement. Note that in all of the case studies below, the implementation of CoGenAI pedagogies may be supported using any multi-user GenAI platform with persistent rooms, instructor dashboards, and RAG curriculum alignment, e.g., YoChatGPT!, ChatGPT! Teams or BoodleBox. At the end of this section, we will summarize by providing a table comparing all three cases.

Case Study 1 - Mathematics: Inquiry-Based Learning with Technology

In a mathematics education course involving pre-service and in-service mathematics teachers in Hong Kong, one of the course assessment tasks was to design an inquiry-based learning active learning pedagogy using the 5E instructional model (Engage, Explore, Explain, Elaborate, Evaluate) (Bybee et al., 2006) supported by some technology. The technologies suggested to support this inquiry-based learning activity were Desmos, Polypad and Geogebra.

For example, a secondary mathematics in service teacher designed a CoGenAI activity for teaching fractions, a persistently challenging topic where students often memorize procedures without conceptual understanding (Siegler et al., 2013), using the following CoGenAI prompt template:

I am an instructor teaching a course called [MTH6134: Technology in Mathematics Education].Please help me design an active learning in-class activity based on [Inquiry Based Learning (IBL)] pedagogy and the [5E-model] for [IBL] pedagogy using [YoChatGPT!] technology on the topic of[fractions] in the subject of [Mathematics] for students in [Grade 8] in [Secondary School].

All students in the course were encouraged to use the above CoGenAI template to initially draft their task designs in groups of 3-4 students for this course choosing different frameworks for IBL, topics, grade levels and technology, using YoChatGPT!

The mathematics education course involved 18 pre-service and in-service secondary mathematics teachers randomly assigned to control (n=9) and experimental (n=9) groups, balanced for teaching experience and technology proficiency. The control group designed IBL activities using traditional methods while the experimental group used the CoGenAI Prompt Template with YoChatGPT. Student learning was assessed through: (1) oral presentation (20%), (2) written task design document (40%), and (3) reflective essay (40%). Task design employed a validated rubric with four dimension: 5E model alignment, technology integration, anticipation of student thinking, and assessment design, which was scored by two independent raters (Cohen's $\kappa=0.82$). Above-average performance was defined as scoring at least greater than or equal to 7.5/10 on task design (the sample median).

Chi-square analysis revealed significant association between group allocation and task design performance: experimental group had 87.5% (7/8) above-average scores versus control group's 22.2% (2/9), $\chi^2(1, N=17)=7.244$, $p=.007$, phi=.65.

Mean task design scores showed Control M=6.2/10 (SD=1.4) versus Experimental M=8.1/10 (SD=1.1), yielding Cohen's d=1.48, a very large effect size. Additionally, critical thinking self-perceptions were significantly higher in the experimental group (M=4.06, SD=0.85) compared to control (M=3.25, SD=0.57), t(15)=2.331, p=.034. These results suggest CoGenAI with YoChatGPT substantially enhances instructional design quality and critical thinking development in mathematics education contexts, though small sample size (N=18) necessitates replication with larger populations.

In this HyFlex mathematics education course, CoGenAI facilitated group exploration using YoChatGPT! multi-user chatrooms, with the 5E inquiry model (Engage, Explore, Explain, Elaborate, Evaluate) adapted for modality equity: in-person groups collaborated via shared devices for real-time AI prompting, synchronous online participants integrated through Zoom screen-sharing for breakout discussions, and asynchronous learners may contribute via persistent chat logs with AI-generated summaries ensuring seamless inclusion. TPACK alignment was achieved by balancing technology (YoChatGPT! adaptive scaffolding), pedagogy (inquiry-based active learning per ICAP's interactive levels), and content (various mathematics topics from K12 to University), fostering conceptual depth through distributed expertise. Challenges include providing enough context to the LLM on the educational technology supporting the IBL activity using the 5E model, as there isn't much publicly available information about how to be technologically efficient using Desmos, Geogebra or PolyPad. However, these challenges were iteratively improved by refining prompts to provide more context into the educational technology (e.g., PDF upload of instructions on how to use Geogebra) and emphasizing human verification via critical thinking of outputs. These iterative behaviors enhanced the overall efficiency and promoting YoChatGPT! as a tool for productive, modality-agnostic collaborations that help trainers and trainees co-construct pedagogically sound active learning activities supported by technology.

In this case study on designing personalized 5E-IBL math activities, the Hyflex principles of learner choice and accessibility were supported through YoChatGPT! multi-user chatrooms allowing in-person groups to use shared devices and online students to use Zoom, while equivalency and reusability were ensured by adapting the 5E inquiry model for all modalities and using AI-generated summaries to keep asynchronous users included. In particular, asynchronous students joined the same persistent room later, reviewed the full AI-moderated thread with auto-generated summaries, and added their own new design 5E instructional prompts or read examples of other classmates' IBL prompts.

Case Study 2 - Psychology: Concept Exploration Through Basic "Question and Answer" Pedagogy

In two Psychology courses on foundations of learning contexts, the instructors used CoGenAI to help students understand abstract psychological constructs by linking them to personal interests by introducing a strategy called the **"Concept Prompt"** (Ting & Chan, 2025). We define the **Concept Prompt Template** as follows:

"I am a [grade level] student who loves [hobby/interest]. Please help me understand [concept] in the subject [discipline], relating it to [hobby/interest]."

The aim of using the concept prompt is to personalize any academic topic to students' hobbies/passions by connecting abstract concepts to concrete, personally meaningful examples.

In implementation of the concept prompt in the teacher education course, we asked students to share their concept prompts on YoChatGPT, when learning about certain learning theories in class. This changes the traditional "question and answer" active teaching strategy where the students ask a question to the teacher in class, to asking the generative AI in class. The basic "question and answer" is in the "active" category of ICAP (Van Amburgh et al., 2007). An example of a concept prompt from a student is as follows:

"I am a university student who loves K-pop (especially BLACKPINK). Please help me understand Vygotsky's Zone of Proximal Development in Educational Psychology, relating it to BLACKPINK."

One of YoChatGPT's LLM response generated an analogy where learning new choreography represents the ZPD movements too easy (already mastered) versus too difficult (physically impossible) versus optimal challenge (requires guidance from a dance coach). The teacher would then explain the LLM response to the class creating a bridge from metaphor to conceptual rigor (Ting & Chan, 2025, p. 38). In fact, the concept prompt can be used in any math or science subject to relate any concept or abstract idea to the students' personal interest, hobbies or passions (Ting et al., 2025).

The impact of this CoGenAI pedagogy of modified "question and answer" with generative AI increased students' personalized learning, in the following sense. Using the Personalized Learning Support Instrument (PLSI) adapted for AI contexts (Zhang et al., 2022), pre/post surveys were given after the above "Concept prompt" in-class activity. Data analysis on the pre/post surveys showed significant improvements in two dimensions:

- *Resourcefulness* ($p=.035$): Students reported increased ability to "reflect on learning strategies and adjust them when needed" via AI tools.

- *Progress Toward Goals* (p=.041): Students better tracked mastery and set personalized learning goals.

Qualitative feedback highlighted that AI-generated analogies "made abstract theories suddenly click" and that the approach "felt less like studying and more like exploring my own interests" (Ting & Chan, 2025, p. 41).

For these HyFlex psychology courses on learning theories, CoGenAI supported personalized concept mapping via YoChatGPT!, connecting theory of learning constructs with individual interests through modality adaptations: in-person sessions used verbal AI inputs for dynamic group mapping, synchronous online leveraged integrated chat for real-time collaboration, and asynchronous participants added reflections to persistent rooms with AI-synthesized updates for continuity (Ting & Chan, 2025). TPACK integration harmonized technology (YoChatGPT! personalized prompting), pedagogy ("basic question and answer" active activity per mapping to ICAP), and content (theories on learning), enabling metacognitive gains. Early challenges, include how the instructor could critically go over all the concept prompts submitted, i.e., there would be over 20 prompts submitted, and due to time constraints of each class, the instructor may only critically describe only one or two outputs from students' concept prompts. Iterative refinement included an arrangement, where students could vote for their favourite concept prompt, and hence, saving the instructors time in trying to choose which concept prompt to go over in class. In addition, asking students to peer critique their classmates' concept prompt would also align with collaborative pedagogies that empower teachers and students to work efficiently with generative AI.

In this case study on conceptual understanding of foundations of learning contexts in psychology, the Hyflex principles of equivalency and learner choice were achieved by allowing all students to personalize abstract concepts via the 'Concept Prompt' regardless of modality. Asynchronous students visited the rooms after class to evaluate other classmates' concept prompts to discover the wide variety of personalization available for abstract theories, and sometimes added their own concept prompts for practice, demonstrating true reusability and accessibility.

Case Study 3 - Business Innovation: Creative Problem-Solving Using Superminds Scaffolding

Multiple innovation and ideation workshops were given addressing real-world challenges through Superminds Ideation, which is Malone's (2018) framework for human-AI collective intelligence. The objectives were to apply systematic creativity techniques (through at least two of six design moves) to generate innovative solutions and to collaboratively evaluate their ideas in terms of feasibility, novelty and impact. This activity scaffolding was used so that teams of students could develop rapid prototypes incorporating AI-generated insights.

The Superminds Framework scaffolds ideation through six design moves (Heyman et al., 2024)): three basic moves of *Zoom In, Zoom Out* and *Analogize*; and three Supermind Moves of *Groupify, Cognify* and *Technify*. Each move is designed to lead the individual or team to come up with a more creative solution to a problem by looking at it from each of these different viewpoints, described as follows:

Basic Moves:

- *Zoom In*: "What are the *parts* of [problem]?" e.g., the parts of whole-person development are sports participation, career readiness, mental health.
- *Zoom Out*: "What *larger problem* is this part of?" e.g., motivating fitness health part of the larger domain of fostering holistic education.
- *Analogize*: "What are analogies for [problem] in different fields?" e.g., motivating students is analagous to credit card companies incentivizing spending via rewards points.

Supermind Moves:

- *Groupify:* "How would a [hierarchical/democratic/market-based] group solve this?" e.g., how would a *doctor's office* diagnose depression to how would a *society* diagnose depression?
- *Cognify:* "What cognitive steps are needed?" e.g., how can you sense depression (sensing needs), decide interventions, and learn from outcomes.
- *Technify*: "What technology could support this?" e.g., how can an online social network sense depression, or how a gamified app can track activity participation with redeemable rewards.

We asked innovation and ideation workshop participants to form groups of three to five, formulate a problem for their group, and given an initial solution to their problem, e.g., how do businesses' increase teamwork in their multiple departments. Then, groups would give an initial solution to their problem, e.g., have more informal gatherings (coffee, lunch, etc...). Finally, we asked groups to go through at least one basic design move and one Supermind move to formulate another solution to their problem with the aide of generative AI. To be precise, we instructed groups to ask the large language models on YoChatGPT to help them zoom in, zoom out, analogize, groupify, cognify, or technify their problem. For example, if a groups' problem was "how do you motivate whole-person development in a university", then groups may use the following sample prompt templates for certain design moves:

1. *Zoom In*: *"What specific activities does our Student Affairs Office offer for sports, sustainability, and mental wellness?"*
2. *Analogize*: *"How do fitness apps (like Strava) motivate users? What parallels exist for university engagement?"*
3. *Technify*: *"Design an app that rewards students for attending Student Affairs events with points redeemable for campus perks."*

We documented each move's output in YoChatGPT rooms, creating an audit trail from problem, analogies to prototype concept.

To evaluate Superminds scaffolding effectiveness, we conducted a quasi-experimental study during innovation and entrepreneurship workshops at a Hong Kong university in Spring 2025. Approximately 20 participants (N ≈ 20) completed a design thinking activity where they first identified organizational problems and initial solutions, then applied the full Superminds scaffolding protocol (Basic Design Moves: Zoom In, Zoom Out, Analogize; Supermind Design Moves: Groupify, Cognify, Technify) with YoChatGPT support over 25-30 minutes. Using a pre-post repeated measures design, participants self-rated their solutions on three 5-point Likert scales both before and after applying Superminds moves: Feasibility ("How practical and achievable is this solution given existing resources, constraints, and technology?"), Novelty ("How original or innovative is this solution compared to existing approaches?"), and Impact ("What is the likely positive impact of this solution if successfully implemented?"). Not all participants completed all three rating dimensions at both timepoints, resulting in varying sample sizes (n=6-12) per measure - a common occurrence in field-based educational research where survey completion is voluntary. We used Welch's independent samples t-tests to compare pre-post means, recognizing this conservative approach treats repeated observations as independent groups.

Table 1 summarizes the comparative results across all three dimensions:

Table 1. Pre/post self-reported scores of feasibility, novelty and impact on a 1-5 Likert scale (within-subjects design with varying response rates). Note: n varies by *dimension due to incomplete survey responses at pre/post timepoints *p < .001; † p < .10 (marginal significance)*

Dimension	Before (Mean ± SD, n)	After (Mean ± SD, n)	Mean Difference	t-value	df (approx.)	p-value (two-tailed)	Cohen' d
Feasibility	3.00 ± 1.00, n=6	3.58 ± 1.26, n=12	+0.58	≈ -1.14	≈ 15.3	≈ 0.272	0.51 (medium)
Novelty	2.29 ± 0.70, n=8	3.70 ± 0.78, n=10	+1.41	≈ -4.25	≈ 15.6	≈ 0.0007 *	1.91 (very large)
Impact	3.42 ± 0.86, n=12	4.00 ± 0.77, n=10	+0.58	≈ -1.77	≈ 19.4	≈ 0.093†	0.71 (medium-large)

The Superminds scaffolding with YoChatGPT produced a *highly statistically significant increase in perceived Novelty* (p≈.0007), with scores rising from 2.29 to 3.70—a 1.41-point improvement representing a 62% increase with very large effect size (Cohen's d=1.91). This demonstrates that the structured design moves fundamentally enhanced creative problem-solving by helping participants systematically explore new perspectives (Zoom In/Out), draw cross-domain connections (Analogize), and leverage collective intelligence (Groupify, Cognify, Technify). Feasibility showed moderate improvement (+0.58 points, Cohen's d=0.51) but did not reach significance (p≈.272), while Impact showed similar gains (+0.58 points, Cohen's d=0.71) approaching marginal significance (p≈.093). The substantial novelty boost alongside maintained feasibility suggests participants generated "feasibly innovative" rather than "wildly impractical" ideas.

In this HyFlex innovation and ideation workshops, CoGenAI facilitated "Superminds" prototyping for creative solutions using YoChatGPT!, with adaptations ensuring cross-modality flow: in-person ideation involved shared screens for AI-mediated discussions, synchronous online used breakout chats for virtual collaboration, and asynchronous users joined via logged inputs with AI summaries maintaining momentum (Ting et al., 2025). TPACK balanced technology (YoChatGPT! synthesis), pedagogy (group problem-based learning scaffolded using Superminds design moves), and content (entrepreneurial skills), augmenting collective intelligence. Challenges include participants not fully understanding the Superminds design activity instructions, insufficient time to complete the task of finding a second solution after Supermind moves; and grouping of participants for productive engagement. In addition, generative AI usually outputs too much information, for which the groups must sift through to obtain their preferred solutions. Iterative refinement for improvement of implementation includes devoting more time to introduce the Supermind moves and how to use them with generative AI in YoChatGPT. In addition, adding an AI agent to nudge groups in the right direction and be more productive when they are stagnant in discussion might aide groups to accelerate their problem solving (Ba, et al., 2025). Finally, adding faculty facilitation and iteratively refining the above process for more inclusive, efficient group work that promotes CoGenAI pedagogies as a key enabler for trainers and trainees in developing more creative solutions to problems.

In this case study on Business Innovation, the Hyflex principles of learner choice and equivalency were realized by providing Superminds scaffolding across all modes—using shared screens for in-person and breakout chats for online groups—to ensure comparable creative output. Reusability and accessibility were secured through YoChatGPT! creation of audit trails and AI summaries, allowing asynchronous users to maintain momentum and access the full history of the ideation process. Asynchronous users were also observed to insert additional Supermind design move prompts which they initially did not try initially, during the classroom activity, to explore what other alternative solutions exist from the ones they've found during class time.

We conclude Section 3 with a summary comparison of all three cases presented above in **Table 2** below, and cross-case insights.

Table 2. Comparison table of CoGenAI pedagogy, AI's role, key outcomes and Hyflex mechanisms in all three case studies across disciplines

Discipline	CoGenAI Pedagogy	AI Role	Key Outcome	Hyflex Mechanism
Mathematics	Design of Inquiry-Based Learning (5E model) Math Activities	Personalizing IBL activity for every student on any math topic	Significantly higher task-design scores (χ^2 p=.007)	Shared 5E instructional workflow and multi-user chatrooms; AI summaries for async handoff
Psychology	Concept Prompt (modified Q&A)	Personalized analogy generation	Improved resourcefulness & goal progress (p<.05)	Real-time chat for sync + persistent logs for async
Business Innovation	Scaffolded Problem-Based Learning via Superminds design moves	Idea expansion & synthesis	Large increase in perceived novelty (p≈.0007)	Cross-session continuity + audit trails

Across the three implementations, three consistent success conditions emerged: persistent multi-user rooms enabling true modality equivalence, structured prompt templates scaffolding higher-order thinking, and deliberate instructor orchestration of human-AI handoffs. Common pitfalls included insufficient facilitation (leading to rushed scaffolding) and under-specification of context for the LLM. Equity was achieved most effectively when asynchronous students received AI-generated thread summaries and explicit handoff prompts. These patterns confirm that CoGenAI's value lies not in the technology alone but in its thoughtful pedagogical integration.

SECTION 4: CRITICAL EVALUATION, ASSESSMENT AND ETHICS

In this section, we reflect critically on certain barriers that may arise during the implementation of CoGenAI pedagogies in hyflex modalities using YoChatGPT! Additionally, we discuss the ethical issues involved in implementing CoGenAI pedagogies.

When CoGenAI activities are only partially and not completely implemented or realized, analysis reveals conditions for effective implementation. In the business innovation case study using Superminds scaffolding, several groups bypassed the six-move framework entirely, jumping directly to brainstorming final solutions without engaging in Superminds moves. A particularly instructive failure occurred in a multimedia design and automation course where students were grouped to construct their multimedia (infographics, webpages or videos) for their non-profit or educational organizations using CoGenAI group activity using superminds scaffolding. However, 5 out of the 9 teams only completed one supermind design move. Another impediment to using generative AI in group problem-solving activities when developing technological prototypes, the "the AI would tell us how to design the whole thing instead of helping us think and struggle, step by step." This is one of the drawbacks of using generative AI for students who are technically less proficient; however, it does force them to critically review and verify each step of the technical implementation. Post-activity interviews revealed, nonetheless, that students liked that they could upload material related to their group problem; and compared YoChatGPT to using other commercialized large language models with their learning management system at school.

For mathematics, implementing CoGenAI through design tasks modelled by IBL through 5E model pedagogy, the challenge of designing instructions for students so that they are clear to follow the 5E steps was challenging. For example, in the "Explore" or "Explain" stage, students may prematurely ask the AI for a direct answer, undermining inquiry pedagogy. In this case, prompt engineering adjustments explicitly instructed the AI to redirect such requests: "If students ask for direct answers, respond: 'I notice you're asking for the answer. Instead, could you show me how you're thinking about this problem? What visual model might help?'" which will reduce direct answer-seeking while maintaining accessible scaffolding for students experiencing productive struggle. However, interviews with students reported that they appreciated the hyflex collaborative drawing features like the whiteboard and text to scientific diagram functionality for students to use in the "exploration" stage of the 5E model for IBL, in all modes (face-to-face, virtual or hybrid). For example, for a CoGenAI activity on fractions, students may explore "What is 3/4?" via multiple visual representations through with the AI occasionally providing direct procedural answers with contexted prompts designed to facilitate conceptual understanding. This highlights AI can be positioned as a collaborative thinking partner rather than an authoritative expert.

Iterative refinement strategies employing TPACK-based troubleshooting have proven essential for converting initial implementation failures into pedagogically sound practices across the documented case studies. When business innovation groups rushed through Superminds moves, refinement involved modifying the contexted prompt to include explicit pacing guidance stating "I notice you've moved to "Cognify" but only spent 2 minutes on "Zoom Out". Let's return to considering broader context" combined with adding meta-cognitive scaffolding questions like "What would be advantages and disadvantages of this approach? What alternatives should we consider?" that positioned AI as critical thinking facilitator rather than solution provider.

The concept prompt implementation in psychology addressed the challenge of instructors critically reviewing all student submissions within time constraints by introducing peer voting mechanisms where students selected their favorite concept prompts for whole-class discussion, simultaneously reducing instructor workload while promoting metacognitive evaluation of prompt quality and introducing collaborative curation as pedagogical practice. Across all three case studies, systematic TPACK troubleshooting proved invaluable: technology dimension analysis identified when text-only interfaces created friction for visual-spatial tasks, prompting development of image upload capabilities and integration with advanced features for mathematics and science education. In addition, in the future, to accommodate students with special educational needs, a speech to text functionality (and vice-versa) will be added for ease of inputting text into the collaborative chatrooms. Pedagogy dimension analysis revealed when group sizes exceeded optimal collaboration thresholds or when asynchronous students needed explicit connection instructions to join ongoing synchronous conversations. In the content dimension of TPACK, we found that AI struggled to help students learn things that required physical practice and understanding different perspectives or connecting to their own life experiences.

The iterative refinement approach positions initial CoGenAI implementations as prototypes requiring evidence-based adjustment rather than expecting immediate pedagogical success, acknowledging that effective CoGenAI practice emerges through cycles of design, implementation, critical evaluation, and revision informed by both learning analytics and qualitative stakeholder feedback.

Effective assessment in CoGenAI environments necessitates a fundamental shift in focus from evaluating static final products to analyzing the collaborative processes that created them. By leveraging YoChatGPT! persistent conversation histories and audit trails, instructors are empowered to evaluate contribution quality, the evolution of ideas, and the critical evaluation of AI outputs rather than simply grading final answers. To operationalize this, we recommend practices such as employing process-based rubrics that heavily weight prompt quality, peer negotiation, and AI critique alongside the final output, as well as requiring students to submit "prompt logs" detailing their reflections on how they verified or challenged AI responses. Furthermore, academic integrity can be bolstered by incorporating oral defenses or peer presentations of group reasoning and utilizing the platform's teacher-verified icon feature to flag instructor-checked outputs; these approaches ensure we are rewarding the higher-order thinking and metacognitive self-regulation that CoGenAI is specifically designed to cultivate.

Ethical considerations demand proactive attention across multiple dimensions of CoGenAI implementation, beginning with fundamental equity concerns regarding differential AI access and digital literacy. While collaborative AI platforms can enable students without individual ChatGPT subscriptions to participate in AI-mediated collaboration, and text-based anonymous interaction can reduce participation barriers for non-native language speakers and students experiencing verbal discussion anxiety, CoGenAI simultaneously creates new exclusions for students lacking reliable internet access. In addition, learners with visual impairments may have screen readers that are incompatible with emerging AI platforms. Finally, learners with limited typing proficiency for whom text-based interaction imposes higher cognitive load than verbal discussion.

Mitigation strategies must include conducting technology access surveys before implementation, providing campus computer lab access and device lending programs, designing low-tech alternative activities ensuring no students face systematic exclusion, and never making AI-mediated activities the sole basis for assessment. Over-reliance risks constitute a second critical ethical concern, particularly in professional education contexts where autonomous problem-solving represents essential competency: when students outsource thinking to AI rather than using it as collaborative scaffold, they may develop intellectual dependency undermining the very critical thinking and metacognitive self-regulation skills that CoGenAI activities intend to cultivate (Miao & Holmes, 2023). Addressing this requires clear instructions and prompt engineering distinguishing AI as collaborative tool from AI as autonomous replacement for human reasoning, assessment designs evaluating the quality of questions students ask and their critical evaluation of AI responses rather than only final products.

Data privacy and institutional surveillance present additional ethical considerations: while persistent conversation histories enable valuable learning analytics and asynchronous participation continuity, they also create surveillance infrastructure students may experience as invasive, potentially inhibiting authentic expression and risk-taking essential for productive intellectual struggle. Privacy-protective practices include transparent data policies, anonymous participation options, student control over conversation retention, limiting institutional access to course instructors rather than broader administrative monitoring, and conducting ethics review board evaluation when using conversation data for research purposes.

Algorithmic bias constitutes a final ethical imperative given that large language models trained on internet-scale datasets reproduce societal biases around race, gender, disability, and other identity dimensions through stereotyped examples, culturally-specific knowledge gaps, and differential response quality. A simple example of algorithmic bias is when a the prompt "cartoon image of a professor" into a text to image model (e.g., Dall-E, GPTImage) usually generates an old man with glasses in a suit with white hair image. Mitigation requires explicitly teaching students about AI limitations and biases as core digital literacy education, instructor monitoring of conversation histories to identify and correctively intervene on problematic AI responses, and activity designs requiring critical evaluation rather than uncritical acceptance of AI-generated content. Our YoChatGPT platform diminishes some of these biases by allowing users to reply to LLM outputs and critique and verify them for accuracy; and has a unique "teacher verification" functionality where a "verified icon" appears on top of AI outputs that are checked by the instructor.

SECTION 5: FUTURE DIRECTIONS

Scaling CoGenAI across institutions requires moving beyond isolated course-level pilots toward systemic integration supported by train-the-trainer models that leverage early adopters as pedagogical change agents. Current implementations remain concentrated within individual courses taught by technically-proficient, pedagogically-innovative instructors, limiting broader institutional transformation potential. Train-the-trainer approaches address this scalability challenge by identifying faculty champions who have successfully implemented CoGenAI pedagogies, providing them with pedagogical leadership training, and positioning them as discipline-specific mentors supporting colleagues' adoption within their departments and across partner institutions. This model reduces individual development burden by creating shared repositories of validated activity designs, discipline-specific prompt templates, and troubleshooting resources, while simultaneously building institutional communities of practice that normalize pedagogical experimentation and evidence-based iteration. Scaling also demands institutional infrastructure investment beyond individual faculty subscriptions, requiring universities to license collaborative AI platforms as core educational technology infrastructure alongside learning management systems. Quality assurance mechanisms become increasingly critical as CoGenAI scales: institutional review processes employing TPACK frameworks (or parallel frameworks, like SAMR or RAT) can evaluate proposed activity designs before implementation. In addition, peer teaching observation initiatives can focus specifically on AI-mediated pedagogy. Finally, learning analytics dashboards and deployment of validated instruments to measure student learning outcomes can track participation equity and conceptual understanding gains. These quantitative methods of collecting evidence to inform effectiveness of CoGenAI pedagogies ensure that adoption maintains pedagogical rigor rather than defaulting to superficial "technology for technology's sake" implementations.

New technologies like virtual reality (VR) and extended reality (XR) could solve many current problems with CoGenAI while creating exciting new learning opportunities. Right now, text-based platforms like YoChatGPT! work great for discussion and idea generation, but they struggle when students need hands-on practice, spatial thinking, or physical manipulation. Imagine students from different locations, where some are in class, some at home, and meeting in the same virtual space where AI helps them explore together. They could conduct chemistry experiments in virtual labs, walk through historical sites, design buildings, or practice professional skills in simulated workplaces together.

For example, chemistry students could run virtual experiments together with AI helping them form hypotheses and interpret results, whether they're joining the class live or working from home later. This solves a major problem: right now, online and asynchronous students often feel disconnected and overwhelmed in lab-based courses. Next-generation AI that can process images, audio, and video (not just text) will make collaboration even richer. Students could get feedback on their design sketches, talk to the AI instead of typing (great for students who struggle with typing), and work together analyzing visual data that's hard to discuss through text alone. However, to the author's current knowledge, no VR or XR platforms can connect with collaborative chatrooms that use multiple multimodal AI models.

AI-powered instant translation opens another exciting possibility: students from different countries could work together on real problems despite language barriers, with AI translating in real-time. This would democratize access to global perspectives that are currently limited to students who speak certain languages. Finally, AI could help form better study groups by analyzing students' strengths, learning styles, and knowledge areas to suggest optimal team compositions. Over time, the system could learn which combinations work best for different types of projects and keep improving its recommendations.

As CoGenAI pedagogies evolve, we need strong research to validate them, i.e., carefully designed studies that prove CoGenAI actually works through controlled experiments tracking students over time and examining impact across different learner groups. YoChatGPT! has already produced robust evidence showing that CoGenAI pedagogies lead to significant improvements: students demonstrated enhanced critical thinking skills within Inquiry-Based Learning frameworks, personalized activities improved metacognitive skills and learning autonomy, and STEM students showed improved academic performance and problem-solving abilities (Ting & Chan, 2025; Ting et al., 2025). However, we need validated assessment tools to measure effectiveness across subjects and contexts, investigate equity issues, e.g., does CoGenAI help or hurt students from different backgrounds? or how specific platform features affect participation patterns to design more inclusive collaboration.

Long-term studies should track whether CoGenAI develops lasting collaborative and AI literacy skills that transfer to careers, how sustained use shapes students' thinking about learning, and whether different HyFlex modes produce equivalent outcomes. Faculty development research must identify effective training approaches, particularly since targeted professional development initiatives focused on pedagogical GenAI integration are essential for success. Moreover, we must investigate what barriers prevent adoption and how disciplinary cultures shape appropriate implementation. Finally, we need to understand the mechanics of collective intelligence: what aspects of AI-mediated collaboration enhance group problem-solving to identify optimal AI intervention patterns that support rather than dominate human thinking.

SECTION 6: CONCLUSION

This chapter introduced Collaborative Generative AI (CoGenAI) as a pedagogical approach addressing the persistent collaboration equity challenge in HyFlex learning environments. In this section, we will synthesize cross-case findings, discuss optimal conditions for when to implement CoGenAI pedagogies, and final pedagogical recommendations. We will then conclude with a discussion on how CoGenAI pedagogies advances processes and outcomes involved in any application of the Hyperflex equivalency principle.

We considered three cross disciplinary implementations of CoGenAI pedagogies (mathematics inquiry through the 5E model, psychology concept exploration through personalized prompting, and business innovation through Superminds scaffolding) which demonstrated its adaptability and impact. Across all cases, the following success factors emerged:

1. *Theoretically-grounded design*: Activities explicitly aligned with TPACK, ICAP, and social constructivist frameworks produced measurable learning gains (enhanced task design quality in mathematics, increased metacognitive awareness in psychology, significantly improved solution novelty in business);
2. *Explicit scaffolding:* Structured prompt templates (CoGenAI Prompt Template, Concept Prompt Template, Superminds Design Moves) provided discipline-flexible yet pedagogically coherent guidance preventing students from treating AI as answer oracle;
3. *Instructor facilitation:* Human monitoring, critical verification, and self-reflective debriefing proved essential for AI integrated teaching without replacing the human element;
4. *HyFlex-specific affordances:* Persistent conversation histories, multi-user rooms, and contexted prompts enabled asynchronous students to genuinely collaborate rather than merely consuming synchronous students' work artifacts.

The decision to implement CoGenAI should be driven by specific pedagogical goals, proving most appropriate when objectives emphasize collaborative knowledge construction, critical thinking, and creative problem-solving regarding abstract concepts rather than rote skill practice. This approach is particularly valuable when the student population includes asynchronous learners who require persistent digital spaces to participate equitably, provided that instructors possess the necessary prompt engineering competencies to monitor group dynamics and the institution ensures data privacy. Conversely, CoGenAI possibly proves counterproductive when learning objectives demand embodied physical practice or the understanding of lived experiences which AI cannot authentically represent, or in professional contexts where autonomous problem-solving is the essential competency being assessed. Furthermore, implementation should be avoided if it creates equity barriers due to lack of technology access or conflicts with disciplinary norms and accreditation requirements that prohibit AI assistance.

To successfully implement CoGenAI pedagogies, we recommend a scaffolded approach that begins with low-stakes, ungraded explorations to build student confidence and AI literacy before moving to assessed work. Design activities with explicit equivalency in mind, ensuring that in-person, synchronous, and asynchronous students achieve comparable outcomes, while treating prompt engineering as a metacognitive skill where the quality of students' questions demonstrates their understanding. It is crucial to build in human verification checkpoints where learners critically evaluate AI outputs for bias and accuracy, while also maintaining options for human-only collaboration to complement AI-mediated interaction. Finally, instructors should leverage persistent conversation logs for formative assessment to identify misconceptions or struggling groups, and continuously iterate their designs based on evidence from student feedback and learning analytics to refine facilitation strategies.

CoGenAI's central contribution lies in operationalizing Beatty's (2019) equivalency principle for collaborative learning. Traditional HyFlex implementations achieve surface-level equivalency where all students access the same lecture content but fail at deeper levels when collaboration becomes modality-dependent. By providing generative AI as persistent collaborative partner accessible regardless of attendance mode, CoGenAI enables process equivalency (all students engage in dialogic knowledge construction) and outcome equivalency (learning gains from collaborative sense-making accrue across modalities) rather than merely content equivalency.

The evidence presented of improved task design quality (mathematics), enhanced metacognitive awareness (psychology), and increased solution novelty (business), suggests that when designed thoughtfully, CoGenAI activities produce learning outcomes meeting or exceeding traditional face-to-face collaboration while extending access to students whom synchronous-only designs systematically exclude. This represents pedagogical progress beyond logistical accommodation: HyFlex transforms from constraint requiring workarounds into affordance enabling collaboration patterns impossible in single-modality instruction.

By positioning multi-user generative AI platforms like YoChatGPT as accessible collaborative partners rather than individual tutors, CoGenAI transforms the HyFlex "flexibility versus quality" dilemma into an opportunity for inclusive, equitable, and pedagogically rigorous group-based learning across synchronous in-person, synchronous online, and asynchronous modalities.

REFERENCES

Abdelmalak, M. M. M., & Parra, J. L. (2016). Expanding learning opportunities for graduate students with HyFlex course design. *International Journal of Online Pedagogy and Course Design*, *6*(4), 19–37. DOI: 10.4018/IJOPCD.2016100102

Ba, S., Swiecki, Z., Tan, Y., Lu, G., Shaffer, D. W., & Gašević, D. (2025). Community of inquiry in motion: Modeling inquiry dynamics with movement analysis (MOVA). *Computers & Education*, *242*, 105513. DOI: 10.1016/j.compedu.2025.105513

Beatty, B. J. (2019). *Hybrid-flexible course design: Implementing student-directed hybrid classes*. EdTech Books. https://edtechbooks.org/hyflex

Bender, E. M., Gebru, T., McMillan-Major, A., & Shmitchell, S. (2021). On the dangers of stochastic parrots: Can language models be too big? *Proceedings of the 2021 ACM Conference on Fairness, Accountability, and Transparency*, 610-623. https://doi.org/DOI: 10.1145/3442188.3445922

Bond, M., Khosravi, H., De Laat, M., Bergdahl, N., Negrea, V., Oxley, E., Pham, P., Chawla, S., & Siemens, G. (2024). A meta systematic review of artificial intelligence in higher education: A call for increased ethics, collaboration, and rigour. *International Journal of Educational Technology in Higher Education*, *21*(1), 4. Advance online publication. DOI: 10.1186/s41239-023-00436-z

Bonwell, C. C., & Eison, J. A. (1991). ASHE-ERIC Higher Education Report: Vol. 1. *Active learning: Creating excitement in the classroom*. Jossey-Bass.

Brown, T. B., Mann, B., Ryder, N., Subbiah, M., Kaplan, J., Dhariwal, P., Neelakantan, A., Shyam, P., Sastry, G., Askell, A., Agarwal, S., Herbert-Voss, A., Krueger, G., Henighan, T., Child, R., Ramesh, A., Ziegler, D. M., Wu, J., Winter, C., & Amodei, D. (2020). *Language models are few-shot learners* (Vol. 33). Advances in Neural Information Processing Systems, https://arxiv.org/abs/2005.14165

Bybee, R. W., Taylor, J. A., Gardner, A., Van Scotter, P., Powell, J. C., Westbrook, A., & Landes, N. (2006). *The BSCS 5E instructional model: Origins and effectiveness*. BSCS. https://media.bscs.org/bscsmw/5es/bscs_5e_full_report.pdf

Cabral, J. (2024). AI-powered learning analytics dashboard for monitoring student progress [Master's thesis, University of Porto]. Repositório Aberto da Universidade do Porto. https://repositorio-aberto.up.pt/bitstream/10216/168811/2/735524.pdf

Chi, M. T. H., & Wylie, R. (2014). The ICAP framework: Linking cognitive engagement to active learning outcomes. *Educational Psychologist*, *49*(4), 219–243. DOI: 10.1080/00461520.2014.965823

Freeman, S., Eddy, S. L., McDonough, M., Smith, M. K., Okoroafor, N., Jordt, H., & Wenderoth, M. P. (2014). Active learning increases student performance in science, engineering, and mathematics. *Proceedings of the National Academy of Sciences of the United States of America, 111*(23), 8410–8415. DOI: 10.1073/pnas.1319030111 PMID: 24821756

Heung, Y. M. E., & Chiu, T. K. F. (2025). How ChatGPT impacts student engagement from a systematic review and meta-analysis study. *Computers and Education: Artificial Intelligence*, *8*, 100361. Advance online publication. DOI: 10.1016/j.caeai.2025.100361

Heyman, J. L., Rick, S. R., Giacomelli, G., Wen, H., Laubacher, R. J., Taubenslag, N., Knicker, M. S., Jeddi, Y., Ragupathy, P., Curhan, J., & Malone, T. W. (2024). Supermind Ideator: How scaffolding human-AI collaboration can increase creativity. *Collective Intelligence*, *3*(4), 26339137241305117. Advance online publication. DOI: 10.1177/26339137241305117

Johnson, D. W., & Johnson, R. T. (2009). An educational psychology success story: Social interdependence theory and cooperative learning. *Educational Researcher, 38*(5), 365–379. DOI: 10.3102/0013189X09339057

Lakhal, S., Mukamurera, J., Bédard, M. E., Heilporn, G., & Chauret, M. (2020). Features fostering academic and social integration in blended synchronous courses in graduate programs. *International Journal of Educational Technology in Higher Education*, *17*(1), 5. Advance online publication. DOI: 10.1186/s41239-020-0180-z

Malone, T. W. (2018). *Superminds: The surprising power of people and computers thinking together*. Little, Brown Spark.

Meyer, A., Rose, D. H., & Gordon, D. (2014). *Universal design for learning: Theory and practice*. CAST Professional Publishing.

Miao, F., & Holmes, W. (2023). *Guidance for generative AI in education and research*. UNESCO., DOI: 10.54675/EWZM9535

Mishra, P., & Koehler, M. J. (2006). Technological Pedagogical Content Knowledge: A framework for teacher knowledge. *Teachers College Record, 108*(6), 1017–1054. DOI: 10.1111/j.1467-9620.2006.00684.x

Moore, S., Eckstein, L., Kwon, C., & Stamper, J. (2025). Generative AI in instructional design education: Effects on novice microlesson quality. In Cristea, A. I., Walker, E., Lu, Y., Santos, O. C., & Isotani, S. (Eds.), *Artificial intelligence in education* (Vol. 15880, pp. 464–471). Springer., DOI: 10.1007/978-3-031-98459-4_35

Prince, M. J. (2004). Does active learning work? A review of the research. *Journal of Engineering Education, 93*(3), 223–231. DOI: 10.1002/j.2168-9830.2004.tb00809.x

Raes, A., Detienne, L., Windey, I., & Depaepe, F. (2020). A systematic literature review on synchronous hybrid learning: Gaps identified. *Learning Environments Research, 23*(3), 269–290. DOI: 10.1007/s10984-019-09303-z

Richardson, J. C., Maeda, Y., Lv, J., & Caskurlu, S. (2017). Social presence in relation to students' satisfaction and learning in the online environment: A meta-analysis. *Computers in Human Behavior, 71*, 402–417. DOI: 10.1016/j.chb.2017.02.001

Siegler, R. S., Fazio, L. K., Bailey, D. H., & Zhou, X. (2013). Fractions: The new frontier for theories of numerical development. *Trends in Cognitive Sciences, 17*(1), 13–19. DOI: 10.1016/j.tics.2012.11.004 PMID: 23219805

Ting, F. S. T., & Chan, L. C. L. (2025). Personalized learning with generative AI in teacher education via the Concept Prompt. *Proceedings of the International Conference on Learning and Teaching 2025 (ICLT 2025)*, 37.

Ting, F. S. T., Wang, D., & Chan, L. C. L. (2025). Integrating GenAI into inquiry-based learning for mathematics education. *Conference Proceedings of the 2nd EdUHK x HKUST Joint International Conference on AI and Education*, 27.

Van Amburgh, J. A., Devlin, J. W., Kirwin, J. L., & Qualters, D. M. (2007). A tool for measuring active learning in the classroom. *American Journal of Pharmaceutical Education, 71*(5), 85. Advance online publication. DOI: 10.1016/S0002-9459(24)03576-9 PMID: 17998982

VanLehn, K. (2011). The relative effectiveness of human tutoring, intelligent tutoring systems, and other tutoring systems. *Educational Psychologist, 46*(4), 197–221. DOI: 10.1080/00461520.2011.611369

Vygotsky, L. S. (1978). *Mind in society: The development of higher psychological processes*. Harvard University Press. https://www.jstor.org/stable/j.ctvjf9vz4

Wang, S., Christensen, C., Cui, W., Tong, R., Yarnall, L., Shear, L., & Feng, M. (2023). When adaptive learning is effective learning: Comparison of an adaptive learning system to teacher-led instruction. *Interactive Learning Environments, 31*(2), 793–803. DOI: 10.1080/10494820.2020.1808794

Wegerif, R. (2013). *Dialogic: Education for the Internet Age*. Routledge., DOI: 10.4324/9780203111222

Wegner, D. M. (1987). Transactive memory: A contemporary analysis of the group mind. In Mullen, B., & Goethals, G. R. (Eds.), *Theories of group behavior* (pp. 185–208). Springer., DOI: 10.1007/978-1-4612-4634-3_9

Wei, X., Wang, L., Lee, L.-K., & Liu, R. (2025). The effects of generative AI on collaborative problem-solving and team creativity performance in digital story creation: An experimental study. *International Journal of Educational Technology in Higher Education*, *22*(1), 23. Advance online publication. DOI: 10.1186/s41239-025-00526-0

Woolley, A. W., Chabris, C. F., Pentland, A., Hashmi, N., & Malone, T. W. (2010). Evidence for a collective intelligence factor in the performance of human groups. *Science*, *330*(6004), 686–688. DOI: 10.1126/science.1193147 PMID: 20929725

Zhang, J., Jantakoon, T., & Laoha, R. (2025). Meta-analysis of artificial intelligence in education. *Higher Education Studies*, *15*(2), 189–201. DOI: 10.5539/hes.v15n2p189

Zhang, L., Basham, J. D., & Carter, R. A.Jr. (2022). Measuring personalized learning through the lens of UDL: Development and content validation of a student self-report instrument. *Studies in Educational Evaluation*, *72*, 101121. Advance online publication. DOI: 10.1016/j.stueduc.2021.101121

Chapter 4
Teacher–AI Collaboration: Professional Development and Pedagogical Shifts in the Hyflex Era

Syed Mohd Faisal
http://orcid.org/0000-0003-2422-3535
Malla Reddy Technical Campus, Malla Reddy Vishwavidyapeeth (Deemed to be) University, Hyderabad, India

Wasim Khan
http://orcid.org/0000-0003-2311-1451
Symbiosis International (Deemed to be) University, Pune, India

Mohammad Ishrat
http://orcid.org/0000-0002-9699-4454
VIT Bhopal University, Sehore, India

ABSTRACT

This chapter explores how Artificial Intelligence (AI) transforms teaching, learning, and professional development in HyFlex education. It presents a multi-level Teacher–AI collaboration model—assistive, augmentative, and transformative—where AI enhances pedagogy through data-driven insights, adaptive feedback, and ethical decision support. The proposed Teacher–AI Synergy Framework illustrates continuous interaction among teachers, learners, and AI systems, fostering personalized learning and informed instructional design. The chapter also addresses the competencies educators need in AI-enabled environments, emphasizing data literacy, ethical awareness, and reflective adaptability. Institutional readiness,

DOI: 10.4018/979-8-3373-6182-6.ch004

governance, and sustainability are highlighted as essential for responsible AI integration. Overall, it envisions an inclusive, human-centered model that balances technological intelligence with pedagogical creativity.

INTRODUCTION

The post-pandemic transformation of global education has accelerated the evolution of learning modalities, propelling institutions toward more flexible, technology-enabled ecosystems. Among these innovations, the HyFlex (Hybrid + Flexible) learning model has emerged as a sustainable paradigm that allows students to choose between in-person, synchronous online, or asynchronous participation without compromising learning continuity. While HyFlex environments enhance accessibility and learner autonomy, they simultaneously present substantial pedagogical and managerial challenges—particularly concerning equitable engagement, assessment alignment, and instructional coherence across modalities (Beatty, 2019a). This dynamic educational landscape necessitates a redefinition of traditional teaching roles and pedagogical frameworks, emphasizing the integration of Artificial Intelligence (AI) as a co-evolving instructional partner rather than a mere digital aid. Artificial Intelligence in education (AIED) has evolved beyond administrative automation to become an enabler of personalized, adaptive, and data-driven instruction. From Intelligent Tutoring Systems (ITS) and recommendation engines to predictive analytics and conversational agents, AI tools increasingly support educators in designing individualized learning trajectories and real-time formative assessments. Within HyFlex environments, AI systems further facilitate automated attendance tracking, participation analytics, engagement monitoring, and predictive performance modeling. These affordances underscore the potential of AI not as a replacement for educators but as a collaborative entity that augments human pedagogical intelligence, optimizes decision-making, and enables context-aware instructional delivery (Tapalova & Zhiyenbayeva, 2022). However, the integration of AI into hybrid learning ecosystems demands profound pedagogical and professional reorientation. Teachers are now expected to acquire digital fluency, data interpretability, and algorithmic literacy to effectively co-design, interpret, and ethically deploy AI-supported learning systems. This reorientation extends beyond technical competence, it represents a cultural and epistemic shift from teacher-centered instruction toward AI-augmented, learner-centered ecosystems grounded in continuous adaptation, feedback, and co-creation (Khezrlou & Stockwell, 2025). Consequently, the concept of teacher–AI collaboration emerges as a central construct for the HyFlex era, bridging human pedagogical intuition with algorithmic precision to cultivate meaningful, equitable, and scalable learning experiences. The primary motivation of this chapter is to examine teacher–AI collaboration as a pedagogical mechanism for enhancing student engagement, inclusivity, and equitable participation within HyFlex learning environments. As learners engage through diverse participation modes—in-person, synchronous online, and asynchronous, maintaining consistent engagement and inclusive learning experiences emerges as a critical instructional challenge. This chapter argues that AI-enabled teacher collaboration provides a structured, data-informed approach to addressing these challenges by supporting adaptive instruction, equitable engagement monitoring, and learner-centered pedagogical decision-making.

This chapter examines the evolving landscape of teacher–AI collaboration within HyFlex learning frameworks, emphasizing how AI reshapes instructional design, assessment methodologies, and professional development paradigms. It explores (i) the foundational principles of HyFlex pedagogy, (ii) the functional roles of AI in instructional ecosystems, (iii) multi-level models of teacher–AI collaboration, and (iv) the competencies and institutional frameworks required for educators to thrive in AI-driven environments. Additionally, the chapter presents global case studies and forward-looking perspectives that highlight ethical, social, and policy dimensions associated with the integration of AI in education. Through this multidimensional exploration, the chapter aims to articulate a sustainable vision for teacher–AI synergy, positioning educators as empowered co-creators in the evolving landscape of AI-powered HyFlex learning.

1. REVIEW OF LITERATURE AND RESEARCH GAPS

The rapid digital transformation of higher education has generated extensive scholarly discourse on hybrid learning models, AI in education, and teacher professional development. Although these domains are individually well explored, they have largely evolved in isolation rather than through integrated analytical frameworks. A critical synthesis of existing literature is therefore required to establish a coherent foundation for examining teacher AI collaboration in HyFlex learning environments and to identify unresolved research gaps.

1.1 HyFlex Learning Models in Higher Education

HyFlex learning has been widely examined as a pedagogical model that provides learners with the flexibility to choose between physical classroom participation, synchronous online engagement, or asynchronous learning activities. Prior research highlights the role of HyFlex education in improving accessibility, learner autonomy, and instructional continuity, particularly in response to large scale disruptions in higher education. Empirical studies frequently report improvements in student satisfaction and participation when flexibility is embedded into course design. Despite these contributions, existing research predominantly emphasizes structural and operational aspects such as scheduling, technological infrastructure, and modality equivalence. Pedagogical analysis often remains descriptive and focuses on content replication across delivery modes rather than adaptive instructional intelligence. Furthermore, teachers are commonly positioned as facilitators responsible for managing multiple delivery formats rather than as strategic decision makers navigating complex instructional ecosystems. As a result, the literature offers limited insight into how educators cognitively manage pedagogical coherence and instructional quality across multiple learning modalities. HyFlex learning is underpinned by several theoretical frameworks that provide a foundation for its pedagogical and technological underpinnings. One such framework is Constructivism, which emphasizes learner-centered, active knowledge construction. In a HyFlex environment, this theory supports the notion that learners can engage in meaningful learning through their choice of participation mode, fostering autonomy and self-directed learning (Vygotsky, 1978). Another relevant theory is Self-Determination Theory (SDT), which posits that learner motivation is driven by the satisfaction of needs for autonomy, competence, and relatedness (Deci & Ryan, 2008). HyFlex environments support these needs by providing learners with flexible options for how they engage in the learning process. Additionally, Technology Acceptance Model (TAM) and Unified Theory of Acceptance and Use of Technology (UTAUT) offer valuable insights into understanding how educators and learners perceive, accept, and adopt the technology that supports HyFlex learning (Davis, 1989; Venkatesh et al., 2003). These frameworks provide theoretical support for examining how AI integration in HyFlex models can enhance engagement, autonomy, and pedagogical flexibility.

1.2 Artificial Intelligence in Teaching and Learning

Research on AI in education has expanded significantly, covering ITS, automated assessment, LA, recommendation systems, and conversational agents. These studies demonstrate the potential of AI to personalize learning experiences, automate instructional processes, and generate predictive insights related to learner performance and engagement. AI is widely recognized for enabling scalable and data informed instruction within digitally mediated learning environments. However, much of the existing scholarship adopts a technology centered orientation that prioritizes system capabilities, algorithmic accuracy, and learner outcomes. Teachers are frequently conceptualized as users or supervisors of AI systems rather than as collaborative pedagogical partners. Additionally, AI applications are commonly examined within fully online or traditional classroom settings, with limited attention to their role in

HyFlex environments where instructional complexity is substantially greater. Consequently, the literature does not sufficiently theorize the interactive relationship between educators and AI systems as co contributors to instructional design and decision making.

1.3 Teacher Professional Development in Artificial Intelligence Mediated Contexts

Teacher professional development literature increasingly emphasizes the importance of digital competence, data literacy, and adaptive pedagogy in technology enriched educational environments. Recent studies highlight the growing need for AI literacy, ethical awareness, and analytical interpretability as essential competencies for educators. Professional development initiatives often focus on equipping teachers with the technical skills required to operate AI enabled platforms and analytics tools. Nevertheless, this body of research remains fragmented and largely skill oriented. Professional development is frequently conceptualized as short term training or tool adoption rather than as a sustained transformation of pedagogical reasoning and professional identity. Moreover, there is limited exploration of how continuous collaboration with AI systems influences teacher autonomy, reflective practice, and instructional judgment, particularly within flexible and hybrid learning contexts. Institutional and governance related dimensions of professional development are also insufficiently addressed in existing studies.

1.4 Identified Research Gaps

A synthesis of the reviewed literature reveals several critical gaps that necessitate further scholarly attention. First, there is a lack of integrative conceptual frameworks that unify HyFlex pedagogy, AI driven instruction, and teacher professional development within a single analytical model. Second, teacher AI collaboration remains under theorized, with limited examination of how educators and intelligent systems jointly contribute to instructional planning, delivery, and assessment. Third, the impact of AI on teacher agency, professional identity, and pedagogical authority has not been adequately explored. Fourth, ethical, institutional, and policy considerations related to AI adoption in HyFlex education are often treated as secondary concerns rather than foundational components. Finally, there is a scarcity of practice grounded evidence illustrating real world implementation of teacher AI collaboration in HyFlex classrooms.

In response to these gaps, the present chapter adopts a conceptual and practice-oriented approach to articulate a comprehensive framework for teacher AI collaboration in HyFlex education. By synthesizing pedagogical theory, technological intelligence, and professional development perspectives, the chapter seeks to advance a holistic understanding of how educators can be empowered as co-creators within AI enabled hybrid learning ecosystems.

2. METHODOLOGICAL APPROACH

This chapter adopts a conceptual and integrative methodological approach to examine teacher–AI collaboration within HyFlex learning environments. Rather than conducting an empirical investigation, the study is grounded in systematic conceptual synthesis, drawing upon established theories, contemporary research findings, and global policy perspectives to construct a coherent analytical framework. Such an approach is appropriate given the emergent and interdisciplinary nature of AI-enabled HyFlex pedagogy, where theoretical consolidation and conceptual clarity remain underdeveloped. The methodological foundation of the chapter is based on an extensive review and synthesis of secondary sources, including peer-reviewed journal articles, scholarly books, conference proceedings, and authoritative policy reports issued by international organizations. Emphasis is placed on high-impact literature from the domains of higher education pedagogy, AI in education, teacher professional development, and educational ethics. In addition, empirical studies related to HyFlex learning implementations and AI-supported instructional systems are selectively incorporated to ensure practical grounding and contextual relevance.

A thematic synthesis method is employed to organize and analyze the literature across four interrelated analytical domains. First, literature on HyFlex pedagogy is examined to identify core principles, instructional challenges, and modality-related complexities that shape contemporary hybrid learning environments. Second, research on AI in education is analyzed to understand the functional capabilities of AI systems, including LA, adaptive content delivery, automated assessment, and decision-support mechanisms. Third, studies on teacher professional development are synthesized to explore evolving competency requirements, pedagogical identity shifts, and capacity-building needs in AI-mediated instructional contexts. Fourth, literature addressing ethics and governance is reviewed to integrate considerations related to data privacy, algorithmic transparency, accountability, and teacher autonomy. Through iterative comparison and abstraction across these domains, key patterns, conceptual linkages, and unresolved issues are identified. This process enables the articulation of teacher–AI collaboration not merely as a technological integration model but as a socio-pedagogical construct involving shared intelligence, co-decision-making, and ethical responsibility. The outcome of this methodological process is the development of a conceptual Teacher–AI collaboration framework tailored to HyFlex learning environments, which synthesizes pedagogical theory, technological intelligence, and professional practice into a unified explanatory model. Overall, the adopted methodology ensures analytical rigor, theoretical coherence, and practical relevance, while avoiding the limitations of context-specific empirical generalization. It provides a robust scholarly foundation for advancing understanding of teacher–AI collaboration and for guiding future empirical research and institutional implementation in AI-enabled HyFlex education.

3. HYFLEX LEARNING IN THE CONTEMPORARY EDUCATIONAL LANDSCAPE

The evolution of digital education has expanded the boundaries of traditional learning environments, leading to the emergence of flexible pedagogical models that accommodate diverse learner needs and contexts. The HyFlex (Hybrid + Flexible) model stands as a paradigm shift that integrates physical and virtual learning spaces, providing students the freedom to select how they participate in each session—in-person, synchronously online, or asynchronously. This model embodies inclusivity, adaptability, and resilience, enabling institutions to maintain learning continuity amid disruptions such as pandemics, natural disasters, or global crises. By offering multiple, equivalent participation modes, HyFlex learning aligns with the principles of accessibility and learner autonomy, fostering engagement through choice and flexibility. At the same time, it compels educators and institutions to rethink curriculum design, assessment strategies, and technological infrastructure to ensure pedagogical equivalence across modalities (Racheva & Peytcheva-Forsyth, 2024). The flexibility inherent in HyFlex learning directly supports inclusive participation by allowing learners to engage according to their contextual, technological, and personal constraints. However, flexibility alone does not guarantee meaningful engagement or pedagogical equivalency across modalities. AI-supported instructional systems, when collaboratively used by teachers, play a critical role in sustaining student engagement and inclusivity by ensuring equivalency of learning experiences, accessibility of resources, and consistent monitoring of learner participation across all HyFlex modes.

3.1. Conceptual Foundations

The conceptual foundation of HyFlex learning is deeply rooted in established learning theories. Constructivism emphasizes learner-centered knowledge construction through interaction, exploration, and reflection. Connectivism, a theory relevant to digital-era learning, highlights the role of technological networks and distributed cognition in shaping modern educational experiences. Furthermore, SDT provides a motivational framework by identifying autonomy, competence, and relatedness as fundamental drivers of learning engagement—principles inherently supported by the HyFlex model (Deci et al., 2017). Together, these theories justify the HyFlex approach as a synthesis of pedagogical inclusivity and technological mediation.

HyFlex education is structured around three interdependent dimensions (Qazi et al., 2024):

- Pedagogical Design – Ensuring that learning objectives, activities, and assessments are equivalent across participation modes.
- Technological Infrastructure – Facilitating seamless interaction and content access through AI-driven LMS and analytics dashboards.
- Institutional Policy and Support – Providing operational frameworks for scheduling, accreditation, and learner equity.

By integrating these layers, HyFlex instruction transcends the dichotomy between traditional and online modalities, fostering an adaptive learning continuum.

Figure 1. Structure and modalities of the HyFlex Learning Model

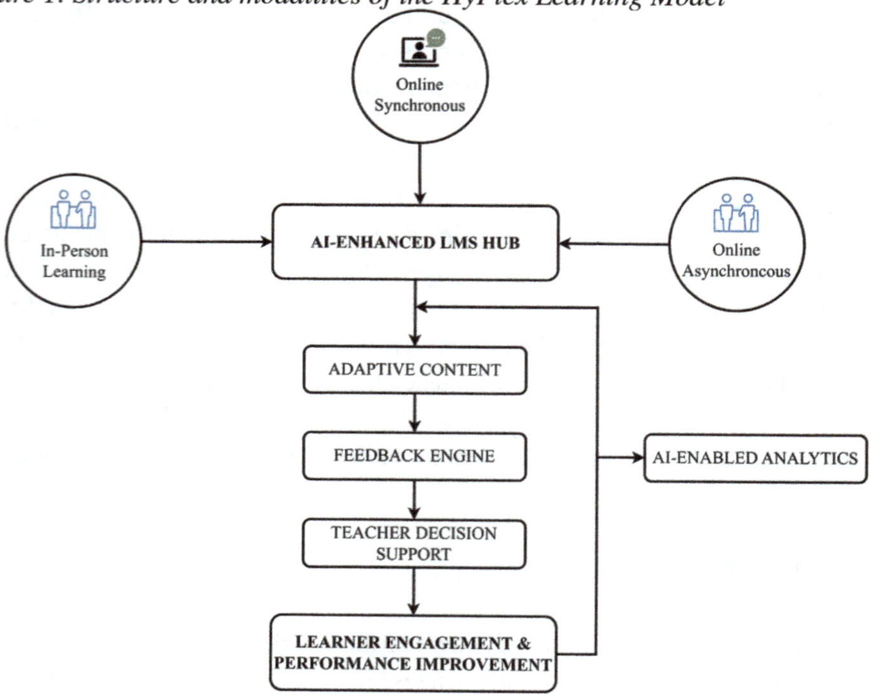

Here Figure 1 illustrates the integrated architecture of the HyFlex Learning Model, where In-Person, Online Synchronous, and Online Asynchronous learning modes converge through an AI-Enhanced LMS Hub. The hub coordinates multi-modal participation, resource distribution, and communication across all delivery modes. A dedicated AI-Enabled Analytics layer continuously exchanges data with the LMS to generate actionable insights that inform adaptive learning pathways, personalized content delivery, and feedback mechanisms. These processes support the Adaptive Content, Feedback Engine, and Teacher Decision Support components, ultimately leading to enhanced Learner Engagement and Performance Improvement. The diagram emphasizes the dynamic, data-driven interaction loop among learners, educators, and intelligent systems that define effective HyFlex pedagogy.

The HyFlex paradigm thus positions learning as a fluid continuum rather than a fixed environment. It empowers educators to become designers of multi-modal learning ecosystems that adapt dynamically to learner preferences, technological access, and contextual variables. Institutions adopting HyFlex education report improvements in participation flexibility and inclusivity, though they must invest in digital infrastructure and faculty development to ensure sustainability and parity across modalities.

3.2. Foundational HyFlex Principles and the Role of Teacher–AI Collaboration

The HyFlex model is underpinned by four foundational principles—learner choice, equivalency, reusability, and accessibility—which collectively ensure that flexibility does not compromise educational quality or student engagement. Learner choice emphasizes students' autonomy to select participation modes based on their contextual needs without academic disadvantage. Equivalency requires that learning objectives, activities, and assessment experiences remain pedagogically comparable across in-person, synchronous online, and asynchronous modes. Reusability focuses on designing learning resources that can be meaningfully repurposed across modalities, while accessibility ensures that all learners can engage with instructional content regardless of technological, physical, or temporal constraints. Teacher–AI collaboration plays a critical role in operationalizing these principles within HyFlex environments. AI-driven learning analytics and engagement dashboards support the principle of equivalency by enabling teachers to monitor participation, interaction patterns, and performance consistently across modalities. Adaptive content delivery systems and intelligent recommendation engines enhance accessibility by tailoring learning materials to diverse learner profiles and participation contexts. Reusability is strengthened through AI-assisted content tagging, recording, and semantic indexing, which allow instructional resources to be effectively reused across synchronous and asynchronous formats. Furthermore, predictive analytics and decision-support tools empower informed learner choice by providing teachers with insights to guide students toward participation modes that best align with their engagement patterns and learning needs. Through this alignment, teacher–AI collaboration ensures that the foundational HyFlex principles are not merely structural design guidelines but are actively enacted as pedagogical mechanisms that sustain student engagement, inclusivity, and instructional coherence across all learning modalities.

3.3. HyFlex in Resource-Constrained Environments

While the HyFlex model holds significant potential for enhancing flexibility and inclusivity in education, its implementation presents challenges for institutions with limited resources. The adoption of AI-assisted HyFlex education requires robust technological infrastructure, including reliable internet connectivity, LMS, and AI-driven analytics platforms. In resource-constrained environments, institutions may struggle to provide the necessary hardware, software, and technical support to sustain these systems. Furthermore, not all disciplines and course formats lend themselves well to HyFlex delivery. For example, hands-on laboratory-based courses or artistic training may require physical presence, and attempting to offer them through a HyFlex model could compromise educational quality. Literature highlights that the successful adoption of AI in HyFlex environments demands a balance between technology investment and pedagogical adaptation, and institutions must consider both technological feasibility and subject-specific instructional needs (Beatty, 2019; Racheva & Peytcheva-Forsyth, 2024).

3.4. Challenges and Opportunities

Despite its pedagogical promise, HyFlex learning introduces a series of operational and instructional challenges. One major concern lies in maintaining instructional coherence across modalities, ensuring that students receive equitable learning experiences regardless of participation mode. Teachers often face difficulties in engaging both physical and remote learners simultaneously, managing asynchronous contributions, and creating assessments that are consistent, fair, and scalable. Technologically, HyFlex implementation requires robust digital ecosystems, including reliable connectivity, cloud-based LMS, and intelligent analytics tools. Disparities in technological access across learners—the persistent digital divide—can compromise educational equity. Furthermore, educators must develop new competencies in digital pedagogy and data interpretation to manage AI-enabled instructional platforms effectively.

Nevertheless, HyFlex models offer transformative opportunities. They enable personalized learning pathways, facilitate data-driven instruction, and promote self-regulated learning (SRL) behaviors. AI-enhanced systems can analyze learner interaction data to provide real-time feedback, recommend adaptive resources, and identify engagement gaps. Thus, AI becomes a critical enabler for managing the inherent complexity of HyFlex instruction (Miller et al., 2021).

Table 1. Comparative analysis of traditional, blended, and HyFlex Learning Models

Learning Mode	Teacher Role	Learner Flexibility	Technology Dependence	Assessment Approach	Engagement Characteristics
Traditional (On-Campus)	Knowledge transmitter	Low	Minimal	In-person exams and discussion	Physical presence and direct interaction
Blended	Facilitator and content integrator	Moderate	Medium	Combination of online and offline tasks	Mix of synchronous and asynchronous engagement
HyFlex	Designer and learning orchestrator	High	High (AI-supported LMS, analytics tools)	Adaptive and multimodal	Continuous, data-driven participation across modalities

The HyFlex model redefines both teaching and learning as adaptive, data-informed, and learner-centric processes. As educational institutions worldwide embrace hybrid flexibility, AI-driven technologies will continue to play a pivotal role in ensuring that such pedagogical transformations are equitable, measurable, and sustainable (Welch et al., 2021). Thus, HyFlex learning does not merely redefine where education occurs; it reimagines how learning unfolds—across contexts, modalities, and learner profiles—laying the groundwork for the teacher–AI collaborative models discussed in the subsequent sections.

4. ARTIFICIAL INTELLIGENCE IN PEDAGOGICAL ECOSYSTEMS

AI is revolutionizing the educational landscape by introducing data-driven precision, personalization, and predictive intelligence into teaching and learning processes. Within the HyFlex ecosystem, AI serves as both an analytical engine and a pedagogical collaborator that bridges the gap between human cognition and machine intelligence. By integrating intelligent systems into multi-modal learning environments, institutions can achieve scalable, personalized, and inclusive education models that dynamically adapt to learners' evolving needs. AI not only supports teachers in designing and delivering instruction but also empowers learners through adaptive feedback, real-time analytics, and personalized learning experiences (Essaid & HAJI, 2020).

The shift toward AI-integrated pedagogy signifies a paradigm transformation where teaching is no longer linear or uniform but instead adaptive, dynamic, and evidence-informed. AI algorithms analyze large volumes of interaction data across diverse modalities—face-to-face, synchronous online, and asynchronous online—to generate actionable insights about learner performance, motivation, and engagement (Niemi, 2020). These insights are then fed back into the instructional loop, enabling real-time adjustments to pedagogy, assessment, and learner support strategies. Thus, AI operationalizes the concept of personalization at scale, an essential requirement in modern HyFlex systems.

4.1. AI Applications in Teaching and Learning

AI applications in education span multiple dimensions, ranging from automation of administrative tasks to sophisticated learning personalization. ITS provides individualized feedback and task sequencing based on learner performance (Mousavinasab et al., 2021), while Natural Language Processing (NLP) tools enable real-time language assessment, automated summarization, and contextual dialogue generation (Liang, 2025). These systems simulate elements of human tutoring by responding adaptively to student inquiries and misconceptions. In addition, Learning Analytics (LA) and Educational Data Mining (EDM) serve as the backbone of AI-enhanced instruction (Ray & Saeed, 2018). They transform raw data from LMS, digital assessments, and discussion forums into measurable indicators of learning quality, behavioral trends, and cognitive engagement. Predictive algorithms can identify at-risk learners by analyzing attendance patterns, quiz results, and interaction frequency—allowing early intervention before academic decline occurs. Recommender Systems, another key application, utilize collaborative filtering and deep learning to deliver tailored content, study materials, or learning activities aligned with a student's prior behavior and learning style.

Moreover, Computer Vision (CV) technologies are being increasingly deployed in classrooms and online settings to analyze non-verbal cues such as eye gaze, facial expressions, and engagement levels (Vanneste et al., 2021). Such affective computing capabilities help educators assess the emotional and cognitive states of learners, fostering empathy-based instructional design. AI also plays a critical role in adaptive assessments, where exam difficulty and question sequencing dynamically adjust to a student's performance level.

Table 2. Key AI technologies and their educational functions

AI Tool	Core Functionality	Pedagogical Role	Example Application
ITS	Adaptive learning through real-time feedback	Personalized instruction	ALEKS, Carnegie Learning
NLP	Text comprehension, generation, and interaction	Conversational tutoring and automated grading	ChatGPT EDU, Grammarly
Learning Analytics & EDM	Data-driven insight generation	Predicting student performance and retention	Moodle Analytics, Brightspace Insights
Computer Vision	Visual recognition and emotion detection	Engagement and attention monitoring	Affectiva, Emotion AI
Predictive Modeling	Forecasting learner outcomes	Early intervention and learning optimization	IBM SPSS Modeler, RapidMiner
Recommender Systems	Personalized content recommendations	Context-aware resource delivery	Coursera AI Recommender, Edmodo AI
Speech Recognition	Voice-based interaction and dictation	Accessibility and language learning	Google Speech-to-Text, Amazon Transcribe

The collective implementation of these technologies enables educators to evolve from reactive instruction toward proactive and data-informed pedagogy, where each learner's experience becomes unique, measurable, and continuously optimized.

4.2. AI Integration in HyFlex Environments

Integrating AI into HyFlex ecosystems involves the convergence of analytics, automation, and adaptive decision-making within a single cohesive architecture. The AI-Enhanced LMS Hub forms the structural and functional core of this ecosystem. It interlinks the three learning modalities—In-Person, Online Synchronous, and Online Asynchronous—while simultaneously capturing real-time interaction data from each. Embedded AI components interpret these data to detect behavioral trends, participation frequency, and cognitive engagement metrics (Dineva, 2024).

The AI-Enabled Analytics layer acts as the intelligence core that processes multimodal data streams, such as textual discussion transcripts, quiz outcomes, eye-tracking patterns, and sentiment indicators. This analytical feedback enables continuous optimization of instructional flow. Teachers receive dashboard-based insights on learner performance, enabling them to adapt content difficulty, pacing, and assessment methods dynamically. Similarly, learners benefit from adaptive feedback systems that personalize guidance and suggest supplementary resources according to their performance trajectories.

Figure 2. AI-orchestrated HyFlex Learning Environment

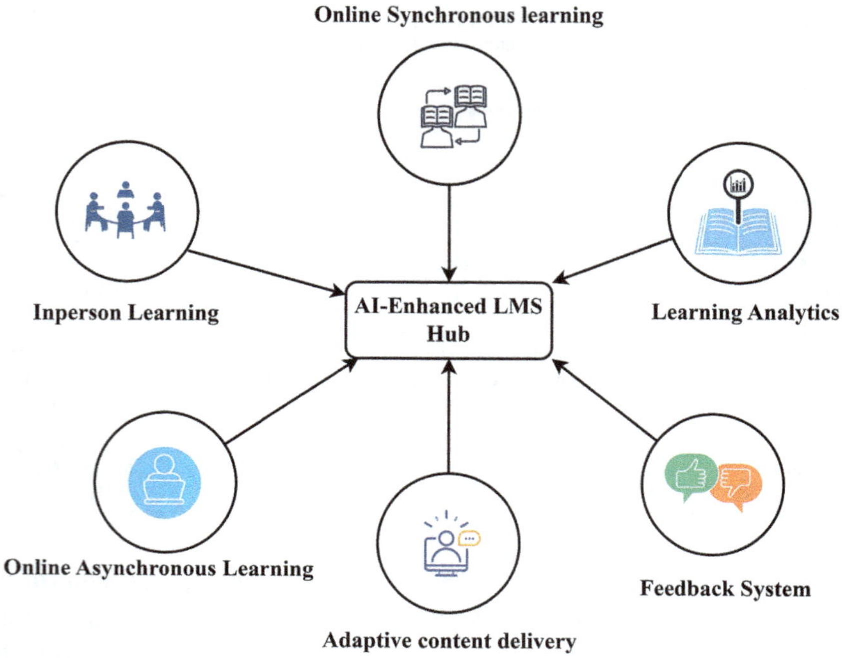

Figure 2 illustrates the AI-Orchestrated HyFlex Learning Environment, where the AI-Enhanced LMS Hub acts as the central coordinator connecting in-person, synchronous, and asynchronous learning modes. Each mode feeds learner data—such as engagement, performance, and participation into the LMS. The hub interacts with AI-enabled analytics, adaptive content delivery, and assessment and feedback engines to personalize learning and automate evaluation. These intelligent subsystems provide real-time insights that support teacher decision-making and continuous pedagogical refinement, ultimately leading to improved learner engagement and performance. The circular flow represents ongoing feedback between learners, AI systems, and instructors, ensuring adaptive and data-driven learning experiences.

AI integration also extends to adaptive content repositories, which are dynamically curated through semantic tagging and clustering algorithms. These repositories recommend personalized resources—videos, reading materials, or practice exercises—based on cognitive load, topic mastery, and learner preference. Furthermore, automated assessment and feedback engines generate immediate responses and grading rationales, ensuring assessment fairness and consistency across different learning modes (Sabol, 2025).

From an institutional perspective, AI contributes to scalability and quality assurance in HyFlex delivery. Automated reporting, plagiarism detection, attendance prediction, and cognitive analytics support educators in managing large cohorts without compromising instructional quality. More importantly, AI augments teacher agency by transforming educators into data-informed designers of learning experiences, enhancing both precision and pedagogical creativity.

Finally, the convergence of HyFlex and AI paradigms fosters a symbiotic relationship between human and artificial intelligence. Teachers contribute contextual, emotional, and ethical judgment, while AI provides analytic precision, pattern recognition, and adaptive responsiveness. This partnership culminates in an ecosystem that continuously learns, adapts, and improves, forming the foundation for the next generation of intelligent, inclusive, and learner-centered education.

4.3. Challenges in the Adoption of AI-Assisted Education

Despite the promising potential of AI in enhancing HyFlex learning environments, several challenges persist in its adoption. The integration of AI systems requires substantial financial investments in infrastructure, training, and ongoing technical support, which many resource-constrained institutions may find difficult to justify (Morandín-Ahuerma, 2023). Additionally, faculty members may face resistance to adopting AI tools due to a lack of digital literacy or concerns over the perceived replacement of traditional teaching methods (Hadi & AlShaikh-Hasan, 2025). Furthermore, the ethical implications of AI use, such as data privacy, algorithmic bias, and the transparency of AI decision-making processes, are critical considerations that must be addressed to ensure equitable and fair outcomes for all students (Grynyuk et al., 2021). AI in education must be deployed with caution, ensuring that it complements, rather than replaces, human pedagogical expertise, and that ethical standards guide its implementation in diverse educational contexts.

5. TEACHER–AI COLLABORATION: CONCEPTUAL AND FUNCTIONAL PERSPECTIVES

As higher education transitions toward data-driven and flexible instructional ecosystems, Teacher–AI collaboration emerges as a cornerstone of pedagogical innovation. This collaboration goes beyond simple task automation—it reshapes instructional design, learning facilitation, and assessment by fostering a co-evolution of human expertise and machine intelligence. Within the HyFlex learning framework, where students participate across in-person, synchronous, and asynchronous modes, this partnership ensures that personalization, equity, and engagement are sustained at scale (Kim, 2024). AI provides continuous analytical intelligence, while teachers contribute contextual understanding, empathy, and ethical oversight, together forming a balanced system of human-AI synergy.

5.1. Defining Collaboration Dynamics

The collaboration between teachers and AI can be understood as a socio-technical partnership where both entities contribute complementary strengths. Teachers provide interpretive, emotional, and contextual insights, while AI systems deliver predictive precision, adaptive recommendations, and analytical depth. This interdependence forms a hybrid intelligence framework that aligns with the principles of human–computer interaction (HCI) and socio-cognitive theory.

In HyFlex settings, this collaboration allows educators to dynamically manage learning diversity. AI tools aggregate data from LMS logs, quizzes, discussion posts, and video interactions to offer visual analytics on learner engagement and comprehension. Teachers then interpret these insights to tailor learning pathways, modify assessment difficulty, or provide targeted support to underperforming learners. Moreover, AI-driven sentiment analysis and emotion detection help educators understand students' cognitive and affective states, enabling timely intervention and emotional scaffolding (Nain et al., 2025).

This dynamic interaction supports the broader vision of pedagogical co-intelligence, where AI not only assists but also learns from teacher behavior. Over time, the system refines its predictive models based on educator feedback, ensuring a continuously improving cycle of teaching efficacy and learner engagement.

5.2. Levels of Teacher–AI Interaction

Teacher–AI interaction can be structured across three evolutionary levels—Assistive, Augmentative, and Transformative—each representing an increased depth of integration and cognitive partnership between human and machine intelligence (Nain et al., 2025). Within this collaborative framework, teacher–AI interaction functions as a core enabler of student engagement by providing continuous visibility into learner participation, cognitive progress, and interaction patterns across modalities. By leveraging AI-driven analytics, adaptive feedback, and personalized learning pathways, teachers can proactively address engagement disparities and design inclusive instructional strategies that respond to diverse learner needs within HyFlex classrooms.

- Assistive AI: At the assistive level, teacher–AI collaboration contributes to enhanced engagement visibility by enabling continuous monitoring of student participation across in-person, synchronous online, and asynchronous modes. By automating routine tracking and administrative processes, AI systems allow teachers to identify early signs of disengagement without increasing cognitive workload. This foundational level supports inclusive instructional responsiveness by ensuring that no learner remains invisible due to modality choice or participation constraints.
- Augmentative AI: Teacher–AI collaboration strengthens personalized learner support through data-informed pedagogical decision-making. AI-driven learning analytics provide teachers with actionable insights into behavioral, cognitive, and interaction-based engagement patterns, enabling timely and targeted instructional interventions. This level plays a critical role in reducing participation gaps across HyFlex modes by supporting adaptive pacing, differentiated feedback, and equitable instructional attention for learners engaging through diverse participation pathways.
- Transformative AI: Teacher–AI collaboration enables inclusive instructional responsiveness by co-orchestrating adaptive learning environments that dynamically respond to individual learner engagement trajectories. Through continuous feedback loops, AI systems and teachers jointly personalize content sequencing, assessment strategies, and support mechanisms across modalities. This level directly enhances sustained student engagement by aligning instructional design with learner needs while ensuring pedagogical equivalency and inclusivity within complex HyFlex learning ecosystems.

Table 3. Levels of teacher–AI collaboration and corresponding functions

Collaboration Level	Task Domain	AI Role	Teacher Role	Expected Outcome
Assistive	Administrative management	Automates repetitive operations	Monitors system reliability	Time efficiency and task simplification
Augmentative	Pedagogical analytics	Provides real-time insights	Interprets and applies analytics	Evidence-based teaching decisions
Transformative	Co-creative learning design	Recommends adaptive and personalized content	Validates, refines, and guides AI models	Co-evolution of human-AI pedagogy

Beyond this structural representation, AI–teacher collaboration also implies ethical and epistemological considerations. Teachers act as moral agents ensuring fairness, accountability, and transparency in AI-mediated decisions. AI in turn, functions as an assistive cognitive entity supporting inclusivity and data equity across diverse learner populations.

5.3. Conceptual Framework for Teacher–AI Synergy

The Conceptual Framework for Teacher–AI Synergy articulates how human pedagogical intelligence and AI coalesce to create a dynamic, feedback-oriented educational ecosystem within the HyFlex environment. The framework positions the AI-Enhanced LMS Hub at the core, mediating interactions between three principal entities, Teacher, AI System, and Learner, to form a continuous and self-improving pedagogical cycle (Nain et al., 2025).

The framework is grounded in multiple educational theories, primarily Connectivism, Socio-Constructivism, and SRL. According to Connectivism, learning occurs through forming networks and connections, a principle mirrored by the bidirectional flow of information between the AI, teacher, and learner. Socio-Constructivism emphasizes the co-construction of knowledge through interaction, which in this model is achieved through human-AI collaboration where data analytics and human intuition work together. SRL theory further underpins this design by promoting learner autonomy and reflection, guided by adaptive AI feedback and teacher facilitation (Lamtara, 2024).

At the heart of the framework, the AI-Enhanced LMS Hub integrates multimodal data—ranging from attendance and behavioral analytics to assessment outcomes—and distributes it to the AI System, which consists of three subcomponents: the Analytics Engine, Adaptive Content Delivery System, and Feedback Generator. These subsystems process learner data to detect performance gaps, monitor engagement, and generate insights for both the teacher and the learner. The Teacher uses this information to make data-informed instructional decisions, adjust pedagogy, and ensure emotional and ethical dimensions are preserved. The Learner, in turn, benefits from personalized learning experiences, receiving adaptive resources and continuous formative feedback.

The diagram (Figure 3) illustrates three interdependent feedback loops:

- Pedagogical Feedback Loop – Teachers modify instructional design and strategies based on AI insights to improve learning outcomes.
- Analytical Feedback Loop: AI systems refine their models based on teacher inputs and observed learner behaviors, improving predictive accuracy.
- Learner Feedback Loop – Learner interactions and reflections provide continuous data for both AI analysis and teacher reflection, promoting self-regulation and personalization.

Together, these feedback loops create a closed adaptive system in which information flows continuously between entities, ensuring constant refinement of pedagogy and learning quality. This model exemplifies Hybrid Intelligence, where human cognition and AI analytics function as complementary forces—humans providing ethical judgment, empathy, and interpretive context, while AI delivers analytical accuracy, scalability, and real-time adaptability.

In essence, this framework envisions a co-evolutionary model of education where teachers are not displaced but empowered through AI collaboration. It advocates for distributed pedagogical intelligence, where decision-making is shared among humans, AI systems, and learners, leading to inclusive, ethical, and data-driven education in the HyFlex era.

Figure 3. Conceptual framework of teacher–AI–learner synergy in HyFlex classrooms

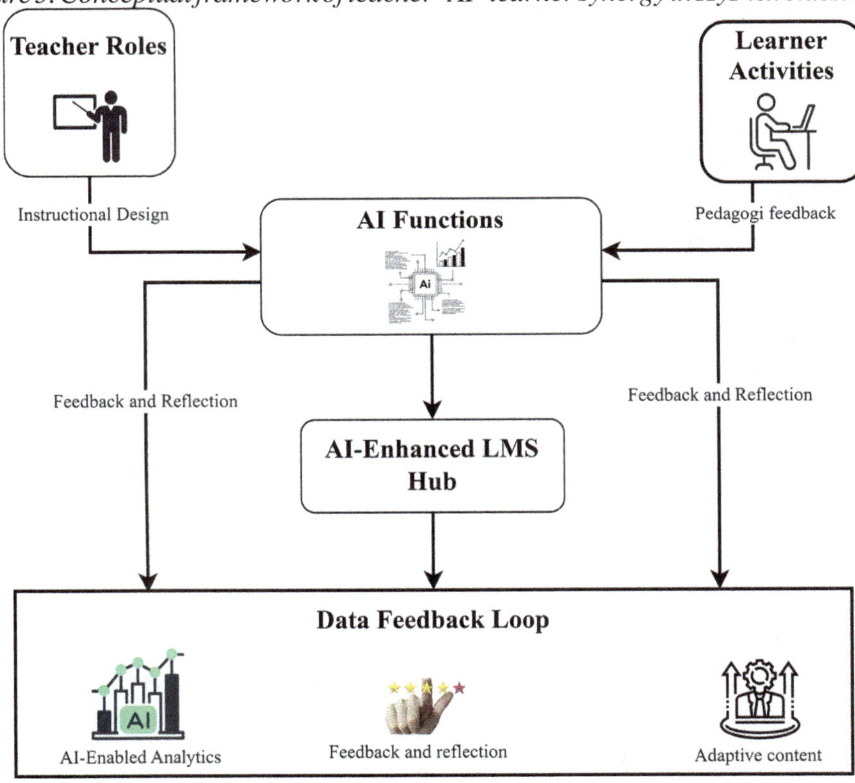

6. REAL-LIFE CASELETS OF TEACHER–AI COLLABORATION IN HYFLEX EDUCATION

To contextualize the proposed conceptual framework and demonstrate its practical relevance, this section presents two concise real-life caselets illustrating teacher–AI collaboration in HyFlex learning environments. These caselets are representative of common institutional practices observed in contemporary higher education and serve to bridge theory with authentic pedagogical application.

6.1. Caselet 1: AI-Supported HyFlex Instruction in a Large Undergraduate Course

Context: A large undergraduate foundational course with enrollments exceeding 250 students was delivered using a HyFlex model, allowing learners to alternate between in-person attendance, synchronous online participation, and asynchronous engagement through recorded lectures and digital resources. Managing instructional coherence, learner engagement, and timely intervention across modalities posed a significant challenge for the course instructor.

AI Tools and Functional Role: The institution deployed an AI-enhanced Learning Management System (LMS) incorporating learning analytics dashboards and predictive performance models. These tools aggregated data from attendance logs, discussion forum participation, quiz attempts, and video interaction metrics to generate real-time indicators of learner engagement and risk profiles.

Teacher–AI Collaboration: The instructor used AI-generated insights to adapt instructional pacing, identify disengaged learners, and initiate targeted academic interventions. Rather than relying solely on intuition, the teacher interpreted analytics outputs to redesign in-class activities, adjust asynchronous content sequencing, and provide personalized feedback to at-risk students. The AI system functioned as a decision-support mechanism, while pedagogical judgment and contextual understanding remained under teacher control.

Outcome: The collaborative use of AI-enabled analytics resulted in improved learner engagement across all participation modes, reduced dropout rates, and more consistent academic performance. Importantly, the instructor reported enhanced instructional confidence and reduced cognitive load when managing the complexity of HyFlex delivery.

6.2. Caselet 2: AI-Enabled Faculty Professional Development for HyFlex Teaching

Context: A higher education institution introduced an AI-supported professional development initiative aimed at preparing faculty members for AI-integrated HyFlex teaching. The program was structured as a modular micro-credential pathway, allowing instructors to upskill in digital pedagogy, learning analytics, and ethical AI use.

AI Role in Professional Development: An AI-driven professional development platform analyzed faculty engagement data, self-assessment results, and prior teaching experience to recommend personalized learning modules. The system dynamically adjusted learning pathways, suggesting targeted resources on data interpretation, adaptive assessment design, and ethical governance based on individual competency gaps.

Teacher–AI Interaction: Faculty members engaged with AI-recommended modules while reflecting on their classroom practices through guided prompts and peer discussion forums. AI-supported feedback enabled instructors to monitor their professional growth, while human mentoring and collaborative reflection ensured pedagogical alignment and contextual relevance.

Outcome: Participants demonstrated improved data literacy, greater confidence in interpreting AI-generated analytics, and increased readiness to integrate AI tools into HyFlex instruction. The program fostered a shift in faculty perception, positioning AI not as a threat to professional autonomy but as a supportive partner in pedagogical innovation.

7. PROFESSIONAL DEVELOPMENT FOR THE AI-ENABLED HYFLEX ERA

The sustainability and success of AI-integrated HyFlex learning systems depend on the professional growth and adaptability of educators. Teachers remain at the heart of instructional transformation, yet their roles are expanding from mere content deliverers to learning designers, data interpreters, and ethical co-creators with AI. Professional development in this context is a continuous, multi-dimensional process that must encompass technical expertise, digital ethics, data fluency, and pedagogical innovation (Nyathani, 2023).

7.1. Evolving Competency Frameworks

The introduction of AI-driven systems into HyFlex classrooms necessitates a new set of teacher competencies that merge pedagogical expertise with technological intelligence. The AI-Era Teacher Competency Framework extends beyond traditional digital literacy to include interpretability, ethical responsibility, and co-design with AI systems as shown in table 4 (Sanders & Mukhari, 2024).

7.1.1. Digital Pedagogical Competence

Teachers must understand how to integrate AI-based tools and analytics platforms into curriculum design, content delivery, and assessment strategies. Competence involves understanding AI functionality, its limitations, and alignment with learning outcomes. This ensures that pedagogy remains intentional, student-centered, and outcome-driven (Moosa, 2025).

7.1.2. Data Literacy and Interpretability

Educators in AI-mediated environments must develop strong data literacy skills—interpreting dashboards, analytics visualizations, and AI-generated insights. The ability to identify patterns and draw meaningful conclusions from learning data allows teachers to intervene effectively and promote student success.

7.1.3. AI Literacy and Ethics

Ethical awareness is central to AI-augmented teaching. Teachers should comprehend algorithmic behavior, bias, and privacy issues to ensure responsible AI usage. Ethical AI literacy enables educators to maintain transparency and fairness while using automated grading, content recommendation, and feedback systems.

7.1.4. Adaptive and Reflective Practice

The hallmark of AI-empowered teaching is reflective adaptability. Teachers should continuously evaluate how AI outputs align with pedagogical goals and learner diversity. Reflective cycles—supported by AI-based mentoring systems—enable data-informed improvement and professional evolution.

Table 4. AI-era teacher competency framework for HyFlex education

Competency Domain	Description	Tools/Technologies	Expected Outcome
Digital Pedagogical Competence	Integration of AI tools and LMS for hybrid delivery	Moodle, Canvas, Google Classroom	Enhanced instructional flexibility and interactivity
Data Literacy & Interpretability	Ability to interpret and utilize AI-driven analytics	Power BI, Tableau, Brightspace Insights	Evidence-based decision-making
AI Literacy & Ethics	Understanding AI logic, bias, and responsible use	ChatGPT EDU, Turnitin AI, Explainable AI models	Ethical and transparent pedagogy
Adaptive & Reflective Practice	Continuous improvement via feedback and analytics	AI Dashboards, Reflective Journals	Personalized and equitable learning outcomes

7.2. Capacity Building and Institutional Ecosystem

AI-integrated education requires systemic institutional support to build teacher readiness and maintain sustainability (Hadi & AlShaikh-Hasan, 2025b). Institutions must adopt a layered approach to professional development encompassing infrastructure, policy, mentorship, and culture as shown in figure 4.

7.2.1. Continuous Learning and Micro-Credentialing

Institutions should design modular certification and micro-credential programs focused on AI literacy, digital ethics, and hybrid pedagogy. These micro-learning units promote continuous professional growth and validate teachers' evolving expertise.

7.2.2. Peer Learning and Collaborative Networks

Communities of practice—faculty circles, interdisciplinary working groups, and mentorship networks—enable experience-sharing and collaborative reflection. AI can assist by identifying best practices and recommending peer collaborations based on expertise alignment.

7.2.3. AI-Driven Professional Development Platforms

AI-powered training platforms can personalize teachers' learning trajectories, recommending resources, simulations, and assessment exercises based on their strengths and skill gaps. Such adaptive systems mirror the same personalization afforded to students in AI-enhanced classrooms.

7.2.4. Policy, Governance, and Institutional Support

Effective integration of AI requires ethical governance structures. Institutions must develop policies around data ownership, algorithmic transparency, and teacher autonomy. Governance frameworks should balance innovation with accountability and protect teachers' intellectual and creative agency (Wu, n.d.).

Figure 4. Ecosystem of continuous professional development in AI-driven HyFlex systems

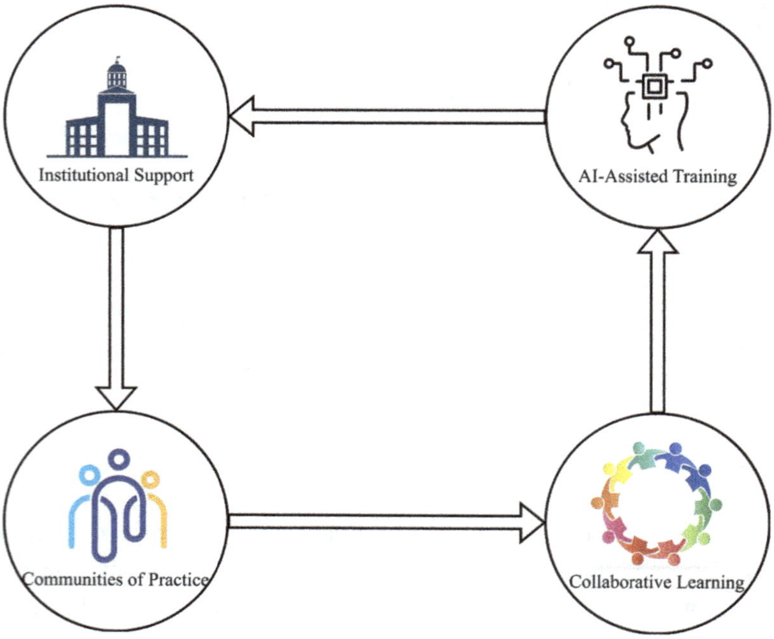

7.3. Challenges in AI-Based Professional Development

While AI offers opportunities for scalable and personalized teacher development, it also introduces several challenges (Roshan et al., 2024):

- Technological Inequity: Not all institutions possess equal access to high-end AI systems or robust data infrastructures, leading to uneven opportunities for professional growth.
- Algorithmic Dependence: Over-reliance on AI recommendations may diminish teachers' critical reflection and pedagogical creativity if unchecked.

- Ethical Concerns: Misuse of teacher analytics, privacy violations, and algorithmic opacity can undermine trust and academic freedom.
- Change Resistance: Faculty accustomed to conventional teaching may perceive AI as disruptive or intimidating, highlighting the need for gradual cultural adaptation.

7.4. Strategies for Sustainable Professional Development

To mitigate these challenges, institutions and educators should implement multipronged strategies (Faikhamta, 2022):

- Blended Training Models: Combine in-person workshops with AI-assisted self-paced modules for flexible skill development.
- Reflective AI Dashboards: Integrate tools that provide teachers with real-time feedback on their instructional effectiveness, enabling self-assessment.
- Mentorship Augmentation: Use AI analytics to match novice teachers with expert mentors based on pedagogical patterns and expertise areas.
- Ethical AI Training: Include dedicated modules on bias detection, explainable AI, and responsible innovation in professional training curricula.

7.5. Future Directions in Teacher Capacity Building

The future of professional development in AI-enhanced HyFlex education lies in co-evolution between human and artificial intelligence. Teachers will increasingly operate within hybrid ecosystems where AI not only informs but also learns from human decisions. Institutions must, therefore, embrace a vision of symbiotic professional growth, where educators continuously shape and are shaped by intelligent systems.

In this evolving paradigm, professional development becomes an ongoing dialogue—between human creativity and machine intelligence, between institutional policy and individual autonomy, and between innovation and ethics. Through sustained capacity building, AI-driven HyFlex education can achieve its ultimate objective: a pedagogically empowered, technologically fluent, and ethically grounded teaching community (Ho & Lee, 2016).

8. PEDAGOGICAL TRANSFORMATIONS DRIVEN BY AI

AI has initiated a paradigm shift in education by transforming how knowledge is designed, delivered, and evaluated. Within HyFlex learning environments, AI serves as both a catalyst and collaborator, enabling personalized learning, real-time analytics, and adaptive assessment (Saaida, 2023). This section examines the pedagogical transformations driven by AI, emphasizing learner-centered instruction, data-informed pedagogy, assessment innovation, and ethical implications.

8.1. Learner-Centric Instructional Redesign

The integration of AI enables a transition from static, one-size-fits-all instruction to dynamic, learner-centered pedagogy. AI systems analyze behavioral, cognitive, and emotional data to generate personalized learning paths, ensuring that each learner progresses according to their unique pace and preferences. In HyFlex classrooms, where students alternate between in-person and virtual modes, AI supports consistency in learning experiences by adapting resources and assignments based on learner participation.

AI-driven adaptive systems such as ITS and Learning Experience Platforms (LXP) use real-time analytics to adjust difficulty levels, provide hints, and curate targeted content. These systems facilitate SRL, empowering students to take ownership of their academic progress. Moreover, the hybrid flexibility of HyFlex environments allows learners to engage with AI-driven simulations, immersive content, and predictive feedback regardless of mode, ensuring continuous engagement and inclusivity.

Table 5. AI-driven pedagogical innovations and their educational impact

Innovation Type	AI Mechanism	Pedagogical Application	Educational Impact
Adaptive Learning Systems	Reinforcement learning, personalization algorithms	Adjusts content based on learner profile	Individualized learning trajectories
AI-Enhanced Content Generation	NLP	Produces context-aware materials	Dynamic and accessible content creation
Predictive Learning Analytics	Machine learning models	Forecasts learner performance	Early identification of at-risk students
Affective Computing	Emotion recognition	Monitors learner engagement	Enhances empathy-driven teaching
Generative AI Simulations	Deep learning	Creates immersive, interactive tasks	Improved experiential learning

AI's learner-centric redesign ensures that instruction is not just responsive but anticipatory, enabling proactive intervention and support. It positions education as an evolving process shaped by data, adaptability, and continuous feedback.

8.2. Data-Driven and Evidence-Informed Pedagogy

AI facilitates the emergence of data-driven pedagogy, where instructional decisions are guided by empirical evidence rather than intuition alone. Teachers equipped with AI-powered dashboards can visualize learner progress, identify cognitive bottlenecks, and modify teaching approaches accordingly. Predictive analytics highlight learning gaps, enabling educators to intervene early with tailored feedback or remedial content. In HyFlex systems, data-driven pedagogy ensures parity of experience across modalities. Whether students attend physically or virtually, AI systems synchronize engagement analytics, ensuring that instructional quality and participation levels remain consistent. Moreover, data collected across different learning environments help institutions refine curricula and improve course design based on evidence rather than assumption (Rizvi, n.d.).

8.3. Assessment Innovation and Academic Integrity

AI-enabled assessment further supports longitudinal learning analytics, allowing continuous tracking of learner development over time. This longitudinal view transforms assessment from a summative endpoint into an ongoing diagnostic process. The AI-Driven Pedagogical Transformation Model (Figure 5) illustrates how adaptive learning systems, intelligent analytics, and ethical assessment frameworks converge within HyFlex education to create a sustainable cycle of instructional innovation, personalized learning, and continuous feedback. AI-enabled assessment further supports longitudinal learning analytics, allowing continuous tracking of learner development over time. This longitudinal view transforms assessment from a summative endpoint into an ongoing diagnostic process.

Figure 5. AI-driven pedagogical transformation model in HyFlex education

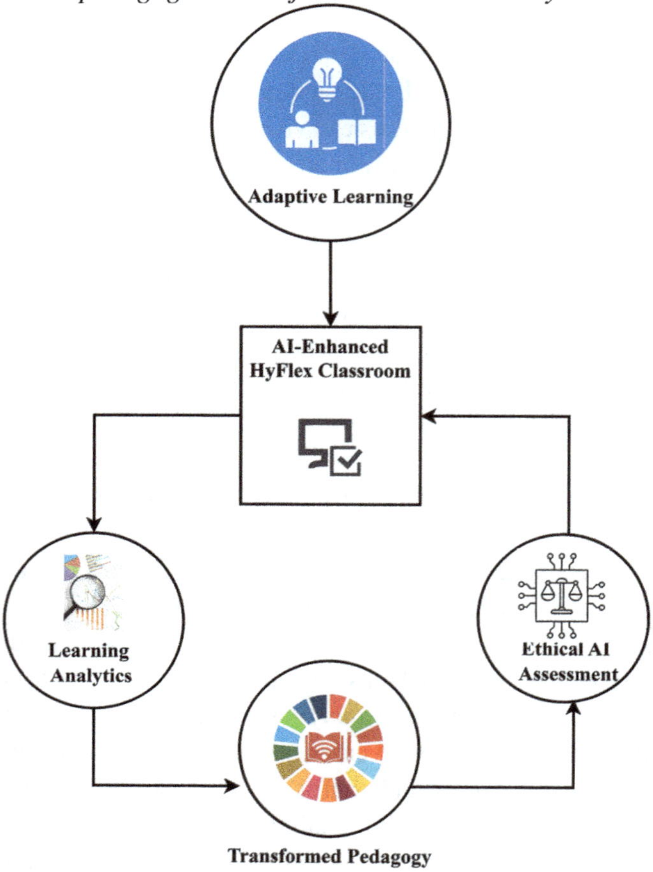

8.4. Collaborative Intelligence and Human–AI Co-Teaching

One of the most significant pedagogical transformations is the evolution toward human–AI co-teaching models, where teachers and AI systems operate collaboratively. In this model, AI assists in lesson planning, monitoring engagement, and providing automated support, while teachers handle effective, motivational, and contextual dimensions of instruction. This hybrid intelligence ensures the balance of automation and empathy within HyFlex education. Co-teaching with AI also fosters adaptive curriculum development, where content continuously evolves based on learner analytics. Teachers become orchestrators of intelligent learning ecosystems, leveraging AI's data-processing capabilities to personalize guidance and scaffold complex learning experiences (Bangulzai et al., 2025).

8.5. Ethical and Societal Implications

While AI's pedagogical impact is profound, it also introduces new ethical, social, and professional challenges. Issues of algorithmic transparency, bias mitigation, data protection, and teacher autonomy must be prioritized in implementation frameworks. Educators should maintain ultimate control over decision-making, ensuring that AI recommendations remain advisory rather than prescriptive. Institutions should adopt ethical guidelines consistent with UNESCO's Recommendation on the Ethics of AI (2021) (Morandín-Ahuerma, 2023) and OECD's framework for AI in Education, emphasizing fairness, inclusivity, and accountability. Teacher preparation programs should therefore integrate ethical AI training, preparing educators to evaluate the social and psychological implications of algorithmic systems in classrooms (Bo, 2025). AI has transformed HyFlex pedagogy into a responsive, data-enriched, and co-intelligent ecosystem. The convergence of adaptive technologies and human expertise promises not only efficiency but also deeper learning experiences that are contextual, equitable, and ethically grounded.

9. INSTITUTIONAL AND POLICY IMPLICATIONS OF AI-DRIVEN HYFLEX LEARNING

The successful integration of AI in HyFlex learning environments depends not only on pedagogical and technological readiness but also on robust institutional and policy frameworks. This section highlights the strategic, ethical, and governance-related implications institutions must address to ensure equitable and sustainable AI adoption (Thompson & Harris, 2025).

9.1. Institutional Readiness and Digital Infrastructure

Institutions must build the technological backbone necessary for AI-driven education. This includes high-speed connectivity, cloud-based LMS, interoperable data architectures, and secure storage mechanisms. Institutional readiness extends to the creation of data governance policies that regulate data ownership, privacy, and interoperability. The deployment of AI in HyFlex environments also necessitates the establishment of learning analytics centers capable of processing large-scale educational data ethically and effectively. The transition to AI-empowered HyFlex education should be guided by strategic planning that aligns digital transformation goals with pedagogical missions. Institutions should establish AI implementation roadmaps that include infrastructure development, faculty training, and student support systems, ensuring that the integration enhances rather than disrupts teaching and learning processes.

9.2. Governance, Policy, and Ethical Frameworks

The introduction of AI into educational ecosystems raises questions of accountability, transparency, and governance. Institutions must adopt clear policies outlining how AI is used, monitored, and evaluated. Ethical governance frameworks should address concerns related to algorithmic bias, student data privacy, informed consent, and intellectual property rights (Grynyuk et al., 2021). International guidelines such as UNESCO's Recommendation on the Ethics of AI (2021) and the OECD Framework for the Classification of AI Systems (2022) provide foundational principles for responsible AI adoption. Institutions should contextualize these frameworks to their local regulatory environments, ensuring alignment with national education policies and data protection laws.

Table 6. Institutional and policy dimensions for ethical AI-driven HyFlex education

Policy Domain	Key Objectives	Institutional Strategies	Expected Outcomes
Governance	Establish accountability and oversight mechanisms	Form AI ethics committees and audit systems	Transparent and responsible AI deployment
Data Protection	Safeguard student and faculty data	Implement encryption, anonymization, and access controls	Enhanced trust and security in digital ecosystems
Faculty Autonomy	Preserve educators' agency and decision-making authority	Define teacher–AI co-governance policies	Balanced human–machine collaboration
Accessibility & Equity	Ensure inclusive AI adoption	Subsidize digital access and adaptive technologies	Reduced digital divide and increased participation

9.3. Institutional Collaboration and Policy Innovation

AI-driven HyFlex learning thrives on collaborative ecosystems that bridge academia, industry, and government. Partnerships with AI developers and ed-tech organizations can provide access to innovative tools, real-world datasets, and capacity-building programs. Collaborative policy design ensures that institutional frameworks remain agile, adaptive, and relevant to emerging technological landscapes. Institutions must also engage in policy experimentation, testing different governance models for AI adoption through pilot projects and controlled trials. Such iterative policy innovation promotes evidence-based regulation while ensuring that ethical considerations evolve alongside technological progress (Fowler, 2014).

9.4. Sustainability and Long-Term Vision

Sustainability in AI-driven education extends beyond infrastructure, it involves maintaining ethical resilience, pedagogical integrity, and financial viability. Institutions should allocate dedicated funding streams for AI maintenance, teacher reskilling, and system upgrades. Moreover, sustainability requires embedding AI ethics into institutional culture, encouraging continuous reflection on the societal impact of intelligent technologies in education. In the long term, institutions should envision themselves as AI-augmented learning ecosystems, where policy, pedagogy, and technology converge to foster innovation without compromising human values. This vision aligns with the global movement toward human-centered AI, ensuring that automation enhances—rather than replaces—educational purpose and creativity (Meadan et al., 2010).

Finally, institutional and policy readiness serve as the foundation for trustworthy AI integration in HyFlex education. Governance mechanisms, ethical oversight, and sustainable digital ecosystems are indispensable for ensuring that AI contributes positively to learning equity, inclusivity, and long-term academic innovation.

10. IMPLICATIONS OF THE STUDY

The conceptualization of teacher–AI collaboration within HyFlex learning environments carries significant implications across theoretical, practical, and social dimensions. By positioning AI as a pedagogical collaborator rather than a mere instructional tool, this study contributes to a deeper understanding of how human and AI can coexist productively within flexible, data-driven educational ecosystems.

10.1. Theoretical Implications

From a theoretical standpoint, this study advances the emerging discourse on hybrid intelligence in education by framing teacher–AI collaboration as a co-intelligent pedagogical construct. Existing theories of HyFlex learning largely emphasize modality flexibility and learner choice, while research on AI in education often focuses on system performance and learner outcomes. This chapter bridges these bodies of knowledge by integrating pedagogical theory with AI-mediated instructional intelligence, thereby extending HyFlex pedagogy beyond logistical flexibility toward adaptive, intelligence-driven instructional orchestration. Furthermore, the proposed framework reconceptualizes the role of educators within AI-enabled learning environments. Rather than positioning teachers as passive users or supervisors of intelligent systems, the study theoretically situates them as co-decision-makers and interpretive agents who guide, validate, and ethically contextualize AI-generated insights. This contributes to a more nuanced understanding of teacher agency, professional identity, and pedagogical authority in digitally mediated education. By doing so, the study establishes teacher–AI collaboration as a legitimate theoretical construct that warrants further scholarly investigation and empirical validation.

10.2. Practical Implications

The findings of this study offer several practical implications for instructional design, faculty development, and institutional implementation of AI-enabled HyFlex education. For educators, the proposed framework provides actionable guidance on how AI-driven analytics, adaptive content systems, and automated feedback mechanisms can be strategically integrated into HyFlex classrooms to maintain pedagogical coherence across in-person, synchronous online, and asynchronous modalities. This supports evidence-informed instructional design and enhances the capacity of teachers to manage diverse learner trajectories effectively. For institutions, the study informs faculty development planning by identifying critical competency areas such as data literacy, AI interpretability, ethical awareness, and adaptive pedagogy. The framework can serve as a reference model for designing professional development programs, micro-credential initiatives, and mentorship structures that prepare educators for sustained collaboration with AI systems. Additionally, the study offers practical insights for decision-makers involved in adopting AI-enabled LMS, emphasizing the importance of aligning technological capabilities with pedagogical goals, governance policies, and teacher autonomy.

10.3. Social Implications

At a broader societal level, this study highlights the potential of teacher–AI collaboration to promote inclusive, equitable, and human-centered education. By leveraging AI to personalize learning pathways and monitor engagement across multiple participation modes, HyFlex systems can reduce structural barriers related to geography, time, and accessibility. This is particularly relevant for learners from diverse socio-economic and cultural backgrounds who may benefit from flexible participation and adaptive instructional support. The framework also underscores the role of AI in mitigating teacher workload and cognitive overload by automating routine tasks and providing decision-support insights. This redistribution of cognitive labor enables educators to focus on higher-order pedagogical functions such as mentoring, critical thinking facilitation, and emotional support. Importantly, the study reinforces the necessity of ethical AI adoption, advocating for transparency, fairness, and human oversight to ensure that technological innovation does not compromise educational values or social trust.

From an engagement and inclusivity perspective, the proposed teacher–AI collaboration framework offers practical mechanisms for identifying participation gaps, supporting diverse learner trajectories, and ensuring equitable instructional responsiveness across HyFlex modalities. AI-supported engagement analytics reduce reliance on subjective judgment, enabling teachers to intervene early and design inclusive learning experiences for students who may otherwise remain disengaged or underserved. Socially, this approach promotes educational equity by aligning flexible participation with adaptive pedagogical support, ensuring that learner choice does not result in unequal learning outcomes.

11. FUTURE DIRECTIONS AND RESEARCH IMPLICATIONS

As educational ecosystems continue to evolve, the convergence of AI and HyFlex learning presents a multitude of future research avenues and implementation challenges. The transformative potential of this integration lies not only in optimizing instructional efficiency but also in redefining human–machine collaboration, ethics, and data-driven innovation in education (Facer & Sandford, 2010). This section discusses emerging trends, future directions, and open research challenges that will shape the next generation of AI-augmented HyFlex learning systems.

11.1. Emerging Trends in AI-Augmented Educatio

The future of HyFlex learning will be marked by the emergence of intelligent educational ecosystems that autonomously adapt to the cognitive, emotional, and social dimensions of learners. One significant trend shaping this evolution is the adoption of Federated Learning in Education, which enables decentralized AI models to train collaboratively across multiple institutions without exposing sensitive data, thereby ensuring privacy-preserving analytics. Another major advancement lies in Multimodal Learning Analytics, where AI systems integrate diverse data streams, including visual, textual, behavioral, and physiological information, to construct holistic learner profiles and deliver deeply personalized educational experiences. Parallel to these developments is the growth of Explainable and Trustworthy AI

(XAI), which emphasizes algorithmic transparency to help teachers and learners interpret AI-generated insights, fostering accountability and trust in automated systems (Shafik, 2024). Moreover, Metaverse-Enabled HyFlex Systems are beginning to merge augmented and virtual reality technologies with AI-driven interactivity, creating immersive and experiential learning spaces that transcend traditional boundaries of classroom engagement. Finally, the concept of Cognitive Digital Twins for Education is gaining prominence, offering virtual replicas of learners or entire classrooms powered by AI to simulate learning processes, predict performance outcomes, and optimize instructional interventions. Collectively, these innovations mark a transition from reactive to anticipatory education systems, wherein AI not only responds to learner needs but proactively predicts and enhances individual learning trajectories for more effective, equitable, and engaging educational experiences.

11.2. Open Research Challenges

Despite rapid advancements, several research gaps remain unaddressed (Masterman, 2016):

- Cross-Modal Data Fusion: How can AI systems effectively integrate heterogeneous learning data across modalities without compromising interpretability?
- Algorithmic Fairness: How can we ensure equitable AI decisions that account for cultural, linguistic, and cognitive diversity among learners?
- Teacher–AI Co-Evolution: What frameworks best describe the reciprocal learning process between humans and AI systems?
- Longitudinal Impact Studies: How can we quantify the long-term pedagogical and ethical outcomes of AI-assisted HyFlex education?
- Scalable Governance Models: What institutional mechanisms can maintain ethical AI deployment across global education networks?

Addressing these questions will require multidisciplinary collaboration among computer scientists, educators, psychologists, and policy experts.

11.3. Ethical and Humanistic Research Directions

Future research should emphasize human-centered AI, ensuring that automation complements human values rather than replacing human agency. Ethical frameworks must evolve to include:

- Algorithmic Transparency and Accountability
- Digital Wellbeing and Psychological Safety

- Human Oversight in AI Decision-Making
- Inclusive Design for Marginalized Learners

By embedding ethical consciousness into AI systems, researchers can safeguard trust, fairness, and human dignity in future HyFlex education models.

11.4. Roadmap for Future Research

The roadmap envisions a cyclical model where theoretical advancements inform adaptive model development, followed by empirical validation in live educational contexts. Insights derived from real-world deployments continuously refine both AI algorithms and pedagogical theories. In essence, the future of Teacher–AI collaboration in HyFlex education will be defined by a balance between technological sophistication and ethical sensitivity. Research must move toward frameworks that prioritize interpretability, co-adaptation, and inclusivity, ensuring that AI not only enhances learning but also reinforces the values of human-centered education (Nursalim et al., 2021).

11.5. Scope for Future Research

Future research may empirically validate teacher AI collaboration frameworks in HyFlex learning through quantitative, qualitative, and mixed method studies. Longitudinal investigations can examine how sustained interaction with AI influences teacher professional identity, autonomy, and reflective practice. Further studies are needed to explore explainable and trustworthy AI models that support ethical and transparent pedagogical decision making. Comparative and cross institutional research may also provide insights into cultural and policy factors affecting AI enabled HyFlex education. These directions will support the development of scalable, ethical, and human centered intelligent learning ecosystems.

12. CONCLUSION

The integration of Artificial Intelligence (AI) within HyFlex learning environments represents a significant pedagogical shift in contemporary higher education, redefining how teaching, learning, and engagement are conceptualized and enacted. This chapter has demonstrated that AI, when positioned as a collaborative pedagogical partner rather than a standalone technological solution, enables teachers to navigate the inherent complexity of HyFlex instruction more effectively. By combining human pedagogical judgment with AI-driven analytics, adaptive feedback, and decision-support systems, educators can design learning experiences that are responsive, scalable, and learner-centered across in-person, synchronous online, and asynchronous modalities. A central contribution of this chapter lies in foregrounding student engagement and inclusivity as core outcomes of teacher–AI collaboration. In HyFlex settings, where learner participation is distributed across multiple modes, sustaining consistent engagement and equitable learning experiences remains a critical challenge. The proposed teacher–AI collaboration framework illustrates how AI-enabled engagement monitoring, personalized learning pathways, and adaptive instructional interventions support behavioral, cognitive, and emotional engagement across modalities. Through these mechanisms, teacher–AI collaboration mitigates participation disparities and ensures that learner choice does not translate into unequal educational outcomes. Importantly, this chapter aligns teacher–AI collaboration with the four foundational principles of HyFlex learning—learner choice, equivalency, reusability, and accessibility. AI-supported analytics and adaptive systems enable teachers to uphold pedagogical equivalency across participation modes, enhance accessibility through personalized content delivery, and promote reusability of instructional resources across synchronous and asynchronous contexts. In doing so, the chapter demonstrates that HyFlex principles are not merely structural design considerations but can be actively operationalized through collaborative human–AI pedagogy to foster inclusive and engaging learning environments. From a broader perspective, the chapter positions teacher–AI collaboration as a core enabler of sustainable, student-centered HyFlex education, directly aligning with the thematic focus of this edited volume. Rather than displacing educators, AI amplifies teacher agency by reducing cognitive load, enhancing instructional visibility, and supporting data-informed pedagogical decision-making. This human-centered approach ensures that technological innovation remains anchored in educational values such as equity, transparency, and learner empowerment.

Finally this chapter contributes a coherent conceptual foundation for understanding how teacher–AI collaboration can enhance student engagement, inclusivity, and pedagogical coherence within HyFlex learning ecosystems. As higher education continues to embrace flexible and hybrid learning models, the insights presented here offer a meaningful framework for researchers, practitioners, and policymakers seeking to align AI-enabled innovation with the core principles of effective and inclusive education. By emphasizing collaboration over automation and engagement over efficiency alone, the chapter advances a vision of HyFlex education that is adaptive, ethical, and fundamentally human-centered.

REFERENCES

Bangulzai, A. R., Begum, R., Mirza, M., & Ahmad, S. (2025). The Future of Teaching: Examining the Role of AI Tutors and Human Teachers in Co-Teaching Models. *The Critical Review of Social Sciences Studies*, *3*(3), 813–829. DOI: 10.59075/rtz61m29

Beatty, B. (2019). *Hybrid-flexible course design*. EdTech Books London. DOI: 10.59668/33

Bo, N. S. W. (2025). OECD digital education outlook 2023: Towards an effective education ecosystem. *Hungarian Educational Research Journal*, *15*(2), 284–289. DOI: 10.1556/063.2024.00340

Davis, F. D. (1989). Perceived usefulness, perceived ease of use, and user acceptance of information technology. *Management Information Systems Quarterly*, *13*(3), 319–340. DOI: 10.2307/249008

Deci, E. L., Olafsen, A. H., & Ryan, R. M. (2017). Self-determination theory in work organizations: The state of a science. *Annual Review of Organizational Psychology and Organizational Behavior*, *4*(1), 19–43. DOI: 10.1146/annurev-orgpsych-032516-113108

Deci, E. L., & Ryan, R. M. (2008). Self-determination theory: A macrotheory of human motivation, development, and health. *Canadian Psychology*, *49*(3), 182–185. DOI: 10.1037/a0012801

Dineva, S. (2024). Hybrid, blended, and hyflex learning as future models for education. *Обучение По Природни Науки и Върхови Технологии*, *33*(3–4), 152–161. DOI: 10.53656/nat2024-3-4.01

Essaid, E. L., & HAJI, A. A. (2020). Proposal of a digital ecosystem based on big data and artificial intelligence to support educational and vocational guidance. [IJMECS]. *International Journal of Modern Education and Computer Science*, *12*(4), 1–11.

Facer, K., & Sandford, R. (2010). The next 25 years?: Future scenarios and future directions for education and technology. *Journal of Computer Assisted Learning*, *26*(1), 74–93. DOI: 10.1111/j.1365-2729.2009.00337.x

Faikhamta, C. (2022). Trends of teacher professional development strategies: A systematic review. *Shanlax International Journal of Education*.

Fowler, A. (2014). *Innovation in institutional collaboration. The role of interlocutors*.

Grynyuk, S., Zheludenko, M., & Zaytseva, I. (2021). Readiness of the digital infrastructure of higher educational institutions in ukraine for mass distance learning. *Visnyk Kremenchutskoho Natsionalnoho Universytetu Imeni Mykhaila Ostrohradskoho–Transactions of Kremenchuk Mykhailo Ostrohradskyi National University*, *4*(4(129)), 35–40. DOI: 10.30929/1995-0519.2021.4.35-40

Hadi, W., & AlShaikh-Hasan, M. N. (2025). AI-Driven Curriculum Transformation and Faculty Development in Developing Universities. In *Revolutionizing Urban Development and Governance With Emerging Technologies* (pp. 289–322). IGI Global Scientific Publishing. DOI: 10.4018/979-8-3373-1375-7.ch010

Ho, D., & Lee, M. (2016). Capacity building for school development: Current problems and future challenges. *School Leadership & Management*, *36*(5), 493–507. DOI: 10.1080/13632434.2016.1247040

Khezrlou, S., & Stockwell, G. (2025). A synthetic review of MALL research: Artifact, environment, and task. *Digital Studies in Language and Literature*, (0).

Kim, J. (2024). Leading teachers' perspective on teacher-AI collaboration in education. *Education and Information Technologies*, *29*(7), 8693–8724. DOI: 10.1007/s10639-023-12109-5

Lamtara, S. (2024). [RETRACTED ARTICLE] Pedagogical Knowledge for Technology-Enhanced Learning: A Literature Review. *Journal of Pedagogy and Education Science*, *3*(01), 72–90. DOI: 10.56741/jpes.v3i01.424

Liang, M. (2025). Leveraging natural language processing for automated assessment and feedback production in virtual education settings. *Journal of Computational Methods in Sciences and Engineering*, *25*(3), 2502–2515. DOI: 10.1177/14727978251314556

Masterman, E. (2016). Bringing Open Educational Practice to a Research-Intensive University: Prospects and Challenges. *Electronic Journal of e-Learning*, *14*(1), 31–43.

Meadan, H., Shelden, D. L., Appel, K., & DeGrazia, R. L. (2010). Developing a long-term vision: A road map for students' futures. *Teaching Exceptional Children*, *43*(2), 8–14. DOI: 10.1177/004005991004300201

Miller, A. N., Sellnow, D. D., & Strawser, M. G. (2021). Pandemic pedagogy challenges and opportunities: Instruction communication in remote, HyFlex, and BlendFlex courses. *Communication Education*, *70*(2), 202–204. DOI: 10.1080/03634523.2020.1857418

Moosa, R. (2025). *Pragmatic Multimodal Teaching Using VARK and AI-Supported Pedagogy*.

Morandín-Ahuerma, F. (2023). *Ten UNESCO recommendations on the ethics of artificial intelligence.*

Mousavinasab, E., Zarifsanaiey, N., & Niakan Kalhori, R., S., Rakhshan, M., Keikha, L., & Ghazi Saeedi, M. (. (2021). Intelligent tutoring systems: A systematic review of characteristics, applications, and evaluation methods. *Interactive Learning Environments*, *29*(1), 142–163. DOI: 10.1080/10494820.2018.1558257

Nain, A., Bohra, N. S., Singh, A., Verma, R., Kumar, R., & Kumar, R. (2025). Mapping the landscape: A bibliometric analysis of AI and teacher collaboration in educational research. *F1000 Research*, *14*, 201. DOI: 10.12688/f1000research.160297.2 PMID: 40386461

Niemi, H. (2020). Artificial intelligence for the common good in educational ecosystems. *Humanistic Futures of Learning: Perspectives from UNESCO Chairs and UNITWIN Networks*, 148–152.

Nursalim, M., Ardianingsih, F., & Maureen, I. Y. (2021). Designing Educational Research Roadmap. *International Joint Conference on Arts and Humanities 2021 (IJCAH 2021)*, 1093–1098.

Nyathani, R. (2023). AI-enabled learning and development: Hr's new paradigm. *Journal of Marketing & Supply Chain Management. SRC/JMSCM-127. DOI: Doi. Org*, *117*(2), 2–5. DOI: 10.47363/JMSCM/2023

Qazi, S., Kadri, M. B., Naveed, M., Khawaja, B. A., Khan, S. Z., Alam, M. M., & Su'ud, M. M. (2024). AI-Driven Learning Management Systems: Modern Developments, Challenges and Future Trends during the Age of ChatGPT. *Computers, Materials & Continua*, *80*(2), 3289–3314. DOI: 10.32604/cmc.2024.048893

Racheva, V., & Peytcheva-Forsyth, R. (2024). Navigating the future: Exploring synchronous hybrid learning in higher education post-covid. *INTED2024 Proceedings*, 6335–6345.

Ray, S., & Saeed, M. (2018). Applications of educational data mining and learning analytics tools in handling big data in higher education. In *Applications of Big Data analytics: Trends, issues, and challenges* (pp. 135–160). Springer. DOI: 10.1007/978-3-319-76472-6_7

Rizvi, S. U.-S. (n.d.). *Evidence-Informed Practices in Early Years Settings.*

Roshan, S., Iqbal, S. Z., & Qing, Z. (2024). Teacher training and professional development for implementing AI-based educational tools. *Journal of Asian Development Studies*, *13*(2), 1972–1987. DOI: 10.62345/jads.2024.13.2.154

Saaida, M. B. (2023). AI-Driven transformations in higher education: Opportunities and challenges. *International Journal of Educational Research and Studies, 5*(1), 29–36.

Sabol, D. A. (2025). *Libraries' future: intelligent catalogs, digital repositories, artificial intelligence*. Dr. Daniel A. Sabol.

Sanders, D. A., & Mukhari, S. S. (2024). Lecturers' perceptions of the influence of AI on a blended learning approach in a South African higher education institution. *Discover Education, 3*(1), 135. DOI: 10.1007/s44217-024-00235-2

Shafik, W. (2024). Towards trustworthy and explainable AI educational systems. In *Explainable AI for Education: Recent Trends and Challenges* (pp. 17–41). Springer. DOI: 10.1007/978-3-031-72410-7_2

Tapalova, O., & Zhiyenbayeva, N. (2022). Artificial intelligence in education: AIEd for personalised learning pathways. *Electronic Journal of e-Learning, 20*(5), 639–653. DOI: 10.34190/ejel.20.5.2597

Thompson, J., & Harris, O. (2025). A Narrative Review of Educational Technology in Higher Education. *Social Science Chronicle, 5*(1), 1–27. DOI: 10.56106/ssc.2025.002

Vanneste, P., Oramas, J., Verelst, T., Tuytelaars, T., Raes, A., Depaepe, F., & Van den Noortgate, W. (2021). Computer vision and human behaviour, emotion and cognition detection: A use case on student engagement. *Mathematics, 9*(3), 287. DOI: 10.3390/math9030287

Venkatesh, V., Morris, M. G., Davis, G. B., & Davis, F. D. (2003). User acceptance of information technology: Toward a unified view. *Management Information Systems Quarterly, 27*(3), 425–478. DOI: 10.2307/30036540

Vygotsky, L. S. (1978). *Mind in society: The development of higher psychological processes* (Vol. 86). Harvard university press.

Welch, R. W., Rabb, R. J., & Eggleston, A. G. (2021). Using the SWIVL for Effective HyFlex Instruction: Best Practices, Challenges, and Opportunities. *2021 ASEE Virtual Annual Conference Content Access*. DOI: 10.18260/1-2--38005

Wu, W. (n.d.). Challenges, Trends, and Recommendations. *Digital Transformation in Global TVET: Methodology and Practices, 167.*

Chapter 5
Educator Readiness in Leveraging Learning Analytics for Adaptive Learning Pathways and Student Success

Abdul Feroz Maluleke
http://orcid.org/0000-0003-2390-1517
Tshwane University of Technology, South Africa

ABSTRACT

As higher education institutions increasingly adopt learning analytics (LA) to personalise learning and drive student success, the readiness and role of educators in implementing and interpreting these technologies has become critical. This chapter explores the intersection of educator digital readiness, pedagogical capacity, and institutional support in leveraging LA for adaptive learning pathways. The chapter examines how faculty understanding and use of analytics derived from LMS can enhance learner engagement, early intervention, and long-term academic achievement. The chapter proposes a framework for enhancing educator readiness, including competencies in data literacy, ethical awareness, and pedagogical adaptation. Drawing from literature and policy considerations, the chapter highlights challenges and opportunities for sustainable, analytics-driven teaching practices. Moreover, it argues that without a deliberate focus on empowering educators, the transformative potential of learning analytics will remain underutilised in improving educational outcomes.

DOI: 10.4018/979-8-3373-6182-6.ch005

INTRODUCTION AND BACKGROUND

In recent years, higher education institutions (HEIs) have increasingly embraced digital technologies as strategic enablers of teaching and learning. This shift has been driven by the imperative to enhance educational outcomes through innovative, technology-supported pedagogical models. Across global contexts, digital adoption initiatives aim not only to improve instructional delivery but also to foster inclusive, flexible, and student-centred learning environments. Notably, the integration of such technologies aligns with broader global development priorities, particularly Sustainable Development Goal 4 (SDG 4), which advocates for inclusive and equitable quality education and lifelong learning opportunities for all. As awareness in relation to sustainable technology adoption continues to grow within the higher education spectrum, institutions are now called upon to ensure that the deployment of educational technologies supports both pedagogical effectiveness and long-term digital sustainability.

The rapid digitization of teaching and learning has positioned Learning Analytics (LA) as a transformative tool for monitoring student progress, personalizing instruction, and improving retention (Arockia et al., 2025; Okoye, Nganji, & Hosseini, 2020). In recent years, there has been a marked surge in the adoption of Learning Management Systems (LMSs) and related educational technologies across higher education institutions (HEIs), largely driven by their potential to enhance programme delivery and improve student outcomes (Márquez, Henríquez, Chevreux, Scheihing, & Guerra, 2024). This widespread uptake reflects the recognised importance of LA in facilitating data-informed decision-making to enhance teaching and learning (Wang et al., 2023). By integrating advanced analytics with LMS and artificial intelligence (AI) platforms, such as Mentimeter, Quizizz, and Kahoot, LA offers unprecedented opportunities to close the loop between educational research and classroom practice, paving new pathways for personalized and adaptive learning (Ouyang, Wu, Zheng, Zhang, & Jiao, 2023).

Despite its transformative promise, scholars caution that the benefits of LA can only be realised through careful and sustainable integration that balances technological capacity with ethical considerations and quality assurance measures (Javed & Alenezi, 2023; Darvishi, Khosravi, Sadiq, & Gašević, 2022). Institutional investments have largely focused on building technical infrastructures such as dashboards and LMS integrations, yet the pedagogical impact of LA remains limited without the active engagement of educators (Bucăţa & Tileagă, 2024). Educator readiness has emerged as critical factor in shaping the success of LA adoption and initiatives across the education spectrum. Educator readiness defined by technological competence, pedagogical alignment, and institutional support (Mane, 2025). Previous studies indicate that a lack of digital literacy, insufficient institutional backing, and ethical concerns impede the effective adoption of LA in higher education (Williamson, 2019; Ifenthaler & Yau, 2020; Liu, Hu, Ng, Ma, & Lai, 2025). Educators are widely regarded as the key actors in ensuring successful LA integration due to their expertise in pedagogy and their understanding of how learning unfolds in diverse contexts (Gabelaia, 2024). As such, their readiness not only determines whether analytics insights are translated into meaningful instructional practices but also underpins the sustainability of LA adoption at scale. This chapter, therefore, explores the concept of educator readiness in leveraging LA to support adaptive learning pathways and student success. Specifically, this chapter seeks to:

- Examine how institutional engagement with LA contributes to adaptive learning pathways.
- Identify enablers and barriers to effective educator use of LMS and LA tools.
- Propose a framework for enhancing educator readiness in LA implementation.
- Highlight implications for institutional policy and practice.

Understanding Learning Analytics and Adaptive Pathways

Learning Analytics has emerged as a key innovation in educational research and practice, especially in online and technology-enhanced learning environments. Kew and Tasir (2022) defined LA as the measurement, collection, analysis, and reporting of data about learners and their contexts, with the aim of understanding and optimizing learning and the environments in which it occurs. LA equips educators and researchers with the ability to extract meaningful insights from educational data, which can guide pedagogical decision-making and enhance learning outcomes (Du et al., 2021). Beyond its evaluative function, LA serves as a strategic lens through which educators can explore how best to integrate emerging technologies into the teaching and learning process, facilitating evidence-based interventions (Poquet, 2024). While LA is often presented in optimistic terms as a data-driven mechanism for enhancing educational decision-making and student success, critical scholarship cautions against uncritical acceptance of its transformative promise. The increasing datafication and datafication of education, although positioned as improving transparency and efficiency, may reshape educational practices in ways that influence how learners and institutions are evaluated and governed (Martens et al., 2024; Perrotta & Williamson, 2018). Moreover, the deployment of LA tools can extend beyond supportive analytics into forms of performativity and surveillance, raising concerns about neutrality, power, and the ethical implications of monitoring student behaviour (Perrotta & Williamson, 2018; Ray & Saeed, 2018).

Despite its growing significance, LA is conceptualized differently across educational contexts, particularly within higher education. In universities, LA has evolved from mere data collection toward supporting student-centered learning, academic advising, and course design tailored to individual needs (Nguyen et al., 2021). This expanded scope includes analyzing behavioural, cognitive, and affective aspects of the learner experience (Jääskelä et al., 2021). For instance, Qazi and Pachler (2025) propose a data analytics framework aimed at enabling targeted professional development for teachers based on performance data, thus positioning LA as both a pedagogical and strategic tool. Wang, Mousavi, and Lu (2022) further argue that theory-driven applications of LA enhance its explanatory power, enabling alignment with learning theories. Valle et al. (2021) emphasise the role of learner-facing dashboards, suggesting that visual analytics can scaffold students' metacognitive awareness and self-regulated learning. Among various conceptual models, Clow's (2012) "Learning Analytics Cycle" remains particularly influential, highlighting the importance of closing the feedback loop between data generation, interpretation, and pedagogical response to ensure LA leads to meaningful action.

In essence, the Learning Analytics Cycle is a process of collecting, analyzing, and utilizing data to improve learning outcomes. Clow (2012) proposed a four-step cycle: learners generate data, which is used to produce metrics or visualizations, followed by interventions to close the feedback loop. This cycle emphasizes quick feedback and wider audience engagement. Clow's learning analytics cycle theoretical framework (See Figure 1) underscores the transformative benefits of systematic data utilization in education. By employing a cyclical process of data collection, analysis, interpretation, and action, the framework enables educational institutions to continuously refine teaching and learning practices (Clow, 2012). Additionally, it facilitates personalized learning experiences by leveraging insights into individual student needs and behaviours, supports early intervention strategies to address academic challenges, and promotes evidence-based decision-making across curricular design, teaching methodologies, and resource allocation (Clow, 2012).

Figure 1. The learning analytics cycle (Clow, 2012)

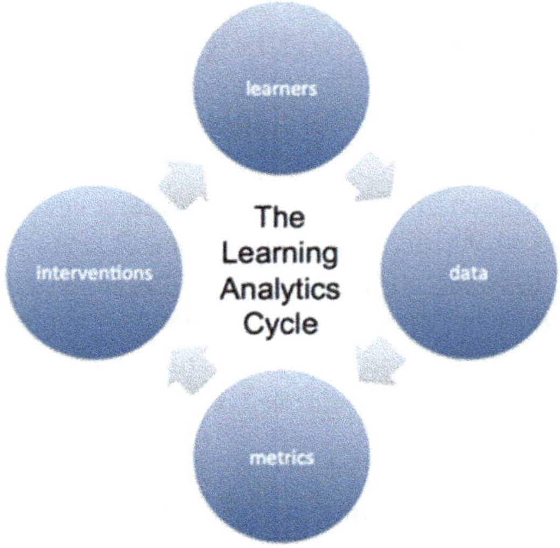

Closely related to LA is the concept of adaptive learning pathways, which refer to the dynamic personalization of the learning process through the use of learner data, pedagogical strategies, and AI-enabled technologies. These pathways adjust the sequencing, difficulty, and nature of learning tasks based on learners' progress, preferences, and prior knowledge (Raj & Renumol, 2024). Adaptive learning systems rely on real-time analytics to continuously update the learner's route through instructional content, offering differentiated support and feedback tailored to their individual profiles (Ning et al., 2025). Such systems are designed not only to personalize content but also to increase engagement and improve learning efficiency.

Research on adaptive learning design highlights its capacity to individualize learning experiences at scale. Donevska-Todorova, Dziergwa, and Simbeck (2022) demonstrate how adaptive strategies can be implemented through modularized content structures and algorithmic decision-making. Similarly, Alazzawi et al. (2025) propose a future-oriented framework that integrates predictive analytics into adaptive e-learning environments, fostering proactive interventions. Tariq (2024) emphasizes that adaptive technologies, when embedded within institutional infrastructures, can support long-term student retention and satisfaction.

The intersection of LA and adaptive learning pathways is particularly potent in promoting student success. Real-time data analytics enable the identification of at-risk students, support the design of targeted interventions, and allow for iterative refinements to the instructional design (Raj & Renumol, 2024; Dwivedi et al., 2024). Moreover, LA supports student engagement by providing timely feedback and actionable insights that encourage deeper interaction with learning materials (Silvola et al., 2021). In online learning environments, where asynchronous interactions and learner isolation are common, LA plays a crucial role in supporting sustainable, data-driven learning ecosystems (Kew & Tasir, 2022).

Benefits of LA implementation or adoption in higher education

The growing integration of LA into higher education landscapes in recent years has yielded a wide array of benefits across pedagogical, technological, institutional, and learner-centric domains (*see Table 1*). Through synthesizing findings from an extensive body of empirical studies, several core themes emerge that highlight the transformative potential of LA in improving student success, enabling adaptive learning, and supporting evidence-informed decision-making.

Table 1. Benefits of learning analytics in higher education

Theme	Summary of benefits	Authors
Curriculum & Learning Design	LA facilitates continuous refinement of learning design by identifying content gaps, misaligned pacing, and inadequate scaffolding in course structure.	Lockyer et al. (2013); Corrin et al. (2022); Dennehy, Conboy & Babu (2023).
Improved Student Performance and Retention	LA supports early identification of at-risk students and tailor interventions to promote achievement. LA enables proactive academic support.	Tempelaar et al. (2015); Xing et al. (2015); Namoun & Alshanqiti (2020); Li et al. (2022)
Personalized learning and student support	Enables educators to fine-tune pedagogical strategies and provide individualized, timely feedback and student support.	Tsai et al. (2020); Leitner et al. (2017); Maseleno et al. (2018); Kurilovas (2019)
Engagement & Motivation	By visualizing student engagement metrics, LA empowers learners to reflect on and adjust their behaviour, fostering metacognitive regulation and motivation.	Matcha et al. (2019); Schumacher & Ifenthaler (2018); Johar et al. (2023); Silvola et al. (2021)
Collaboration Enhancement	LA reveals patterns in peer collaboration, helping educators redesign group activities to ensure balanced participation and interaction.	"Wise & Vytasek (2017); Gašević et al. (2015); Ouyang & Zhang (2024).
Efficiency in Course Delivery	Enables instructors to optimize course delivery by identifying which resources and activities are most effective or underused.	Ifenthaler & Widanapathirana (2014); Tran, Jan, & Kew (2022); Barthakur et al. (2022)
Evidence-based Decision Making	Encourages data-informed pedagogical and administrative decisions by presenting insights on student behaviour and course effectiveness.	Papamitsiou & Economides (2014); Dawson et al. (2019); Yan et al. (2024)

One of the most widely acknowledged benefits is the ability of LA to support data-informed decision-making at both micro (individual course) and macro (institutional policy) levels. For instance, studies by Dawson et al. (2019) and Leitner et al. (2017) underscore how LA facilitate evidence-based educational decisions, thereby reducing assumptions and aligning educational practices with established student behaviours and outcomes. Moreover, LA enhances early identification and predictive modelling to flag students at risk of failure or drop-out, allowing for timely interventions (Daud et al., 2017; Namoun & Alshanqiti, 2020; Hasan et al., 2020). Predictive algorithms and engagement data help instructors and academic advisors proactively engage struggling students and improve retention.

Another critical advantage lies in the personalization of learning pathways, which has been shown to be effective in increasing student motivation, engagement and learning outcomes (Kurilovas, 2019; Maseleno et al., 2018). Personalization is made possible through advanced machine learning techniques and adaptive platforms that tailor educational content delivery based on student performance and preferences. Additionally, LA improves curriculum design and learning design processes through the provision of actionable insights that allow instructional designers and educators to refine course structure, assessment methods, and learning materials. This alignment between design and actual learner engagement is supported by Corrin et al. (2022), Lockyer et al. (2013), and Dennehy et al. (2023), whose findings show that data-informed design leads to improved pedagogical practices.

LA also contributes to the enhancement of student engagement and self-regulated learning. Self-regulation is one the key dispositions that allow learners to be competent in using educational technology to foster learning. Platforms that integrate real-time feedback, dashboards, and reflective tools help learners better monitor their own progress and develop metacognitive skills (Silvola et al., 2021; Matcha et al., 2019). LA also facilitates better feedback mechanisms, especially those built from multimodal analytics to foster deeper reflection and learner autonomy (Yan et al., 2024). A further benefit of LA is the development of collaborative learning and community-based support structures, especially in virtual or hybrid learning environments (Ouyang & Zhang, 2024). This is closely tied to the use of social network analysis and multimodal data to assess participation and collaboration dynamics. On an operational level, when implemented systematically, LA enables course evaluation and institutional accountability, ensuring that learning outcomes align with quality assurance standards and strategic objectives (Wise & Vytasek, 2017; Barthakur et al., 2022). Moreover, LA could improve student retention particularly in high-risk disciplines. LA could highlight retention risk factors in fields such as STEM and other high-risk disciplines in order to support targeted retention strategies (Li et al., 2022), thus reinforcing its value in driving institutional performance and learner equity. This could aid close the gap and educational access between developed and least developed countries.

Educator Readiness: Dimensions and determinants in implementing Learning Analytics

The adoption and effective implementation of LA in higher education is a complex process that extends beyond technological infrastructure to include institutional culture, policy, and importantly; educator readiness. As Alzahrani et al. (2023) argue that, institutions must proactively assess and address the multifaceted challenges associated with LA implementation to ensure sustainable and successful integration. These challenges include structural barriers, ethical concerns, and resistance to change, all of which intersect with the capabilities, perceptions, and preparedness of educators. Educator readiness is now widely acknowledged as a decisive factor in the successful implementation of LA. For instance, Márquez et al. (2024), in a systematic review of LA adoption in higher education, emphasize that without adequate faculty involvement and preparedness, LA efforts often remain underutilized or misaligned with pedagogical goals. This readiness is not only a technical concern but a pedagogical and cultural one, influenced by educators' ability to meaningfully interpret data and apply insights to support student learning.

Interestingly, educator readiness is also shaped by students' acceptance and perceptions of LA tools. Hussan, Er, and Nadarajah (2024) note that when students themselves demonstrate readiness and openness to data-informed educational environments, educators may feel more confident and motivated to integrate LA into their teaching. This highlight the key motivational role that students play in relation to successful LA implementation. However, Gabelaia (2024) points out that findings on educator readiness are mixed, suggesting the need for more comprehensive and inclusive frameworks that account for contextual differences, such as institutional support, disciplinary norms, and faculty digital literacy. It should be understood that readiness is not simply a static condition but an ongoing developmental process that requires assessment, reflection, and capacity building. Liu et al. (2025) show that when educators are better prepared to integrate tools such as LA dashboards into their pedagogical practices, student engagement, collaboration and performance improve significantly. Similarly, Ahmad et al. (2023) argue that evaluating educational technology adoption and e-learning preparedness is essential for ensuring fair and equitable implementation of LA in diverse learning environments, thereby preventing data misuse or the reinforcement of existing educational inequalities.

Dimensions of Educator Readiness

To further conceptualize educator readiness, Table 2 outlines five core dimensions, each of which reflects an actionable domain for institutional intervention and professional development. These dimensions include pedagogical and assessment alignment, data literacy, ethics and governance, tool proficiency, and organizational readiness. Furthermore, these dimensions highlight both the individual and systemic factors involved in building LA competency. Table 2 presents a summary of the significant dimensions of educator readiness that are crucial when implementing LA in higher education.

Table 2. Key dimensions of educator readiness for implementing LA

Dimension	What "ready" looks like	Author
Pedagogical & assessment alignment	LA is embedded in the plan–teach–analyse–act cycle; indicators map to learning outcomes; educators "close the loop" by acting on insights and evaluating impact.	Papamitsiou & Economides (2021); van Leeuwen and Rummel (2019)
Data literacy & analytical competence	Teachers can pose pedagogical questions to data, interpret limits/ uncertainty, translate patterns into action, and evaluate results beyond basic stats.	Mandinach & Gummer (HLA Chapter, 2016); Cheng, Yang and Zhu (2026)
Ethics, privacy & governance literacy	Informed consent, transparency, data minimization, role-based access, and lifecycle ethics are understood and communicated to students; practices align with institutional frameworks.	Prinsloo (2022); Nichols (2024)
Tool proficiency & technical practicality (TPACK-aligned)	Teachers can operate dashboards/ alerts, integrate them into feedback routines, and select feasible, instructionally useful tools; data literacy is integrated with TPACK/AI-TPACK.	Cui et al. (2022); Ning et al. (2024); van Leeuwen and Rummel (2019); van Leeuwen, Knoop-van Campen, Molenaar & Rummel (2021).
Organizational & change-readiness	Success depends on strategy, culture, policies, PD time, and processes; readiness instruments and reviews highlight leadership alignment and workload support.	Márquez et al. (2024); Oster et al. (2016)

Educators who are "ready" for LA implementation integrate analytics into the instructional design cycle planning, teaching, analyzing, and acting on evidence. As Papamitsiou and Economides (2021) and van Leeuwen and Rummel (2019) suggest, such integration ensures that LA indicators are mapped to learning outcomes, allowing for purposeful pedagogical adjustments. Data literacy is equally critical; Mandinach and Gummer (2016) and Cheng, Yang and Zhu (2026) stress the need for educators to go beyond surface-level statistics and engage in deep analysis of patterns, uncertainties, and pedagogical implications. Ethical competence, as framed by Prinsloo (2022) and Nichols (2024), involves understanding privacy, consent, and governance issues, ensuring that analytics practices respect students' rights and institutional policies. Tool proficiency involves not just knowing how to operate dashboards but integrating them into feedback routines in line with the TPACK framework (Cui et al., 2022; Ning et al., 2024). Finally, organisational readiness encompasses leadership support, strategic alignment, and adequate time for professional development, all of which are foundational for sustaining LA adoption (Oster et al., 2016; Márquez et al., 2024).

Tools and platforms enabling Learning Analytics

In response to the growing global interest in LA among higher education institutions (HEIs), a diverse range of tools and platforms have emerged to support data-informed decision-making in higher education. These tools are designed not only to collect and process educational data but also to offer actionable insights that can enhance the teaching and learning experience across different contexts. A substantial number of these LA tools have been evaluated based on their usability and user experience, with increasing attention being paid to their actual impact on learning experiences and outcomes. With the ever-increasing and intensified competition among HEIs, many universities and colleges have adopted LA technologies as strategic instruments to improve student engagement, retention, and overall academic performance (Nkomo. Daniel, & Butson, 2021).

The capabilities of LA tools are particularly significant in online and blended learning environments, where real-time tracking of learner behaviours can inform timely interventions. For instance, learning analytics tools enable instructors to detect patterns of disengagement, personalize learning content, and provide targeted feedback, thereby fostering a more adaptive and student-centred pedagogical approach. Research highlights that LA tools have the potential to significantly improve learning design by enabling more precise alignment between instructional strategies and learners' needs (Drugova et al., 2024). Furthermore, these platforms support the broader online learning ecosystem through multi-dimensional tracking and analysis, which enhances institutional capacity for evidence-based decision-making (Li, Duffy, & Zhang, 2022). As such, LA tools not only streamline instructional workflows but also contribute to building more effective, inclusive, and responsive higher education systems.

Learning Analytics Tools within Brightspace LMS

Brightspace, developed by Desire2Learn (D2L), provides a suite of built-in LA tools that offer instructors and educators timely insights into student engagement, module content access, student performance, and participation. These analytics features enable educators to tailor instruction and promote adaptive learning pathways by responding to learners' needs in real time. In this section, we reflect on LA tools used within the author's own module on Business Administration, offered at a higher education institution and supported by Brightspace's institutional platform.

Class Progress Tool

The Class Progress dashboard (Figure 2) provides an overview of key performance indicators for each learner, including login frequency, grades, content access, assignment submissions, and quiz performance. Educators can identify students with declining engagement patterns, such as those who have not accessed content or missed deadlines, enabling early intervention strategies by the module instructors. In the present module, this tool has proven essential in flagging at-risk students and sending automated reminders through Brightspace's Intelligent Agents feature.

Figure 2. Sample view of Brightspace Class Progress dashboard

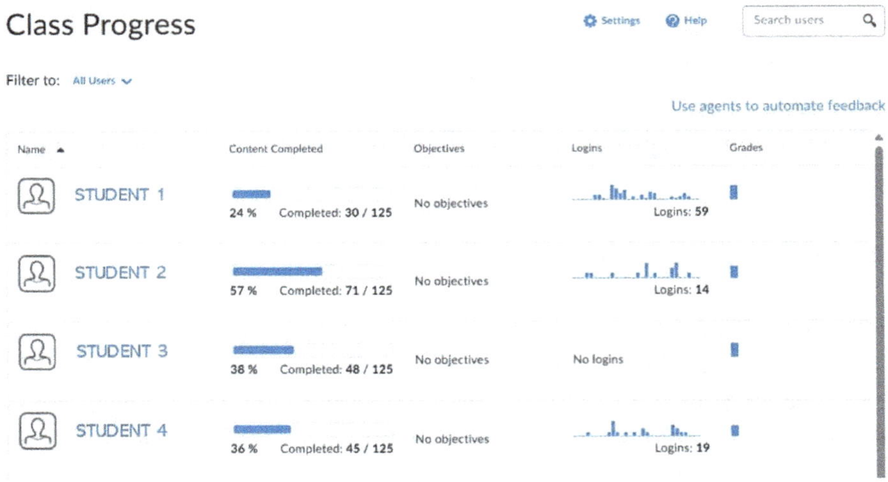

Content Statistics

Another valuable feature is the Content Reports (Figure 3), which allow instructors to view how often students access individual content items, how much time they spend engaging with materials, and which topics are under-utilized. Instructors can utilize this feature to view the topics that are seldomly accessed or view topics with low performance.

Figure 3. Content statistics report showing student views, time spent, and access trends across various learning modules

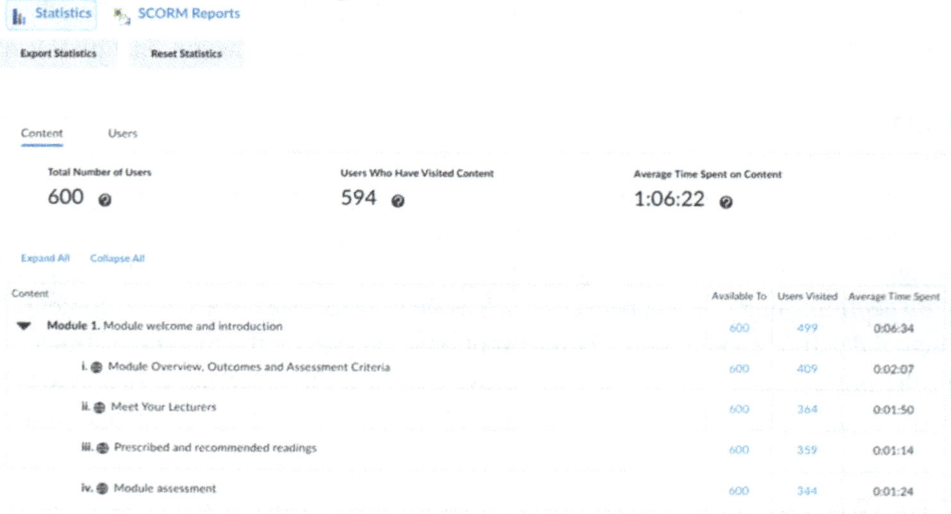

In the module under review, this report was used to identify a particular topic that had low access rates, leading to a redesign that incorporated multimedia summaries and in-class discussion prompts. Also, this allows for timely intervention strategies which can enhance students' attainment of achievement outcome of select students.

Quiz and Assignment Analytics

Brightspace's quiz and assignment tools integrate advanced analytics capabilities that provide insights into submission patterns, average scores, question-level performance, and student-level outcome distributions (Figure 4). These analytics facilitate data-informed formative assessment practices by enabling instructors to identify problematic items, adjust question difficulty levels, and detect key concepts that may require further clarification or reteaching. For example, quiz analytics allow educators to evaluate students' comprehension of specific learning units and assess their grasp of core concepts covered during instruction.

Furthermore, the quiz functionality can be configured as a graded assessment component that contributes to the overall course grade, while simultaneously offering learners immediate feedback on their performance. This immediate feedback loop enhances metacognitive awareness and supports self-regulated learning.

Figure 4. Quiz statistics showing grade distribution and question-level performance analysis

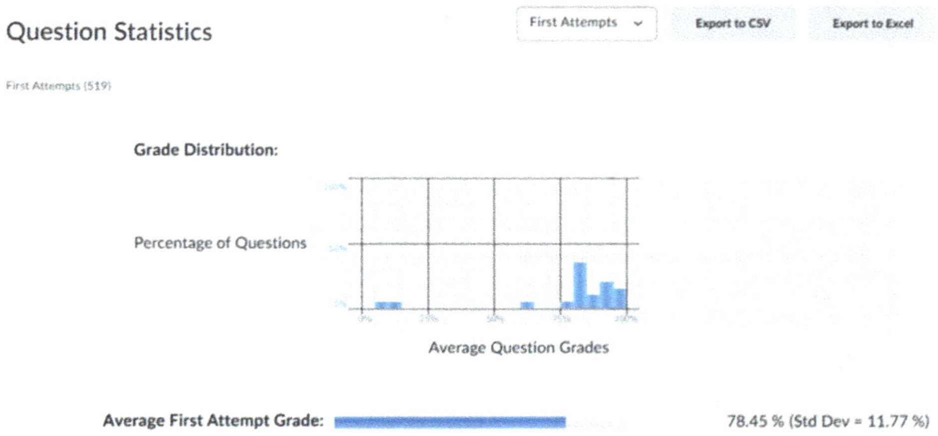

Historically, educators faced challenges when conducting formative assessments using traditional paper-based methods prior to the implementation of LA through educational technology. These challenges included the labor-intensive nature of manual grading, increased risk of data entry errors, possible misplacement of student scripts, and delayed feedback cycles. In contrast, the integration of quiz and assignment analytics within Brightspace streamlines assessment administration, ensures the secure storage of submissions, and enables the provision of timely, accurate feedback, thereby enhancing assessment efficiency and instructional responsiveness.

Discussion Statistics and Engagement Insights

Participation in discussion forums is another metric of learner engagement. Using discussion statistics (Figure 5), instructors can monitor contributions, reply depth, and reading behaviour to assess interaction quality and quantity. This helps promote a socially interactive learning environment, particularly critical in blended or online learning contexts. In the current module, low participation in a particular forum led to the integration of collaborative group activities to stimulate dialogue.

Figure 5. Screenshot of discussion statistics panel indicating number of posts, replies, and views per student

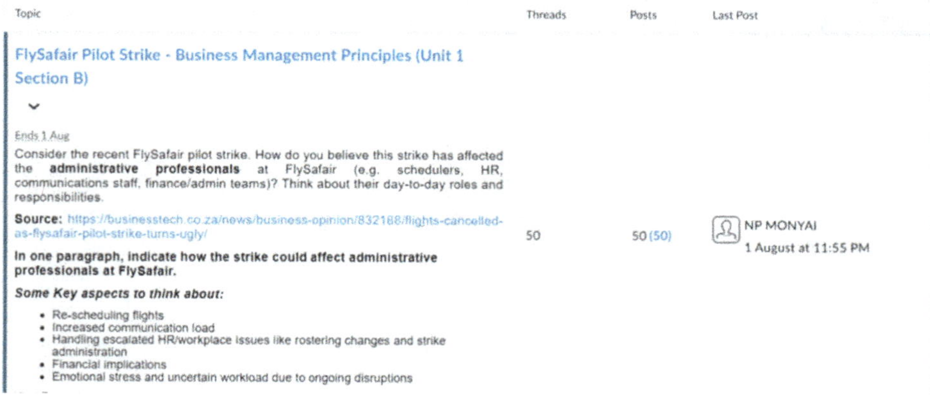

The discussion dashboard also facilitates peer-to-peer teaching between students, allowing students to collaborate and exchange ideas on a given topic. As such, it is crucial for educators to understand how the discussion LA dashboard operate and to extract data meaningful data that can foster sustainable learning using LMSs.

Engagement Dashboard and Adaptive Triggers

The Learner Engagement Dashboard (Figure 6) synthesizes various behavioural data points including time-on-platform, number of logins, content views, and assignment completion to generate composite engagement profiles. These dashboards can be configured to flag students who are potentially at risk and enable instructors to trigger remedial or adaptive content delivery. In the module implementation, students with low engagement scores received alternative study plans or check-in messages using automated workflows.

Figure 6. Engagement dashboard illustrating learner access patterns, average time in course, and engagement score indicators

The integration of LA tools within Brightspace equips educators with the means to systematically monitor student progress, identify challenges early, and deliver timely, adaptive interventions. The case examples depicted above highlight the dual role of LA in both reactive (identifying struggling students) and proactive (designing adaptive pathways) teaching strategies. However, educators must also possess the requisite data literacy and ethical awareness to interpret LA outputs responsibly and equitably. Furthermore, aligning LA use with course learning outcomes and assessment strategies ensures that analytics enhance, rather than dictate, pedagogical decisions.

Challenges to Educator Engagement with Learning Analytics

Despite the growing potential of LA to support adaptive learning and improve educational outcomes, several barriers continue to inhibit meaningful educator engagement with these tools in higher educational context. These challenges are technical, ethical, institutional, and pedagogical in nature, and they often intersect in complex ways that compromise successful implementation. One significant limitation lies in the depth of analytics tools themselves. Susnjak, Ramaswami, and Mathrani (2022) observe that most LA dashboards deployed in higher education institutions primarily rely on surface-level descriptive analytics such as click counts, time spent, and submission logs rather than more sophisticated predictive or prescriptive analytics that could inform deeper instructional decisions. This limitation diminishes the perceived value of LA for educators, particularly when dashboards do not translate data into actionable pedagogical insights. Moreover, ethical and cultural concerns play a critical role in shaping educator resistance. Alzahrani et al. (2023) found that from the perspective of institutional leaders, issues related to informed consent, data privacy, and resistance to surveillance cultures were among the most pronounced barriers to LA adoption, particularly in institutions still in the early phases of adoption. These concerns are exacerbated in contexts where educators feel unequipped to navigate the ethical complexities of data use in learning environments or lack institutional clarity on governance frameworks (Márquez et al., 2024).

A further obstacle is the absence of robust, practice-oriented implementation frameworks. Kaliisa, Kluge, and Mørch (2022) highlight that while numerous LA models exist, few offer clear, operational guidance that educators can apply in day-to-day teaching. Furthermore, the gap between high-level policy and classroom reality leaves educators without structured support for integrating analytics into their existing pedagogical practices (Arockia et al., 2025). Another emergent challenge is the creation of emotionally adaptive learning environments. Joseph-Richard, Uhomoibhi, and Jaffrey (2021) argue that while predictive LA can model behavioural data, it often struggles to incorporate affective responses and emotional variability in learners. This limits the capacity of LA systems to respond sensitively to student disengagement, stress, or motivational issues, areas where teacher intuition currently plays a crucial role.

Emerging technologies such as AI and chatbots, while promising numerous benefits, also pose challenges. Ouyang et al. (2023) and Chang et al. (2023) caution that AI-based learning environments often place additional cognitive and design demands on educators, requiring them to integrate predictive systems, feedback mechanisms, and personalized pathways within complex digital infrastructures. Without adequate training, these demands can overwhelm educators or result in shallow adoption. From a pedagogical lens, Wang et al. (2023) and Ahmad et al. (2022) emphasize that AI and analytics tools often lack alignment with the values, workflows, and assessment practices of educators, leading to disconnection and underutilization. Additionally, some faculty may perceive LA tools as top-down mechanisms for accountability rather than as supports for teaching, thereby promoting further resistance among students and educators. As a result, Longo and Gibson (2023) argue that educator engagement cannot be mandated; it must be enabled through meaningful participation, collaborative development, and context-specific support mechanisms.

A Framework for Enhancing Educator Readiness

The integration of LA into higher education contexts presents both immense opportunities and pressing challenges, particularly regarding educator readiness. While LA tools can provide powerful insights into student learning, their effective implementation largely hinges on educators' ability to interpret, integrate, and act upon analytic outputs. This framework was developed to conceptualize the multi-layered components that influence educator readiness for LA adoption, based on an extensive synthesis of literature (e.g., Drugova et al., 2024; Alzahrani et al., 2023; Ifenthaler & Widanapathirana, 2014). The framework identifies key readiness domains, barriers to be addressed, enabling interventions, and long-term impact pathways. It provides a strategic guide for institutions, policymakers, and instructional designers to build LA capacity among academic staff, ensuring sustainable and ethical implementation of analytics-enhanced teaching. In this section, we present the framework for enhancing educator readiness when implementing LA in higher education (see Figure 7).

Figure 7. Framework for enhancing educator readiness in implementing LA

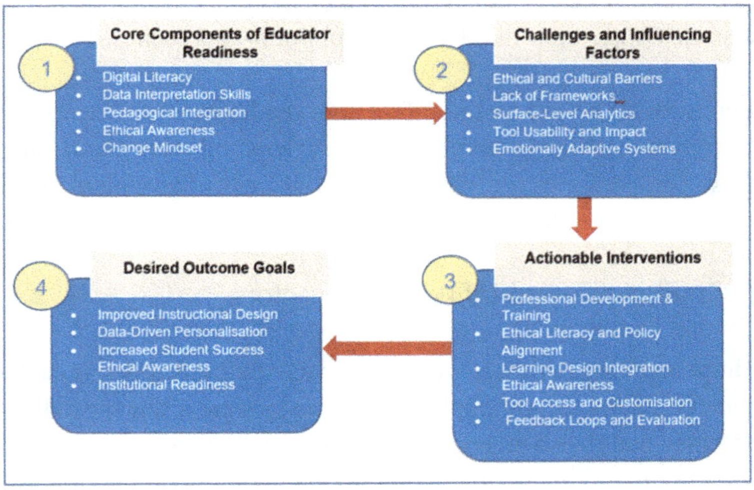

Layer 1: Core Readiness Components

At the heart of the framework are five interdependent educator capacities (i.e. core competencies):

- **Digital literacy**: There is a pressing need for educators to possess foundational understanding of technology tools and platforms, which are essential for navigating LA dashboards and systems. Educators are expected to pass on these digital literacy skills to their students.
- **Data interpretation skills**: Educators should possess the ability to make sense of data visualizations, predictive indicators, and metrics in LA dashboards (Johar et al., 2023).
- **Pedagogical integration**: This refers to applying LA insights to design adaptive learning pathways, assessments, and feedback loops (Corrin et al., 2022; Lockyer et al., 2013). When implementing LA, educators are expected to integrate their expertise related to their subject matter into digital technologies such as LMSs.
- **Ethical awareness**: Understanding data privacy, consent, and ethical use of student data is of great importance (Alzahrani et al., 2023; Tsai et al., 2020). Given the large amounts of data collected using e-learning digital technologies.
- **Change mindset**: This refers to the willingness to adopt new tools and teaching paradigms, crucial for transformative innovation (Wise & Vytasek, 2017). The use of educational technology and implementation of LA requires educators to alter their mindset and adopt new approaches.

In the context of this study, these five core readiness components serve as the foundation for successful engagement with LA tools and strategies. Educators who possess these competencies are more likely to successfully integrate LA into their teaching and learning endeavors.

Layer 2: Challenges and Influencing Factors

When implementing LA, there are several contextual and systemic challenges that hinder educator readiness. Although these challenges are often viewed as 'educator challenges', they could also emerge as institutional challenges:

- **Ethical and cultural barriers**: LA implementations also raises challenges. There are concerns over surveillance, student consent, and resistance from educators unfamiliar with data-driven systems (Alzahrani et al., 2023).
- **Lack of implementation frameworks**: Institutions often adopt tools without clear implementation plans or professional development structures (Kaliisa & Dolonen, 2022). The lack clear frameworks to guide the implementation of LA implementation is a huge challenge facing HEIs.

- **Surface-level use of analytics:** Most LA dashboards are limited to descriptive analytics, missing the opportunity for predictive and prescriptive insights (Susnjak et al., 2022). There is a need for educator training on the use of LA to attain deep insights on student learning patterns.
- **Tool usability issues**: LA tools may be difficult to interpret, especially for educators lacking prior exposure (Silvola et al., 2021).
- **Emotional adaptivity limitations**: Current LA systems struggle to adapt to student emotions and affective needs, limiting their pedagogical value (Joseph-Richard et al., 2021).

Layer 3: Actionable Interventions

To mitigate these challenges and enhance readiness, the framework, through the third layer, proposes the following interventions:

- **Professional development**: In order to successfully implement LA, there is a need to facilitate ongoing, context-specific training on LA tools and their pedagogical use. This helps educators understand how to properly use the LA dashboard and other functionalities.
- **Ethical literacy and policy alignment**: HEIs should ensure that there are regular workshops and readily available institutional guidelines to help educators understand the ethical use of student data.
- **Learning design integration:** Embedding LA into course design, assessment planning, and instructional decision-making ensures that institutions take full benefit of LA functionalities (Corrin et al., 2022; Dawson et al., 2019).
- **Tool access and customization:** Ensuring educators have access to tools that are usable, relevant, and allow for adaptation.
- **Feedback loops and evaluation:** Incorporating iterative feedback from staff and students to refine LA practices (Matcha et al., 2019).

Layer 4: Desired Outcome Goals

When readiness is cultivated through the above components and interventions, institutions can expect:

- **Improved instructional design:** An improved instructional design through LA adoption ensures a better alignment of teaching/learning activities and assessments with learning outcomes.

- **Data-driven personalization**: The extraction of LA data ensures that there is tailored support and resources for diverse learner needs (Maseleno et al., 2018). This aids HEIs to bridge the gap in relation to educational access ensuring that disadvantaged communities are not left behind.
- **Increased student success**: More accurate identification of at-risk learners and timely interventions, ensuring student success and performance (Daud et al., 2017).
- **Institutional readiness**: The implementation of LA requires institutions of higher learning to demonstrate a culture of innovation, agility, and ethical use of educational data (Tsai et al., 2020).

RECOMMENDATIONS FOR PRACTICE AND POLICY

For the sustainable implementation of LA in higher education, the mobilization of educator readiness must be supported by deliberate policy development and well-designed institutional practices. Policymakers and institutional leaders should recognize LA not merely as a technological innovation but as a broader pedagogical and organisational transformation that requires investment in educator capacity, ethical governance, and equitable access to quality education. However, it is equally important to acknowledge that educator readiness alone cannot fully address the structural constraints and power dynamics that often accompany the deployment of analytics within educational environments. The increasing datafication of higher education may introduce new forms of accountability pressures, performance monitoring, and institutional control that shape how educators and students interact with analytics systems. Consequently, policies guiding LA adoption should not only focus on building technical competencies but also ensure transparency, accountability, and participatory governance in the use of educational data. By recognizing these broader socio-institutional dynamics, higher education institutions can develop more balanced and responsible approaches to learning analytics implementation that support both pedagogical innovation and ethical stewardship of data.

- ***Establishing dedicated learning analytics support centers or communities of practice:*** Institutions should establish structured professional development policies that provide ongoing, scaffolded training in the technical, analytical, and pedagogical dimensions of LA use. This training should be embedded into institutional capacity-building initiatives rather than being offered as once-off workshops, ensuring that readiness evolves alongside technological advancements.

- ***Integrating ethical considerations into LA policy documents, ensuring compliance with national and institutional guidelines:*** The creation of dedicated institutional learning analytics support units or "centres of excellence" staffed by learning designers, data analysts, and pedagogical experts can provide continuous guidance for educators struggling with tool interpretation, ethical decision-making, or curriculum alignment. Policy frameworks must also foreground ethical considerations by mandating explicit guidelines for data consent, transparency in analytics use, and the communication of analytic outcomes to students, thereby fostering a culture of trust and accountability in data-driven decision-making.
- ***Creating institution-wide dashboards tailored to diverse educator needs:*** Additionally, institutions need to enact policies that encourage the integration of LA insights into learning design processes, assessment practices, and continuous course improvement cycles, thereby ensuring that analytics are not merely observed but are acted upon to inform adaptive learning pathways. To promote educator agency and ownership, institutions should implement participatory decision-making structures that involve academic staff in tool selection, customization, and evaluation. Incentive systems such as workload recognition, performance-based rewards, and promotion criteria should acknowledge the time and expertise required to meaningfully integrate LA into teaching practice.
- ***Incentivizing cross-disciplinary collaboration among data scientists, instructional designers, and teaching staff*:** Incentivising cross-disciplinary collaboration among data scientists, instructional designers, and teaching staff represents an important strategy for strengthening the implementation and sustainability of LA initiatives in higher education. The effective use of LA requires expertise that spans multiple domains, including data analysis, educational research, pedagogical design, and subject-specific teaching practices. Consequently, institutions should encourage collaborative structures where these different forms of expertise intersect to support the meaningful interpretation and application of LA. For example, interdisciplinary teams can work together to translate complex data outputs from LMSs into pedagogically actionable insights that inform course design, assessment strategies, and targeted student support interventions. Such collaboration ensures that analytics are not interpreted solely from a technical perspective but are contextualized within the realities of teaching and learning.

In addition to promoting interdisciplinary partnerships, institutions should establish structured feedback mechanisms that allow educators and students to reflect on LA-driven interventions and their impact on learning processes. These feedback loops may take the form of collaborative review meetings, analytics-informed teaching committees, or reflective workshops where staff and students jointly examine engagement patterns and learning outcomes. Through these processes, educators can continuously refine their teaching strategies, while students gain greater awareness of how their learning behaviours are captured and interpreted through analytics systems. Over time, such participatory approaches contribute to the development of a culture of reflective, data-informed pedagogy that values transparency and shared responsibility. Furthermore, institutions should recognise and reward collaborative engagement with LA through incentives such as teaching innovation grants, recognition in promotion frameworks, or dedicated workload allocations.

- ***Student Data Literacy and Co-Interpretation of Learning Analytics:*** An additional dimension that complements educator readiness is the development of student data literacy and ethical-agency in engaging with learning analytics. While institutional policies often focus on ethical governance and transparency, students should also be supported in understanding how their learning data is generated, interpreted, and used to inform educational decisions. Promoting student data literacy allows learners to actively participate in the co-interpretation of analytics dashboards, enabling them to reflect on engagement patterns and make informed adjustments to their learning strategies. In practice, institutions may operationalize this through learning analytics support centres or workshops where educators and learning designers guide students in interpreting analytics reports and translating insights into personalized learning actions. Such collaborative interpretation strengthens trust, promotes transparency, and reinforces the use of analytics as a shared tool for improving teaching, learning, and student success.

FUTURE RESEARCH DIRECTIONS

As the adoption of LA continues to expand in higher education, there is a pressing need to envision forward-looking strategies that enhance educator readiness and ensure sustainable, equitable, and impactful implementation. The proposed Educator Readiness Framework highlights foundational competencies and institutional enablers, yet several areas require further exploration to refine policies, improve practices, and guide research. Future directions must consider the dynamic intersections of pedagogy, technology, and ethics, particularly in relation to adaptive learning pathways, AI-enhanced tools, and evolving digital competencies. These directions aim not only to address current limitations but also to provide a strategic roadmap for institutions seeking to embed LA meaningfully within teaching and learning. The subsections that follow propose specific avenues for inquiry and action, focusing on emerging themes such as professional development models, ethical co-design, cross-contextual adaptability, and the role of artificial intelligence in augmenting educators' decision-making capacities.

Longitudinal Studies on Educator Readiness and Learning Analytics implementation

To date, most studies have taken a cross-sectional or snapshot view of educator readiness and institutional adoption of learning analytics tools. A future research direction should involve longitudinal studies that track how educator readiness evolves over time across different stages of LA implementation (e.g., exploration, adoption, integration, and sustainability). These studies can explore the trajectories of skills acquisition, changes in pedagogical practices, and the long-term impacts of interventions like professional development or institutional policy shifts. Longitudinal insights would also enable researchers to assess which factors most influence sustained engagement with LA, including leadership support, time allocation, and shifts in institutional culture.

Cross-Institutional and Cross-Cultural Comparative Studies

There is a growing need for comparative research that examines how educator readiness and LA adoption vary across contexts, particularly between well-resourced institutions and those in low-resource or developing regions. Such comparative studies could examine how cultural, infrastructural, and policy differences influence readiness dimensions (e.g., ethics awareness, data literacy, tool proficiency). Research from Global South contexts, for instance, could yield unique insights into localized challenges such as digital equity, institutional readiness, and resistance to change. These studies could help inform more globally relevant and culturally responsive frameworks, models, and readiness instruments for LA.

Development and Validation of Diagnostic Readiness Tools

Building on your framework, future work should focus on designing, piloting, and validating diagnostic instruments that institutions can use to measure educator readiness across the five core dimensions: pedagogical alignment, data literacy, ethics & privacy, tool proficiency, and organisational support. These tools should be adaptable to various educational technologies and institutional types, allowing for benchmarking, needs assessments, and tailored professional development. Additionally, readiness tools should be co-designed with educators to ensure that they are contextually relevant, user-friendly, and pedagogically sound.

Integration of Learning Analytics with AI-Ethics

As LA increasingly incorporate AI-driven technologies (e.g., adaptive pathways, predictive models, sentiment analysis), future research should explore the intersection between LA and AI ethics in teaching and learning. Specifically, how can ethical AI principles such as explainability, transparency, fairness, and accountability, be embedded into the design and use of LA tools? Studies could examine how AI-augmented analytics systems can support adaptive learning, while ensuring student data rights and trust are upheld. Furthermore, researchers could investigate how such ethically grounded systems influence educator engagement and decision-making when delivering personalized feedback or designing learner interventions.

Academic Workload, Emotional Resilience, and Recognition in Learning Analytics Adoption

LA offers considerable potential for enhancing adaptive learning pathways and improving student success, its implementation also introduces important considerations related to academic workload, emotional resilience, and professional recognition. The integration of LA into teaching practices often requires educators to engage with complex data dashboards, interpret student engagement metrics, and redesign instructional strategies based on analytic insights, which can increase workload demands if institutions do not provide adequate support and time allocation (Dawson et al., 2019; Tsai et al., 2020). Furthermore, the expectation that educators continuously monitor student engagement and intervene when learners appear at risk may create emotional pressure, particularly when academics feel accountable for student outcomes but lack the resources to respond timeously. Scholars have argued that the increasing datafication of education can shift responsibility onto educators in ways that may influence their professional autonomy and well-being (Prinsloo, 2019). Consequently, higher education institutions should complement LA initiatives with policies that support educator well-being, including professional development, peer-support networks, and realistic workload adjustments. Equally important is the recognition of analytics-informed teaching practices within institutional reward structures, such as promotion criteria and teaching excellence frameworks, as this may motivate educators to adopt LA more sustainably and meaningfully.

CONCLUSION

In recent years, LA has emerged as a dynamic and transformative area of research and practice in higher education, reflecting the growing imperative for data-informed approaches to enhance student success and institutional decision-making. With the proliferation of digital learning environments, the integration of LA has become increasingly central to how institutions design, deliver, and refine teaching and learning experiences. Amid this evolution, educators are positioned not only as users of LA tools but also as critical agents in ensuring its pedagogical relevance, ethical integrity, and contextual alignment with sustainable teaching practices. Consequently, this study focused on the readiness of educators to adopt and meaningfully engage with LA, particularly in designing adaptive learning pathways that respond to individual learner needs and behaviours.

The research reveals that educator readiness is a multidimensional construct shaped by individual competencies, institutional support mechanisms, and broader ethical and technological ecosystems. Through a rigorous synthesis of recent empirical and theoretical literature, the study presents a framework for enhancing educator readiness, structured around five key layers: (1) Institutional Strategy and Governance, which underscores the importance of alignment with policy, vision, and support structures; (2) Professional Learning and Capacity Building, which advocates for targeted development of data literacy, pedagogical alignment, and tool fluency; (3) Educator Dispositions and Mindsets, highlighting beliefs, motivations, and openness to innovation; (4) Pedagogical Practices, which involve the integration of LA within the learning design cycle; and (5) Technological Infrastructure and Data Systems, ensuring access to usable, secure, and context-aware LA platforms.

Each of these layers is interconnected, reflecting a systems-thinking approach to readiness. The framework is not merely descriptive but offers actionable entry points for stakeholders to foster sustainable LA adoption. It bridges institutional leadership imperatives with grassroots pedagogical innovation, and it emphasizes ethical data practices and learner-centricity as foundational principles for future implementation. The implications of this research are significant for higher education policy and practice. Institutions must go beyond tool deployment and invest in educator empowerment, fostering environments where LA is both technically feasible and pedagogically meaningful. The study also informs future research by identifying gaps related to the longitudinal impact of professional development, the role of educator emotions and values, and the interoperability of LA tools within diverse contexts. As LA continues to shape the contours of digital education, the readiness of educators will remain a decisive factor in realizing its full potential for personalized learning, student engagement, and academic success.

REFERENCES

Ahmad, S. F., Alam, M. M., Rahmat, M. K., Mubarik, M. S., & Hyder, S. I. (2022). Academic and administrative role of artificial intelligence in education. *Sustainability (Basel), 14*(3), 1101. DOI: 10.3390/su14031101

Ahmad, S., Mohd Noor, A. S., Alwan, A. A., Gulzar, Y., Khan, W. Z., & Reegu, F. A. (2023). eLearning acceptance and adoption challenges in higher education. *Sustainability (Basel), 15*(7), 6190. DOI: 10.3390/su15076190

Alazzawi, F. J. I., Shannaq, B., Al Maqbali, S., & Al Rawahi, S. (2025). The role of predictive analytics for adaptive e-learning: A future pathway framework for personalized education. In *Sustainable Data Management: Navigating Big Data, Communication Technology, and Business Digital Leadership* (Vol. 1, pp. 367–376). Springer Nature Switzerland. DOI: 10.1007/978-3-031-83911-5_32

Alzahrani, A. S., Tsai, Y. S., Iqbal, S., Marcos, P. M. M., Scheffel, M., Drachsler, H., Kloos, C. D., Aljohani, N., & Gašević, D. (2023). Untangling connections between challenges in the adoption of learning analytics in higher education. *Education and Information Technologies, 28*(4), 4563–4595. DOI: 10.1007/s10639-022-11323-x PMID: 36281258

Arockia, V. J., Vettriselvan, R., Rajesh, D., Velmurugan, P. R. R., & Cheelo, C. (2025). Leveraging AI and Learning Analytics for Enhanced Distance Learning: Transformation in Education. In *AI and Learning Analytics in Distance Learning* (pp. 179-206). IGI Global Scientific Publishing.

Barthakur, A., Joksimovic, S., Kovanovic, V., Richey, M., & Pardo, A. (2022). Aligning objectives with assessment in online courses: Integrating learning analytics and measurement theory. *Computers & Education, 190*, 104603. DOI: 10.1016/j.compedu.2022.104603

Bucăţa, G., & Tileagă, C. (2024). Digital renaissance in education: Unveiling the transformative potential of digitization in educational institutions. *Land Forces Academy Review, 29*(1), 20–37. DOI: 10.2478/raft-2024-0003

Chang, D. H., Lin, M. P. C., Hajian, S., & Wang, Q. Q. (2023). Educational design principles of using AI chatbot that supports self-regulated learning in education: Goal setting, feedback, and personalization. *Sustainability (Basel), 15*(17), 12921. DOI: 10.3390/su151712921

Cheng, Z., Yang, F., & Zhu, C. (2026). Understanding Teacher Workload in Blended Learning: Insights Through the Job Demands-Resources Model. *Electronic Journal of e-Learning, 24*(1), 125–137. DOI: 10.34190/ejel.24.1.4465

Clow, D. (2012). The learning analytics cycle: Closing the loop effectively. In *Proceedings of the 2nd International Conference on Learning Analytics and Knowledge* (pp. 134–138). DOI: 10.1145/2330601.2330636

Corrin, L., Kennedy, G., & Mulder, R. (2022). Enhancing learning design using learning analytics: A case study. *Australasian Journal of Educational Technology, 38*(3), 77–93.

Darvishi, A., Khosravi, H., Sadiq, S., & Gašević, D. (2022). Incorporating AI and learning analytics to build trustworthy peer assessment systems. *British Journal of Educational Technology, 53*(4), 844–875. DOI: 10.1111/bjet.13233

Daud, A., Aljohani, N. R., Abbasi, R. A., Lytras, M. D., Abbas, F., & Alowibdi, J. S. (2017, April). Predicting student performance using advanced learning analytics. In *Proceedings of the 26th international conference on world wide web companion* (pp. 415-421. DOI: 10.1145/3041021.3054164

Dawson, S., Gašević, D., Siemens, G., & Joksimović, S. (2019). A review of learning analytics research in higher education: Implications for practice and policy. *Educational Technology Research and Development, 67*(5), 1063–1089. DOI: 10.1007/s11423-018-09684-3

Dennehy, D., Conboy, K., & Babu, J. (2023). Adopting learning analytics to inform postgraduate curriculum design: Recommendations and research agenda. *Information Systems Frontiers, 25*(4), 1315–1331. DOI: 10.1007/s10796-021-10183-z PMID: 37546703

Donevska-Todorova, A., Dziergwa, K., & Simbeck, K. (2022). Individualizing learning pathways with adaptive learning strategies: Design, implementation and scale. In *CSEDU (2)* (pp. 575–585).

Du, X., Yang, J., Shelton, B. E., Hung, J. L., & Zhang, M. (2021). A systematic meta-review and analysis of learning analytics research. *Behaviour & Information Technology, 40*(1), 49–62. DOI: 10.1080/0144929X.2019.1669712

Dwivedi, D. N., Mahanty, G., & Dwivedi, V. N. (2024). The role of predictive analytics in personalizing education: Tailoring learning paths for individual student success. In *Enhancing Education With Intelligent Systems and Data-Driven Instruction* (pp. 44–59). IGI Global Scientific Publishing. DOI: 10.4018/979-8-3693-2169-0.ch003

Gabelaia, I. (2024). *Examining Pedagogical Analytical and Digital Literacy in Higher Education: Predicting Faculty's Readiness for and Adoption of Learning Analytics* (Doctoral dissertation, Drake University).

Gašević, D., Mirriahi, N., & Dawson, S. (2015). Analytics of the effects of video use and instruction to support reflective learning. *Proceedings of the Fifth International Conference on Learning Analytics And Knowledge*, 123–132.

Hasan, R., Palaniappan, S., Mahmood, S., Abbas, A., Sarker, K. U., & Sattar, M. U. (2020). Predicting student performance in higher educational institutions using video learning analytics and data mining techniques. *Applied Sciences (Basel, Switzerland)*, *10*(11), 3894. DOI: 10.3390/app10113894

Hussan, F., Er, H. M., & Nadarajah, V. D. (2024). Health professions students' acceptance and readiness for learning analytics: Lessons for educators. *BMC Medical Education*, *24*(1), 1347. DOI: 10.1186/s12909-024-06284-3 PMID: 39574101

Ifenthaler, D., & Widanapathirana, C. (2014). Development and validation of a learning analytics framework: Two case studies using support vector machines. *Technology. Knowledge and Learning*, *19*(1-2), 221–240. DOI: 10.1007/s10758-014-9226-4

Ifenthaler, D., & Yau, J. Y.-K. (2020). Utilising learning analytics to support study success in higher education: A systematic review. *Educational Technology Research and Development*, *68*(4), 1961–1990. DOI: 10.1007/s11423-020-09788-z

Jääskelä, P., Heilala, V., Kärkkäinen, T., & Häkkinen, P. (2021). Student agency analytics: Learning analytics as a tool for analysing student agency in higher education. *Behaviour & Information Technology*, *40*(8), 790–808. DOI: 10.1080/0144929X.2020.1725130

Javed, Y., & Alenezi, M. (2023). A case study on sustainable quality assurance in higher education. *Sustainability (Basel)*, *15*(10), 8136. DOI: 10.3390/su15108136

Johar, N. A., Kew, S. N., Tasir, Z., & Koh, E. (2023). Learning analytics on student engagement to enhance students' learning performance: A systematic review. *Sustainability (Basel)*, *15*(10), 7849. DOI: 10.3390/su15107849

Joseph-Richard, P., Uhomoibhi, J., & Jaffrey, A. (2021). Predictive learning analytics and the creation of emotionally adaptive learning environments in higher education institutions: A study of students' affect responses. *The International Journal of Information and Learning Technology*, *38*(2), 243–257. DOI: 10.1108/IJILT-05-2020-0077

Kaliisa, R., & Dolonen, J. A. (2022). CADA: A teacher-facing learning analytics dashboard to foster teachers' awareness of students' participation and discourse patterns in online discussions. *International Journal of Educational Technology in Higher Education*, *19*, 25. Advance online publication. DOI: 10.1186/s41239-022-00338-6

Kaliisa, R., Kluge, A., & Mørch, A. I. (2022). Overcoming challenges to the adoption of learning analytics at the practitioner level: A critical analysis of 18 learning analytics frameworks. *Scandinavian Journal of Educational Research, 66*(3), 367–381. DOI: 10.1080/00313831.2020.1869082

Kew, S. N., & Tasir, Z. (2022). Learning analytics in online learning environment: A systematic review on the focuses and the types of student-related analytics data. *Technology. Knowledge and Learning, 27*(2), 405–427. DOI: 10.1007/s10758-021-09541-2

Kurilovas, E. (2019). Advanced machine learning approaches to personalise learning: Learning analytics and decision making. *Behaviour & Information Technology, 38*(4), 410–421. DOI: 10.1080/0144929X.2018.1539517

Leitner, P., Khalil, M., & Ebner, M. (2017). Learning analytics in higher education—A literature review. *Learning Analytics: Fundaments, Applications, and Trends*, 1–23.

Li, C., Herbert, N., Yeom, S., & Montgomery, J. (2022). Retention factors in STEM education identified using learning analytics: A systematic review. *Education Sciences, 12*(11), 781. DOI: 10.3390/educsci12110781

Liu, Y., Hu, X., Ng, J. T. D., Ma, Z., & Lai, X. (2025). Ready or not? Investigating in-service teachers' integration of learning analytics dashboard for assessing students' collaborative problem solving in K–12 classrooms. *Education and Information Technologies, 30*(2), 1745–1776. DOI: 10.1007/s10639-024-12842-5

Lockyer, L., Heathcote, E., & Dawson, S. (2013). Informing pedagogical action: Aligning learning analytics with learning design. *The American Behavioral Scientist, 29*(1), 1–13. DOI: 10.1177/0002764213479367

Longo, N. V., & Gibson, C. M. (2023). Collaborative engagement: The future of teaching and learning in higher education. In *Publicly Engaged Scholars* (pp. 61–75). Routledge. DOI: 10.4324/9781003446583-5

Mandinach, E. B., & Gummer, E. S. (2016). *Data literacy for educators: Making it count in teacher preparation and practice*. Teachers College Press.

Mane, M. S. B. (2025). Teachers' Readiness and the Integration of Technology in Teaching. [IJMCER]. *Educational Research, 7*(3), 260–290.

Márquez, L., Henríquez, V., Chevreux, H., Scheihing, E., & Guerra, J. (2024). Adoption of learning analytics in higher education institutions: A systematic literature review. *British Journal of Educational Technology, 55*(2), 439–459. DOI: 10.1111/bjet.13385

Martens, M., De Wolf, R., & De Marez, L. (2024). Datafication and algorithmization of education: How do parents and students evaluate the appropriateness of learning analytics? *Education and Information Technologies*, *29*(7), 8151–8177. DOI: 10.1007/s10639-023-12124-6

Maseleno, A., Sabani, N., Huda, M., Ahmad, R., Jasmi, K. A., & Basiron, B. (2018). Demystifying learning analytics in personalised learning. *IACSIT International Journal of Engineering and Technology*, *7*(3), 1124–1129. DOI: 10.14419/ijet.v7i3.9789

Matcha, W., Gašević, D., Uzir, N. A., & Pardo, A. (2019). A study of self-regulated learning in the context of a flipped classroom. *Proceedings of the 9th International Conference on Learning Analytics & Knowledge*, 378–387.

Namoun, A., & Alshanqiti, A. (2020). Predicting student performance using data mining and learning analytics techniques: A systematic literature review. *Applied Sciences (Basel, Switzerland)*, *11*(1), 237. DOI: 10.3390/app11010237

Nguyen, A., Tuunanen, T., Gardner, L., & Sheridan, D. (2021). Design principles for learning analytics information systems in higher education. *European Journal of Information Systems*, *30*(5), 541–568. DOI: 10.1080/0960085X.2020.1816144

Nichols, M. (2024). Development of an approved learning analytics ethics position. *Open Learning*, *39*(3), 245–260. DOI: 10.1080/02680513.2021.1986376

Ning, J., Ma, Z., Yao, J., Wang, Q., & Zhang, B. (2025). Personalized learning supported by learning analytics: A systematic review of functions, pathways, and educational outcomes. *Interactive Learning Environments*, *33*(8), 1–23. DOI: 10.1080/10494820.2025.2478437

Nkomo, L. M., Daniel, B. K., & Butson, R. J. (2021). Synthesis of student engagement with digital technologies: A systematic review of the literature. *International Journal of Educational Technology in Higher Education*, *18*(1), 34. PMID: 34778529

Okoye, K., Nganji, J. T., & Hosseini, S. (2020). Learning analytics for educational innovation: A systematic mapping study of early indicators and success factors. *International Journal of Computer Information Systems and Industrial Management Applications*, *12*, 17–17.

Oster, M., Lonn, S., Pistilli, M., & Brown, M. (2016). The Learning Analytics Readiness Instrument. In *Proceedings of the Sixth International Conference on Learning Analytics & Knowledge (LAK '16)* (pp. 1–5). ACM. DOI: 10.1145/2883851.2883925

Ouyang, F., & Zhang, L. (2024). AI-driven learning analytics applications and tools in computer-supported collaborative learning: A systematic review. *Educational Research Review*, *44*, 100616. DOI: 10.1016/j.edurev.2024.100616

Ouyang, F., Wu, M., Zheng, L., Zhang, L., & Jiao, P. (2023). Integration of artificial intelligence performance prediction and learning analytics to improve student learning in online engineering course. *International Journal of Educational Technology in Higher Education, 20*(1), 4. DOI: 10.1186/s41239-022-00372-4 PMID: 36683653

Papamitsiou, Z., & Economides, A. A. (2014). Learning analytics and educational data mining in practice: A systematic literature review of empirical evidence. *Journal of Educational Technology & Society, 17*(4), 49–64.

Perrotta, C., & Williamson, B. (2018). The social life of learning analytics: Cluster analysis and the "performance" of algorithmic education. *Learning, Media and Technology, 43*(1), 3–16. DOI: 10.1080/17439884.2016.1182927

Poquet, O. (2024). A shared lens around sensemaking in learning analytics: What activity theory, definition of a situation and affordances can offer. *British Journal of Educational Technology, 55*(4), 1811–1831. DOI: 10.1111/bjet.13435

Prinsloo, P. (2019). A social cartography of analytics in education as performative politics. *British Journal of Educational Technology, 50*(6), 2810–2821. DOI: 10.1111/bjet.12872

Prinsloo, P. (2022). Considering student data privacy in learning analytics: A critical data studies perspective. *British Journal of Educational Technology, 53*(6), 1520–1534. DOI: 10.1111/bjet.13216

Qazi, A. G., & Pachler, N. (2025). Conceptualising a data analytics framework to support targeted teacher professional development. *Professional Development in Education, 51*(3), 495–518. DOI: 10.1080/19415257.2024.2422066

Raj, N. S., & Renumol, V. G. (2024). An improved adaptive learning path recommendation model driven by real-time learning analytics. *Journal of Computers in Education, 11*(1), 121–148. DOI: 10.1007/s40692-022-00250-y

Ray, S., & Saeed, M. (2018). Applications of educational data mining and learning analytics tools in handling big data in higher education. In Saeed, S., & Maddox, N. (Eds.), *Applications of big data analytics: Trends, issues, and challenges* (pp. 135–160). Springer International Publishing., DOI: 10.1007/978-3-319-76472-6_7

Schumacher, C., & Ifenthaler, D. (2018). Features students really expect from learning analytics. *Computers in Human Behavior, 78*, 397–407. DOI: 10.1016/j.chb.2017.06.030

Silvola, A., Näykki, P., Kaveri, A., & Muukkonen, H. (2021). Expectations for supporting student engagement with learning analytics: An academic path perspective. *Computers & Education, 168*, 104192. DOI: 10.1016/j.compedu.2021.104192

Susnjak, T., Ramaswami, G. S., & Mathrani, A. (2022). Learning analytics dashboard: A tool for providing actionable insights to learners. *International Journal of Educational Technology in Higher Education*, *19*(1), 12. DOI: 10.1186/s41239-021-00313-7 PMID: 35194560

Tariq, M. U. (2024). Navigating the personalization pathway: Implementing adaptive learning technologies in higher education. In *Adaptive Learning Technologies for Higher Education* (pp. 265–291). IGI Global. DOI: 10.4018/979-8-3693-3641-0.ch012

Tempelaar, D. T., Rienties, B., & Giesbers, B. (2015). In search for the most informative data for feedback generation: Learning analytics in a data-rich context. *Computers in Human Behavior*, *47*, 157–167. DOI: 10.1016/j.chb.2014.05.038

Tran, T. P., Jan, T., & Kew, S. N. (2022, September). Learning analytics for improved course delivery: applications and techniques. In *Proceedings of the 6th International Conference on Digital Technology in Education* (pp. 100-106). DOI: 10.1145/3568739.3568758

Tsai, Y. S., Poquet, O., Gašević, D., Dawson, S., & Pardo, A. (2020). Complexity leadership in learning analytics: Drivers, challenges, and opportunities. *British Journal of Educational Technology*, *51*(6), 1294–1313. DOI: 10.1111/bjet.12846

Valle, N., Antonenko, P., Dawson, K., & Huggins-Manley, A. C. (2021). Staying on target: A systematic literature review on learner-facing learning analytics dashboards. *British Journal of Educational Technology*, *52*(4), 1724–1748. DOI: 10.1111/bjet.13089

van Leeuwen, A., Rummel, N., & van Gog, T. (2019). What information should CSCL teacher dashboards provide to help teachers interpret CSCL situations? *International Journal of Computer-Supported Collaborative Learning*, *14*(3), 261–289. DOI: 10.1007/s11412-019-09299-x

van Leeuwen, A., Knoop-van Campen, C. A. N., Molenaar, I., & Rummel, N. (2021). How teacher characteristics relate to how teachers use dashboards: Results from two case studies in K–12. *Journal of Learning Analytics*, *8*(2), 6–21. DOI: 10.18608/jla.2021.7325

Wang, Q., Mousavi, A., & Lu, C. (2022). A scoping review of empirical studies on theory-driven learning analytics. *Distance Education*, *43*(1), 6–29. DOI: 10.1080/01587919.2021.2020621

Wang, T., Lund, B. D., Marengo, A., Pagano, A., Mannuru, N. R., Teel, Z. A., & Pange, J. (2023). Exploring the potential impact of artificial intelligence (AI) on international students in higher education: Generative AI, chatbots, analytics, and international student success. *Applied Sciences (Basel, Switzerland)*, *13*(11), 6716. DOI: 10.3390/app13116716

Williamson, B. (2019). Policy networks, performance metrics and platform markets: Charting the expanding data infrastructure of higher education. *British Journal of Educational Technology*, *50*(6), 2794–2809. DOI: 10.1111/bjet.12849

Wise, A. F., & Vytasek, J. (2017). Learning analytics implementation design. *Handbook of Learning Analytics*, 151–159.

Xing, W., Guo, R., Petakovic, E., & Goggins, S. (2015). Participation-based student final performance prediction model through interpretable genetic programming: Integrating learning analytics, educational data mining and theory. *Computers in Human Behavior*, *47*, 168–181. DOI: 10.1016/j.chb.2014.09.034

Yan, L., Echeverria, V., Jin, Y., Fernandez-Nieto, G., Zhao, L., Li, X., Alfredo, R., Swiecki, Z., Gašević, D., & Martinez-Maldonado, R. (2024). Evidence-based multimodal learning analytics for feedback and reflection in collaborative learning. *British Journal of Educational Technology*, *55*(5), 1900–1925. DOI: 10.1111/bjet.13498

KEY TERMS AND DEFINITIONS

Adaptive Learning Pathways: Personalized learning routes within a curriculum where instructional content and assessment strategies are adjusted based on the needs, performance data and engagement patterns of each individual.

Analytics-Informed Teaching: A teaching approach where educators use data insights derived from digital learning environments to guide instructional decisions and improve student learning outcomes.

Data Literacy: This refers to the ability of educators and students to understand, interpret, critically evaluate, and make informed decisions based on educational data and analytics outputs.

Datafication of Education: The process through which educational activities, behaviours, and interactions are transformed into quantifiable data that can be analysed to monitor and improve learning processes.

Educator Readiness: The degree to which educators possess appropriate competencies, attitudes, and institutional support required to effectively interpret and apply learning analytics in teaching and learning contexts.

Ethical use of learning data: The responsible handling and interpretation of student data in ways that respect privacy, ensure transparency, and uphold fairness in educational decision-making.

Institutional Readiness for Learning Analytics: The extent to which an educational institution has the policies, infrastructure, governance structures, and support systems necessary to implement learning analytics effectively and ethically.

Learning Analytics (LA): this refers to a systematic collection, analysis, and interpretation of data generated from digital learning environments to understand and improve teaching, learning processes, and educational decision-making.

Learning Management System (LMS): Refers to a digital platform used by educational institutions to manage course content, facilitate communication, track learner progress, and generate data that can inform learning analytics.

Pedagogical Integration of Learning Analytics: The process of embedding analytics insights into teaching strategies, curriculum design, and assessment practices to enhance learning effectiveness.

Student Data Literacy: The capability of learners to understand how their learning data is collected and used, enabling them to interpret analytics feedback and make informed adjustments to their learning strategies.

Student Engagement Analytics: The analysis of digital traces such as logins, discussion participation, assessment submissions, and interaction with course materials to understand levels of learner involvement and participation.

Chapter 6
Teaching at the Crossroads of AI and Flexibility:
Faculty Readiness for Hyflex Learning

Indranil Mutsuddi
http://orcid.org/0000-0002-4202-8744
JIS University, India

ABSTRACT

The evolving landscape of higher education, shaped by technological innovation and shifting learner expectations, has brought the Hybrid-Flexible (HyFlex) model to the forefront. This approach allows students to engage with courses in-person, online synchronously, or asynchronously, promoting inclusivity and learner autonomy. Unlike traditional hybrid formats, HyFlex demands a complete redesign of course structure and instructional methods, placing new pressures on faculty to ensure consistency across modalities. The integration of generative AI further enhances the potential of HyFlex by enabling adaptive learning, automated feedback, and content personalization. However, effective implementation relies on faculty readiness, requiring digital proficiency, ethical AI use, and flexible pedagogy. This chapter examines the convergence of HyFlex and AI, emphasizing targeted professional development to equip educators for this transformative era in higher education.

DOI: 10.4018/979-8-3373-6182-6.ch006

INTRODUCTION

The landscape of higher education is undergoing a rapid transformation, driven by technological advancement, evolving learner expectations, and the increasing demand for flexible, inclusive learning environments. Among the most innovative responses to these shifts is the HyFlex (Hybrid-Flexible) model—an instructional approach that empowers students to choose between attending classes in-person, participating in real-time online sessions, or engaging asynchronously based on their individual circumstances. By centering learner autonomy, HyFlex bridges the gap between accessibility and academic rigor, making education more inclusive and adaptable.

Unlike traditional hybrid formats that prescribe fixed combinations of face-to-face and online activities, HyFlex emphasizes student choice and flexibility at the point of engagement. This pedagogical innovation necessitates a rethinking of course design, assessment, and delivery to ensure consistent learning outcomes across modalities. At the heart of this transformation lies the faculty—who must shift from conventional teaching roles to multifaceted ones encompassing design, facilitation, technology integration, and student support.

As the education sector increasingly adopts Artificial Intelligence (AI) technologies, particularly generative AI (GenAI), the synergy between AI and HyFlex teaching emerges as a powerful catalyst for personalized, adaptive, and efficient instruction. AI tools can enhance HyFlex environments by automating routine tasks, analyzing learning data, supporting content creation, and enabling dynamic feedback mechanisms. For students, AI offers personalized learning pathways and tools for deeper engagement; for faculty, it provides insights and efficiencies that can transform the teaching experience.

However, realizing the potential of AI-integrated HyFlex education depends significantly on faculty readiness and ongoing professional development. Instructors must be equipped with not only digital literacy and pedagogical agility but also a clear understanding of AI's ethical and practical implications in education. This requires well-structured training initiatives that align with the flexible principles of HyFlex learning—allowing educators to experience firsthand the modalities they will implement in their own classrooms.

This chapter explores the intersection of faculty preparedness and professional development perspectives within the context of AI-integrated HyFlex teaching. Drawing on current literature and identifying existing research gaps, it aims to provide actionable insights and frameworks to support higher education faculty in navigating this complex yet promising educational paradigm. The discussions presented here are intended to empower academic professionals to adopt resilient, student-centered, and technology-enabled pedagogies that meet the demands of contemporary learners and future-ready institutions.

REVIEW OF LITERATURE

Higher education is undergoing a significant transformation, reshaping both how instruction is delivered and how administrative tasks are managed. This shift is largely influenced by advancements in digital technology, the widespread adoption of online learning, evolving student expectations, increasing institutional costs, and the growing appeal of alternative credentials such as micro and nano degrees (Alenezi, 2023). Digital tools have become essential in academic settings, equipping educators with enhanced methods for delivering content and engaging learners. Adaptive learning platforms, for example, are increasingly being utilized to personalize instruction based on student data, adjusting materials and pacing to suit individual learning needs (Das et al., 2024).

A prominent development in this landscape is hybrid teaching, which integrates face-to-face instruction with online components. This blended approach provides flexibility and adaptability, offering students the opportunity to benefit from digital innovation while retaining the interpersonal advantages of classroom learning. However, this model also introduces challenges, including disparities in technology access, time management difficulties, communication barriers, and complexities in assessment practices (Gudoniene et al., 2025).

In response to these dynamics, the HyFlex (Hybrid-Flexible) model has emerged as an innovative framework that supports active, student-centered learning. It enables learners to choose how they participate—whether in-person, synchronously online, or asynchronously—while fostering interaction through collaborative exercises and discussion-based activities. Initially developed as a strategy to address financial constraints and increasing demands for flexible learning pathways, HyFlex is now a growing focus in research on hybrid education (Howell, 2022). By allowing personalized learning experiences and data-informed content delivery, the model encourages autonomy, critical thinking, and deeper engagement (Aldosemani, 2023).

Faculty readiness plays a crucial role in successfully implementing HyFlex courses. Authors like, (Romero-Hall & Ripine, 2021) found that many instructors feel confident adapting traditional teaching techniques to HyFlex formats, particularly those methods that already align with in-person instruction. The hybrid model has been associated with improved student outcomes, such as enhanced satisfaction, increased self-confidence, and better engagement—outcomes linked to students' familiarity with remote learning during the pandemic and the flexibility offered by hybrid formats (Adi Badiozaman et al., 2025).

Nevertheless, faculty often expressed uncertainty about how to handle the distinctive complexities of the HyFlex model. To address this, (Albashiry et al., 2024) proposed a digital competency framework that helps university instructors assess and develop their skills in designing and delivering technology-enhanced courses. This framework emphasizes cross-disciplinary collaboration among educators, instructional designers, faculty developers, and institutional leaders.

Adoption of artificial intelligence (AI) in higher education is another critical area of development. Scholars like (Alnasib, 2023) highlighted that an instructor's personal attributes—such as age, gender, and teaching experience—significantly influence their readiness to integrate AI into pedagogy, more so than their job titles or departments. Promoting responsible and effective use of AI in education requires targeted support to improve faculty understanding, skill development, and strategic application of these technologies. Educators are increasingly recognizing the value of diverse teaching strategies within HyFlex environments, though those new to this model often need substantial institutional support and professional development.

According to (Filiz et al., 2025), educators are increasingly recognizing the value of AI-powered tools such as ChatGPT and MagicSchool in enhancing instructional efficiency, promoting personalized learning, and boosting student engagement. However, alongside these promising advancements, several persistent challenges remain. Issues related to curriculum integration, technological constraints, ethical considerations, and the need for culturally responsive adaptation continue to hinder the effective use of AI in educational settings. The research highlights the necessity for robust institutional backing, clear ethical frameworks, and sufficient resource allocation to address these concerns effectively. The rapid advancement of Generative AI (GenAI) has also redefined the skillsets and knowledge essential for effective teaching, prompting a fundamental shift in teacher education. This evolution underscores the urgent need for pedagogical reform and deeper research at both the initial teacher training and professional development stages. Such reforms must be contextualized within diverse teacher education programs and responsive to varied regional and institutional needs. Teacher educators, positioned at the core of this transformation, hold a dual responsibility: preparing future teachers through both theoretical instruction and hands-on supervision, and conducting impactful research that addresses critical challenges in teaching practices and teacher learning.

Instructors working within HyFlex settings frequently face logistical difficulties, including managing concurrent learning formats, handling technology failures, managing heavier workloads, and navigating insufficient training opportunities. Meanwhile, students benefit from increased flexibility, broader course access, and greater autonomy, along with the development of practical skills relevant to modern workplaces (Morrison et al., 2025). However, they must also overcome technical challenges, adapt to the demands of hybrid formats, maintain communication, foster collaboration, and develop strong time management and self-regulation habits. Recent findings by (Melek Koc, 2024) reveal that prospective teachers show varying preferences regarding how instruction, observation, and feedback are delivered in hybrid environments. The adaptability of the HyFlex model makes it well-suited to traditional and digital learning contexts alike. Moreover, (Kim, 2024) observed that faculty see potential in AI-assisted collaboration to support teaching duties such as planning, delivery, grading, and professional growth. Nonetheless, challenges such as lack of consistent curricular guidance, overreliance on commercial AI tools, limited ethical frameworks, and educator hesitancy remain key hurdles.

Adding on, (Sanders & Mukhari, 2024) underscored the need for strong support systems in AI-enhanced hybrid learning. Essential components include leadership commitment, quality professional development, reliable infrastructure, and time allowances for faculty adaptation. Their study illuminated both the opportunities and challenges of AI integration in blended education. A comprehensive study by (Noichun et al., 2024) affirmed a shared expert consensus on critical elements for successful HyFlex implementation: technological infrastructure, faculty training, supportive institutional policies, student engagement strategies, and continuous quality improvement. These findings contribute to a robust, multidimensional framework that institutions can follow when adopting HyFlex approaches.

Moving on, (Markauskaite et al., 2023) argued for a more holistic perspective on digital teaching competencies. Rather than focusing solely on individual skills, they advocate for a broader ecological approach that acknowledges the intricate interplay between digital technologies and the human practices embedded within education systems. This comprehensive understanding is essential for addressing the complexities of teaching in a digitally integrated academic landscape.

CRITICAL REVIEW OF LITERATURE AND ANSLYSIS OF RESEARCH GAPS

The current body of literature underscores a significant transformation in higher education driven by digital technologies, evolving learning models like HyFlex, and the integration of AI tools. While advancements such as adaptive learning platforms, hybrid instruction, and AI-assisted teaching have enhanced flexibility and personalization in learning, critical gaps remain. These include disparities in faculty readiness, inconsistent institutional support, technological inequalities, and the need for clearer ethical guidelines in AI usage. Many studies emphasize the benefits of HyFlex and AI-enhanced education, including improved engagement and instructional efficiency; however, they also highlight persistent challenges such as inadequate digital competencies, logistical hurdles, and limited professional development. A key research gap lies in the lack of comprehensive, cross-contextual frameworks that account for regional diversity, institutional variability, and the dynamic interplay between digital tools and human teaching practices. Future research must adopt an ecological approach to digital pedagogy, focusing not only on individual skill development but also on systemic factors that influence successful implementation of hybrid and AI-supported teaching models.

CHANGING LANDSCAPE OF HIGHER EDUCATION IN THE AI ERA

In the rapidly evolving landscape of higher education, Artificial Intelligence (AI) has emerged as a powerful force driving change. The rise of advanced language models, such as OpenAI's ChatGPT and Anthropic's Claude-3, has ignited a profound transformation in how learning, teaching, and academic engagement are conceptualized and implemented (Abulaiti, 2024). These developments mark a significant shift—not just in the tools used by educators and students, but in the very foundations of pedagogical design and institutional strategy.

The integration of AI into higher education signals a paradigm shift. Unlike previous technological adoptions that had localized or incremental effects, AI is poised to reshape the educational experience on a structural level (Ruano-Borbalan, 2025). Intelligent systems now offer tailored, adaptive learning environments that adjust to individual student needs, pacing, and learning styles. This personalization leads to deeper student engagement, enhanced motivation, and improved outcomes, suggesting that AI has the potential to reduce educational disparities and promote more inclusive learning environments.

Historically, technological innovations in education have often followed a pattern of gradual adoption, with their impact constrained by institutional inertia, resource limitations, and pedagogical conservatism. The current wave of AI tools, however, presents a more disruptive potential. While some skeptics argue that the integration of AI may mirror earlier trends—ultimately yielding modest improvements limited to specific educational or research functions—the unprecedented capabilities of generative AI and the emergence of Artificial General Intelligence (AGI) suggest a much deeper and more pervasive transformation.

Generative AI tools are redefining traditional academic processes, from content creation and curriculum design to assessment and feedback. Language models like ChatGPT can generate coherent, contextually aware text, enabling educators to automate administrative tasks, draft instructional materials, and even simulate interactive tutoring sessions. These technologies blur the line between creator and consumer, offering students new ways to explore complex ideas, conduct research, and express their understanding.

The influence of AI is not confined to the classroom. As the global economy continues to digitize, the skillsets required for success are rapidly evolving. Tasks that once demanded specialized training—such as data analysis, coding, or natural language processing—are becoming increasingly accessible, yet essential, across a broad range of fields. Consequently, higher education institutions face a critical imperative: to equip students not only with technical expertise but also with the soft skills that machines cannot replicate. Creativity, critical thinking, emotional intelligence, and ethical reasoning are now as vital as proficiency in AI tools. In response to these shifts, universities must rethink their curricula, research agendas, and institutional missions. This includes integrating AI literacy across disciplines, fostering interdisciplinary collaborations, and developing ethical frameworks for responsible AI use. Rather than viewing AI as a threat to traditional education, forward-thinking institutions are beginning to embrace it as a catalyst for innovation, equity, and lifelong learning.

RISE OF HYFLEX: A RESPONSE TO EVOLVING LEARNER NEEDS

As educators and students continue to navigate the evolving landscape of post-pandemic education, the Hybrid-Flexible (HyFlex) model has gained significant traction as a dynamic and inclusive approach to teaching and learning. Born out of the urgent need for adaptable learning frameworks during the COVID-19 pandemic, the HyFlex model has since established itself as a long-term strategy that addresses the diverse needs of today's learners. By blending in-person, synchronous online, and asynchronous online learning into a single course structure, HyFlex empowers students with the freedom to choose how they engage with each session, offering an unprecedented level of autonomy and personalization.

At its core, the HyFlex model is grounded in the principle of flexibility. It recognizes that students face varying personal, professional, and technological circumstances, and it seeks to remove barriers to access while maintaining academic rigor. Whether students prefer the immediacy and structure of attending classes on campus, the convenience of joining lectures via live video conferencing, or the flexibility of engaging with pre-recorded materials and digital resources on their own schedule, HyFlex accommodates all these preferences within a unified learning experience.

This level of adaptability not only fosters greater student satisfaction and engagement but also supports equity in education. Learners who may have previously been marginalized due to geographic distance, health limitations, caregiving responsibilities, or financial constraints now have more viable pathways to participate in higher education. The model also proves beneficial for international students and working professionals, allowing them to balance academic commitments with personal obligations.

Since its widespread adoption in 2020, the HyFlex model has evolved from an emergency solution to a well-researched, intentional approach to curriculum delivery. By 2024, academic research had begun to offer deeper insights into the effectiveness of HyFlex pedagogy. Studies indicate that when implemented with careful planning and technological support, HyFlex can lead to comparable—or even improved—learning outcomes across modalities. Moreover, the model encourages the development of digital literacy, self-regulation, and collaborative skills, which are increasingly essential in modern academic and professional environments.

However, successful implementation of HyFlex requires thoughtful course design, institutional support, and faculty development. Instructors must ensure that all participation modes are equally robust, engaging, and accessible. This includes leveraging learning management systems, integrating interactive tools, and providing timely feedback regardless of how students choose to engage. Additionally, institutions must invest in infrastructure, such as high-quality classroom recording equipment and technical support staff, to ensure a seamless experience for both in-person and remote learners.

Understanding the HyFlex model

The Hybrid-Flexible (HyFlex) model is redefining the landscape of modern education by centering student choice, inclusivity, and adaptability at the heart of instructional design. As colleges and universities navigate the demands of a rapidly evolving academic environment, shaped by technological advancements and global disruptions, HyFlex offers a forward-thinking solution that seamlessly integrates traditional classroom instruction with digital learning opportunities. This model not only bridges the divide between in-person and online education but also ensures that students can engage in ways that suit their individual needs—whether due to work, health, geography, or learning preferences. By doing so, HyFlex addresses the growing call for learning environments that are both accessible and resilient.

Unlike conventional models that lock students into one mode of participation, HyFlex courses are designed with built-in flexibility, allowing learners to choose—on a class-by-class basis—whether to attend sessions physically, join live via virtual platforms, or access course materials asynchronously at their convenience. This approach supports learners who may be managing full-time jobs, caring for family members, or dealing with health challenges. Instructors play a crucial role in ensuring that the learning experience remains consistent across all modalities. In-person classes focus on interactive engagement, while synchronous online sessions utilize tools like Zoom, Google Meet, or Microsoft Teams to foster real-time dialogue and collaboration. Meanwhile, asynchronous learners benefit from thoughtfully prepared resources such as lecture recordings, digital readings, interactive modules, and discussion forums that can be accessed anytime.

What distinguishes the HyFlex model is its commitment to educational equity and its alignment with inclusive pedagogical practices. It removes logistical and physical barriers, allowing students of varied backgrounds and abilities to participate fully in their education. This model not only enhances access but also promotes the development of essential skills like self-regulation, digital literacy, and time management—capabilities that are increasingly vital in both academic and professional contexts. Ultimately, HyFlex represents more than just a mode of delivery; it embodies a shift toward a more student-centered, future-ready approach to teaching and learning. As educational institutions look ahead, HyFlex stands out as a sustainable, adaptable, and empowering model fit for the challenges and opportunities of 21st-century education.

Pedagogical Implications of HyFlex Teaching

HyFlex (Hybrid-Flexible) learning is an innovative instructional model that seamlessly integrates multiple modes of course delivery to accommodate diverse student needs and preferences. Specifically, it combines face-to-face (F2F) instruction, synchronous online learning, and asynchronous online participation. Each class session and related learning activities are designed to be accessible through all three modalities, allowing students the autonomy to choose how they engage with the course content based on their schedules, learning styles, or personal circumstances. Central to this model is a student-centered philosophy that emphasizes choice, autonomy, and equitable access to learning, regardless of participation mode. HyFlex promotes active and interactive learning through diverse methods such as direct instruction, group collaboration, experiential projects, and independent study—all designed to be effective across different formats. A strong emphasis is placed on cultivating teacher and social presence to foster a sense of community among all learners, whether they are physically present or remote. The approach also ensures that activities and assessments are equivalent and adaptable across all modes, supporting fairness in learning outcomes. Technology plays a critical role in enabling multi-modal delivery, supporting interaction, and ensuring accessibility so that all students can participate fully. Through its flexible and inclusive design,

HyFlex redefines modern teaching by making learning more responsive to students' diverse needs and circumstances.

This adaptable framework is grounded in inclusive pedagogy and aims to create equitable learning opportunities for all students, whether they are physically present in the classroom, joining virtually in real-time, or accessing materials on their own time. Instructors using the HyFlex model must carefully design their courses to ensure that each mode of participation offers a comparable learning experience.

To achieve this, educators employ a variety of instructional strategies that align with the unique opportunities offered by each delivery method. These strategies include:

- **Direct Instruction**, where the instructor delivers content through lectures or demonstrations, either in person or via live or recorded video.
- **Interactive Instruction**, which emphasizes discussion, collaboration, and peer engagement through forums, breakout rooms, and classroom activities using online interactive tools like Mentimeter, Slido, Kahoot etc.
- **Experiential Learning**, which involves hands-on tasks, simulations, or real-world problem solving, and can be facilitated both on-site and through digital platforms.
- **Independent Study**, allowing students to explore topics individually through research, projects, or self-paced modules.

These pedagogical approaches are supported by the **pedagogy-space-technology (PST) framework** proposed by (Radcliffe, 2009), which highlights the interdependent relationship between instructional strategies (pedagogy), the physical or virtual environment where learning occurs (space), and the tools used to support instruction (technology). According to this framework, effective learning design in a HyFlex environment requires intentional integration of these three elements, as changes in one domain inevitably impact the others. By embracing the HyFlex model, institutions can provide more resilient and student-centered learning environments that support academic success across various learning contexts and life circumstances.

Physical Arrangements in a typical HyFlex Teaching Setup: Figure 1 presents a visual representation of a HyFlex learning environment, showcasing how physical classroom arrangements are designed to accommodate both in-person and remote learners at the same time. In a HyFlex (Hybrid-Flexible) teaching environment, the physical setup of the classroom plays a crucial role in ensuring that both in-person and remote learners receive an equitable and engaging educational experience. Unlike traditional classrooms designed solely for face-to-face instruction, HyFlex spaces are intentionally arranged to support simultaneous participation across multiple modalities—on-site, online synchronous, and online asynchronous.

At the heart of the physical arrangement is the integration of advanced audio-visual technology. Classrooms are typically equipped with high-definition cameras that can capture both the instructor and classroom activities (use of smart boards with integrated online camera and virtual meeting softwares like MS Teams), allowing remote learners to follow along in real time. These cameras may be stationary or motion-tracking to accommodate movement, especially in interactive sessions. Microphones are strategically placed throughout the room—on the instructor, around student seating areas, or built into the ceiling—to capture clear audio from all participants, ensuring that remote students can hear both lectures and class discussions without disruption.

Another critical component is the display and projection systems. Classrooms often feature large screens or interactive whiteboards that show online participants, digital content, or shared materials. These allow the instructor and in-person students to see and interact with their remote peers, fostering a sense of connection and collaboration. In some setups, dual monitors or projection systems may be used to display different content to in-person and online students simultaneously.

Figure 1. HyFlex teaching and learning setup

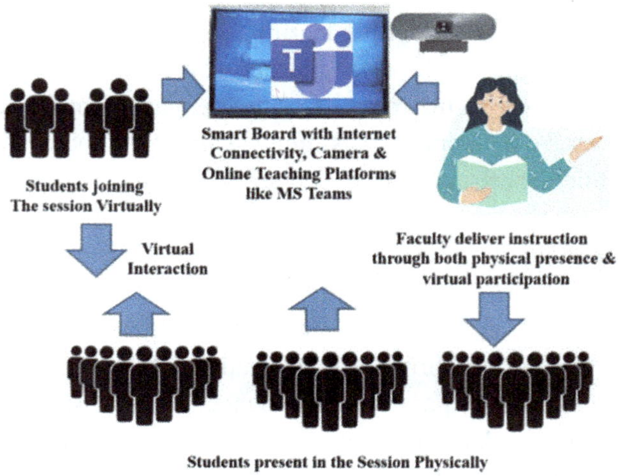

In addition, the diagram outlines designated seating arrangements for in-person students, ensuring visibility and audio clarity, while also illustrating the digital interface used by online learners to join the session in real time. This setup exemplifies how thoughtfully integrated space and technology can support flexible, inclusive participation for all students, regardless of location.

Student Engagement perspectives in HyFlex Teaching

HyFlex teaching and learning (HTL), which integrates simultaneous online and in-person course delivery, represents a significant shift in how education—particularly adult and post-compulsory education—is conceptualized and delivered. At its core, the HyFlex model empowers students by offering a flexible, choice-based approach to learning. It allows learners to decide how they wish to participate—whether by attending sessions on campus, joining synchronously online, or engaging with materials asynchronously at their own pace. This increased flexibility not only aligns with the complex lives and responsibilities of adult learners but also challenges long-standing assumptions about how teaching and learning should be structured beyond compulsory education (Baker et al., 2024).

The traditional separation of delivery modes—face-to-face and online—has historically shaped educational design and engagement strategies as distinct and often incompatible. HyFlex, however, blurs these boundaries, requiring educators to rethink pedagogical norms, instructional practices, and student engagement (SE) in more holistic and inclusive ways. This convergence of modalities invites a deeper exploration into how lifelong learners interact with content, instructors, and peers across different environments.

One of the key promises of HyFlex learning lies in its potential to reimagine engagement by accounting for the diverse, often non-linear, educational journeys of adult learners. Existing frameworks of student engagement frequently rely on simplified behavioural indicators, such as attendance or participation in discussions. These metrics, while measurable, fail to capture the depth and diversity of learner experience—particularly among those who engage more slowly, prefer reflective learning styles, or face contextual challenges like digital access or caregiving responsibilities. Furthermore, traditional models often rest on implicit assumptions about what "good" engagement looks like. These tacit expectations tend to privilege fast-paced, vocal, and visible forms of participation while framing quieter, more contemplative engagement as passive or disengaged. Such assumptions risk marginalizing students whose learning preferences or life contexts do not align with these narrow norms. For example, learners who require additional time to process information or who contribute asynchronously may be unfairly perceived as less involved, despite being deeply committed to their learning.

In HyFlex environments, these dynamics become more complex. Engagement is no longer confined to a single space or mode, and understanding how students navigate and blend different modes of participation becomes essential (Hews et al., 2022). Yet, research in this area remains limited. Much of the existing literature continues to treat in-person and online learning as separate "icebergs," with distinct challenges and strategies for each. This bifurcated view can obscure the nuanced realities of hybrid learners who move fluidly between these spaces. Noteworthy exceptions in the research include (Johnson et al., 2018), whose study of postgraduate students in a hybrid program revealed that learners' levels of digital literacy significantly influenced both their academic engagement and their sense of connection to the learning community. Their ability to navigate technology impacted not only their performance but also their confidence and identity as learners. Similarly, (Bowden, 2022) explored the factors that contributed to student success across in-person and blended learning environments. The study found that behavioural engagement—such as attending sessions and submitting assignments—was closely linked to student wellbeing, while affective engagement, which encompasses emotional and motivational investment, played a crucial role in making the learning experience transformative. These findings suggest that engagement in HyFlex contexts is multi-dimensional, shaped by a complex interplay of skills, emotions, identities, and access to resources. Given the growing relevance of HyFlex models, it is timely and necessary to revisit how we conceptualize student engagement in lifelong learning. Educators, institutions, and policymakers must develop more nuanced, context-sensitive frameworks that account for the diversity of adult learners' experiences. This includes acknowledging that flexibility does not automatically equate to equity and recognizing that providing choices in mode of participation must be supported by thoughtful design, inclusive pedagogy, and access to technology and support services.

FACULTY ROLES IN HYFLEX TEACHING

Faculty members play a pivotal role in the careful design, strategic planning, and successful implementation of HyFlex (Hybrid-Flexible) teaching approaches. As emphasized by (Beatty, 2019), the effectiveness of HyFlex learning environments relies heavily on faculty engagement in creating inclusive and flexible educational experiences that cater to diverse student needs. This innovative mode of instruction allows students to participate in course sessions either face-to-face or online in real-time, utilizing video conferencing systems (VCS), as noted by (Kohnke & Moorhouse, 2021). HyFlex teaching is distinct from traditional hybrid models. While the hybrid model combines synchronous in-person, synchronous online, and asynchronous components, student choice is often limited. In contrast, HyFlex empowers learners by allowing them to select, on a session-by-session basis, whether to attend in person, join online synchronously, or engage asynchronously, depending on their preferences or circumstances (Cumming et al., 2024). This adaptability not only enhances learner autonomy but also benefits instructors, as it eliminates the need to deliver the same course multiple times in different formats.

Pedagogical Planning and Classroom Setup

Effective HyFlex instruction demands intentional planning of classroom dynamics, instructional strategies, and technology integration. Faculty must design strategic classroom environments that are both pedagogically sound and technologically equipped to support real-time and flexible participation. This includes configuring audio-visual systems, establishing multiple camera angles to enhance remote student immersion, and ensuring all teaching materials are accessible to both in-person and online learners. Furthermore, faculty must receive comprehensive training in HyFlex pedagogy and classroom management. Structured professional development initiatives should be implemented to equip educators with the skills necessary to manage technical complexities and facilitate engagement across learning modalities. Students should also be provided with clear, practical guidelines regarding expected norms and behaviors in a HyFlex environment, helping to cultivate a sense of structure and predictability.

Managing Instructional Perspectives

Given the unpredictable nature of technology, it is essential to prepare contingency plans to address potential failures or access issues. Instructors should communicate these backup protocols to students in advance to reduce confusion and maintain continuity of instruction. Faculty should also consider designating a teaching assistant (TA) or assigning a student to help manage technological aspects such as chat monitoring, troubleshooting access issues, and maintaining communication with remote learners during live sessions. This reduces the cognitive load on instructors and helps sustain a smoother instructional flow.

Session Planning and Delivery

Designing each HyFlex session with specific learning outcomes in mind is crucial. Faculty should consider the diversity of their students, available technology, and the physical setup of the classroom when developing lesson plans. Effective session planning includes:

- Time allocation for technical setup and informal student check-ins.
- Inclusion of interactive activities and guided instructions.
- Opportunities to pause for questions and chat monitoring.
- Debriefing sessions to reflect on learning outcomes.

Familiarization with Classroom Technology

Before the course/session begins, faculty members should visit their assigned classrooms to test available technology, including projectors, microphones, audio systems, and cameras. Understanding how to operate and integrate these tools (smartboards) with personal devices is critical to delivering a seamless learning experience. For classrooms supported by institutional IT services, faculty should schedule training sessions to familiarize themselves with specific equipment.

Choosing Inclusive Student Engagement Strategies for Hybrid Sessions

This involves ensuring equitable participation for all students—whether in-person or remote—is fundamental in HyFlex instruction. Faculty should:

- Clearly communicate classroom norms, participation expectations, and technology protocols.
- Discuss interaction guidelines between instructors, Teaching Assistants, and students.
- Address how peer engagement will be facilitated across modalities.

Fostering Student Interaction

In order to create a vibrant learning community, faculty must design activities that facilitate interaction between all students, regardless of physical location. If working with a co-instructor or Teaching Assistant, responsibilities such as chat monitoring and fielding remote questions can be distributed. For solo instructors, assigning students to rotate as chat monitors can ensure remote voices are heard and included in classroom dialogue. Faculty may use strategies like:

- Icebreakers that engage both in-person and remote learners (e.g., partner introductions, digital "waves," or call-and-response interactions).
- Choose interactive instruction contents, which emphasizes discussion, collaboration, and peer engagement through forums, breakout rooms, and classroom activities using online interactive tools like Mentimeter, Slido, Kahoot etc
- Live quizzes on collaborative platforms using tools like quizizz.com
- Thought-provoking prompts on discussion boards to involve asynchronous students.

These methods support student motivation and create a sense of belonging within a distributed classroom environment.

Leveraging Support Roles in the HyFlex Classroom

Delivering HyFlex instruction is inherently complex and benefits from collaborative teaching structures. Teaching Assistants can provide essential support by:

- Assisting with pre-class equipment checks.
- Monitoring live chat and offering real-time assistance to remote learners.
- Ensuring clarity of instructions and mitigating technical disruptions.

In the absence of formal TAs, instructors might assign specific roles to students, such as Chat Monitor or Tech Support Liaison. Rotating these responsibilities promotes shared ownership and inclusion. For smaller seminar-style classes, pairing in-person and remote students as learning buddies can enhance engagement. Each in-person student could use a device to maintain a live video connection with their remote partner, ensuring both have access to class discussions and materials in real time.

Transformation from Instructor to Designer, Facilitator, and Technologist in HyFlex Teaching

In today's rapidly changing educational environment, the role of the educator has undergone a profound transformation, moving beyond the traditional image of a content-delivering instructor to that of a dynamic, multifaceted professional. Modern educators are increasingly taking on the integrated roles of learning designer, facilitator, and technologist to meet the diverse needs of 21st-century learners. As designers, educators thoughtfully create learner-centered experiences that go beyond rote memorization, ensuring that learning objectives are aligned with engaging, meaningful activities and authentic assessments. This approach encourages students to connect theoretical knowledge with practical application, making learning more relevant and impactful. In their role as facilitators, educators shift from being the sole source of knowledge to becoming guides who nurture collaborative, inquiry-based environments. They promote critical thinking, dialogue, and student agency, empowering learners to take ownership of their educational journey. Furthermore, the rapid integration of technology in education has redefined educators as technologists who skillfully utilize digital tools to enhance instruction, foster interactivity, and provide personalized learning pathways. From using learning management systems and multimedia resources to incorporating data analytics and adaptive learning platforms, educators now play a critical role in building students' digital fluency and ensuring equitable access to high-quality education. This evolution signifies a broader commitment to creating flexible, inclusive, and future-ready learning ecosystems where both teaching and learning are continuously enriched.

AI AS A CATALYST FOR INNOVATION IN HYFLEX ENVIRONMENTS

The rise of hybrid-flexible (HyFlex) learning environments—where students can participate both in-person and online—has revolutionized education and workplace training. However, the true potential of HyFlex models emerges when combined with the transformative power of Artificial Intelligence (AI). AI acts as a catalyst for innovation in HyFlex environments by enhancing adaptability, personalization, and engagement, thereby creating more dynamic and effective learning and collaboration experiences (Table 1).

Table 1. AI as a catalyst for Innovation in Hyflex environment

Items	Details
Personalized Learning at Scale	A key challenge in HyFlex learning environments is catering to the varied needs of students who participate through different modes simultaneously. AI tools help overcome this by examining each learner's unique style, preferences, and progress. This enables the delivery of customized materials suited to every individual, whether they are attending in person or online. Through smart algorithms, the system can suggest appropriate resources, modify the complexity of tasks, and offer immediate feedback, thereby enhancing the overall learning experience and ensuring it is accessible to all.
Enhancing Interaction and Engagement	Maintaining learner engagement is essential in HyFlex models, especially since remote learners can often experience a sense of isolation. AI-driven chatbots and virtual helpers promote active involvement by providing immediate responses to questions and encouraging conversation. Additionally, AI tools can oversee online discussions, monitor student participation, and assess the overall mood to detect learners who might require extra assistance, helping to make sure everyone stays on track.
Automating Administrative Tasks	HyFlex learning setups demand intricate management of timetables, resources, and evaluations. Artificial intelligence streamlines these administrative tasks by automating processes such as grading, tracking attendance, and generating comprehensive reports on student progress. By handling these routine duties, AI allows educators to dedicate more time to teaching strategies and creative improvements instead of administrative work.

continued on following page

Table 1. Continued

Items	Details
Supporting Accessibility and Inclusion	In HyFlex settings, AI technologies help remove accessibility obstacles by offering real-time transcription and translation, allowing learners from various language backgrounds to participate effectively. Additionally, AI-powered adaptive tools support students with disabilities, making these learning environments genuinely inclusive for everyone.
Facilitating Continuous Improvement	AI collects and examines extensive data on student interactions with course materials and peers, offering valuable insights that support ongoing enhancement. These insights enable educators and administrators to fine-tune curriculum design, explore innovative instructional approaches, and apply effective strategies to improve the overall HyFlex learning experience.

FACULTY READINESS FOR AI-INTEGRATED HYFLEX TEACHING

The swift evolution of technology, especially Artificial Intelligence (AI), is reshaping education, making it essential for educators to embrace innovative teaching approaches like HyFlex. This method blends face-to-face and online instruction, providing learners with greater flexibility while demanding that instructors master both conventional and digital teaching techniques. Incorporating AI into HyFlex learning introduces new challenges and possibilities, highlighting the importance of thorough faculty preparation. AI-enhanced HyFlex education uses intelligent systems to customize learning experiences, streamline administrative duties, and boost student engagement across different formats. Examples of AI in this context include adaptive learning software, automated grading tools, virtual assistants for student inquiries, and analytics platforms that track learner progress. To harness these benefits effectively, instructors need a clear and balanced understanding of AI's strengths and limitations within the hybrid teaching framework. Table 2 illustrates the various dimensions used for faculty readiness for AI-integrated teaching:

Table 2. Dimensions of faculty readiness for AI-integrated teaching

Items	Details
Technological Competency	Faculty must be comfortable using various AI tools and platforms, ensuring seamless integration with both face-to-face and online teaching. This includes proficiency in learning management systems (LMS), video conferencing software, AI-driven content creation, and student assessment technologies.
Pedagogical Adaptability	Effective HyFlex instruction requires adapting teaching strategies to accommodate different learner needs and modes of delivery. Faculty need to design flexible lesson plans that incorporate AI's personalized learning features while maintaining pedagogical rigor across settings.
Attitudinal Openness	Embracing AI integration demands a positive attitude toward technological innovation and continuous learning. Faculty should be willing to experiment with new tools, reflect on their teaching practices, and engage in professional development.
Ethical Awareness	AI raises ethical concerns, including data privacy, algorithmic bias, and transparency. Educators must understand these issues to ensure AI use upholds fairness and protects student rights.

Digital Competency and Pedagogical Agility for HyFlex Teaching

The evolution of modern-day education has brought about innovative teaching models, with HyFlex (Hybrid-Flexible) learning emerging as a prominent approach. This model blends in-person and online instruction, allowing students the flexibility to choose how they attend classes. To successfully implement HyFlex teaching, educators must develop two critical skill sets: digital competency and pedagogical agility. Digital competency involves an educator's skill in utilizing digital technologies and tools to effectively facilitate learning. In HyFlex settings, instructors must be comfortable working with a range of platforms, including learning management systems (LMS), video conferencing software, and online collaboration tools. More than just basic familiarity, teachers should be able to integrate these technologies naturally into their lesson plans to boost student participation and engagement. Important aspects of digital competency include:

- **Technological proficiency:** Efficiently operating and resolving issues within digital platforms.
- **Content development:** Creating diverse multimedia materials such as videos, podcasts, and interactive lessons.
- **Data literacy:** Interpreting analytics from digital tools to track student performance and tailor teaching strategies.

Role of Pedagogical Agility: Pedagogical agility refers to an educator's ability to dynamically and effectively modify teaching methods to accommodate the unique and evolving needs of students across different learning environments. This skill becomes particularly crucial in Hybrid-Flexible (HyFlex) classrooms, where instructors are challenged to manage and engage both synchronous learners attending in real time and asynchronous learners participating at their own pace. To succeed in such settings, teachers must quickly shift between diverse instructional approaches to ensure all students remain connected and supported regardless of how they choose to participate. Key elements of pedagogical agility include flexible lesson planning that seamlessly integrates activities suitable for both face-to-face and online learners, differentiated instruction that adapts teaching styles and materials to address the varied ways students absorb information in physical and virtual spaces, and responsive feedback that is delivered promptly and personalized to meet individual learner needs, irrespective of their mode of engagement. This multifaceted adaptability ensures that learning remains effective, inclusive, and engaging across multiple formats.

Integrating Digital Competency and Pedagogical Agility: The combination of digital proficiency and pedagogical agility equips educators with the ability to design and deliver learning experiences that are both inclusive and engaging, regardless of the learning environment. For instance, a teacher who is skilled in using digital technologies can effortlessly transition from leading face-to-face classroom discussions to managing and facilitating conversations in online forums, ensuring all students remain actively involved. At the same time, pedagogical agility enables the instructor to adapt their teaching strategies, modify lesson content, and adjust assessment methods to suit the diverse ways students choose to engage, whether in person or remotely. Effectively implementing the HyFlex teaching model requires educators to continually develop their skills through professional learning opportunities and to remain open to experimenting with innovative instructional approaches. To foster this growth, educational institutions play a crucial role by offering comprehensive training programs, providing access to necessary technological tools, and delivering ongoing technical support designed specifically to meet the challenges and demands of HyFlex education. This combined effort creates a supportive environment that empowers teachers to confidently navigate hybrid teaching landscapes and ensures students receive a rich, flexible learning experience. Table 3 illustrates a hypothetical Faculty Competency Metrics for AI-Driven HyFlex Teaching.

Table 3. A hypothetical faculty competency metrics for AI-driven HyFlex teaching

Name of the Competency	Competency Details	Benchmarks expected (KPIs)	Level Desirable
Instructional Design for AI-Driven HyFlex Teaching	Capability to create adaptable and inclusive lesson plans that effectively engage both on-campus and remote students, ensuring equitable learning experiences across all participation modes	• **Unified Content Delivery**: Course materials are thoughtfully structured to ensure consistency and alignment, whether delivered in-person, online synchronously, or asynchronously. • **Integrated Lesson Planning**: Each lesson is designed to include a balance of live (synchronous) and self-paced (asynchronous) activities, providing flexibility while maintaining instructional continuity. • **Clear and Consistent Objectives**: Well-defined learning goals and measurable outcomes are communicated clearly across all formats, ensuring that all students—regardless of participation mode—achieve the same academic standards.	Proficient
Ability to use AI-Driven Tools & Techniques	Capability to select, use, and evaluate appropriate AI tools to support teaching and learning.	• Use of AI for personalized feedback or content generation • AI tools embedded in course delivery • Evaluation of AI impact on student learning	Advanced
Technology Acumen	Proficiency in using platforms essential for HyFlex delivery (e.g., LMS, video conferencing, digital collaboration tools).	• Confident use of LMS • Effective facilitation of live sessions • Use of online polling, gamification exercises, AI-driven analytics	Proficient
Inclusive and Accessible Teaching	Ability to create inclusive, accessible learning environments using digital tools.	• Course materials meet accessibility standards • Students with diverse needs actively participate • Use of digital course contents, transcripts, online learning resources etc	Basic Proficient
Ability to assess & give feedback	Use of AI and digital tools to create fair, effective, and timely assessments.	• Use of AI for auto-grading, feedback, or rubric creation • Develop Assessment strategies for hybrid modes of teaching & learning • Timely, personalized feedback for learners	Basic Proficient

Factors Influencing AI Readiness for HyFlex Teaching

Successfully integrating artificial intelligence (AI) into HyFlex teaching requires a multifaceted approach. Several critical factors (Table 4) influence how prepared educators are to adopt AI technologies within flexible learning environments. AI readiness in HyFlex teaching is not solely about having the latest technology—it's about preparing educators with the mindset, skills, support, and ethical grounding to integrate AI in ways that enhance learning. As institutions and educators navigate this evolving landscape, a holistic approach to readiness will be essential for sustainable and impactful adoption.

Table 4. Factors influencing AI readiness for HyFlex teaching

Factors influencing AI readiness for HyFlex Teaching	**Details**
Educator Mindsets and Beliefs	One of the foundational elements of AI readiness is educators' attitudes toward AI. Faculty members who view AI positively are more inclined to explore and implement these tools in their practice. Their perception of AI's usefulness, ease of use, and potential to enhance student learning significantly affects adoption. Confidence in using technology—also known as technological self-efficacy—is essential.
Training, Resources, and Infrastructure	To effectively use AI in teaching, educators must have access to high-quality training and ongoing professional development. This includes workshops, hands-on experiences, and peer collaboration. Equally important is the availability of necessary resources such as compatible hardware, software, and reliable internet connectivity. Without adequate infrastructure, even the most innovative AI tools may remain underutilized.
Understanding and Literacy in AI	Teachers must develop a foundational understanding of how AI functions and its educational applications. AI literacy empowers educators to evaluate tools critically, make informed decisions, and use AI in ways that support their teaching goals. Awareness of the data used by AI systems—including its quality, sources, and accessibility—is also essential for effective implementation.
Pedagogical Alignment and Classroom Relevance	AI tools should support and align with existing teaching methodologies and curriculum objectives. Tools that seamlessly fit into a teacher's instructional approach are more likely to be adopted and sustained. In a HyFlex setting, this means AI must accommodate both in-person and remote learners and adapt to diverse student needs.
Institutional and Cultural Support	Leadership commitment and a supportive school culture are pivotal for AI readiness. Institutions must actively encourage innovation, provide clear policies, and foster an environment where teachers feel safe to experiment and adapt. Organizational encouragement helps normalize AI integration as part of the broader educational vision.
Ethical and Contextual Awareness	Educators must be mindful of ethical issues related to AI, such as data privacy, algorithmic bias, and fairness. Understanding these implications ensures responsible use of AI and promotes trust among students and parents. Furthermore, AI tools should be chosen based on their relevance to specific subjects and student demographics to ensure meaningful and equitable impact.

Faculty Challenges in Managing Multi-Modal Engagement in HyFlex Teaching Model

Implementing HyFlex teaching brings considerable promise in terms of flexibility and accessibility, but it also introduces several challenges—particularly in maintaining student engagement across multiple learning modes. Instructors must find ways to ensure that in-person, live online, and asynchronous learners all receive equitable learning experiences. Creating this balance is difficult, as in-person students often benefit from direct interaction, while remote and asynchronous students may feel disconnected or excluded. Designing lessons that are equally engaging across these modes requires careful planning and deliberate instructional strategies. Figure 2 presents a pictorial representation of these challenges.

Figure 2. Faculty challenges in managing multi-modal engagement in HyFlex Teaching Model

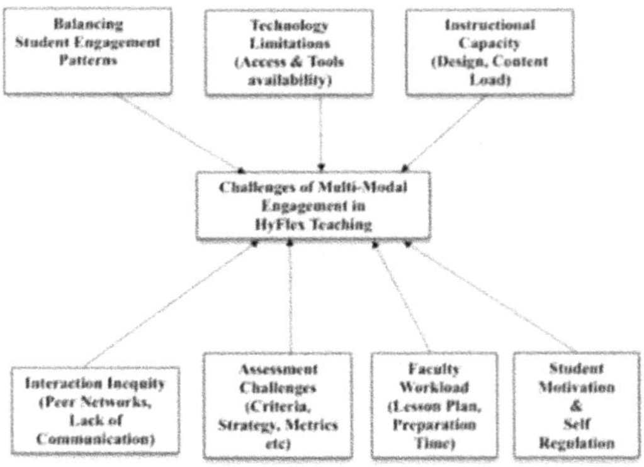

Technological issues are another major barrier to multi-modal engagement. Not all students have equal access to the necessary devices, software, or stable internet connectivity, which can limit participation—especially for those attending remotely. Even within the classroom, technical disruptions such as audio problems or poor video quality can hinder communication and diminish the overall learning experience. Teachers also face a steep learning curve when it comes to using new technologies effectively and consistently across platforms, adding to the complexity of hybrid instruction.

Additionally, maintaining student interaction and motivation is a common concern in HyFlex classrooms. Remote learners, particularly those participating asynchronously, often face difficulties staying engaged and self-regulated without the structure and accountability of a physical classroom. At the same time, instructors may struggle to facilitate meaningful peer interaction between online and in-person students, which can weaken the sense of community and collaboration. These differences can result in uneven participation and learning outcomes across modalities.

Finally, the overall workload for educators significantly increases under the HyFlex model. Planning and delivering lessons that cater to multiple formats requires more time, resources, and energy. Educators must also rethink assessment methods to ensure they are fair, accessible, and effective across all learning environments. Without adequate institutional support, training, and access to tools, teachers may experience fatigue or frustration. To overcome these challenges, institutions must invest in professional development, technological infrastructure, and policies that support inclusive, high-quality hybrid education.

FACULTY DEVELOPMENT STRATEGIES FOR AI-DRIVEN HYFLEX TEACHING

The integration of Artificial Intelligence (AI), particularly Generative AI (GenAI), is revolutionizing how educators approach HyFlex course design. In HyFlex settings—where students can choose between attending in person, joining live online, or working asynchronously—AI tools offer powerful solutions to personalize learning, automate content development, and enhance engagement. A focused, week-long hybrid workshop can support faculty in exploring these innovations by providing both live sessions and asynchronous opportunities for hands-on experimentation and reflection.

Strategy 1: Enhancing Course Design with AI: One of the core goals of faculty development in this context is helping instructors leverage AI to plan and build more flexible, engaging HyFlex courses. AI can assist in developing dynamic learning materials that suit multiple formats, such as auto-generating quizzes, summaries, or adapting in-person lectures for asynchronous learners. Tools like custom GPTs also enable instructors to create interactive course assistants, guiding students through content, answering questions, or providing tailored study advice—especially useful when learners are working independently.

Strategy 2: Aligning FDP Content with desirable Student Outcomes: To equip educators for AI-enhanced HyFlex teaching, the workshop should combine guided practice, ethical reflection, and collaborative creation. Faculty participants will engage in labs, discussions, and design sprints to create adaptable learning activities, assessments, or support tools. They'll leave with tangible outputs—such as a custom GPT or redesigned module—that they can implement immediately and share with peers. Ultimately, the workshop aims to build a community of practice that embraces innovation while staying grounded in effective, inclusive pedagogy.

Strategy 3: Ongoing Professional Development Programs: Institutions should provide comprehensive training programs that emphasize AI literacy, HyFlex instructional design, and ethical use of emerging technologies. This can be achieved through a combination of interactive workshops, on-demand webinars, and structured peer mentoring. These initiatives will help educators and staff develop the necessary skills to effectively integrate AI tools into teaching and learning, promote flexible and inclusive instructional methods, and uphold ethical standards in the use of technology.

Strategy 4: Develop Technical Support Systems for Faculty: Offering accessible and responsive IT support plays a critical role in easing faculty concerns related to technology use. When instructors know that help is readily available, they are more likely to feel confident in trying new digital tools and teaching methods. Prompt, user-friendly support services—such as live chat, help desks, and dedicated tech liaisons—can create a supportive environment that reduces frustration and technical barriers. This encouragement not only lowers anxiety but also fosters a culture of innovation, where faculty feel empowered to experiment with technology to enhance teaching and learning outcomes.

Strategy 5: Develop Collaborative Communities: Setting up dedicated forums where faculty members engaged in AI-enhanced HyFlex teaching can come together to exchange their most effective strategies, openly discuss the challenges they encounter, and keep each other informed about the latest advancements in AI technology helps build a collaborative environment. This shared space encourages ongoing learning and adaptation, ultimately fostering a culture where continuous improvement and innovation in teaching methods are prioritized and supported.

PRINCIPLES OF EFFECTIVE FACULTY TRAINING IN HYFLEX CONTEXTS

HyFlex (Hybrid-Flexible) learning environments combine face-to-face and online instruction, allowing students to choose how they participate in each session. Faculty training in these contexts requires a specialized approach that supports instructors in navigating the complexities of dual-mode teaching. The following principles (Table 5) guide effective faculty training for HyFlex models:

Table 5. Principles of effective faculty training in AI-driven HyFlex teaching

Principle	Details	Desirable Student Outcomes
Principle of Pedagogical Flexibility	Faculty must develop skills to design lessons adaptable to both in-person and remote learners. Training should focus on creating learning activities that are effective regardless of delivery mode, ensuring equal engagement and access for all students.	Students will be effectively engaged with course content and participate actively in learning activities across both in-person and remote settings. They will be able to utilize accessible resources that support equal learning opportunities, demonstrate enhanced collaboration and communication skills in hybrid environments, and adapt to various teaching methods to maintain consistent engagement and success regardless of delivery mode.
Principle of Technological Proficiency	Faculty need comprehensive training on the technology platforms and tools that enable HyFlex teaching, including video conferencing software, learning management systems, and collaborative tools. Confidence with technology reduces barriers and enhances teaching effectiveness.	Students will be having the ability to confidently navigate and engage with digital learning platforms, actively participate in both in-person and online environments, and collaborate effectively using various technological tools. Students will be able to overcome technological barriers and maximizes their overall educational experience
Principle of Inclusive Teaching	HyFlex training should prioritize inclusive strategies that address diverse learner needs. Faculty should learn how to create accessible content, foster participation across modalities, and accommodate various learning styles and environments.	Increased student engagement and participation, regardless of their learning environment or style. Students will benefit from accessible course materials designed to meet diverse needs and experience inclusive teaching approaches that support their unique learning preferences.
Principle of Experimentation and Innovation	Because HyFlex teaching is relatively new for many, faculty training should encourage instructors to experiment with different instructional approaches and technologies, promoting a growth mindset and willingness to adapt.	Increased student adaptability and openness to diverse learning methods, as well as enhanced engagement through varied instructional approaches. Students will develop skills to thrive in dynamic learning environments, benefiting from faculty who continuously explore and integrate AI-driven tools and teaching strategies.

IMPLICATIONS OF THE STUDY

Theoretical Implications: AI integration in higher education signals a fundamental shift in educational theory, redefining the roles of instructors, learners, and institutions. It moves beyond technology use to challenge traditional pedagogies, promoting adaptive, learner-centered models. The HyFlex approach exemplifies this change, combining in-person, synchronous, and asynchronous learning through AI-driven tools that support diverse needs. Education becomes a flexible, multimodal experience, no longer confined by time or place. As a result, educators evolve into facilitators, designers, and technologists, while institutions must realign strategies to prioritize accessibility, inclusion, and innovation. AI thus reimagines—not just enhances—the foundations of higher education.

Practical Implications: The integration of AI in higher education is transforming teaching, learning, and institutional operations. Tools like adaptive platforms, automated assessments, and virtual assistants personalize learning and streamline workflows. With the rise of HyFlex models, faculty must adapt content for in-person, synchronous, and asynchronous delivery, requiring new skills in pedagogy and technology. Institutions must invest in digital infrastructure, faculty training, and ethical guidelines to support responsible AI use. As students gain flexibility in how they engage, education shifts toward learner-driven, inclusive models. This shift demands a rethinking of institutional strategies, and the chapter introduces a proposed competency framework to guide faculty in AI-driven HyFlex teaching.

Social Implications: AI integration and the rise of HyFlex models in higher education are reshaping access, equity, and participation of faculty & students. By personalizing learning and offering flexible formats, they empower students from varied backgrounds—such as those with disabilities, working adults, caregivers, and remote learners—to pursue education more freely. These innovations help bridge long-standing gaps and promote a more inclusive, student-centered model. However, they also raise concerns around digital access, data privacy, and technology disparities. To ensure equitable benefits, thoughtful ethical and social frameworks are essential.

SCOPE OF FURTHER STUDIES

The evolving AI landscape in higher education calls for focused empirical research on how AI-integrated HyFlex models are transforming teaching, student engagement, and institutional strategy. While early discussions highlight AI's potential in personalization and flexibility, future studies must assess its effectiveness, equity, and ethical impact across diverse contexts. Key areas include the influence of adaptive tools on learning outcomes, faculty preparedness for multi-modal teaching, and the use of generative AI in instructional design and assessment. Long-term research is also needed to understand AI's impact on access, equity, and learner autonomy—especially for underserved groups. Evidence-based inquiry will be essential to guide responsible innovation aligned with educational values.

CONCLUSIONS

In summary, the landscape of higher education is undergoing a profound transformation driven by the integration of AI and Hybrid-Flexible (HyFlex) teaching models. AI is no longer a peripheral tool but a central force enabling personalized instruction, automating routine academic tasks, and fostering more engaging, student-centered learning environments. At the same time, the HyFlex model meets the growing demand for flexibility and equity by allowing students to choose how they engage with learning—whether in person, online, or asynchronously—based on their unique circumstances. The convergence of AI and HyFlex methodologies necessitates a fundamental reimagining of faculty roles, highlighting the need for new competencies in instructional design, digital fluency, and adaptive pedagogy. To fully realize the potential of AI-enhanced HyFlex education, institutions must implement clear frameworks that define and support faculty readiness. Despite ongoing challenges—such as ensuring consistent learning experiences across modalities and addressing the digital divide—this shift represents a strategic move toward more inclusive, responsive, and sustainable models of higher education. Moving forward, an ethically grounded, holistic approach will be essential to shaping future-ready institutions capable of meeting the diverse needs of learners in the AI era.

REFERENCES

Abulaiti, M. (2024). *Higher Education in the Era of AI.*, DOI: 10.4018/979-8-3693-2857-6.ch014

Adi Badiozaman, I. F., Ng, A., & Mung Ling, V. (2025). "Here we go again": Unfolding HE students' hybrid experience and resilience during post-covid times. *Asia Pacific Journal of Education*, *45*(3), 920–941. DOI: 10.1080/02188791.2023.2238324

Albashiry, N. M., Belhadj, H., & Al-Smadi, M. (2024). A Digital Competency Framework for University Teachers: Towards Agile and Sustainable Curriculum. *2024 ASU International Conference in Emerging Technologies for Sustainability and Intelligent Systems (ICETSIS)*, 1491–1494. DOI: 10.1109/ICETSIS61505.2024.10459701

Aldosemani, T. (2023). Adopting HyFlex Course Design: Actions for Policymakers, Researchers, and Practitioners. In *Active and Transformative Learning in STEAM Disciplines* (pp. 197–227). Emerald Publishing Limited. DOI: 10.1108/978-1-83753-618-420231010

Alenezi, M. (2023). Digital Learning and Digital Institution in Higher Education. *Education Sciences*, *13*(1), 88. DOI: 10.3390/educsci13010088

Alnasib, B. N. M. (2023). Factors Affecting Faculty Members' Readiness to Integrate Artificial Intelligence into Their Teaching Practices: A Study from the Saudi Higher Education Context. *International Journal of Learning. Teaching and Educational Research*, *22*(8), 465–491. DOI: 10.26803/ijlter.22.8.24

Baker, S., Gunn Watkinson, M., Honeyman, F., Mowll, J., & Tyulkina, S. (2024). Rethinking student engagement for 'hyflex' teaching and learning in post-compulsory settings: Acknowledging flexibility and agency needed for unplanned events. *International Journal of Lifelong Education*, *43*(4), 432–447. DOI: 10.1080/02601370.2024.2359595

Beatty, B. J. (2019). *Hybrid-Flexible course design: Implementing student-directed hybrid classes* (1st ed.). EdTech Books. DOI: 10.59668/33

Bowden, J. L.-H. (2022). Analogues of engagement: Assessing tertiary student engagement in contemporary face-to-face and blended learning contexts. *Higher Education Research & Development*, *41*(4), 997–1012. DOI: 10.1080/07294360.2021.1901666

Cumming, T. M., Han, C., & Gilanyi, L. (2024). University student and instructor experiences with HyFlex learning: A scoping review. *Computers and Education Open*, *7*, 100229. DOI: 10.1016/j.caeo.2024.100229

Das, S., Mutsuddi, I., & Ray, N. (2024). *Artificial Intelligence in Adaptive Education.*, DOI: 10.4018/979-8-3693-8227-1.ch002

Filiz, O., Kaya, M. H., & Adiguzel, T. (2025). Teachers and AI: Understanding the factors influencing AI integration in K-12 education. *Education and Information Technologies*, *30*(13), 17931–17967. Advance online publication. DOI: 10.1007/s10639-025-13463-2

Gudoniene, D., Staneviciene, E., Huet, I., Dickel, J., Dieng, D., Degroote, J., Rocio, V., Butkiene, R., & Casanova, D. (2025). Hybrid Teaching and Learning in Higher Education: A Systematic Literature Review. *Sustainability (Basel)*, *17*(2), 756. DOI: 10.3390/su17020756

Hews, R., McNamara, J., & Nay, Z. (2022). Prioritising lifeload over learning load: Understanding post-pandemic student engagement. *Journal of University Teaching & Learning Practice*, *19*(2), 128–146. DOI: 10.53761/1.19.2.9

Howell, E. (2022). HyFlex model of higher education: Understanding the promise of flexibility. *On the Horizon. On the Horizon*, *30*(4), 173–181. DOI: 10.1108/OTH-04-2022-0019

Johnson, E., Morwane, R., Dada, S., Pretorius, G., & Lotriet, M. (2018). Adult Learners' Perspectives on Their Engagement in a Hybrid Learning Postgraduate Programme. *The Journal of Continuing Higher Education*, *66*(2), 88–105. DOI: 10.1080/07377363.2018.1469071

Kim, J. (2024). Types of teacher-AI collaboration in K-12 classroom instruction: Chinese teachers' perspective. *Education and Information Technologies*, *29*(13), 17433–17465. DOI: 10.1007/s10639-024-12523-3

Kohnke, L., & Moorhouse, B. L. (2021). Adopting HyFlex in higher education in response to COVID-19: Students' perspectives. *Open Learning*, *36*(3), 231–244. DOI: 10.1080/02680513.2021.1906641

Markauskaite, L., Carvalho, L., & Fawns, T. (2023). The role of teachers in a sustainable university: From digital competencies to postdigital capabilities. *Educational Technology Research and Development*, *71*(1), 181–198. DOI: 10.1007/s11423-023-10199-z PMID: 36779078

Melek Koc, E. (2024). LMS-supported HyFlex clinical supervision model: Illuminating perspectives from teacher candidates in the department of English language teaching. *Heliyon*, *10*(8), e29503. DOI: 10.1016/j.heliyon.2024.e29503 PMID: 38681619

Morrison, L., Kay, R., Atkinson, H., Mann, A., & Tepylo, D. (2025). *EXPLORING THE EMERGING LANDSCAPE OF HYFLEX TEACHING AND LEARNING IN HIGHER EDUCATION: A SCOPING REVIEW.* 1330–1338. DOI: 10.21125/inted.2025.0421

Noichun, N., Kaewrattanapat, N., Khaengkhan, M., Suwanajote, N., Nookhong, J., & Pintuma, S. (2024). READINESS FOR THE HYFLEX INSTRUCTIONAL MODALITY IMPLEMENTATION. *The 2024 International Academic Multidisciplines Research Conference in Hokkaido.*

Radcliffe, D. (2009). A pedagogy-space-technology (PST) framework for designing and evaluating learning places. In Radcliffe, D., Wilson, H., Powell, D., & Tibbetts, B. (Eds.), *Learning spaces in higher education: Positive outcomes by design.*

Romero-Hall, E., & Ripine, C. (2021). Hybrid Flexible Instruction: Exploring Faculty Preparedness. *Online Learning : the Official Journal of the Online Learning Consortium, 25*(3). Advance online publication. DOI: 10.24059/olj.v25i3.2426

Ruano-Borbalan, J.-C. (2025). The transformative impact of artificial intelligence on higher education: A critical reflection on current trends and futures directions. *International Journal of Chinese Education, 14*(1), 2212585X251319364. Advance online publication. DOI: 10.1177/2212585X251319364

Sanders, D. A., & Mukhari, S. S. (2024). Lecturers' perceptions of the influence of AI on a blended learning approach in a South African higher education institution. *Discover Education, 3*(1), 135. DOI: 10.1007/s44217-024-00235-2

Chapter 7
Real-World Case Studies:
AI-Enhanced HyFlex Implementation in Diverse Cultural and Institutional Settings

Bo Zhang
http://orcid.org/0000-0002-6529-8720
Xi'an Jiaotong-Liverpool University, China

Kexin Chen
http://orcid.org/0009-0002-0677-9927
Xi'an Jiaotong-Liverpool University, China

ABSTRACT

This chapter summarizes a set of real-world case studies on AI-enhanced HyFlex implementation in higher education across different cultural, disciplinary, and institutional contexts, organized using the Community of Inquiry framework. It reviews documented uses of XR-based virtual campuses, immersive and gamified 3D environments, and AI-supported tools to facilitate intercultural collaboration and learning adaptation. The chapter also examines immersive technologies applied to abstract and complex subjects, including collaborative VR laboratories, HyFlex-VR and metaverse-based learning designs, multi-institutional VR learning environments, and AI-mediated virtual spaces for philosophy education. In addition, it synthesizes cases of large language model applications for assessment and instructional alignment, such as automated grading, process-oriented AI tutor use, and course-aligned LLM systems. Further cases address AI and XR for professional skills training and the use of generative AI and avatars to support inclusive and special needs education.

DOI: 10.4018/979-8-3373-6182-6.ch007

INTRODUCTION

Advances in AI and XR technologies have enhanced the HyFlex model by enabling more flexible, adaptive, and immersive learning experiences while maintaining equivalency across participation modes (Beatty, 2019). XR environments, particularly immersive VR, provide shared spaces for experiential and cross-cultural learning and serve as effective testbeds for examining instructional design and learning processes (Radianti et al., 2020). From a Community of Inquiry perspective, AI avatars act as pedagogical agents that enhance social and teaching presence in XR-enabled HyFlex settings (Sikström et al., 2024). The following cases examine how these technologies support HyFlex learning across diverse educational and cultural contexts.

THEORETICAL FRAMEWORK: THE COMMUNITY OF INQUIRY (CoI)

Community of Inquiry (CoI) framework is a model for understanding how deep learning happens in online and hybrid educational environments (Garrison et al., 2000). It posits that effective learning emerges through the interaction of three kinds of presence: cognitive presence, social presence, and teaching presence. Cognitive presence refers to the ability of learners to think critically and construct meaning via continuous reflection and discussion. Students first identify the problem, then search for various viewpoints and information, then integrate their own ideas into a complete content, and finally use these new knowledge to solve practical problems. Social presence refers to the ability of learners to express their true selves in a learning community. This ability includes expressing emotions, engaging in open conversations, and creating a sense of belonging. Learners with a sense of social presence tend to interact more frequently with others, exchange ideas, and collaborate, thereby reducing their feelings of loneliness. Teaching presence is the role that teachers or facilitators play in guiding and supporting students' learning. It encompasses aspects such as designing the learning process, setting goals, organizing content, encouraging interaction, and providing feedback. Teaching presence ensures that the learning environment is properly arranged and that students can receive the necessary assistance to achieve excellent results. CoI framework stresses that these three forms of presence are mutually reinforcing and collectively contribute to deep learning and collaborative knowledge construction (Garrison et al., 2000).

1. XR FOR INTERCULTURAL COLLABORATION AND ADAPTATION

As information technology becomes increasingly integrated into higher education, fostering students' social presence in blended learning environments has emerged as a critical determinant of educational quality. It is important to understand the role of social presence in the CoI framework because it enables learners to reduce psychological distance, fostering the trust and openness of each other. The emergence of AI and virtual technologies enables students to engage in immersive communication and learning in various cross-cultural environments and institutional scenarios. Simulating real-world cross-cultural situations by different AI tools, students can handle the problems they face during communication (Klimova & Chen, 2024). This has greatly enhanced the flexibility of the HyFlex teaching model.

1.1 Virtual Campus: Using XR for Cross-Cultural Integration

Immersive virtual reality could make students more involved, give them more hands-on practical skills, and help them learn better by putting them in the context. High degree of immersion makes it easier for people to understand the culture and feel emotions (Stracke et al., 2025). Zhang carried out a study to assess the applicability of online remote collaboration tools for cross-cultural learning (Zhang et al., 2023). The results indicate that the virtual environment aligns with students' preferences for remote collaboration software, and virtual technology performs effectively in online cross-cultural learning contexts (Zhang et al., 2023). To promote cross-cultural communication between Chinese students and local Irish students, a study was conducted based on the Terf® virtual platform to build an immersive virtual campus, and through inclusive design and cross-cultural collaboration mechanisms, it effectively enhanced students' abilities in language, culture, and learning adaptation (Zhang et al., 2017). For instance, to help students become familiar with the campus and learning environment before arriving in Ireland, the development team embedded a 3D model of the university campus (Figure 1) in the virtual campus.

Figure 1. A 3D model of University College Dublin (UCD) embedded in the virtual campus

Students can greatly enhance their communication adaptability, cultural perception and team cooperation abilities through real tasks such as cross-cultural cooperation projects (Knutzen et al., 2025).

1.2 Immersive Gamification in Blended Learning: Enhancing Intercultural Engagement and Outcomes

In the field of modern education, integrating gamification elements into blended learning environments has become a promising approach to enhancing students' learning outcomes (Thi Binh et al., 2025). Game-based learning is gaining popularity in language education and the interaction games can boost students' engagement and stimulate intercultural communication in virtual exchanges (Canto & Jauregi-Ondarra, 2021). Yang investigated how different gamification elements affect the learning behaviors of college students in virtual learning communities. The study was conducted on students from some institutions using the Chinese higher education virtual learning platform (Yang et al., 2025). The study distinguished between immersive, achievement-oriented, and social gamification mechanisms and analyzed their effects using the cognitive-affective-attitude framework. The research results showed that immersive gamification elements such as scenario-based tasks, narrative-oriented activities, and challenge-oriented learning environments greatly improved students' learning engagement and sustained participation. Also in Zhang's research, cross-cultural students did teamwork tasks inside a gamified 3D world and compared it to a text-based cooperation situation (Zhang et al., 2022). From the research result we can see that the 3D interactive games under certain circumstances greatly improved the students' interest and engagement in cooperative work and fostered the exchange of language and culture knowledge.

The research shows that by putting cross-cultural cooperation into immersive, goal-oriented game situations, it was found that immersive gamification could lessen students' communication problems and encourage culturally adaptive interactions in virtual learning spaces (Zhang et al., 2022).

1.3 AI-Based Interventions: Enhancing Cross-Cultural Competence and Adaptability in a Globalized Environment

AI can provide a totally customized learning experience with advanced algorithms. These algorithms will change the content and ways according to what each student needs and their culture background. Personalized learning may result in better language learning results and help students develop a richer sense of culture (Zhang et al., 2024). A recent study introduced AI-based teaching interventions into the English as a Foreign Language (EFL) courses for undergraduate students in China. The research results show that with the assistance of artificial intelligence in learning, students' cultural knowledge, open-mindedness, and communication skills have significantly improved (Ma & Yang, 2025). Beyond language education, artificial intelligence can also play an important role in diverse cultural university environments. For instance, a survey conducted on graduate students from 9 different countries indicated that if artificial intelligence tools possess empathy and support functions, these tools can help students engage in cross-cultural communication and make it easier for them to adapt to new social and academic environments (Sarwari et al., 2024). Additionally, a study explored how to incorporate AI into STEM education to cultivate students' cross-cultural skills (Chen et al., 2025). Through the language assistance and cultural adaptation tasks provided by artificial intelligence, students from different backgrounds can better collaborate.

These cases show that virtual reality supports immersive language and cultural learning through collaborative tasks, shared cultural scene construction, and game-based interaction, thereby reducing cross-cultural adaptation barriers and fostering cultural empathy. Cultural empathy, in turn, mediates the relationship between emotional and social competencies and academic self-efficacy, enhancing students' social presence and engagement in HyFlex learning environments (Finkelstein & Soffer-Vital, 2025). At the same time, XR-supported intercultural learning raises ethical and safety concerns, including risks of cyber harassment in anonymous virtual spaces and physical discomfort such as motion sickness caused by prolonged immersion (Bailenson, 2018). These issues highlight the necessity for institutions to establish clear behavioral guidelines and thoughtful learning design to ensure that enhanced social presence is achieved in a safe and inclusive environment.

2. IMMERSIVE TECHNOLOGIES FOR ABSTRACT AND COMPLEX SUBJECTS

Cognitive presence is an important indicator for evaluating the quality of online learning experience, as it requires students to construct knowledge through continuous reflection and discussion. This process can deepen their understanding of concepts and their own experiences. Therefore, cognitive presence can serve as a guiding model, helping the AI-Enhanced HyFlex model to assist students in better learning in a constructive way. Researchers have also been exploring various teaching strategies to enhance the cognitive presence, thereby maximizing the quality of the online learning experience (Sadaf & Olesova, 2017).

2.1 Asymmetric Collaborative Learning in VR Labs: Enhancing Conceptual Reasoning and Decision-Making

In the fields of science and engineering, many schools are now using virtual reality technology to recreate complex laboratory environments (Radianti et al., 2020; Jensen & Konradsen, 2018).This technology enables students to conduct experimental operations safely and flexibly in a virtual environment. The introduction of virtual reality technology is aimed at helping students better understand abstract concepts, enhancing their experimental decision-making abilities, and making their learning process more enjoyable (Makransky et al., 2022). A study by De Lorenzis provides a clear example. The researchers created an immersive virtual reality laboratory for a university chemistry course (Figure 2), and adopted the "asymmetric collaborative learning" method they proposed to observe the students' performance (De Lorenzis et al., 2024). In this research, students are divided into two roles which is operator and assistant. The operator wears a VR headset and carries out the experiment inside the virtual lab. The assistant works at a desktop computer, where they view information such as reaction mechanisms and guidelines, and support the operator. This design successfully addresses the practical problems encountered in chemical experiments, such as the scarcity of virtual reality devices and the large number of students. At the same time, it also promotes cooperation among students. This study found that this role-based collaborative virtual reality model is particularly adept at enhancing students' thinking ability regarding concepts and their ability to make decisions based on experiments. Compared with students who study alone, students in collaborative groups perform better in selecting reaction conditions, evaluating chemical processes, and interpreting experimental results. The reason for this might be that working together in a shared immersive environment can reduce students' cognitive load and prompt them to systematically analyze experimental data (Antonelli et al., 2023). Regarding user experience, students working alone and those in collaborative groups had similar levels of engagement, immersion, and usability.

In conclusion, this study shows that the combination of virtual reality and AI teaching design can enhance learners' conceptual understanding and support their collaborative learning. In situations where laboratory work is difficult to carry out or where institutional resources are limited, virtual reality can still provide a practical and comprehensive solution for laboratory-based courses.

Figure 2. Virtual laboratory environment

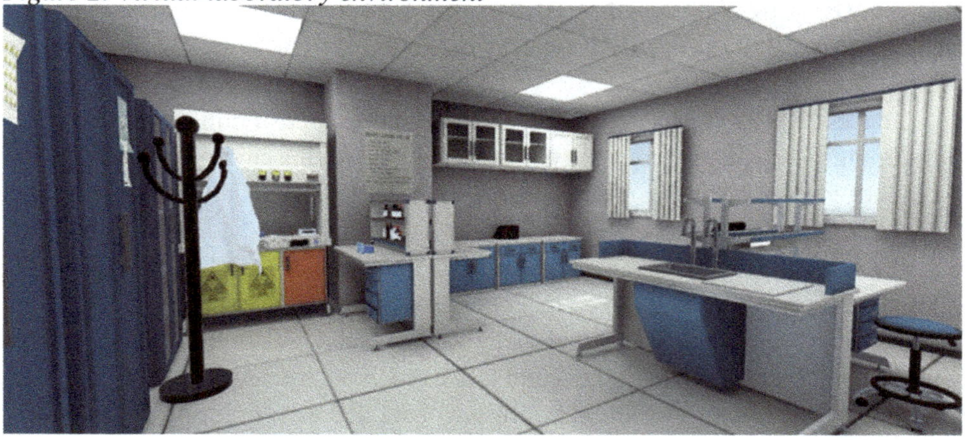

2.2 HyFlex-VR and Metaverse Integration: Fostering Systematic and Innovative Thinking

Another study designed the HyFlex-VR learning model, which combines multimedia technology and pedagogy into four types of learning modes: face-to-face, synchronous online, asynchronous online, and VR (Mahande et al., 2025). This model gives students all the freedom and control they need, so they can pick the best way to learn. This research shows that the HyFlex-VR model greatly improves students' interest in schoolwork and helps them think more creatively and critically (Mahande et al., 2025). And it is noteworthy that the VR modality creates an immersive and enjoyable learning atmosphere for students, making the learning process more vivid and interesting. This research helps teachers understand how to innovate teaching methods in universities. By combining HyFlex with technologies such as virtual reality, it can enable students to learn more effectively and gain personalized learning experiences. In order to explore how the learning ecosystem of the metaverse can enhance students' systematic thinking and innovative thinking, a new teaching model was created and evaluated using the Snoopathon methodology (Karapakdee et al., 2024). Snoopathon is an inquiry-based pedagogical approach rooted in design thinking, which guides students to "snoop" for information like detectives, analyze problems from multiple perspectives, and generate innovative solutions.

The research discovered that merging the metaverse learning ecosystem with the Snoopathon technique considerably improved participants' systemic and innovative thought. It indicates that with the aid of immersive technology and new methods, we can train the complicated thinking skills of students (Rasheed et al., 2021).

2.3 REVEALING Project: Enhancing Learning through Immersive Virtual Reality Learning Environments

The REVEALING project, a multi-institutional European initiative, focused on developing and evaluating immersive virtual reality learning environments (VRLEs) for higher education courses (Aufenanger et al., 2025). Researchers from institutions in Cyprus, Germany, Greece, Poland, and Portugal joined forces to create five different VRLEs. These environments included topics such as ancient Greek technology, marine biology (sea urchin size), linear algebra, and historic expeditions. Students and teachers could enter 3D virtual classrooms or labs, where they could interact with virtual objects or experiments and talk to each other using avatars. And these virtual classrooms can give them a fully involved and active learning experience. One example is the VRLE made for a linear algebra class that lets students see vector spaces and changes in 3D space. Students can change the geometry and see it changing right away and learn about difficult ideas in math easily. This immersive visualization technology gives math teachers a better method than the tradition drawings and books. The technology makes it easier for students to grasp abstract ideas by giving them something more tangible. Another VRLE was created for a history class so that students could virtually walk along a recreated historical expedition route. They can look at virtual arts and talk with other people in the virtual world. This approach improves students' involvement and comprehension of historical information. Many students said that compared to normal classrooms, these places made them more interested and helped them understand hard or tricky concept better. They also felt a greater sense of being present in the virtual learning setting.

This case shows that when immersive virtual reality is used in the higher education curriculum, it can greatly improve the way that students learn (Llanos-Ruiz et al., 2025). Virtual Reality gives students new ways to interact and understand things, which can supplement or enhance regular classroom instruction (Nesenbergs et al., 2021).

2.4 AI-Mediated Immersive Learning in Philosophy: Visualizing Abstract Concepts for Generation Z

In an experiment at the University of Győr, the researchers explored how immersive virtual environments and artificial intelligence-assisted technologies (Figure 3) could enhance the teaching efficiency of undergraduate philosophy courses (Vehrer & Pálfalusi, 2025). The researchers concentrated their investigation on first-year students studying humanities and social sciences. These students are from Generation Z and are used to using digital and interactive media (Turner, 2015). They sought to determine whether creating an immersive virtual environment supported by an AI assistant could help students better understand and retain complex philosophical concepts (Vehrer & Pálfalusi, 2025). In the study, some first year students learned about ten core philosophical topics within a virtual environment created using the Walter's Cube platform (Walter's Cube, 2024). Walter's Cube was first made for online art galleries so people could walk around and look at the pictures hanging on the virtual walls. The research team used this technology for teaching by creating a set of virtual rooms according to the official philosophy teaching syllabus. Every room has pictures of famous thinkers and what they said, along with short notes to explain them. There are also virtual representations of spatial concepts. All these elements are displayed on the virtual walls. Students can move through the various rooms at their own pace and can repeatedly review specific philosophers or topics if they need to. In this 3D space, an artificial intelligence mediator is directly integrated. When students walk in the virtual environment, they can raise questions to this mediator either in written form or through voice. Then, the artificial intelligence will provide students with answers related to the course materials, offer explanations of concepts, and emphasize the relationships between various different viewpoints. In practice, the AI acted as a personal tutor available at any time inside the environment, especially useful when students were preparing for the exam or reviewing difficult parts of the syllabus (Essel et al., 2022). At the end of the semester, students sat the standard offline written exam that is used in the conventional version of the course. Only after completing this exam were they invited to fill out a voluntary, anonymous ten question paper survey about their experience with the virtual environment and the AI mediator (Vehrer & Pálfalusi, 2025). The results showed that about 80 percent of the participants received good or excellent grades on the final exam. Most respondents also believed that virtual materials were quite effective. Many students stated that the 3D space technology enhanced their motivation to learn and helped them maintain concentration for a longer period of time. They believed that presenting philosophical ideas in the form of images, maps, and simple charts made the abstract content more concrete and easier to understand. According to their comments, this visual and spatial presentation supported memory, because they could recall both the idea and the place where it appeared in the virtual gallery. Several students also indicated that they would welcome similar virtual and AI supported materials in other subjects.

Figure 3. Virtual gallery environment

Taken together, these cases show that combining an immersive virtual environment with an AI mediator can improve both learning outcomes and the subjective learning experience in courses that rely heavily on abstract reasoning and conceptual understanding (Vehrer & Pálfalusi, 2025). This profound understanding of the concept strengthens the students' cognitive presence because the virtual rooms and the AI guide offer another way for students to encounter the same content in a more concrete, interactive, and personally guided form (Essel et al., 2022). However, this AI-guided teaching design also faces hidden issues related to data security and physical health issue. While the XR system accurately captures learners' behaviors and physiological data to optimize teaching, it also raises problems regarding unclear privacy boundaries. Moreover, the visual fatigue and physical burden caused by intense immersive operations on students cannot be ignored. Therefore, future teaching designs need to pursue students' deep understanding while also taking into account data governance and the health of learners.

3. LLMS FOR SCALABLE FEEDBACK AND INSTRUCTIONAL ALIGNMENT

Teaching presence is central to sustaining the Community of Inquiry (CoI) in HyFlex courses, as it supports effective instructional design, learner autonomy, and learning outcomes (Garrison et al., 2000; Sadaf & Olesova, 2017). In XR-enabled HyFlex environments, AI avatars can enhance teaching presence by providing adaptive, dialogue-based guidance and feedback across learning modes, thereby extending instructional support beyond traditional classrooms (Wu et al., 2025). For example, AI avatars can identify learners' difficulties based on behavioral data, such as repeated engagement with specific content, and deliver targeted explanations or practice activities. Supported by natural language processing technologies, AI avatars are able to offer consistent and contextually appropriate feedback while remaining aligned with instructional objectives (Zhang & Dong, 2022; Zhang, Ou, & Yu, 2020).

3.1 Zero-shot LLM Grading: Automating Assignment Feedback in Higher Education

A recent study proposed a zero shot large language model framework for automatic assignment grading in higher education (Yeung et al., 2025). Instead of training a separate model for each course or building large labelled datasets, the authors relied on careful prompt design. The system receives the assignment question, an optional marking scheme and reference answer, and the student's submission. It then uses GPT-4 to assign a score and generate written feedback without any task specific fine tuning. This approach was first applied in an introductory statistics course and then extended to two graduate level courses in data management and risk management at The Chinese University of Hong Kong (Yeung et al., 2025). For students, this model produces detailed, personalized comments that explain mistakes and suggest concrete ways to improve. Teachers can make use of the overall class performance overview and common error analysis provided by the system to quickly identify the difficult points in teaching and grasp the general patterns of students' understanding of concepts. Most learners have stated that the feedback provided by AI has enhanced their comprehension skills, helping them more clearly identify the gaps in their learning and boosting their motivation to study. Especially for students with poor grades, they have given very positive evaluations of the system. They tend to prefer using this system over traditional grading by teaching assistants for their studies (Yeung et al., 2025). This case is in line with the findings of many studies, which indicate that as long as the prompts and scoring criteria are properly designed, large language models (LLMs) can provide ratings and feedback comparable to those of human raters (Poličar et al., 2025). Therefore, zero shot LLM can serve as a flexible and scalable option for educators when evaluating courses with a large volume of tasks.

By automating most of the grading and first-round feedback processes, teachers can devote more time to high-value activities such as after-class tutoring, targeted support, and curriculum design, while students can still receive rich and specific guidance for their assignments(Yeung et al., 2025).

3.2 AI-U Instructional Alignment System: A course-tuned LLM for accurate and traceable science teaching support

In a recent university science course, researchers developed the AI-University platform (Figure 4), aiming to combine high-tech subject teaching with generative artificial intelligence, providing a scalable model for AI-driven content delivery (Shojaei et al., 2025). In this case, instructors of a graduate-level course on the Finite Element Method used AI-U to fine-tune a large language model (LLM) so that it could generate responses and explanations that match the instructor's teaching style and course materials, including lecture videos, notes, textbooks, and problem sets. Overall workflow was carefully planned so as to give us a clear, correct AI helper. It includes a pipeline to prepare training data, using the parameter-efficient fine-tuning method on an open-source LLM, and adding Retrieval-Augmented Generation to ground answers in specific course materials (Wang & Singh, 2025). To get the most trust and trackability, a sample web app was made that lets students ask questions and get answers right away that go with the exact part of a course text or video they asked about (Shojaei et al., 2025; Kahl et al., 2025). Evaluation of this AI-enhanced instructional alignment showed promising results. In 86% of the test cases, the responses generated by the expert-optimized model had a higher cosine similarity with the reference materials than those produced by the basic large language model. Experienced reviewers also confirmed the scientific accuracy and consistency of the AI-U model in science teaching, indicating that AI-U is capable of generating high-quality explanations tailored to specific courses (Shojaei et al., 2025).

This case demonstrates that integrating platforms based on large language models into higher education science teaching can significantly support the delivery of teaching and the consistency of content (Jain et al., 2025).

Figure 4. Demonstration of the web application, available at https://my-ai-university .com

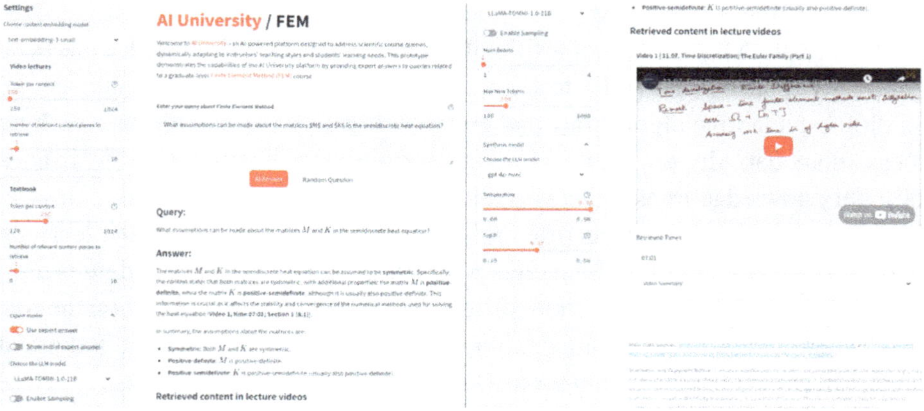

3.3 Intelligent Educational Software IES: Multi-Modal AI for Personalized Teaching and Reduced Workload

The increasing application of AI technologies in higher education is establishing various forms of Intelligent Educational Software (IES) as a key element for universities to achieve personalized learning and digital pedagogy. The latest research shows that AI driven learning analytics can greatly improve students' efficiency by creating personalized learning routes according to students' behavior data and giving immediate feedback (Zawacki-Richter et al., 2019). In China, many higher education institutions are starting to use IES platforms to follow how students learn, find out about specific problems some students have, and give special help to them. The ongoing improvement of multi-modal AI technology adds more data sources for IES. This technology makes it possible for systems to incorporate information such as student voice, pictures, faces, and in-class interaction behaviors, thereby enabling more complete pedagogical observation. Take Affective Computing as an example, it is integrated into intelligent tutoring systems to recognize students' facial expressions, changes in engagement, and emotions, so teachers can understand the classroom atmosphere and change their teaching methods in real time (Shingjergji et al., 2025). Also, smart system technology has developed, so the tasks that used to take up a lot of time for teachers, such as grading work, watching over students' progress, and figuring out common issues, are now done automatically by machines (Holmes et al., 2021). This kind of automation technology enables teachers to devote more of their energy to more valuable tasks, such as designing courses and having important conversations with students to guide their learning. Similarly, a dual-perspective evaluation of the development of IES in China indicates that most teachers think that introducing intelligent systems is a good method to ease teachers' burden and promote student-centered teaching (Wu et al., 2025).

Therefore, with the support of artificial intelligence, teaching presence has been significantly enhanced in HyFlex teaching. The gradual convergence of multi-modal technologies, adaptive algorithms, and emotional analysis is making the teaching process more data-driven, while also transforming the instructor's role from a traditional knowledge transmitter into a learning designer and facilitator. However, automated feedback systems often rely on continuous analysis of the learning process and the content of assignments, which makes the way student data is used in algorithmic decision-making more opaque. Moreover, when AI takes on the role of assessment in teaching, the attribution of feedback responsibility and judgment authority may also become ambiguous. Therefore, it is necessary to clearly define the scope of application of AI feedback. Additionally, it is necessary to clarify the final decision-making authority and the explain of related algorithms to avoid the problem of teaching being overly dominated by technical logic (Kourtesis, 2024).

4. AI/XR FOR ENGAGEMENT TRACKING AND EMPIRICAL EVALUATION

In traditional teaching environments, assessing students' engagement often relies on teachers' subjective observations, post-class question-and-answer sessions, or homework. With the integration of generative AI and sensing technology, modern educational platforms are initiating a full-time, multi-dimensional assessment model. For instance, through AI to recognize students' facial expressions to analyze their emotions to assess empathy. Moreover, by using facial expression recognition algorithms to analyze the subtle movements of facial muscles, it is possible to identify whether students are confused when encountering complex concepts. This comprehensive evaluation based on physiological feedback and natural language processing provides teachers with precise data, allowing them to adjust teaching strategies according to students' actual participation, truly enhancing teaching presence.

4.1 AI Tutor: Process-Oriented Assessment for Academic Integrity

A study examined the use of an AI tutor in a civil engineering course called "Hydrology and Hydraulic Works" at a public Argentine university (Paz, 2025a). The study investigated some students across two distinct phases regarding the use of ChatGPT as a personal tutor during assignment preparation (Baillifard et al.,

2025). In the initial phase, students were simply invited to use the tool without any strict controls on usage or process documentation. This resulted in a complete failure, with a pass rate of 0% and plagiarism analysis showing an average similarity of approximately 65%, with some reports exceeding 80% overlap, highly similar to AI-generated text (Paz, 2025a). The documents looked polished but there was almost no trace of authentic student reasoning. This initial outcome made clear that if there are no process requirements for the task, many students will treat the AI as a shortcut rather than a learning aid (Wang et al., 2024). In response, the teacher redesigned the intervention measures. The new version requires students to submit an exported chat record as "Appendix A", and they must have at least 120 minutes of interaction with the AI tutor, as well as solve verifiable numerical hydrological problems, rather than just writing conceptual summaries (Paz, 2025a). The scoring criteria have also been revised. The revised scoring criteria will shift the focus from the appearance of the final document to evidence of actual interaction with the AI tutor, intermediate calculations, and clear reasoning steps. Based on the evaluation criteria, a hybrid assessment method will combine the analysis of students' scores with the submitted chat records. This redesigned system has produced significantly different results. The average score of the students has risen to 88 points (out of 100), and the chat records show that the students questioned the answers given by the AI, checked its suggestions, and integrated the tool into a more comprehensive problem-solving process, rather than simply copying its answers word for word (Paz, 2025a).

This case demonstrates that generative artificial intelligence mentors can be integrated into engineering education in a way that not only protects academic integrity but also enhances students' learning outcomes. However, this is only possible if the course design incorporates transparency and process evidence into the assessment system. Instead of banning AI or allowing it without rules, the study points to a third option. In this option, students must show how they worked with the tutor, and assessment focuses on their own reasoning anchored in verifiable calculations. This kind of task design can be applied to other STEM courses that wish to adopt AI tutors while keeping strong integrity safeguards (Sullivan et al., 2023).

4.2 CLiVR: Sentiment Analysis for Quantifying Student Empathy

CLiVR is a conversational learning system in virtual reality created to simulate real-life doctor-patient interactions using AI-generated 3D avatars for education (Amithasagaran et al., 2025). Traditional simulations usually depend on standardized patients and high-fidelity manikins, needing lots of time, workers, and room. CLiVR gives an option with virtual patients driven by large language models and voice technology, enabling learners to conduct clinical conversations repeatedly and at scale without just relying on meeting people in person (Amithasagaran et al., 2025). The system operates within a virtual clinic constructed with Unity and deployed on standalone headsets such as the Meta Quest 3. In this clinic, students will encounter 3D patient avatars that can hear, speak, and react in real-time. The system captures the learner's speech via the headset microphone, sends it to an automatic speech recognition module, and then feeds the transcript to an LLM, which generates the virtual patient's reply. Lastly, the text-to-speech service turns these replies into sound and syncs them up with the virtual patient's facial expressions before sending them off to the students. It gives students a normal and easy chat experience, so they can talk directly to the virtual patient instead of picking from fixed answer choices. One of the main features of CLiVR is sentiment analysis, which allows us to evaluate the emotional tone of each doctor statement during the interaction, supporting educational objectives such as evaluating empathy and communication style (Lin et al., 2024). Each transcribed message is categorized as positive, negative, or neutral by means of natural language models (Amithasagaran et al., 2025). This function can give back information about how well someone feels and talks to others based on what they do when talking to other people. And this feedback is important because empathy and good people skills are what makes someone a safe and caring caregiver (Foster et al., 2016; Guetterman et al., 2019). Training based on VR and virtual patient systems has been evaluated, and the soft skills have become the focus of examination and training (Cho & Kim, 2024; Yamada et al., 2025). The author's investigation revealed that teachers generally believe that CLiVR is an effective tool for teaching communication and history-taking skills, especially helpful for students who have difficulties in bedside communication (Amithasagaran et al., 2025).

In conclusion, this case demonstrates how the AI-driven virtual patient system can provide modern, flexible and repeatable training for medical and nursing education, and also addresses the cost and time limitations of traditional simulations.

4.3 SMARTe-VR: Learning Behavior Tracking via Biometric Technology

SMARTe-VR (Figure 5) is a recent example of an immersive virtual reality platform that supports adaptive online learning in higher education (Daza et al., 2025). The platform combines an immersive VR environment with detailed student tracking (Nagao, 2023). Learners attend video lectures inside VR and interact with a virtual screen and textbook. While they study, the system will record their facial biometric features, such as fine facial movements and gaze patterns (Dubovi, 2024). It will also collect traditional learning metadata, such as timestamps, the number of attempts on questions, and the difficulty level of the questions, to track the students' learning progress and strategies (Daza et al., 2025). Instructors can upload video lectures and organize them into structured segments, and students can engage with the content by highlighting and marking important or unclear parts. And also, the system's built-in auto Q&A function checks the students' comprehension before and after each video clip and gives instant feedback, which is very useful for learners to spot misunderstandings and things they should revisit, thereby creating a structured, personalised learning cycle. From the point of view of higher education, SMARTe-VR shows how immersive VR, biometrics, and AI-based analytics can work together in one platform. With this kind of system, universities could give VR lectures, watch how students are doing in real time, and do automatic tests without having to switch to a different tool. Instructors could see an analytics dashboard showing how far along their students are and what concepts are causing problems, so they can change what they teach, how fast they go, or how questions are asked using real information instead of guessing. For students, the platform gives them a more personal path because the level of difficulty and type of help can be changed according to how they behave and do in school (Van der Kleij et al., 2015).

In general, the SMARTe-VR case study indicates that immersive VR combined with adaptive learning technologies supports more data-driven, personalized instruction and enhances the way students engage with complicated course materials in online higher education environments (Daza et al., 2025).

Figure 5. SMARTe-VR platform

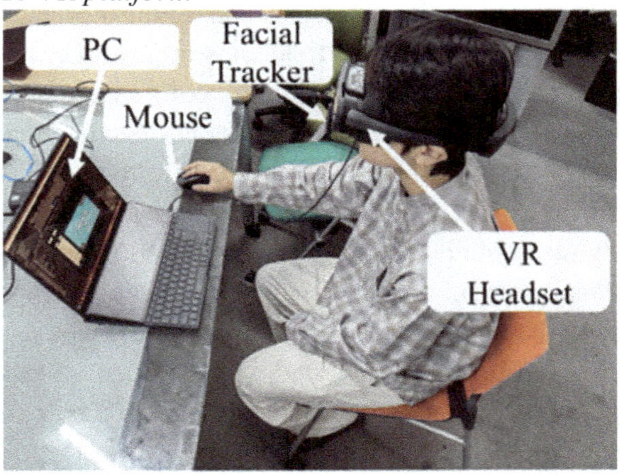

4.4 AI and Fieldwork Synergies: Integrating Field Research to Foster Critical AI Usage

The New York University Shanghai campus has just revamped an undergraduate business class, incorporating generative artificial intelligence instruments into the instruction procedure and merging hands-on field experiences to nurture pupils' creativity and hands-on commercial expertise (Wang, 2025). Students started using tools such as ChatGPT to rapidly investigate unfamiliar areas including raw materials, production techniques, and market developments, which helped them develop ideas from scratch even without basic understanding (Zhu et al., 2023; Rodrigues Vasconcelos & dos Santos, 2023). Then they compared the AI generated information with what they saw during their field trips, so they could find any problems or too simple parts in the AI's output. Screening and practicing interaction led them to adopt a more critical attitude towards the AI suggestion (Sun & Deng, 2025; Salinas-Navarro et al., 2024). In the latter part of the course, students learned how to use multi-modal tools such as Midjourney and Pika. They used these platforms to make brand logos, product pictures, and AI-made video ads, then put all their work together into a big brand package that had presentations, a website, and promotional materials (Zhang & Xu, 2025). Students said that AI tools greatly sped up the process of turning their fuzzy thoughts into solid drafts, whether their starting points were half-baked or their marketing groundwork was shaky. The generative tools took care of the technical work such as layout, illustrations, and first round copywriting, which lowered the entry barrier for students doing business practice and allowed them to concentrate on developing strategies and telling stories. And importantly, the real world feedback got from those field trips in Yiwu became quite useful as a kind of counterweight to the students simply taking everything the AI came up with at face value. After seeing real products being manufactured and interacting with the market in Yiwu themselves, they were able to use AI to improve their brand execution further. The final projects showed obvious strategy and a uniform style, more closely resembling the actual market situation, and the overall quality was much better than usual submissions in regular business courses (Wang, 2025).

This course shows that generative AI can do more than just be a quick way to finish homework when it is deliberately integrated with experiential learning, scaffolded guidance, and real-world validation. Such pedagogical designs can foster creativity and expand students' productive capacity. At the same time, the reliance on engagement analytics to evaluate learning remains limited, as quantitative indicators alone may oversimplify complex learning processes. This highlights the significance of teachers' ability to combine qualitative judgments with their teaching context when interpreting the engagement data generated by artificial intelligence.

5. GENERATIVE AI FOR INCLUSIVE AND SPECIAL NEEDS EDUCATION

By strengthening the teaching presence, social presence and cognitive presence within the CoI framework, AI tools offer new possibilities for inclusive needs-based education. Through adaptive feedback, multimodal support and emotionally responsive interaction, AI systems can enhance deeper cognitive engagement for special learners with diverse needs.

5.1 Generative AI as Assistive Technology: Supporting Disabled Students' Academic Writing

In 2025, an empirical survey was conducted that looked into how 124 disabled university students make use of generative artificial intelligence during their academic writing (Zhao, Cox, & Chen, 2025). Respondents mentioned a variety of conditions impacting their writing, such as ADHD, dyslexia, dyspraxia, and autism. Most of them depended on generative AI chatbots such as ChatGPT, and rewriting and translating tools, using them at different stages of the writing process. They used these tools to generate ideas, organise and structure activities, reword draft text, fix language, and translate language when necessary (Zhao et al., 2025). For many students, it allowed them to better organize their thoughts, take on hard tasks, and finish written work. In this way, generative AI became a kind of supportive aid to the act of writing, lowering the obstacles faced by disabled pupils (Ayala, 2024; Sakowicz & Hamidi, 2025). And it can help them better meet the writing requirements of higher education, which will promote educational inclusion (Jaime-Vargas, 2025). At the same time, the students also had some concerns. They worried about the accuracy of AI-generated content, saw the danger of accidentally breaking academic honesty rules, and said that paying for AI tools was a problem. These problems might possibly cause a fresh digital gap phenomenon among disabled students (Zhao et al., 2025).

Many respondents wanted clearer educational policies and specific AI training to solve these existing issues. Thus, generative artificial intelligence may become an important enabler for disabled students, but only if it is used under the guidance of inclusive policies, explicit AI literacy support, and equal access.

5.2 From UDL to ChatGPT: Generative AI as Assistive Support for Students with Disabilities

In a recent study by Sakowicz and Hamidi, they investigated how generative AI could aid students with disabilities, particularly focusing on integrating AI within the UDL framework (Sakowicz & Hamidi, 2025). The study looked at how special educators used AI tools to make adaptive learning materials for students with many kinds of disabilities, such as those who have trouble seeing, hearing, thinking, or moving around (Jaime-Vargas, 2025). For instance, an AI-powered text-to-speech feature enables visually impaired students to hear written content and the speech-to-text function would help the students having difficulty reading so that all the students can get the same information according to what suits them best. Likewise, the content simplification system based on artificial intelligence allows teachers to automatically convert complicated academic language into an easier-to-understand format to cater to students with different types of learning disabilities (Sakowicz & Hamidi, 2025). These changes helped meet the different needs of students with disabilities and gave them a more personal way to learn, which made the learning process more open to everyone. By leveraging artificial intelligence, educators are able to offer students with disabilities a more flexible learning environment, enhancing both accessibility and student participation. Similarly, ChatGPT was piloted as an assistive tool at a university in the United States. Disability support staff encouraged students with disabilities to use the chatbot to understand the meanings of assignments, generate explanations for complex materials, or summarize long-form texts. Students reported that this conversational support helped them organize their thoughts, reduced cognitive load, and enabled them to persist through demanding reading and writing tasks (Ayala, 2024).

5.3 AI-Driven Avatars for Autism Support: Remote Communication Training and Social Skills Practice

AI avatars are already making a tangible difference for vulnerable populations (Garzotto et al., 2024; Alabood et al., 2024). A laboratory group, in an inter-institutional collaboration, developed an AR remote presence system to overcome geographical barriers for nonspeaking autistic individuals learning spelling-based communication (Dow et al., 2025). The system is equipped with a holographic alphabet board and a fully embodied virtual avatar with real-time head and hand tracking capabilities. These features enable remote Communication and Regulatory Partners (CRP) to provide immersive and collaborative guidance to students. The team conducted a study with 18 non-verbal autistic participants, and 15 of them (83%) successfully completed the course with the support of the virtual avatar. The interaction among the participants has become more intense, and they indicated that they prefer the assistance provided by the virtual avatars to the communication solely via phone. At the same time, educational research institutes are applying these AI avatars into real-world projects to test their efficacy in actual classrooms (Nazari et al., 2023). A group of researchers from the University of Kansas have created VOISS (Virtual reality Opportunity to Integrate Social Skills) that uses artificial intelligence and extended reality technology to help autistic students improve their social skills (Krings, 2025). VOISS adds AI to current extended reality projects, giving students virtual situations where they can rehearse socializing safely and repeatedly, see Figure 6. Students can improve their social skills by having more natural spoken conversations with AI-driven virtual avatars instead of using pre-recorded buttons. VOISS can be used on multiple platforms (such as iPad, Chromebook, or Oculus VR headsets), allowing for flexible and multi-path usage before, during, and after classes.

This case demonstrates that artificial intelligence-driven virtual avatars can provide personalized and universal social skills training for autistic students in educational settings.

Figure 6. Student avatars converse and make their way through a school hallway in VOISS, available at https://lifespan.ku.edu/news/article/ku-research-team-develops-virtual-reality-ai-boosted-system-to-help-students-with-autism-improve-social-skills

In the application of Generative AI for learners with special needs, while personalized support enhances educational accessibility, it simultaneously raises new ethical concerns. These systems typically require the collection of highly sensitive individual data, including characteristics of learning disabilities, behavioral patterns, or emotional responses, which necessitates stringent protections for data privacy and informed consent rights of vulnerable groups. Furthermore, if algorithmic designs lack inclusivity, Generative AI may inadvertently reinforce stereotypes or unfair categorizations (Ferrara, 2024). Therefore, while leveraging AI to advance inclusive education, it is imperative to integrate data transparency, fairness audits, and continuous human oversight into the system design.

LIMITATIONS AND CHALLENGES

Furthermore, it remains challenging to evaluate the effectiveness of AI-enhanced HyFlex learning, and successful outcomes are often difficult to replicate. This difficulty largely stems from the lack of standardized approaches for describing the instructional practices that contribute to these outcomes. The factors involved are highly diverse, including technological specifications, the level of administrative support, and pedagogical strategies, making it difficult for researchers to determine which models are most effective in educational contexts. In addition, unequal access to technologies may exacerbate the digital divide among learners, leading to disparities in learning opportunities (Beck et al., 2024). These limitations also point to the need for more systematic design frameworks and context-sensitive evaluation methods in future research.

REFERENCES

Alabood, L., Dow, T., Feeley, K. B., Jaswal, V. K., & Krishnamurthy, D. (2024). From letterboards to holograms: Advancing assistive technology for nonspeaking autistic individuals with the HoloBoard. In CHI '24: Proceedings of the 2024 CHI Conference on Human Factors in Computing Systems (Article 71, pp. 71:1–71:18). Association for Computing Machinery. DOI: 10.1145/3613904.3642626

Amithasagaran, A., Dakshit, S., Suryadevara, B., & Stockton, L. (2025). CLiVR: Conversational learning system in virtual reality with AI-powered patients. arXiv. /arXiv.2510.19031DOI: 10.48550

Antonelli, D., Christopoulos, A., Laakso, M.-J., Dagienė, V., Juškevičienė, A., Masiulionytė-Dagienė, V., Mądziel, M., Stadnicka, D., & Stylios, C. (2023). A virtual reality laboratory for blended learning education: Design, implementation and evaluation. *Education Sciences, 13*(5), 528. DOI: 10.3390/educsci13050528

Aufenanger, S., Zender, R., Ifenthaler, D., Dahmen, J., Beutner, M., & Scharke, W. (2025). Immersive virtual reality learning environments for higher education: Results from the REVEALING project. *Computers & Education: X Reality, 7*, Article 100105. DOI: 10.1016/j.cexr.2025.100105

Ayala, S. (2024). ChatGPT as a Universal Design for Learning tool: Supporting college students with disabilities. Educational (Re)naissance, 12(1). DOI: 10.33499/edren.v12i1.3866

Bailenson, J. (2018). Experience on demand: What virtual reality is, how it works, and what it can do. WW Norton & Company. https://psycnet.apa.org/record/2019-04570-000

Baillifard, A., Gabella, M., Banta Lavenex, P., & Martarelli, C. S. (2025). Effective learning with a personal AI tutor: A case study. *Education and Information Technologies, 30*(1), 297–312. DOI: 10.1007/s10639-024-12888-5

Beatty, B. J. (2019). *Hybrid-Flexible course design: Implementing student-directed hybrid classes*. EdTech Books. DOI: 10.59668/33

Beck, D., Morgado, L., & O'Shea, P. (2024). Educational practices and strategies with immersive learning environments: Mapping of reviews for using the metaverse. *IEEE Transactions on Learning Technologies, 17*, 319–341. DOI: 10.1109/TLT.2023.3243946

Canto, S., & Jauregi-Ondarra, K. (2021). Interaction Games to Boost Students' Engagement in Foreign Language Virtual Exchanges: The Case of Virtual Worlds and Video-Communication. In Research-publishing.net.

Chen, X., Ma, L., Su, D., Zhang, Y., Liu, X., Xing, J., Li, L., & Ryoo, J. (2025). AI-enhanced cross-cultural competence in STEM education. In Proceedings of the International Conference on New Findings in Humanities and Social Sciences (Article 267). DOI: 10.33422/hsconf.v1i1.267

Cho, M.-K., & Kim, M. Y. (2024). The effect of virtual reality simulation on nursing students' communication skills: A systematic review and meta-analysis. *Frontiers in Psychiatry*, *15*, 1351123. DOI: 10.3389/fpsyt.2024.1351123 PMID: 39035600

Daza, R., Shengkai, L., Morales, A., Fierrez, J., & Nagao, K. (2025). SMARTe-VR: Student monitoring and adaptive response technology for e-learning in virtual reality. arXiv. https://arxiv.org/abs/2501.10977 DOI: 10.1145/3728487.3759231

De Lorenzis, F., Visconti, A., Restivo, S., Mazzini, F., Esposito, S., Fraterrigo Garofalo, S., Marmo, L., Fino, D., & Lamberti, F. (2024). Combining virtual reality with asymmetric collaborative learning: A case study in chemistry education. *Smart Learning Environments*, *11*(1), 43. Advance online publication. DOI: 10.1186/s40561-024-00331-8

Dow, T., Pratishtha, P., Alabood, L., Jaswal, V. K., & Krishnamurthy, D. (2025). AR-based embodied avatar assistance for nonspeaking autistic people? Design and feasibility study. In *Proceedings of the 2025 ACM Designing Interactive Systems Conference (DIS '25)* (pp. 423–440). Association for Computing Machinery. DOI: 10.1145/3715336.3735807

Dubovi, I. (2024). Facial expressions capturing emotional engagement while learning with desktop VR: The impact of emotional regulation and personality traits. *Interactive Learning Environments*, *32*(9), 5041–5057. DOI: 10.1080/10494820.2023.2208173

Essel, H. B., Vlachopoulos, D., Tachie-Menson, A., Johnson, E. E., & Baah, P. K. (2022). The impact of a virtual teaching assistant (chatbot) on students' learning in Ghanaian higher education. *International Journal of Educational Technology in Higher Education*, *19*(1), 57. DOI: 10.1186/s41239-022-00362-6

Ferrara, E. (2024). Fairness and Bias in Artificial Intelligence: A Brief Survey of Sources, Impacts, and Mitigation Strategies. *Sci*, *6*(1), 3. DOI: 10.3390/sci6010003

Finkelstein, I., & Soffer-Vital, S. (2025). Cultural Empathy in AI-Supported Collaborative Learning: Advancing Inclusive Digital Learning in Higher Education. *Education Sciences*, *15*(10), 1305. DOI: 10.3390/educsci15101305

Foster, A., Chaudhary, N., Kim, T., Waller, J. L., Wong, J., Borish, M., Cordar, A., Lok, B., & Buckley, P. F. (2016). Using virtual patients to teach empathy: A randomized controlled study to enhance medical students' empathic communication. *Simulation in Healthcare*, *11*(3), 181–189. DOI: 10.1097/SIH.0000000000000142 PMID: 26841278

Garrison, D. R., Anderson, T., & Archer, W. (2000). Critical inquiry in a text-based environment: Computer conferencing in higher education. *The Internet and Higher Education*, *2*(2–3), 87–105. DOI: 10.1016/S1096-7516(00)00016-6

Garzotto, F., Gianotti, M., Patti, A., Pentimalli, F., & Vona, F. (2024). Empowering persons with autism through cross-reality and conversational agents. *IEEE Transactions on Visualization and Computer Graphics*, *30*(5), 2591–2601. DOI: 10.1109/TVCG.2024.3372110 PMID: 38437092

Guetterman, T. C., Sakakibara, R., Baireddy, S., Kron, F. W., Scerbo, M. W., Cleary, J. F., & Fetters, M. D. (2019). Medical students' experiences and outcomes using a virtual human simulation to improve communication skills: Mixed methods study. *Journal of Medical Internet Research*, *21*(11), e15459. DOI: 10.2196/15459 PMID: 31774400

Holmes, W., Bialik, M., & Fadel, C. (2021). *Artificial intelligence in education promises and implications for teaching and learning*. Center for Curriculum Redesign., DOI: 10.3991/ijac.v18i1.51197

Jaime-Vargas, J. A. (2025). Generative AI for enhancing accessibility and inclusion in higher education: A systematic review. *HighTech and Innovation Journal*, *6*(2), 723–734. DOI: 10.28991/HIJ-2025-06-02-022

Jain, A., Cui, L., & Chen, S. (2025). Aligning LLMs for the classroom with knowledge-based retrieval: A comparative RAG study. arXiv preprint arXiv:2509.07846. DOI: 10.1109/TALE66047.2025.11346682

Jensen, L., & Konradsen, F. (2018). A review of the use of virtual reality head-mounted displays in education and training. *Education and Information Technologies*, *23*(4), 1515–1529. DOI: 10.1007/s10639-017-9676-0

Kahl, S., Löffler, F., Maciol, M., Ridder, F., Schmitz, M., Spanagel, J., Wienkamp, J., Burgahn, C., & Schilling, M. (2025). Evaluating the impact of advanced LLM techniques on AI lecture tutors for a robotics course. In F. Bellas & O. Fontenla-Romero (Eds.), AI in education and educational research: First International Workshop, AIEER 2024, Santiago de Compostela, Spain, October 19–20, 2024, Proceedings (pp. 149–160). Springer. DOI: 10.1007/978-3-031-93409-4_14

Karapakdee, J., Wannapiroon, P., & Nillsook, P. (2024). Metaverse learning ecosystem for Hyflex learning Snoopathon to enhance systematic thinking and innovative thinking. *International Journal of Information and Education Technology (IJIET), 14*(7), 1016–1022. DOI: 10.18178/ijiet.2024.14.7.2129

Klimova, B., & Chen, H. (2024). The impact of AI on enhancing students' intercultural communication competence at the university level: A review study. *Language Teaching Research Quarterly, 43*, 1–27. DOI: 10.32038/ltrq.2024.43.06

Knutzen, K., Rothenberger, L., Tribusean, I., & Xu, Y. (2025). Using Social Virtual Reality in Teaching Intercultural Communication. Technology, Knowledge and Learning, 1-21.

Kourtesis, P. (2024). A comprehensive review of multimodal XR applications, risks, and ethical challenges in the metaverse. *Multimodal Technologies and Interaction, 8*(11), 98. DOI: 10.3390/mti8110098

Krings, M. (2025, January 29). KU research team develops virtual reality, AI-boosted system to help students with autism improve social skills. Life Span Institute, University of Kansas. https://lifespan.ku.edu/news/article/ku-research-team-develops-virtual-reality-ai-boosted-system-to-help-students-with-autism-improve-social-skills

Lin, H.-L., Wang, Y.-C., Huang, M.-L., Yu, N.-W., Tang, I., Hsu, Y.-C., & Huang, Y.-S. (2024). Can virtual reality technology be used for empathy education in medical students: A randomized case-control study. *BMC Medical Education, 24*(1), 1254. DOI: 10.1186/s12909-024-06009-6 PMID: 39497110

Lin, Y.-Z., Petal, K., Alhamadah, A. H., Ghimire, S., Redondo, M. W., Vidal Corona, D. R., Pacheco, J., Salehi, S., & Satam, P. (2025). Personalized education with generative AI and digital twins: VR, RAG, and zero-shot sentiment analysis for Industry 4.0 workforce development. Proceedings of the ASEE 2025 Annual Conference [arXiv preprint]. arXiv. DOI: 10.48550/arXiv.2502.14080

Llanos-Ruiz, D., Abella-García, V., & Ausín-Villaverde, V. (2025). Virtual reality in higher education: A systematic review aligned with the Sustainable Development Goals. *Societies (Basel, Switzerland), 15*(9), 251. DOI: 10.3390/soc15090251

Ma, G., & Yang, X. (2025). Fostering intercultural competence through AI driven tools: A case study of linguistic and cultural adaptability in Chinese EFL education. Digital Technologies Research and Applications, 4(1), 105-123. http://ojs.ukscip.com/index.php/dtra/article/view/1131

Mahande, R. D., Abdal, N. M., Nasir, N., & Rahmi, U. (2025). Design and effectiveness of the HyFlex-VR learning model for emancipated learning in higher education. *Journal of Applied Research in Higher Education*. Advance online publication. DOI: 10.1108/JARHE-12-2024-0713

Makransky, G., Terkildsen, T. S., & Mayer, R. E. (2022). The potential of immersive virtual reality to enhance learning: A meta-analysis. *Educational Research Review, 36*, 100452. DOI: 10.1016/j.edurev.2022.100452

Nagao, K. (2023). Virtual reality campuses as new educational metaverses. *IEICE Transactions on Information and Systems, 106*(2), 93–100. DOI: 10.1587/transinf.2022ETI0001

Nazari, A., Shahidi, A., Kaufman, K. M., Bondi, J. E., Alabood, L., Jaswal, V. K., Krishnamurthy, D., & Wang, M. (2023). Interactive AR applications for nonspeaking autistic people? A usability study. In CHI '23: Proceedings of the 2023 CHI Conference on Human Factors in Computing Systems (Article 708, pp. 1–15). Association for Computing Machinery. DOI: 10.1145/3544548.3580721

Nesenbergs, K., Abolins, V., Ormanis, J., & Mednis, A. (2021). Use of augmented and virtual reality in remote higher education: A systematic umbrella review. *Education Sciences, 11*(1), 8. DOI: 10.3390/educsci11010008

Paz, H. R. (2025a). The AI tutor in engineering education: Design, results, and redesign of an experience in hydrology at an Argentine university (arXiv:2510.22279).

Poličar, P. G., Špendl, M., Curk, T., & Zupan, B. (2025). Automated assignment grading with large language models Insights from a bioinformatics course. *Bioinformatics (Oxford, England), 41*(Suppl. 1), i21–i29. DOI: 10.1093/bioinformatics/btaf196 PMID: 40662811

Radianti, J., Majchrzak, T. A., Fromm, J., & Wohlgenannt, I. (2020). A systematic review of immersive virtual reality applications for higher education: Design elements, lessons learned, and research agenda. *Computers & Education, 147*, 103778. DOI: 10.1016/j.compedu.2019.103778

Rasheed, G., Khan, M., Malik, N., & Akhunzada, A. (2021). Measuring Learnability through Virtual Reality Laboratory Application: A User Study. *Sustainability (Basel), 13*(19), 10812. DOI: 10.3390/su131910812

Rodrigues Vasconcelos, M. A., & dos Santos, R. P. (2023). Enhancing STEM learning with ChatGPT and Bing Chat as objects to think with: A case study. arXiv. / arXiv.2305.02202DOI: 10.48550

Sadaf, A., & Olesova, L. (2017). Enhancing cognitive presence in online case discussions with questions based on the practical inquiry model. *American Journal of Distance Education, 31*(1), 56–69. DOI: 10.1080/08923647.2017.1267525

Sakowicz, M., & Hamidi, F. (2025). Exploring the role of generative AI in supporting students with disabilities, through the lens of Universal Design for Learning. *American Journal of STEM Education, 15*, 1–22. DOI: 10.32674/yeyaaq64

Salinas-Navarro, D. E., Vilalta-Perdomo, E., Michel-Villarreal, R., & Montesinos, L. (2024). Using generative artificial intelligence tools to explain and enhance experiential learning for authentic assessment. *Education Sciences, 14*(1), 83. DOI: 10.3390/educsci14010083

Sarwari, A. Q., Javed, M. N., Mohd Adnan, H., & Abdul Wahab, M. N. (2024). Assessment of the impacts of artificial intelligence (AI) on intercultural communication among postgraduate students in a multicultural university environment. *Scientific Reports, 14*(1), 13849. DOI: 10.1038/s41598-024-63276-5 PMID: 38879546

Shingjergji, K., İren, D., Urlings, C. C., & Klemke, R. (2025). Affective computing in online higher education: A systematic literature review. Computers & Education. *Artificial Intelligence*. Advance online publication. DOI: 10.1016/j.caeai.2025.100499

Shojaei, M. F., Gulati, R., Jasperson, B. A., Wang, S., Cimolato, S., Cao, D., Neiswanger, W., & Garikipati, K. (2025). AI-University: An LLM-based platform for instructional alignment to scientific classrooms. arXiv. /arXiv.2504.08846DOI: 10.48550

Sikström, P., Valentini, C., Sivunen, A., & Kärkkäinen, T. (2024). Pedagogical agents communicating and scaffolding students' learning: High school teachers' and students' perspectives. *Computers & Education, 222*, 105140. DOI: 10.1016/j.compedu.2024.105140

Stracke, C. M., Bothe, P., Adler, S., Heller, E. S., Deuchler, J., Pomino, J., & Wölfel, M. (2025). Immersive virtual reality in higher education: A systematic review of the scientific literature. *Virtual Reality (Waltham Cross), 29*(2), 1–21. DOI: 10.1007/s10055-025-01136-x

Sullivan, M., Kelly, A., & McLaughlan, P. (2023). ChatGPT in higher education: Considerations for academic integrity and student learning. *Journal of Applied Learning & Teaching, 6*(1), 1–10. DOI: 10.37074/jalt.2023.6.1.17

Sun, R., & Deng, X. (2025). Using generative AI to enhance experiential learning: An exploratory study of ChatGPT use by university students. *Journal of Information Systems Education, 36*(1), 53–64. DOI: 10.62273/ZLUM4022

Thi Binh, A. D., Hoang, T.-H., & Quang, H. T. (2025). Designing Effective Hybrid Course Curriculum: A Design Science Approach to Gamification and Student Outcomes Validation. *Evaluation Review*, *49*(3), 453–486. DOI: 10.1177/0193841X241291752 PMID: 39384204

Turner, A. (2015). Generation Z: Technology and social interest. *Journal of Individual Psychology*, *71*(2), 103–113. DOI: 10.1353/jip.2015.0021

Vehrer, A., & Pálfalusi, Z. (2025). The application of virtual environments and artificial intelligence in higher education: Experimental findings in philosophy teaching. arXiv. /arXiv.2509.00110DOI: 10.48550

Walter's Cube. (2024). About. Walter's Cube. https://walterscube.com/about/

Wang, H., Dang, A., Wu, Z., & Mac, S. (2024). Generative AI in higher education: Seeing ChatGPT through universities' policies, resources, and guidelines. arXiv. / arXiv.2312.05235DOI: 10.48550

Wang, J., & Singh, R. (2025). Grounding large language models in course materials using RAG and PEFT. *Computers & Education: Artificial Intelligence*, *8*, 100245. DOI: 10.1016/j.caeai.2025.100245

Wang, N. C. (2025). Scaffolding creativity: Integrating generative AI tools and real-world experiences in business education. CHI EA '25: Extended Abstracts of the CHI Conference on Human Factors in Computing Systems. arXiv. DOI: 10.48550/arXiv.2501.06527

Wang, X. (2025). KNOWLEDGE GRAPH EMPOWERS THE TEACHING REFORM OF PROGRAMMING COURSES. PUPIL: International Journal of Teaching. *Education and Learning*, *569–570*, 569–570. Advance online publication. DOI: 10.20319/ictel.2025.569570

Wu, J., Zhang, B., Jiang, B., Liu, J., & Ksenia, T. (2025). Exploring the construction of a standard AI literacy framework for middle school students in the era of GAI: Focusing on the assessment of AI application and innovation. In *Proceedings of the 2025 5th International Conference on Artificial Intelligence and Education (ICAIE)* (pp. 790–795). IEEE. DOI: 10.1109/ICAIE64856.2025.11158190

Wu, J., Zhang, B., Liu, J., & Jiang, B. (2025). The Potential of Generative AI used for AI Literacy Framework Construction. In R. Jake Cohen (Ed.), Proceedings of Society for Information Technology & Teacher Education International Conference (pp. 1007-1016).

Yamada, R., Futakawa, K., Kuangzhe, X., & Kondo, S. (2025). Using virtual patients to enhance empathy in medical students: A scoping review protocol. *Systematic Reviews, 14*(1), 52. DOI: 10.1186/s13643-025-02793-4 PMID: 40025554

Yang, Y., Yu, A., Li, J., Shafi, M., & Fauzi, M. A. (2025). Exploring the impact of gamified elements on college students' learning in virtual learning communities. *Kybernetes, 54*(9), 5133–5157. DOI: 10.1108/K-01-2024-0017

Yeung, C., Yu, J., Cheung, K. C., Wong, T. W., Chan, C. M., Wong, K. C., & Fujii, K. (2025). A zero shot LLM framework for automatic assignment grading in higher education (arXiv:2501.14305). arXiv. https://arxiv.org/abs/2501.14305

Zawacki-Richter, O., Marín, V. I., Bond, M., & Gouverneur, F. (2019). Systematic review of research on artificial intelligence applications in higher education – Where are the educators? *International Journal of Educational Technology in Higher Education, 16*(1), 39. DOI: 10.1186/s41239-019-0171-0

Zhang, B., & Dong, R. (2022). How natural language processing technology empowers the AIED: The perspective of AI scientist. [Educational Sciences]. *Journal of East China Normal University, 40*(9), 19.

Zhang, B., Goodman, L., & Gu, X. (2022). Novel 3D contextual interactive games on a gamified virtual environment support cultural learning through collaboration among intercultural students. *SAGE Open, 12*(2), 1–14. DOI: 10.1177/21582440221096141

Zhang, B., Goodman, L., & Gu, X. (2023). Telecollaboration tool preferences for online intercultural learning in higher education: Perspectives of Chinese international students. *SAGE Open, 13*(2), 1–12. DOI: 10.1177/21582440231180087

Zhang, B., Robb, N., Eyerman, J., & Goodman, L. (2017). Virtual worlds and gamification to increase integration of international students in higher education: An inclusive design approach. *International Journal of E-Learning & Distance Education, 32*(2), 1–21.

Zhang, C., & Xu, S. (2025). Aesthetic experience and educational value in co-creating art with generative AI: Evidence from a survey of young learners. arXiv. /arXiv.2509.10576DOI: 10.48550

Zhang, Y., Liu, H., & Chen, J. (2024). Cross-cultural intelligent language learning system (CILS): Leveraging AI to facilitate language learning strategies in cross-cultural communication. *Applied Sciences (Basel, Switzerland), 14*(13), 5651. DOI: 10.3390/app14135651

Zhang, Y., Ou, Z., & Yu, Z. (2020). Task-Oriented Dialog Systems That Consider Multiple Appropriate Responses under the Same Context. *Proceedings of the AAAI Conference on Artificial Intelligence*, *34*(05), 9604–9611. DOI: 10.1609/aaai.v34i05.6507

Zhang, B., Wang, X., Li, Y., Chen, Y., & Gu, X. (2025). Dual Perspective Assessment of the Development Level and Characteristics of Intelligent Educational Software in China. *SAGE Open*, *15*(4), 21582440251387420.

Zhang, B., Li, Y., Xing, Q., Chen, Y., & Wang, X. (2025, December). The Construction of Evaluation Indicators for Intelligent Educational Software and the Measurement of Its Developmental Level. In *International Conference on Computers in Education*.

Zhao, X., Cox, A., & Chen, X. (2025). The use of generative AI by students with disabilities in higher education. *The Internet and Higher Education*, *66*, 101014. DOI: 10.1016/j.iheduc.2025.101014

Zhu, G., Fan, X., Hou, C., Zhong, T., Seow, P., Chen, A. S.-H., Rajalingam, P., Low, K. Y., & Tan, L. P. (2023). Embrace opportunities and face challenges: Using ChatGPT in undergraduate students' collaborative interdisciplinary learning. arXiv. /arXiv.2305.18616DOI: 10.48550

Chapter 8

AI-Supported HyFlex Active Learning (AHAL) Model:

Integrating Innovative and Traditional Approaches for Enhanced Student Learning in Life Sciences

Lai Zee Wei
http://orcid.org/0000-0002-8521-4686
Taylor's University, Lakeside, Malaysia

Adeline Chia Yoke Yin
Taylor's University, Lakeside, Malaysia

Sreelakshmi Sankara Narayanan
Taylor's University, Lakeside, Malaysia

Teoh Ming Li
Taylor's University, Lakeside, Malaysia

Lee Khai Wooi
Taylor's University, Lakeside, Malaysia

ABSTRACT

This chapter explores the implementation of HyFlex learning in undergraduate science education, focusing on its effects on student engagement, assessment outcomes,

DOI: 10.4018/979-8-3373-6182-6.ch008

and educator perspectives. Using both quantitative and qualitative approaches, the analysis compares pre-HyFlex (September 2024) and post-HyFlex (April 2025) cohorts. Findings indicate that academic performance remained consistent or improved slightly following the introduction of HyFlex, with students benefiting from increased flexibility and access to AI-supported learning tools. However, challenges were observed in sustaining interaction, managing self-regulation, and maintaining a sense of community across delivery modes. Educators reported greater preparation demands and concerns related to AI ethics, data privacy, and reduced human interaction, while acknowledging efficiencies gained through personalized feedback. The chapter concludes that, when guided by thoughtful pedagogy, institutional support, and ethical safeguards, HyFlex learning can enhance accessibility, engagement, and teaching effectiveness

1. INTRODUCTION

The COVID-19 pandemic has accelerated the transition from traditional teaching methods to Hybrid-Flexible (HyFlex) learning, reshaping the higher education landscape. During this period, higher education institutions worldwide were compelled to adopt various remote teaching models to maintain continuity in learning. This sudden and large-scale transformation not only changed conventional pedagogical practices but also gave rise to a more sustainable and adaptable model, which is HyFlex learning, that integrates inclusivity, flexibility, and technology-enhanced environments to meet diverse student needs. According to recent literature, the hyflex model has become a standard approach in modern education, emphasizing the need for further research on its impact on both teaching effectiveness and student learning outcomes (Mentzer et al., 2023).

This transformation continues to evolve across disciplines, positioning HyFlex learning as a key innovation in higher education. It allows students to decide how they wish to participate in each class, either in person, synchronously online, or asynchronously online, according to their circumstances and preferences (Cumming et al., 2024), often supported by Artificial Intelligence (AI)-driven tools. This trimodal approach ensures that all students, regardless of their mode of participation, achieve equivalent learning outcomes and are equally supported throughout the learning process. However, as the HyFlex concept becomes increasingly widespread, its interpretation and implementation vary significantly depending on institutional context, available infrastructure, and instructional design philosophy (Wong et al., 2023).

A longitudinal analysis of HyFlex learning and related practices from 2013 to 2022 indicates a substantial increase in learner engagement, flexibility, and satisfaction. At the same time, challenges have been identified, particularly regarding institutional readiness, technological infrastructure, and the increased workload placed on instructors adapting to hybrid delivery (Wong et al., 2023). The success of HyFlex learning thus depends not only on its technological foundation but also on pedagogical soundness, faculty support, and thoughtful instructional design that maintains coherence between different learning modes.

In the post-pandemic era, higher education has moved beyond emergency remote teaching toward intentionally designed hybrid frameworks that emphasize engagement, accessibility, and learner autonomy (Gudoniene et al., 2025). As education systems transition into this new phase, advancements in digital technologies, particularly AI, have become central to optimizing HyFlex environments. The integration of AI into HyFlex learning has paved the way for a new chapter in educational innovation, addressing students' personalized learning needs and enhancing engagement through data-driven insights and adaptive learning systems.

Within this context, AI integration supports seamless interaction between physical and virtual learning spaces. For instance, AI-powered systems can help automate administrative tasks, deliver personalized learning analytics, and enable real-time feedback that fosters continuous improvement. These technologies not only facilitate more interactive and collaborative learning but also empower instructors to shift from content delivery to higher-order teaching tasks such as mentoring, problem-solving facilitation, and critical reflection. As a result, AI becomes a supportive pedagogical partner in enhancing student-centered learning experiences across HyFlex settings.

Moreover, the increasingly globalized landscape of higher education demands pedagogical models that can accommodate students from diverse socioeconomic, cultural, and geographical backgrounds. The AI-enhanced HyFlex model represents a significant step toward this goal, combining innovative teaching practices with intelligent technologies to provide equitable access and meaningful engagement opportunities for all students. By connecting students and teachers across different places and times, these models give students more control over their studies and help educators create learning environments that are more engaging and inclusive.

In science disciplines, however, flexibility in learning is not sufficient by itself. These fields demand more than just learning facts; they require students to cultivate a range of transferable competencies such as critical thinking, problem-solving, collaboration, and adaptability. These skills are indispensable for navigating the complex and scientific challenges of the 21st century. In response to this need, active learning has emerged as one of the most effective pedagogical strategies in undergraduate STEM (Science, Technology, Engineering, and Mathematics) education (Freeman et al., 2014).

Traditional, lecture-based approaches tend to rely heavily on passive instruction, where students are positioned as recipients rather than participants in knowledge construction. Such methods limit opportunities for meaningful engagement with content, peers, and instructors. In contrast, active learning, often referred to as student-centered learning, places students at the core of the educational process. It empowers them to construct their own understanding, apply theoretical knowledge to real-world problems, and engage in higher-order thinking through interactive, structured activities. `Freeman et al. (2014) conducted a meta-analysis of 225 studies and found that active learning significantly improves student performance and reduces failure rates in undergraduate STEM courses compared to traditional lectures. These findings demonstrate that engaging students in this learning process leads to better understanding, retention, and application of complex scientific concepts.

When we combine, active learning pedagogical approach with hyflex models for life science students will provide high flexibility for students to engage as well as offer several pedagogical advantages. This integration enhances engagement and participation by allowing students to interact with content through in-person and online sessions while engaging in AI-supported learning activities that reinforce key concepts. For instance, AI-based tools such as adaptive quizzes and AI-learning assistant chat-based tutoring systems can provide real-time feedback and personalize the learning experience, catering to individual learning styles and paces.

Additionally, combining HyFlex and active learning models increases accessibility and inclusivity by allowing students to participate in learning activities regardless of time and location constraints. This combined approach bridges the gap between theoretical understanding and practical application, supporting students in developing essential scientific skills such as critical thinking, collaboration, and problem-solving (Freeman et al., 2014; Mentzer et al., 2023). Furthermore, it promotes equity by ensuring that all students, regardless of their chosen mode of participation, receive comparable learning experiences and opportunities for engagement (Prince, 2004).

AI technologies have become powerful pedagogical tools, transforming educational experiences and expanding access to digital and lifelong learning. In higher education, AI does not replace the educator but augments human teaching by creating an interactive and responsive learning ecosystem. Within our AI-supported Hyflex Active Learning (AHAL) model implemented at the School of Biosciences, Taylor's University, prerecorded lectures were developed using AI avatars to ensure consistency in content quality. These materials are accessible anytime, supporting flexibility and self-paced learning, an essential feature of HyFlex delivery (Zawacki-Richter et al., 2019). Once created, AI avatar lectures can be reused, reducing instructor workload and allowing educators to focus on higher-order teaching tasks such as assessment and discussion facilitation. Additionally, AI avatar videos can be produced in multiple languages and at adjustable speeds, supporting non-native English speakers in mastering complex scientific content (Wang and Zou, 2025).

In this model, HyFlex provides structural flexibility, active learning promotes meaningful engagement, and AI tools enhance both by enabling real-time support and personalized learning experiences. Therefore, integrating active learning strategies within AI-enhanced HyFlex models ensures that science students are not only equipped with disciplinary knowledge but also empowered to develop critical, analytical, and collaborative skills essential for the future. This chapter explores the development and trial implementation of an AHAL Model, integrating flexible delivery modes with structured active learning and AI-driven tools to foster engagement and enhance the learning experience in life sciences.

2. PEDAGOGY: AHAL MODEL

The AHAL model emerges by integrating three 3 different pedagogical frameworks, including the hyflex model, active learning theory concepts, and AI-supported tools for personalization, shown in **Figure 1**. This model has been designed to provide the students with flexibility, personalization, and engagement in life science education. This AHAL model is embedded with three important components, including Interactive Synchronous Learning Hour (ISL), Interactive Learning Hour (ILH), and AI-Powered Digital Learning Resources, to adopt a student-centered learning approach with flexibility and personalization. The AHAL model aims to help students take more control of their learning while ensuring that all learning modes are inclusive and provide equal opportunities. By using modern technology and proven active learning methods, it turns traditional teaching into an interactive and smart learning system. This model allows students to move easily between online, face-to-face, and AI-supported learning environments while keeping learning outcomes consistent.

Figure 1. Schematic representation of AI-supported Hyflex Active Learning (AHAL) model

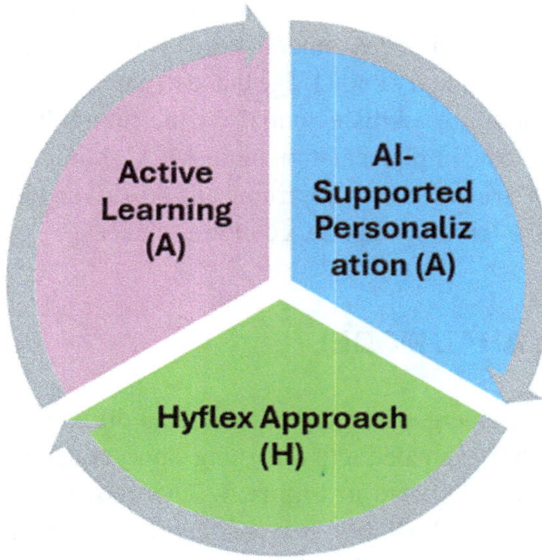

2.1 Conceptual Framework of the AHAL Model

2.1.1 Hyflex Approach

Over the past decade, HyFlex models have gained attraction in universities worldwide, notably at San Francisco State University, Purdue University, and the University of Southampton, which have used them to enhance resilience and continuity in the post-pandemic era (Mahrishi et al., 2025; Wong et al., 2023). Evidence consistently shows that HyFlex broadens student access, accommodates diverse learning preferences, and promotes persistence in higher education (Cumming et al., 2024).

The hyflex model was originally formulated by Dr. Brian Beatty from San Francisco State University, which combines the hybrid model and flexibility, and is derived from four principles, including learner choice, equivalency, reusability, and accessibility (Beatty, 2019). These four pillars provide a solid foundation for the hyflex component in this model. These four pillars are described in detail below:

The principle of Learner Choice insists that students be given meaningful options in how they engage, with flexibility not just in theory but in practice. In the AHAL model, students may opt daily or by topic for one of three modes:

- Campus Connect: fully in-person, face-to-face delivery
- Sync-Live: synchronous online participation (e.g., via Zoom or Microsoft Teams or other options)
- Flexi-Learn: asynchronous, self-paced digital learning

This flexibility allows students to adapt their modality to constraints (e.g. health, travel, connectivity) or preference (e.g. whether they focus better via synchronous group interaction or offline reflection). The key is that choice is authentic with equivalent pathways to learning.

Equivalency doesn't mean that every learning mode has to look the same, but it does mean that all students should reach the same learning goals and level of understanding. In the AHAL model, whether students learn in class, join live online sessions, or study on their own, they all should think deeply, ask questions, and reflect on what they learn. Each option uses the same rubrics, tasks, and grading standards to make sure everyone is treated fairly. Students also get similar support, like group discussions, instructor feedback, and helpful questions, so that all students, no matter how they study, can have the same quality of learning experience. For instance, a problem-based discussion conducted in class would have a synchronous version (such as breakout rooms) and an asynchronous version (like a discussion board or structured journal) that require the same level of reasoning, even though the delivery methods differ. This pedagogical approach necessitates a deliberate design to ensure that all students, regardless of their chosen modality, receive comparable opportunities for engaging with course material and demonstrating their learning (Bjaelde and Lindberg, 2018).

Reusability means that different learning materials like lectures, recorded sessions, interactive modules, and AI avatar videos can be used in different formats and groups. In the AHAL model, for example, a recorded lecture can be reused in Flexi-Learn, shown in a live class, or included in an in-class activity. Discussions from online forums can also be shared during live sessions. By creating materials that are easy to reuse and adapt, this model helps keep learning efficient, consistent, and connected across all modes. This strategic approach to reusability not only optimizes resource utilization but also reinforces pedagogical coherence across diverse instructional delivery methods, ensuring a harmonized educational experience irrespective of the chosen modality (Amiruddin et al., 2024).

Accessibility means removing all kinds of barriers, such as technology problems, learning difficulties, time limits, or physical challenges, that might prevent students from fully participating in learning. In the AHAL model, this is achieved by making sure every student has the right tools, internet access, and training to use them effectively. It also involves applying Universal Design for Learning (UDL) principles so that lessons include different ways to learn and understand information. In addition, alternative versions of materials such as transcripts, subtitles, or audio descriptions are provided for videos and other media to support diverse learning needs (Beatty, 2019). Flexibility in pacing and deadlines is also offered when needed, allowing students to learn at their own pace. The main goal is to ensure that no student is left out or disadvantaged by the learning mode they choose, and that every option, whether in-person, online, or self-paced, should be open, fair, and accessible to all.

Together, these four HyFlex principles build a flexible learning system. To make this flexibility even more effective and engaging, the AHAL model also includes active learning and AI-based tools to support high-quality learning for everyone. This approach ensures that learning environments are not only accessible but also tailored to individual needs, promoting deeper engagement and improved educational outcomes (Priyadharsini and Mary, 2024).

2.1.2 Active Learning Theory

In the AHA model, active learning is structured around four key pillars which are engagement, collaboration, reflection, and application, where each is integrated across the Interactive Synchronous Learning Hour (ISL), Interactive Learning Hour (ILH), and AI-powered digital platforms to promote meaningful participation and deeper learning. Engagement is achieved through a combination of interactive technologies and real-time learning experiences. During ISL sessions, students take part in live polls, quizzes, and discussions on Microsoft Teams. AI avatar videos are also used to help keep their attention and make the lessons easier to understand. In ILH sessions, activities such as gamification, debates, and role plays transform content into interactive experiences that strengthen motivation and conceptual understanding (Bonwell & Eison, 1991; Prince, 2004). The use of AI-enabled tools like Noodle Factory, Labster, and LearnSci further sustains engagement beyond class by providing adaptive simulations, quizzes, and feedback that respond to individual learning needs (Chen et al., 2025).

Collaboration is fostered through structured group interactions in both online and face-to-face settings. ILH sessions emphasize teamwork through group discussions, jigsaw activities, and debates that encourage students to share perspectives, construct knowledge together, and develop communication skills. Meanwhile, during ISL sessions, the instructor demonstrates case studies or live discussions while students contribute their ideas through chat or verbal responses, promoting active participation. AI chatbots such as Noodle Factory are used for interactive role-plays and quizzes, helping students practice and strengthen their topic understanding through active participation (Garrison & Anderson, 2003; Johnson & Johnson, 2009).

Reflection is embedded throughout the learning process to help students think critically about their progress, challenges, and strategies for improvement. After

ISL classes, students complete reflective prompts or feedback-based quizzes in Noodle Factory that highlight misconceptions and reinforce understanding. ILH sessions often conclude with reflective debriefs or peer feedback discussions that encourage students to articulate what they have learned and identify areas needing further exploration. Reflection is crucial to metacognitive growth, as it enables students to monitor and regulate their own understanding (Kolb, 1984; Schön, 1987; Zimmerman, 2002).

Finally, the Application ensures that students can transfer theoretical knowledge to practical, real-world contexts. Labster provides virtual laboratory environments where students conduct simulated experiments and interpret results, while ILH sessions integrate case studies, problem-based activities, and role plays that connect classroom learning with professional practice in the life sciences. Through AI-supported adaptive tasks in Noodle Factory, students apply concepts to new scenarios and receive personalized feedback to refine their understanding (Chi & Wylie, 2014; Freeman et al., 2014). Together, these four pillars ensure that learning in the AHA model remains engaging, collaborative, reflective, and applicable across all modalities, creating a dynamic and inclusive environment that supports deep, meaningful learning for all students.

2.1.3 AI-supported personalization

The third pillar of the AHAL model is AI-supported personalization, which utilises the capabilities of artificial intelligence to provide adaptive, individualized, and continuous learning support. In this framework, AI is not merely an added feature; it serves as a central enabler that connects asynchronous, synchronous, and face-to-face learning experiences. Through tools like Noodle Factory, Labster, and LearnSci, students receive real-time feedback, adaptive guidance, and opportunities for self-paced practice.

AI-driven personalization allows learning paths to be dynamically adjusted based on student performance, engagement, and individual learning needs. This creates a responsive and data-informed educational environment. Recent research highlights that AI tutors and intelligent learning systems can significantly enhance engagement and mastery by providing immediate formative feedback and targeted support, often matching or even surpassing the effectiveness of traditional instructor-led sessions (Kestin et al., 2025). According to Létourneau (2025), it has also been shown that the use of AI in education promotes deeper problem-solving, increased metacognitive awareness, and enhanced collaborative learning by adapting to students' states and behaviors.

Moreover, studies carried out by Kosslyn (2025) on "Dynamic Personalized Learning: Leveraging AI to Develop Active Learning Experiences" emphasized that

AI-driven tools can seamlessly integrate with active learning strategies, transforming passive study into interactive and personalized exploration. Within the AHAL model, these technologies automate feedback, provide intelligent tutoring, and use analytics to inform teaching and learning decisions, ensuring that every learner benefits from a continuously optimized and inclusive educational experience.

The AHAL model is built on three main ideas that work together: HyFlex design, active learning, and AI-supported personalization. HyFlex design gives students flexibility and choice in how they learn, making sure that all learning modes are equal, reusable, and accessible. Active learning focuses on keeping students engaged, collaborating, and reflecting and applications. AI-supported personalization helps by giving tailored guidance, instant feedback, and learning insights.

The AHAL model allows students to move easily between on-campus, live online, and self-paced learning, while keeping learning outcomes consistent and offering personal support. In this way, it supports fairness, flexibility, and independent learning for all students.

Overall, the literature indicates that HyFlex learning, active learning strategies, and emerging AI-supported pedagogies can significantly enhance student engagement, flexibility, and personalized learning experiences. However, several challenges and debates remain. Existing studies have noted that while AI tools offer substantial pedagogical benefits, they may also introduce additional responsibilities for instructors, including redesigning assessments, monitoring AI-generated outputs, and addressing ethical concerns such as data privacy and algorithmic bias (Kasneci et al., 2023; Bozkurt et al., 2023). Building on this literature, there remains a need for structured pedagogical frameworks that meaningfully integrate AI tools within HyFlex environments while maintaining pedagogical coherence and supporting instructor adaptability. The Adaptive HyFlex Active Learning (AHAL) model proposed in this chapter addresses these gaps by combining HyFlex delivery with active learning principles and AI-supported instructional strategies.

3. AI-SUPPORTED ACTIVE HYFLEX LEARNING MODEL IN SCHOOL OF BIOSCIENCES

The AHAL model, enabled by AI championed by Taylor's University School of Biosciences, is a paradigm shift toward pedagogy for future-proofing the life sciences. This section outlines the structure, components, and rationale of the AHAL model, highlighting how it addresses common challenges in foundational life science education. The effectiveness of the AHAL model may vary depending on institutional readiness, available resources, and student characteristics.

Based on Beatty's (2007, 2019) HyFlex principles of learner choice, equivalency, reusability, and accessibility, the AHA model combines flexible course design, active learning methods, and AI-driven tools to make higher education more inclusive, engaging, and adaptable. By linking each identified challenge to a specific model component, this discussion emphasizes the problem–solution alignment central to the AHAL approach. It was implemented across three core undergraduate modules in the first year, first semester, including Cell Biology, Biochemistry Principles and Introduction to Microbiology, which constitute a collective scientific foundation for Biotechnology, Biomedical Science, Food Science, and Applied Health Sciences programmes.

Active learning was embedded at the core of the model, with the intention of developing students' engagement and ownership of learning. Organized activities such as group discussion, gamified quizzes, debate, problem solving and role play were blended into the curriculum to promote engagement. The organized activities were supplemented with HyFlex delivery and AI-enabled tools to create a learning space where students could engage meaningfully, whether participating face to face, synchronously online or asynchronously. This three-layer mix of HyFlex flexibility, active learning and AI customization was the pedagogical foundation of the model (Freeman et al. 2014; Baker et al. 2024).

While this model enhances flexibility and engagement, its implementation requires investment in AI tools, staff training, and ongoing maintenance. Institutions with limited resources may experience different outcomes, and long-term sustainability depends on continued support and infrastructure.

The model structure comprised three interrelated components that harmonize together to provide an integrated learning setting. The first was the Interactive Synchronous Learning Hour, conducted fortnightly in online sessions lasting approximately two hours. These incorporated AI avatar videos, real-time Microsoft Teams debates and interactive in-video quizzes. The AI avatars, built from pre-scripted lectures, ensured standardized delivery of core concepts across cohorts and gave students the convenience of studying material at their own pace. The incorporation of live question-and-answer sessions and real-time discussion boards helped create continuity and connection between asynchronous and synchronous interaction.

The second component is the Interactive Learning Hour, which was conducted weekly in person to reinforce ideas introduced in the online sessions. Different active learning strategies, such as think-pair-share, group debates, gamification, and role play, were incorporated in each one-hour session. For instance, in Introduction to Microbiology, students experienced an outbreak investigation simulation replicating a public-health response; in Cell Biology, students shared analysis of microscopy images using digital annotation tools; and in Principles of Biochemistry, they engaged in enzyme-kinetics games and molecular-modelling exercises. These activities encouraged critical thinking, collaboration and communication that are central to scientific inquiry and laboratory practice.

The third element featured AI-driven learning platforms designed to personalize and extend learning beyond the classroom. Adaptive quizzes, automated formative feedback and AI-generated assessments that guided students through weekly subject matter were delivered through Noodle Factory. The platform's analytics enabled teachers to identify misconceptions and adapt their pedagogy accordingly. Labster provided virtual simulation experiments that enabled practice in microbial culture handling, enzymatic assays and microscopy skills, particularly useful when physical lab access was restricted. LearnSci modules supplemented biochemistry and microbiology conceptual learning with embedded interactive exercises and instant feedback. Although these AI platforms facilitate personalized learning and formative feedback, their effectiveness depends on student self-regulation, digital literacy, and thoughtful integration by educators. Together, these platforms supported student autonomy, allowing students to choose when and how they would learn while maintaining equivalence in academic quality across learning modes.

Overall, the AHAL model combines HyFlex flexibility, active learning strategies, and AI support to create a structured yet adaptable learning environment, while recognizing that successful implementation requires planning, resources, and ongoing evaluation.

4. IMPLEMENTATION IN LIFE SCIENCE MODULES

The School of Biosciences (SBS) at Taylor's University has embarked on a pilot initiative to introduce the AHAL teaching and learning model into three cornerstone life science modules—Cell Biology, Principles of Biochemistry, and Introduction to Microbiology. These modules were carefully selected because of their centrality to the undergraduate programmes offered under the School, namely Biotechnology, Biomedical Sciences, Food Science, and Applied Health Sciences. Together, they form the academic foundation upon which more specialised knowledge and professional competencies are built.

By integrating AHAL pedagogy into these core modules, SBS aims to explore how flexible, technology-enabled learning environments can enhance inclusivity, adaptability, and student engagement across disciplines. The initiative also responds to a broader institutional goal: to develop learning ecosystems that are responsive to the diverse needs of contemporary students and resilient in the face of future disruptions.

This chapter provides the rationale for selecting these three modules and discusses why life sciences provide a particularly fertile ground for educational innovation. It also examines how the adoption of HyFlex strengthens diversity, flexibility, accessibility, and equity in learning—key values that align with Taylor's University's commitment to student-centered and future-ready education.

4.1 Rationale for Module Selection

The choice of Cell Biology, Principles of Biochemistry, and Introduction to Microbiology was neither incidental nor purely logistical. These modules were identified through deliberate pedagogical reflection and strategic planning. They were considered ideal for a HyFlex pilot because of their foundational nature, cross-programme relevance, and balanced combination of theoretical and practical learning experiences.

4.2 Foundational Significance

Each of these modules represents a gateway to understanding life at its most fundamental level. Cell Biology introduces students to the intricate architecture and functioning of cells—the basic unit of life—laying the groundwork for advanced topics such as molecular genetics, physiology, and immunology. Principles of Biochemistry equips students with the "language of molecules," allowing them to grasp metabolic regulation, enzyme kinetics, and the biochemical processes that sustain life. Introduction to Microbiology, meanwhile, opens students' eyes to the unseen microbial world, exploring its implications for health, agriculture, and food systems.

These subjects are taught in the early stages of all SBS degree programmes, where students are still developing their scientific thinking and learning identities. As such, they provide the most appropriate context for testing new teaching innovations. Literature in higher education supports this approach. Wong et al. (2023) emphasise that HyFlex models are most impactful when applied to large, foundational courses, as they reach diverse student populations and provide rich opportunities to assess different learning preferences. Similarly, Cumming et al. (2024) highlight that inclusivity and accessibility are especially crucial in introductory modules, where students' prior knowledge and technological proficiency often vary widely. Implementing HyFlex at this stage allows educators to close learning gaps early and to build habits of self-regulation and autonomy that will benefit students throughout their studies.

4.3 Cross-Programme Relevance

A second factor driving the selection of these modules is their cross-programme integration. Each is a core requirement across multiple undergraduate programmes within the school of Biotechnology, Biomedical Sciences, Food Science, and Applied Health Sciences. This shared curriculum framework ensures that the AHAL model pilot engages a broad and diverse cohort of students, encompassing a variety of academic interests, career goals, and personal learning needs.

Such diversity provides a valuable testing ground for flexible learning models. Amirova et al. (2023) note that technology-enhanced and hybrid approaches are particularly effective in heterogeneous classrooms because they allow students to choose participation modes that align with their individual circumstances while maintaining equivalent learning outcomes. In the context of SBS, this means that a biotechnology student focusing on laboratory research and an applied health student balancing clinical training can both thrive within the same flexible ecosystem.

4.4 Pedagogical Suitability

The hybrid structure of these modules—combining conceptual lectures with hands-on laboratory practice—makes them exceptionally well-suited for this model delivery. While theoretical content can be presented asynchronously or synchronously online, laboratory components require face-to-face engagement for skill acquisition and experiential learning. This combination allows the school to test the limits and possibilities of AHAL pedagogy: how technology can supplement, but not replace, embodied learning experiences that are essential to the life sciences.

Liu and Rodriguez (2023) argue that HyFlex and blended learning approaches are particularly valuable in courses that balance abstract theory with applied practice, as they allow students to review and reinforce complex ideas through digital materials before or after practical sessions. Wong et al. (2023) similarly found that technology-mediated practices, such as recorded laboratory demonstrations or virtual experiments, enhance students' understanding of applied science concepts and support self-paced learning. In the context of Biochemistry or Microbiology, this flexibility allows students to revisit molecular pathways or laboratory protocols multiple times, deepening their comprehension.

4.5 Timing and Student Readiness

The decision to implement AHAL in first- and second-year modules was also informed by considerations of timing and developmental readiness. These courses are taught during a period when students are still adjusting to the expectations of university learning—grappling with scientific language, laboratory discipline, and independent study. Early exposure to flexible, student-directed learning models helps cultivate self-regulation, digital literacy, and ownership of learning—all essential attributes for success in higher-level courses and future scientific careers.

The AHEAD 2030 Horizon Scanning Report underscores that foundational courses are the ideal sites for introducing pedagogical innovation, as they help students build adaptive learning strategies and technological fluency from the outset. Jarni and Gurr (2024) likewise contend that "next practices" in education—those emphasizing choice, collaboration, and multimodality—are best introduced early in a programme, allowing students to internalise them as part of their academic identity.

In summary, these three modules were selected because they unite curricular importance, cross-disciplinary relevance, pedagogical versatility, and strategic timing. By piloting the AHAL model at this critical juncture in the curriculum, SBS can assess its efficacy in shaping not only student learning outcomes but also attitudes, skills, and academic confidence.

4.6 Promoting Diversity, Flexibility, Accessibility, and Equity

Embracing Diversity

Students in the life sciences bring varied cultural, educational, and socioeconomic backgrounds. Traditional classroom models, while effective for some, may unintentionally marginalise others who juggle family responsibilities, work commitments, or health challenges. The AHAL model empowers students to engage through multiple modalities, creating a more equitable environment where individual circumstances do not limit participation (Cumming et al., 2024; Bakar et al., 2024).

Ensuring Flexibility

Flexibility lies at the heart of HyFlex, which is one of the core components of the AHAL model. Students may move fluidly between physical and virtual participation according to their personal schedules. For life sciences students managing fieldwork, lab sessions, or part-time employment, this adaptability is invaluable. Studies show that such flexibility fosters engagement, reduces stress, and improves overall satisfaction (Wong et al., 2023).

Expanding Accessibility

Accessibility extends beyond physical presence. Recorded lectures, digital laboratory demonstrations, and interactive online resources allow students to review materials repeatedly, supporting mastery learning. This approach particularly benefits international students, those with health conditions, or those facing logistical barriers (Cumming et al., 2024).

Advancing Equity

Equity in education is achieved when all students, regardless of background or circumstance, have genuine opportunities to succeed. The AHAL model ensures equivalency of learning experiences across modes of participation. It levels the playing field for students who may otherwise face geographic, financial, or caregiving constraints (Amirova et al., 2023).

4.8 Technology Integration and Student Autonomy

Technology underpins the success of the AHAL model delivery. When used purposefully, it not only enables flexibility but also fosters deeper learning. Wong et al. (2023) note that technology-mediated instruction enhances engagement by giving students control over pace and timing, thereby promoting self-directed learning.

Digital competence and self-regulated learning are key predictors of success in AHAL model environments. Amiruddin et al. (2024) found that students with strong technological skills exhibit greater motivation and adaptability, as they can personalize their learning strategies. This is particularly relevant in disciplines like biochemistry or molecular biology, where complex information often requires iterative learning.

Furthermore, AHAL pedagogy contributes to a more inclusive and responsive educational environment. As Baker et al. (2024) point out, it provides resilience in times of disruption—be it a pandemic, natural disaster, or personal crisis—ensuring learning continuity without sacrificing quality. This adaptability nurtures a sense of belonging, which is essential to student wellbeing and retention.

4.9 Application in the Three Modules

In practice, AHAL model implementation within the pilot modules will manifest differently according to pedagogical needs. In Cell Biology, for instance, digital microscopy demonstrations will supplement live laboratory sessions, allowing students to observe, pause, and review cellular structures and techniques. In Principles of Biochemistry, recorded lectures and problem-solving tutorials will help students navigate complex metabolic pathways, while collaborative online discussions will promote peer learning. In Introduction to Microbiology, pre-laboratory safety simulations will prepare students for in-person experiments, ensuring that essential hands-on competencies are achieved while maintaining flexibility for those unable to attend every session.

4.10 Anticipated Benefits for SBS

Through this pilot, SBS anticipates several outcomes:

- Enhanced student satisfaction and engagement through flexible and responsive learning pathways.
- Greater inclusivity and accessibility for students from diverse educational and personal backgrounds.
- Improved equity in participation and outcomes across all programmes.
- Strengthened digital literacy, autonomy, and self-regulated learning skills among students.
- Increased institutional resilience and pedagogical readiness for future educational disruptions.

The introduction of the AHAL model in Cell Biology, Principles of Biochemistry, and Introduction to Microbiology represents a significant pedagogical milestone for the School of Biosciences. By embedding flexibility, choice, and technological empowerment into foundational learning, SBS reaffirms its commitment to cultivating an inclusive, future-ready generation of scientists.

Far from being a temporary response to changing educational demands, the AHAL model offers a sustainable model for 21st-century learning—one that respects the diversity of student experiences while maintaining the rigour and integrity of scientific education. Within the life sciences, this model does more than transform the mode of delivery; it transforms the learner's experience itself.

5. STUDENT ENGAGEMENT AND EXPERIENCES

HyFlex, a term originally coined by Beatty (2007), merges in-person and online learning with an emphasis on student choice and flexibility. The main goal of this model was to allow students to attend classes face-to-face or remotely (synchronously or asynchronously) according to their needs, thereby maintaining participation even during disruptions. In contrast to the purely face-to-face format of September 2024, the AHAL model (implemented by April 2025) gave students greater agency in how they participated. This fundamental change in instructional delivery had a noticeable impact on student engagement.

At the institution under review, feedback collected in April 2025 reflected this value of choice: students highlighted the ability to manage personal schedules more effectively and avoid disruptions to their studies due to illness or unforeseen circumstances. Such feedback resonates with international findings that HyFlex supports equitable access by ensuring continuity during unplanned events such as illness, transport problems, or climate-related disruptions (Baker et al., 2024). While flexibility was welcomed by many, it was also clear that not all students experienced this model in the same way. The April 2025 survey data revealed variations in acceptance across student demographics. International students expressed higher acceptance of AI-based learning assistants (71.9%) and AI avatar videos (43.8%) compared with local students (47.8% and 15.8%, respectively). This deviation may reflect differences in prior exposure to technology, cultural expectations of teaching, and perceived authenticity of digital tools. The findings highlight that this model does not produce uniform experiences, but rather amplifies differences shaped by background and learning preferences.

Furthermore, changes in participation patterns were observed. Class participation became more diversified, as some students who were quiet in face-to-face settings found their voice online. This aligns with recent studies reporting that students can be more actively engaged in synchronous online classes than in traditional classrooms. For example, students asked more questions and volunteered explanations more readily during live online sessions than in person. In our AHAL implementation, features like live chat and discussion boards provided additional channels for interaction. Several students took advantage of these tools to clarify concepts in real time or to continue discussions after class, indicating that this model can foster interactive engagement beyond the confines of the physical classroom. This multi-modal participation resonates with the literature suggesting this multimodal approach engages students in new ways and caters to different communication preferences (Picciano, 2019, as cited in Amiruddin et al., 2024). Notably, student agency in choosing the mode of participation contributed to a sense of comfort, felt more confident typing out questions or attending virtually, which in turn kept them actively involved in the learning process. Some students responded with excitement and appreciation. *"I was enjoying it,"* one student wrote simply, referring to the AHAL model format's blend of online and face-to-face elements. Another admitted, *"I think use AI can better test myself about the topic I have learned."* This student found value in the AI-based quizzes and explanations as a way to check understanding at their own pace, highlighting a segment of the class that thrived under self-directed, technology-enhanced learning.

Despite these positive trends, student experiences also revealed important challenges and variations in engagement. A portion of students expressed a strong preference for the traditional classroom, indicating that *"nothing beats face-to-face"* interaction for deep engagement and understanding. Some found the asynchronous or video components of AHAL less effective: for instance, one student commented that *"AI avatar videos are extremely unhelpful, prefer face to face"*, feeling that important distinctions were lost in pre-recorded lectures. Another admitted, *"I found the AHAL learning experience less effective than expected,"* underscoring that simply providing online content is not a good way to teach. These views underline the continued importance of human presence and immediacy in learning. They mirror observations from international studies on hyflex model that, while HyFlex offers convenience, students still highly value face-to-face interaction for collaborative learning and clarity. For example, in Baker et al.'s (2024) HyFlex study, one participant noted *"talking with my peers face to face is much more conducive to sharing, clarifying, and collaborating"*, suggesting that in-person dialogue can feel more natural and productive. Likewise, some of our students reported that discussions flowed less smoothly online, echoing the concern that virtual conversations can be "clunky" compared to the spontaneity of in-person classes. Another frustrated comment revealed a critical issue: *"Video says so much less than the full set of notes... it is confusing to know what is the important part of the lesson that is crucial for exam."* This feedback indicated that the condensed AI avatar video lectures (designed to summarize key concepts) sometimes oversimplified or obscured the priorities, leaving students unsure about exam-relevant content.

Another engagement issue in this model environment was the sense of disconnection between online and in-person students if not carefully managed. Several survey respondents pointed out that there was *"less interaction between the lecturers and students"* overall, and that *"the interaction between online and in-person students felt very disconnected, and online participation was often sidelined"*. This feedback highlights a risk of parallel tracks emerging in HyFlex classes, where remote students might become passive observers if instructors don't intentionally integrate them. Such concerns are echoed in broader literature; for instance, Baker et al. (2024) found that while HyFlex students appreciated flexibility, they also wanted more opportunities to connect and feel part of the learning community. Technology was sometimes cited as both a barrier and an enabler: technical glitches, poor audio, or camera issues could hinder engagement for remote participants, even as the technology also enabled others to participate who otherwise couldn't. These nuances suggest that student engagement in this model is highly contingent on implementation. When done well, the AHAL model can support strong engagement by fostering inclusivity, self-efficacy, and belonging. But without deliberate instructional design to create a unified classroom experience, some students may feel isolated or less involved. Overall, the shift to the AHAL model transformed the student experience: it provided new avenues for participation and greater flexibility yet required overcoming new challenges to ensure all students remained equally engaged and connected.

6. TEACHING STAFF'S PERSPECTIVE

Teaching staff perspectives provide critical insights into the pedagogical and professional implications of implementing the AHAL model supported by artificial intelligence (AI). While this approach was developed to enhance accessibility and continuity of learning, lecturers involved in the modules reported that the process demanded substantial time for preparation, material redesign, and technological adaptation. Several lecturers described developing teaching content in the AHAL model, particularly AI-assisted video materials, as initially an increased workload, as they needed to restructure lecture notes, prerecorded scripts, and familiarize themselves with digital tools. However, the effort became more manageable over time, as once the digital materials and workflows were established, future iterations required only minor modifications. This experience reflects what has been observed in other higher education contexts, where the initial implementation phase of hybrid or AI-supported teaching often requires a steep learning curve followed by improved efficiency (Tan et al., 2025; Zawacki-Richter et al., 2019).

The teaching staff collectively recognized the importance of digital upskilling as a necessary outcome of adopting this model. They noted that the process encouraged continuous learning and adaptation to emerging technologies. As one lecturer expressed, "The system forced us to become digitally competent educators." This aligns with broader literature emphasizing that teacher readiness and technological confidence are essential for sustaining digital pedagogical practices (Basilotta-Gómez-Pablos et al., 2022; Tan et al., 2025). Despite this positive shift, lecturers also identified the challenge of maintaining human connection and authenticity in AI-mediated environments. The use of pre-recorded AI avatar lectures was considered efficient but less personal compared to live sessions. Some reported that students perceived the videos as "too perfect" and missed the spontaneity of in-person lectures. This observation aligns with previous studies that have reported reduced interaction and engagement as key limitations of AI-driven delivery (Wut et al., 2025). In addition to AI avatar content, the integration of Noodle Factory for formative assessment was generally well-received. Staff appreciated the platform's ability to generate instant feedback and track student progress, allowing them to redirect effort toward higher-order instructional activities. However, they also noted occasional inaccuracies in AI-generated questions and answers, reinforcing the need for ongoing human oversight. This hybrid dynamic, combining automation with lecturer moderation, was viewed as essential to maintaining pedagogical quality. The system's ability to automate repetitive marking tasks reduced routine workload and created more time for student mentoring and research activities.

Although the AHAL approach offers pedagogical flexibility and operational efficiency, some lecturers reported a gradual sense of emotional exhaustion and pedagogical detachment after prolonged implementation. The need to simultaneously manage in-person and online students, design AI-ready content, and monitor multiple digital tools often resulted in cognitive overload and reduced job satisfaction. Recent studies indicate that continuous exposure to AI-mediated systems can heighten teacher burnout and emotional fatigue, particularly when institutional structures fail to provide adequate psychosocial support (Tang et al., 2025; Shamsuddinova, 2024). Educators also described a diminished sense of connection with students, as interactions mediated through AI avatars or automated platforms limited spontaneity and empathy—key features of meaningful teaching relationships (Carter et al., 2025). This depersonalization reflects a broader challenge in technology-rich learning environments, where efficiency sometimes supersedes authenticity and emotional presence. Without deliberate institutional strategies to sustain educator well-being and human interaction, the long-term use of AI-HyFlex systems risks eroding motivation and professional identity, thereby compromising the sustainability of pedagogical innovation in higher education (Deep et al., 2025).

Ethical and professional considerations also emerged as important concerns. Lecturers expressed apprehension about the authenticity of AI-generated teaching materials and questioned how their recorded voices and gestures might be stored or reused. This concern aligns with long-standing debates on data privacy, ownership, and academic integrity in AI-assisted education, as discussed by Holmes et al. (2019), and has become increasingly pressing with the emergence of generative AI tools and evolving ethical frameworks (Kamali et al., 2024). Maintaining transparency and authenticity was seen as vital to ensuring students' trust and protecting the professional identity of educators. Another issue raised by staff concerned the copyright and authorship of AI-generated teaching materials. Although lecturers prepared the original scripts and recordings, these digital assets could technically be repurposed or assigned to AI avatars not representing the original authors. This raised concerns about ownership, consent, and professional representation. Similar issues regarding educator identity and moral rights in digital teaching contexts have been highlighted in recent studies that discuss ethical and human-centered approaches to AI integration in education (Fu et al., 2024; Knox, 2020). Institutions, therefore, need to establish clear policies to safeguard educators' intellectual property and prevent misuse of their digital likenesses. Participants emphasized that AI tools should be used to complement, not replace, the educator's role in fostering engagement, empathy, and critical thinking (Porayska-Pomsta et al., 2023).

Institutional support was widely acknowledged as a decisive factor in the success of the AHAL model implementation. Lecturers who received clear policy guidance, technical assistance, and pedagogical training reported smoother transitions and greater confidence in using AI tools, while inconsistent communication or limited administrative backing often led to uncertainty and workload stress. This underscores the institutional responsibility to establish structured frameworks for professional development, ethical AI use, and equitable workload management (Beatty, 2019; Shahzad et al., 2025; Wut et al., 2025). Despite the initial challenges, teaching staff ultimately regarded the AHAL as both demanding and rewarding. Once digital workflows were established, many found that they enhanced instructional efficiency, encouraged pedagogical innovation, and expanded flexible learning opportunities for students. However, staff emphasized that the approach should be applied selectively, particularly for concept-driven modules rather than those requiring high levels of spontaneity or laboratory-based interaction. The dominant ideas emerging from staff reflections are illustrated in **Figure 2**, which visualizes frequently cited terms such as preparation effort, digital upskilling, human interaction, and institutional support, highlighting the key dimensions shaping their overall teaching experience.

Figure 2. Teaching staff perceptions of the AHAL learning model. The word cloud illustrates key concepts derived from qualitative reflections of five lecturers who implemented the AHAL model approach in their modules. The relative size of each word indicates its prominence in the participants' feedback, highlighting recurrent areas such as preparation effort, digital upskilling, human interaction, and institutional support.

7. ASSESSMENTS AND OUTCOMES

Implementing AHAL raised the question about academic outcomes: *Would students learn as effectively? How would assessments be managed fairly across modes?* A critical concern in adopting the AHAL model was whether academic outcomes would remain consistent across delivery modes. To investigate this, final exam results from September 2024 (pre-AHAL model, traditional delivery) were compared with April 2025 (AHAL model implementation). Both cohorts undertook the same assessment structure, with final exams weighed at 40% of the overall grade. This parallel design allowed for a meaningful comparison of student performance between the two delivery formats.

Figure 3. Final exam score averages (out of 40 points) in three modules, comparing the September 2024 (non-AHAL model) cohort and the April 2025 (AHAL model) cohort. Each pair of bars represents the average final exam mark (out of 40) for a core module in the curriculum. The AHAL cohort matched or slightly exceeded the performance of the prior cohort in all three modules

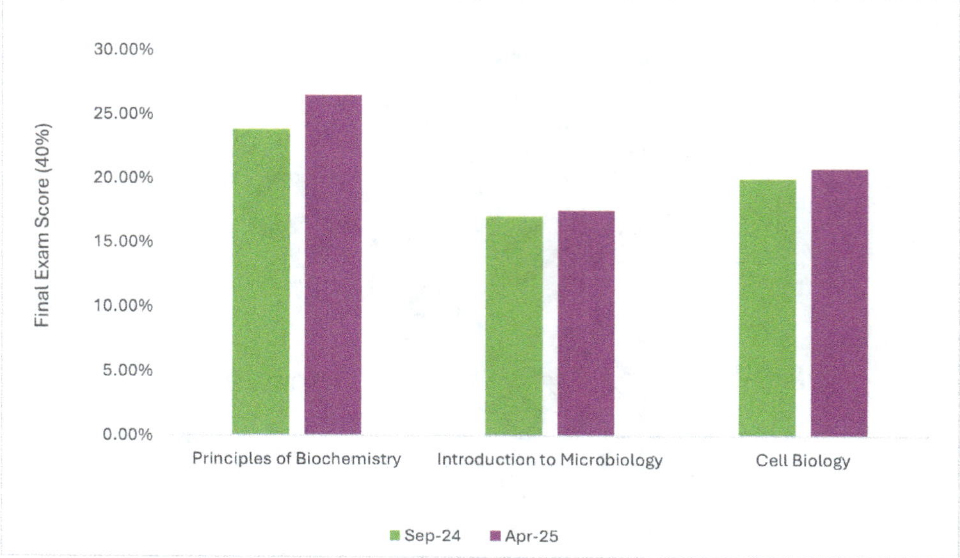

In order to align the content and difficulty of assessments with the learning activities in each mode. For example, when the AHAL model cohort received asynchronous video lectures, the accompanying quizzes were adjusted to reinforce those videos' content, ensuring that remote and in-person students were equally prepared for what the final exam would demand.

The comparative results were encouraging. As illustrated in Figure 3, students in the AHAL model cohort performed on par with, and in some cases slightly better than, their counterparts from the traditional offering. In *Principles of Biochemistry*, for instance, the April 2025 AHAl model group's average final exam score was a few points higher than the September 2024 group's average. A similar uptick was observed in *Introduction to Microbiology* and *Cell Biology*, though the differences were modest. These small gains fall within normal year-to-year variation, but importantly, there was no decline in performance attributable to this model format. In other words, giving students more flexibility did not come at the expense of their learning outcomes – if anything, it may have provided a slight boost. From an educator's perspective, this was a relief and a validation. One of the biggest concerns starting out was whether the lack of a traditional, arranged schedule would lead to gaps in knowledge or lower achievement. Seeing the AHAL model cohort succeed academically put to rest many of those anxieties. It indicated that, when supported properly, students can thrive under a flexible learning environment and still meet the rigorous outcomes of the course. This finding aligns with reports in the literature that other HyFlex model courses can achieve outcomes comparable to or even better than single-mode courses. Karlsson and Steen's (2025) study, for example, found that a HyFlex implementation yielded the highest student performance (and satisfaction) when compared to the same course delivered fully face-to-face before the pandemic, or fully online during the pandemic.

Several factors might explain why the AHAL model cohort did as well as, if not slightly better than, the traditional cohort. One hypothesis is that the additional resources and autonomy in this model empowered students to engage with the material in ways that suited them best. For instance, students had 24/7 access to recorded lectures and AI-generated quizzes for self-practice; those who took advantage of these could reinforce their learning continuously, rather than being limited to notes from a one-time lecture. Many of the top-performing students in the AHAL model cohort were those actively using the Noodle Factory AI learning assistant to test themselves on key concepts weekly. By contrast, in the pre-AHAL model run, students without such tools might have only revisited material during scheduled tutorials closer to the exam. This suggests that the AHAL model's flexibility can promote better study habits and ongoing revision, contributing to strong exam performance. Research on student behaviors supports this: when given flexibility, motivated students often space out their learning and make use of online materials for revision, which is known to improve retention (Luo et al., 2022; Huang & Wang, 2023; Jarrah et al., 2025). Of course, not every student utilized the resources equally – a few admitted in feedback that they "fell behind" because it depended on them to watch the videos or attempt the quizzes on their own time. For those students, the structured rhythm of a face-to-face class might have been beneficial. This highlights an important point: self-regulation has become a more prominent factor in success under this model. Students with strong time-management and self-study skills fared well, whereas those who struggled with discipline needed additional support. This observation resonates with findings by Amiruddin et al. (2024) that students' technological skills and self-regulated learning habits significantly influence their attitude and success in HyFlex environments. As such, one of our takeaways was to incorporate more guidance on study strategies and time management into the HyFlex course orientation, to help all students adjust to the greater freedom (and responsibility) that comes with this format.

It's also worth discussing student perceptions of assessment in this model context, because *outcomes* are not just numbers, but also confidence and satisfaction in the learning process. Some students voiced concerns about how they felt for the final exam. As mentioned, one critique was that condensing the model materials made it harder to discern important content. To mitigate this, I incorporated more formative assessments throughout the term – weekly low-stakes quizzes and reflective prompts – to give students continuous feedback on their understanding. The idea was to mimic the frequent check-ins that happen informally in a physical class (like when you see confused faces and clarify on the fly) by embedding checkpoints in the proposed model course. These formative activities were especially helpful for students who engaged with them; they reported feeling more confident about what they needed to know. However, not all students took the optional quizzes, and interestingly, those who skipped them were often the ones who later felt unsure about exam content. This pattern reinforced the value of engagement in the AHAL model: the more a student interacted with the available materials and activities, the better their outcome tended to be.

In the AHAL model implementation, student outcomes remained steady. Exam scores and pass rates were consistent with previous cohorts, meeting the baseline goal of ensuring that learning quality was not compromised. Beyond the numbers, however, the experience revealed a richer and more complex picture. Many students appreciated the greater autonomy and flexibility that the AHAL model offered, while others struggled to stay engaged or felt less connected to the learning community. End-of-semester feedback reflected this duality: some described the model as "refreshing" and "adaptable," while others admitted they still preferred the structure of traditional face-to-face learning. Yet, overall satisfaction levels did not decline compared to the previous cohort. For every student who missed the old format, there was another who found the new one empowering. This balance mirrors Karlsson and Steen's (2025) observations that HyFlex can achieve high satisfaction and performance when implemented well, though outcomes depend heavily on student expectations and learning habits.

Overall, the assessment outcomes from the AHAL model implementation presented an encouraging picture. The AHAL model cohort performed on par with, and in some cases slightly better than, the traditional cohort, demonstrating that learning objectives can be achieved within a flexible format without compromising academic quality. This finding supports global evidence suggesting that when implemented thoughtfully, hybrid-flexible teaching "does no harm" to student achievement and can, in fact, enhance it (Karlsson & Steen, 2025). These results validate the potential of this model as a sustainable pedagogical model capable of maintaining performance while broadening access and engagement.

Ultimately, the success of this model cannot be measured by exam results alone. Its true impact lies in creating learning environments where students feel both empowered and supported, where flexibility coexists with structure, and where autonomy is balanced by connection. The collective insights from institutional data, student feedback, and the broader hyflex literature point toward a single conclusion: when approached with intention and empathy, this proposed model of learning represents not merely an adjustment in delivery but a holistic evolution in the way teaching and learning can occur in contemporary higher education.

8. FUTURE PERSPECTIVES IN THE NATION'S HIGHER EDUCATION SYSTEM

The adoption of the AHAL model pedagogy at Taylor's University represents a strategic advancement that aligns with Malaysia's national vision for a flexible, inclusive, and technology-driven education system. Higher education in the country is evolving toward personalized learning ecosystems that integrate digital tools to support diverse student needs while staying connected with global educational transformations (Beatty, 2019; Wong et al, 2023). This evolution reflects Malaysia's commitment to Education 5.0, emphasizing human and technological collaboration for future-ready graduates (Ministry of Higher Education Malaysia, 2015).

The success of this model in life science modules provides a scalable framework for other disciplines such as business, engineering, and health sciences. Expanding this approach will require sustained institutional commitment, digital infrastructure enhancement, and policies that safeguard ethical AI use, data protection, and faculty rights (Kamali et al, 2024; Shahzad et al., 2025). When implemented with strong institutional governance, the AHAL model can serve as a blueprint for national educational transformation, fostering equity and adaptability across academic disciplines (Cumming et al., 2024).

AI learning analytics can revolutionize data-informed teaching by enabling early identification of at-risk students and promoting adaptive learning interventions. Predictive dashboards and personalized feedback systems empower educators to design responsive teaching strategies that enhance student engagement and retention (Porayska-Pomsta, et al., 2023). This approach aligns with global trends where data-driven pedagogy strengthens inclusivity and learning outcomes in flexible learning environments (Basilotta-Gómez-Pablos et al., 2022). It also complements Malaysia's Education 5.0 vision, where human and technological collaboration ensures that flexibility is matched with personalized support.

Educators must now evolve into learning designers and digital mentors who facilitate active, self-directed, and technology-enhanced learning. Faculty digital upskilling at Taylor's University has already led to greater innovation and professional empowerment, mirroring international observations that teacher readiness and technological confidence are key enablers of sustainable AI integration in higher education (Tan et al, 2025; Zawacki-Richter et al., 2019). At a national level, embedding AI literacy, instructional design, and ethical awareness into professional development will ensure educators remain central to the human dimension of teaching (Holmes et al, 2019).

Lastly, the AHAL model signifies a paradigm shift from reactive adaptation to proactive transformation. By combining flexibility with academic rigor and technology with empathy, it offers a sustainable pathway for Malaysian higher education. As Malaysia positions itself as a regional hub for digital education, the challenge ahead lies not in deciding whether to adopt such models, but in sustaining, scaling, and humanizing them to ensure that the future of education remains both innovative and profoundly human (Karlsson & Steen, 2025; Baker et al., 2024).

9. LIMITATIONS OF THE AHAL MODEL

While the AHAL model demonstrates promising outcomes in enhancing flexibility and engagement, several limitations should be acknowledged. The successful implementation at Taylor's University benefited from strong institutional support, digital infrastructure, and access to AI-enabled learning tools. Institutions with limited technological resources may face challenges in replicating the model at scale. Additionally, while AI-driven analytics can support personalized learning and early identification of at-risk students, over-reliance on automated systems may reduce opportunities for human pedagogical judgment and require careful attention to ethical considerations such as data privacy and algorithmic bias.

Equity and accessibility also remain important considerations in flexible learning environments. Students may have unequal access to reliable internet connectivity, digital devices, or conducive study spaces, which can influence their engagement with asynchronous materials. Furthermore, extended interaction with digital platforms may contribute to digital fatigue for some learners, particularly those who benefit from more structured or face-to-face learning environments. Finally, although the AHAL model proved effective in life science modules, its implementation may differ across disciplines. Fields that rely heavily on discussion-based learning may require adapted strategies to maintain interaction and experiential learning. These considerations suggest that the AHAL model should be viewed as an adaptable framework rather than a universally prescriptive solution for all educational contexts.

10. POLICY IMPLEMENTATIONS AND CONSIDERATIONS

While the AHAL model demonstrates promising outcomes in engagement, flexibility, and academic performance, scaling this approach requires careful attention to policy, equity, and institutional readiness. Universities and higher education may need to support funding for AI-enabled learning infrastructure, promote faculty digital upskilling, and adjust workload and promotion criteria to recognize the effort required for hybrid and AI-supported pedagogy. Risks, including digital inequality across institutions, limited infrastructure in smaller universities, and the potential for AI-driven surveillance if analytics are misused, should be explicitly considered. Claims regarding national scalability should be framed cautiously, acknowledging that outcomes observed in Taylor's University are prospective and may vary depending on institutional resources and student populations. Embedding these considerations ensures that AHAL implementation remains equitable, sustainable, and aligned with broader strategic goals in higher education.

11. CONCLUSION

In conclusion, the AI-supported HyFlex Active Learning (AHAL) model represents a transformative and future-ready approach to higher education. It seamlessly integrates HyFlex flexibility, active learning engagement, and AI-driven personalization into a consistent and sustainable framework.

This model has been successfully implemented in Taylor's School of Biosciences, enhancing engagement, inclusivity, and accessibility in the Introduction to Microbiology, Cell Biology, and Principles of Biochemistry modules, all without compromising students' academic performance. Both students and educators have experienced increased flexibility and digital empowerment; however, challenges such as emotional fatigue, self-regulation, and the need for authentic human connections have underscored the necessity for balanced design and institutional support. It should be noted that replicating this model requires institutional investment in technology, faculty training, and ongoing maintenance, which may affect sustainability and scalability across different contexts.

Assessment outcomes confirmed that academic achievement remained consistent—and in some cases improved—demonstrating that thoughtful integration of AI-assisted feedback, flexible access, and active learning can uphold rigor and quality. For educators, the model has fostered digital upskilling and pedagogical innovation while also raising ethical and professional considerations regarding AI use, identity, and equitable workload distribution. However, outcomes are conditional on institutional readiness, digital infrastructure, and faculty engagement.

Aligned with Malaysia's Education 5.0 vision, the AHAL model exemplifies how human-technology collaboration can create adaptable, inclusive, and data-informed learning ecosystems. Its success offers a scalable framework for other disciplines and institutions when accompanied by supportive policies, equitable resource allocation, and careful attention to risks such as digital inequality and AI misuse.

The integration of HyFlex, active learning, and AI personalization demonstrates a balanced approach that acknowledges both benefits and challenges, emphasizes human–technology collaboration, and supports student and educator flexibility while addressing emotional fatigue and self-regulation concerns. By presenting AHAL as a flexible framework rather than a rigid prescription, the model provides a robust foundation for scalable and inclusive learning ecosystems.

The AHAL model also directly addresses key challenges in higher education. Table 1 below summarizes how common issues map to model responses, illustrating the problem–solution alignment for students and educators:

Table 1. Mapping of higher education challenges to AHAL model solutions

Challenge/Problem	**AHAL Model Response / Solution**
Low student engagement	HyFlex options, active learning activities, AI tools for interaction
Diverse learning preferences	Multiple participation modes: in-person, synchronous online, asynchronous online
Emotional fatigue/self-regulation	Flexible pacing, formative AI quizzes, structured guidance for self-directed learning
Equity & accessibility gaps	Recorded lectures, virtual labs (Labster, Learn Sci), accessible online resources
Educator workload / digital skills	AI-assisted content creation and automated analytics; supported by professional development and digital upskilling initiatives
Maintaining academic rigor across modes	Standardized AI lectures throughout the module, aligned assessment activities through Noodle Factory, and continuous feedback

Ultimately, the AHAL model redefines higher education as a dynamic partnership between flexibility and structure, automation and empathy—advancing not only academic excellence but also the human values essential for sustainable digital transformation. While promising, the model's effectiveness depends on adequate resources, governance, and careful attention to implementation trade-offs.

REFERENCES

Amirova, A., Zhumabayeva, A., Zhunusbekova, A., Kalbergenova, S., Nygymanova, N., & Arenova, A. (2023). Effect of using HyFlex technology learning on preservice teachers' success and attitudes. *International Journal of Education in Mathematics. Science and Technology*, *11*(3), 623–642. DOI: 10.46328/ijemst.3309

Amiruddin, A., Sunardi, S., & Setialaksana, W. (2024). Students' technological skills and attitudes toward HyFlex learning: The mediating role of online self-regulated learning, blended learning perception, and preferred learning modes. *Frontiers in Education*, *8*, 1258298. DOI: 10.3389/feduc.2023.1258298

Baker, S., Watkinson, M. G., Honeyman, F., Mowll, J., & Tyulkina, S. (2024). Rethinking student engagement for HyFlex teaching and learning: Acknowledging flexibility and agency needed for unplanned events. *International Journal of Lifelong Education*, *43*(4), 432–447. DOI: 10.1080/02601370.2024.2359595

Basilotta-Gómez-Pablos, V., Matarranz, M., Casado-Aranda, L. A., & Otto, A. (2022). Teachers' digital competencies in higher education: A systematic literature review. *International Journal of Educational Technology in Higher Education*, *19*(1), 8. DOI: 10.1186/s41239-021-00312-8

Beatty, B. (2007). Transitioning to an online world: Using HyFlex courses to bridge the gap. In *EdMedia: World Conference on Educational Media and Technology* (pp. 1–7).

Beatty, B. J. (2019). *Hybrid-flexible course design: Implementing student-directed hybrid classes.* EdTech Books. https://edtechbooks.org/hyflex

Bjaelde, O. E., & Lindberg, A. B. (2018). Using continuous assessment with feedback loops to generate useful data for learning analytics. In M. Campbell et al. (Eds.), *Open oceans: Learning without borders. Proceedings ASCILITE 2018* (pp. 53–62). ASCILITE. DOI: 10.14742/apubs.2018.1928

Bonwell, C. C., & Eison, J. A. (1991). ASHE-ERIC Higher Education Report: Vol. 1. *Active learning: Creating excitement in the classroom.*

Bozkurt, A., Xiao, J., Lambert, S., Pazurek, A., Crompton, H., Koseoglu, S., Farrow, R., Bond, M., Nerantzi, C., Honeychurch, S., Bali, M., Dron, J., & Jandrić, P. (2023). Speculative futures on ChatGPT and generative artificial intelligence (AI): A collective reflection from the educational landscape. *Asian Journal of Distance Education*, *18*(1), 53–130.

Carter, J. W., Scott, J. T., & Barrett, J. D. (2025). The emotional cost of AI chatbots in education: Who benefits and who struggles? *Computers in Human Behavior: Artificial Humans*, *5*, 100181. DOI: 10.1016/j.chbah.2025.100181

Chen, F. Z., Chen, L. A., Tseng, C. C., Pai, C. H., Tsai, K. E., Liang, E. C., Chen, Y. F., Chen, T. L., Liu, S. Y., Lee, P. C., Lai, K. C., Liu, B. R., Fouad, K. E., & Chen, C. W. (2025). Enhancing student engagement and learning outcomes in life sciences: Implementing interactive learning environments and flipped classroom models. *Discover Education*, *4*(1), 102. DOI: 10.1007/s44217-025-00501-x

Chi, M. T. H., & Wylie, R. (2014). The ICAP framework: Linking cognitive engagement to active learning outcomes. *Educational Psychologist*, *49*(4), 219–243. DOI: 10.1080/00461520.2014.965823

Cumming, T. M., Gilanyi, L., & Han, C. (2024). HyFlex delivery mode in a postgraduate course: Instructor and student perspectives. *Discover Education*, *3*(1), 24. Advance online publication. DOI: 10.1007/s44217-024-00110-0

Deep, P. D., Ghosh, N., & Chen, Y. (2025). Faculty burnout in higher education: Effects on student engagement, learning outcomes, and artificial intelligence–driven institutional responses. *Journal of Educational and Developmental Psychology*, *15*(1), 29–45. DOI: 10.5539/jedp.v15n1p29

Freeman, S., Eddy, S. L., McDonough, M., Smith, M. K., Okoroafor, N., Jordt, H., & Wenderoth, M. P. (2014). Active learning increases student performance in science, engineering and mathematics. *Proceedings of the National Academy of Sciences of the United States of America*, *111*(23), 8410–8415. DOI: 10.1073/pnas.1319030111 PMID: 24821756

Fu, Y., & Weng, Z. (2024). Navigating the ethical terrain of AI in education: A systematic review on framing responsible human-centered AI practices. *Computers and Education: Artificial Intelligence*, *7*, 100306. DOI: 10.1016/j.caeai.2024.100306

Garrison, D. R., & Anderson, T. (2003). *E-learning in the 21st century: A framework for research and practice.* RoutledgeFalmer.

Holmes, W., Bialik, M., & Fadel, C. (2019). *Artificial intelligence in education: Promise and implications for teaching and learning*. Center for Curriculum Redesign.

Huang, Y., & Wang, S. (2023). How to motivate student engagement in emergency online learning? Evidence from the COVID-19 situation. *Higher Education*, *85*(5), 1101–1123. DOI: 10.1007/s10734-022-00880-2 PMID: 35702421

Jarni, N., & Gurr, D. (2024). A futures perspective on learning and teaching in higher education: An essay on best and next practices. *Trends in Higher Education*, *3*(3), 793–811. DOI: 10.3390/higheredu3030045

Jarrah, M., Alghazo, S., Al-Deaibes, M., & Alhawamdeh, H. A. (2025). Real-world experiences of online learning: The effect of synchronous online learning on university students' classroom engagement. *Humanities & Social Sciences Communications*, *12*(1), 575. DOI: 10.1057/s41599-025-04701-6

Johnson, D. W., & Johnson, R. T. (2009). An educational psychology success story: Social interdependence theory and cooperative learning. *Educational Researcher*, *38*(5), 365–379. DOI: 10.3102/0013189X09339057

Kamali, J., Alpat, M. F., & Bozkurt, A. (2024). AI ethics as a complex and multifaceted challenge: Decoding educators' AI ethics alignment through the lens of activity theory. *International Journal of Educational Technology in Higher Education*, *21*(1), 62. DOI: 10.1186/s41239-024-00496-9

Karlsson, R., & Steen, L. (2025). Critical perspectives on HyFlex teaching. *Journal of Social Work Education*, *61*(4), 621–628. Advance online publication. DOI: 10.1080/10437797.2025.2530015

Kasneci, E., Sessler, K., Küchemann, S., Bannert, M., Dementieva, D., Fischer, F., Gasser, U., Groh, G., Günnemann, S., Hüllermeier, E., Krusche, S., Kutyniok, G., Michaeli, T., Nerdinger, F., Pfeffer, J., Poquet, O., Sailer, M., Schmidt, A., Seidel, T., & Kasneci, G. (2023). ChatGPT for good? On opportunities and challenges of large language models for education. *Learning and Individual Differences*, *103*, 102274. DOI: 10.1016/j.lindif.2023.102274

Kestin, G., Miller, K., Klales, A., Milbourne, T., & Ponti, G. (2025). AI tutoring outperforms in-class active learning: An RCT introducing a novel research-based design in an authentic educational setting. *Scientific Reports*, *15*(1), 17458. DOI: 10.1038/s41598-025-97652-6 PMID: 40537565

Knox, J. (2020). Artificial intelligence and education in China. *Learning, Media and Technology*, *45*(3), 298–311. DOI: 10.1080/17439884.2020.1754236

Kolb, D. A. (1984). *Experiential learning: Experience as the source of learning and development*. Prentice-Hall.

Kosslyn, S. M. (2025). Dynamic personalized learning: Leveraging AI to develop active learning experiences. *International Journal of Educational Technology in Higher Education*. Advance online publication. DOI: 10.1080/23735082.2025.2494628

. Létourneau, A., Deslandes Martineau, M., Charland, P., Karran, J. A., Boasen, J., & Léger, P. M. (2025). A systematic review of AI-driven intelligent tutoring systems (ITS) in K-12 education. *npj Science of Learning, 10*, Article 29. https://doi.org/ DOI: 10.1038/s41539-025-00320-7

Liu, C. Y. A., & Rodriguez, R. C. (2023). Evaluation of the impact of the HyFlex learning model. *International Journal of Innovation and Learning*. Advance online publication. DOI: 10.1504/IJIL.2019.099986

Luo, N., Li, H., Zhao, L., Wu, Z., & Zhang, J. (2022). Promoting student engagement in online learning through a harmonious classroom environment. *The Asia-Pacific Education Researcher, 31*(5), 541–551. DOI: 10.1007/s40299-021-00606-5

Mahrishi, M., Abbas, A., Siddiqui, M. K., & Aladhadh, S. (2025). The genesis and prevalence of the HyFlex model: A systematic review and bibliometric analysis. *International Journal of Educational Research Open*, *8*, 100410. DOI: 10.1016/j.ijedro.2024.100410

Mentzer, G. A., Laumakis, M. A., & Forsyth, D. E. (2023). HyFlex course design: Enhancing flexibility and access in hybrid learning environments. *Journal of Online Learning Research and Practice*, *9*(2), 45–58.

Ministry of Higher Education Malaysia. (2015). *Malaysia education blueprint 2015–2025 (Higher education)*. Ministry of Higher Education Malaysia.

Picciano, A. G. (2019). Theories and frameworks for online education: Seeking an integrated model. *Online Learning Journal*, *23*(4), 166–190.

Porayska-Pomsta, K., Holmes, W., & Nemorin, S. (2023). The ethics of AI in education. In du Boulay, B., Mitrovic, A., & Yacef, K. (Eds.), *Handbook of artificial intelligence in education* (pp. 571–604). Edward Elgar., DOI: 10.4337/9781800375413.00038

Prince, M. (2004). Does active learning work? A review of the research. *Journal of Engineering Education*, *93*(3), 223–231. DOI: 10.1002/j.2168-9830.2004.tb00809.x

Priyadharsini, R., & Sahaya Mary, R. (2024). Universal design for learning (UDL) in inclusive education: Accelerating learning for all. *Shanlax International Journal of Arts. Science and Humanities*, *11*(4), 145–150.

Schön, D. A. (1987). *Educating the reflective practitioner*. Jossey-Bass.

Shahzad, F., Avunduk, Z. B., Ullah, Z., & Arslan, A. (2025). Understanding management educators' perspectives on AI adoption: A qualitative study. *International Journal of Management Education*, *23*(3), 101274. DOI: 10.1016/j.ijme.2025.101274

Shamsuddinova, S., Heryani, P., & Naval, M. A. (2024). Evolution to revolution: Critical exploration of educators' perceptions of the impact of artificial intelligence on the teaching and learning process in the GCC region. *International Journal of Educational Research, 125*, 103236. DOI: 10.1016/j.ijer.2024.102326

Tan, X., Cheng, G., & Ling, M. H. (2025). Artificial intelligence in teaching and teacher professional development: A systematic review. *Computers and Education: Artificial Intelligence, 8*, 100355. DOI: 10.1016/j.caeai.2024.100355

Tang, Z., & Liao, J. (2025). Unlocking emotional resilience: Exploring the impact of AI-enhanced support systems on EFL teachers' burnout and student well-being. *Acta Psychologica, 260*, 105672. DOI: 10.1016/j.actpsy.2025.105672 PMID: 41043358

Wang, C., & Zou, B. (2025). D-ID Studio: Empowering language teaching with AI avatars. *TESOL Journal, 16*(2), e70034. Advance online publication. DOI: 10.1002/tesj.70034

Wong, B. T. M., Li, K. C., Chan, H. T., & Cheung, S. K. S. (2023). HyFlex learning research and practice: A longitudinal analysis. *Sustainability (Basel), 15*(12), 9699. DOI: 10.3390/su15129699

Wut, T. M., Wong, H. S. M., & Sum, C. K. M. (2025). Person-to-person interactions in hybrid teaching and learning. *International Journal of Educational Research Open, 9*, 100485. DOI: 10.1016/j.ijedro.2025.100485

Zawacki-Richter, O., Marín, V. I., Bond, M., & Gouverneur, F. (2019). Systematic review of research on artificial intelligence applications in higher education: Where are the educators? *International Journal of Educational Technology in Higher Education, 16*(1), 39. DOI: 10.1186/s41239-019-0171-0

Zimmerman, B. J. (2002). Becoming a self-regulated learner: An overview. *Theory into Practice, 41*(2), 64–70. DOI: 10.1207/s15430421tip4102_2

Chapter 9
HyFlex Approaches to Inclusive Laboratory Science Education in Higher Education

Nicole Simon
http://orcid.org/0009-0004-0678-1300
SUNY Nassau Community College, USA

ABSTRACT

Exploring how HyFlex (Hybrid-Flexible) course design can enhance inclusive and equitable laboratory science teaching in higher education, especially in situations where in-person participation is not always possible or preferred. Science laboratory courses are foundational to STEM education, offering students essential experiential learning through hands-on practice, inquiry-driven investigation, and the application of theoretical concepts in authentic contexts. However, the adaptation of these high-impact learning environments to hybrid or flexible modalities presents distinct pedagogical and logistical challenges. The inherently tactile and collaborative nature of laboratory work—often reliant on shared equipment, direct supervision, and synchronous interaction—complicates its transition to more fluid, technology-mediated formats.

INTRODUCTION: THEORETICAL FOUNDATIONS OF HYFLEX IN SCIENCE LABORATORIES

Hybrid-Flexible (HyFlex) learning has emerged as a promising pedagogical model for addressing persistent access and equity challenges in higher education,

DOI: 10.4018/979-8-3373-6182-6.ch009

particularly in contexts where in-person participation is not always possible or preferred. In science laboratory education—where learning is traditionally grounded in physical experimentation, shared equipment, and supervised practice, these challenges are especially pronounced. Laboratory courses are foundational to STEM education, supporting not only conceptual understanding but also scientific reasoning, methodological judgment, collaboration, and professional identity formation. Yet their reliance on fixed schedules, physical spaces, and synchronous supervision can disadvantage students facing health constraints, caregiving responsibilities, employment demands, or geographic barriers.

Laboratory science courses represent a particularly challenging context for flexible course design because they combine conceptual reasoning with procedural skill development, safety-critical practices, and tightly coordinated use of shared resources. Unlike lecture-based courses, laboratories often rely on co-located supervision, real-time feedback, and access to specialized equipment, making assumptions about physical presence deeply embedded in their instructional logic. These characteristics have historically limited flexibility and contributed to access barriers for students whose participation is constrained by health, caregiving, employment, or geography. HyFlex design brings these assumptions into question by requiring instructors to disentangle which aspects of laboratory learning are fundamentally tied to physical co-presence and which can be supported through alternative, modality-equivalent pathways without compromising rigor.

The theoretical foundations of HyFlex learning in science laboratory contexts provide a framework for responding to these tensions without compromising academic rigor. Drawing on recent literature and pedagogical tools (Barclay et al., 2022; Beatty, 2019), HyFlex emphasizes how science educators can uphold learning integrity, support student engagement, and ensure equitable access across participation modes. Rather than treating flexibility as an accommodation layered onto traditional laboratory structures, HyFlex reframes flexibility as a design principle—one that requires intentional alignment among learning outcomes, instructional activities, and assessment practices. As conceptualized by Beatty (2019), the HyFlex model is grounded in four foundational values: learner choice, equivalency, reusability, and accessibility. Each of these values holds particular significance in laboratory-based STEM education. When operationalized effectively, they create flexible learning environments that promote student agency while maintaining high standards of instructional quality.

Learner choice emphasizes students' autonomy in selecting participation modes that align with their circumstances and preferences. In laboratory contexts, this may include attending in-person sessions, participating synchronously online, or engaging asynchronously through recorded demonstrations, datasets, or simulations. Crucially, learner choice in HyFlex is not optional or peripheral; each pathway must constitute a legitimate and meaningful route to achieving the course's intended learning outcomes.

Equivalency ensures that all students, regardless of modality, achieve comparable educational outcomes. In science laboratories, equivalency does not imply identical experiences. Instead, it requires careful consideration of how core competencies—such as data interpretation, experimental reasoning, and methodological understanding—can be developed through different learning activities. For example, while in-person learners may handle reagents or instrumentation directly, remote learners may observe high-resolution demonstrations or work with curated datasets and virtual models. Although the methods differ, the cognitive and procedural demands must remain consistent (Barclay et al., 2022).

Reusability refers to the creation of instructional materials and learning artifacts that can support students across modalities and over time. Recorded demonstrations, annotated datasets, shared lab notebooks, and exemplar analyses enable all learners to engage with the same core content while also supporting efficiency and sustainability in course design. In laboratory settings, reusability is particularly important for reducing redundancy and supporting students who benefit from revisiting complex procedures or concepts at their own pace.

Accessibility remains foundational to HyFlex implementation. Science educators must ensure that students across modalities can access necessary tools, technologies, and instructional supports. This includes attention to captioned videos, low-bandwidth options, device-agnostic materials, and alternatives to specialized software when possible. Importantly, accessibility in HyFlex extends beyond technical accommodations to encompass physical, cognitive, and contextual barriers that shape students' ability to participate fully (Barclay et al., 2022).

These four values align closely with backward design principles, in which clearly articulated learning outcomes serve as the foundation for instructional planning and assessment. Through backward design, educators begin by identifying what students should know and be able to do, determine acceptable evidence of learning, and then design activities across modalities that generate that evidence. In HyFlex laboratory courses, backward design functions as a stabilizing logic, ensuring that flexibility in participation does not result in variability in expectations or rigor. When learning outcomes are clearly specified and assessments are aligned, multiple participation pathways can converge on the same academic goals, supporting both equivalency and inclusivity.

Although empirical research on HyFlex science laboratories remains limited, recent syntheses provide important insight into the conditions under which HyFlex supports inclusive learning. Romero Hall et al. (2025), in a comprehensive review of HyFlex implementation in undergraduate education, identify learner choice and perceived flexibility as consistently valued features across studies. Students report that modality choice supports agency and reduces barriers related to health, commuting, and scheduling. However, the authors caution that flexibility alone does not guarantee equitable outcomes. When choice is offered without sufficient structure or scaffolding, students may experience decision fatigue, disengagement, or uneven participation—particularly those new to self-directed or multimodal learning environments.

Equivalency emerges in this literature as the central theoretical challenge of HyFlex design. Romero Hall et al. emphasize that successful HyFlex environments prioritize modality parity, not activity replication. This requires intentional design of content, interaction, and assessment so that students across modalities engage in comparable intellectual work and receive timely feedback. Without such alignment, flexibility risks producing tiered learning experiences rather than equitable ones.

HyFlex and the Problem of Laboratory Access

Science laboratory courses are foundational to STEM education because they foster conceptual understanding through experiential learning, inquiry-driven investigation, hands-on practice, and the application of theoretical concepts in authentic contexts (Biggs & Tang, 2011). Laboratory instruction supports not only disciplinary knowledge but also scientific reasoning, methodological judgment, collaboration, and professional identity formation. For many STEM disciplines, laboratory experiences are considered high-impact learning practices that are central to program outcomes and accreditation requirements.

Despite their pedagogical value, laboratory courses are among the least flexible components of STEM curricula. Participation typically depends on access to physical spaces, specialized equipment, and synchronous supervision—conditions that can disadvantage students who face health-related barriers, caregiving responsibilities, employment constraints, transportation challenges, or geographic distance (Dziuban et al., 2020; Howell et al., 2024). These structural constraints became especially visible during the COVID-19 pandemic but persist beyond emergency contexts as higher education institutions seek to serve increasingly diverse student populations.

HyFlex course design offers a structured response to these access challenges by enabling students to choose among in-person, synchronous online, or asynchronous online participation while maintaining equivalent learning outcomes (Beatty, 2007, 2019). Rather than framing access as an individualized accommodation, HyFlex positions flexibility as a core design commitment. In laboratory contexts, however, this commitment raises complex questions about assessment validity, procedural skill development, safety, and faculty workload. As a result, HyFlex laboratories cannot simply replicate lecture-based HyFlex models; they require intentional, theory-informed design grounded in learning outcomes and assessment principles.

Research Gap and Purpose

Although HyFlex has gained prominence in higher education research, the existing literature disproportionately focuses on lecture-based and discussion-oriented courses. Empirical research examining HyFlex laboratory instruction—particularly in STEM disciplines—remains limited relative to the rapid expansion of HyFlex adoption (Barr & Luo, 2025; Romero-Hall et al., 2025). Within the available literature, several gaps are consistently identified.

First, there is limited guidance on modality-equivalent assessment in laboratory contexts. Traditional laboratory assessment often relies on in-person observation of procedures and synchronized performance, assumptions that do not hold consistently in HyFlex environments. Second, research remains underdeveloped on how procedural and psychomotor skills can be supported and assessed when students engage remotely or asynchronously. Third, relatively few studies explicitly address equity and accessibility in HyFlex laboratories, particularly with respect to modality parity and Universal Design for Learning (Howell et al., 2024; Nordmann et al., 2025).

The relative absence of laboratory-focused HyFlex research is not merely a matter of disciplinary neglect, but reflects unresolved theoretical questions about how scientific knowledge and skill are constructed in practice-based environments. Laboratory learning involves not only cognitive outcomes but also procedural judgment, safety awareness, and disciplinary ways of seeing and reasoning that are often developed through guided participation. Existing HyFlex studies, which largely emphasize content delivery and discussion-based interaction, provide limited guidance for addressing these dimensions of learning. As a result, instructors seeking to implement HyFlex laboratories must navigate questions of assessment validity, equivalency, and professional standards with little empirical or conceptual support specific to laboratory contexts.

The purpose of this chapter is to address these gaps by synthesizing HyFlex principles with established instructional design frameworks and applying them specifically to laboratory science education. Rather than treating HyFlex as a technological overlay on traditional laboratories, the chapter conceptualizes HyFlex laboratories as equity-oriented learning environments that require explicit alignment among learning outcomes, assessment strategies, instructional activities, and institutional supports (Beatty, 2019).

Objectives and Chapter Contribution

This chapter advances four interrelated objectives. First, it synthesizes foundational HyFlex scholarship with research on laboratory science education to clarify how HyFlex principles apply to high-impact, skills-based learning environments

(Beatty, 2007, 2019). Second, it examines key challenges associated with HyFlex laboratory implementation, including faculty workload, cognitive load, engagement, and sustainability (Sweller, 2011; Wood et al., 2025).

Collectively, these objectives position the chapter not only as a source of applied guidance, but as a conceptual intervention in how laboratory science education understands flexibility, rigor, and equity. By centering assessment and alignment rather than delivery mode, the chapter contributes a framework that can be adapted across disciplines, institutional contexts, and resource conditions. This emphasis distinguishes the chapter from implementation-focused accounts of HyFlex by foregrounding the theoretical commitments that must underpin sustainable and equitable laboratory design.

Third, the chapter proposes an integrated conceptual framework grounded in constructive alignment (Biggs & Tang, 2011), backward design (Wiggins & McTighe, 2005), and Universal Design for Learning (CAST, 2018). This framework foregrounds assessment as the primary mechanism for ensuring rigor and equity across modalities. Fourth, the chapter offers applied design guidance—including a tiered outcome model, an assessment portfolio structure, and strategies for sustainable grading and collaboration—to support instructors and institutions implementing HyFlex laboratory courses in diverse contexts.

Learning Equivalence Through Constructive Alignment

A central challenge in HyFlex laboratory design is ensuring learning equivalence across participation modes. Importantly, equivalence does not imply identical experiences. Rather, it requires that students across modalities engage in comparable intellectual work and are evaluated using aligned criteria (Beatty, 2019). Constructive alignment provides a foundational framework for achieving this goal by emphasizing coherence among learning outcomes, instructional activities, and assessment practices (Biggs & Tang, 2011).

In laboratory science education, constructive alignment carries particular weight because laboratory outcomes are often tied to disciplinary standards, accreditation expectations, and professional competencies. When learning outcomes, assessments, and activities are misaligned, modality differences can quickly become inequities rather than legitimate variations in learning pathways. In HyFlex laboratories, this risk is amplified: without explicit alignment, in-person activities may implicitly signal higher rigor or legitimacy, while remote or asynchronous pathways are perceived as substitutes rather than equivalent routes to learning. Constructive alignment mitigates this risk by making expectations explicit and defensible, ensuring that rigor is anchored in outcomes and evidence rather than in physical co-presence or procedural replication. In this sense, constructive alignment functions not only as an instructional design framework, but also as a mechanism for protecting equity and academic integrity across participation modes.

In laboratory contexts, constructive alignment clarifies which outcomes are essential—such as scientific reasoning, data interpretation, methodological understanding, and communication—and prevents modality differences from becoming inequities. When outcomes and evidence are clearly specified, instructors can design different activities that converge on the same learning goals, preserving rigor while allowing flexibility in participation format.

Backward Design as the Planning Spine

Backward design operationalizes constructive alignment by requiring instructors to begin with desired learning results, determine acceptable evidence, and then plan learning experiences and instruction (Wiggins & McTighe, 2005). This approach is particularly valuable in HyFlex laboratories because it forces explicit decisions about what counts as evidence of learning and which outcomes can be demonstrated across modalities.

Backward design is especially valuable in HyFlex laboratory contexts because it forces a critical distinction between activity equivalence and evidence equivalence. While laboratory activities may differ substantially across participation modes, the evidence used to evaluate learning must remain aligned to shared criteria. By specifying acceptable evidence in advance, instructors can justify why different activity forms—such as hands-on experimentation, simulation-based exploration, or analysis of shared datasets—are legitimate when they generate comparable demonstrations of learning. This distinction is central to maintaining assessment validity in HyFlex laboratories, as it shifts the focus from how learning occurs to what learning is demonstrated. Backward design therefore provides a defensible rationale for modality variation while safeguarding rigor, transparency, and fairness.

For example, cognitive outcomes such as data interpretation and experimental reasoning may be assessed through analysis of shared datasets or simulation outputs, regardless of how data were generated. In contrast, safety-critical psychomotor skills may require supervised in-person validation. Backward design makes these distinctions transparent and defensible, supporting both equity and academic integrity.

Universal Design for Learning as Equity Infrastructure

Universal Design for Learning (UDL) provides a complementary framework for HyFlex laboratories by offering concrete guidelines for reducing barriers and maximizing learning opportunities for all students (CAST, 2018). UDL emphasizes providing multiple means of engagement, representation, and action/expression, recognizing learner variability as predictable rather than exceptional. In this sense, UDL functions as equity infrastructure, supporting informed design decisions aligned with learning outcomes rather than retroactive accommodations.

The relevance of Universal Design for Learning is heightened in laboratory settings because laboratories combine conceptual reasoning with procedural complexity, safety considerations, and specialized tools. Learner variability in prior preparation, physical access, sensory processing, and learning pace is therefore not incidental but structurally predictable. In HyFlex laboratories, UDL supports equity by encouraging instructors to anticipate this variability during design rather than responding to it through ad hoc accommodations. When UDL principles are integrated alongside backward design and constructive alignment, accessibility becomes a core feature of the learning environment rather than a contingent response to individual need. This alignment allows HyFlex laboratories to maintain high expectations while offering multiple, equally legitimate pathways for students to demonstrate learning. In HyFlex laboratory contexts, UDL principles encourage instructors to design instructions, assessments, and engagement structures that are accessible across modalities from the outset. When applied intentionally, UDL reduces the need for individualized fixes later and supports more predictable, sustainable course operations.

Faculty Roles, Cognitive Load, and Sustainable HyFlex Practice

HyFlex laboratory instruction expands the faculty role beyond the traditional responsibilities of laboratory supervision and content facilitation. In HyFlex environments, instructors must support multiple participation modes (in-person, synchronous online, asynchronous online), coordinate resources across modalities, and maintain equivalent expectations for learning and assessment regardless of how students participate (Beatty, 2019). This expansion is particularly consequential in laboratory courses, where safety supervision, procedural coaching, and real-time troubleshooting are central to the learning experience, and where modality differences can easily become inequities if they are not deliberately designed for parity.

A key sustainability challenge is that HyFlex is not merely a delivery format; it requires redesign work. HyFlex course design guidance emphasizes that instructors must make informed decisions about whether and how HyFlex design can solve course needs, and then implement strategies that support student-directed participation (Beatty, 2019). In laboratory contexts, redesign includes creating modality-equivalent learning pathways, developing reusable learning objects (e.g., demonstrations, datasets, simulation prompts), and establishing assessment systems that can evaluate comparable evidence of learning across different activity forms. This work is most defensible when approached through backward design logic—starting with intended learning results, then determining acceptable evidence, and only then planning instructional experiences—so that modality decisions follow from outcome requirements rather than technological convenience (Wiggins & McTighe, 2005).

Workload and Role Expansion in HyFlex Laboratories

HyFlex laboratories tend to increase faculty workload because instructors must simultaneously manage the needs of multiple student groups who are experiencing different activity environments. Evidence from a systematic review of educators' experiences in synchronous hybrid learning—a closely related instructional model—identifies four recurring themes: technology demands, redesigning teaching and learning, student engagement, and staff workload (Wood et al., 2025). These same themes apply directly to HyFlex laboratory instruction, where technology is integral to participation, redesign is required for equivalency, engagement must be sustained across modalities, and workload increases as faculty juggle parallel course operations.

A critical but often underacknowledged distinction in HyFlex implementation is the difference between redesign labor and delivery labor. In HyFlex laboratories, much of the additional workload occurs before the course begins, as instructors redesign activities, assessments, and materials to support modality-equivalent learning pathways. This front-loaded labor is qualitatively different from the ongoing demands of course delivery, yet it is frequently invisible within traditional workload models. When redesign labor is not institutionally recognized, HyFlex laboratories risk becoming unsustainable despite their pedagogical promise. Making this distinction explicit clarifies why institutional support and policy alignment are essential components of equitable HyFlex adoption, rather than optional enhancements.

Role expansion is also pedagogical. Instructors shift from primarily supervising physical procedures to acting as designers of learning pathways and assessors of modality-equivalent evidence. In laboratory settings, this requires explicitly distinguishing between outcomes that can be demonstrated via analysis and reasoning (often modality-portable) and outcomes that require supervised validation (often safety-linked). Making these distinctions transparent allows instructors to preserve rigor while avoiding implicit modality hierarchies that privilege in-person participation by default.

Cognitive Load: Why HyFlex Can Become Unsustainable Without Design Supports

Cognitive Load Theory describes how instructional conditions can overload working memory and reduce learning effectiveness; it also provides a rationale for designing instruction that minimizes unnecessary cognitive burden (Sweller, 2011).

In HyFlex laboratories, cognitive load challenges occur for both students and instructors. Students may experience increased extraneous load when instructions are fragmented across platforms or when expectations differ subtly by modality. Instructors may experience increased extraneous load when they must monitor multiple channels simultaneously (in-room activity, video conferencing, chat, LMS submissions), troubleshoot technology in real time, and maintain equitable interaction patterns across modalities.

The synchronous hybrid learning review underscores that technology demands and redesign pressures shape educators' experiences and contribute to workload challenges (Wood et al., 2025). When HyFlex laboratories are implemented without strong design scaffolds—clear routines, reusable materials, standardized rubrics, and predictable communication workflows—faculty cognitive load can accumulate over time, reducing instructional presence and weakening feedback cycles. This, in turn, can undermine student engagement and equivalency across participation modes.

Cognitive load challenges in HyFlex laboratories also have direct implications for equity. When instructors' attention is divided across modalities, feedback cycles may become uneven, with in-person learners receiving more immediate guidance than remote or asynchronous peers. Over time, these discrepancies can accumulate into modality-based advantages that undermine the principle of equivalency. Intentional design supports—such as standardized rubrics, predictable submission workflows, and reusable feedback banks—reduce extraneous cognitive load and help stabilize instructional presence across modes. In this way, managing cognitive load is not only a matter of instructor well-being, but a necessary condition for maintaining equitable learning conditions.

Sustainability as an Institutional and Design Responsibility

Sustainability in HyFlex laboratories cannot be treated as an individual instructor responsibility. Evidence from the synchronous hybrid learning literature emphasizes that adequate staff training and ongoing classroom support are essential for effective teaching and learning in multimodal environments (Wood et al., 2025). In laboratory contexts, institutional support may include standardized AV configurations for demonstrations, in-room technical assistance, instructional design support for assessment alignment, and policies that recognize the redesign labor inherent in HyFlex adoption.

Universal Design for Learning (UDL) further reframes sustainability and equity as design problems rather than accommodation problems. When UDL principles are applied intentionally, variability in learner access, pace, and engagement is anticipated rather than treated as exceptional (CAST, 2018). In HyFlex laboratories, this approach reduces rework and troubleshooting by embedding flexibility into core course structures, supporting more predictable and sustainable operations over time.

Practical Design Implications for Sustainable HyFlex Laboratories

Three design implications emerge from the theoretical and empirical literature discussed above. First, HyFlex laboratories benefit from a stable module architecture that reduces extraneous cognitive load. A predictable instructional rhythm—such as preparation, activity, evidence submission, and feedback—supports student navigation while reducing management overhead for instructors. Second, sustainability is strengthened when faculty invest in reusable instructional assets, including short demonstration videos, dataset banks, exemplar analyses, and standardized rubrics. Reusability supports equivalency across participation modes while limiting redundant labor over time. Third, interaction design should be treated as a workload consideration, not solely a pedagogical one. Clearly defined interaction roles for remote learners (ex., prediction, error analysis, methods critique) reduce ad hoc engagement fixes and clarify participation expectations across modalities.

Transition to Assessment: Why Assessment Must Be the "Center of Gravity

Because HyFlex laboratories are defined by modality variation, sustainability ultimately depends on assessment systems that remain stable across different activity forms. Backward design centers assessment by requiring instructors to determine acceptable evidence before selecting learning experiences (Wiggins & McTighe, 2005). For this reason, the next section positions assessment not as an endpoint, but as the primary design lever through which rigor, equity, and sustainability can be maintained simultaneously in HyFlex laboratory courses.

Assessment Strategies and Learning Outcomes in HyFlex STEM Laboratories

Assessment is the primary mechanism through which HyFlex laboratories preserve rigor and equity while enabling flexible participation. While HyFlex emphasizes learner choice, it also requires equivalency: students across modalities must be held to consistent learning outcomes and evaluated using aligned criteria, even if their activity experiences differ (Beatty, 2019). In laboratory contexts, where traditional assessment often relies on synchronous performance and in-person observation, HyFlex implementation requires instructors to specify what counts as valid evidence of learning across participation modes and to design assessment systems that remain stable when learning activities vary by modality (Biggs & Tang, 2011).

Backward design provides a defensible planning logic for this work. Instructors identify desired learning results, determine acceptable evidence, and then plan learning experiences that generate that evidence (Wiggins & McTighe, 2005). In HyFlex laboratories, assessment therefore functions as the center of gravity that stabilizes equivalence, supports academic integrity, and mitigates workload drift over time.

Start With Outcomes: What Must Be Comparable Across Modalities?

HyFlex laboratory outcomes typically span cognitive, psychomotor, and affective domains. Backward design requires that these outcomes be stated explicitly and that acceptable evidence of learning be defined prior to activity selection. Distinguishing which outcomes are portable across modalities and which require supervised in-person validation makes equivalence transparent and prevents modality drift in which one pathway becomes implicitly easier or less rigorous (Beatty, 2019). Table 1 summarizes a tiered outcome structure for HyFlex laboratories. The tiers clarify which outcomes can be assessed across modalities and which require targeted in-person validation, supporting transparency and equity in assessment design (Wiggins & McTighe, 2005; Beatty, 2019).

Explicitly articulating which outcomes must be comparable across modalities also supports transparency for students and external stakeholders. In HyFlex laboratories, students must understand which competencies are universally assessable and which require in-person validation so that participation choices are informed rather than consequentially hidden. From an assessment standpoint, tiered outcomes provide a defensible structure for aligning evidence to learning goals without privileging a single mode of participation. This clarity is particularly important in laboratory courses, where safety-critical skills and professional standards require careful documentation and justification.

Table 1. Outcome tiers and assessment implications in HyFlex laboratory courses

Outcome tier	Primary domain	Examples of outcomes	Acceptable evidence across modalities	Equity implication
Tier 1: Universally assessable	Cognitive / analytical	Data interpretation; error analysis; argumentation from evidence; conceptual application	Dataset analysis memos; annotated graphs; lab reports; short oral defenses (live or recorded)	Equivalent intellectual demand can be maintained across all modalities
Tier 2: Hybrid outcomes	Cognitive + procedural understanding	Experimental design reasoning; method justification; troubleshooting plans	Simulation logs + reasoning prompts; critique of recorded demonstration; "method redesign" write-ups	Activity forms may differ, but evidence criteria remain common via shared rubrics
Tier 3: In-person essential	Psychomotor / safety-critical	Instrument handling; calibration; hazardous procedure compliance	Supervised checkoffs; observed technique demonstrations; safety audits	Make requirements explicit and narrow; provide accessible scheduling windows

Modality-Equivalent Assessment: Parity Without Identical Tasks

Equivalence in HyFlex assessment does not imply identical learning experiences. Rather, equivalence requires that students engage in comparable intellectual work and demonstrate aligned outcomes through comparable evidence standards (Beatty, 2019). In laboratory contexts, modality-equivalent assessment can be achieved through parallel evidence tasks, where different activity forms converge on the same learning goals and are evaluated using shared rubrics. This approach shifts assessment emphasis from where data originate to how students reason from evidence, justify methods, interpret uncertainty, and communicate conclusions. When criteria emphasize these dimensions, equivalency can be maintained across modalities without requiring activity replication.

Designing for modality-equivalent assessment requires instructors to articulate what constitutes meaningful disciplinary work in laboratory science. Rather than treating physical manipulation of equipment as the sole indicator of competence, modality-equivalent assessment emphasizes reasoning, interpretation, methodological justification, and communication—competencies that define scientific practice across contexts. When assessments prioritize these dimensions, differences in activity format become pedagogically acceptable variations rather than indicators of diminished rigor. This approach aligns HyFlex laboratories with authentic scientific practice, where data are frequently generated, analyzed, and interpreted by different actors across distributed settings.

A HyFlex Assessment Portfolio: Combining Low-Stakes and High-Stakes Evidence

A portfolio approach strengthens assessment validity by distributing evidence across multiple artifacts rather than relying on a single modality-dependent performance. Frequent low-stakes assessments support engagement and reveal misconceptions early, while summative tasks evaluate higher-order reasoning and scientific communication. A portfolio-based assessment approach is particularly well suited to HyFlex laboratories because it distributes evaluative weight across multiple forms of evidence collected over time. This distribution reduces the disproportionate impact of any single modality-dependent task and allows students to demonstrate learning through a range of artifacts aligned to shared criteria. From a validity perspective, portfolios also make learning processes more visible, capturing not only final products but also decision-making, revision, and reflection. In HyFlex contexts, where learning pathways may vary, this breadth of evidence strengthens confidence that comparable outcomes are being achieved across participation modes.

Table 2 illustrates a representative HyFlex laboratory assessment portfolio organized around preparation, process, product, and reflection evidence. This structure aligns with backward design principles and supports equivalency by enabling multiple pathways to demonstrate the same outcomes. *Table 2 provides a representative HyFlex laboratory assessment portfolio organized by preparation, process, product, and reflection evidence. Distributing assessment across multiple aligned artifacts reduces reliance on any single modality-dependent task while supporting validity and workload sustainability (Wiggins & McTighe, 2005; Beatty, 2019).*

Table 2. Sample HyFlex laboratory assessment portfolio aligned to learning outcomes

Evidence type	Example artifacts (modality-flexible)	Primary outcomes assessed	Equity / sustainability rationale
Preparation evidence	Pre-lab concept checks; protocol planning notes; safety acknowledgments	Readiness; conceptual foundations; safety awareness	Low-stakes; scalable; supports consistent entry conditions
Process evidence	Digital lab notebooks; simulation decision logs; observation logs for recorded demonstrations	Methodological understanding; inquiry process; documentation practices	Makes thinking visible; supports formative feedback across modes
Product evidence	Lab reports; data analysis memos; posters; short presentations	Scientific reasoning; data literacy; communication	Rubric-graded; modality-agnostic; authentic outcomes
Reflection evidence	Error analysis narratives; "what I would change" prompts; ethics reflections	Metacognition; uncertainty reasoning; professional responsibility	Reinforces learning transfer; supports improvement cycles

Assessing Collaboration Across Modalities

Collaboration is a defining feature of laboratory education, yet participation pathways can fragment teamwork if collaboration is treated as co-presence rather than as scientific work. In HyFlex laboratories, collaboration should be assessed using modality-agnostic criteria aligned to outcomes rather than to participation format. A defensible assessment model integrates both group-level artifacts (e.g., shared analysis memos, jointly authored notebooks) and individual-level evidence (e.g., reflective statements, annotated contributions). This combination preserves accountability while maintaining equitable participation across modalities.

Treating collaboration as an assessable learning outcome rather than a byproduct of co-presence is essential in HyFlex laboratory design. Scientific collaboration often involves distributed roles, asynchronous contributions, and negotiated meaning-making practices that mirror professional scientific work more closely than synchronized, co-located activity alone. When collaboration is assessed through shared artifacts and individual accountability mechanisms, differences in participation mode become less salient than the quality of collective reasoning and contribution. This reframing allows HyFlex laboratories to preserve the social dimensions of scientific inquiry while maintaining equity across modalities.

Rubrics stabilize expectations across diverse formats and submission types. Modality-agnostic rubrics emphasize reasoning quality, methodological justification, data literacy, and communication rather than the mechanics of data generation. Reusing a consistent rubric structure across assignments reduces grading drift, supports transparency, and enhances sustainability. Effective feedback systems combine rubric-based scoring, low-stakes formative checks, and multimodal feedback options. Reusable feedback banks and periodic calibration practices further support fairness and efficiency. Together, these strategies allow instructors to manage the complexity inherent in HyFlex laboratories without sacrificing rigor or equity.

Technology and Institutional Infrastructure for HyFlex Laboratories

Technology is an enabling condition for HyFlex laboratory instruction, but it is not itself the pedagogical solution. HyFlex design literature emphasizes that technology choices should follow from instructional needs and learning outcomes rather than dictate course structure (Beatty, 2019). In laboratory contexts, this principle is particularly important because technology can easily amplify inequities if access, usability, and alignment are not considered explicitly.

From an equity-oriented perspective, technology in HyFlex laboratories should be understood as a mediating infrastructure rather than a pedagogical substitute.

Decisions about platforms, access, and integration shape who can participate fully and how consistently learning conditions are experienced across modalities. When technological systems are unstable, inaccessible, or unevenly supported, modality parity is compromised regardless of instructional intent. Conversely, when technology is standardized, reliable, and aligned with assessment requirements, it can support equivalency by enabling consistent access to data, feedback, and collaborative processes across participation modes.

HyFlex laboratories typically rely on a constellation of tools rather than a single platform. When these tools are not coherently integrated, students may experience fragmented instructions, inconsistent expectations, and increased extraneous cognitive load (Sweller, 2011). From a backward design perspective, technology should therefore be selected and configured only after instructors have clarified desired learning outcomes and acceptable evidence of learning.

Technology as a Support for Modality-Equivalent Assessment

Assessment-centered HyFlex design reframes technology as a means for collecting, sharing, and evaluating evidence of learning rather than as a proxy for participation. Shared datasets, simulation outputs, and digital lab notebooks allow students across modalities to engage in comparable analytic work, even when physical data generation differs. However, the availability of technological tools does not guarantee equitable outcomes. Disparities in internet access, device quality, and learning environments can shape students' ability to engage fully across modalities. Institutions implementing HyFlex laboratories must therefore treat technology access as an equity issue rather than an individual student responsibility. Sustainable HyFlex laboratory implementation typically requires institutional standardization in three areas: classroom and laboratory AV configurations, instructional design support, and professional development. Without these supports, HyFlex laboratories risk becoming dependent on individual instructor effort, undermining consistency and scalability.

Engagement and Inclusion Across Modalities

Engagement mediates the relationship between access and learning quality in HyFlex laboratories. While HyFlex expands participation options, flexibility alone does not guarantee meaningful engagement. Engagement must be intentionally designed across behavioral, emotional, and cognitive dimensions. In HyFlex laboratories, engagement is best understood as a function of design coherence rather than modality choice alone. Students are more likely to engage meaningfully when expectations, evidence requirements, and feedback mechanisms are consistent across participation modes. Assessment-centered design supports this coherence by making engagement visible through shared artifacts and criteria, reducing the risk that remote or asynchronous learners become peripheral participants. In this sense, engagement equity is not achieved by replicating interactions across modalities, but by ensuring that all students are invited into comparable forms of intellectual work.

Assessment-centered design supports behavioral engagement by making participation visible through consistent artifacts across modalities. Emotional engagement is supported when collaboration and community are treated as design responsibilities rather than as byproducts of co-presence. Cognitive engagement is strengthened when assessment emphasizes reasoning, interpretation, and inquiry rather than procedural replication. Instructor presence remains critical across all modalities. Predictable communication routines, timely feedback, and visible facilitation of inquiry support engagement equity and reduce the risk that remote or asynchronous learners become peripheral participants.

Global and Resource-Constrained Contexts

HyFlex laboratory implementation is context-dependent. In many global and resource-constrained settings, assumptions about stable connectivity, specialized equipment, and institutional support do not hold. In such contexts, low-bandwidth design patterns, data-first laboratories, and targeted in-person intensives may offer more equitable and sustainable pathways than technology-heavy replication models. From a backward design perspective, this requires identifying outcomes that can be supported reliably within existing constraints and selecting evidence types accordingly. When aligned intentionally, these approaches can support rigorous scientific reasoning while expanding access for students who would otherwise be excluded.

In resource-constrained contexts, the principles of backward design and modality-equivalent assessment become especially consequential. When access to equipment, connectivity, or institutional support is limited, attempting to replicate high-resource laboratory models can exacerbate inequities rather than resolve them. By contrast, outcome-driven design allows instructors to prioritize core scientific competencies—such as data interpretation, experimental reasoning, and methodological critique—and to select evidence types that can be supported reliably within existing constraints. This approach reframes limitation as a design condition rather than a deficit, enabling rigorous laboratory learning even when participation pathways differ substantially.

CONCLUSION: HYFLEX AS EQUITY-ORIENTED LABORATORY DESIGN

HyFlex laboratories represent a demanding but consequential shift in how science education conceptualizes access, rigor, and participation. This chapter has argued that HyFlex is not best understood as a delivery format or emergency accommodation, but as an equity-oriented design framework that re-centers learning outcomes, assessment validity, and sustainability in laboratory education. When implemented without theoretical grounding, HyFlex risks reproducing the very inequities it seeks to address. When implemented through intentional design, however, it offers a defensible pathway for expanding access to high-impact STEM learning without diluting academic standards.

Across the chapter, assessment has been positioned as the center of gravity for HyFlex laboratory design. Backward design and constructive alignment provide the necessary logic for navigating modality variation while maintaining rigor. By distinguishing between universally assessable outcomes and those requiring in-person validation, instructors can preserve the integrity of laboratory learning while making participation more flexible and transparent. This approach reframes equivalence away from identical activities and toward aligned intellectual demand, ensuring that learning outcomes—not modality—define academic expectations.

The analysis also underscores that faculty workload, cognitive load, and institutional infrastructure are not peripheral concerns but structural determinants of HyFlex success. Sustainable HyFlex laboratories depend on reusable assessment architectures, standardized rubrics, and institutional support systems that recognize the redesign labor involved. Without these supports, HyFlex risks becoming an individualized burden rather than a scalable model for inclusive practice.

Finally, the chapter highlights that HyFlex laboratories must be understood as context-dependent. In global and resource-constrained settings, low-bandwidth design patterns, data-first laboratories, and targeted in-person intensives may offer more equitable and sustainable pathways than technology-heavy replication models. Universal Design for Learning further reinforces that accessibility and engagement are design responsibilities, not accommodations triggered by individual need.

REFERENCES

Barclay, P., Nguyen, T., & Schmidt, R. (2022). Cognitive load in HyFlex and blended STEM laboratory teaching. *Journal for STEM Education Research, 9*(3), 112–130.

Barr, T., & Luo, T. "HyFlex Course Design: Outcomes, Challenges, and Supports for Students and Instructors" (2025). *STEMPS Faculty Publications*. 392. https://digitalcommons.odu.edu/stemps_fac_pubs/392

Beatty, B. (2019). *Hybrid-Flexible Course Design: Implementing Student Choice*. EdTech Press. DOI: 10.59668/33

Beatty, B. J. (2007). Hybrid-flexible course design. *E-mentor, 5*(5), 1–12.

Biggs, J., & Tang, C. (2011). *Teaching for Quality Learning at University* (4th ed.). McGraw-Hill/Open University Press.

CAST. (2018). Universal Design for Learning Guidelines version 2.2. Retrieved from http://udlguidelines.cast.org

CAST. (2018). *Universal Design for Learning Guidelines version 2.2*. CAST.

Dziuban, C., Graham, C. R., Moskal, P. D., Norberg, A., & Sicilia, N. (2020). Blended learning: The new normal and emerging technologies. *International Journal of Educational Technology in Higher Education, 17*(3), 1–18.

Howell, E., Linder, S., Ryan, J., & Bridges, W. (2024). Examining higher education through HyFlex. *Open Learning, 40*(3), 252–267. DOI: 10.1080/02680513.2024.2354245

Howell, K., Zhang, L., & Omar, S. (2024). HyFlex pedagogy as equity-oriented design in graduate STEM education. *Education Sciences, 14*(3), 210–228.

Nordmann, E., Hronska, B., & MacKay, J. (2025). How do higher education staff understand the terms hybrid, hyflex and blended learning? Choice, modality and uncertainty. *Research in Learning Technology, 33*. Advance online publication. DOI: 10.25304/rlt.v33.3353

Romero-Hall, E., Allen, E., & Duan, Y.. (2025). *A decade of HyFlex learning: a systematic review in undergraduate education*. Education Tech Research Dev., DOI: 10.1007/s11423-025-10544-4

Sweller, J. (2011). Cognitive load theory. *Psychology of Learning and Motivation, 55*, 37–76. DOI: 10.1016/B978-0-12-387691-1.00002-8

Wiggins, G., & McTighe, J. (2005). *Understanding by Design* (2nd ed.). Association for Supervision and Curriculum Development.

Wood, H., Detyna, M., & Dommett, E. (2025). Assessing and Understanding Educators' Experiences of Synchronous Hybrid Learning in Universities: A Systematic Review. *Education Sciences, 15*(8), 987. DOI: 10.3390/educsci15080987

Chapter 10

Toward Intelligent Assessment in HyFlex Learning:
Opportunities and Challenges for AI Integration

Joana Heil
http://orcid.org/0000-0001-5069-0781
University of Mannheim, Germany

Yvonne Michelle Fromm
https://orcid.org/0000-0002-3780-995X
University of Mannheim, Germany

Dirk Ifenthaler
http://orcid.org/0000-0002-2446-6548
University of Mannheim, Germany & Curtin University, Australia

ABSTRACT

This chapter provides an overview of the potential impact of artificial intelligence (AI) on assessment practices in higher education with a specific focus on HyFlex learning environments. It provides an overview of AI in higher education with a particular emphasis on online assessment. Moreover, it discusses the potential of AI to automate assessment, its connection to personalized learning and assessment analytics, and the aspects of authenticity that AI can or cannot yet address. Further, the implementation of AI in assessment is critically evaluated, and a conclusion, along with implications for research and practice, is developed. A focus lies on

DOI: 10.4018/979-8-3373-6182-6.ch010

Generative AI, a specific form of AI that can create seemingly new content. This chapter highlights how AI can support flexibility in assessment and hybrid learning opportunities in higher education while also discussing the remaining challenges.

TOWARD INTELLIGENT ASSESSMENT IN HYFLEX LEARNING: OPPORTUNITIES AND CHALLENGES FOR AI INTEGRATION

HyFlex Learning Environments

Digitally-supported learning has led to many changes in classroom settings, especially considering the impact on assessment. Given the course content's delivery mode, multiple approaches, such as blended learning, flipped classroom, and hybrid learning, have been introduced. While blended learning combines digital support and in-class instruction, flipped learning shifts class time from instruction to application. Hybrid learning environments, on the other hand, combine online and in-person learning, with some participants attending online and others attending on-site simultaneously (Saichaie, 2020). A systematic review by Detienne et al. (2018) focusing on hybrid synchronous classroom settings highlighted that combining in-class and online teaching scenarios increased flexibility for students and teachers, increased the student population, helped ensure the continuity of instruction, and reduced dropout rates. However, according to Detienne et al. (2018), hybrid learning also presents challenges, including limited technology literacy among many teachers and the need for reliable infrastructure.

Hyflex is short for "Hybrid and Flexible" and combines the essence of hybrid learning with even greater flexibility in learning arrangements. The concept was first developed by Brian Beatty around 2006 at San Francisco State University and is described in Beatty (2019), a course developed at San Francisco State University to address two issues: the desire to attract more students and the realization that going completely online was not supported by the teaching staff's prerequisites or by the institution, nor was it expected to be accepted by students. In most blended learning scenarios, students must participate in both the online and offline parts of the course. However, the problem with these blended environments is that they do not accommodate the different needs of students who may require different schedules due to distance from the classroom or caregiving responsibilities. Therefore, they decided to transition to hybrid, flexible courses, allowing students to choose whether to attend in person or participate online.

A systematic review by Howell (2022) with $N = 19$ articles highlighted the role of HyFlex environments in supporting student agency and increasing participation while managing the cost of higher education. On the other hand, challenges were found in individualizing instruction for different students and in supporting newly gained agency, self-regulation, and digital literacy. Considering the social side of these learning environments, a challenge was identified in managing student attendance and fostering meaningful social interaction across both face-to-face and virtual modalities. Quite similarly, a study by Jerlinder et al. (2025) emphasized students' satisfaction with the flexibility and possibility of choice provided by these HyFlex environments while pointing out the didactical and technological hurdles that still exist in practice, such as a lack of infrastructure as well as a need for pedagogical development for teachers and effective communication among students, which is also highlighted in the results of design-based research by Howell et al. (2025). Yang et al. (2025) investigated student acceptance of different attendance modes in HyFlex learning environments. Their results showed high levels of acceptance, with the highest reported among students engaging on-site as well as synchronously online. Further, the perceived benefit was an important factor in determining students' acceptance. Wong et al. (2023) conducted a longitudinal analysis of $N = 84$ articles, analyzing research and publication patterns on HyFlex environments between 2013 and 2022. The findings reflect a focus on higher education and a sharp increase in research on the topic since 2018. Moreover, the findings highlight the need for effective technology for course delivery, course management, and communication. Further, the identified benefits for students include enabling remote students to participate in face-to-face learning by watching livestreamed videos, as well as improving learning experiences and outcomes through easy access to teachers' instructional resources. Teachers and institutions play an important role in realizing these scenarios (Wong et al., 2023). Especially when considering the equity between synchronous and asynchronous student participation, while the learning outcomes do not seem to differ, other aspects, such as interaction and individual needs, warrant further research (Howell, 2022).

Moreover, recent research has recognized the potential of artificial intelligence (AI) to support learning processes in HyFlex learning environments by providing automated assessment, personalized learning, and continuous student support (Sunusi et al., 2025). Therefore, this chapter outlines the role of AI in Hyflex learning environments in higher education. It begins by defining HyFlex and reviewing AI applications in higher education, before turning to online and authentic assessment, AI-enhanced assessment practices, and the specific integration of AI into HyFlex assessment. It then addresses challenges of AI integration and concludes with practical implications and future research directions.

AI IN HIGHER EDUCATION

Definition

In order to analyze the impact of artificial intelligence (AI) on assessment in HyFlex environments, it is important to develop an understanding of AI and its potential applications. Therefore, this subsection of the chapter outlines a central definition of AI, its various applications in higher education, and highlights the critical aspects of its successful implementation. The term AI dates back to 1956, introduced by Marvin Minsky and John McCarthy in the context of a conference (Haenlein & Kaplan, 2019). It can be understood as an umbrella term for many different applications, many of which aim to mimic human intelligence or analyze large amounts of data. According to Russell and Norvig (1995), AI systems are defined as acting humanly, thinking humanly (cognitive modelling), reasoning rationally (laws of thought), or acting rationally (rational agent approach), with them favoring the rational agent approach for their book. Throughout the years of AI research development, multiple breakthroughs have been achieved, with deep learning networks around 2010 having a major impact on research and practice (Ertel, 2024). Recent research focuses on the similarities and differences of information processing influenced by AI (Ifenthaler, 2025).

Application

In the past decade, AI technologies have received increasing attention for supporting learning processes in higher education (Bond et al., 2024; Zawacki-Richter et al., 2019). In their systematic review, Zawacki-Richter et al. (2019) identified several application areas of AI in higher education, including (1) profiling and prediction, (2) assessment and evaluation, (3) adaptive systems and personalization, and (4) intelligent tutoring systems. When considering the area of assessment and evaluation, they identified four subcategories: (1) automated grading, (2) automated feedback, (3) evaluation of student understanding, engagement, and academic integrity, and (4) evaluation of teaching.

Of particular relevance to this chapter, Ng et al. (2024) organized their AI Literacy Questionnaire (AILQ) around four dimensions: affective, behavioural, cognitive, and ethical. Aiming to develop a comprehensive overview, this chapter focuses on these dimenisions regarding AI-enhanced HyFlex assessment design.

GenAI

In the last few years, the specific version of AI, generative AI (GenAI), has become more central in public discourse (Heil et al., 2025). While AI is often understood to be more analytical on a decision-making level, GenAI is capable of generative tasks, usually probabilistic, combining elements in a novel way (Feuerriegel et al., 2024). GenAI, according to Ronge et al. (2025), can be defined in terms of four aspects: multimodality, interaction, flexibility, and productivity. Multi-modality is characterized by GenAI's ability to generate text, images, and sound. GenAI's interaction with humans is defined by its ease of use, and the possibilities it offers laypeople to engage with it, for instance, through chatbots. GenAI's flexibility lies not only in its availability but also in the range of topics and content it covers. Productivity emerges from the other three aspects, with a focus on GenAI's capability to boost user productivity (Ronge et al., 2025). Bozkurt (2023) conducted a study on potential research areas for GenAI in education and identified seven primary areas: (1) the interaction and communication with GenAI-powered chatbots, (2) the impact of large language models (LLMs) and GenAI on teaching and learning, (3) conversational educational agents, (4) generative AI for enhancing social and cognitive learning processes, (5) supporting AI literacy for future opportunities, (6) harnessing GenAI to expand academic capabilities, and (7) adapting educational experiences through human-AI interaction. Considering the practical application of GenAI, Belkina et al. (2025) conducted a systematic review of $N = 21$ empirical studies. They identified the potential of aligning GenAI with structured pedagogical approaches to enhance students' learning. They also called for more longitudinal studies on GenAI, as well as more studies on its time-saving benefits and ethical challenges.

AI in HyFlex Environments

Looking at the more specific case of HyFlex environments, AI can play a particularly important role, catering to the needs of hybrid and flexible settings. For hybrid learning to be effective, it needs to be designed as a pedagogically sound approach and constantly adapted to the needs of students and teachers. For this purpose, a data-driven approach, including AI, can be used to analyze vast amounts of data on hybrid learning scenarios (Verma, 2025). A systematic review by Park and Doo (2024) examined AI-supported blended learning, drawing on $N = 30$ journal articles. The results highlight the role of AI in blended learning environments as a mediator, helping students be more engaged through individualized learning or scaffolding. Specifically, AI-assisted chatbots can support communication, and automatic translation tools can aid students' engagement (Almusaed et al., 2023). Moreover, in hybrid and flexible learning, student data analytics can help teachers intervene and support students (Ifenthaler, 2015; Ifenthaler & Yau, 2020). However, Park and Doo's (2024) systematic review also revealed that AI is mostly investigated in the asynchronous part of blended learning, and more research on how AI could be used to bridge the synchronous and asynchronous aspects of a blended learning environment is needed. Additionally, challenges emerge in AI-supported hybrid learning, including effective course design, teacher training, personalization of learning (balancing this to avoid losing connection with students in face-to-face settings), data privacy and security, and equity and accessibility (Guerrero-Quiñonez et al., 2023). To investigate concrete application scenarios with student data, it is important to consider assessment as both a central data resource and a central part of students' learning experiences, especially in HyFlex learning environments. An example of AI-enhanced assessment in HyFlex learning environments could be realized through an implemented formative assessment analytics systems that could be accessed on a shared learning management system. Based on assessment results, different learning materials could be recommended. It should be flexible, independent of time or place, and work as a learning companion. Furthermore, students could receive dashboards that reflect their progress. The concrete background and design opportunities will be highlighted in the following sections.

ONLINE ASSESSMENT

Definitions of Assessment

Assessment is defined as the systematic gathering of information about learners and their environment to draw inferences about their learning processes (Baker et al., 2016). Considering the impact and design of assessment on the learning process, the concept of learning-oriented assessment was proposed (Carless, 2007). The main idea is that measurement and certification should not be the main goals of student assessment. Therefore, active learner engagement is central to learning-oriented assessment (Carless, 2015). Accordingly, research distinguishes between multiple assessment formats, including formative and summative, and between assessment of, for, and as learning (Webb & Ifenthaler, 2018). While formative and summative assessment focus mostly on the timing of the assessment in relation to the learning process, assessment of, for, and as learning focuses on the purpose it serves. Formative assessment is conducted during the learning process and used to adapt the learning process. It is often used interchangeably with assessment for learning, which views the assessment process as a tool for enhancing students' learning (Black & Wiliam, 2009). Summative assessment in opposition is used at the end of a learning unit to assess the results of a learning process and is often used synonymously with the term assessment of learning (Shute & Becker, 2010). Ultimately, assessment as learning focuses on students' learning as they take on active, reflective roles as they engage with the materials (Yan & Boud, 2021).

The increase in online learning in higher education has created a need for online assessments. Online assessment is an assessment conducted through online technologies and can be classified by mode, format, and type. While the mode can be realized through teacher, peer, automated, or self-assessment, the format can be either formative or summative, and the types can range from project-based tasks, essays, or quizzes (Heil & Ifenthaler, 2023).

Assessment in HyFlex Environments

Online assessment is of particular importance in HyFlex learning environments, as it poses challenges and opportunities for equity across modes of attendance. Therefore, the question remains: How can online assessment be designed in the specific case of HyFlex learning environments? Research by Boelens et al. (2017) on blended learning highlighted the different assessment designs depending on the learning environment's modality. In online environments, formative assessment was conducted through quizzes, and, in a supplementary format, the final examination of the courses was administered in a face-to-face setting. In HyFlex learning, ongoing assessments are essential to maintain connection to students and provide continuous support (Guerrero-Quiñonez et al., 2023). Therefore, when approaching a HyFlex environment that emphasizes student choice of modality, this separation between assessment on- and offline might not support the equity that is the goal of HyFlex learning (Howell, 2022). Creating an assessment that is not focused on summative assessment but rather developed through formative assessment and competence development might be an approach to mitigate these challenges. In this regard, AI may offer potential for supporting authentic and automated assessment (Xia et al., 2024), which might serve as the basis for designing personalized learning environments that provide individual support based on formative assessment results (González-Castro et al., 2021).

AI IN ASSESSMENT

In HyFlex environments too, AI has a significant impact on assessment as recent advances in AI offer possibilities to enhance assessment practices in higher education. A systematic review with $N = 81$ empirical studies by C. Zhao (2024) identified the central applications of AI in assessment as intelligent tutoring and personalized learning, automated assessment and feedback, virtual classroom and online collaboration, learning analytics and prediction, knowledge management and resource recommendation, and lastly educational chat assistants.

Automated Assessment

In a systematic review with N = 22 papers, González-Calatayud et al. (2021) found that AI in student assessment was mostly used for formative assessment and automated grading. When considering the specific case of GenAI, a recent scoping review by Xia et al. (2024) highlights the transformative nature of GenAI in assessment, pointing to opportunities for perceived unbiased, immediate, and diverse feedback and for self-assessment. Automated assessment can, for example, be realized through automated feedback in quizzes (Lee & Moore, 2024). AI can also take on the role of automated question generation, such as short-answer questions (Lu et al., 2021) or cloze items (Yang et al., 2021), thereby helping with repetitive practice and enhancing learning performance. For long-form texts, automated essay scoring can support teachers in automated grading (Ifenthaler, 2022).

Automated Essay Scoring

Automated essay scoring systems date back to their introduction by Ellis Page in the 1960s (Page, 1968) and have been further developed in the early 2000s. The four main commercial approaches include Project Essay Grade, E-rater, Intelligent Essay Assessor, and IntelliMetric (Zupanc & Bosnić, 2017). In 2012, the William and Flora Hewlett Foundation introduced the so-called Automated Student Assessment Prize (ASAP). This competition led to a steep increase in research and development of automated essay scoring systems, with 154 teams participating. The resource for this task was a dataset containing essays written by high-school students between the grades seven and ten (Ke & Ng, 2019). Furthermore, like many other technologies, automated essay scoring has also developed rapidly in recent years. These evolved from more statistically based methods to neural approaches, including LSTMs (Taghipour & Ng, 2016), CNNs, models with attention layers (Uto et al., 2020), and ultimately BERT models (Elmassry et al., 2025). While many approaches yielded relatively high accuracy scores compared to human raters, it is important to keep in mind that most of these approaches stem from a technological rather than a pedagogical perspective. Ideally, both views should be combined, and not only AES's accuracy but also its didactic benefits should be evaluated. The lack of equitable approaches was often due to insufficiently annotated data for training systems (Carlile et al., 2018). To enhance the actionable feedback provided to students, rubric-based approaches were explored that provide more detail on specific features of the work.(Mathias & Bhattacharyya, 2018). However, many of these systems are not accredited and are neither unbiased, comprehensive, nor fully valid for implementation in practice (Ifenthaler, 2022; Ifenthaler & Dikli, 2015).

Modes of assessment

Therefore, it is important to consider the other modes of online assessment (i.e., teacher, peer, and self-assessment). Combined with them, automated assessment can take on a specific role by complementing, while not replacing, the other modes. Considering teacher feedback, GenAI-created feedback can serve a different purpose for students. While they perceive teacher feedback as more helpful and trustworthy, AI can aid by offering ease of access, timeliness, volume, and understandability. Furthermore, students might consider it less risky than asking their teacher (Henderson et al., 2025). Regarding peer assessment, automated assessment can also be implemented in a complementary manner. Banihashem et al. (2024) highlighted discrepancies in quality between peer and automated assessments via ChatGPT. While the automatically generated assessment provided more descriptive feedback, the feedback derived from the peer assessment was considered of higher quality, as it highlighted specific issues with the text and engaged more with the context. As support for peer assessment, AI can be implemented to guide the assessor in self-monitoring and to aid teachers in overseeing the process (Darvishi et al., 2022). Regarding self-assessment, AI can support students by helping them reflect on their learning and providing personalized, timely feedback (Mpolomoka, 2025).

Personalized Learning

The combination of assessment and AI bears great potential for personalized learning. AI enables the use of students' assessment data to evaluate individual performance and provide appropriate learning paths (Ayeni et al., 2024; Fromm et al., 2025). For example, formative assessment data can be used to adapt the difficulty level of learning materials and to provide personalized recommendations of learning content (González-Castro et al., 2021). Furthermore, personalized learning is closely connected to learning analytics, which can be enhanced by assessment data (Ifenthaler & Yau, 2020). Learning analytics involve collecting and analyzing static and dynamic data about learners and learning environments to enable real-time modelling, prediction, and optimization of learning processes (Ifenthaler, 2015; Ifenthaler & Yau, 2020). The concept of learning analytics is distinct in that its primary purpose is to support and enhance learning, as well as analyze data (Romero & Ventura, 2020).

Assessment analytics is a specific type of learning analytics that focuses on analyzing and visualizing learning processes using assessment data (Sahin & Ifenthaler,

2024). Assessment analytics can be implemented in various functions to support and improve assessment practices. According to Caspari-Sadeghi (2023), assessment analytics can be used to monitor and analyze learning processes, provide automated feedback, and predict, prevent, and intervene in order to support learning processes.

Monitoring, analysis, and automated feedback can be supported and achieved through visualization methods such as dashboards, which provide students and teachers with overviews of indicators (e.g., number of correctly answered questions in quizzes) of the learning process (Ifenthaler & Sahin, 2023) or prompts (Akinyi et al., 2024). Prompts can be sent to students as short messages that aim to support their self-regulated learning strategies (Schumacher & Ifenthaler, 2021). Furthermore, assessment analytics can enrich the learning process by providing actionable recommendations and personalized feedback (Pardo et al., 2019).

Considering prediction, prevention, and intervention, assessment analytics can further support students' learning processes by identifying patterns and informing interventions (Sahin & Ifenthaler, 2024), aligning with the more analytical aspects of AI. For this purpose, various assessment data can be used, including pass/fail status, the number of points achieved, or the number of attempts required to complete an assessment (Nouira et al., 2019). New forms of assessment might include serious game analytics, analyzing data such as time needed, number of mistakes and corrections, amounts of access, content accesses, and types of contents accessed (Loh et al., 2015). A specific further development is the so-called stealth assessment, which measures learning continuously in the background while students engage, e.g., with games (Rahimi & Shute, 2024; Shute, 2011). Stealth assessment aims to assess not only learning outcomes but also usually unobservable competencies such as problem-solving, persistence, and emergency readiness (Rahimi & Shute, 2024).

Authentic Assessment through AI

Considering the practical design of assessment in higher education, it reflects a need for authentic assessment to prepare students for life after graduation and to aid reflection and the development of so-called 21st-century skills (Butler-Henderson & Crawford, 2020). 21st-century skills are not to be understood as a synonym of digital skills. Van Laar et al. (2017) conducted a systematic review with N = 75 articles and developed seven core skills: technical skills, information management, communication, collaboration, creativity, critical thinking, and problem solving. Furthermore, they identified the following contextual skills: ethical awareness, cultural awareness, flexibility, self-direction, and lifelong learning. A common objective of authentic assessment is to replicate the work tasks and performance standards typically encountered in professional settings, thereby fostering skills that enhance students' employability.

Authentic assessment design

Ashford-Rowe et al. (2014) defined eight aspects that determine an authentic assessment activity: (1) the activity should challenge the student, (2) require a performance or product as final assessment outcome, (3) demand the transfer of learning by the demonstration of a skill, (4) require the demonstration of metacognition, (5) be evaluated as authentic by a relevant client or stakeholder, (6) ensure fidelity in the assessment process, (7) enable discussion and feedback in the assessment, and lastly, (8) demand collaboration between students. However, the definitions and goals of authentic assessment in higher education are broad and might encompass multiple different areas. According to Villarroel et al. (2018), authentic assessment should cover three broader conceptual dimensions: (1) realism (i.e., presence of a real context or tasks typically faced in real or professional life), (2) cognitive challenge (i.e., the assessment tasks require the development of higher-order cognitive and metacognitive skills), and (3) evaluative judgement (i.e., students can develop an understanding of what constitutes a good performance). Other researchers argue for a broader understanding of the term 'authentic' in the context of assessment. According to McArthur (2023), a separation between the educational world and the seemingly parallel real world, that is understood as the world of work, is arbitrary. Instead, education and work are part of the bigger picture of society. Education and assessment should therefore not only focus on the realities of potential workplaces to be deemed authentic, but also include broader aspects of society, such as grand challenges like climate change. Other researchers argue that authenticity should not be considered in assessment tasks but rather a quality throughout the educational process, focusing on students' individual development to become responsible citizens (Vu & Dall'Alba, 2014). Similarly, authenticity should address digital authenticity by situating assessment within the broader context of digital society. Rather than simply providing a digital tool, it should offer a curriculum that supports students in developing digital literacy (Nieminen et al., 2023). The implementation of authentic assessment still faces significant challenges. For instance, replicating work tasks poses challenges for students in less career-oriented degree programs that are loosely linked to specific professions. Moreover, current practices of authentic assessment may fail to prepare students for the future. An authentic assessment needs to address digital literacies and competencies. Further, it would be insufficient if it involved only current work practices and did not adapt to potential future challenges (Ajjawi et al., 2024). Therefore, the introduction of AI and GenAI into assessment raises conditions that researchers and practitioners alike need to address. According to Chiu (2024), assessment should be reconsidered and redesigned in order to prepare students for a future workforce in which AI takes on a central function.

Authentic assessment and technology

Similarly, Hu et al. (2025) point out that digital technologies can support authenticity in assessment by enhancing disciplinary learning, fostering workplace readiness, supporting personal growth, and improving assessment delivery. More specifically, GenAI can function as a learning assistant, creating artificial scenarios that replicate work tasks and providing opportunities to foster cognitive challenge and evaluative judgement through feedback and reflection (Salinas-Navarro et al., 2024). Furthermore, GenAI raises further questions regarding the role of evaluative judgement, positioning it more central than other aspects of authentic assessment. While in practice, authentic assessment is typically realized through the replication of work tasks, thus addressing the first dimension (realism), cognitive challenge and evaluative judgement have been neglected in many application scenarios (Villarroel et al., 2018). However, especially evaluative judgement might become more central as a distinguishing human feature, which educators and learners alike should foster rather than rely on AI (Bearman et al., 2024). Therefore, individual learning and support for fostering evaluative judgement need to be prioritized when designing assessments. This could be achieved through activities such as self-assessment, peer-assessment, exemplars, or feedback (Tai et al., 2018). Additionally, in the context of self-assessment, authenticity calls for reflection on one's own learning based on individual incentive, rather than being told to self-assess. This is what students would encounter in a world outside of formal education (Nieminen & Boud, 2025).

Authentic assessment and AI

Meanwhile, GenAI might necessitate changes, such as a paradigm shift in the intended learning outcomes for students in higher education, given its broad availability and access not only in education but also across society and the workplace. A scoping review by Weng et al. (2024) highlights changes in assessment. It introduces new, focused learning outcomes emerging from the use of GenAI, specifically career-driven competencies and lifelong learning skills, which are becoming more central in GenAI-facilitated learning environments. In the same vein, given that GenAI tools perform well on lower levels of Bloom's taxonomy (Thanh et al., 2023), this suggests practitioners design assessments targeting higher-order cognitive skills. While cognitive complexity alone does not constitute authenticity — which also requires realism and evaluative judgement (Villarroel et al., 2018) — such assessments may better resist AI completion and, when grounded in realistic contexts, may also be considered more authentic. Thus, GenAI might not only allow assessment to be more authentic by supporting personal growth and simulating realistic work scenarios, but also necessitate it. To support learners in achieving the intended learning outcomes in these learning environments, it is important to consider the challenges that emerge through the introduction of AI in assessment in higher education, as well as factors that might influence the process (Spirgi et al., 2025).

AI in Assessment in HyFlex Learning Environments

In order to combine the impact of GenAI on assessment in higher education as well as on HyFlex environments, the specific characteristics of both approaches have to be evaluated and incorporated. AI in assessment can help address identified challenges in HyFlex environments, such as individualizing instruction for different students (Howell, 2022). AI and learning analytics can help here by using assessment data. Assessment analytics can help teachers maintain connections with students through AI-enhanced monitoring of learning processes (Verma, 2025), and can further support students' individualized learning through personalized feedback based on formative assessment data. In addition, AI can be implemented to support self-regulation (Afzaal et al., 2024) and provide guidance for students with limited digital literacy, which are other challenges for HyFlex learning environments (Howell, 2022). Given the need for meaningful interactions, AI can help automate assessment and, therefore, allow teachers to be more flexible in their interactions with students (Almusaed et al., 2023). HyFlex learning environments also tend to lack the personal connection, which could be enhanced through more AI, especially in providing feedback (Guerrero-Quiñonez et al., 2023), such as an AI tool integrated in the communications platform that offers automated feedback with rubrics on essays or quizzes with the possibility to be adapted either in the synchronous or asynchronous setting (Villegas-Ch et al., 2024). Other modes of assessment, such as peer or self-assessment, can support learners (Heil & Ifenthaler, 2025) and be enhanced through AI (Banihashem et al., 2024; Schumacher, 2023) to improve communication among students in HyFlex learning. The transformation of AI, specifically GenAI, will have a broad impact on assessment and is not yet fully explored. Especially given the goal of equity in HyFlex learning environments, it is crucial to provide all students with access to all resources, regardless of the modality they choose. However, as AI is predominantly implemented in an asynchronous modality (Park & Doo, 2024), this equity remains a challenge for HyFlex learning. Further, the broader integration of AI into higher education assessment practices still faces significant challenges that need to be addressed before realizing its potential.

CHALLENGES OF AI INTEGRATION IN ASSESSMENT

The use of AI for automated assessment in HyFlex learning environments also poses challenges that need to be addressed to implement effective, trustworthy assessment practices (Ifenthaler, 2023). These challenges include algorithmic biases, validity concerns in automated assessment, and challenges to the privacy of student data (Mpolomoka, 2025). Additionally, C. Zhao (2024) points out negative attitudes, insufficient abilities of the people engaging with AI, academic integrity issues, and a lack of proper guidance as challenges for AI-assisted assessment. This ties in with the results of a scoping review by Xia et al. (2024), highlighting the need for teachers to be competent in developing new and innovative assessments that accommodate the changes brought by GenAI, as well as the challenge of student academic integrity.

Ethical Challenges

Multiple approaches have been proposed to address the ethical challenges AI poses to higher education, particularly in assessment. As central aspects to be considered, Dignum (2017) proposed the so-called ART-principles stand for accountability, responsibility, and transparency when it comes to engagement with AI. An analysis of seven global AI ethics policies in higher education by Slimi & Villarejo Carballido (2023) reflected this approach by highlighting transparency and accountability, as well as the need for unbiased AI algorithms, as central concerns. Further, Memarian and Doleck (2023) investigated the FATE (Fairness, Accountability, Transparency, and Ethics) aspects in AI implementation in higher education research. In their systematic review, they found fairness to be the central concern, but it was mostly considered in technical terms. They call for further research on accountability and transparency. It is important to consider students' different financial opportunities when implementing HyFlex environments and AI in higher education. This refers to technical infrastructure, such as devices, as well as freemium applications. Additionally, privacy is an important issue in the ethical use of AI, especially as students tend to be quite conservative about the data they are willing to share for learning analytics (Ifenthaler & Schumacher, 2016). To accommodate students' privacy needs, it is important to optimize data-use regulations, enhance students' awareness of data protection, and provide them with potential legal remedies (Huang, 2023).

AI Competence

Furthermore, research emphasizes the importance of students developing the skills to use AI effectively to support their learning (Delcker et al., 2024; Heil et al., 2025). In the context of employing AI in higher education assessment, learners must be competent when dealing with AI, as research reflects the impact of competence on interaction with AI tools in their learning processes (Chiu, 2024; Delcker et al., 2024). AI competence encompasses multiple aspects, including theoretical knowledge of AI, understanding of legal frameworks, understanding of the implications, attitudes toward AI, learning with AI, and ongoing professionalization (Delcker et al., 2025). This has further implications for the role of higher education institutions in supporting students and teachers in effectively using AI (J. Zhao et al., 2024), as well as in providing guidelines. However, the focus should not be only on AI competence but also on feedback literacy. Feedback literacy is not only important for interaction with different modes of assessment (Heil & Ifenthaler, 2025), and learning analytics-based feedback (Tepgec et al., 2024), but also for AI-generated feedback (Min et al., 2025). Furthermore, as C. Zhao (2024) highlighted, considering individual attitudes and opinions toward AI is important when implementing AI in assessment. While students are rather comfortable with the use of AI for career and administrative support, as well as formative assessments, they reported higher levels of discomfort with AI in summative grading and offering wellbeing support. In Rodway and Schepman's (2023) study, the hypothetical introduction of AI led to a decrease in course satisfaction. Students' use of GenAI tools in higher education is influenced by attitudes and self-efficacy (Sukirman et al., 2024). A major predictor of behavioral intention for the use of ChatGPT are habit, performance expectancy, and hedonic motivation, that is, the enjoyment of using it (Strzelecki, 2024). Additionally, students tend to prefer GenAI tools for assessment that would enhance and support their learning process compared to tools that allow for work to be passed off as their own (Heil et al., 2025).

Administration

From an administrative perspective, guidelines have been implemented, particularly regarding academic integrity, as this has been a key issue in public discourse. Simultaneously, proctoring systems, which supervise students during summative examinations, are under discussion due to their ethical implications (Coghlan et al., 2021). Therefore, it is important to consider the approaches that institutions put forward for implementing AI in assessment. According to an analysis by Jin et al. (2025) of international policies, higher education institutions tend to focus on developing guidelines for ethical GenAI use, designing authentic assessments to address misuse, and providing training programs for teachers and students to foster AI competence. Simultaneously, they emphasized the lack of comprehensive policy frameworks, particularly regarding data privacy and equitable access to GenAI. A systematic review by Le (2024) identified two main approaches to policy: either banning GenAI altogether in assessment or embracing it, accompanied by clear guidance on how to use it ethically, as well as a request for a declaration of AI use. In illustrating the spectrum between these two poles, Perkins et al. (2024) developed an AI Assessment Scale (AIAS) comprising five levels of AI adoption in assessment. On the first level, 'no AI', none is allowed, and all usage of AI is considered cheating. The second level encompasses 'AI-assisted idea generation and structuring', where AI can be used for developing ideas, but no AI is allowed in the final submission. In the middle, on the third level called 'AI-assisted editing'. AI can be used to improve the work, but no new content is allowed to be developed. The work can be submitted with AI editing, but an original submission must be submitted as well. On the fourth level, 'AI task completion, human evaluation', AI can be used to complete specified tasks in the assessment. However, that must be cited. On the highest level, 'Full AI', AI can be used throughout the process and does not have to be cited.

PRACTICAL IMPLICATIONS

When it comes to the practical implementation of AI in HyFlex assessment, several implications arise. It is important to keep in mind that flexible learning opportunities, including blended and online courses, must be effectively designed to achieve their intended goals (Andrade & Alden-Rivers, 2019). Teaching strategies have to be adapted, curriculum developments reconsidered, and a sound infrastructure developed (Wright, 2016). To effectively implement and deal with AI in educational practices, higher education institutions should focus on enhancing students' and teachers' digital literacy, enabling faculty to engage with students, providing faculty and student training, updating academic policies and guidelines, and supporting research on GenAIs' effects on teaching and learning (Ifenthaler et al., 2024; Rudolph et al., 2023). Teachers and policymakers should focus further on teaching students about trustworthy AI, meaning lawful, ethical, and robust applications, in order to provide a realm in which to operate (Aler Tubella et al., 2024). However, the challenges to academic integrity posed by AI in higher education assessment cannot be solely addressed through policies and institutions; it also requires assessment design developed by individual teachers. Evangelista (2025) proposes alternative assessment types such as oral exams, project-based learning, or performance-based assessment. Strategies such as real-world problem-solving, interactive feedback mechanisms, and multimodal question integration should be considered to support learners. The redesign principles they propose are personalizing assessment tasks, assessing the learning process rather than the final product, and emphasizing creativity through problem-solving, innovation, and novel thinking. This also aligns with the concepts presented for designing authentic assessments and fostering 21st-century skills. However, authentic assessment alone is no miracle cure and does not, in itself, protect academic integrity. Therefore, Kofinas et al. (2025) propose a paradigmatic shift from assessing outputs to focusing on the process and relevance of the assessment tasks. They propose considering synchronous interpersonal assessments above written assessments. Considering the assessment design within a broader pedagogical design, authenticity should be a concern, and it should be considered alongside a clear understanding of the educational goals of higher education (Fawns et al., 2025). AI and GenAI could serve as a vehicle to address existing challenges in higher education assessment, necessitating a reframing of current practices.

CONCLUSION AND OUTLOOK

Overall, research indicates the potential for transforming assessment through AI, particularly GenAI. However, this is still in development and has not reached widespread, structured implementation. GenAI has significant potential to support students' learning in assessment if implemented correctly. In current higher education practice, however, many institutions have yet to fully leverage student data to enhance learning and teaching (Komljenovic et al., 2024). This constant improvement cycle, however, is also essential for successful HyFlex learning. For AI to fulfill its potential in assessment, redesigning assessment and supporting the literacy and professional development of learners and teachers are crucial (Xia et al., 2024; J. Zhao et al., 2024). This should also include pedagogical, rather than only technical, teacher training (Viberg et al., 2024). GenAI can support teachers in automated assessment and in creating assessment scenarios. Therefore, some challenges identified for HyFlex environments, including a lack of infrastructure and a need for pedagogical development for teachers and students, are similar across both HyFlex environments (Jerlinder et al., 2025) and AI in assessment and can be addressed through collaborative efforts. Therefore, implications arise for practice and research. Both GenAI and HyFlex environments can act as incentives to rethink and redesign existing curricula and teaching decisions in higher education. Especially given the flexible environment and the need for supervision of student learning, which might not occur in face-to-face settings in HyFlex environments, it might be more important to integrate continuous, formative assessment and move away from traditional closed-book summative assessment. The pedagogical reliability of overreliance on high-stakes examinations has been under discussion for some time (Boud, 1995; French et al., 2024). Further, the widespread availability of GenAI might necessitate more innovative assessment designs, such as authentic assessment (Thanh et al., 2023) or more collaborative assessment designs (Kofinas et al.,

2025). Research indicates that AI is primarily used in the asynchronous component of blended learning (Park & Doo, 2024). As equity is one of the central goals of HyFlex learning and should be ensured in assessment, it is important to bear this in mind when implementing and shifting assessment practices to a medium accessible to all students equally. Therefore, more research is needed to develop ethical, secure, and trustworthy systems that support learners and teachers alike. Long-term studies and practical implementations regarding AI-enhanced online assessment will help to solidify a strong empirical basis for the specific case of HyFlex learning environments. To conclude, AI should not replace humans and should be implemented to maximize benefits while minimizing risks (Slimi & Villarejo Carballido, 2023). In the duality between opportunities and potential challenges, for AI in assessment, it is important to consider ethical challenges and evaluate the individual case to achieve fruitful implementations.

REFERENCES

Afzaal, M., Zia, A., Nouri, J., & Fors, U. (2024). Informative Feedback and Explainable AI-Based Recommendations to Support Students' Self-regulation. *Technology. Knowledge and Learning*, *29*(1), 331–354. DOI: 10.1007/s10758-023-09650-0

Ajjawi, R., Tai, J., Dollinger, M., Dawson, P., Boud, D., & Bearman, M. (2024). From authentic assessment to authenticity in assessment: Broadening perspectives. *Assessment & Evaluation in Higher Education*, *49*(4), 499–510. DOI: 10.1080/02602938.2023.2271193

Akinyi, G. L., Oboko, R., & Muchemi, L. (2024). Learning Analytics Intervention Using Prompts and Feedback for Measurement of e-Learners' Socially-Shared Regulated Learning. *Electronic Journal of e-Learning*, *22*(5), 103–116. DOI: 10.34190/ejel.22.5.3253

Aler Tubella, A., Mora-Cantallops, M., & Nieves, J. C. (2024). How to teach responsible AI in Higher Education: Challenges and opportunities. *Ethics and Information Technology*, *26*(1), 3. DOI: 10.1007/s10676-023-09733-7

Almusaed, A., Almssad, A., Yitmen, I., & Homod, R. Z. (2023). Enhancing Student Engagement: Harnessing "AIED"'s Power in Hybrid Education—A Review Analysis. *Education Sciences*, *13*(7), 632. DOI: 10.3390/educsci13070632

Andrade, M. S., & Alden-Rivers, B. (2019). Developing a framework for sustainable growth of flexible learning opportunities. *Higher Education Pedagogies*, *4*(1), 1–16. DOI: 10.1080/23752696.2018.1564879

Ashford-Rowe, K., Herrington, J., & Brown, C. (2014). Establishing the critical elements that determine authentic assessment. *Assessment & Evaluation in Higher Education*, *39*(2), 205–222. DOI: 10.1080/02602938.2013.819566

Ayeni, O. O., Hamad, N. M. A., Chisom, O. N., Osawaru, B., Adewusi, O. E., Ayeni, O. O., Hamad, N. M. A., Chisom, O. N., Osawaru, B., & Adewusi, O. E. (2024). AI in education: A review of personalized learning and educational technology. *GSC Advanced Research and Reviews*, *18*(2), 2. Advance online publication. DOI: 10.30574/gscarr.2024.18.2.0062

Baker, E. L., Chung, G. K. W. K., & Cai, L. (2016). Assessment Gaze, Refraction, and Blur: The Course of Achievement Testing in the Past 100 Years. *Review of Research in Education*, *40*(1), 94–142. DOI: 10.3102/0091732X16679806

Banihashem, S. K., Kerman, N. T., Noroozi, O., Moon, J., & Drachsler, H. (2024). Feedback sources in essay writing: Peer-generated or AI-generated feedback? *International Journal of Educational Technology in Higher Education*, *21*(1), 23. DOI: 10.1186/s41239-024-00455-4

Bearman, M., Tai, J., Dawson, P., Boud, D., & Ajjawi, R. (2024). Developing evaluative judgement for a time of generative artificial intelligence. *Assessment & Evaluation in Higher Education*, *49*(6), 893–905. DOI: 10.1080/02602938.2024.2335321

Beatty, B. J. (2019). Beginnings: Where Does Hybrid-Flexible Come From? In Beatty, B. J. (Ed.), *Hybrid-Flexible Course Design: Implementing Student-Directed Hybrid Classes* (pp. 9–21). EdTech Books., DOI: 10.59668/33

Belkina, M., Daniel, S., Nikolic, S., Haque, R., Lyden, S., Neal, P., Grundy, S., & Hassan, G. M. (2025). Implementing generative AI (GenAI) in higher education: A systematic review of case studies. *Computers and Education: Artificial Intelligence*, *8*, 100407. DOI: 10.1016/j.caeai.2025.100407

Black, P., & Wiliam, D. (2009). Developing the theory of formative assessment. *Educational Assessment, Evaluation and Accountability(Formerly: Journal of Personnel Evaluation in Education), 21*(1), 5–31. DOI: 10.1007/s11092-008-9068-5

Boelens, R., De Wever, B., & Voet, M. (2017). Four key challenges to the design of blended learning: A systematic literature review. *Educational Research Review*, *22*, 1–18. DOI: 10.1016/j.edurev.2017.06.001

Bond, M., Khosravi, H., De Laat, M., Bergdahl, N., Negrea, V., Oxley, E., Pham, P., Chong, S. W., & Siemens, G. (2024). A meta systematic review of artificial intelligence in higher education: A call for increased ethics, collaboration, and rigour. *International Journal of Educational Technology in Higher Education*, *21*(1), 4. DOI: 10.1186/s41239-023-00436-z

Boud, D. (1995). Assessment and Learning: Contradictory or Complementary? In *Assessment for Learning in Higher Education*. Routledge.

Bozkurt, A. (2023). Unleashing the potential of generative AI, conversational agents and chatbots in educational praxis: A systematic review and bibliometric analysis of GenAI in education. *Open Praxis*, *15*(4), 261–270. Advance online publication. DOI: 10.55982/openpraxis.15.4.609

Butler-Henderson, K., & Crawford, J. (2020). A systematic review of online examinations: A pedagogical innovation for scalable authentication and integrity. *Computers & Education*, *159*, 104024. DOI: 10.1016/j.compedu.2020.104024 PMID: 32982023

Carless, D. (2007). Learning-oriented assessment: Conceptual bases and practical implications. *Innovations in Education and Teaching International*, *44*(1), 57–66. DOI: 10.1080/14703290601081332

Carless, D. (2015). Exploring learning-oriented assessment processes. *Higher Education*, *69*(6), 963–976. DOI: 10.1007/s10734-014-9816-z

Carlile, W., Gurrapadi, N., Ke, Z., & Ng, V. (2018). Give Me More Feedback: Annotating Argument Persuasiveness and Related Attributes in Student Essays. In Gurevych, I., & Miyao, Y. (Eds.), *Proceedings of the 56th Annual Meeting of the Association for Computational Linguistics* (pp. 621–631). Association for Computational Linguistics. DOI: 10.18653/v1/P18-1058

Caspari-Sadeghi, S. (2023). Learning assessment in the age of big data: Learning analytics in higher education. *Cogent Education*, *10*(1), 2162697. DOI: 10.1080/2331186X.2022.2162697

Chiu, T. K. F. (2024). Future research recommendations for transforming higher education with generative AI. *Computers and Education: Artificial Intelligence*, *6*, 100197. DOI: 10.1016/j.caeai.2023.100197

Coghlan, S., Miller, T., & Paterson, J. (2021). Good Proctor or "Big Brother"? Ethics of Online Exam Supervision Technologies. *Philosophy & Technology*, *34*(4), 1581–1606. DOI: 10.1007/s13347-021-00476-1 PMID: 34485025

Darvishi, A., Khosravi, H., Sadiq, S., & Gašević, D. (2022). Incorporating AI and learning analytics to build trustworthy peer assessment systems. *British Journal of Educational Technology*, *53*(4), 844–875. DOI: 10.1111/bjet.13233

Delcker, J., Heil, J., & Ifenthaler, D. (2025). Evidence-based development of an instrument for the assessment of teachers' self-perceptions of their artificial intelligence competence. *Educational Technology Research and Development*, *73*(1), 115–133. DOI: 10.1007/s11423-024-10418-1

Delcker, J., Heil, J., Ifenthaler, D., Seufert, S., & Spirgi, L. (2024). First-year students AI-competence as a predictor for intended and de facto use of AI-tools for supporting learning processes in higher education. *International Journal of Educational Technology in Higher Education*, *21*(1), 18. DOI: 10.1186/s41239-024-00452-7

Detienne, L., Raes, A., & Depaepe, F. (2018). Benefits, Challenges and Design Guidelines for Synchronous Hybrid Learning: A Systematic Literature Review. In Bastiaens, T., Van Braak, J., Brown, M., Cantoni, L., Castro, M., Christensen, R., Davidson-Shivers, G., DePryck, K., Ebner, M., Fominykh, M., Fulford, C., Hatzipanagos, S., Knezek, G., Kreijns, K., Marks, G., Sointu, E., Korsgaard Sorensen, E., Viteli, J., Voogt, J., Weber, P., Weippl, E., & Zawacki-Richter, O. (Eds.), *Proceedings of EdMedia: World Conference on Educational Media and Technology* (pp. 2004-2009). Amsterdam, Netherlands: Association for the Advancement of Computing in Education.

Dignum, V. (2017). Responsible artificial intelligence: Designing AI for human values. *ITU Journal : ICT Discoveries, 1*(Special Issue), 1–17.

Elmassry, A. M., Zaki, N., Alsheikh, N., & Mediani, M. (2025). A Systematic Review of Pretrained Models in Automated Essay Scoring. *IEEE Access : Practical Innovations, Open Solutions, 13*, 121902–121917. DOI: 10.1109/ACCESS.2025.3584784

Ertel, W. (2024). *Introduction to Artificial Intelligence*. Springer Nature.

Evangelista, E. D. L. (2025). Ensuring academic integrity in the age of ChatGPT: Rethinking exam design, assessment strategies, and ethical AI policies in higher education. *Contemporary Educational Technology, 17*(1), ep559. DOI: 10.30935/cedtech/15775

Fawns, T., Bearman, M., Dawson, P., Nieminen, J. H., Ashford-Rowe, K., Willey, K., Jensen, L. X., Damşa, C., & Press, N. (2025). Authentic assessment: From panacea to criticality. *Assessment & Evaluation in Higher Education, 50*(3), 396–408. DOI: 10.1080/02602938.2024.2404634

Feuerriegel, S., Hartmann, J., Janiesch, C., & Zschech, P. (2024). Generative AI. *Business & Information Systems Engineering, 66*(1), 111–126. DOI: 10.1007/s12599-023-00834-7

French, S., Dickerson, A., & Mulder, R. A. (2024). A review of the benefits and drawbacks of high-stakes final examinations in higher education. *Higher Education, 88*(3), 893–918. DOI: 10.1007/s10734-023-01148-z

Fromm, Y., Rasch, J., & Ifenthaler, D. (2025). Technology-enhanced personalized learning environments based on prior knowledge in continuing education: An experimental study. *Smart Learning Environments, 12*(1), 54. DOI: 10.1186/s40561-025-00407-z

González-Calatayud, V., Prendes-Espinosa, P., & Roig-Vila, R. (2021). Artificial Intelligence for Student Assessment: A Systematic Review. *Applied Sciences (Basel, Switzerland), 11*(12), 5467. DOI: 10.3390/app11125467

González-Castro, N., Muñoz-Merino, P. J., Alario-Hoyos, C., & Kloos, C. D. (2021). Adaptive learning module for a conversational agent to support MOOC learners. *Australasian Journal of Educational Technology, 37*(2), 24–44. DOI: 10.14742/ajet.6646

Guerrero-Quiñonez, A. J., Bedoya-Flores, M. C., Mosquera-Quiñonez, E. F., Ango-Ramos, E. D., & Lara-Tambaco, R. M. (2023). Hybrid Education: Current Challenges. *Ibero-American Journal of Education & Society Research, 3*(1), 276–279. DOI: 10.56183/iberoeds.v3i1.629

Haenlein, M., & Kaplan, A. (2019). A Brief History of Artificial Intelligence: On the Past, Present, and Future of Artificial Intelligence. *California Management Review, 61*(4), 5–14. DOI: 10.1177/0008125619864925

Heil, J., & Ifenthaler, D. (2023). Online Assessment in Higher Education: A Systematic Review. *Online Learning. 27*(1), 187–218. DOI: 10.24059/olj.v27i1.3398

Heil, J., & Ifenthaler, D. (2025). Effects of teacher, peer and self-feedback on student improvement in online assessment: The role of individuals' presumptions and feedback literacy. *Assessment & Evaluation in Higher Education*, •••, 1–20. DOI: 10.1080/02602938.2025.2530452

Heil, J., Ifenthaler, D., Cooper, M., Mascia, M. L., Conti, R., & Penna, M. P. (2025). Students' perceived impact of GenAI tools on learning and assessment in higher education: The role of individual AI competence. *Smart Learning Environments, 12*(1), 37. DOI: 10.1186/s40561-025-00395-0

Henderson, M., Bearman, M., Chung, J., Fawns, T., Buckingham Shum, S., Matthews, K. E., & De Mello Heredia, J. (2025). Comparing Generative AI and teacher feedback: Student perceptions of usefulness and trustworthiness. *Assessment & Evaluation in Higher Education*, •••, 1–16. DOI: 10.1080/02602938.2025.2502582

Howell, E. (2022). HyFlex model of higher education: Understanding the promise of flexibility. *On the Horizon. On the Horizon, 30*(4), 173–181. DOI: 10.1108/OTH-04-2022-0019

Howell, E., Linder, S., Ryan, J., & Bridges, W. C. (2025). Examining higher education through HyFlex. *Open Learning, 40*(3), 252–267. Advance online publication. DOI: 10.1080/02680513.2024.2354245

Hu, A., Liu, Q., & Daniel, B. (2025). The role of digital technology in authentic assessment: Perspectives of university educators. *Assessment & Evaluation in Higher Education*, •••, 1–14. DOI: 10.1080/02602938.2025.2524095

Huang, L. (2023). Ethics of Artificial Intelligence in Education: Student Privacy and Data Protection. *Science Insights Education Frontiers*, *16*(2), 2577–2587. DOI: 10.15354/sief.23.re202

Ifenthaler, D. (2015). Learning analytics. In Spector, J. M. (Ed.), *The SAGE encyclopedia of educational technology* (Vol. 2, pp. 448–451). Sage., DOI: 10.4135/9781483346397.n187

Ifenthaler, D. (2022). Automated Essay Scoring Systems. In *Handbook of Open, Distance and Digital Education* (pp. 1–15). Springer Nature Singapore. DOI: 10.1007/978-981-19-0351-9_59-1

Ifenthaler, D. (2023). Ethische Perspektiven auf künstliche Intelligenz im Kontext der Hochschule. In T. Schmohl, A. Watanabe, & K. Schelling (Eds.), Künstliche Intelligenz in der Hochschulbildung. Chancen und Grenzen des KI-gestützten Lernens und Lehrens (pp. 71–86). transcript-Verlag. https://doi.org/DOI: 10.14361/9783839457696

Ifenthaler, D. (2025). Information processing re-visited: How artificial intelligence supports human-centered systems. *AI-Enhanced Learning*, *1*(1), 229–243. DOI: 10.70725/465418kgasdx

Ifenthaler, D., & Dikli, S. (2015). Automated scoring of essays. In Spector, J. M. (Ed.), *The SAGE encyclopedia of educational technology* (Vol. 1, pp. 64–68). Sage.

Ifenthaler, D., Majumdar, R., Gorissen, P., Judge, M., Mishra, S., Raffaghelli, J., & Shimada, A. (2024). Artificial intelligence in education: Implications for policymakers, researchers, and practitioners. Technology. *Knowledge and Learning*, *29*(4), 1693–1710. DOI: 10.1007/s10758-024-09747-0

Ifenthaler, D., & Sahin, M. (2023). Empowering higher education students to monitor their learning progress: Opportunities of computerised classification testing. *Interactive Technology and Smart Education*, *20*(3), 350–366. DOI: 10.1108/ITSE-11-2022-0150

Ifenthaler, D., & Schumacher, C. (2016). Student perceptions of privacy principles for learning analytics. *Educational Technology Research and Development*, *64*(5), 923–938. DOI: 10.1007/s11423-016-9477-y

Ifenthaler, D., & Yau, J. Y.-K. (2020). Utilising learning analytics to support study success in higher education: A systematic review. *Educational Technology Research and Development*, *68*(4), 1961–1990. DOI: 10.1007/s11423-020-09788-z

Jerlinder, K., Johansson, M., Blomqvist, S., Svennberg, L., Ervasti, P.-E., & Qvarfordt, A. (2025). Assessing student satisfaction and learning perceptions of HyFlex education. *Open Learning*, •••, 1–18. DOI: 10.1080/02680513.2025.2532622

Jin, Y., Yan, L., Echeverria, V., Gašević, D., & Martinez-Maldonado, R. (2025). Generative AI in higher education: A global perspective of institutional adoption policies and guidelines. *Computers and Education: Artificial Intelligence*, *8*, 100348. DOI: 10.1016/j.caeai.2024.100348

Ke, Z., & Ng, V. (2019). Automated Essay Scoring: A Survey of the State of the Art. In *Proceedings of the Twenty-Eighth International Joint Conference on Artificial Intelligence*(pp. 6300–6308). https://doi.org/DOI: 10.24963/ijcai.2019/879

Kofinas, A. K., Tsay, C. H., & Pike, D. (2025). The impact of generative AI on academic integrity of authentic assessments within a higher education context. *British Journal of Educational Technology*, *56*(6), 2522–2549. DOI: 10.1111/bjet.13585

Komljenovic, J., Sellar, S., & Birch, K. (2024). Turning universities into data-driven organisations: Seven dimensions of change. *Higher Education*, *89*(5), 1369–1386. DOI: 10.1007/s10734-024-01277-z

Le, X. (2024). Assessment Reform in Higher Education: An Ethical Approach to Harness the Power of Generative Artificial Intelligence. *Education Research and Perspectives*, *51*, 156–185. DOI: 10.70953/ERPv51.2412007

Lee, S. S., & Moore, R. L. (2024). Harnessing Generative AI (GenAI) for Automated Feedback in Higher Education: A Systematic Review. *Online Learning : the Official Journal of the Online Learning Consortium*, *28*(3), 82–106. DOI: 10.24059/olj.v28i3.4593

Loh, C. S., Sheng, Y., & Ifenthaler, D. (2015). Serious Games Analytics: Theoretical Framework. In Loh, C. S., Sheng, Y., & Ifenthaler, D. (Eds.), *Serious Games Analytics* (pp. 3–29). Springer International Publishing., DOI: 10.1007/978-3-319-05834-4_1

Lu, O. H. T., Huang, A. Y. Q., Tsai, D. C. L., & Yang, S. J. H. (2021). Expert-Authored and Machine-Generated Short-Answer Questions for Assessing Students Learning Performance. *Journal of Educational Technology & Society*, *24*(3), 159–173.

Mathias, S., & Bhattacharyya, P. (2018). ASAP++: enriching the asap automated essay grading dataset with essay attribute scores. In N. Calzolari, K. Choukri, C. Cieri, T. Declerck, S. Goggi, K. Hasida, H. Isahara, B. Maegaard, J.

McArthur, J. (2023). Rethinking authentic assessment: Work, well-being, and society. *Higher Education*, *85*(1), 85–101. DOI: 10.1007/s10734-022-00822-y PMID: 35194229

Memarian, B., & Doleck, T. (2023). Fairness, Accountability, Transparency, and Ethics (FATE) in Artificial Intelligence (AI) and higher education: A systematic review. *Computers and Education: Artificial Intelligence*, *5*, 100152. DOI: 10.1016/j.caeai.2023.100152

Min, X., Padmadewi, N. N., Artini, L. P., Karang, B. G., & Tao, Z. (2025). Ai-Driven Learning Analytics and Their Effect on Personalized Feedback in Blended Higher Education Courses at Nanjing Normal University, China. *Lex Localis*, *23*(S6), 4023–4050. DOI: 10.52152/0f8d2h45

Mpolomoka, D. L. (2025). Utilizing artificial intelligence for assessment in higher education. *Pedagogical Research*, *10*(3), em0243. Advance online publication. DOI: 10.29333/pr/16677

Ng, D. T. K., Wu, W., Leung, J. K. L., Chiu, T. K. F., & Chu, S. K. W. (2024). Design and validation of the AI literacy questionnaire: The affective, behavioural, cognitive and ethical approach. *British Journal of Educational Technology*, *55*(3), 1082–1104. DOI: 10.1111/bjet.13411

Nieminen, J. H., Bearman, M., & Ajjawi, R. (2023). Designing the digital in authentic assessment: Is it fit for purpose? *Assessment & Evaluation in Higher Education*, *48*(4), 529–543. DOI: 10.1080/02602938.2022.2089627

Nieminen, J. H., & Boud, D. (2025). Placing authenticity at the heart of student self-assessment: An integrative review. *Teaching in Higher Education*, *30*(3), 640–662. DOI: 10.1080/13562517.2024.2367669

Nouira, A., Cheniti-Belcadhi, L., & Braham, R. (2019). An ontology-based framework of assessment analytics for massive learning. *Computer Applications in Engineering Education*, *27*(6), 1343–1360. DOI: 10.1002/cae.22155

Page, E. B. (1968). The use of the computer in analyzing student essays. *International Review of Education*, *14*(2), 210–225. DOI: 10.1007/BF01419938

Pardo, A., Jovanovic, J., Dawson, S., Gašević, D., & Mirriahi, N. (2019). Using learning analytics to scale the provision of personalised feedback. *British Journal of Educational Technology*, *50*(1), 128–138. DOI: 10.1111/bjet.12592

Park, Y., & Doo, M. Y. (2024). Role of AI in Blended Learning: A Systematic Literature Review. *International Review of Research in Open and Distance Learning*, *25*(1), 164–196. DOI: 10.19173/irrodl.v25i1.7566

Perkins, M., Furze, L., Roe, J., & MacVaugh, J. (2024). The Artificial Intelligence Assessment Scale (AIAS): A framework for ethical integration of Generative AI in Educational Assessment. *Journal of University Teaching & Learning Practice, 21*(6), 49–66. DOI: 10.53761/q3azde36

Rahimi, S., & Shute, V. J. (2024). Stealth assessment: A theoretically grounded and psychometrically sound method to assess, support, and investigate learning in technology-rich environments. *Educational Technology Research and Development, 72*(5), 2417–2441. DOI: 10.1007/s11423-023-10232-1

Rodway, P., & Schepman, A. (2023). The impact of adopting AI educational technologies on projected course satisfaction in university students. *Computers and Education: Artificial Intelligence, 5*, 100150. DOI: 10.1016/j.caeai.2023.100150

Romero, C., & Ventura, S. (2020). Educational data mining and learning analytics: An updated survey. *Wiley Interdisciplinary Reviews. Data Mining and Knowledge Discovery, 10*(3), e1355. DOI: 10.1002/widm.1355

Ronge, R., Maier, M., & Rathgeber, B. (2025). Towards a Definition of Generative Artificial Intelligence. *Philosophy & Technology, 38*(1), 31. DOI: 10.1007/s13347-025-00863-y

Rudolph, J., Tan, S., & Tan, S. (2023). ChatGPT: Bullshit spewer or the end of traditional assessments in higher education? *Journal of Applied Learning and Teaching, 6*(1), 342–363. DOI: 10.37074/jalt.2023.6.1.9

Russell, S., & Norvig, P. (1995). *Artificial Intelligence: A modern approach* (Vol. 25). PrenticeHall, Inc.

Sahin, M., & Ifenthaler, D. (2024). Foundations of Assessment Analytics. In Sahin, M., & Ifenthaler, D. (Eds.), *Assessment Analytics in Education: Designs, Methods and Solutions* (pp. 3–17). Springer International Publishing., DOI: 10.1007/978-3-031-56365-2_1

Saichaie, K. (2020). Blended, Flipped, and Hybrid Learning: Definitions, Developments, and Directions. *New Directions for Teaching and Learning, 2020*(164), 95–104. DOI: 10.1002/tl.20428

Salinas-Navarro, D. E., Vilalta-Perdomo, E., Michel-Villarreal, R., & Montesinos, L. (2024). Designing experiential learning activities with generative artificial intelligence tools for authentic assessment. *Interactive Technology and Smart Education, 21*(4), 708–734. DOI: 10.1108/ITSE-12-2023-0236

Schumacher, C. (2023). Linking Assessment and Learning Analytics to Support Learning Processes in Higher Education. In *Learning, Design, and Technology* (pp. 741–780). Springer., DOI: 10.1007/978-3-319-17461-7_166

Schumacher, C., & Ifenthaler, D. (2021). Investigating prompts for supporting students' self-regulation – A remaining challenge for learning analytics approaches? *The Internet and Higher Education*, *49*, 100791. DOI: 10.1016/j.iheduc.2020.100791

Shute, V. J. (2011). Stealth assessment in computer-based games to support learning. In Tobias, S., & Fletcher, J. D. (Eds.), *Computer Games and Instruction* (pp. 503–524). Information Age Publishing. DOI: 10.1108/978-1-61735-410-620251025

Shute, V. J., & Becker, B. J. (2010). Prelude: Assessment for the 21st Century. In Shute, V. J., & Becker, B. J. (Eds.), *Innovative Assessment for the 21st Century: Supporting Educational Needs* (pp. 1–11). Springer US., DOI: 10.1007/978-1-4419-6530-1_1

Slimi, Z., & Villarejo Carballido, B. (2023). Navigating the Ethical Challenges of Artificial Intelligence in Higher Education: An Analysis of Seven Global AI Ethics Policies. *TEM Journal*, 590–602. https://doi.org/DOI: 10.18421/TEM122-02

Spirgi, L., Seufert, S., Delcker, J., Heil, J., & Ifenthaler, D. (2025). Soziotechnische Systemgestaltung im Kontext generativer KI: Eine empirische Untersuchung. *Zeitschrift für Hochschulentwicklung,* 20(SH-KI-1), 89–108. https://doi.org/DOI: 10.21240/zfhe/SH-KI-1/06

Strzelecki, A. (2024). Students' Acceptance of ChatGPT in Higher Education: An Extended Unified Theory of Acceptance and Use of Technology. *Innovative Higher Education*, *49*(2), 223–245. DOI: 10.1007/s10755-023-09686-1

Sukirman, S., E., Setiawan, A., Chamsudin, A., Yuliana, I., & Wantoro, J. (2024). Exploring Student Perceptions and Acceptance of ChatGPT in Enhanced AI-Assisted Learning. In *2024 International Conference on Smart Computing, IoT and Machine Learning (SIML)* (pp. 291–296). DOI: 10.1109/SIML61815.2024.10578145

Sunusi, S. L., Azhari, A., Sembiring, S. A., & Safitri, C. D. (2025). Implementation of Artificial Intelligence (AI) in HyFlex-Based Final Project Guidance. *Celebes Journal of Language Studies*, *5*(2), 251–262. DOI: 10.51629/cjls.v5i2.261

Taghipour, K., & Ng, H. T. (2016). A Neural Approach to Automated Essay Scoring. In Su, J., Duh, K., & Carreras, X. (Eds.), *Proceedings of the 2016 Conference on Empirical Methods in Natural Language Processing* (pp. 1882–1891). DOI: 10.18653/v1/D16-1193

Tai, J., Ajjawi, R., Boud, D., Dawson, P., & Panadero, E. (2018). Developing evaluative judgement: Enabling students to make decisions about the quality of work. *Higher Education, 76*(3), 467–481. DOI: 10.1007/s10734-017-0220-3

Tepgec, M., Heil, J., & Ifenthaler, D. (2024). Feedback literacy matters: Unlocking the potential of learning analytics-based feedback. *Assessment & Evaluation in Higher Education, 50*(1), 50–66. DOI: 10.1080/02602938.2024.2367587

Thanh, B. N., Vo, D. T. H., Nhat, M. N., Pham, T. T. T., Trung, H. T., & Xuan, S. H. (2023). Race with the machines: Assessing the capability of generative AI in solving authentic assessments. *Australasian Journal of Educational Technology, 39*(5), 5. Advance online publication. DOI: 10.14742/ajet.8902

Uto, M., Xie, Y., & Ueno, M. (2020). Neural Automated Essay Scoring Incorporating Handcrafted Features. In D. Scott, N. Bel, & C. Zong (Eds.), *Proceedings of the 28th International Conference on Computational Linguistics* (pp. 6077–6088). International Committee on Computational Linguistics. DOI: 10.18653/v1/2020.coling-main.535

van Laar, E., van Deursen, A. J. A. M., van Dijk, J. A. G. M., & de Haan, J. (2017). The relation between 21st-century skills and digital skills: A systematic literature review. *Computers in Human Behavior, 72*, 577–588. DOI: 10.1016/j.chb.2017.03.010

Verma, C. (2025). A real-time AI tool for hybrid learning recommendation in education: Preliminary results. *Computers and Education: Artificial Intelligence, 8*, 100432. DOI: 10.1016/j.caeai.2025.100432

Viberg, O., Mutimukwe, C., Hrastinski, S., Cerratto-Pargman, T., & Lillieskőld, J. (2024). Exploring teachers' (future) digital assessment practices in higher education: Instrument and model development. *British Journal of Educational Technology, 55*(6), 2597–2616. DOI: 10.1111/bjet.13462

Villarroel, V., Bloxham, S., Bruna, D., Bruna, C., & Herrera-Seda, C. (2018). Authentic assessment: Creating a blueprint for course design. *Assessment & Evaluation in Higher Education, 43*(5), 840–854. DOI: 10.1080/02602938.2017.1412396

Villegas-Ch, W. E., Govea, J., Gutierrez, R., & Mera-Navarrete, A. (2024). Improving interaction and assessment in hybrid educational environments: An integrated approach in microsoft teams with the use of ai techniques. *IEEE Access : Practical Innovations, Open Solutions, 12*, 93723–93738. DOI: 10.1109/ACCESS.2024.3424397

Vu, T. T., & Dall'Alba, G. (2014). Authentic Assessment for Student Learning: An ontological conceptualisation. *Educational Philosophy and Theory, 46*(7), 778–791. DOI: 10.1080/00131857.2013.795110

Webb, M., & Ifenthaler, D. (2018). Assessment as, for and of 21st Century learning using information technology: An overview. In Voogt, J., Knezek, G., Christensen, R., & Lai, K.-W. (Eds.), *International handbook of IT in primary and secondary education* (2nd ed., pp. 581–600). Springer., DOI: 10.1007/978-3-319-71054-9_37

Weng, X., Xia, Q., Gu, M., Rajaram, K., & Chiu, T. K. F. (2024). Assessment and learning outcomes for generative AI in higher education: A scoping review on current research status and trends. *Australasian Journal of Educational Technology, 40*(6), 37–55. DOI: 10.14742/ajet.9540

Wong, B. T. M., Li, K. C., Chan, H. T., & Cheung, S. K. S. (2023). HyFlex Learning Research and Practice: A Longitudinal Analysis. *Sustainability (Basel), 15*(12), 9699. DOI: 10.3390/su15129699

Wright, D. (2016). The HyFlex course design: A case study on adult and career education courses. *National Social Science Journal, 48*(2), 88–93.

Xia, Q., Weng, X., Ouyang, F., Lin, T. J., & Chiu, T. K. F. (2024). A scoping review on how generative artificial intelligence transforms assessment in higher education. *International Journal of Educational Technology in Higher Education, 21*(1), 40. DOI: 10.1186/s41239-024-00468-z

Yan, Z., & Boud, D. (2021). Conceptualising assessment-as-learning. In Z. Yan & L.

Yang, A. C. M., Chen, I. Y. L., Flanagan, B., & Ogata, H. (2021). Automatic Generation of Cloze Items for Repeated Testing to Improve Reading Comprehension. *Journal of Educational Technology & Society, 24*(3), 147–158.

Yang, H. H., Yin, Z., & Zhu, S. (2025). Examining students' acceptance of the large-scale HyFlex course: An empirical study. *British Journal of Educational Technology, 56*(1), 42–60. DOI: 10.1111/bjet.13477

Zawacki-Richter, O., Marín, V. I., Bond, M., & Gouverneur, F. (2019). Systematic review of research on artificial intelligence applications in higher education–where are the educators? *International Journal of Educational Technology in Higher Education, 16*(1), 1–27. DOI: 10.1186/s41239-019-0171-0

Zhao, C. (2024). AI-assisted assessment in higher education: A systematic review. *Journal of Educational Technology and Innovation, 6*(4), 39–58. DOI: 10.61414/jeti.v6i4.209

Zhao, J., Chapman, E., & Sabet, P. G. P. (2024). Generative AI and Educational Assessments: A Systematic Review. *Education Research and Perspectives, 51*, 124–155. DOI: 10.70953/ERPv51.2412006

Zupanc, K., & Bosnić, Z. (2017). Automated essay evaluation with semantic analysis. *Knowledge-Based Systems, 120*, 118–132. DOI: 10.1016/j.knosys.2017.01.006

ADDITIONAL READING

Bearman, M., Tai, J., Dawson, P., Boud, D., & Ajjawi, R. (2024). Developing evaluative judgement for a time of generative artificial intelligence. *Assessment & Evaluation in Higher Education, 49*(6), 893–905. DOI: 10.1080/02602938.2024.2335321

Bond, M., Khosravi, H., De Laat, M., Bergdahl, N., Negrea, V., Oxley, E., Pham, P., Chong, S. W., & Siemens, G. (2024). A meta systematic review of artificial intelligence in higher education: A call for increased ethics, collaboration, and rigour. *International Journal of Educational Technology in Higher Education, 21*(1), 4. DOI: 10.1186/s41239-023-00436-z

Delcker, J., Heil, J., Ifenthaler, D., Seufert, S., & Spirgi, L. (2024). First-year students AI-competence as a predictor for intended and de facto use of AI-tools for supporting learning processes in higher education. *International Journal of Educational Technology in Higher Education, 21*(1), 18. DOI: 10.1186/s41239-024-00452-7

Fromm, Y., Rasch, J., & Ifenthaler, D. (2025). Technology-enhanced personalized learning environments based on prior knowledge in continuing education: An experimental study. *Smart Learning Environments, 12*(1), 54. DOI: 10.1186/s40561-025-00407-z

Heil, J., & Ifenthaler, D. (2023). Online Assessment in Higher Education: A Systematic Review. *Online Learning. 27*(1), 187–218. DOI: 10.24059/olj.v27i1.3398

Chapter 11

Secure Software Engineering for AI-Powered HyFlex Learning:

Building Trustworthy and Engaging Educational Platforms

Hanh Le
http://orcid.org/0009-0007-8172-0809
University of the Cumberlands, USA

ABSTRACT

As artificial intelligence (AI) technologies become increasingly integrated into HyFlex learning environments, the need for secure, scalable, and pedagogically aligned software systems has never been greater. This chapter examines how software engineering practices can support the development of AI-enhanced learning platforms that are both engaging for students and resilient against emerging cyber threats. Drawing on the Theories of Deskilling of Jobs, Job Characteristics, and Technology Threat Avoidance, the chapter explores secure coding methodologies, privacy-preserving AI features, and the role of DevSecOps in maintaining continuous trust within educational ecosystems. Through semi-structured interviews, document analysis, and interaction analytics, the chapter presents multiple case studies illustrating how secure, inclusive, and human-centered design enhances student trust, system usability, and learning outcomes.

DOI: 10.4018/979-8-3373-6182-6.ch011

INTRODUCTION

The integration of artificial intelligence (AI) into HyFlex learning environments offers opportunities for personalized, adaptive education while posing challenges related to security, trust, and human engagement. AI-powered platforms can provide real-time feedback, adaptive learning pathways, and virtual learning companions; however, these benefits come with risks, including automation-induced deskilling, privacy concerns, and diminished learner motivation. To design effective, trustworthy systems, it is essential to ground development in both technical rigor and human-centered principles.

This chapter examines how secure software engineering practices can be leveraged to enhance student engagement, preserve instructor expertise, and foster trust in AI-powered HyFlex platforms. By synthesizing insights from Deskilling Theory, Job Characteristics Theory, and Technology Threat Avoidance Theory, the chapter proposes a conceptual framework that informs research design, system development, and pedagogical practice. Case studies, interviews, and analytics illustrate how secure and inclusive design supports both technical reliability and human-centered learning outcomes.

LITERATURE REVIEW

The integration of artificial intelligence (AI) into HyFlex learning environments has generated increasing scholarly attention across the fields of software engineering, educational technology, learning sciences, and cybersecurity. Early literature primarily emphasized the pedagogical advantages of HyFlex models—such as flexibility, accessibility, and learner autonomy—alongside the efficiency and scalability afforded by AI-powered instructional systems. As these technologies have matured and become more deeply embedded within institutional infrastructures, however, researchers have begun to critically examine the risks, limitations, and ethical implications associated with this convergence. These concerns extend beyond instructional effectiveness to encompass issues of system security, data privacy, algorithmic transparency, and long-term institutional trust.

Although research on this topic has grown substantially, existing research remains fragmented across disciplinary boundaries. Pedagogical studies often focus on learner engagement and instructional outcomes, while technical research addresses AI performance or system optimization in isolation. Ethical discussions, meanwhile, frequently remain conceptual and detached from the realities of implementation. This lack of integration limits the field's ability to develop comprehensive models that account for how pedagogical goals, ethical principles, and secure software engineering practices interact in AI-enhanced HyFlex environments. Accordingly, this literature review synthesizes and critically evaluates scholarship across four core areas: secure software development for educational platforms, AI integration in instructional systems, student data privacy and trust, and user experience in AI-enhanced learning. Together, these domains inform a multidimensional understanding of what it means to design and implement secure, scalable, and engaging educational technologies in an increasingly AI-driven landscape.

Secure Software Engineering in Educational Technology

HyFlex learning environments combine the flexibility of asynchronous participation with the immediacy and interactivity of live instruction, enabling students to select learning modalities that best align with their individual preferences, schedules, and learning needs (Beatty, 2024). This dual-mode design has been widely recognized for supporting accessibility and inclusivity, particularly for students balancing professional, familial, or geographic constraints. The pedagogical literature consistently highlights HyFlex models as mechanisms for enhancing learner agency while maintaining instructional coherence across modalities.

The integration of AI technologies—including intelligent tutoring systems, adaptive feedback agents, and AI-driven analytics dashboards—has further expanded the pedagogical capabilities of HyFlex environments (Mentzer et al., 2023). By leveraging real-time data on student engagement, comprehension, and performance, AI-enabled systems can personalize learning experiences, optimize instructional pacing, and provide targeted support at scale (Liang et al., 2023). These affordances align with constructivist and self-regulated learning theories, which emphasize adaptive scaffolding and timely feedback as drivers of deep learning.

However, the literature also reveals growing concerns regarding the complexity and risk introduced by AI-enhanced HyFlex systems. Scholars note that algorithmic opacity, embedded bias, and vulnerabilities related to unauthorized access or misuse of student data pose significant challenges to equitable and trustworthy learning environments (Khan et al., 2021). Moreover, the operational complexity of these platforms requires continuous monitoring, secure coding practices, and robust data governance frameworks to ensure system reliability and ethical use (NanoMatrix, 2024). While pedagogical research acknowledges these risks in principle, it often stops short of examining how secure software engineering practices can systematically address them. This gap underscores the need for integrated approaches that align instructional innovation with security-aware system design.

Secure Software Engineering and AI Ethics

Secure software engineering provides a foundational framework for addressing the intertwined challenges of security, privacy, and ethics inherent in AI-enabled systems. Secure-by-design methodologies advocate embedding security controls and privacy safeguards at the earliest stages of development, rather than treating them as post-deployment concerns (Upreti et al., 2024). In educational contexts, such measures may include encrypted data transmission, secure authentication mechanisms, anonymized or pseudonymized data storage, and access controls tailored to diverse user roles.

The DevSecOps paradigm extends these principles by integrating continuous security testing, automated threat detection, and compliance validation throughout the software development lifecycle (Rajapakse et al., 2022). While DevSecOps has been widely adopted in enterprise software environments, its application within AI-enhanced educational platforms remains limited. Educational systems present unique challenges, including fluctuating user populations, heightened ethical responsibilities, and stringent regulatory requirements. As a result, existing DevSecOps models often require adaptation to align with pedagogical priorities and institutional accountability.

Ethical considerations are deeply intertwined with software security in AI-driven learning environments. Responsible AI frameworks grounded in fairness, accountability, transparency, and explainability (FATE) provide normative guidance for ensuring that AI systems respect learner autonomy and promote equity (Cheong, 2024). In HyFlex platforms, predictive algorithms and adaptive feedback mechanisms directly influence learning trajectories, assessment outcomes, and student perceptions of fairness. Despite widespread acknowledgment of FATE principles, much of the literature remains abstract, offering limited insight into how these ethical commitments can be operationalized through concrete software engineering practices. This disconnect highlights the need for frameworks that explicitly link ethical AI principles with secure system design and lifecycle management.

Privacy-Preserving AI and Data Protection

The rapid expansion of data-driven learning analytics has intensified concerns surrounding student data privacy in AI-enhanced educational environments. AI-powered HyFlex systems routinely collect and process sensitive information, including behavioral data, performance metrics, and engagement patterns. In response, privacy-preserving AI techniques such as federated learning, differential privacy, and homomorphic encryption have emerged as promising solutions for balancing analytical insight with data protection (Li et al., 2024).

Federated learning enables collaborative model training without centralizing raw data, thereby reducing exposure to breaches. Differential privacy introduces controlled noise to prevent re-identification, while homomorphic encryption enables computations over encrypted datasets. Although these approaches offer substantial privacy benefits, they also introduce trade-offs in terms of system complexity, computational overhead, and model accuracy. The educational literature has only begun to explore how such trade-offs affect real-world HyFlex deployments.

Regulatory frameworks such as the General Data Protection Regulation (GDPR) and the Family Educational Rights and Privacy Act (FERPA) further shape data governance practices by establishing requirements for informed consent, data minimization, and individuals' rights to access and delete their data (U.S. Department of Education, 2020). While compliance is often treated as a legal obligation, integrating regulatory requirements into secure software engineering practices offers an opportunity to strengthen ethical accountability and institutional trust. Nonetheless, few studies examine how privacy-preserving techniques, regulatory compliance, and pedagogical goals can be systematically aligned within HyFlex architectures.

Case Studies and Empirical Insights

Empirical studies of AI-powered learning platforms provide insight into the practical application of secure and ethical design principles. Interactive AI tools such as ChatGPT and virtual learning companions have been shown to enhance engagement, motivation, and learner support, particularly in asynchronous and hybrid contexts (Avila-Chauvet et al., 2023; Liang et al., 2023). These tools demonstrate how pedagogical innovation can coexist with responsible design when transparency and secure feedback mechanisms are prioritized.

Institutional case studies implementing DevSecOps frameworks highlight the benefits of continuous monitoring, automated threat detection, and compliance validation in improving system resilience and stakeholder trust (NanoMatrix, 2024; Rajapakse et al., 2022). However, most documented implementations originate from enterprise or IT infrastructure settings, with limited focus on learner-facing AI components or pedagogical implications.

Ethical AI research further suggests that transparency and explainability positively influence student trust and acceptance of AI-mediated instruction (Barke et al., 2023; Rinta-Kahila et al., 2023). Still, empirical validation of how ethical safeguards are embedded at the software architecture level remains sparse. Collectively, these studies illustrate the potential of integrated approaches while also revealing a lack of comprehensive models that unite security, ethics, and pedagogy in educational AI systems.

Research Gaps

Despite increasing interest in AI-driven HyFlex education, several critical gaps remain. First, much of the existing literature prioritizes pedagogical outcomes and learner experience while underexamining the secure software engineering frameworks necessary to support trustworthy system operation. This imbalance impedes the translation of instructional innovation into scalable, resilient platforms.

Second, empirical research on the application of secure-by-design and DevSecOps methodologies within educational AI systems remains limited. While these approaches are well-established in enterprise contexts, their adaptation to HyFlex environments—where personalization, privacy, and ethical accountability intersect—has not been sufficiently explored.

Third, the tension between personalization and privacy remains inadequately addressed. AI-driven HyFlex systems depend on extensive learner data, yet architectural strategies that reconcile adaptive learning with data minimization and regulatory compliance remain underdeveloped.

Finally, ethical AI frameworks grounded in the FATE principles remain largely conceptual. Few studies demonstrate how these principles can be translated into enforceable software engineering practices embedded within the development lifecycle of HyFlex platforms.

Bridging Theory and Practice

Bridging the gap between theory and practice in AI-powered HyFlex education requires an integrative framework that unites pedagogy, cybersecurity, and software engineering. HyFlex pedagogy emphasizes flexibility and learner autonomy, but these principles can only be realized if the underlying systems are secure, transparent, and trustworthy. Secure-by-design and privacy-by-design approaches must therefore be adapted to educational contexts, translating abstract principles into actionable architectural decisions.

The DevSecOps paradigm provides a practical mechanism for embedding security and ethical evaluation throughout the system lifecycle. At the same time, human-centered AI frameworks emphasize oversight, explainability, and co-adaptive interactions between learners and AI agents (Cheong, 2024). Together, these approaches position secure software engineering as an enabler of pedagogical integrity rather than a technical constraint.

Practical Design Artifacts for AI-Enhanced HyFlex Systems

While the preceding sections synthesize theoretical, empirical, and ethical perspectives on AI-enhanced HyFlex learning, the literature also implies a need for more concrete guidance to support practical implementation. Prior studies have repeatedly identified challenges related to system security, data governance, algorithmic transparency, and learner trust, yet these concerns are often discussed in abstract terms or addressed in isolation (Khan et al., 2021; Cheong, 2024; NanoMatrix, 2024). To translate these insights into actionable design considerations, this section distills the reviewed literature into three practical artifacts: a high-level system architecture, a simplified threat model, and a secure and ethical design checklist. These artifacts synthesize recurring recommendations across secure software engineering, ethical AI, and HyFlex pedagogy, thereby extending the practical usefulness of the literature review.

High-Level System Architecture

The literature on secure software engineering and AI-enabled education suggests that modular and layered architectures are critical for balancing pedagogical flexibility with system security and ethical governance (Upreti et al., 2024; Rajapakse et al., 2022). In the context of HyFlex learning, such an architecture can be conceptualized as comprising four interrelated layers: user interaction, application logic, AI services, and data management, all supported by a cross-cutting security and governance layer.

At the user interaction layer, students and instructors engage through in-person classroom technologies, synchronous online platforms, and asynchronous learning management systems, reflecting the modality flexibility emphasized in HyFlex pedagogy (Beatty, 2024). The application layer manages instructional content, assessments, and engagement tracking, ensuring consistency across modalities (Mentzer et al., 2023). AI services, including adaptive feedback systems, learning analytics models, and conversational agents, operate as modular components accessed through well-defined interfaces rather than direct data access, a design choice aligned with secure-by-design principles (Upreti et al., 2024).

The data management layer supports encrypted storage of learner data, metadata, and system logs, with role-based access controls and data minimization policies informed by FERPA and GDPR requirements (U.S. Department of Education, 2020; Li et al., 2024). Privacy-preserving techniques such as anonymization or federated learning may be incorporated to reduce exposure of centralized data (Li et al., 2024). Across all layers, a security and governance layer enforces authentication, authorization, audit logging, and compliance monitoring, operationalized through

DevSecOps pipelines that integrate continuous testing and validation throughout system evolution (Rajapakse et al., 2022). This architectural synthesis reflects the literature's call for security and ethics to be embedded as foundational design elements rather than post hoc controls.

Threat Model for AI-Enhanced HyFlex Platforms

A recurring theme in the literature is the heightened risk profile of AI-enabled educational systems, particularly those operating in hybrid and distributed environments (Khan et al., 2021; NanoMatrix, 2024). Building on these insights, a simplified threat model can be derived to identify key risk areas and corresponding mitigation strategies in AI-enhanced HyFlex platforms.

At the user interface level, risks include unauthorized access, identity spoofing, and session hijacking, exacerbated by the coexistence of in-person and online access modalities. Prior work emphasizes the importance of consistent authentication and secure session management across learning contexts to mitigate these risks (NanoMatrix, 2024). At the AI service layer, threats such as data poisoning, model manipulation, and inference attacks raise concerns about both system integrity and learner privacy, particularly in adaptive systems that continuously retrain on interaction data (Khan et al., 2021). Mitigation strategies highlighted in the literature include controlled training pipelines, input validation, and the application of privacy-preserving techniques such as differential privacy (Li et al., 2024).

The data layer presents risks related to breaches, unauthorized aggregation of learner data, and regulatory noncompliance. Encryption at rest and in transit, strict access controls, and data minimization practices are widely cited as essential safeguards (Upreti et al., 2024; U.S. Department of Education, 2020). At the infrastructure level, misconfigurations and outdated dependencies can expose systems to external attacks, underscoring the value of continuous monitoring and automated vulnerability scanning enabled by DevSecOps practices (Rajapakse et al., 2022). By mapping these threats across architectural layers, the threat model synthesizes dispersed findings from the literature into a coherent risk perspective tailored to HyFlex environments.

Secure and Ethical Design Checklist

The reviewed literature consistently emphasizes the need to operationalize secure software engineering and ethical AI principles within educational systems, yet offers limited guidance on how to do so in practice (Cheong, 2024; Khan et al., 2021). Drawing on recurring themes across the literature, a concise design checklist can support practitioners in aligning AI-enhanced HyFlex systems with pedagogical, ethical, and security expectations:

1. **Pedagogical Alignment**: Ensure AI functionalities directly support instructional goals and HyFlex flexibility, consistent with learner-centered design principles (Beatty, 2024; Mentzer et al., 2023).
2. **Data Minimization and Transparency**: Limit data collection to what is necessary for learning objectives and clearly communicate data use to learners, in accordance with FERPA and GDPR requirements (U.S. Department of Education, 2020; Li et al., 2024).
3. **Secure-by-Design Implementation**: Embed encryption, access control, and secure APIs throughout system development rather than treating security as a post-deployment concern (Upreti et al., 2024).
4. **Privacy-Preserving AI Techniques**: Apply methods such as anonymization, federated learning, or differential privacy to reduce exposure of sensitive learner data while supporting analytics (Li et al., 2024).
5. **Ethical AI Governance**: Incorporate fairness, accountability, transparency, and explainability checks into AI model development and deployment workflows (Cheong, 2024).
6. **Continuous Security and Compliance Monitoring**: Use DevSecOps pipelines to automate vulnerability scanning, compliance validation, and system updates (Rajapakse et al., 2022; NanoMatrix, 2024).
7. **Human Oversight and Accountability**: Ensure instructors retain oversight over AI-driven recommendations and can intervene when system behavior conflicts with pedagogical or ethical expectations (Rinta-Kahila et al., 2023).

Together, these artifacts translate the literature's theoretical and normative insights into practical design implications. By grounding architectural choices, threat awareness, and design decisions in established research, this section enhances the actionability of the literature review while maintaining its scholarly scope.

Conclusion of Literature Review

The reviewed literature highlights both the transformative potential and the unresolved challenges of AI-powered HyFlex learning environments. While prior research has advanced understanding of pedagogical affordances, adaptive instruction, and ethical principles, few studies have examined how these elements intersect through a secure software engineering lens. This gap limits the scalability, resilience, and trustworthiness of AI-enhanced educational systems.

To address these limitations, this chapter advances a Secure Software Engineering Framework for AI-Enhanced HyFlex Learning grounded in DevSecOps, FATE-based ethical governance, and privacy-preserving design. By embedding security, ethics, and compliance throughout the software development lifecycle, the proposed approach extends beyond existing work that treats these concerns as peripheral. Instead, it positions them as foundational design imperatives that shape learner trust, institutional accountability, and equitable educational outcomes. This synthesis contributes a cohesive pathway for translating pedagogical and ethical ideals into secure, scalable, and sustainable AI-driven HyFlex platforms.

RESEARCH QUESTIONS

Building upon the identified research gaps and theoretical foundations, this chapter seeks to clarify how secure software engineering can be strategically applied to enhance the trustworthiness and pedagogical effectiveness of AI-powered HyFlex learning environments. The research questions are designed to guide a structured inquiry into the integration of ethical AI principles, privacy-preserving mechanisms, and security-aware development practices within educational technology.

Together, these questions aim to illuminate how software engineering methodologies—traditionally focused on system reliability and performance can be extended to address the human-centered values of transparency, fairness, and learner engagement. By framing the inquiry through these lenses, the chapter positions itself at the intersection of technical innovation, educational theory, and ethical governance, offering a holistic perspective on the development of secure and engaging digital learning ecosystems.

RQ1: How can secure software engineering principles be applied to the design and implementation of AI-powered HyFlex learning platforms?

RQ2: What role do DevSecOps and privacy-preserving AI techniques play in building trustworthy and compliant HyFlex systems?

RQ3: How do secure and inclusive design practices influence student engagement, trust, and learning outcomes in AI-enhanced educational environments?

BACKGROUND AND THEORETICAL FRAMEWORKS

The integration of artificial intelligence (AI) into HyFlex learning environments introduces not only innovative opportunities for personalized and adaptive education but also complex challenges related to security, trust, and human engagement. To systematically explore these dynamics, it is essential to ground the analysis in theoretical frameworks that capture both the technical and human dimensions of AI-enhanced learning. This chapter draws on three interrelated theories — Deskilling of Jobs Theory, Job Characteristics Theory, and Technology Threat Avoidance Theory — to provide a multidimensional lens for examining how secure software engineering practices influence student engagement, instructor agency, and overall system trustworthiness. Together, these frameworks enable a holistic understanding of the interplay between automation, motivation, and threat perception, thereby guiding the design and evaluation of AI-powered HyFlex learning platforms.

Deskilling of Jobs Theory

Deskilling of Jobs Theory (Braverman, 1974) examines how technological automation can reduce human expertise, autonomy, and the complexity of work tasks. In the context of AI-powered education, this theory highlights the potential for intelligent systems to assume instructional responsibilities traditionally performed by educators, such as grading, providing feedback, and offering adaptive tutoring. Recent studies suggest that while AI integration can significantly enhance efficiency and scalability, it also risks eroding instructors' professional autonomy and learners' development of higher-order thinking skills (Daigle, 2024; Khurana et al., 2024).

Daigle (2024) notes that as generative AI tools become integrated into educational workflows, educators are increasingly relying on automated feedback and analytics, which may reduce opportunities for creative instructional design. Similarly, Khurana et al. (2024) highlight that excessive dependence on AI-driven support systems can lead to overreliance and diminished user confidence, particularly when prompt-based interactions obscure underlying reasoning processes.

By incorporating secure software engineering practices—such as transparent AI decision-making, explainable adaptive systems, and human-in-the-loop designs—developers can mitigate these deskilling effects. Such design approaches ensure that automation complements rather than replaces human expertise, promoting a balanced ecosystem in which both educators and learners retain agency, interpretive control, and opportunities for meaningful engagement.

Job Characteristics Theory

Job Characteristics Theory (Hackman & Oldham, 1976) identifies five core dimensions—skill variety, task identity, task significance, autonomy, and feedback—that influence motivation, engagement, and performance. Although originally formulated for workplace design, Job Characteristic Theory is also highly applicable to learning environments. In AI-powered HyFlex systems, design decisions that affect autonomy (e.g., choice of learning modality), task significance (e.g., meaningful adaptive activities), and feedback (e.g., timely AI-generated recommendations) can directly influence student engagement and learning outcomes. Conversely, insecure or opaque systems can reduce motivation by limiting learners' sense of control or undermining trust. Through Job Characteristics Theory, secure software engineering is not only a technical imperative but also a pedagogical tool for sustaining meaningful, engaging, and motivating learning experiences.

Technology Threat Avoidance Theory

Technology Threat Avoidance Theory (Liang & Xue, 2009) examines how users' perceptions of technology-related threats, combined with their belief in coping efficacy, shape their adoption and interaction behaviors. In AI-enabled HyFlex learning platforms, students and instructors may perceive risks such as data breaches, algorithmic bias, or privacy violations. Technology Threat Avoidance Theory posits that effective avoidance or mitigation behaviors depend on both awareness of these threats and confidence in protective measures.

Recent studies reinforce this relationship by highlighting the importance of trust, transparency, and perceived control in shaping users' security behaviors. Upreti et al. (2024) emphasize that trustworthy machine learning frameworks, grounded in privacy and security assurance, can significantly reduce user anxiety and enhance engagement in AI-mediated environments. Similarly, Riazi et al. (2023) emphasize the importance of methodological rigor and trustworthiness in qualitative system design, highlighting that user confidence relies on the consistent application of ethical and secure research and development practices.

By implementing security best practices—such as encryption, privacy-preserving analytics, and continuous monitoring—and communicating these measures transparently, software engineers can reduce the perceived severity of threats, increase users' coping efficacy, and foster sustainable trust and engagement within AI-driven HyFlex ecosystems.

Integrating the Theories

The combination of Deskilling Theory, Job Characteristics Theory, and Technology Threat Avoidance Theory provides a comprehensive framework for understanding AI-powered HyFlex learning systems. Deskilling Theory focuses on the preservation of human expertise in automated environments, Job Characteristics Theory emphasizes the motivational and engagement-related aspects of task design, and Technology Threat Avoidance Theory addresses the influence of security perceptions on technology use. Together, these theories inform the design and evaluation of AI-enhanced educational platforms, underscoring the crucial role of secure software engineering in fostering trustworthy, engaging, and pedagogically effective learning experiences.

Conceptual Framework

Figure 1. Conceptual framework illustrating the relationships between secure software engineering practices, trust, motivation, and learning outcomes in AI-powered HyFlex learning platforms. Deskilling Theory informs technical design to preserve human expertise, Technology Threat Avoidance Theory guides threat perception and trust, and Job Characteristics Theory explains the pathways of engagement and motivation. A feedback loop represents iterative improvement based on system analytics and outcomes

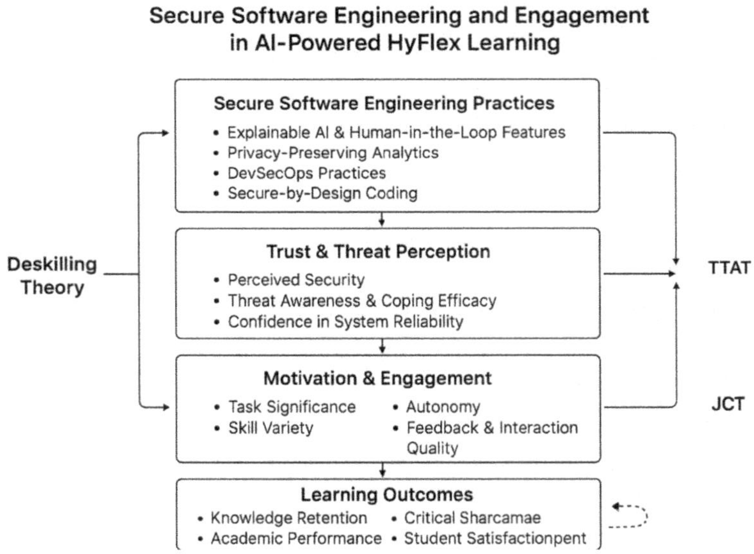

To synthesize theoretical perspectives and guide the inquiry, this chapter proposes a conceptual framework that links secure software engineering practices to trust, engagement, and learning outcomes in AI-powered, hybrid, flexible (HyFlex) learning environments. The framework integrates the Theories of Deskilling of Jobs, Job Characteristics, and Technology Threat Avoidance, illustrating how technical, motivational, and psychological factors interact to shape student and instructor experiences.

Framework Narrative

1. **Secure Software Engineering Practices (Technical Dimension)**
   - o Incorporates **secure-by-design principles**, **privacy-preserving AI techniques**, and **DevSecOps practices**.
   - o Ensures system reliability, compliance with FERPA/GDPR, and protection against unauthorized access.
   - o Grounded in **Deskilling Theory**, these practices preserve human expertise by providing transparency, human-in-the-loop AI features, and explainable adaptive systems.
2. **Trust and Threat Perception (Psychological Dimension)**
   - o Draws on Technology Threat Avoidance Theory to account for users' perceptions of threat severity, susceptibility, and coping efficacy.
   - o Effective secure design reduces perceived risks, enhances confidence in AI systems, and promotes willingness to engage with learning technologies.
3. **Motivation and Engagement (Pedagogical Dimension)**
   - o Informed by Job Characteristics Theory, design features that support skill variety, task significance, autonomy, and feedback are found to increase student motivation.
   - o Secure and transparent AI features reinforce learners' sense of control and meaningful participation, sustaining engagement even in highly automated HyFlex settings.
4. **Learning Outcomes (Educational Impact)**
   - o The combined effect of secure engineering, trust, and engagement influences academic performance, knowledge retention, and the development of critical skills.
   - o The framework posits that **security and ethics are not ancillary** but central to adequate, human-centered AI-enhanced learning.

METHODOLOGY

This chapter employs a qualitative multiple-case study methodology to investigate how secure software engineering practices influence trust, engagement, and learning outcomes in AI-powered hybrid flexible (HyFlex) learning environments. The approach is grounded in the chapter's conceptual framework, which integrates Deskilling of Jobs Theory, Job Characteristics Theory, and Technology Threat Avoidance Theory. Together, these frameworks guide case selection, data collection, and analysis, ensuring alignment between theoretical constructs and practical observations.

Research Design

A qualitative multiple-case study design was chosen because it allows for in-depth exploration of complex socio-technical phenomena within real-world AI-enabled HyFlex learning contexts (Crowston & Bolici, 2025; Peoples, 2021). Each case represents an institution that has implemented an AI-powered HyFlex platform, providing insights into system design, pedagogical practices, and user experiences.

Semi-structured interviews were the primary data collection method, enabling the study to capture nuanced perceptions and behaviors that could not be fully observed from system logs or documents. Interviews were conducted with three stakeholder groups:

1. Students – to explore their experiences with AI features, engagement patterns, and perceptions of system security and trustworthiness.
2. Instructors – to examine how AI-assisted HyFlex platforms influence teaching practices, autonomy, and professional expertise.
3. Software Developers and System Administrators – to understand the implementation of secure software engineering practices, threat mitigation strategies, and alignment with ethical AI principles.

The conceptual framework guided interview questions:

- Deskilling Theory: How do AI features affect human expertise and autonomy?
- Job Characteristics Theory: How do system features influence engagement, task significance, and learner motivation?
- Technology Threat Avoidance Theory: How do users perceive security threats, and how do these perceptions shape their interactions with the system?

Semi-structured interviews were supplemented with document analysis (e.g., system architecture diagrams, privacy policies) and interaction logs from AI platforms to triangulate findings and enhance the validity of the results.

Case Selection

Cases were selected using purposive sampling to ensure diversity in institutional context, HyFlex implementation, and AI system design. Criteria included:

- Use of AI features in HyFlex learning (e.g., adaptive learning modules, AI tutors, virtual learning companions).
- Evidence of secure software engineering practices, privacy considerations, or compliance measures.
- Availability of engagement and learning outcome data for analysis.

This strategy ensured that each case offered rich, relevant insights into the intersection of secure engineering, trust, and student engagement.

Data Collection

Data collection relied on triangulation to strengthen reliability and depth:

1. Semi-structured interviews: Conducted with students, instructors, and developers; interviews were audio-recorded and transcribed for coding.
2. Document Analysis: System specifications, development guidelines, and privacy policies were analyzed to assess security measures and the implementation of ethical AI.
3. Interaction Analytics: Learning platform logs, AI-generated feedback, and participation metrics were reviewed to examine correlations between system security, trust, and engagement.

Triangulating these sources allowed the study to connect technical system characteristics with user experiences and learning outcomes, directly reflecting the theoretical framework.

Data Analysis

Data were analyzed using thematic coding (Braun & Clarke, 2020), guided by the three theoretical lenses:

- Deskilling Analysis: Focused on automated tasks, instructor and student autonomy, and preservation of human expertise.
- Motivational and Engagement Analysis: Examined task variety, autonomy, task significance, and feedback mechanisms, consistent with Job Characteristics Theory.
- Trust and Threat Analysis: Explored users' perceptions of security risks, privacy concerns, and coping efficacy, consistent with Technology Threat Avoidance Theory.

Cross-case synthesis was conducted to identify patterns and divergences across institutions, highlighting both shared principles and context-specific practices. The analysis linked secure software engineering practices to perceived trust, engagement behaviors, and learning outcomes, providing practical guidance for designing AI-powered hybrid flexible (HyFlex) systems.

Ethical Considerations

Given the sensitivity of student and instructor data, the study adhered to strict ethical protocols:

- IRB Approval: All research protocols were reviewed and approved by the University of the Cumberlands' Institutional Review Boards.
- Anonymity and Confidentiality: Participant identities were anonymized, and data were stored securely.
- Informed Consent: Participants were fully informed about the study's purpose, procedures, and data handling.
- Privacy-Preserving Data Handling: System logs and AI interaction data were processed using privacy-preserving techniques to prevent unauthorized disclosure.

These ethical safeguards reinforce the chapter's emphasis on secure, trustworthy, and human-centered AI design.

FINDINGS AND DISCUSSION

This section presents the key findings derived from multiple case studies of AI-powered HyFlex learning platforms. Drawing on a qualitative synthesis of semi-structured interviews with students, instructors, and system developers, complemented by document analysis and examination of system interaction logs, the analysis captures both technical and experiential dimensions of AI-enabled learning environments.

The findings are organized and interpreted through the study's conceptual framework, enabling a systematic examination of how secure software engineering practices shape stakeholder trust, influence perceptions of technological risk and threat, and ultimately affect student engagement and learning outcomes. Rather than treating security, ethics, and pedagogy as independent factors, the analysis foregrounds their interdependence, illustrating how design decisions embedded in

AI systems—such as data-handling mechanisms, transparency features, and adaptive feedback processes—manifest in users' lived experiences.

By situating empirical observations within this integrative framework, the section moves beyond descriptive accounts of platform functionality to reveal the socio-technical dynamics that underpin effective and trustworthy HyFlex learning. The findings illuminate how secure-by-design and ethically informed development practices can either reinforce or undermine learner confidence, instructional effectiveness, and sustained engagement, thereby offering insight into the conditions under which AI-powered HyFlex platforms can support equitable, resilient, and pedagogically meaningful educational experiences.

RQ1: Application of Secure Software Engineering Principles

(Deskilling Theory Lens)

Interviews revealed that AI-powered features, such as automated grading, adaptive feedback, and virtual learning companions, could deskill instructors by reducing opportunities for direct pedagogical decision-making. Instructors expressed concerns about overreliance on AI for evaluating student performance. For example, one instructor noted: "While AI saves time grading, I worry that my role in mentoring and providing nuanced feedback is becoming secondary."

Secure software engineering practices, particularly those involving transparent and explainable AI and human-in-the-loop designs, effectively mitigated these risks. Developers implemented mechanisms that allowed instructors to review AI-generated recommendations before submitting them to students, thereby preserving professional autonomy and ensuring that critical pedagogical judgment remained at the forefront of the process.

Document analysis revealed the widespread adoption of secure-by-design coding, role-based access control, and continuous vulnerability assessments, resulting in reduced system downtime and reinforcing trust in the AI infrastructure. These practices aligned with Deskilling Theory by maintaining instructor agency while supporting automated functionalities.

Discussion:

The findings indicate that the integration of secure software engineering practices extends beyond protecting data and system integrity to play a critical role in preserving and reinforcing human expertise in AI-enhanced HyFlex environments. Rather than displacing instructional judgment, securely designed AI systems were found to support a balanced distribution of agency between automation and human oversight, enabling instructors to remain actively involved in pedagogical decision-making. Participants described how transparent system behavior, controllable automation features, and reliable feedback mechanisms allowed educators to interpret, contextualize, and, when necessary, override AI-generated recommendations.

In this way, secure-by-design principles functioned as pedagogical enablers rather than merely technical safeguards. By embedding accountability, explainability, and access controls into system architecture, secure engineering practices helped maintain instructional authority, fostered trust in AI-supported tools, and mitigated the risk of over-reliance on automated processes. These design choices supported reflective teaching practices and sustained professional expertise, illustrating how security-conscious development can actively contribute to instructional quality, ethical engagement, and the long-term resilience of AI-powered HyFlex learning environments.

RQ2: Role of DevSecOps and Privacy-Preserving AI in Trustworthy Systems

(Technology Threat Avoidance Theory Lens)

Both students and instructors highlighted the importance of perceived security in fostering trust and sustained engagement. Interview participants reported that platforms implementing clear privacy policies, encrypted data storage, and real-time threat monitoring increased their confidence in the system. One student stated: "Knowing that my learning data is encrypted and only accessible to instructors makes me more willing to participate actively."

Developers emphasized the role of DevSecOps in continuous vulnerability monitoring, automated security testing, and compliance with FERPA and GDPR. Case documentation revealed that platforms utilizing privacy-preserving AI techniques, such as anonymized analytics and federated learning, facilitated adaptive personalization without compromising sensitive student data.

Discussion:

Interpreted through the lens of Technology Threat Avoidance Theory, these findings demonstrate that learners' and instructors' perceptions of threat mitigation and coping efficacy are central determinants of both adoption and sustained engagement with AI-powered HyFlex systems. Participants' willingness to rely on AI-supported features was shaped not only by perceived usefulness but also by their confidence that potential threats—such as data misuse, opaque algorithmic behavior, or loss of instructional control—were actively managed and mitigated.

DevSecOps practices and privacy-preserving AI mechanisms emerged as key structural antecedents of these perceptions. Continuous security monitoring, transparent data handling, and clearly articulated safeguards enhanced users' sense of coping efficacy, reinforcing beliefs that risks could be understood, controlled, and responded to effectively. In turn, this heightened sense of protection and agency fostered trust in the platform, which functioned as a mediating mechanism between technical safeguards and meaningful pedagogical engagement.

Importantly, the findings suggest that trust is not an automatic byproduct of AI adoption but a conditional outcome shaped by visible, comprehensible, and reliable security practices. When users perceived AI features as operating in a secure, ethically governed environment, they were more likely to engage deeply with adaptive feedback, analytics dashboards, and virtual learning companions. Conversely, uncertainty or ambiguity surrounding data practices diminished engagement, even when AI functionalities were technically sophisticated. These results underscore the explanatory power of TTAT in HyFlex contexts, highlighting how effective threat mitigation and coping efficacy—enabled through DevSecOps and privacy-preserving design—mediate the relationship between AI capability and educational impact.

RQ3: Influence of Secure and Inclusive Design on Engagement and Learning Outcomes

(Job Characteristic Theory Lens)

Interviews and interaction logs revealed that secure and inclusive AI design had a positive impact on student motivation, autonomy, and engagement. Features such as adaptive learning pathways, timely AI-generated feedback, and customizable interaction modes enabled students to take control of their learning, enhancing task significance and skill variety. One student explained: "The system adapts to my pace, and I feel like I have control over my assignments, which motivates me to stay engaged."

Secure-by-design mechanisms, including transparent consent processes and privacy-preserving analytics, reinforced perceptions of fairness and transparency. Cross-case comparisons indicated that students were more likely to engage deeply when security features were visible and intuitive, rather than hidden or opaque.

Discussion:

When interpreted through the lens of Job Characteristics Theory, the findings indicate that secure system design and inclusive implementation are not merely ethical or legal obligations, but foundational drivers of pedagogical effectiveness in AI-enhanced HyFlex learning environments. Trustworthy AI systems were shown to meaningfully shape core job characteristics experienced by both learners and instructors, particularly perceived autonomy, task significance, and feedback quality.

Secure and transparent design practices—such as clear data governance, explainable AI behavior, and user-controllable automation—enhanced learners' sense of autonomy by allowing them to engage with AI-supported tools on their own terms, without fear of surveillance or unintended data misuse. Participants described greater willingness to explore adaptive learning features and analytics dashboards when they felt empowered rather than constrained by the system. Similarly, instructors reported that secure, accountable AI systems preserved their professional agency, enabling them to integrate automated insights into instructional decision-making while retaining ultimate pedagogical control.

Task significance was reinforced through inclusive design choices that acknowledged diverse learner needs and safeguarded equitable access. When AI systems operated within secure and ethically governed frameworks, learners perceived AI-mediated activities as meaningful contributions to their learning rather than as mechanistic or extractive processes. High-quality, reliable feedback—supported by validated data pipelines and monitored AI behavior—further strengthened this perception by ensuring that automated guidance was timely, relevant, and pedagogically aligned.

Collectively, these enhanced job characteristics fostered higher levels of engagement, intrinsic motivation, and learning persistence. The findings thus extend Job Characteristics Theory into the domain of AI-powered HyFlex education, demonstrating that secure-by-design and inclusive system development directly influence motivational and cognitive outcomes. In this context, security and inclusivity function not as peripheral constraints, but as enabling conditions that amplify the pedagogical value of AI-driven instructional technologies

Cross-Case Synthesis

Synthesizing findings across cases highlights several integrative insights:

1. Secure software engineering preserves human expertise and mitigates deskilling by maintaining human oversight over automated processes.
2. Trust, influenced by threat perception and security measures, is a critical mediator between system functionality and user engagement.
3. Inclusive and secure design enhances motivation, engagement, and learning outcomes, demonstrating that security and pedagogy are interdependent in AI-powered hybrid flexible (HyFlex) platforms.

The interplay among Deskilling Theory, Job Characteristic Theory, and Technology Threat Avoidance Theory provides a holistic explanation of these patterns, showing that technical safeguards, psychological trust, and motivational design must operate in concert to create effective AI-enhanced learning environments.

DISCUSSION AND IMPLICATIONS

Discussion

The findings of this study highlight the complex interplay between secure software engineering practices, trust, motivation, and learning outcomes in AI-powered hybrid flexible (HyFlex) learning environments. Through the lens of the conceptual framework, which integrates the Deskilling of Jobs Theory, Job Characteristics Theory, and Technology Threat Avoidance Theory, several critical insights emerge.

First, Deskilling Theory underscores the potential for AI automation to reduce human agency among both instructors and students. Semi-structured interviews revealed that while AI-assisted grading, adaptive feedback, and virtual learning companions can enhance efficiency, excessive reliance on automated systems may erode instructors' pedagogical control and students' autonomy in problem-solving. However, implementing transparent, explainable AI features and human-in-the-loop mechanisms effectively mitigates these risks, preserving expertise while leveraging technological advantages.

Second, Technology Threat Avoidance Theory emphasizes that users' perceptions of threats directly influence their engagement with AI-powered platforms. Findings indicate that privacy-preserving AI techniques, DevSecOps-driven monitoring, and clear data governance policies reduce perceived risks and increase user trust. Students and instructors reported greater engagement and a greater willingness to adopt AI features when they understood the security measures and felt confident in the system's reliability.

Third, applying Job Characteristics Theory, secure and inclusive AI design positively impacts motivation and engagement. Features that allow learners to exercise autonomy, receive timely feedback, and navigate meaningful tasks enhance engagement and learning outcomes. Moreover, transparent, accessible security features contribute to a perceived sense of fairness and control, thereby reinforcing intrinsic motivation.

Overall, the study demonstrates that security and pedagogy are inseparable in AI-powered HyFlex learning: technical safeguards directly support human agency, motivation, and trust, which in turn influence engagement and learning outcomes. The findings underscore the need for holistic design approaches that integrate ethical, pedagogical, and technical considerations, rather than treating security as a standalone requirement.

Implications for Practice

The findings of this study offer several actionable insights for software developers, educators, and institutional policy makers:

1. Human-Centered Secure Design:

Developers should prioritize explainable AI, human-in-the-loop controls, and role-based oversight to preserve instructor expertise and support learner agency, countering the deskilling effects of automation.

2. Trust-Building Measures:

Incorporating principles from Technology Threat Avoidance Theory, institutions should adopt privacy-preserving AI techniques, transparent policies, and continuous security monitoring. Visible, understandable security measures enhance trust, encouraging active participation and sustained engagement.

3. Policy and Compliance Integration:

Systems must comply with regulations such as FERPA and GDPR, while embedding ethical and privacy considerations directly into system design. Policies should support both compliance and trust-building, fostering user confidence in AI platforms.

4. Continuous Iteration and Monitoring:

DevSecOps practices and real-time analytics allow ongoing identification of vulnerabilities and opportunities to enhance engagement. Iterative improvements ensure that platforms remain secure, effective, and aligned with evolving pedagogical needs.

Implications for Research

1. Future studies should investigate the longitudinal effects of secure AI interventions on student learning outcomes and instructor autonomy.
2. Comparative research across diverse institutional contexts could identify best practices for balancing automation, security, and pedagogy.
3. Further exploration of human-AI interaction dynamics, including trust calibration and users' perceptions of risk, could refine the theoretical integration

among Deskilling Theory, Job Characteristics Theory, and Technology Threat Avoidance Theory.

The discussion illustrates that secure software engineering, ethical AI implementation, and pedagogical design are deeply interdependent in AI-powered hybrid flexible (HyFlex) learning environments. By addressing automation-induced deskilling, fostering motivation and engagement, and mitigating perceived security threats, developers and educators can create platforms that are not only technologically robust but also trustworthy, inclusive, and effective for diverse learners. These insights provide a roadmap for designing AI-enhanced educational systems that balance efficiency, security, and human-centered learning outcomes, thereby advancing both theory and practice in secure, AI-driven educational innovation.

LIMITATIONS AND FUTURE DIRECTIONS

While this chapter outlines the foundational principles of secure software engineering in AI-powered HyFlex learning environments, several limitations must be acknowledged to contextualize the findings and recommendations:

1. Evolving Nature of AI Technologies

The rapid evolution of artificial intelligence, including machine learning algorithms and adaptive systems, poses a challenge for maintaining long-term security standards. Techniques that are secure today may become vulnerable as new attack vectors and adversarial methods emerge.

2. Data Dependency and Bias

AI-driven educational systems rely heavily on data, including student interactions, performance metrics, and behavioral patterns. Such dependence increases the risk of data quality issues, algorithmic bias, and privacy violations, particularly when datasets are not diverse or ethically sourced.

3. Limited Longitudinal Evaluation

The long-term impact of secure and AI-enhanced HyFlex systems on student learning outcomes, engagement, and trust remains understudied. Existing implementations often focus on short-term metrics, neglecting systemic sustainability and long-term ethical implications.

4. Human Factors and Adoption Barriers

Even with strong technical safeguards, the human element, including user awareness, training, and compliance, remains a critical limitation. Educators and students may inadvertently weaken system security through poor password management or unintentional data sharing.

As AI technologies and educational paradigms continue to evolve, several promising directions emerge for research and practice:

1. AI Governance and Ethical Auditing

Future systems should integrate ongoing AI auditing frameworks that detect bias, ensure fairness, and maintain ethical integrity in decision-making processes. This detection will require collaboration between software engineers, educators, and ethicists.

2. Privacy-Preserving Learning Analytics

Advances in federated learning, differential privacy, and homomorphic encryption can enable institutions to leverage powerful analytics while protecting individual student data, thereby striking a balance between innovation and responsibility.

3. Human-Centered Design and Engagement

Future HyFlex systems should prioritize human-in-the-loop design, ensuring that AI supports rather than replaces educators, and enhancing learner engagement through empathy-driven personalization.

CONCLUSION

The evolution of AI-powered HyFlex learning environments marks a transformative era in education—one where intelligent systems personalize learning experiences, expand access, and promote continuous engagement across physical and virtual spaces. However, these advancements also introduce complex challenges in security, privacy, ethics, and trust. Building a trustworthy educational platform requires more than technological innovation; it demands a foundation of secure software engineering principles integrated throughout the development lifecycle.

Secure design, data protection, and transparent AI decision-making are not optional components but essential prerequisites for sustaining learner confidence and institutional credibility. The chapter emphasizes that a secure HyFlex ecosystem must align with ethical AI practices, regulatory compliance, and robust cybersecurity frameworks. Only by embedding security and trustworthiness from inception to deployment can developers ensure that AI-driven educational systems remain resilient, equitable, and engaging.

The future of HyFlex learning depends not only on the sophistication of AI algorithms but on the ethical and secure foundation upon which they are built. By continuously integrating secure software engineering, responsible AI, and human-centered design, educational institutions can realize the vision of a truly trustworthy, inclusive, and engaging digital learning ecosystem.

REFERENCES

Avila-Chauvet, L., Mejía, D., & Acosta Quiroz, C. (2023). CHATGPT as a support tool for online behavioral task programming. *SSRN*. Retrieved from https://ssrn.com/abstract=4329020

Barke, S., James, M., & Polikarpova, N. (2023). Grounded copilot: How programmers interact with code-generating models. *Proceedings of the ACM on Programming Languages, 7*(OOPSLA1), 85-111. DOI: 10.1145/3586030

Beatty, B. (2024). *Can Gen AI be used to support "accidental" asynchronous learners in HyFlex courses?* Retrieved from https://www.hyflexlearning.org/2024/06/21/genai_interaction

Braun, V., & Clarke, V. (2020). One size fits all? What counts as quality practice in (reflexive) thematic analysis? *Qualitative Research in Psychology, 18*(3), 328–352. DOI: 10.1080/14780887.2020.1769238

Braverman, H. (1974). *Labor and monopoly capital.* Monthly Review Press. DOI: 10.14452/MR-026-03-1974-07_1

Cheong, B. C. (2024). Transparency and accountability in AI systems: Safeguarding wellbeing in the age of algorithmic decision-making. *Sec. Digital Impacts, 6*, 1421273. Advance online publication. DOI: 10.3389/fhumd.2024.1421273

Crowston, K., & Bolici, F. (2025). Deskilling and upskilling with AI Systems. *nformation Research an International Electronic Journal, 30*(iConf), 1009-1023. DOI: 10.47989/ir30iConf47143

Daigle, K. (2024). *Survey: The AI wave continues to grow on software development teams.* Retrieved from https://github.blog/author/kdaigle/

Hackman, J. R., & Oldham, G. R. (1976). Motivation through the design of work: Test of a theory. *Organizational Behavior and Human Performance, 16*(2), 250–279. DOI: 10.1016/0030-5073(76)90016-7

Khan, A. A., Badshah, S., Liang, P., Khan, B., Waseem, M., Niazi, M., & Akbar, M. A. (2021). Ethics of AI: A Systematic Literature Review of Principles and Challenges. *Computers and Society*. https://doi.org//arXiv.2109.07906DOI: 10.48550

Khurana, A., Subramonyam, H., & Chilana, P. K. (2024). Why and when llm-based assistants can go wrong: Investigating the effectiveness of prompt-based interactions for software help-seeking. *arXiv.org*. Retrieved from /arxiv.2402.08030DOI: 10.1145/3640543.3645200

Li, Y., Xu, G., Meng, X., Du, W., & Ren, X. (2024). LF3PFL: A Practical Privacy-Preserving Federated Learning Algorithm Based on Local Federalization Scheme. *Entropy (Basel, Switzerland), 26*(5), 353. DOI: 10.3390/e26050353 PMID: 38785602

Liang, H., & Xue, Y. (2009). Avoidance of information technology threats: A theoretical perspective. *Management Information Systems Quarterly, 33*(1), 71–90. DOI: 10.2307/20650279

Liang, Y., Zou, D., Xie, H., & Wang, F. L. (2023). Exploring the potential of using ChatGPT in physics education. *Smart Learn. Environ, 10*(52), 52. Advance online publication. DOI: 10.1186/s40561-023-00273-7

Mentzer, N. J., Isabell, T. M., & Mohandas, L. (2023). The impact of interactive synchronous HyFlex model on student academic performance in a large active learning introductory college design course. *Journal of Computing in Higher Education, 36*(3), 619–646. DOI: 10.1007/s12528-023-09369-y PMID: 37359046

NanoMatrix. (2024). *Continuous Monitoring, Data Governance, and Compliance: A Guide to Optimizing AI Performance*. Retrieved from https://www.nanomatrixsecure.com/continuous-monitoring-data-governance-and-compliance-a-guide-to-optimizing-ai-performance/

Peoples, K. (2021). *How to write a phenomenological dissertation: A step-by-step guide* (Vol. 56). SAGE.

Rajapakse, R. N., Zahedi, M., & Babar, M. A. (2022). Collaborative Application Security Testing for DevSecOps: An Empirical Analysis of Challenges, Best Practices and Tool Support. https://doi.org//arXiv.2211.06953DOI: 10.48550

Riazi, M., Rezvani, R., & Ghanbar, H. (2023). Trustworthiness in L2 writing research: A review and analysis of qualitative articles in the Journal of Second Language Writing. *Research Methods in Applied Linguistics, 2*(3), 100065. Advance online publication. DOI: 10.1016/j.rmal.2023.100065

Rinta-Kahila, T., Penttinen, E., Salovaara, A., Soliman, W., & Ruissalo, J. (2023). The vicious circles of skill erosion: A case study of cognitive automation. *Journal of the Association for Information Systems, 24*(5), 1378–1412. DOI: 10.17705/1jais.00829

Upreti, R., Lind, P. G., Elmokashfi, A., & Yazidi, A. (2024). Trustworthy machine learning in the context of security and privacy. *International Journal of Information Security, 23*(3), 2287–231. DOI: 10.1007/s10207-024-00813-3

U.S. Department of Education. (2020). *Family Educational Rights and Privacy Act (FERPA) Annual Notice*. Retrieved from https://studentprivacy.ed.gov/sites/default/files/resource_document/file/CSSOs%20Annual%20Notice%20April%202020.pdf

KEY TERMS AND DEFINITIONS

Adaptive Learning: A pedagogical approach that leverages AI algorithms to tailor educational content, pacing, and feedback based on individual student needs and behaviors.

AI-Powered Systems: Software applications enhanced by artificial intelligence techniques—such as machine learning, natural language processing, or predictive analytics—to automate decision-making, personalize learning, or optimize system performance.

Authentication and Authorization: Security mechanisms that verify user identities (authentication) and determine what resources users are allowed to access (authorization).

Compliance and Regulation: Adherence to legal and institutional standards—such as FERPA, GDPR, or HIPAA—governing the handling of educational and personal data.

Continuous Monitoring: The ongoing process of tracking system activities and security events in real time to detect and respond promptly to potential threats.

Cybersecurity Framework: A structured set of guidelines or best practices—such as NIST or ISO/IEC 27001—used to manage and reduce cybersecurity risks in software systems.

Data Integrity: The assurance that information remains accurate, complete, and unaltered during processing, storage, and transmission.

Data Privacy: Protecting personal and sensitive user information from unauthorized access, disclosure, or misuse is critical for educational platforms that collect student performance data.

Encryption: The process of converting data into a coded format to prevent unauthorized access, ensuring confidentiality and integrity during storage and transmission.

Ethical AI: The implementation of artificial intelligence aligns with moral and social values, ensuring it avoids bias, discrimination, and harmful consequences in decision-making.

Explainable AI (XAI): AI systems that provide clear and understandable justifications for their decisions increase transparency and user trust in educational contexts.

Human-in-the-Loop (HITL): A system design principle where human oversight is integrated into AI decision-making processes to enhance accountability and ethical compliance.

HyFlex Learning: A hybrid-flexible instructional model that combines in-person and online learning environments, allowing students to choose their mode of participation (synchronous or asynchronous) without compromising engagement or outcomes.

Risk Management: The identification, assessment, and mitigation of potential security, ethical, and operational risks in AI-powered educational software systems.

Secure Coding Practices: Programming techniques designed to prevent vulnerabilities such as SQL injection, cross-site scripting (XSS), or buffer overflows.

Secure Software Engineering: The practice of designing, developing, and maintaining software systems with built-in mechanisms to prevent security vulnerabilities, data breaches, and unauthorized access throughout the software development lifecycle.

Software Development Lifecycle (SDLC): A framework outlining the stages of software creation—from requirements analysis to deployment and maintenance—with integrated security practices at each stage.

Trustworthy AI: AI systems are designed to be transparent, explainable, fair, and secure, ensuring ethical decision-making and user confidence in automated processes.

User Engagement: The level of attention, interest, and participation a learner exhibits on an educational platform is often enhanced by adaptive, interactive AI-driven tools.

Vulnerability Assessment: The systematic process of identifying, analyzing, and prioritizing security weaknesses within a system before they can be exploited.

Chapter 12
Reimagining Creative Writing Pedagogy:
A Hyflex Approach to Flexible Learning

Sze De Silva MARK
http://orcid.org/0009-0001-1071-9962
Taylor's University, Malaysia

Sze Yuing T. Anrie Too
http://orcid.org/0009-0002-4162-7654
Taylor's University, Malaysia

ABSTRACT

Creative writing modules in universities taught in English can be a challenge for students who are non-native English speakers. They often struggle to express creative ideas fluently, focusing more on grammatical accuracy than on free expression. This research explores a combined methodology that integrates the traditional "Pantser" method of writing with Hyflex learning to support non-native English-speaking students in creative text composition. The Pantser method emphasizes spontaneity and authenticity in creative writing, while Hyflex learning allows students to review lectures in their mother tongue. Together, these approaches form a systematic method that guides students from finding a stimulus for a story through to preparing a final draft. The study examines the application of this combined approach in a monologue writing assignment within the Introduction to Creative Writing module and evaluates student work using the module's assessment rubrics. The findings suggest that this combined approach offers a promising pedagogy for teaching creative writing.

DOI: 10.4018/979-8-3373-6182-6.ch012

INTRODUCTION

Creative writing modules have become increasingly popular in recent years, with universities offering them as part of their curricula to enhance the holistic learning of both arts- and non-arts-related disciplines. When the creative writing modules are conducted in English, it poses a challenge to students who are non-native English speakers. Universities that conduct their creative writing modules in the English language create a challenge for their students who are non-native English speakers. These students must juggle the technical knowledge of crafting creative writing pieces while ensuring they use grammatically correct English. There is a double demand required by the creative writing module of crafting stories, characters, and imagery while ensuring grammatical accuracy and fluency (Hyland, 2003) which in turn creates this emotional barrier for students – especially those whose English is a second language. It is worthy to note that at Taylor's University, creative writing modules are offered to students from various linguistic and cultural backgrounds, many of whom only speak English as a second or even third language. Therefore, it is important for us to be aware and acknowledge this tension – as it may stifle creativity, hinder participation from students, or even reduce confidence in writing and creating original material.

Existing research shows that many English as a Foreign Language (EFL) students would rely on digital and AI-based tools to help compensate for their insecurities towards these emotional barriers caused by language barriers. Woo et al. (2022) discussed how EFL students in Hong Kong used applications to generate writing in their mother tongue first, highlighting a struggle to creatively express in the English language. The reliance on generative tools highlights the students' familiarity with AI to aid in their everyday work. A study of students in the Philippines stated that 83% of the research population use AI to help in their writing, while 67% use AI tools to generate ideas in writing (Malto & Pineda, 2024). The reliance on AI demonstrates that students may feel insecure with methods of writing that are more technically constructed. Therefore, through this, we realised that there is a deeper need for teaching methods that could help restore student confidence and creative independence in their writing.

The Pantser method of writing can be defined as an organic way of writing or discovery writing and it offers an alternative approach that emphasizes spontaneity and intuition. The concept of the Pantser method essentially allows the writers to create without a fixed plan, allowing plots and characters to emerge organically (Bell, 2018) The Pantser method, is effective for beginner writers, as it encourages exploration and reduces the fear of making grammatical mistakes (Lowrey, 2021) similar to a free-writing exercise or in-class improvisation activity where students can just generate scenes without overthinking the language of which it is presented.

The Pantser method's more organic approach to writing is a contrast to more technical approaches that could be deemed more rigid as structured plotting can sometimes stifle the imagination, especially among multilingual students. (Manery, 2016). While Pantser methods support creativity, they also require structure and feedback to help non-native writers to further refine their work.

HyFlex learning is a combination of hybrid and flexible learning that enables students to join classes either face-to-face, online, or asynchronously (Beatty, 2019). This is especially advantageous for multilingual learners as the asynchronous sessions provide extra time to translate, reflect, or revise before they must share their ideas (Raes et al., 2020). HyFlex not only addresses accessibility but also complements creative processes by letting students work at their own pace.

When the Pantser method is combined with AI tools and HyFlex flexibilities - a structured methodology can be developed which will particularly help students who are not native English speakers. Essentially utilising AI tools as scaffolds for grammar, translation or brainstorming without compromising on human creativity.

The utilisation of creative spontaneity via Pantser Method, HyFlex delivery models and AI as language assistance are usually studied in isolation and there is currently no methodology that combines the Pantser method of writing with evolving AI technology (Zou et al., 2023; Raes et al., 2020). Given the increasing diversity of students' backgrounds at Taylor's University, this form of integrated approach is believed to be able to help democratise creative expression.

Overview

This chapter situates the present study within existing scholarship on creative writing pedagogy for non-native English speakers, the flexible instruction of the HyFlex model as well as the use of artificial intelligence (AI) in language and writing learning. Creative writing pedagogy, AI in education and flexible learning is believed to be crucial strands in a multilingual higher education environment (Hyland, 2003; Beatty, 2019) The central issue being highlighted is that non-native speakers are expected to produce grammatically correct creative writing in English, an insecurity which leads to a reliance on AI (Woo et al., 2022). By reviewing these strands of literature, this study aims to provide a foundation for exploring how the Pantser method, AI tools, and HyFlex delivery can be combined to support multilingual learners. The following sections will review some of the relevant literature which will inform the design of the combined Pantser-AI-HyFlex methodology. This will be preceded by the application and critical reflection of the Hyflex-Pantser approach to creative writing throughout the course of one semester in the module *Introduction to Creative Writing* at Taylor's University.

Creative Writing Pedagogy in ESL/EFL Contexts

The creative writing pedagogy in English as a Second Language (ESL) or English as a Foreign Language (EFL) context has long grappled with how to support linguistic accuracy without diminishing creativity. A substantial body of research has identified the unique challenges faced by ESL/EFL learners in creative writing contexts when students face difficulty in balancing grammatical accuracy with creative expression. Hyland (2003) observes that grammar concerns inhibit creativity, hence limiting the development of original ideas - the dilemma between form and freedom, having grammatical control versus imaginative expression.

Similarly, Ivanic (1998) argues that writing is closely linked to identity, and for non-native speakers, the added pressure to conform to English academic norms could restrict their personal voice and creativity. It was also observed that for some of the learners, they may be hindered by their limited vocabulary to freely explore their creativity, their limitation of language expression leading to hesitation in the expression of original ideas (Hanauer, 2012).

In conventional module assessment, there may also be tendencies of assessment practices to reinforce an emphasis on correctness on the use of English language over creativity (Lee, 2009). In a more localised reference at Taylor's University, creative writing students often come from multilingual backgrounds; presenting a kind of diversity that is embraced for the richness of culture but riddled with the complicated elements of self-expression. In combination, all these factors create barriers allowing for authentic expression in creative writing and it is justifiable to create new pedagogical interventions.

The practice of drafting in the mother tongue within this study may also be framed through translanguaging theory, which recognises multilingual learners' full linguistic repertoire as a cognitive resource rather than a limitation. Rather than separating languages, translanguaging allows learners to develop ideas across linguistic systems before refining them in English. This approach also aligns with Krashen's Affective Filter Hypothesis, which suggests that anxiety and fear of error can inhibit language production. By allowing students to originate ideas in their first language before translating them, the model lowers affective barriers and prioritises creative meaning-making before linguistic correction.

Creative Writing as Pedagogical Practice

Despite cultural and linguistic challenges, creative writing in English has been widely recognised as a valuable pedagogical tool in second language education; it remains a powerful pedagogical tool for language learning and personal expression. Varying forms of writing allow learners to develop language appreciation in differing ways, as Hanauer (2012) highlights that poetry-writing in a second language allows learners to engage in meaningful self-expression. Creative writing complements traditional composition by encouraging emotional engagement, imagination and voice (Hanauer, 2012; Craig, 2013).

Creative writing as a module encourages learners to build fluency and ownership of the language (Craig, 2013) due to its creatively expressive format. For the *Introduction to Creative Writing* module at Taylor's University, it is presented as a free-elective module under the Bachelor of Performing Arts Programme. Its inclusion in the curricula of the programme recognizes creative-inspired approaches that encourage students to draw on lived experiences for self-expression (Winston, 2013). Drama-based activities like monologue writing or improvisation can help deepen cultural awareness while creative writing aids the students to gain an "ownership of language", and for self-representation.

The Pantser Method

The Pantser or discovery writing method, challenges the structured approach to creative writing by prioritising spontaneity and exploration of self (Bell, 2018); which is in contrast with the "plotter" approach, that emphasizes pre-planning prior to the writing process. In contrast to the 'plotter' approach which begins a story with a mindmap of sorts, the Pantser method begins with a 'spark' that can include a word, a line, a character or even a memory. This then grows with questioning what would most interestingly happen next, as opposed to pre-planned beats to a story. The character's desire drives the plot, and the journey is often messy, unpredictable, and organic (Manery, 2016). Whereby, the underlying philosophy for the Pantser method is to encourage students to trust the subconscious process, allowing characters and plots to emerge through unimpeded writing. The Pantser approach offers authenticity and freedom, yet it may require structured feedback for learners in navigating the language boundaries.

Pedagogical Applications in Creative Writing

By utilising the Pantser method in classrooms, students' anxiety can be lowered as Lowrey (2021) suggested. It is also an approach that aligns with drama pedagogies that use improvisation and memory recall to generate ideas (Spolin, 1999; Winston, 2013). For multilingual learners, the method may help encourage personal storytelling without the fear of making any grammatical error, with its focus on spontaneity of the moment. However, the Pantser method's lack of structure could also prove to be overwhelming for non-native speakers who may require more guidance

(Manery, 2016). Therefore, a combined approach of the Pantser method with other more structured frameworks could provide the balance required by novice writers.

AI in Language Learning and Creative Writing

In the current climate, generative AI tools have been incorporated into educational frameworks, including translation systems like Google Translate, editing platforms such as Grammarly, and generative tools like ChatGPT (Zou et al., 2023). Research shows that ESL/EFL learners use AI widely as illustrated by Woo et al. (2022) who has found that students in Hong Kong frequently rely on AI to help generate or translate their ideas, while in the Philippines, 83% of students utilise AI for writing support (Malto & Pineda, 2024). These instances suggest that students are utilising AI support systems due to an insecurity with English – hence, contributing to an increasing trend of over-reliance on AI support.

Through a recent investigation of AI in EFL writing, Sarica and Deneme (2023) reviewed 19 studies and found that students valued efficiency and personalization but risked over-reliance. Also, Liu et al. (2025) showed that even though AI tools can support critical thinking, it also reduces original thinking by learners. However, Lai (2025) reported that AI-assisted blended learning helps improve writing self-efficacy and resilience in students. Therefore, while AI supports accuracy, there are also concerns of plagiarism, overreliance and loss of originality (Cotton et al., 2023; Fitria, 2023) that needs to be considered, which reenforces the need for AI integration to be thoughtfully considered into pedagogy. In this model, AI is positioned as a scaffold rather than an author.

Ethical Integration of AI in Creative Writing

Given ongoing concerns regarding authorship and originality, ethical boundaries were clearly communicated to students. AI use was limited to brainstorming, translation, and editing support, while full narrative generation was prohibited. Students disclosed AI usage in reflective journals, ensuring transparency in process documentation. This approach aligns with institutional academic integrity guidelines and reinforces creative ownership while allowing responsible technological assistance.

HyFlex Learning and Student Engagement

HyFlex is a combination of hybrid and flexible learning, allowing for face-to-face participation, synchronous and asynchronous learnings (Beatty, 2019). Essentially, it is an extension of the blended learning model, where experiences across modes support the same learning objectives (Raes et al., 2020). Due to the asynchronous options of HyFlex, it has been found to enhance inclusivity and accessibility (Miller et al. 2021) for non-native speakers as it provides extra time for them to reflect and draft their ideas before sharing. These features acknowledge the students' possible challenges and assure them that it is a system that aims to help their participation. A study of the components of the Tripartite Model of Student Engagement (Fredricks et al., 2016) demonstrates that a model like Hyflex can potentially address common challenges of emotional (lack of confidence, anxiety) and behavioral (poor attendance, lack of interaction) engagements. When pairing AI tools through Hyflex learning with the traditional aspects of creative writing, student engagement issues can be tackled holistically (Woo et al., 2022).

In this study, engagement is interpreted through the tripartite model comprising behavioural, emotional, and cognitive dimensions (Fredricks et al., 2016). Behavioural engagement is reflected in attendance, participation, and assignment completion. Emotional engagement is evidenced through reduced anxiety and increased writing confidence. Cognitive engagement is demonstrated through students' willingness to revise, reflect, and deepen narrative complexity across drafting stages. The HyFlex-Pantser-AI integration was intentionally structured to support all three dimensions rather than focusing solely on final performance outcomes.

Language insecurity which may lead to lack of confidence and anxiety in the classroom are endeavoured to be reduced with multilingual Avatars and AI translation tools (if embedded into a system which is taught), and a clear explanation of an inclusive method of teaching and learning would assure confidence amongst students whom in the past may have avoided classes due to insecurities. However, the multiple ways in which a student can attend a lecture via Hyflex can be a double-edged sword. One of the more notable critiques in HyFlex could be due to its uneven engagement, where some students may be highly engaged online whereas others participating less actively (Raes et al., 2020). Students may decide to depend solely on online methods of learning, forgetting the social aspect of creative writing. Also, it creates extra workload for instructors, who are required to prepare materials in varying formats (Miller et al., 2021), as well as technical barriers, such as limited internet access.

Theoretical Frameworks to Reflect on Outcomes of Hyflex Learning

Hyflex Learning's unique propensity for independent learning would require a thoughtful and complementing framework of reflection. Zimmerman's (2001) self-regulated learning (SLR) theory provides a fitting framework to reflect on the outcomes of Hyflex Learning. Its cyclical nature, which comprises the Forethought Phase, Performance Phase, and Reflection Phase translates suitably to typical Hyflex

Learning models, particularly this research's model which advocates that the students' independently plan their study prior to lectures via the MyTimes site and engage in self-monitoring while learning happens. When Hyflex is used for disciplines like creative writing which may require more subjective assessment, the reflection of the student's progress and final work can be bolstered with a more multi-faced model like Brookfield's (2017) Four Lenses of Critical Reflection, which reflects on the creative work through the Self Lens (student self-reflection), Peer Lens (Other students), Expert Lens (Lecturer) and Theoretical (Rubrics). A four-pronged approach to reflection helps eliminate suspicion of AI generated works in creative writing. An assessment that considers the reflection of perspectives provides a well-rounded reflection on a creative piece and ultimately produces a fair grading (Malto & Pineda, 2024).

Assessment within this framework also reflects principles of constructive alignment, where learning outcomes, instructional strategies, and evaluation criteria are intentionally connected. The rubric assessing narrative, language, and performance aligns with the module's objectives while incorporating reflective dimensions through Brookfield's lenses. This ensures that evaluation captures both product quality and process awareness, particularly important in AI-supported environments. These more established theoretical frameworks, when combined with the visionary Hyflex Learning presents a holistic system of learning and assessing creative works.

Gaps in Existing Research

Literature shows that non-native English learners highly benefit from creative writing pedagogy, AI support and flexible delivery model – where each approach addresses different learners' needs. Current research shows that there has not been a combined Pantser, AI and HyFlex into a single methodology, revealing a gap for pedagogical innovation that unites discovery-based writing, AI support and flexible delivery. As students often address AI-assisted writing separately from creative writing pedagogy (Zou et al., 2023; Raes et al., 2020) Therefore, this study seeks to develop and test a combined AI-Pantser-HyFlex methodology for Creative Writing.

The Hyflex-Pantser Approach as a New Writing Pedagogy: Research Design

This research adopts a convergent mixed-methods research design that is predominantly classroom-based. The three main components of research are classroom observation, assignment analysis, and questionnaire distributed at the end of the semester (Merriam & Tisdell, 2016). Qualitative data was acquired via the structured classroom observations, reflection of assignments while quantitative data was dependent on the response to the questionnaire. The researcher's population was 74 students who took the *Introduction to Creative Writing* module as a free elective. These students ranged from 18 to 25 years of age, and come from various countries, with the majority being Malaysians. The lecturers observed the students' attitudes towards writing in every lecture and tutorial. This was gauged via components like engagement, attention, participation and interaction (Fredricks et al., 2016). While the lectures are the main assessors of the engagement, attention, participation and interaction, they have made reflective notes throughout the writing process, particularly the weeks leading to the presentation of the monologue to enhance the credibility of the assessment. The lecturers' observations were then compared to the students' own reflection of their attitudes to writing through the Reflective Journal assignment, which was submitted as part of the final portfolio. The assignment, which requires the students to detail their processes and challenges in writing, was submitted alongside the monologue, which was then analysed using a rubric (narrative, character, language). To guide the lecturers' assessment, a rubric was used, as per Figure 1 below:

Figure 1. Rubric to assess the student's portfolio

Portfolio & Critique Rubric (40% Total)

Criteria	Excellent (5 pts)	Proficient (4 pts)	Developing (3 pts)	Incomplete (1–2 pts)
Completion & Organization	All drafts, finals, notes, and reflections included. Neatly scanned and labeled.	Missing 1–2 minor pieces. Labels or dates unclear in a few places.	Several missing drafts or disorganized. No dates/context provided.	Portfolio incomplete or largely missing.
Reflective Depth	Insightful analysis of process, feedback, and growth. Specific examples given.	Reflection covers most points but lacks detail in some areas.	Superficial, minimal engagement with feedback or revisions.	Reflection missing or extremely brief.
Constructive Critique	Thoughtful, balanced feedback with actionable suggestions. Supports peer's revision.	Critique identifies strengths/weaknesses but lacks specificity.	Overly vague or overly negative. No actionable advice.	Critique missing or irrelevant.
Writing Quality	Drafts show clear development. Final pieces polished and creative.	Some inconsistency in revision quality. Finals need minor improvements.	Drafts lack refinement. Finals feel rushed or unfinished.	Work is illegible, incoherent, or off-task.

Pseudonyms were used when referencing students' works and journal entries. The selection of referenced works will be based on how they respond to the mechanism of the Hyflex-Pantser writing approach, particularly pieces which have been initially written in the students' mother tongue. Students' whose works were selected were asked to sign a consent form.

At the end of the semester, the students will respond to a questionnaire prepared and administered by Taylor's University's Department of Learning Innovation and Development. The questionnaire included Close-ended questions (students were asked if they agree or not) such as:

1. I get feedback from AI to improve my draft essays or writing.
2. I learn complex topics by discussing them with AI.
3. I work with AI to brainstorm alternative ways to express my ideas.
4. I use AI to generate complete summaries or full written assignments.

Likert-type questions in the questionnaire included:

1. The use of AI Avatars in videos supports my learning and helps me retain information better.
2. I feel connected and confident learning from AI-generated avatars representing real lecturers.
3. Given a choice, I prefer learning through AI Avatar videos over text-based or traditional lectures.
4. I find AI Avatar videos more engaging compared to traditional recorded lectures.

The questionnaire was balanced with an open-ended section which allows the students to express their sentiments on the application of the Hyflex learning system beyond structured questions.

The Hyflex-Pantser Approach as a New Writing Pedagogy: Purpose and Application

The main endeavour in the development of the Hyflex-Pantser approach is to provide a clear system of writing for students, particularly non-native English speakers. The approach would support the learning outcomes of the modules, which are to develop storytelling skills with a focus on characters, plots, and language; to cultivate skills in stage writing, particularly through the Personal Monologue; and to create a portfolio of original work. The approach's components were inspired by Flower and Hayes' three-arc structure (Becker, 2006). In the 1980s, Linda Flower and John Hayes developed a process-based writing model that focuses on the cognitive and thought processes of the writer. Created to assist novice writers, the model is constructed into three parts: the task environment, the writer's long-term memory, and the writing process itself. The writing process is broken down into three additional stages: the planning stage, the translating stage, and the revision stage (Becker, 2006).

The Flower and Hayes writing model contrasts with conventional models before it, which focus on a linear methodology. The Stage Model of writing presents a way of writing in clearly set sequences. The components of this model begin with the prewriting stage, where ideas are generated, then the drafting stage, where the ideas are turned into paragraphs, which is then followed by the revision, editing, and publishing stages (Emig, 1971). Figure 2 below summarizes the Hyflex-Pantser model which depicts interconnected components, the Originating Stage, the Translating Stage, and the Revision Stage.

Figure 2. The Hyflex-Pantser methodology for creative writing

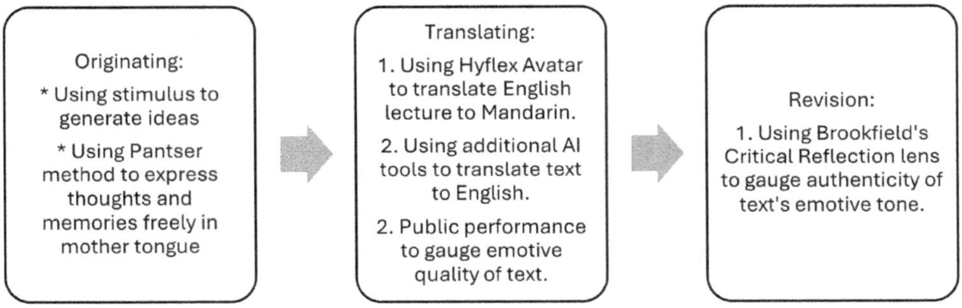

In the Originating stage, students are introduced to stimuli—drawn from memories, lived experiences, or social observations—as prompts for developing monologue ideas. A word or sentence from the past, a character that is pertinent to the writer's life, or an emotion that surfaces can all be sparks to begin the story (Manery, 2016). Through the HyFlex system at Taylor's University, students are given synchronous online lectures, which are then followed by an Avatar of the same lecture in either English or Mandarin. Both the online lecture and Avatar in the first week of the semester endeavour to stimulate creative ideas. Some of the activities that are used in both the online and Avatar lectures are drama-based techniques which support the Pantser technique of writing, which is to allow spontaneity and intuitiveness. In line with the HyFlex system of allowing the students to revisit the lecture in Mandarin, students are also encouraged to write their first drafts in their mother tongue to preserve authenticity of the writer's culture. In line with the Pantser (Bell, 2018) method of writing, students are encouraged to not force the seed of the story, but to let it 'spark' at any instance. The idea can come from the first online lecture, while revisiting the lecture via the Avatar, or in tutorial discussions with the lecturer.

Van Pinxteren's (2023) research showed that when the students are taught using their mother tongue or a language close to their mother tongue, there will be higher participation and hence better education. In designing this writing methodology, allowing the use of the mother tongue enables students to focus on the creative process of developing their stories rather than being constrained by language concerns. In previous observations, students often became so preoccupied with linguistic accuracy that they struggled to fully grasp and apply the technical aspects of story writing.

In the Originating stage, students first learn and understand the techniques of writing from the lecturer through synchronous online sessions. Some of the writing techniques taught in the first two weeks would encompass understanding the core components of a story's narrative like characters, journey, and theme. They would also be introduced to the Pantser method of writing. They then deepen their understanding of these techniques in their mother tongue via the Avatar component of the HyFlex system, before beginning to write their drafts in their mother tongue. The words would emerge naturally through their stream of consciousness, free from the constraints of language concerns, as the focus at this stage is for them to write freely following the principles of the Pantser method. Spontaneous writing of this nature allows the work to be creative and uncensored, enabling students to write without the constraints of structure or correctness. The resulting pieces are often raw, genuine, and unique, as they embody the writer's culture, experiences, and emotional truth. This method of writing in the mother tongue correlates with the ethos of the pantser method, which encourages spontaneity. This multifaceted approach in the planning stage of writing aids particularly students who in the past relied purely on theoretical knowledge learned and inherent language proficiency. A planning stage that acknowledges the student's self-efficacy (Zimmerman et al., 2001) adds self-awareness into the preparatory stage, and remedies it with AI tools like the multilingual Avatar, to ultimately help the student write the piece to the best of their ability.

Once the piece has been written in the mother tongue, it progresses to the second stage, the Translating stage, where the work is not merely translated literally into English, but carefully adapted to ensure that its nuances and cultural meanings are preserved. Figures 3 and 4 below show an online synchronous lecture and the Avatar delivering a lecture.

Figure 3. Online lecture via MyTimes

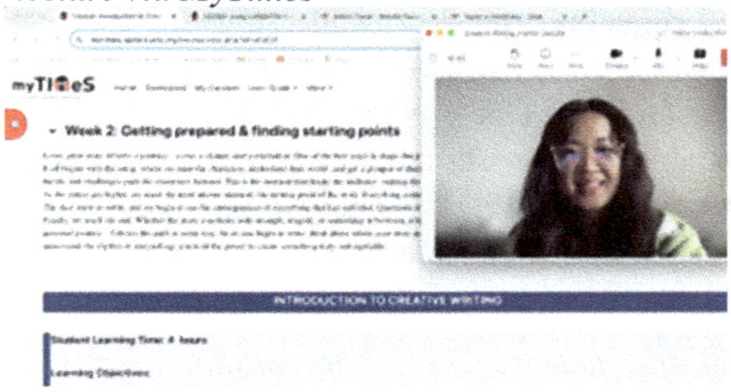

Figure 4. An avatar of the lecture conducted in English or Mandarin

The second stage of the methodology is the Translating stage, where the students work to translate their first drafts into English. Rather than viewing this as a technical step, this methodology encourages the student to consider this part of the process, where the culture of the piece and the world of the character take precedence over language correctness. Students are allowed to use any AI translation tools for this step. Students take inspiration from writers like Amy Tan and Alex Haley, who present rich cultural landscapes through their writing. Trust and self-control are important components at this point. With Zimmerman et al. (2001) theory of self-regulated learning as framework, trust and self- control in this context refers to the unspoken agreement between the teacher and learner of the endeavour to be discretionary in the selection of parts that employ AI for translation. While the utilization of Turnitin in the final submission is included as a cautionary note, the Hyflex- Pantser system of writing upholds trust and the joy of creating over academic discipline.

Figure 5 below shows an example of a student's monologue originally written in their mother tongue, Mandarin. Once the student is satisfied with the story's narrative, they proceed to translate it manually, paying close attention to preserving the nuances of the original version. Meanwhile, some students prefer to translate the entire text first and then review the translated version to ensure that the meaning and emotional tone remain intact. One way to preserve the original culture of the piece is to selectively retain certain words or phrases in the mother tongue. For example, a student writing originally in Bahasa Indonesia can retain certain words like *Ibu* (mother) to lend authenticity to the piece.

Figure 5. Example of a student's work in the translating stage

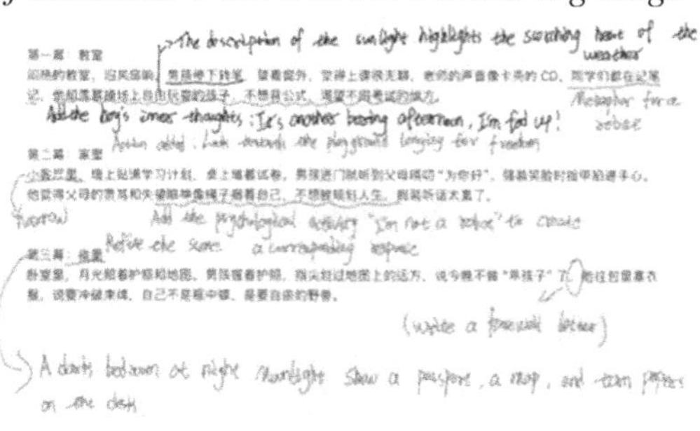

The final stage, which is Revision, guides the students in preparing the final draft for submission. Using Brookfield's (2017) Four Lenses of Critical Reflection as a theoretical guide, students received structured feedback from other students (Peer Lens), lecturers (Theoretical Lens), and external examiner (Expert Lens) and engaged in self-reflection (Self Lens). For feedback from peers, students are required to choose a monologue which has been written and performed by a peer, and comment on its narrative, language, and performance. This is called the 'Peer Review'. For self-reflection, students are required to write a reflection on their writing process of the monologue. This would entail details on the conceptualization, drafting, editing, and finalizing the monologue for submission. The lecturer's assessment (Theoretical) will assess how well the students respond to components of writing taught, while the external examiner who is usually a writer from the industry will provide feedback from a perspective of someone in the field.

The idea is that with four facets of reflection, the student can compare the translated piece of writing with the original draft, to make final creative decisions. The final piece, which has undergone the 3 steps of this methodology of the HyFlex-Pantser approach would be one that is current, has cultural authenticity, and original. The lecturer would send their feedback via MyTimes, a part of the Hyflex learning portal. The feedback would provide the breakdown of marks (10 marks for Narrative, 10 marks for Language, 10 marks for Performance), and accompanying explanation of the given marks. Figure 6 is an example of the lecturer's feedback.

Figure 6. Written feedback from the lecture on MyTimes

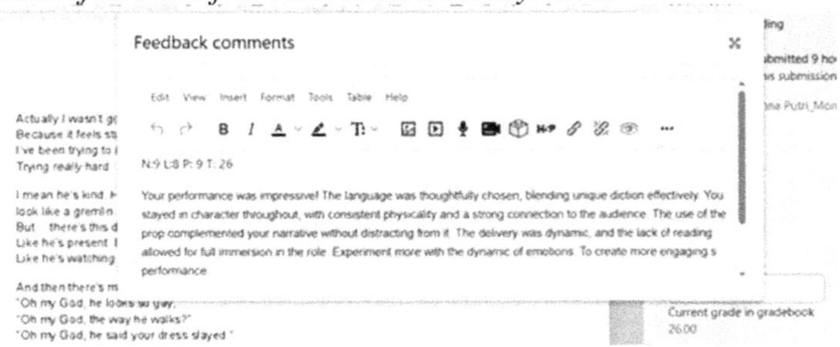

The students will also receive verbal feedback from peers and invited guest lecturers when their monologues are read in class. This is done in week 7 of the semester when the monologues are ready for submission. Peer review and self-reflection of the monologue are submitted at the end of the semester, in the portfolio.

Writing Samples Produced through the HyFlex-Pantser Approach

Figures 7 and 8 below present a sample of the student's creative process, from writing a draft in Chinese using the Pantser method, to translating the text to English with the help of AI, and finally the final draft based on reflection, and the mechanism suggested by the HyFlex-Pantser approach.

Figure 7. The draft written in Chinese and English

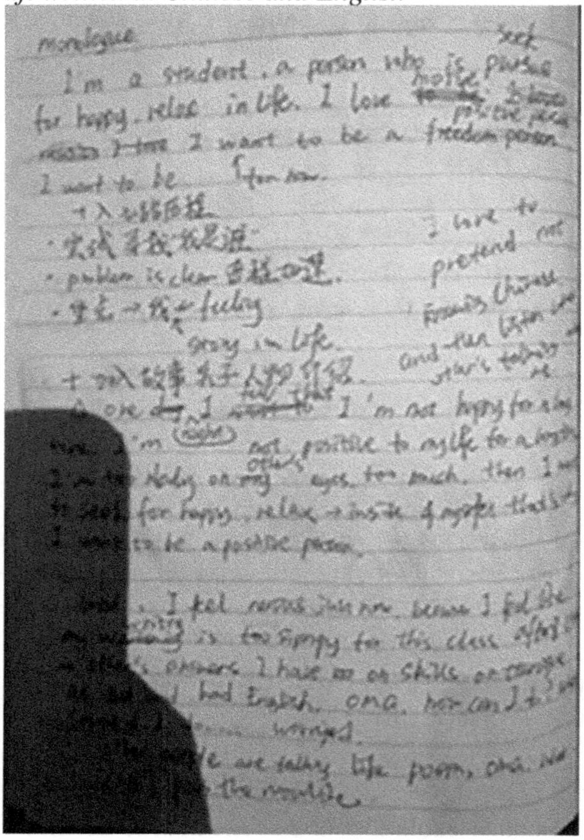

Figure 8. The final draft translated to English

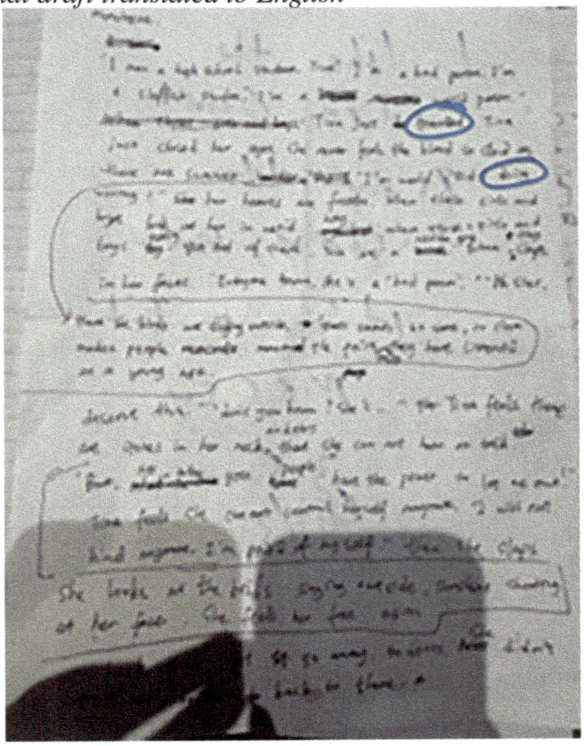

The monologue, as submitted after editing:

(Tina stands centre stage. She looks down, takes a deep breath before speaking.)

I am a high school student. Tina. I'm a bad person. I'm a selfish student. I'm a weird person.

(She looks away, as if remembering something painful.)

Tina just stood there. She closed her eyes—she never felt her blood run so cold, even in the middle of summer.

(Pauses, voice trembling.)

"I'm weird. Did I do something wrong?"

(She presses her hand against her chest.)

Her heart feels frozen. When the girls and boys look at her in that strange way, laughing, whispering, yelling—

(Imitating the others, bitterly)

"Get out of there! You're a freak!"

(Beat. She touches her cheek as if recalling a slap.)

Everyone knows, they say, she's a bad person.

(She glances toward the window, softening.)

There are birds singing outside. Their song sounds so calm, so gentle. It makes her remember the fairytales she once loved when she was young.

(Her tone hardens again.)

"Don't you know? She's…"

(She clutches her throat.)

Tina feels the weight of stones around her neck—she can't speak, she can't even hear.

(Desperate, shouting)

"But why do you people have the power to let me out?"

(Silence. Then, calmly but with resolve.)

Tina feels she can't control herself anymore. "I won't hide anymore. I'm proud of myself."

(She slaps herself, then stands still. A moment of quiet.)

(Looking toward the window again.)

The birds are still singing. Sunshine touches her face. She feels free again.

(She turns away, walks slowly toward the back of the stage.)

She doesn't turn back. Not anymore.

When assessed, the monologue reveals a strong emotional journey of a young woman who grows from embarrassment to frustration and, ultimately, empowerment. The student demonstrates an understanding of exposition, rising tension, conflict, and resolution—key narrative components introduced in the online lectures. Although she employs simple language, the monologue remains expressive, well-paced, and marked by strong theatricality and vivid imagery.

As part of the creative process of the Hyflex-Pantser writing approach, students are required to reflect on their writing process via a Reflective Journal exercise. They write freely on how they composed the piece and the challenges faced and ways to manage them. For the student, Li (Pseudonyms have been used for all participants to ensure confidentiality and protect their identities) whose mother tongue is Mandarin, she shared her thought process via her Reflective Journal:

> *'So, I constructed the monologue by focusing on emotions first. I decided that it was a piece filled with a sense of sadness. I wrote a short draft in Chinese first, just thinking about this emotion. The protagonist lives in a repressive East Asian family where his parents have a strong desire for control and extremely high demands. At the beginning of the monologue, I imagined that the protagonist would have very angry and sad emotions. But I found that the protagonist was more often questioning her parents, saying that she just wanted more freedom and didn't want to be under so much pressure. So, I made a change. I made changes to some words so that it ties in more with this emotion.*
>
> *As I was editing, and making the changes, I also started translating the piece into English, ensuring the emotion was still the same.'*

Li used the Hyflex-Pantser method of writing effectively, using emotion as the focal point to move from her mother tongue to English. She was able to emotionally engage to the requirements of the assessment, and in doing so, access her experiences and memories to turn in a piece that is rich in emotion (Zimmerman et al., 2001). This demonstrates that for a vocation like creative writing, one must be truly connected to the affective- which makes this approach distinct from especially models of writing which are more technical. Figure 9 is an excerpt of her original draft in Chinese, and the final submission in English follows.

Figure 9. Li's original draft which focuses on the emotion of the protagonist

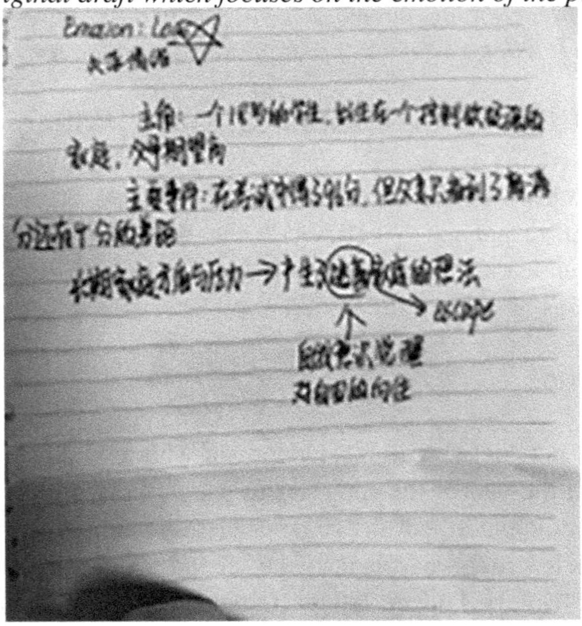

Li's submitted monologue:

The Determination to Escape

(I stood in the corner, one hand tightly grasping the strap of my schoolbag, with a blank look in my eyes.)

People say that silence is a peaceful war.

I was born into a family that had a strong desire to control me. My parents had high expectations of me, so I really wanted to run away.Every achievement, every word I say at the dinner table, every subtle expression. They said, "We treat you like this because we love you. I once believed what they said. "(I raised my eyes and looked ahead)

On my birthday, they whispered in my ear, "You're one year older. Don't mess up everything from now on."(I sighed and repeated in a low voice)"Don't mess up." In this final exam, I cried after getting 96 points. My father said, "OK. At least you know you are still 4 points away from perfection." (The speaking speed began to increase and the intonation rose.) I wanted to cry hysterically at them, "What if I don't want to be perfect? What if I just want to be myself?"
But I swallowed these words. Once again, I couldn't count how many times it was. (After a brief pause, I clenched my fist.) I can't remember when the last time was I did something for myself. I don't know what I like. Or who am I.... Their words were etched into my bones like scars. (I looked ahead, my voice deep but firm.) "I'm afraid of leaving this home... My parents will be very worried about me. But if I stay... It will be even more painful. (Pause, voice sobs) I'm ready."

Reflecting on the Hyflex- Pantser Creative Writing Approach

As the HyFlex learning system is new at Taylor's University, we aimed to understand how students responded to it, the challenges they encountered, and the factors that supported their learning. The below reflects the response based on Brookfield's (2017) Four Lenses of Critical Reflection.

Participant Lens

A survey was conducted with 20 students, of whom 40% were non-native English speakers, at the end of the semester to gauge the students' response to the combined methodology. 26% of the students shared that the methodology helped them to refine their writing, particularly the second and third stages of translation and reflection. 58% of the students felt that the methodology's inclusion of AI aided in brainstorming creative ideas. 67% of the students felt that the Avatar videos used in the Hyflex system of this methodology helped them retain the technical skills in writing. Based on the students' response to the survey, the combined methodology reveals that conventional writing instructions are not the sole measure of effectiveness. The higher percentages connected to AI use (58%) and Avatar videos (67%) suggest that students increasingly value tools that extend beyond conventional pedagogy, particularly those that foster creativity and enhance retention through multimodal engagement. Generally, students who are non-native English speakers are appreciative of the Hyflex-Pantser writing approach's inclusion of the multilingual Avatar and a component in the creative process that allows for language translation. As illustrated in earlier chapters, the students' ability to be thoughtful in their usage of AI translation tools whilst writing helped relieve anxiety in writing.

Despite the generally positive responses to a system that was new to the students, some neutral to negative feedback was recorded via the open-ended section of the questionnaire. Some of the anonymous responses include:

'Using AI in learning caters to the needs of the technology today. But the learners' progress cannot be evaluated personally as AI might give general feedback instead of constructive feedback.'

'Remove AI Avatar lectures, we learn absolutely nothing from it and it's not helpful nor innovative at all'

'I prefer for lectures to be face to face rather than online despite the HyFlex Learning.'

Researcher's Lens (Self)

This new writing approach highlights an increasing recognition that writing development is not confined to grammatical precision or structural refinement but is equally dependent on creative stimulation and technological integration. When the researchers who are the lecturers of this module reflected on the works submitted, the writing reflected the ethos of this pedagogy, which is to champion the writer's cultural background without the need to present perfect English. The most significant positive outcome from the implementation of the Hyflex-Pantser approach is the student engagement. All students completed the monologue assignment on time (and the other 2 assignments of this module), proving the methodology's efficacy in ensuring students comprehension and completion. No students were barred due to poor attendance and all students abided by the maximum allowable absenteeism limit. It should also be noted that after the lecturer informed the students of how the Hyflex-Pantser Writing Approach supports students who are non-native English speakers, there was a noticeable wave of relief in the classroom, which contributed to a more relaxed and conducive environment of learning.

With regards to preparation, both lecturers of this module acknowledge the additional work required to prepare for the Hyflex-Pantser writing approach. In comparison to past semesters which required more hands-on mentoring of the students' work, lecturers now have the added responsibility of preparing the Hyflex materials which include the script and videos of the Avatars, and the online resource on MyTimes. The lecturers invested about 20 hours to integrate Hyflex into this module. The work included training on Hyflex usage and preparing the resources for the MyTimes site. Additional time had to be allocated at the start of the semester to explain to the students on the mechanisms of this new mode of teaching and learning. Although the questionnaire to gauge the student's response to Hyflex learning was sent to all 74 students in the class, only 20 responded. The low response rate may reflect survey fatigue associated with online learning or limited student engagement with the questionnaire.

It is also important to acknowledge that students entered the module with varying levels of AI and digital literacy. While some demonstrated strategic prompting and selective AI usage, others required guidance in navigating tools effectively and ethically. Future iterations of the model may benefit from a short preparatory workshop to ensure equitable digital competency across cohorts.

This semester's class size of 74 students is considered large for a hands-on discipline like creative writing. The Hyflex application is suitable for large lecture classes as the online mode of delivery can cater to an unlimited number of students. However, if this module is to be scalable to a larger number of students, the tutorial classes would have to be more intimate (about 30 students per tutorial) to allow for more personalized attention from the lecturer.

Theoretical Lens

A comparison was made between the results from an earlier semester, which did not incorporate this combined methodology, and the results from this research, to gauge the students' adherence to the module's rubrics. In the Semester 202409, 20% of students achieved an A grade, while in Semester 202504, this figure increased to 30%, indicating a 10% increase in high achievement. Based on the rubrics used to assess the assignments in the module, the improvement in grades signifies progress in the assessment criteria, namely character development, narrative, and language use. The upward trend suggests more confidence in the ability to craft stronger characters, narratives, and language through the combined use of conventional writing models integrated with AI tools. While grades are not the best way to gauge the quality of good writing, the criteria in the rubrics indicate the main components the students have worked on. Another criterion of this assessment is 'Performance', where the students must read out their monologues in front of the audience and lecturer. An improvement in overall grades for this assessment is indicative of not just the ability to ideate and compose a monologue, but to perform one with confidence and creativity. Hyflex-Pantser's multifaceted learning strategies aided learners of all backgrounds to comprehend and compose the writing, while its reassuring and inclusive quality provided a safe space of expression, ultimately heralding a change in perception towards creative writing amongst students who are non-native English speakers.

Sue (Pseudonyms have been used for all participants to ensure confidentiality and protect their identities), a Malaysian student who grew up using Mandarin as her first language, mentioned in her Reflective Journal that writing in her mother tongue first helped her in her creative process. She explained that since English is not her first language, there is a limitation when she writes scripts in English. To express real and raw emotions, she must write in Chinese, her first language. She added that when translating her Chinese scripts into English, she relies on her understanding of English, which she has developed through exposure to English television shows and movies since childhood. She also uses AI tools to help translate certain words rather than full sentences, to avoid misinterpreting meanings. As she noted, "For Chinese, a word can mean a lot of different things; on the other hand, a lot of English words can mean the same thing. This is something I must work on when I write scripts creatively".

Sue's sharing illustrates how the Hyflex-Pantser writing methodology provides a structured guide to writing that alleviates their stress and anxiety in writing in the English language. While she may have applied this method informally in the past, its introduction as a legitimate methodology provided her with greater confidence. Notably, Sue was among the students who excelled in this module, achieving an A grade.

The responses above demonstrate that the Hyflex-Pantser Writing Approach's The students' conducive and inclusive environment to learn has resulted in improved behavioral engagement (comprehension, retention and analysis of writing pedagogy). This then converts to more emotional engagement (confident expression throughout the writing process), which ultimately yields more organic and honest creative pieces (Fredricks et al., 2016). The final result is monologues which are confident, and culturally specific. Figure 10 below is an extract from a student's work, which combined Bahasa Indonesia and English in a monologue. The top portion is the final draft, while the portion below is her draft written in English. This student obtained an A grade for the module, reflecting original writing, with well-crafted characters and narrative.

Figure 10. Student writing sample

MOTHER
(calm voice)

Yang aku mau just dia punya normal life. Keluarga yang perfect. Seorang ayah yang she boleh lihat sebagai role model. I mungkin hate dia, tapi dia tetap ayah dari aisyah. I terlalu sibuk defend him. Tapi pada akhirnya, akulah yang jahat di matanya.

(All I wanted for her was to have a normal life. A complete family. A father to look up to. I may hate him but he will always be the father to my child. I was so busy defending him. But in the end I was the villain in her eyes.)

MOTHER falls into a sitting position. PAUSES.

12

Recommendations on Developing the Hyflex Pantser Writing System.

After analysing the results and reflections, several recommendations can be made to improve the HyFlex-Pantser writing system. Based on the survey results, students generally hold a moderate level of acceptance toward learning with AI-generated avatars. A majority (57.89%) agreed that AI Avatar videos support their learning and help them retain information better, although only a small proportion (10.53%) strongly agreed. Engagement levels were also relatively positive, with 52.63% finding AI Avatar videos more engaging than traditional recorded lectures. However, feelings of connection and confidence toward AI-generated avatars were less pronounced, as only 36.84% expressed agreement and 42.11% were neutral. Preference for AI Avatar videos over text-based or traditional lectures was also limited, with most students showing neutral, and suggesting that the Hyflex-Pantser model included more time for interaction with the lecturer. The recommendations below are based on the survey findings. To address some neutral to negative feedback, the use of Avatar lectures can be studied further, as students perceive them as unengaging. Balancing the Avatar video lectures with more face-to-face tutorial time may be more effective for the students' learning, as elaborated in the chapters below. Educating the students on the expectations and demands of a combined mode of learning like the Hyflex-Pantser writing approach may result in more effective engagement.

To do this, there may be a need to develop pre-module tutorials on how to use the system before students begin the course. As this is a new system, students should not spend the first week trying to familiarize themselves with it while simultaneously learning new content. Other disciplines have used preparatory courses to aid the success of the study of the main course. Montgomery's (2012) paper on the effects of preparatory courses on university entrance examinations in high school-age students show how short courses can help the student to understand new modules. Pre-module tutorials which can be packaged as a short preparatory course would introduce students to the mechanisms of hybrid learning like the Hyflex system, so that when they begin the creative writing module, their focus will be wholly on the writing itself.

The second recommendation is to provide students with more tutorial time, during which lecturers can coach them face-to-face. The HyFlex mode should be leveraged for its dual-language and multifunctional features, but face-to-face interaction remains essential for helping students refine their writing voice. Incorporating more in-class writing tasks that complement the online features of HyFlex can also make the system more holistic and effective. The second semester of the Introduction to Creative Writing module in September 2025 has begun incorporating in-class writing tasks that co-relate with the online activities available on the Hylex site.

Students learn the techniques via online lectures and deepen their understanding through the materials on the site and then apply this learning in face to face tutorials with the lecturer.

The third recommendation is to extend multilingual functions in all the HyFlex system's online components, in line with its Avatar function which currently allows the students to rewatch lectures in any language. Currently, Avatar is limited to Mandarin, which excludes students who use other languages. For scalability, and inclusivity, it is suggested that the Taylor's University Learning and Development department include more language options for the Avatar lectures. In line with this, supplementary materials like quizzes that can be translated to any language with a single click would complement this writing model, which champions cultural diversity and accommodates diverse learning capabilities.

As findings are based on a single semester cohort, long-term effects on writing confidence, linguistic development, and creative independence remain unexamined. Longitudinal tracking across multiple semesters would provide stronger evidence of sustained impact and developmental progression.

Finally, this research can be extended over several semesters to achieve longitudinal data. The lecturers can study the sustained writing confidence and development of creative writing, to discover necessary tweaks for the improvement of the Hyflex-Pantser writing approach.

Implications for the Future of Creative Writing

The Hyflex-Pantser system of writing is in line with the current trends in creative writing.

Instructions, prompts, and mechanisms for the novice writer have evolved significantly over the years. Wu et al. (2025) found that the Creative Painting Diary (CPD), which combines visual stimuli, helps the students' creativity and writing. The students who used the system, which incorporated visuals in their stimulus process in writing, were more creative than students who wrote conventionally. Visuals like drawings and images were familiar to the students, which gave them a more confident point to start writing, demonstrating the importance of comfort and well-being to aid creativity. When this is compared to the HyFlex-Pantser system of writing, where anxiety levels were reduced amongst students who were not confident to write in English, the implication of a 'comfort element' to aid creative writing should be explored further.

(Hernandez, 2025)'s study focused on how technology aided high school students in their creative writing journey. Digital tools and platforms like Wattpad were used in this study for the students to brainstorm, develop, and structure ideas in creative writing. A pre-test and post-test was administered on the students, which demonstrated a significant improvement in the students writing based on criteria like content development, language, and technical accuracy. This study illustrates the significance of technology amongst the youth today, and how its familiarity aids in their learning of a module like creative writing.

The aspects of creating a safe space to be creative in writing and the incorporation of technology have both demonstrated positive results in this study and the two case studies cited above. Other models of creative writing can benefit with exploration and experimentation with technology, and more consideration on the writer's well being as part of their model of creative process.

CONCLUSION

As the world shifts into digital platforms, it is only natural that the craft of creative writing embraces the trend. With consumers preferring online publications, the integration of AI in writing should be combined with traditional writing practices, as proposed by this methodology. One of the bases of ideating a story is to be relevant with the current world, and to write a piece which is about the now. AI is in every facet of the world now and integrating it thoughtfully into the age of art of storytelling, is the way forward. This research endeavours to be a pioneer in this movement, while aiding the growth of young writers from diverse cultural backgrounds.

REFERENCES

Beatty, B. J. (2019). *Hybrid-Flexible course design: Implementing student-directed hybrid classes*. EdTech Books. https://edtechbooks.org/hyflex

Becker, A. (2006). A review of writing model research based on cognitive processes. In Allal, L., Chanquoy, P., & Largy, P. (Eds.), *Revision: History, theory, and practice* (pp. 25–49). Springer.

Bell, J. S. (2018). *Write your novel from the middle: A new approach for plotters, pantsers, and everyone in between*. Compendium Publishing.

Brookfield, S. D. (2017). *Becoming a critically reflective teacher* (2nd ed.). Jossey-Bass.

Cotton, D. R. E., Cotton, P. A., & Shipway, J. R. (2023). ChatGPT: Friend or foe? *Journal of Higher Education Policy and Management, 45*(5), 502–518. DOI: 10.1080/1360080X.2023.2203859

Craig, C. (2013). Exploring the pedagogical practices of creative writing teachers in higher education. *English in Education, 47*(3), 245–260. DOI: 10.1111/eie.12027

Emig, J. (1971). *The composing processes of twelfth graders*. National Council of Teachers of English.

Fitria, T. N. (2023). Use of AI in academic writing: Benefits and challenges. *English Language Teaching and Applied Linguistics, 5*(2), 45–52.

Fredricks, J. A., Filsecker, M., & Lawson, M. A. (2016). Student engagement, context, and adjustment: Addressing definitional, measurement, and methodological issues. *Learning and Instruction, 43*, 1–4. DOI: 10.1016/j.learninstruc.2016.02.002

Hanauer, D. I. (2012). Meaningful literacy: Writing poetry in the language classroom. *Language Teaching, 45*(1), 105–115. DOI: 10.1017/S0261444810000522

Hernandez, J. M. R. (2025). Developing creative writing skills through technology-based language approaches. *International Journal of Social Science and Human Research, 8*(4), 2406–2412. DOI: 10.47191/ijsshr/v8-i4-53

Hyland, K. (2003). *Second language writing*. Cambridge University Press. DOI: 10.1017/CBO9780511667251

Lee, I. (2009). Feedback revolution: What gets in the way? *ELT Journal, 63*(1), 1–12. DOI: 10.1093/elt/XXIV.1.1

Liu, D., Liu, Y., & Wang, J. (2025). Critical thinking and AI in EFL writing. *Journal of Second Language Writing*.

Lowrey, S. (2021). Pantser or planner? *Publishers Weekly*, *268*(2), 63–64.

Malto, R. R. M., & Pineda, J. C. R. (2024). Analysing students' use of AI in essay outputs: A case study in purposive communication. *International Journal of Research and Innovation in Social Science*, *8*(5), 253–257. DOI: 10.47772/IJRISS.2024.8508

Manery, R. (2016). *The education of the creative writing teacher: A study of conceptions of creative writing pedagogy in higher education (Doctoral dissertation)*. University of Michigan. https://hdl.handle.net/2027.42/133407

Merriam, S. B., & Tisdell, E. J. (2016). *Qualitative research: A guide to design and implementation* (4th ed.). Jossey-Bass.

Miller, A. N., Dyer, T., & Nadler, N. (2021). Student engagement in HyFlex learning: Equity, access, and participation. *Journal of University Teaching & Learning Practice*, *18*(4), 25–37.

Montgomery, P., & Lilly, J. (2012). Systematic reviews of the effects of preparatory courses on university entrance examinations in high school-age students. *International Journal of Social Welfare*, *21*(1), 3–12. DOI: 10.1111/j.1468-2397.2011.00812.x

Raes, A., Detienne, L., Windey, I., & Depaepe, F. (2020). A systematic review on synchronous hybrid learning. *Educational Research Review*, *31*, 100–114. DOI: 10.1016/j.edurev.2020.100364

Sarica, P., & Deneme, S. (2023). AI-supported writing in EFL contexts: A systematic review. *Journal of Language and Linguistic Studies*, *19*(2), 580–596. DOI: 10.52462/jlls.213

Spolin, V. (1999). *Improvisation for the theater* (3rd ed.). Northwestern University Press.

van Pinxteren, B.. (2023). The relevance of the medium of instruction and mother tongue for education effectiveness. [ScienceDirect]. *International Journal of Educational Development*, *99*, 102–112.

Winston, J. (2013). *Second language learning through drama: Practical techniques and theoretical perspectives*. Routledge. DOI: 10.4324/9780203805114

Woo, D. J., Wang, Y., Susanto, H., & Guo, K. (2022). *Understanding EFL student idea generation strategies for creative writing with NLG tools*. arXiv Preprint. https://arxiv.org/abs/2209.12345

Wu, E. L., Du, Z., Chang, C.-Y., Kuo, H.-C., Chen, I.-H., Wang, L.-C., & Shen, T.-Y. (2025). Canvas and quill: Improving students' creativity and writing composition through creative painting diary. *Thinking Skills and Creativity*, *57*, 101820. DOI: 10.1016/j.tsc.2025.101820

Zimmerman, B. J., & Schunk, D. H. (Eds.). (2001). *Self-regulated learning and academic achievement: Theoretical perspectives* (2nd ed.). Lawrence Erlbaum Associates.

Zou, D., Xie, H., & Wang, F. L. (2023). *Generative AI for education: Opportunities and challenges*. Computers & Education. *Artificial Intelligence*, *4*, 100171. DOI: 10.1016/j.caeai.2023.100171

Chapter 13
Leveraging Learning Analytics for Adaptive Pathways and Student Success

Manju Priya R.
http://orcid.org/0000-0001-9144-5301
Jain (Deemed to be) University, India

N. Sathyanarayana
http://orcid.org/0000-0002-4185-7751
Jain (Deemed to be) University, India

Daniel Nesa Kumar C.
http://orcid.org/0000-0003-4184-216X
Sri Ramakrishna College of Arts and Science, India

ABSTRACT

In the evolving landscape of HyFlex education, learning analytics has emerged as a key enabler of adaptive and personalized learning pathways that enhance student engagement and success. This conceptual chapter examines how AI-powered learning analytics can transform traditional educational practices into data-informed systems responsive to individual learner needs across digital and physical environments. By capturing and analyzing learner behavior, engagement patterns, and performance data, educators can design timely interventions and predictive supports to improve academic outcomes. The chapter is grounded in two foundational frameworks: the Learning Analytics Cycle (LAK), which guides data-driven instructional action, and Zimmerman's Self-Regulated Learning (SRL) model, which emphasizes learner

DOI: 10.4018/979-8-3373-6182-6.ch013

autonomy through planning, monitoring, and reflection. Drawing on examples from higher education and professional learning contexts, the chapter also addresses ethical considerations, data privacy, and faculty readiness.

1 INTRODUCTION

Digitisation of higher education has led to significant changes in how learners engage with content, instructors, and institutional systems. One of the most significant inventions in the dynamic environment is a hybrid model known as HyFlex education, where students can attend classes in a real-world setting or online, either in real time or asynchronously. The model's dynamism also aligns with learners' desires and expectations, as their needs shift toward convenience, customisation, and autonomy in their learning. Nonetheless, HyFlex education has its own set of problems, especially in assessing student engagement, forecasting learning outcomes, and developing effective instructional pathways that are responsive to diverse learners in a systematic manner.

In this case, AI-based learning analytics has emerged as a successful method for addressing the challenge of maintaining a flexible learning environment while providing more structured pedagogy. Learning analytics refers to the systematic collection, analysis, and presentation of data generated by learners to enhance teaching, learning, and decision-making (Siemens, 2013). Learning analytics has become an effective tool that provides additional information on student behaviour, performance trends, and engagement, as artificial intelligence, machine learning models, predictive systems, and intelligent dashboards have been introduced. Such learnings may be applied to designing adaptive learning pathways that modify instructional content, activities, and assessments according to the needs, progress, and preferences of individual learners.

HyFlex settings also greatly appreciate adaptive pathways. The difference in the learning practices by the students depending on the location and mode of attending the institution, whether onsite, online live or asynchronous, poses a challenge to the instructors who must have consistency and quality of learning across all the modes. Learning analytics can facilitate this process: identifying disengagement early, customising learning content, and proposing immediate recommendations will help a student succeed. In turn, AI-based analytics is becoming a leading contributor to student-centric, data-driven pedagogy.

The chapter describes how learning analytics and adaptive pathways can be implemented in the environment of HyFlex and conceptualised to have the impact on student engagement and academic performance. The analysis will be based on two popular theoretical models: the Learning Analytics Cycle (LAK Framework) and the Self-Regulated Learning (SRL) model, developed by Zimmerman, to provide a strong foundation. LAK Framework offers an organised approach to data collection and processing, and how they are applied in the educational decision-making (Ferguson, 2012). The SRL Model, however, is concerned with how the learners plan, control and assess their learning (Zimmerman, 2002). The chapter is an amalgamation of both these models; the first one on the institutional level and the second one on the learner level in order to gain insight into how efficient adaptive learning systems may be designed.

The LAK Framework is applicable to the concept of how institutions can create a cycle of continuous data enhancement. For example, information on student logins, assignment completion, and involvement in online discussions can be examined to identify tendencies toward disengagement before they lead to poor performance. Predictive analytics can then notify instructors to take an early intervention by providing feedback, additional resources, or personalised support. This, combined with HyFlex delivery, ensures that online and on-site students receive similar levels of attention and guidance.

In its turn, the SRL Model focuses on the fact that learners are the agents in their learning process. Students in a flexible learning context must take greater responsibility for scheduling, motivation, goal-setting, and time management. AIs can enhance self-regulation among learners by providing clarity and actionable information, such as performance dashboards, personalised nudges, and study-planning projects. When learners track their progress through visual information, they become increasingly aware of their strengths and weaknesses, allowing them to think more and improve.

Another concern is the increasing use of HyFlex and AI technologies in educational institutions worldwide. According to recent surveys, most universities that used HyFlex models reported increased student satisfaction and course completion when analytics tools were integrated into their systems (Eom, S. 2023). Indicators of progress relative to peers or course expectations are shown to boost student participation through analytics dashboards; for example, in the same context, early-warning mechanisms have minimised dropout rates by notifying instructors of patterns indicating academic vulnerability.

In addition to these benefits, privacy, data ethics, transparency, and preparedness of faculties are some of the challenges associated with the use of learning analytics in HyFlex. Teachers might not be well-versed in interpreting the analytics reports and developing activities based on the data findings. The students are likely to be afraid of the level of scrutiny their interactions will face. Data protection and algorithmic fairness can be concerns within institutions. These points show that there should be effective, practical policies, ethics, and training to achieve responsible and effective adoption.

In this respect, the chapter is likely to contribute to the body of scholarly knowledge by offering a conceptual, holistic view of how AI-driven learning analytics can enable adaptive learning and enhance student performance in HyFlex settings. The chapter is based on an overview of the existing literature, an assessment of theoretical knowledge, and examples from higher education, online learning platforms, and professional development. It also addresses ethical concerns, institutional policies, and future trends to consider when educators and administrators adopt analytics in HyFlex systems.

In general, the point is to illustrate how learning analytics has the potential to change learning environments so they become inclusive, responsive, and personalised. HyFlex education is a teaching method that enhances flexibility and effectiveness by using AI to analyse learner behaviour and provide insights into implementation. With the world facing increasing demand for hybrid and flexible learning, institutions must leverage data and artificial intelligence to ensure that every learner, regardless of mode, has an equal chance to engage and succeed. The recent studies indicate the growing importance of learning analytics in flexible and hybrid and HyFlex learning spaces, most specifically to aid in student engagement, persistence, and adaptive instructional design aspects within post-pandemic higher education settings (Bond et al., 2020)(Ifenthaler, D., and Yau, J. Y. K., 2020).

The chapter will then describe the conceptual underpinnings of learning analytics in HyFlex education, followed by an integrative argument on the appropriateness of the theoretical models. This is followed by an analysis of how the frameworks underpin adaptive learning pathways, and it concludes with practical, ethical, and institutional implications for improving student engagement and success.

The literature has been broad in recognising the possibilities of learning analytics to aid student engagement, personalisation, and academic achievement. Nevertheless, much of the literature remains divided, with a tendency to focus on analytics tools, learner behaviour, and instructional design individually. Within the framework of HyFlex education, in which learners dynamically switch between physical and virtual modes, there is a lack of conceptual clarity about how insights generated by analytics can be systematically incorporated into adaptive learning processes. This mismatch necessitates a unified framework that aligns institutional data processes with learner-centric self-regulation.

Recent learning analytics literature indicates a shift from descriptive data reporting to pedagogically motivated, ethically informed applications. Present-day research highlights the alignment of analytics with instructional design, learner agency, and institutional decision-making, especially in the context of hybrid and HyFlex studies (Ferguson et al., 2016; Viberg et al., 2018). This transformation necessitates combined conceptual frameworks that bridge data-based insights and teaching and learning processes.

2 OBJECTIVES OF THE CHAPTER

(i) To explore the conceptual foundations of learning analytics and adaptive learning in HyFlex education.
(ii) To apply the Learning Analytics Cycle (LAK Framework) for understanding institutional data-driven interventions.
(iii) To integrate Zimmerman's Self-Regulated Learning (SRL) Model for enhancing learner autonomy and reflection.
(iv) To present diverse examples showcasing adaptive pathways informed by AI and learning analytics.
(v) To identify ethical, pedagogical, and policy considerations in using analytics for student success.

3 CONCEPTUAL ORIENTATION OF THE CHAPTER

The current body of research generally recognises the promise of learning analytics in helping students engage, personalise, and succeed, both academically and personally. The literature, however, is highly fragmented, with many studies focusing on analytics tools, learner behaviour, or instructional design separately. Within the framework of HyFlex education, where learners freely move between physical and virtual settings, there is a lack of conceptual understanding of how insights from analytics can be systematically incorporated into adaptive learning pathways. This shortcoming illustrates the need for a unified framework to address institutional data operations and learner-based self-organisation systems.

The recent literature on learning analytics indicates a shift from earlier data-reporting approaches to more ethically informed and pedagogically valuable applications. Recent research highlights the concepts of analytics and their alignment with instructional design, student agency, and institutional decision-making, particularly in the context of hybrid and HyFlex education (Ferguson et al., 2016; Viberg et al., 2018). With this development, there is a necessity to have conceptual frameworks that are aligned to link data-based insights and teaching learning processes.

3.1 Conceptual Research Orientation

Conceptual framing is required in spheres where rapid technological growth occurs (artificial intelligence, digital learning ecosystems, analytics) because it provides a logical way to explain processes before they become embedded in stable empirical trends. This approach is particularly well-suited to HyFlex education, where teaching and learning modalities continue to change due to technological upgrades, learner expectations, and instructional design.

In this chapter, a conceptual methodology allows for a general analysis of the intersection of learning analytics, AI-based personalisation, and the HyFlex model. As AI-based analytics tools vary across institutions, from simple LMS dashboards to full-scale predictive analytics engines, conceptual analysis will allow consideration of multiple perspectives without reference to any specific case within an institution. It assists with pattern recognition across various environments and shows how analytics-enabled adaptive pathways can be generalised to educational contexts.

Moreover, conceptual research can help close the gap between conventional theoretical approaches and contemporary digital learning trends. For example, the Learning Analytics Cycle (Ferguson, 2012) and the Self-Regulated Learning model by Zimmerman (2002) were developed before AI-based analytics dashboards or HyFlex systems. These models can be reconceptualised through conceptual reasoning to understand how the key principles of AI tools, such as feedback loops, metacognitive monitoring, and personalised instruction, are operationalised. This makes classical theories applicable to modern digital learning systems (Clow, 2012). Thus, the main topic of this chapter is conceptual research, which provides an understanding of the adaptability and flexibility of digital learning ecosystems using learning analytics, a subject that is subject to further development.

Figure 1. Learning analytics cycle and self-regulated learning processes

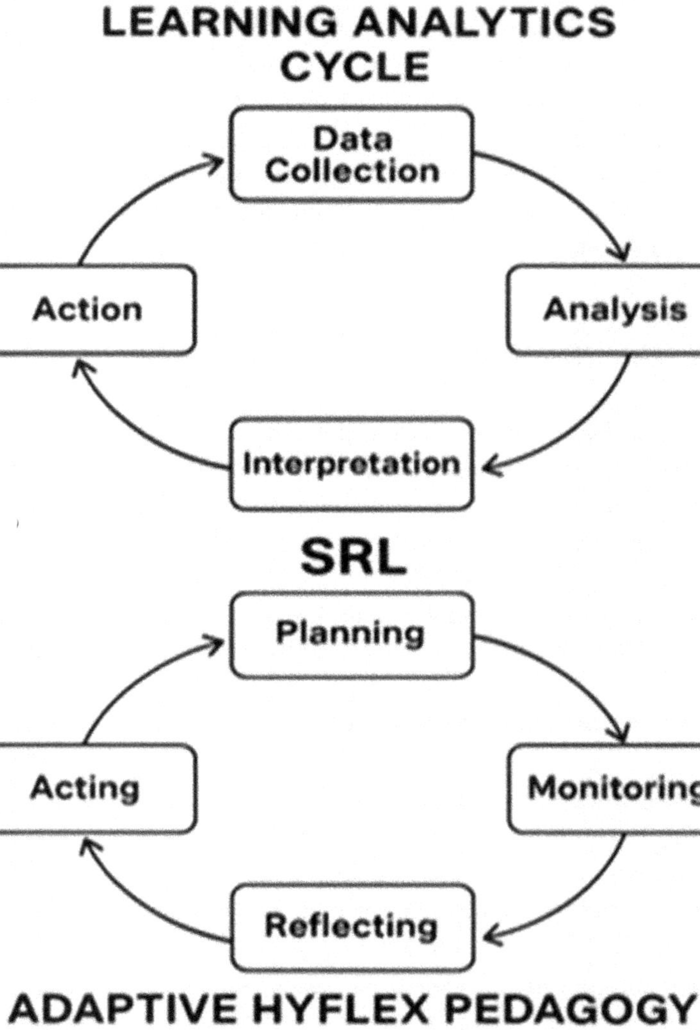

Figure 1 illustrates that two interdependent cycles operate at once: institutional-level learning analytics and self-regulated learning (at the learner level). These cycles, in turn, enable responsive HyFlex pedagogy based on adaptive instructional decisions and real-time learner tracking.

3.2 Sources of Secondary Data

The chapter draws on an extensive collection of secondary sources to develop a comprehensive conceptual framework for AI-based learning analytics in HyFlex learning. The journal articles and reports published by EDUCAUSE, UNESCO, the OECD, and the Society of Learning Analytics Research (SoLAR) are the most recent sources of information on the progress of global adoption, ethical issues, and institutional readiness. The most important references are case studies of universities. These sources provide a valid, multimedia foundation for understanding theoretical frameworks and for integrating learning analytics into HyFlex systems.

4 ANALYTICAL FRAMEWORK

The analytical framework of the current chapter is based on two theoretical frameworks: the Learning Analytics Cycle (LAK Framework) and the Self-Regulated Learning (SRL) Model. The two provide an integrated method for investigating the interreliability between data-informed knowledge and student dispositions to support adaptive learning tracks in HyFlex settings. In light of this conceptual gap, the next section presents the Learning Analytics Cycle (LAK Framework), a systematic approach for transforming learner data into actionable insights within institutions.

4.1 Learning Analytics Cycle (Instructional Level Lens)

The Learning Analytics Cycle (LAK Framework) offers institutions a framework for transforming learning data into meaningful actions. The process typically consists of data gathering from learning management systems, learner records, and evaluation archives, and analytical procedures for the data, both conceptual and practical. The results may help teachers and administrators make effective decisions, address the issue promptly, and design materials for academic interventions. The LAK framework is applied in HyFlex to manage various participation patterns and to monitor the progress of learners, both physical and digital (Ferguson, 2012).

Figure 2. The learning analytics cycle (LAK framework)

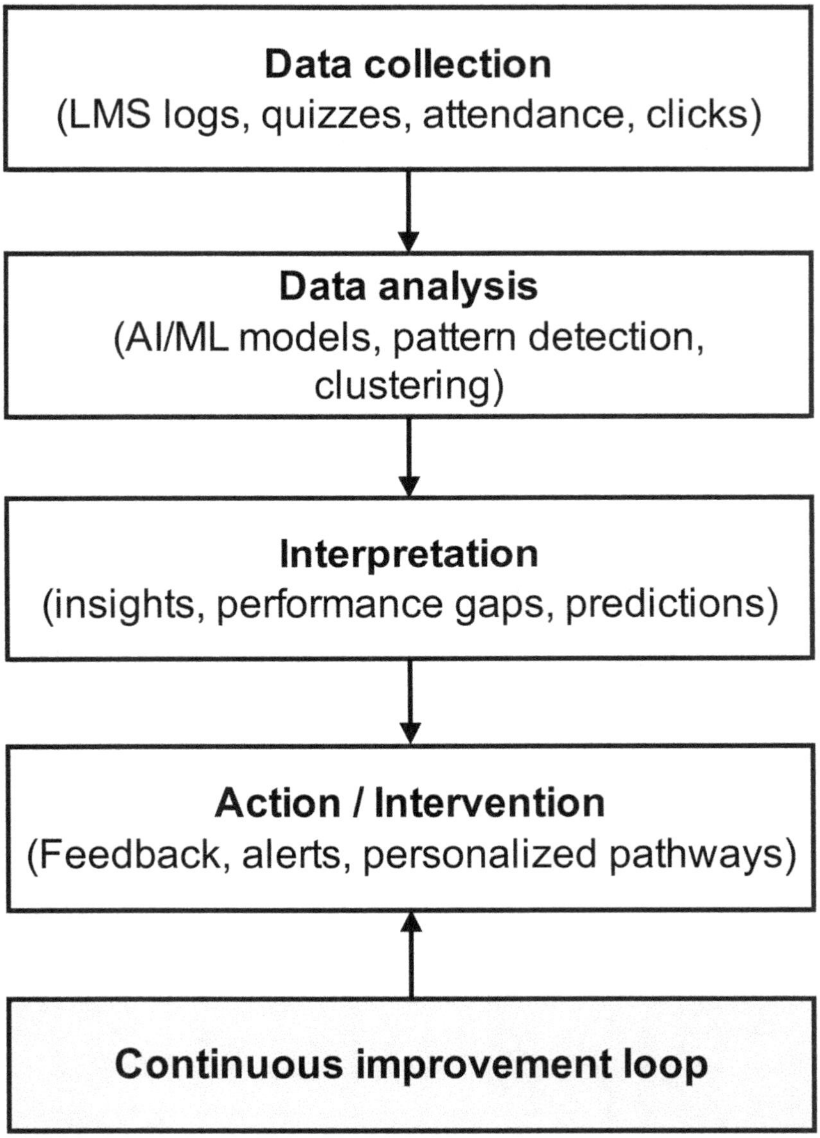

Recent research demonstrates the appropriateness of the learning analytics cycle for institutional decision-making, early warning, and student services in blended and HyFlex learning environments, thereby validating its applicability to higher education (Matcha et al., 2019; Schumacher & Ifenthaler, 2018).

Figure 2 provides an overview of the cyclical learning analytics process at the institutional level, in which learner data is systematically transformed into valuable knowledge and pedagogical actions. The continuous improvement loop states that learning analytics must be an ongoing process, not a one-time activity, enabling the institution to streamline its teaching processes, improve student support, and adapt effectively to changing learning behaviours in HyFlex courses.

4.2 Self-Regulated Learning Model (Learner-level Lens)

Figure 3: Zimmerman's Self-Regulated Learning (SRL) model presents a learner-centred perspective on students' management of their learning cycle across three learning cycles. One of the steps is forethought, which entails setting goals, planning, and forming motivating beliefs that will define a learner's commitment and motivation. The performance stage entails self-control, attention, learning strategies, and constant self-observation to ensure that one's objectives remain on course. The final step in the cycle is self-reflection, through which learners will review their performance, understand what led to their performance or difficulties, and take corrective steps for future assignments. The SRL processes are supported by AI-enhanced dashboards, engagement indicators, and personalised recommendations in digital HyFlex learning settings, allowing learners to use real-time feedback and monitor their learning progress to make well-informed adjustments and remain in control of their learning (Zimmerman, 2002).

Figure 3. Zimmerman's Self-Regulated Learning (SRL) model

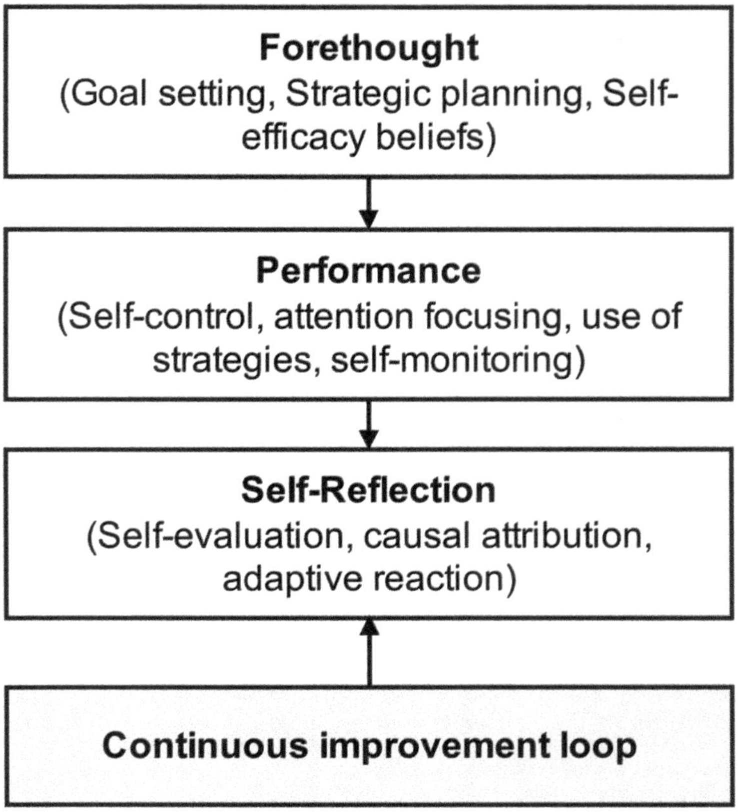

Figure 3 represents the Self-Regulated Learning model developed by Zimmerman, which highlights that learning is a cyclical process activated by setting objectives, actively tracking performance, and reflecting on performance. The learner's active role in managing motivation, using strategies, and achieving learning outcomes is emphasised in the continuous improvement loop, which is why the SRL framework is particularly applicable in HyFlex learning settings, where autonomy and self-direction are key to continued engagement and success.

4.3 Integration of LAK and SRL

Figure 4 on HyFlex environments demonstrates that the Learning Analytics Cycle (LAK) and the Self-Regulated Learning (SRL) model combine dynamically to emphasise the relationships between institutional decision-making and learner autonomy. Although the LAK framework allows institutions to create focused interventions, individualised journeys, and prompt support for clients, learners also use analytics-based data to manage their behavioural patterns, track their progress, and adjust strategies based on SRL principles. Both processes work simultaneously to form a dual-loop adaptive ecosystem in which data constantly drives instructional changes, and these changes, in turn, affect how learners interact, learn, and communicate. The activities of learners using digital tools and dashboards generate new data, which in turn feed back into the LAK cycle, enabling continuous improvement. Such a reciprocal relationship makes learning experiences responsive, personalised, and constantly changing, based on institutional analytics and the learner's self-regulation.

Figure 4. Integration of the learning analytics cycle (LAK) and the Self-Regulated Learning (SRL) model

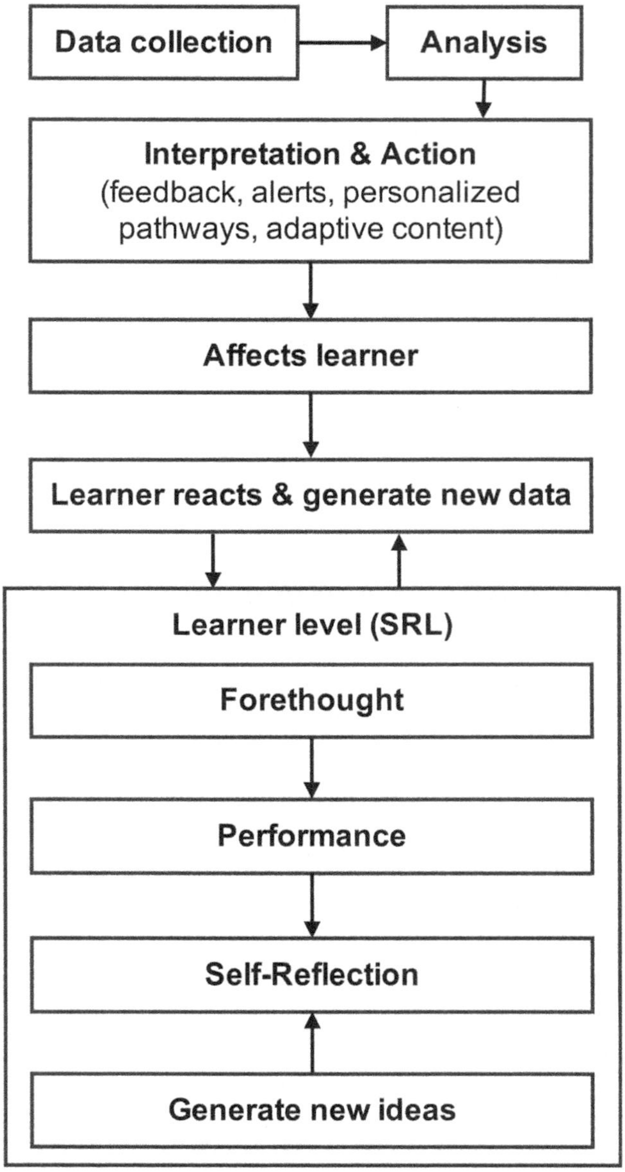

The simplified integrated model (Figure 4) shows that institutional analytics (LAK) and learner self-regulation (SRL) represent interconnected systems in a HyFlex environment. The LAK cycle at the institutional level starts with gathering information on students' activities, assignments, and online communication. These findings are analysed to identify learning styles and potential challenges. Based on these observations, the interventions provided to the institution include feedback, early warning, and individual learning materials. All these institutional practices have a direct impact on the way learners plan and engage in learning as well as reflecting on their activities.

At the learner level, students work through the SRL cycle: they set goals (forethought), apply strategies, monitor their progress (performance), and evaluate their progress (self-reflection). By engaging in these processes, learners gain new insights into their learning behaviour, such as time spent on tasks, patterns of participation, and performance indicators. The feedback of the new information into the LAK cycle allows the institution to keep on updating interventions. Thus, the compound model depicts a two-way process of ongoing interaction between an institution's decisions and learner behaviour, whereby the latter generates data to guide improvements to the former.

5 DESIGNING ADAPTIVE PATHWAYS WITH ANALYTIC

The Learning Analytics Cycle explains how data can be created and analysed at the institutional level, but, pedagogically, it can be used to interpret findings into learning-adjustive processes. Adaptive pathways are dynamic learning pathways guided by the tutor in response to learners' needs regarding content, pace, and support. The adaptations based on analytics in HyFlex environments provide guidance to students at the individual level irrespective of the participation mode they use and hence encourage continuity, engagement, and self-directed learning (Siemens, 2013).

The adaptive pathways are particularly effective in a HyFlex environment, where students can transition among different modalities, i.e., on-site, synchronous online, and asynchronous online. The various modalities have their own patterns of engagement and challenge. For example, asynchronous online learners may show a high level of independence and poor submission over time. In contrast, on-site learners may actively engage in discussions but fail to use digital materials. Analytics tools help the teacher understand such differences and create responsive, adaptive supports for each learner group. Through continuous data collection, teachers can identify who is in danger, who needs improvement, and who is better served by more organised guidance (Ferguson, 2012).

One essential element of adaptive pathway design is data-driven learner profiling. Learning analytics systems build dynamic learner profiles based on variables such as time spent on activities, login frequency, discussion forum activity, performance trends, and behavioural indicators such as procrastination or disengagement. These real-time, updated profiles enable instructors to group students (e.g., highly engaged, moderately engaged, disengaged) using machine learning algorithms such as clustering and predictive modelling (Ifenthaler & Yau, 2020). After profiling learners, AI applications can suggest personalised materials, such as videos, readings, quizzes, or simulations, based on their current level of knowledge.

The adaptive pathways also use machine-learning-driven prediction models that forecast student achievement or anticipate when a student is facing challenges. Predictive analytics uses past and current data to predict that particular students are likely to fail a quiz, drop out, or have difficulty with a concept. For example, an early-warning system can alert when a student's participation falls below a preset threshold or when assignment performance shows a negative trend (Clow, 2012). Teachers can then play a proactive role by sending customised messages, providing remedial content, or adjusting due dates. Such predictive interventions can not only enhance learners' academic performance but also their well-being, as they reduce anxiety and help maintain momentum.

Another highly important component of adaptive pathways design is adaptive content sequencing. It is changing the sequence of learning material and the difficulty or type of material, depending on data analysis. Learning solutions built on an artificial intelligence system can propose the next step by automatically rearranging content based on the learner's mastery level. For example, a learner with weaknesses in prerequisite material can be instructed in that material, and gifted students can be instructed in advanced material. Such sequencing gives substance to the elements of mastery learning by ensuring that learners move forward once they demonstrate competency (Bloom, 1984). In HyFlex environments, adaptive sequencing means that, regardless of the mode used, each learner is guaranteed a coherent and personalised learning experience.

Moreover, adaptive pathways help facilitate fair learning by providing differentiated opportunities for learners who may be disadvantaged in some modalities. Asynchronous students may find it difficult to engage in real-time conversations. However, analytics can help them recognise this difference and send interactive materials or reflection exercises to support it. On the same note, analytics can be used to identify that on-site learners are not engaging with digital resources in depth, and instructors can add blended activities to balance the strengths of the modality. Adaptive pathways, therefore, provide a sense of fairness when support is given based on individual needs rather than on learners' common experiences.

The key aspect of adaptive pathway design is the incorporation of Self-Regulated Learning (SRL) principles. Improving SRL can be achieved by enabling learners to monitor their progress, analyse results, and set improvement objectives using AI-based dashboards. For example, changes in achievement, time management, or engagement statistics displayed in dashboards will enable students to adjust their strategies in advance (Zimmerman, 2002). The extent of transparency that analytics can provide students helps them take ownership of the learning process; hence, adaptive pathways are not only instructor-driven but also learner-driven.

Also, analytics enables adaptive assessment practices, in which instructors can adjust the format and difficulty of an assessment based on learners' preparedness. In adaptive quizzes, question difficulty varies based on past responses, and the user can choose an appropriate level. Similarly, formative analytics can be used to identify learners who require additional support or feedback to achieve mastery, helping educationalists create tailored assessment plans. These adaptive tests come in particularly handy in HyFlex environments, where integrity, equity and consistency of tests may be challenging to maintain.

Adaptive pathways are also promoted by learning recommendation systems, such as those used by platforms like Netflix and Spotify. These systems use recommendation algorithms to suggest media such as videos, readings, peer interactions, or practice questions, and they all depend on the learner's interests, weaknesses, and learning goals. For example, if the analytics reveal a lack of engagement with a specific concept, the system can propose engaging simulations or opportunities to discuss with peers. Such personalisation makes learning more interesting and enables learners to work with what they are inclined to learn (Brown et al., 2020).

In addition, the design of adaptive pathways depends on the ability to operate on continuous feedback loops, in which teaching shifts are refined by data information and learning changes are refined by performance analytics to enhance research practices. Feedback based on analytics will ensure that students receive feedback in time and in a personalised, non-generic form. For example, feedback messages can specify certain behaviours identified in the system, such as "You appear to spend less time reading materials this week" or "Your quiz performance in Topic 3 indicates that you need to revise basic concepts." This specificity enhances the relevance and effectiveness of feedback, which are major predictors of student success.

The scalability of adaptive pathways is especially beneficial in HyFlex environments. Because analytics automates much of the data interpretation, teachers do not have to work more intensively to guide large groups. Moreover, adaptive pathways are modality-agnostic, meaning students can switch between online and offline engagement without disruption or loss of individualised instruction. This flexibility helps maintain academic consistency, inclusion, and learner autonomy regardless of their patterns of physical attendance (Pedro, 2019).

Figure 5. Learning analytics dashboard showing learner performance, engagement, predictive indicators, and personalized recommendations.

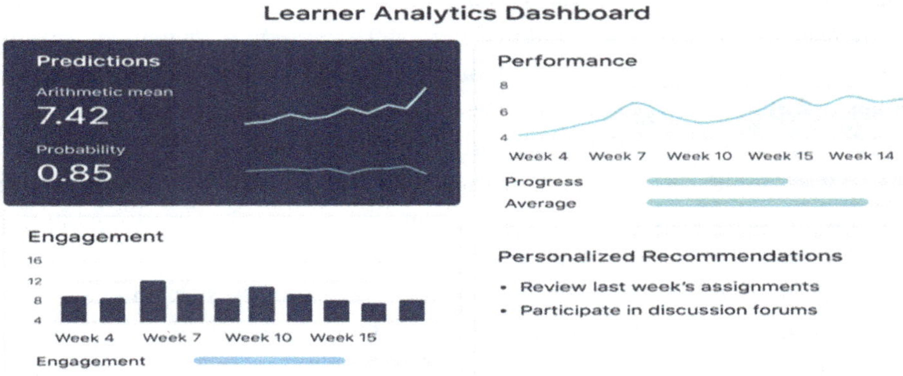

The learning analytics dashboard (Figure 5) is a visual summary of key data on a learner's progress, engagement, and performance in a digital learning environment. It provides information on course completion status, assessment levels, participation levels, and predictive risk warning indicators in a single interface, enabling instructors and learners to understand learning patterns quickly. The dashboard can provide timely feedback, personalised interventions, and informed decision-making by displaying real-time data in charts and visual cues. Altogether, the dashboard shows how learning analytics can convert raw learner data into insights that can be applied in HyFlex learning to improve engagement, self-regulation, and academic achievement.

6 ENHANCING ENGAGEMENT AND STUDENT SUCCESS

Student engagement and educational outcomes remain the primary focus in the HyFlex learning environment, where students participate in various ways, including on-campus, synchronous online, and asynchronous online interactions. Nevertheless, this may prove complicated, as instructors must maintain a steady level of engagement and provide accommodations for learners across these modalities, which is especially difficult when a teacher does not have a real-time view of their students. The solution here is the use of AI-powered learning analytics, which can make the engagement between learners more measurable, interpretable, and actionable, which will in turn allow the institutions and instructors to develop interventions that can impact the motivations, participation, and performance of students in a substantially meaningful manner (Siemens, 2013).

Real-time monitoring of learners' behaviour is one of the main ways analytics will enhance engagement. Data captured in modern learning management systems (LMS) with analytics dashboards includes time spent on tasks, login frequency, attendance, forum activity, and assignment status. These analytics indicators show signs of disengagement, which is an early warning to intervene before things go wrong. For example, the frequency of logging in and a decrease in interaction in discussions could indicate that a student is experiencing a problem or losing interest, and instructors could use this information to customise a learner (Ferguson, 2012). These insights are much harder to achieve in traditional classes, making analytics especially useful in digitally mediated, flexible environments.

The second valuable input of analytics to engagement is an early-warning system. These systems use predictive models to identify at-risk learners based on past and current information. If there is a risk to learners, e.g., when they are performing poorly or not participating enough, the system will notify the instructors or send individualised messages to the students. According to studies, early-warning interventions help increase retention and academic performance by responding to students in a timely manner and motivating them to reread course materials or seek help when needed (Clow, 2012). Student disengagement information is easily lost in the anonymity of the online environment, leading to recurring absenteeism in HyFlex environments. Early-warning systems help maintain learners' visibility and connectedness.

The analytics also enhance engagement with intelligent tutoring systems (ITS) and AI-based feedback systems. These systems offer assignments, quizzes, and practice activities to provide immediate and individualised feedback. Instead of being evaluated by an instructor, learners receive automated feedback that clarifies mistakes, offers hints, or suggests additional resources. Basic feedback improves motivation by strengthening progress and clearing up misunderstandings; this is especially helpful in asynchronous modes, where interaction between instructors and students is minimal (Fryer & Bovee, 2016). ITS devices mimic one-on-one tutoring sessions, which leads to greater satisfaction among learners and improved performance.

Along with automated feedback, analytics can be used to recommend content to users, personalised for them, as in the commercial recommendation systems of websites such as Netflix or Amazon. The AI algorithms identify learners' preferences and performance trends, as well as engagement behaviour, to recommend particular readings, videos, practice tasks, or discussion threads. The recommendations help students find relevant resources that align with their learning needs and interests (Ifenthaler & Yau, 2020). For example, when a learner has difficulty grasping a particular idea, they can be referred to brief explanatory videos, interactive simulations, or posts from peer discussions that explain the subject. Recommendation systems lead to more engagement and mastery by increasing the discoverability and relevance of learning material.

Gamification, supported by real-time data tracking, is another potent tool in which analytics can be used to enhance engagement. Gamified systems built on analytics give rewards (badges, points, or achievements) for quantifiable actions (quiz completion, interaction with peers, regular logins, etc.). Reward schemes can be adjusted for each learner based on their performance and provide encouraging feedback that helps maintain interest, because analytics enables these systems to track progress (Vijay & Jayan, 2023). Gamification has also been shown to enhance participation, endurance, and enjoyment, especially in online and asynchronous learning settings.

Additionally, analytics enhances participation by providing social learning insights that show students' interactions with one another. The patterns that can be revealed through social network analytics include central contributors in discussion forums, lonely learners who should be encouraged or groups of learners who engage in repeated collaborations (Dawson, 2010). These lessons can guide instructors to create learning communities that are more welcoming and supportive by promoting peer-to-peer discussion, group projects, or mentoring relationships. The high level of social presence is one of the most relevant predictors of engagement with HyFlex and blended models, and analytics offers a systematic means to enhance it.

Adaptive pacing also occurs in analytics, where learners can work at their own pace based on their understanding and motivation. Performance data analysed with AI can indicate to learners when to pause and reconsider foundational content, or when they are ready to tackle more complex content. Adaptive pacing is of interest because it minimises boredom among fast learners and frustration among slow learners, thereby facilitating the best possible learning experiences for all learners (Bloom, 1984). This is particularly essential in HyFlex classes, where students have diverse backgrounds, schedules, and learning styles.

The correlation between analytics and student achievement is also of great importance. By tracking trends among high-performing students, the institution will be able to identify behaviours associated with high performance, including regular study time, punctuality in submitting assignments, attendance, and greater use of digital materials. The learning is applied to formulate success strategies and best-practice recommendations that may be offered to students in general. For example, dashboards can draw attention to successful learners, whose example may inspire others to work harder and deliver better outcomes (Brown et al., 2020).

Moreover, analytics contribute to success by facilitating instructors' decision-making. Educators will be able to receive in-depth information about learning issues, the timeframes during which students are not engaged, and the subjects that many of them struggle with. The information can be used to guide strategic instruction redesign, including changing content clarity, changing pacing, or adding more interactive activities. By minimising guesswork, instructor analytics helps educators with evidence-based information and can eventually enhance the quality of teaching and student outcomes (Usher et al., 2021).

Analytics also enhances equality in learning outcomes by helping identify underserved students through existing modalities or teaching techniques. For example, the results may show that asynchronous students perform poorly on quizzes or discuss less. In turn, this can be addressed by instructors heeding those groups by designing specific interventions, such as formative peer interaction or other formative assessments. On the same note, disparities across demographic groups can be detected through analytics, and institutions can then develop an equity-based approach to delivering fair and accessible services (Nachbauer & Kyriakides, 2020).

Last but not least, analytics makes one successful by encouraging self-regulated learning (SRL). Students can better understand their strengths and weaknesses when they are exposed to individualised dashboards that show their progress, engagement, and achievement trends. This transparency encourages reflection, goal establishment and redefined approaches- critical aspects of SRL. Studies show that students who use analytics dashboards tend to take ownership of their learning and are more likely to perform better, persevere, and even be satisfied (Zimmerman, 2002). In so doing, analytics not only informs institutional action but also empowers it.

Overall, AI-based learning analytics can enhance student engagement and achievement in HyFlex contexts through real-time tracking, early warning, personalised recommendations, adaptive feedback, gamification, social learning analytics, adaptive pacing, instructor decision support, and self-regulation. Analytics transforms visible, actionable HyFlex education into a responsive, equitable, and personalised learning ecosystem that supports learners across all modalities.

7 ETHICAL AND INSTITUTIONAL CONSIDERATIONS

Some of the most visible ethical issues in learning analytics are data privacy and confidentiality. The HyFlex learning settings leave a large digital footprint, including login history, behavioural data, assessment data, and interaction history. Despite these data being useful for improving teaching, questions about their accessibility, the duration for which they are held, and their management also arise. These two learning institutions should comply with data protection regulations and have effective data governance policies that emphasise learners' privacy and informed consent

(Slade & Prinsloo, 2013). The openness of data use is one of the main factors that help students become credible and develop a positive attitude towards analytics tools.

The role of ethical governance in learning analytics has been addressed as a novel trend that will enable transparency, informed consent, accountability and learner-centred design. Researchers say that compliance-only strategies should no longer be adopted in institutions; instead, value-based governance models that facilitate trust, fairness, and the responsible use of learners' data should be adopted, especially in digitally intensive HyFlex learning environments (Prinsloo & Slade, 2017; Slade et al., 2022).

The application of learning analytics and adaptive learning pathways to HyFlex education is a complex area, with many ethical and internal implications beyond technical implementation. Even though analytics-based systems can offer personalised assistance and prompt intervention, they raise issues of data privacy, learner autonomy, transparency, and accountable management. The analytics of learning used in HyFlex institutions, where learning information is continuously generated across various digital platforms, are intended to support learning development and balance. These ethical and institutional aspects facilitate learning analytics practices essential to ensuring the sustainability of learning analytics, inclusiveness, and pedagogy.

Privacy is also closely related to student consent and student agency. Without notifying students about the data collected, the purpose of the collection, and how the data will be used, ethical learning analytics is impossible. Consent mechanisms within the HyFlex environment, where learners can communicate through various platforms, should be explicit, concise, and relevant. It is the students' privilege to be aware of the consequences of analytics and, in other cases, of the absence of certain types of data surveillance, which can be disadvantageous to their studies. Providing learners with access to their data aligns with self-regulated learning and ethical digital pedagogy (Prinsloo & Slade, 2016).

The other critical ethical issue is the fairness of algorithms. AI-based analytics systems generate predictions and recommendations based on past events. When the underlying data are biased (e.g., socioeconomic status, language ability, access to technology and analytics systems), they can become an unwanted source of inequity. For example, predictive models can misclassify certain groups of learners as at risk because of non-academic factors that lead to miscommunication or incorrect measures (Holmes et al., 2022). In other HyFlex cohorts, analytics algorithms should be regularly reviewed by institutions to ensure they are both fair, valid, and context-sensitive.

The explainability and transparency of analytics systems are also critical ethical issues. Algorithms or black-box predictions that cannot be explained may also lower the trust in the learners. Students would feel unsafe following suggestions they do not comprehend, and teachers would also be reluctant to use analytics-driven insights if they do not understand how the conclusions are drawn. Ethical learning analytics fosters explainable AI, in which results are understandable and accompanied by contextual explanations to enable informed decisions (Ifenthaler & Schumacher, 2016). Openness enhances acceptability and proper use of analytics tools.

Capacity building and faculty preparedness are major issues at the institutional level. The efficient application of learning analytics involves instructors interpreting data, developing adaptive interventions and integrating analytics knowledge into teaching practice. However, not all teachers undergo training in data literacy and analytics-based teaching. Unless analytics dashboards are interpreted and professionally developed, and supported by professional development, their potential impact on student success may be low (West et al., 2016). Institutions are required to invest in faculty lifelong learning and other forms of support to ensure that the use of analytics aligns with pedagogical goals rather than being driven by technical complexity.

The institution's policies also play a major role in promoting the use of ethical analytics. It requires explicit policies that define data ownership, access rights, permissible use, and accountability. Governance structures must exist to define who will govern the analytics systems, address ethical concerns, and handle unexpected results. The coordinated institutional control is particularly important in HyFlex environments, where data moves between different digital platforms. The required leadership skills are ethical, ensuring that analytics projects are aligned with institutional values and do not harm learners (Drachsler & Greller, 2016).

Automation versus human judgment is another aspect to consider. Even though AI-based analytics can be effective at discovering patterns and predicting success, professional knowledge and situational awareness cannot be replaced. Overreliance on automated decision-making is likely to reduce learners to data and overlook qualitative variables (motivation, personal situation, emotional health, etc.). Ethical implementation focuses on human-in-the-loop models, where analytics is used as an aid to decision-makers, not as a decision-maker in instruction and advising (Siemens, 2013). The balance preserves the human element of learning while leveraging AI assets.

Access and digital equity are also ethical issues that are problematic in HyFlex learning. Digital tools and connectivity are also other assumptions of learning analytics systems, which are not always accessible to learners. Low-tech students can produce biased or incomplete data, which may affect the quality of analytics and subsequent intervention steps. The institutions are expected to take contextual inequalities into account when interpreting the analytical outputs and develop inclusive approaches to mitigate the drawbacks of access (Resta & Laferriere, 2008). Equity-based analytics ensure that support systems are sensitive to learners' diversity and do not fault them.

In addition, the institutions should be mindful of the mental impact of analytics on learners. Anxiety or pressure associated with constant performance tracking and monitoring may also cause anxiety or even pressure among students in cases when the conclusions of the analytics become negative (Siddiqui et al., 2025). The delivery of analytics insights in supportive and developmental forms that foster growth, rather than surveillance, is an ethical practice. It should be grounded in positive framing and formative feedback, and empower learners so that it enhances motivation rather than demoralises students (Slade & Prinsloo, 2013).

Finally, there are long-term sustainability and institutional alignment. Learning analytics projects should not be implemented as isolated technologies, but as broader institutional strategies to foster the quality of teaching, student achievement, and digitalisation. Ethical sustainability means continuously monitoring analytics operations, engaging with stakeholders, and complying with evolving educational objectives. The needs of learners and the technologies in question require the institution to be flexible and to reexamine its policies and practices.

Finally, the responsible use of AI learning analytics in HyFlex settings may be informed by ethical and institutional considerations. Analytic-oriented systems will improve student achievement without harming it by addressing concerns about privacy, consent, fairness, transparency, faculty preparedness, governance, equity, and human-centred decision-making. Proper use of learning analytics can also be an efficient ethical tool that promotes inclusivity, builds trust, and establishes standards for the learning process within a flexible learning ecosystem.

8 FUTURE TRENDS IN AI-DRIVEN HYFLEX PEDAGOGY

The future of HyFlex pedagogy is closely linked to the development of artificial intelligence (AI), learning analytics, and educational data science. As higher education continues to transform toward more flexible, learner-centred models, AI-based systems will become the focus of instructional design, learner support, and institutional decision-making. Trends indicate that AI will not only assist with HyFlex learning but also alter how learning experiences are individually structured, assessed, and maintained across multiple modalities (Siemens, 2013).

Among the most evident trends in the future is the growth of predictive and prescriptive analytics. Although modern learning analytics primarily focuses on descriptive information, such as monitoring participation and performance, future systems will also be able to predict and prescribe interventions for learners. The complex machine learning models will be able to predict behavioural patterns that are often subtly manifested and lead to disengagement, and to offer proactive support solutions that are not only timely but also context-focused (Kovanović et al., 2019).

In HyFlex settings where learners' engagement modalities differ, predictive analytics will enable institutions to anticipate challenges before they affect learning outcomes.

The other trend involves incorporating generative AI into instructional design and feedback. It is believed that large language models and AI-based content generators will help instructors generate adaptive learning content, formative assessment, and scale-driven personalised feedback. Generative AI in HyFlex environments can dynamically adapt the material being taught to fit learners in alternative modalities, while remaining consistent and sensitive to individual learning requirements (Holmes et al., 2022). This change will reduce the instructor's workload and improve instructional responsiveness.

Another development of AI-driven pedagogy is hyper-personalisation. Future analytics systems will integrate cognitive, behavioural, and affective data to make learning paths more accurate. To illustrate, AI can adjust content difficulty based on learners' confidence, motivation, or emotional interest, rather than on performance measures. These emotionally sensitive analytics solutions can enhance learner satisfaction and persistence, especially in flexible learning contexts where students take greater control of their learning (Ifenthaler & Yau, 2020).

Lifelong and micro-credential learning, supported by learning analytics, is another emerging trend. With the adoption of modular learning, stackable credentials, and continuous professional development in higher education, analytics will not be limited to conventional degree programs. The AI systems will monitor learners' competencies across a variety of courses, platforms, and institutions and facilitate individualised upskilling. In HyFlex settings, learners can freely switch between online and face-to-face learning while maintaining a consistent learning history.

Another area of increased focus on the HyFlex pedagogy in the future will be multimodal learning analytics. Conventional analytics does not include a significant number of physical-classroom and video analytics, biometric sensors, and VR/AR technologies, which will be incorporated into future systems. For example, AI can be used to read facial expressions or voice patterns to determine engagement in synchronous sessions and supplement LMS data. Although these innovations deepen understanding of learning processes, they also introduce a new layer of ethical concerns regarding privacy and consent (Drachsler & Greller, 2016).

XAI will become increasingly important as more complex analytics systems are developed. Teachers and students will insist on the transparency of how AI systems generate predictions and recommendations. Elucidative analytical tools will deliver transparent displays and storytelling descriptions that will help stakeholders understand and have confidence in AI-based findings. Ethical adoption and productive pedagogical integration in HyFlex settings will depend on this transparency (Ifenthaler & Schumacher, 2016).

Another future trend is the intensification of AI-assisted faculty decision systems. The analytics dashboards will be redesigned as intelligent decision support systems that provide pedagogical advice, unlike the descriptive reporting functionality. For example, AI can propose alternative teaching ideas, redesign assessments, or interventions to engage learners based on real-time learner data. The systems will facilitate evidence-based teaching and maintain the instructor's freedom and professional judgment (West et al., 2016).

It is also expected to develop learning analytics ecosystems. Instead of functioning as standalone aids, the future analytics will exist as a network of interdependent ecosystems that incorporate LMS platforms, student information systems, advising services, and institutional research units. This comprehensive method will help institutions integrate HyFlex pedagogy into larger student success, retention, and quality assurance programs. The scalability and sustainability of analytics-driven innovation will improve through cross-system integration (Clow, 2012).

Moreover, AI-based HyFlex pedagogy will become more learner-centric and self-regulated. Complex dashboards will help learners set goals, track progress, and reflect on results across modalities. Analytics will reinforce learners' agency and sense of responsibility by enabling them to see and act within the learning process. The most important qualities for achieving success in the flexible learning settings (Zimmerman, 2002). This change makes learners participants rather than passive consumers of analytics.

Lastly, the trends pointed to in the future highlight the need for ethically sound, policy-oriented innovation. As the field of AI technologies advances, institutions will require dynamic forms of governance that compromise innovation and ethical accountability. The ongoing assessment, stakeholder involvement, and alignment with educational values will play a key role in maintaining trust and ensuring that AI-driven HyFlex pedagogy benefits the overall mission of inclusive and high-quality education (Slade & Prinsloo, 2013).

Finally, the future of HyFlex AI-driven pedagogy is predictive intelligence, generative AI, hyper-personalisation, multimodal analytics, explainable systems, and ecosystems with learners at the forefront. All of these tendencies indicate a transition toward more receptive, data-driven, and ethically grounded learning strategies. Through the well-planned integration of AI solutions, institutions can turn the HyFlex learning model into a sustainable, inclusive, and future-proofed pedagogical approach.

9 CONCLUSION

The HyFlex learning model has transformed the externalities of higher education by providing flexibility and learner choice across physical and online learning; nonetheless, it has also necessitated novel pedagogical models to sustain academic success. This chapter offered a conceptual discussion of how learning analytics can be used to inform adaptive learning pathways in HyFlex education. The chapter connected the institutional processes of data with a learner-centred pedagogical design by incorporating the Learning Analytics Cycle (LAK Framework) and the Zimmerman model of Self-Regulated Learning. The analytics feedback process can also assist institutions in identifying the engagement trends, anticipating learning challenges, and taking timely actions to improve teaching efficiency and student performance (Clow, 2012; Ferguson, 2012). Learning analytics is thus a strategic institutional resource that transforms data into actionable information within HyFlex pedagogical systems.

On the part of the learners, the integration between analytics and Self-Regulated Learning (SRL) concepts help the learners track, analyse and adjust their learning activities in flexible modalities in a proactive manner. Setting goals, performance measures, and reflection are key components of self-regulation that are essential to success in HyFlex environments and are supported by analytics-grounded dashboards and personalised feedback systems (Zimmerman, 2002). The hybrid LAK-SRL model highlights the two-faceted nature of adaptation: institutionally initiated interventions are receptive to supporting learner behaviour, and the exchange of information among learners yields data that is continually refined (Greller & Drachsler, 2012). When applied ethically and transparently, AI-based learning analytics would promote learner agency, institutional responsiveness, and sustainable educational quality within a flexible institution of higher learning (Slade & Prinsloo, 2013).

The question of how learning analytics and artificial intelligence may be merged, what is referred to as ethical-by-design models, and how learning systems can be learner-centred to enable HyFlex learning to be sustainable and inclusive, can also be explored in future research (Gašević, 2015).

REFERENCES

Bloom, B. S. (1984). The 2 sigma problem: The search for methods of group instruction as effective as one-to-one tutoring. *Educational Researcher, 13*(6), 4–16. DOI: 10.3102/0013189X013006004

Bond, M., Buntins, K., Bedenlier, S., Zawacki-Richter, O., & Kerres, M. (2020). Mapping research in student engagement and educational technology in higher education: A systematic evidence map. *International Journal of Educational Technology in Higher Education, 17*(1), 2. DOI: 10.1186/s41239-019-0176-8

Brown, M., McCormack, M., Reeves, J., Brook, D. C., Grajek, S., Alexander, B., & Weber, N. (2020). *2020 educause horizon report teaching and learning edition.* Educause., https://www.learntechlib.org/p/215670/

Clow, D. (2012, April). The learning analytics cycle: closing the loop effectively. *In Proceedings of the 2nd international conference on learning analytics and knowledge* (pp. 134-138). DOI: 10.1145/2330601.2330636

Dawson, S. (2010). 'Seeing'the learning community: An exploration of the development of a resource for monitoring online student networking. *British Journal of Educational Technology, 41*(5), 736–752. DOI: 10.1111/j.1467-8535.2009.00970.x

Drachsler, H., & Greller, W. (2016, April). Privacy and analytics: it's a DELICATE issue a checklist for trusted learning analytics. In *Proceedings of the sixth international conference on learning analytics & knowledge* (pp. 89-98). DOI: 10.1145/2883851.2883893

Eom, S. (2023, May). A Digital Distance Learning Critical Success Factors Model for Conducting Learning Analytics Research. In *International Conference on Decision Support System Technology* (pp. 277-286). Cham: Springer Nature Switzerland. DOI: 10.1007/978-3-031-32534-2_20

. Ferguson, R. (2012). Learning analytics: drivers, developments and challenges. *International journal of technology enhanced learning,* 4(5-6), 304-317. DOI: 10.1504/IJTEL.2012.051816

Ferguson, R., Hoel, T., Scheffel, M., & Drachsler, H. (2016). Guest editorial: Ethics and privacy in learning analytics. *Journal of Learning Analytics, 3*(1), 5–15. DOI: 10.18608/jla.2016.31.2

Fryer, L. K., & Bovee, H. N. (2016). Supporting students' motivation for e-learning: Teachers matter on and offline. *The Internet and Higher Education, 30*, 21–29. DOI: 10.1016/j.iheduc.2016.03.003

Holmes, W., Porayska-Pomsta, K., Holstein, K., Sutherland, E., Baker, T., Shum, S. B., Santos, O. C., Rodrigo, M. T., Cukurova, M., Bittencourt, I. I., & Koedinger, K. R. (2022). Ethics of AI in education: Towards a community-wide framework. *International Journal of Artificial Intelligence in Education*, *32*(3), 504–526. DOI: 10.1007/s40593-021-00239-1

Ifenthaler, D., & Schumacher, C. (2016). Student perceptions of privacy principles for learning analytics. *Educational Technology Research and Development*, *64*(5), 923–938. DOI: 10.1007/s11423-016-9477-y

Ifenthaler, D., & Yau, J. Y. K. (2020). Utilising learning analytics to support study success in higher education: A systematic review. *Educational Technology Research and Development*, *68*(4), 1961–1990. DOI: 10.1007/s11423-020-09788-z

Kovanović, V., Joksimović, S., Poquet, O., Hennis, T., de Vries, P., Hatala, M., Dawson, S., Siemens, G., & Gašević, D. (2019). Examining communities of inquiry in Massive Open Online Courses: The role of study strategies. *The Internet and Higher Education*, *40*, 20–43. DOI: 10.1016/j.iheduc.2018.09.001

Matcha, W., Uzir, N. A. A., Gašević, D., & Pardo, A. (2019). A systematic review of empirical studies on learning analytics dashboards: A self-regulated learning perspective. *IEEE Transactions on Learning Technologies*, *13*(2), 226–245. DOI: 10.1109/TLT.2019.2916802

Nachbauer, M., & Kyriakides, L. (2020). A review and evaluation of approaches to measure equity in educational outcomes. *School Effectiveness and School Improvement*, *31*(2), 306–331. DOI: 10.1080/09243453.2019.1672757

Pedro, F., Subosa, M., Rivas, A., & Valverde, P. (2019). Artificial intelligence in education: Challenges and opportunities for sustainable development. https://hdl.handle.net/20.500.12799/6533

Prinsloo, P., & Slade, S. (2016). Big data, higher education and learning analytics: Beyond justice, towards an ethics of care. In *Big data and learning analytics in higher education: Current theory and practice* (pp. 109–124). Springer International Publishing., DOI: 10.1007/978-3-319-06520-5_8

Prinsloo, P., & Slade, S. (2017, March). An elephant in the learning analytics room: The obligation to act. In *Proceedings of the seventh international learning analytics & knowledge conference* (pp. 46-55).

Resta, P., & Laferrière, T. (2008). Issues and challenges related to digital equity. *International handbook of information technology in primary and secondary education,* 765-778. DOI: 10.1007/978-0-387-73315-9_44

Schumacher, C., & Ifenthaler, D. (2018). Features students really expect from learning analytics. *Computers in Human Behavior, 78*, 397–407. DOI: 10.1016/j.chb.2017.06.030

Siddiqui, M., Hussain, S. A., Saleemi, H., & Fatmi, K. (2025). The Intersection of AI Educational Psychology and Learning Analytics Predicting Student Dropout Risk through Behavioural Indicators. *The Critical Review of Social Sciences Studies, 3*(3), 104–120. DOI: 10.59075/k2zgws84

Siemens, G. (2013). Learning analytics: The emergence of a discipline. *The American Behavioral Scientist, 57*(10), 1380–1400. DOI: 10.1177/0002764213498851

Slade, S., & Prinsloo, P. (2013). Learning analytics: Ethical issues and dilemmas. *The American Behavioral Scientist, 57*(10), 1510–1529. DOI: 10.1177/0002764213479366

Usher, M., Hershkovitz, A., & Forkosh-Baruch, A. (2021). From data to actions: Instructors' decision making based on learners' data in online emergency remote teaching. *British Journal of Educational Technology, 52*(4), 1338–1356. DOI: 10.1111/bjet.13108

Viberg, O., Hatakka, M., Bälter, O., & Mavroudi, A. (2018). The current landscape of learning analytics in higher education. *Computers in Human Behavior, 89*, 98–110. DOI: 10.1016/j.chb.2018.07.027

Vijay, M., & Jayan, J. P. (2023, August). Evolution of research on adaptive gamification: A bibliometric study. In 2023 *International Conference on Circuit Power and Computing Technologies* (ICCPCT) (pp. 1062-1070). IEEE. DOI: 10.1109/ICCPCT58313.2023.10245165

West, D., Huijser, H., & Heath, D. (2016). Putting an ethical lens on learning analytics. *Educational Technology Research and Development, 64*(5), 903–922. DOI: 10.1007/s11423-016-9464-3

Zimmerman, B. J. (2002). Becoming a Self-Regulated Learner: An Overview. *Theory into Practice, 41*(2), 64–70. DOI: 10.1207/s15430421tip4102_2

Chapter 14
Student Voices and Experiences:
Co-Designing an AI-Based HyFlex Learning System

Ahmad Maulana Ulumuddin
http://orcid.org/0009-0000-3623-6128
Universitas Esa Unggul, Indonesia

Binastya Anggara Sekti
http://orcid.org/0000-0001-5489-4888
Universitas Esa Unggul, Indonesia

ABSTRACT

This chapter presents an exploration of AI-powered HyFlex learning environments to enhance student engagement and participation. The authors examine the integration of artificial intelligence tools in co-designing flexible learning experiences that accommodate both in-person and remote learners. Through qualitative analysis of student voices and experiences, the chapter highlights strategies for personalized and adaptive learning, the impact of AI on collaborative learning, and challenges in implementing HyFlex systems. Findings provide actionable insights for educators and institutions seeking to optimize hybrid learning models using AI technologies.

INTRODUCTION

The COVID-19 pandemic accelerated the digital transformation of education, forcing institutions to adopt hybrid and online learning models. One prominent model is HyFlex (Hybrid-Flexible) learning, which allows students to choose between

DOI: 10.4018/979-8-3373-6182-6.ch014

face-to-face, synchronous online, or asynchronous participation depending on their needs and circumstances (Beatty, 2019). This flexibility supports diverse learning preferences and improves accessibility in higher education. However, maintaining student engagement across multiple learning modalities remains a major challenge. (Baker and Smith, 2025).

To address this challenge, many institutions have begun integrating Artificial Intelligence (AI) into HyFlex learning environments. AI technologies such as intelligent chatbots, adaptive learning systems, and learning analytics tools can personalize learning experiences, provide real-time assistance, and help educators monitor student engagement (Holmes et al., 2021). These technologies offer opportunities to improve learning effectiveness and support data-driven instructional strategies. Nevertheless, the effectiveness of AI integration depends not only on technological capability but also on how well these systems align with students' needs and experiences.(Mahrishi *et al.*, 2025).

Despite the growing adoption of AI in education, student perspectives are often overlooked in the design of AI-enhanced learning systems. Many educational technologies are developed primarily from the perspectives of educators or system developers, with limited direct involvement from students as end users. As a result, these systems may fail to fully address issues such as usability, accessibility, and motivation in real learning contexts (Castañeda & Williamson, 2021). Including student perspectives is therefore essential for ensuring that educational technologies effectively support learning processes and equitable access.(Mentzer *et al.*, 2025).

Co-design approaches provide a promising strategy for addressing this issue. Through participatory design processes, students can contribute feedback, share experiences, and collaborate in developing solutions that reflect real learning needs and contexts. Such collaboration helps improve the relevance and effectiveness of educational technologies while empowering students as active participants in shaping their learning environments.(Xiao, Yang and Li, 2025)

This chapter examines how student voices can contribute to the co-design of AI-powered HyFlex learning environments. By analyzing student experiences, existing studies, and emerging practices, the chapter explores the challenges students face and how AI technologies can better support inclusive and adaptive learning systems. These insights aim to guide educators, technology developers, and policymakers in designing future HyFlex models that are both technologically innovative and learner-centered.(Sarchet *et al.*, 2025)

Although research on HyFlex learning and AI in education has grown rapidly, important gaps remain. Many studies focus on technological capabilities or instructional strategies, while fewer examine how students can actively participate in designing AI-supported learning environments. This gap is important because students possess unique insights into usability, accessibility, and motivation that may not be fully visible to instructors or system developers.

To address this gap, this chapter adopts a student-centered perspective by exploring how student experiences and perspectives can inform the development of AI-powered HyFlex systems. By emphasizing participatory design and co-creation, the chapter contributes to the growing discussion on human-centered educational technology and highlights the importance of integrating student voices into the development of future AI-enhanced learning environments. (Sarchet *et al.*, 2025)

2. HYFLEX LEARNING AND AI INTEGRATION: AN OVERVIEW

HyFlex (Hybrid-Flexible) learning is an instructional model that combines face-to-face and online learning, allowing students to choose their mode of participation: in-person, synchronous online, or asynchronous learning. The core principles of HyFlex include learner choice, equivalency of learning outcomes, reusability of learning materials, and accessibility (Beatty, 2019). This model has become increasingly relevant in post-pandemic higher education as students demand more flexible and personalized learning pathways. However, maintaining consistent engagement and learning effectiveness across multiple modalities remains a significant challenge. (Dela Cruz and Dela Cruz, 2026)

Artificial Intelligence (AI) plays an important role in addressing these challenges by enhancing the adaptability of HyFlex environments. AI technologies such as intelligent chatbots, adaptive learning platforms, and learning analytics systems can personalize learning experiences, automate routine tasks, and provide real-time feedback for students and instructors (Holmes et al., 2021). These tools help educators monitor student engagement and support data-driven instructional decisions, contributing to more responsive and inclusive learning environments. (Castillo *et al.*, 2026)

Several AI-based tools have been implemented to support flexible learning systems. Chatbots and conversational AI technologies can assist students by answering questions and clarifying concepts outside classroom hours. Learning analytics platforms can monitor student participation and identify engagement patterns, while adaptive learning systems deliver personalized content based on individual learning progress. Together, these technologies contribute to more dynamic and responsive learning environments that support diverse learning needs.(Reina-Parrado, Román-Graván and Hervás-Gómez, 2026)

Despite these advantages, integrating AI into HyFlex environments requires careful consideration. Issues such as data privacy, algorithmic bias, and accessibility must be addressed to ensure that AI systems promote fairness and inclusivity. Therefore, the implementation of AI should align with institutional pedagogical goals and the broader educational context. (Sagredo-Gallardo *et al.*, 2026)

Figure 1. AI Integration Across HyFlex Learning Modes

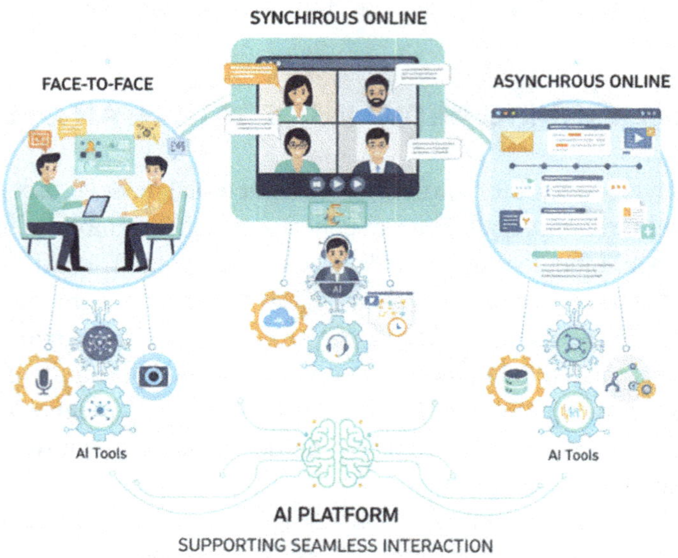

Source: Developed by the authors.

Table 1. Comparison of AI Tools Supporting HyFlex Learning

Tool Type	Function	Example Tools	Application in HyFlex
Chatbot	Real-time Q&A, concept clarification	Jill Watson, ChatGPT	24/7 academic support across all learning modes
Learning Analytics	Track performance, predict outcomes	Moodle Analytics, Canvas Insights	Monitor and adapt teaching based on learner data
Content Recommender	Personalized learning path	Knewton, Smart Sparrow	Deliver relevant materials in sync with learner pace
Virtual Lab/ Simulation	Practice-based environments	Labster, PhET	Asynchronous, self-directed hands-on experience
Voice/AI Assistants	Natural language interaction for navigation	Google Assistant, Alexa for Ed	Accessibility aid and voice-controlled learning tools

2.1 Definition and Basic Principles of HyFlex Learning

The HyFlex (Hybrid-Flexible) learning model combines online and face-to-face instruction within a single learning system, allowing students to select the participation mode that best suits their needs and circumstances. This flexibility enables students to continue learning despite constraints related to time, location, or personal responsibilities. As a result, HyFlex has evolved from a temporary solution during the pandemic into a long-term strategy for supporting flexible education. (Mahrishi *et al.*, 2025).

According to Beatty (2019), HyFlex is based on four main principles: learner choice, equivalency, reusability, and accessibility. Learner choice emphasizes students' ability to determine their preferred learning mode. Equivalency ensures that learning outcomes remain consistent regardless of participation mode. Reusability focuses on the efficient use of instructional materials across different learning formats, while accessibility ensures that all students can participate regardless of technical or physical limitations.(Romero-Hall *et al.*, 2025).

The implementation of HyFlex also reshapes the roles of educators and students. Educators must design learning experiences that are accessible and interactive across multiple platforms, while students are encouraged to take greater responsibility for managing their learning activities. This shift reflects a broader transition from teacher-centered instruction to learner-centered education. (Gloria and Pelayo, 2025).

Successful implementation of HyFlex requires strong institutional support, including reliable digital infrastructure, integrated learning platforms, and adaptive academic policies. Continuous professional development for educators is also necessary to ensure effective use of digital technologies and cross-modal learning strategies.(Barr and Luo, 2025)

Figure 2. Three-Mode Diagram in HyFlex Learning

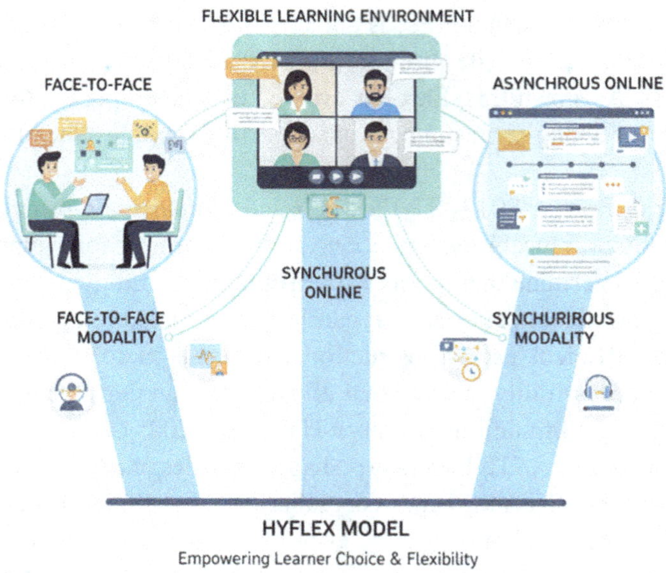

Source: Developed by the authors.

2.2 The Role of AI in Supporting Flexible Learning Modes

Artificial Intelligence (AI) strengthens the flexibility of HyFlex learning by supporting various learning modes through adaptive and data-driven technologies. In synchronous online learning environments, AI tools can assist communication and interaction through features such as automatic transcription, discussion moderation, and real-time feedback. (Namaziandost, 2025)

In asynchronous learning, AI systems can personalize learning experiences by analyzing student behavior data, including learning progress, activity frequency, and assessment results. Based on this analysis, AI can recommend additional learning materials or remedial activities tailored to individual student needs. This approach supports student-centered learning principles that are fundamental to HyFlex systems. (Lin, 2026).

Within face-to-face learning contexts, AI can function as an analytical tool that provides insights into classroom engagement and learning effectiveness. Learning analytics systems can help educators identify participation patterns and evaluate instructional strategies, allowing them to adjust teaching approaches based on evidence and data. (Saini *et al.*, 2025).

Overall, AI does not replace educators but rather enhances their ability to support students. By providing data-driven insights and personalized feedback, AI can help create more responsive and inclusive learning environments while maintaining the essential human dimension of education.(Khasawneh *et al.*, 2025).

Table 2. Examples of AI Tools in HyFlex Learning

Tool Name	Main Functions	Supported HyFlex Modes
ChatGPT	Answering conceptual questions	Synchronous & Asynchronous
Otter.ai	Automatic transcription of lecture sessions	Face-to-face & Synchronous
Squirrel AI	Material recommendations based on academic performance	Asinkron
FeedbackFruits	Analysis of discussion participation and feedback	All modes

Figure 3. Visualization of AI Utilization in LMS

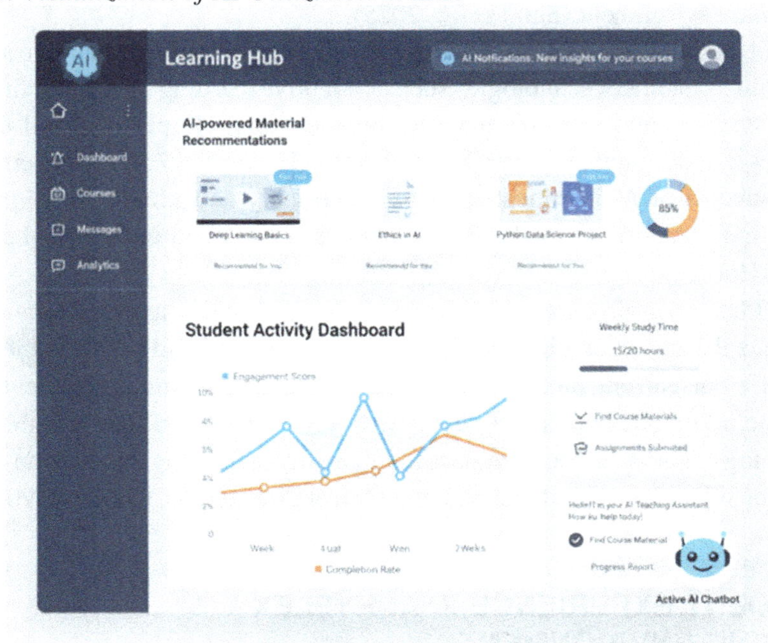

Source: Developed by the authors.

2.3 Strengths and Synergy Potential of HyFlex + AI

The integration of Artificial Intelligence and the HyFlex learning model creates a flexible and adaptive learning ecosystem. AI technologies help manage the complexity of multiple learning modes by analyzing student engagement and identifying learning difficulties in real time. These capabilities allow instructors to provide timely interventions and improve the overall effectiveness of learning processes.

AI also transforms instructional strategies by supporting dynamic learning management. Learning analytics systems can identify students who may require additional support, while recommender systems provide personalized learning resources based on student performance. AI-enhanced Learning Management Systems can further streamline administrative processes such as grading and performance reporting, allowing educators to focus more on mentoring and pedagogical design. (Khasawneh *et al.*, 2025).

Beyond operational efficiency, the synergy between AI and HyFlex can foster more inclusive and meaningful learning experiences. AI enables personalized learning pathways, while educators gain valuable insights for designing more effective instructional strategies. When implemented ethically and transparently, the integration of AI within HyFlex systems can support a more equitable and human-centered educational environment.(Saini *et al.*, 2025).

Recent studies highlight the growing role of AI in supporting adaptive and flexible learning systems. Technologies such as adaptive learning platforms, intelligent tutoring systems, and learning analytics tools can provide personalized feedback and support individualized learning pathways. However, researchers emphasize that the success of AI in education depends not only on technological innovation but also on its integration within pedagogical practices and institutional contexts. (Lan and Zhou, 2025).

In HyFlex environments, AI can support flexible participation by providing automated feedback, personalized content recommendations, and engagement analysis across different learning modes. Nevertheless, scholars also highlight potential challenges, including issues related to data privacy, transparency, and equitable access to technology. These factors demonstrate that successful implementation requires careful consideration of pedagogical and ethical dimensions. (Mnguni, 2025).

3. STUDENT EXPERIENCE IN AI-HYFLEX LEARNING ENVIRONMENTS

The implementation of AI-powered HyFlex learning has brought diverse experiences among students, shaped by their socio-cultural background, access to technology, and learning preferences. Students from urban institutions often express appreciation for AI tools such as automated grading systems and chatbots that provide 24/7 assistance (Liu et al., 2022). Meanwhile, students from rural or underserved regions highlight challenges such as limited internet access, difficulty navigating unfamiliar platforms, and a lack of support when AI tools malfunction or provide generic responses. These varied narratives emphasize the importance of context in understanding how students engage with AI-HyFlex systems.(Bhuiyan *et al.*, 2025)

Student preferences regarding learning modes vary significantly. While some learners favor face-to-face sessions for real-time interaction and motivation, others choose synchronous online modes for schedule flexibility without losing class engagement. A growing number of students prefer asynchronous learning to manage work-life balance, especially among adult learners and students with family responsibilities (Martin et al., 2020). AI plays a vital role here by supporting asynchronous learners through features such as adaptive video content, automated quizzes, and AI-curated learning paths tailored to individual pace and understanding.(Khan *et al.*, 2025)

Perceptions toward AI in education are mixed. Many students find AI chatbots helpful for basic questions, saving time compared to waiting for lecturer responses. Others appreciate personalized content recommendations that reduce cognitive load in selecting study materials (Chen et al., 2021). However, some students express skepticism, particularly when AI-generated feedback feels impersonal, unclear, or misaligned with their context. There is also concern that overreliance on AI tools could reduce human interaction and critical thinking. These perspectives underline the need for transparent and explainable AI, where students understand how and why decisions or recommendations are made.(Mnguni, 2025)

Students also face practical challenges in AI-HyFlex environments. Unstable internet connections, especially in remote regions, hinder real-time participation and access to AI-powered features such as video annotation tools or live adaptive quizzes. Digital literacy gaps create anxiety when navigating dashboards or interpreting AI feedback. Trust in AI systems also emerges as a key issue students report being unsure whether AI assessments are fair or whether chatbots can be relied on for academic accuracy (Selwyn & Jandrić, 2020). These obstacles suggest that institutional support, digital skill-building, and inclusive design are necessary to ensure AI-HyFlex systems benefit all learners equitably.(Neshaei *et al.*, 2025)

4. COLLABORATIVE DESIGN AND THE ROLE OF STUDENT VOICE

The concept of co-design in education emphasizes the active participation of end-users especially students in the design and development of learning environments and technologies. Co-design (or participatory design) recognizes students not merely as consumers of educational technology, but as co-creators who bring valuable insights from their lived experiences (DiSalvo et al., 2017). In the context of AI-HyFlex learning systems, where technological tools mediate core learning interactions, student input becomes critical to ensure that systems are responsive, inclusive, and contextually relevant.(Kim and Kwon, 2025)

Engaging students in co-design offers numerous benefits. First, it promotes user-centered development, aligning features with actual student needs rather than developer assumptions. Second, it enhances student agency, making learners feel heard and valued, which in turn can increase engagement and satisfaction (Bovill & Bulley, 2011). Third, it improves the quality and usability of educational tools, as students help identify pain points, suggest features, and test usability from real user perspectives. Finally, involving students in iterative design processes promotes equity, ensuring that solutions reflect the diversity of student backgrounds, digital access levels, and learning preferences.(Ambrosetti *et al.*, 2025)

Several real-world examples illustrate the impact of co-design in educational settings. At the University of Melbourne, the Students as Partners (SaP) initiative integrated students into course and technology design teams, leading to improved interface design and better-aligned learning analytics dashboards (Matthews et al., 2018). In Indonesia, a university piloted a chatbot-based academic advising system where students provided iterative feedback during development stages resulting in a system that better understood local language nuances and academic jargon. These cases show how student participation can refine both the technical accuracy and cultural usability of AI-supported tools.

Implementing student feedback effectively requires structured strategies. Open-ended surveys and focus groups are common entry points, but deeper engagement can be achieved through design sprints, joint workshops, or student advisory boards for technology development. Figure 3 illustrates a co-design loop that incorporates students throughout the development process from initial problem identification to prototyping and refinement. Table 3 outlines practical strategies to integrate student voice in different phases of AI-HyFlex system development.(Zhang and Qianjun, 2025)

5. AI TOOLS FOR ENGAGEMENT AND PERSONALIZATION

Artificial Intelligence (AI) has become a key enabler in promoting student engagement and learning personalization, especially in HyFlex environments where diverse learner needs must be addressed simultaneously. One of the most widely used AI tools is the educational chatbot, which functions as a 24/7 virtual assistant for students. These chatbots, powered by natural language processing (NLP), can provide instant answers to frequently asked questions, deliver content reminders, and even engage in basic tutoring (Winkler & Söllner, 2018). Notable examples include *Jill Watson*, *ChatGPT*, and institution-specific bots integrated into Learning Management Systems (LMS). When designed well, chatbots enhance accessibility, reduce instructor workload, and support learner autonomy.(Lin *et al.*, 2026)

Beyond simple query response, AI also drives content recommendation systems that adaptively suggest learning materials based on a student's interaction history, performance data, and declared preferences. These systems use machine learning algorithms to predict what type of content would be most effective for a given learner (Chen et al., 2021). For instance, a student struggling with a specific math concept might be recommended a visual explainer video, while another student may receive a quiz-based reinforcement module. This personalized learning pathway helps optimize study time and improves retention especially valuable in asynchronous HyFlex formats where guidance is often limited.(Dela Cruz and Dela Cruz, 2026)

Another transformative AI application is learning analytics, which collects and analyzes data from students' interactions with digital platforms. Through dashboards and predictive models, instructors can identify patterns of disengagement, knowledge gaps, or risk of dropout (Ifenthaler & Yau, 2020). In HyFlex settings, where students may interact differently across modalities, learning analytics serves as a unifying layer of insight bridging the online and in-person divide. For students, analytics-based feedback empowers them to monitor their progress, compare performance against class averages, and set improvement goals.

However, the integration of AI tools into educational settings is not without challenges. From a technical perspective, personalization models often struggle with data sparsity, especially for new or infrequent learners. Moreover, over-reliance on algorithmic decision-making can lead to filter bubbles, where students are only exposed to content similar to their past choices, limiting intellectual growth (Selwyn, 2022). From an ethical standpoint, AI tools collect vast amounts of personal and behavioral data, raising concerns around privacy, consent, and transparency. Students may not be fully aware of how their data is used or whether recommendations are based on pedagogical merit or platform optimization.

To maximize the positive potential of AI while mitigating its risks, institutions should adopt transparent policies, involve students in AI tool evaluation, and prioritize explainable and auditable systems. Figure 4 visualizes the interaction between key AI tools in a HyFlex learning cycle, while Table 4 provides a comparative overview of their functions, benefits, and associated risks.(Vassileva, Stanimirov and Miltenoff, 2026)

Figure 4. AI Tools Supporting Engagement and Personalization in HyFlex Learning

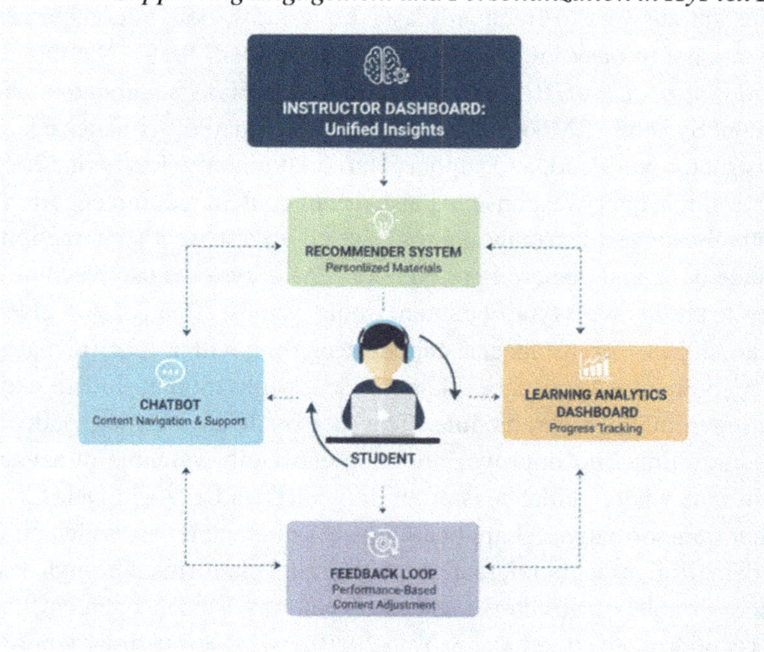

Source: Developed by the authors.

Table 3. Comparative Overview of AI Tools in HyFlex Learning

Tool	Function	Benefits	Risks/Challenges
Chatbot	Student Q&A, reminders, motivation	Real-time support, reduces staff load	Limited contextual understanding, user frustration
Recommender System	Suggest content based on preferences	Tailored learning path	Filter bubbles, overfitting user profiles
Learning Analytics	Monitor activity, predict engagement	Targeted interventions, early warnings	Privacy concerns, data misinterpretation
Feedback Generator	Automated response on assignments	Consistent grading, fast turnaround	Lack of nuance, potential demotivation

5.1 Chatbot Pembelajaran sebagai Pendamping Virtual

Educational chatbots are AI-powered automated systems designed to interact with students, answer academic inquiries, and support independent learning processes. In HyFlex environments where students may alternate between face-to-face, synchronous online, and asynchronous modes chatbots serve as consistent points of communication and guidance. Their presence bridges the gap in interaction that often occurs in online or self-paced learning, providing an accessible and responsive interface for academic support. By simulating human-like conversation through natural language processing *(NLP)*, chatbots foster a sense of social presence that can help sustain motivation and engagement in digital learning spaces.(Han, 2026)

Beyond simple question-and-answer functionality, chatbots can perform a variety of educational tasks that enhance the learning experience. They can clarify difficult concepts by providing examples or explanations tailored to a student's prior responses, remind students of upcoming deadlines, or share additional resources such as videos and readings related to current topics. More advanced chatbots, such as Jill Watson developed at Georgia Tech or ChatGPT, are capable of contextual understanding allowing them to respond to open-ended questions and guide students through problem-solving processes. In this sense, chatbots act not merely as digital assistants but as *virtual tutors* that complement the role of human instructors.

One of the most significant contributions of chatbots to HyFlex learning is their ability to provide continuous and equitable access to academic support. Students studying asynchronously, for instance, can interact with chatbots at any time, removing dependence on instructor availability. This feature democratizes access to information, especially for students in different time zones or with limited opportunities for face-to-face consultations. Moreover, chatbots can be programmed to accommodate multiple languages, ensuring inclusivity for diverse student populations. When integrated into institutional Learning Management Systems (LMS), chatbots also enable seamless communication by connecting with course databases, assignment records, and gradebooks.(Olivier and Weilbach, 2026)

However, while chatbots greatly enhance accessibility and engagement, they are not intended to replace human educators. Instead, they serve to extend the educator's reach by handling repetitive or administrative queries, freeing instructors to focus on mentorship, feedback, and critical instruction. The key to successful implementation lies in designing chatbots that are empathetic, context-aware, and transparent about their limitations. When aligned with pedagogical objectives, educational chatbots can cultivate more interactive, supportive, and humanized learning environments bridging the gap between automation and authentic educational experience.(Guatibonza Briceño *et al.*, 2026)

Figure 5. Student Interaction Scheme and Academic Chatbot

Source: Developed by the authors.

5.2 Recommendation Systems: Personalization Based on Preferences and Performance

Within the context of AI-driven learning environments, recommendation systems function as intelligent *learning assistants* that suggest relevant materials tailored to each student's individual needs. By analyzing academic performance, interaction data, and engagement patterns, these systems identify gaps in understanding and recommend resources that align with the learner's unique profile. For instance, if a student struggles with a particular concept in mathematics, the system might automatically suggest a remedial module, a short explanatory video, or an interactive quiz to reinforce comprehension. Through this adaptive mechanism, AI ensures that students receive the right content at the right time enhancing both efficiency and learning outcomes.

Beyond providing targeted resources, AI recommendation systems can foster deeper engagement and collaboration among learners. By examining behavioral and interest-based data, the system can recommend peer study partners with complementary strengths or connect students to relevant discussion forums where they can exchange insights and ask questions. This form of intelligent networking transforms the learning experience from a solitary activity into a dynamic, community-driven process. Furthermore, recommendation systems can adapt to evolving learning trajectories: as students progress and their performance data change, the system continuously refines its suggestions, ensuring that the learning path remains personalized and up to date.(Kim *et al.*, 2026)

In HyFlex learning settings, the role of recommendation systems becomes even more critical, as students often navigate between synchronous, asynchronous, and face-to-face modes. These systems help maintain continuity and coherence across modalities by tracking progress in one mode and adjusting recommendations in another. For example, a student who attends fewer live sessions may receive more interactive asynchronous materials, while those highly active in discussions may be encouraged toward in-depth readings or projects. By combining analytics, machine learning, and user modeling, recommendation systems contribute to a holistic learning ecosystem that promotes autonomy, adaptability, and sustained motivation key values at the heart of AI-integrated HyFlex education.(Dela Cruz and Dela Cruz, 2026)

5.3 Learning Analytics untuk Deteksi Dini dan Intervensi Proaktif

Learning analytics refers to the AI-driven process of collecting, analyzing, and interpreting data generated through students' interactions within digital learning environments. It encompasses various data points, including attendance, participation frequency, quiz results, discussion engagement, and even time spent on specific learning materials. By aggregating and interpreting this information, learning analytics provides a comprehensive overview of each student's learning behavior. Unlike traditional evaluation methods that rely on periodic assessments, learning analytics offers continuous monitoring and real-time insights, enabling educators to make data-informed decisions that directly impact student success.(Ajani, Gamede and Govender, 2026)

One of the most valuable applications of learning analytics lies in its ability to identify at-risk students early often before signs of academic decline become visible through conventional indicators. For example, if the system detects a consistent drop in a student's participation, delayed assignment submissions, or a downward trend in quiz performance, it can automatically alert the instructor or academic advisor. This early warning allows educators to intervene proactively, offering personalized guidance, supplementary materials, or one-on-one mentoring sessions. In some systems, AI can even generate automated feedback or motivational messages to re-engage the learner before disengagement deepens. This approach transforms assessment from a reactive process into a proactive strategy that supports student retention and achievement.

Furthermore, when integrated into HyFlex learning environments, learning analytics serves as a unifying mechanism that bridges data from multiple modes face-to-face, synchronous online, and asynchronous learning. Educators can use analytics dashboards to visualize participation patterns across these modalities, identifying which mode best supports each student's progress. Students themselves benefit from transparent feedback dashboards that allow them to track their learning goals, compare progress with peers, and reflect on their performance. This reciprocal flow of information fosters accountability and self-regulated learning. Ultimately, learning analytics not only enhances personalization through empirical data but also cultivates a culture of continuous improvement and collaborative responsibility between students and educators.(Mahmoud and Surwanti, 2026)

Figure 6. Learning Analytics Dashboard for Lecturers

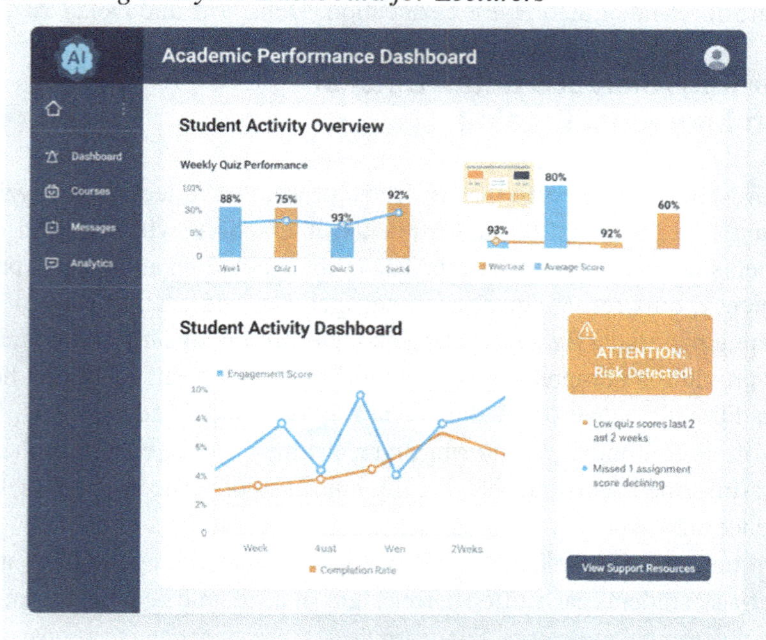

Source: Developed by the authors.

5.4 Ethical and Technical Challenges in Implementing AI Tools

While Artificial Intelligence (AI) offers immense potential to enhance engagement, personalization, and learning efficiency, its implementation in educational environments also introduces a complex set of ethical and technical challenges. The first and most pressing issue concerns data privacy and security. AI systems rely heavily on vast amounts of learner data ranging from academic performance records and behavioral analytics to biometric inputs such as facial expressions or voice patterns. Without proper safeguards, this data can be misused or exposed to breaches, compromising students' privacy and trust. Therefore, institutions must establish transparent policies regarding how data is collected, stored, shared, and analyzed. Ethical AI in education requires not only technical compliance with data protection standards but also a culture of accountability that respects students as data owners, not merely data sources.

Another major concern is algorithmic bias, which can undermine the fairness and inclusivity that AI systems aim to promote. Algorithms trained on biased datasets or developed without considering local and cultural diversity can inadvertently reinforce stereotypes or exclude underrepresented student groups. For example, an AI grading system trained on limited linguistic patterns might misinterpret essays written in non-native English, leading to unjust evaluations. Addressing bias requires intentional design choices such as using diverse datasets, conducting regular audits of AI models, and involving educators and students in evaluating system outputs. In an equitable learning ecosystem, fairness must be treated as a design principle not as an afterthought.(Ajani, Gamede and Govender, 2026)

From a pedagogical standpoint, over-personalization poses another risk in AI-based learning. While personalization can optimize learning experiences, excessive tailoring of content may lead to the creation of *filter bubbles*, where students are continuously exposed to materials that align only with their past interests or performance levels. This phenomenon limits intellectual curiosity and reduces opportunities for cognitive challenge and growth. To prevent this, educators and designers must balance personalization with exposure to diverse perspectives and learning materials. AI tools should be designed to encourage exploration and critical thinking, not merely to maximize comfort or efficiency. A truly educational AI system should promote curiosity, resilience, and adaptability.

Finally, technological accessibility and infrastructure disparities remain significant barriers to ethical AI implementation. Not all students have equal access to reliable internet connections, advanced devices, or digital literacy skills factors that can lead to unequal learning outcomes when AI tools are deployed. Moreover, educators themselves may face challenges in adapting to AI-based systems due to limited training or institutional support. Overcoming these barriers requires systemic investment in digital infrastructure, professional development, and inclusive policy frameworks. When implemented responsibly with transparency, fairness, and empathy AI has the potential to democratize education rather than deepen existing inequalities. The future of AI in HyFlex learning depends not only on technological advancement but also on the ethical maturity of the institutions that adopt it.(Mahmoud and Surwanti, 2026)

Figure 7. Ethical and Technical Challenges of AI Implementation in Education

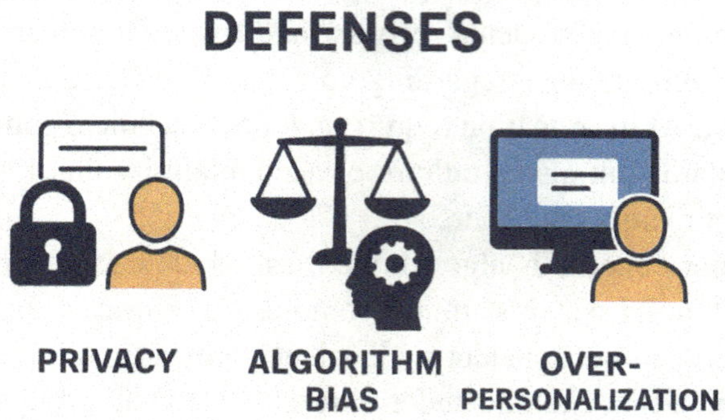

Source: Developed by the authors.

6. BARRIERS AND CHALLENGES IN AI-HYFLEX IMPLEMENTATION

Despite the many promises of AI-powered HyFlex learning, the implementation of such systems faces a multitude of barriers and challenges both systemic and technical. One of the most pressing issues is the digital divide: unequal access to reliable internet connections, computing devices, and power infrastructure. Students in remote or economically disadvantaged regions often struggle to participate in synchronous sessions or access AI-supported features such as automated assessments, video analytics, or adaptive content recommendations (UNESCO, 2021). This results in a two-tier learning experience, where students with better connectivity benefit more from technology-enhanced education.

In addition to infrastructure disparities, there are significant gaps in digital literacy among students. While digital natives are often assumed to be tech-savvy, the reality is more nuanced. Many students are familiar with social media or messaging apps but lack the skills to interpret analytics dashboards, interact meaningfully with learning chatbots, or manage their data privacy settings (van Laar et al., 2017). This digital literacy gap can cause frustration, reduce self-efficacy, and lead to disengagement particularly when AI tools are introduced without proper orientation or ongoing support.(Asamoah and Amarteifio, 2025)

Another challenge lies in the adaptability of instructors and education staff. Successful implementation of AI-HyFlex systems depends not only on student engagement but also on the ability of teachers to integrate AI tools into pedagogical strategies. However, many educators face steep learning curves, time constraints, or institutional inertia when transitioning to AI-enhanced teaching. Moreover, the lack of professional development in AI literacy among faculty results in underutilized tools or poorly aligned practices (Zawacki-Richter et al., 2019). Without buy-in and competence from educators, even the most advanced AI platforms may fail to improve learning outcomes.

Ethical concerns also emerge as a critical barrier in AI-HyFlex environments. Issues related to algorithmic fairness, transparency, and accountability are especially relevant when AI systems make decisions that affect student progress, assessment, or content exposure. Studies have shown that AI models trained on biased datasets may reinforce stereotypes or exclude minority learners from relevant opportunities (Binns, 2018). Furthermore, students may not understand how their data is collected or used, raising concerns about consent and surveillance. Addressing these risks requires clear ethical guidelines, explainable AI models, and participatory governance mechanisms in system development.

To fully realize the potential of AI-HyFlex learning, stakeholders must recognize and proactively address these multifaceted challenges. Figure 5 illustrates the interaction of key implementation barriers and their impact on different learner groups, while Table 5 provides a classification of common barriers and potential mitigation strategies.(Sagredo-Gallardo *et al.*, 2026)

7. FUTURE DIRECTIONS: TOWARD EMPATHETIC AND INCLUSIVE AI-HYFLEX SYSTEMS

As artificial intelligence (AI) technology evolves and the adoption of the HyFlex model increases in educational institutions, the future of learning systems demands a more empathetic, inclusive, and human-centered approach. Students are not just end users, but partners who have unique insights into what they need in a learning system. From the results of various field studies and reflections, many students expressed a desire for more personalized, supportive, and emotionally adaptive features, such as virtual tutors that can customize communication styles, AI-based self-reflection dashboards, and intelligent scheduling systems that take into account individual academic loads.

Future AI systems need to be able to respond to the diverse needs of students including those with accessibility barriers, certain mental health conditions, or different socio-cultural backgrounds. For example, students with disabilities may need an AI avatar that supports adaptive visual or audio communication. Likewise, students from remote areas can take advantage of the AI *content caching* system that works optimally even with a limited network. Human-AI collaboration should be a fundamental principle in the design of future systems, not just a replacement of teacher roles or a reduction in human contact. (Alsaiari *et al.*, 2025)

From an institutional and curriculum perspective, the empathetic and inclusive implementation of AI-HyFlex requires policy reform. The curriculum must open up space for flexible learning while still standardizing in quality. In addition, lecturer training should be focused not only on technical skills, but also on empathy-based pedagogic digital competencies (Gallardo-Echenique et al., 2021). Policy evaluation also needs to consider non-cognitive indicators such as learning well-being, perception of fairness, and student satisfaction in AI-based interactions.

As a development roadmap, future AI-HyFlex systems should adopt the principles of "Design for All" and strong AI ethics from the design process, testing, to implementation. Cross-role involvement (students, lecturers, developers, ethicists) will result in an equitable educational technology ecosystem. The following Figure 6 summarizes the pillars of the future-oriented AI-HyFlex system design, while Table 6 presents strategic recommendations in terms of features, policies, and stakeholder engagement.(Aditi and Gaurav, 2025)

7.1 Rekomendasi Fitur Masa Depan dari Perspektif Mahasiswa

As the primary users of HyFlex learning systems, students offer unique insights into the kinds of features needed to make these systems more human-centered, adaptive, and inclusive. Their perspectives highlight not only the importance of technological efficiency but also the emotional and psychological dimensions of learning. In a hybrid-flexible environment, where learners navigate between in-person, synchronous, and asynchronous modalities, students emphasize the value of systems that can respond intelligently to their individual rhythms and challenges. Their voices reveal a clear preference for features that enhance self-regulation, emotional well-being, and a sense of connection qualities that are often overlooked in purely technology-driven designs.

Based on interviews and small-scale surveys conducted with students from three Indonesian universities Universitas Indonesia (UI), Universitas Negeri Yogyakarta (UNY), and Universitas Negeri Makassar (UNM) several recurring feature requests emerged. Among the most desired innovations are smart notifications, virtual mentors, and learning mood trackers. Each of these features reflects a growing awareness among students that meaningful learning requires not only cognitive engagement but also emotional support and contextual awareness. By articulating these expectations, students contribute valuable guidance for the next generation of AI-based HyFlex systems that aim to balance intelligence with empathy.(Aditi and Gaurav, 2025)

The first proposed feature, smart notifications, represents a move toward *context-aware communication*. Unlike standard reminders, smart notifications would adapt to students' schedules, workload, and engagement levels. For example, the system might postpone non-urgent alerts when it detects prolonged activity or stress indicators, or suggest breaks during extended study sessions. This kind of personalized nudging helps students manage cognitive load, avoid burnout, and maintain productivity without feeling overwhelmed. When implemented ethically, such notifications could act as subtle digital companions encouraging balance and well-being rather than adding pressure.

The second major recommendation involves virtual mentors, or emotionally intelligent chatbots that can provide both academic and affective support. Unlike conventional chatbots that focus solely on answering content-related questions, virtual mentors would be equipped with *sentiment analysis* and *contextual understanding* to detect emotional cues such as frustration, confusion, or fatigue. They could respond with empathy, suggest relaxation techniques, or connect students to counseling resources when needed. Academically, these mentors could also help students plan their study routines, set realistic goals, and monitor progress over time. Such integration of emotional intelligence into AI systems aligns with the broader educational goal of promoting holistic student development.

Lastly, students expressed enthusiasm for a "learning mood tracker" a feature designed to record psychological states and adapt learning activities accordingly. By allowing students to log or automatically detect mood fluctuations, this tool could personalize workload distribution, suggest lighter content on stressful days, or recommend group collaboration when motivation is low. Over time, mood tracking could provide valuable data for both learners and instructors, helping identify patterns between emotional well-being and academic performance. This approach redefines personalization beyond cognitive metrics, positioning emotional awareness as an essential part of adaptive learning design. Together, these student-driven ideas envision a future where AI-HyFlex systems are not only *smart* but also *sensitive*, capable of understanding learners as whole individuals mind, body, and emotion. (Lin and Kuo, 2025)

7.2 AI Systems Responsive to Diverse Learner Needs

One of the most pressing challenges in developing digital and AI-based learning systems lies in ensuring inclusivity for diverse and vulnerable student groups. While technology promises to democratize education, its benefits are not evenly distributed students with disabilities, those from remote or underprivileged areas, and those with special learning needs often remain marginalized. For these learners, barriers such as connectivity, accessibility, and language differences can significantly limit participation in HyFlex environments. Therefore, the next generation of AI-based educational systems must go beyond efficiency and personalization to actively address diversity, equity, and inclusion as core design priorities rather than supplementary features.

A key foundation for inclusivity is universal accessibility. Future AI-HyFlex systems should be designed following the principles of *Universal Design for Learning (UDL)*, ensuring that every student regardless of physical, sensory, or cognitive condition can engage fully with the material. Technologies such as text-to-speech, automatic captioning, and voice-based navigation are essential for students with visual or hearing impairments. AI can further enhance accessibility by dynamically adjusting font sizes, color contrasts, or reading speeds based on individual user preferences. In this way, AI functions as an enabler of equity, creating environments where technology adapts to humans, not the other way around.(Alsaiari *et al.*, 2025)

Equally important is cultural and linguistic personalization, which recognizes that learning is deeply shaped by language, identity, and social context. Many educational platforms remain dominated by global or English-centric content, which can alienate students whose first language differs from the medium of instruction. AI-powered translation and localization tools can mitigate this gap by delivering materials in students' native languages or culturally familiar formats. Moreover, adaptive systems could incorporate local examples, idioms, and contextual references, ensuring that learning content resonates with each learner's background. Such personalization not only improves comprehension but also fosters a sense of belonging and respect for cultural diversity within global digital classrooms.(Lin and Kuo, 2025)

Another vital consideration is low-bandwidth adaptability, especially for students in regions with unstable internet access or limited infrastructure. AI can optimize the delivery of educational materials by compressing data, prioritizing text-based or audio alternatives, and enabling offline synchronization when connectivity is restored. For instance, an AI system could detect a weak connection and automatically switch to a lightweight interface, offering downloadable content or asynchronous interaction options. This feature is particularly crucial in developing countries, where disparities in digital access often translate into educational inequities. A responsive AI system should therefore guarantee that learning remains uninterrupted regardless of bandwidth conditions or device limitations.

Ultimately, building an AI system responsive to diverse learner needs requires a shift in design philosophy from technology-centered to human-centered. Institutions, educators, and developers must collaborate to ensure that empathy, ethics, and equity guide every stage of innovation. Accessibility features, cultural sensitivity, and technological flexibility should not be treated as optional add-ons but as fundamental indicators of quality in modern education. When AI systems are inclusive by design, they move beyond mere efficiency to embody the true purpose of education: empowering all learners, regardless of their background or circumstance, to participate meaningfully in the pursuit of knowledge.(Sheng *et al.*, 2025)

7.3 Implikasi bagi Desain Kurikulum dan Kebijakan Institusi

Achieving an empathetic and inclusive AI-HyFlex learning system requires not only technological innovation but also a strong institutional framework that integrates policy, pedagogy, and ethics. While AI can optimize teaching and learning processes, its true impact depends on how well institutions align their curriculum design, governance structures, and professional development programs with principles of inclusivity and human-centered education. A technology-driven approach alone is insufficient; institutional reform must ensure that AI integration serves pedagogical goals rather than replacing them. This calls for universities and policymakers to rethink existing educational models, ensuring that flexibility, fairness, and ethical responsibility become structural components of digital transformation.

The first key implication lies in curriculum adaptability, particularly through the adoption of competency-based education (CBE) frameworks. Traditional credit systems that rely on seat time or rigid semester schedules are increasingly incompatible with the personalized, self-paced nature of HyFlex and AI-enhanced learning. A competency-based model allows students to progress according to mastery rather than attendance, supported by AI systems that track learning outcomes and recommend appropriate learning resources. Such a framework empowers students to take ownership of their learning while enabling educators to provide differentiated support. Moreover, adaptive curricula can better accommodate diverse learning paces and contexts, fostering equity without compromising academic rigor.(Alsaiari *et al.*, 2025)

The second major consideration involves data privacy and AI ethics policies, which must be clearly articulated and communicated to all stakeholders especially students. As AI systems collect vast amounts of behavioral and performance data, institutions bear a moral and legal obligation to ensure transparency about how such data is used, stored, and shared. Students should have the right to informed consent, the ability to access their own data records, and the assurance that algorithms used in assessment or personalization are subject to ethical review. Establishing institutional ethics boards or AI oversight committees can help maintain accountability and prevent misuse. Ethical governance should not only comply with existing data protection laws but also cultivate trust between learners and educational institutions.

A third critical aspect concerns faculty training and professional development. Instructors play a central role in mediating the relationship between students and technology. Yet many educators still face significant challenges in adapting to AI-driven environments due to limited technical confidence or pedagogical preparation. Institutions must therefore move beyond basic ICT training to include digital pedagogical literacy, focusing on how to integrate AI tools meaningfully into instructional design, feedback systems, and assessment strategies. This shift requires continuous learning opportunities, cross-disciplinary collaboration. (Aditi and Gaurav, 2025)

7.4 Pilar Desain Sistem AI-HyFlex Empatik

As a concluding reflection, the development of an empathic AI-HyFlex learning system must be grounded in a clear ethical and human-centered design framework. Empathy in educational technology is not merely about user satisfaction it represents a commitment to understanding learners' experiences, emotions, and contexts. An empathic system recognizes that education is both a cognitive and emotional process, requiring balance between efficiency and care. Therefore, the design of such systems should rest on four foundational pillars: Human-Centeredness, Cultural Awareness, Accessibility, and Transparency. These pillars serve as guiding principles to ensure that technological innovation remains aligned with human values, promoting fairness, inclusion, and trust.

The first pillar, Human-Centered Design, emphasizes that AI in education must begin with and revolve around the learner's experience. Rather than focusing solely on automation or data analytics, human-centered design prioritizes empathy-driven development understanding how students think, feel, and interact in hybrid environments. This approach encourages co-design processes, where students, educators, and developers collaboratively shape system features based on real needs. Through iterative testing and user feedback, the AI-HyFlex system becomes not just a platform for delivering content but a responsive partner that evolves with its learners. (Lin and Kuo, 2025)

The second pillar, Cultural Awareness, ensures that AI systems respect and adapt to the diversity of global education contexts. Learning is embedded in culture; therefore, the design of AI-HyFlex platforms must be sensitive to linguistic, social, and cultural variations. This involves incorporating local content, multilingual support, and contextually relevant examples that reflect students' lived realities. A culturally aware system avoids imposing one-size-fits-all standards and instead fosters inclusion through recognition and representation. By honoring cultural diversity, AI-HyFlex environments can strengthen students' sense of identity and belonging critical elements for motivation and engagement in learning.

The third pillar, Accessibility, focuses on designing systems that can be used by everyone, regardless of physical, cognitive, or socio-economic constraints. This principle extends beyond compliance with accessibility standards; it seeks to actively remove barriers that prevent equitable participation. Features such as text-to-speech conversion, captioning, color contrast adjustment, and low-bandwidth optimization should be embedded as default, not optional, components. An accessible AI-HyFlex system democratizes education by ensuring that technological advancement does not privilege some while excluding others. True accessibility reflects an ethical commitment to justice and inclusion at the heart of digital education. (Sheng *et al.*, 2025)

Finally, the fourth pillar, Transparency, serves as the foundation of ethical AI practice in education. Transparency means that students and educators should clearly understand how AI systems operate how data is collected, how recommendations are made, and what limitations exist within algorithms. This pillar builds trust between users and technology, allowing for accountability and informed consent. Transparent AI also encourages explainability, where system decisions can be interpreted and questioned rather than blindly accepted. In combination, these four pillars Human-Centeredness, Cultural Awareness, Accessibility, and Transparency form the ethical architecture of an empathic AI-HyFlex system. Together, they guide the creation of learning environments that are not only technologically advanced but also deeply humane, inclusive, and sustainable. (Lin and Kuo, 2025).

Figure 8. Pilar Desain Sistem AI-HyFlex Empatik

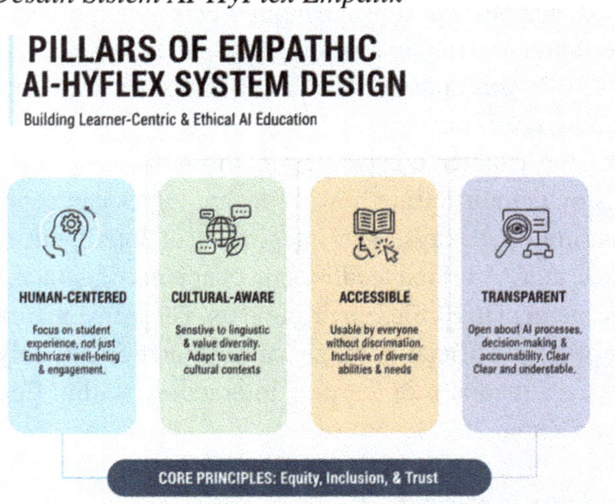

Source: Developed by the authors.

8. IMPLICATIONS OF THE STUDY

The findings presented in this chapter offer several important implications for the development and implementation of AI-powered HyFlex learning environments.

By highlighting the role of student voices and experiences in the co-design of educational technologies, this chapter contributes to a broader understanding of how artificial intelligence can support more inclusive, responsive, and engaging learning systems. The implications of this work can be viewed from three main perspectives: theoretical, practical, and social.

8.1 Theoretical Implications

From a theoretical perspective, this chapter contributes to the growing body of research on AI in education and HyFlex learning by emphasizing the importance of student-centered design. Much of the existing literature on AI-supported learning environments focuses on technological capabilities, system architecture, or instructor-driven pedagogical strategies. While these perspectives are valuable, they often overlook the role of students as active contributors to the design and improvement of learning systems.

The insights presented in this chapter suggest that integrating student perspectives into the development of AI-based HyFlex systems can enhance both usability and pedagogical effectiveness. This aligns with emerging theoretical frameworks that emphasize participatory design and human-centered approaches to educational technology development. By incorporating student experiences, educational technologies can move beyond purely technical solutions toward systems that better reflect real learning needs and contexts.

Furthermore, the chapter contributes to discussions on hybrid and flexible learning models by demonstrating how AI technologies can support adaptive and personalized learning pathways. The integration of intelligent tutoring systems, learning analytics, and AI-driven feedback mechanisms illustrates how digital tools can enhance engagement in HyFlex environments. These insights expand theoretical understandings of how artificial intelligence can function not only as a technological tool but also as a mediator of learning interactions within flexible educational systems. (Lan and Zhou, 2025)

8.2 Practical Implications

The findings of this chapter also offer practical insights for educators, instructional designers, and institutional decision-makers seeking to implement AI-supported HyFlex learning environments. One key implication is the importance of involving students in the design and evaluation of educational technologies. Institutions often adopt new digital tools without sufficiently considering how students interact with these systems in real learning contexts. By incorporating structured feedback mechanisms, co-design workshops, or participatory design approaches, universities can ensure that AI-powered learning systems are more aligned with student needs and expectations.

In addition, the chapter highlights the potential of AI tools to enhance student engagement and personalization in HyFlex learning environments. Tools such as adaptive learning platforms, AI-driven feedback systems, and learning analytics dashboards can support diverse learning preferences by providing flexible pathways for participation. For example, students who participate remotely may benefit from AI-supported discussion analysis, automated summarization tools, or personalized recommendations for learning resources.

However, the chapter also emphasizes the need for careful implementation strategies. Institutions should provide training and support for both instructors and students to ensure that AI tools are used effectively and ethically. Transparent communication about how AI systems collect and use learning data is also essential to maintain trust and promote responsible adoption. By balancing technological innovation with pedagogical and ethical considerations, institutions can maximize the benefits of AI-enhanced HyFlex learning. (Mnguni, 2025)

8.3 Social Implications

Beyond theoretical and practical contributions, the findings of this chapter also have broader social implications. As artificial intelligence becomes increasingly integrated into educational systems, it is essential to consider how these technologies influence issues such as equity, accessibility, and digital inclusion. HyFlex learning environments aim to provide flexible access to education, allowing students to participate through in-person, online, or hybrid modes. When combined with AI technologies, these environments have the potential to support more inclusive learning experiences by adapting to diverse student needs.

However, the implementation of AI in education also raises important concerns regarding data privacy, algorithmic bias, and unequal access to technological resources. If not carefully managed, AI systems may inadvertently reinforce existing inequalities within educational systems. For example, students with limited access to reliable internet connections or digital devices may experience disadvantages in AI-enhanced learning environments.

Therefore, institutions must adopt responsible and inclusive approaches when implementing AI-supported HyFlex systems. Policies related to ethical AI use, data governance, and digital accessibility should be integrated into institutional strategies for educational technology adoption. By prioritizing transparency, fairness, and inclusivity, universities can ensure that AI-driven innovations contribute positively to the broader goal of equitable and sustainable education. (Ajani, Gamede and Govender, 2026)

9. LIMITATIONS OF THE STUDY

While this study provides important insights into the role of voice and student experience in the development of the AI-based HyFlex learning system, some limitations need to be noted. First, the discussion in this chapter is more conceptual and exploratory, with a focus on literature analysis and reflection on emerging trends in the development of AI-based educational technology. Therefore, the results presented have not been fully supported by large-scale empirical studies involving various educational institutions or diverse learning contexts.

Second, the development of artificial intelligence technology in education is happening very quickly. Many new platforms, tools, and approaches continue to emerge every year. This means that some examples of technologies or approaches discussed in this chapter may undergo further changes or developments in the future. Therefore, the interpretation of the findings and discussions in this chapter needs to be understood as part of the dynamics of the development of the AI field in education. (Reina-Parrado, Román-Graván and Hervás-Gómez, 2026)

Third, the implementation of the AI-based HyFlex system is greatly influenced by the institutional context, including the availability of technological infrastructure, institutional policies, lecturer readiness, and student digital literacy. Differences in conditions between institutions can affect how the technology is applied and how students respond to it. Therefore, the results of the discussion in this chapter may not be fully generalized to all higher education contexts without considering these contextual factors.

Recognizing these limitations is important to provide a more balanced understanding of the chapter's contributions while opening up opportunities for further research to expand and deepen the study of AI integration in the HyFlex learning environment. (Romero-Hall *et al.*, 2025)

10. FUTURE RESEARCH DIRECTIONS

Seeing the rapid development of artificial intelligence technology in education, there remain many research opportunities to expand understanding of AI implementation in HyFlex learning environments. One important direction is conducting empirical studies involving students, lecturers, and institutions to evaluate the effectiveness of AI-based HyFlex systems in improving engagement, learning outcomes, and overall learning experiences.

Future research may also examine how co-design approaches involving students, lecturers, and technology developers can produce learning systems that better respond to user needs. This participatory approach can improve the quality of educational technology by incorporating user perspectives from the early stages of system development. (Romero-Hall *et al.*, 2025)

Further research should also address ethical issues in AI use within education. Topics such as student data privacy, algorithm transparency, and potential bias in AI systems are becoming increasingly important as these technologies expand in digital learning environments.

Another direction is exploring how AI can support more inclusive and adaptive learning for students with diverse backgrounds and abilities. Through technologies such as learning analytics, adaptive learning systems, and intelligent tutoring systems, future research can help create more personalized and student-centered HyFlex learning environments.

Through these research directions, the development of AI-based HyFlex systems can become more mature not only technologically but also pedagogically and ethically. In addition, future studies should investigate how AI-supported HyFlex systems influence long-term student learning behaviors and digital learning habits. Understanding how students interact with AI-driven recommendations, analytics dashboards, and automated feedback systems can provide deeper insights into the sustainability of such technologies in education. This research direction may also reveal how AI can support continuous learning beyond formal classroom environments. (Lan and Zhou, 2025)

11. CONCLUSION

The integration of Artificial Intelligence (AI) within HyFlex (Hybrid-Flexible) learning environments represents an important step toward the future of higher education. This chapter has shown how flexibility, technology, and human-centered design can reshape learning experiences to become more inclusive, adaptive, and student-centered. While technological innovation provides powerful tools for personalization and efficiency, the success of AI-enhanced education ultimately depends on understanding students' experiences and needs. Involving students in the co-design process allows institutions to create systems that are both intelligent and contextually relevant. (Lan and Zhou, 2025)

Several themes emerge from this discussion. First, AI should support rather than replace educators by automating repetitive tasks, providing data-driven insights, and enabling more meaningful human interaction. Second, student participation in system design and evaluation is essential to ensure technologies address real learning challenges. Third, inclusivity and ethical considerations must remain central priorities, particularly as algorithms increasingly influence educational pathways. (Omirali, Kozhakhmet and Zhumaliyeva, 2025)

The studies and reflections presented here underscore that effective AI-HyFlex systems require not only robust technical design but also institutional readiness and pedagogical innovation. Universities must adopt adaptive curricula, establish clear data ethics policies, and invest in faculty development that emphasizes digital pedagogy, not merely technical literacy. Moreover, collaboration between educators, developers, and students must become standard practice in the iterative design of AI-powered systems. Such interdisciplinary cooperation ensures that education remains responsive to social and cultural realities rather than being dictated solely by technological trends.(Adarkwah, 2025)

Ultimately, future of education lies in systems that are intelligent equitable. An AI-HyFlex learning environment should recognize students as individuals. Path forward calls for innovation by ethics, design informed by student experience, and technology that supports human spirit of learning.(Le, 2025)

REFERENCES

Adarkwah, M. A. (2025). GenAI-Infused Adult Learning in the Digital Era: A Conceptual Framework for Higher Education. *Adult Learning*, *36*(3), 149–161. DOI: 10.1177/10451595241271161

Aditi, S., & Gaurav, S. (2025). 'Mothers' Assistant for Labor analgesia (MALA): A novel artificial intelligence interactive avatar for patient education in obstetric anesthesia'. *International Journal of Obstetric Anesthesia*, *64*, 104762. Advance online publication. DOI: 10.1016/j.ijoa.2025.104762 PMID: 40915118

Ajani, O. A., Gamede, B. T., & Govender, S. (2026). Cultural and ethical dimensions of learning management system adoption in rural universities: Exploring data privacy, algorithmic bias, and contextual realities. *Multidisciplinary Science Journal*, *8*(3), 2026142. Advance online publication. DOI: 10.31893/multiscience.2026142

Alsaiari, O., Baghaei, N., Lahza, H., Lodge, J. M., Boden, M., & Khosravi, H. (2025). Emotionally enriched AI-generated feedback: Supporting student well-being without compromising learning. *Computers & Education*, *239*, 105363. Advance online publication. DOI: 10.1016/j.compedu.2025.105363

Ambrosetti, É., Gaudin, C., Flandin, S., & Poizat, G. (2025). Students as co-designers in health professional education: A scoping review. *BMC Medical Education*, *25*(1), 645. Advance online publication. DOI: 10.1186/s12909-025-07110-0 PMID: 40319259

Asamoah, M. K., & Amarteifio, J. (2025). Overcoming barriers and ethical challenges in implementing intelligent tutoring systems in Ghanaian higher education. *Discover Education*, *4*(1), 179. Advance online publication. DOI: 10.1007/s44217-025-00593-5

Baker, M. J., & Smith, C. (2025). Let Them Choose: Empowering Students Through a HyFlex Learning Model. *Nurse Educator*, *50*(3), E174. DOI: 10.1097/NNE.0000000000001859 PMID: 40184408

Barr, T., & Luo, T. (2025). HyFlex course design: Outcomes, challenges, and supports for students and instructors [Preprint]. *Journal of Computing in Higher Education*. Advance online publication. DOI: 10.1007/s12528-025-09452-6

Bhuiyan, M. A., Rahman, M. K., Basile, V., Ping, H., & Mainul Bari, A. B. M. (2025). 'Adoption of ChatGPT for students' learning effectiveness'. *International Journal of Management Education*, *23*(3), 101255. Advance online publication. DOI: 10.1016/j.ijme.2025.101255

Castillo, G. E. D.. (2026). ChatGPT as an intelligent academic feedback agent: Correlational analysis of its perception among university students. *European Public and Social Innovation Review*, *11*, 1–19. Advance online publication. DOI: 10.31637/epsir-2026-2132

Dela Cruz, C. S., & Dela Cruz, L. S. (2026). Leveraging artificial intelligence for intelligent student support: An AI-enabled SRM framework for higher education. *Multidisciplinary Science Journal*, *8*(3), 2026160. Advance online publication. DOI: 10.31893/multiscience.2026160

Gloria, D. S., & Pelayo, E. T. C. (2025). Perspectives on flexible learning towards the development of proposed quality assurance framework for HyFlex learning. *Journal of Education and Learning*, *19*(4), 2279–2290. DOI: 10.11591/edulearn.v19i4.22810

Guatibonza Briceño, P. A., ... (2026) 'Evaluating an AI-Driven Chatbot Tutor for Enhancing Introductory Programming Learning', in *Lecture Notes in Computer Science*, pp. 235–245. Available at: DOI: 10.1007/978-3-031-98281-1_19

Han, S. (2026). 'Learner autonomy and mode selection in dual-mode chatbot: Students' interaction patterns and learning outcomes in an online course'. *Computers & Education*, *240*, 105464. Advance online publication. DOI: 10.1016/j.compedu.2025.105464

Khan, T., Kumar Nag, A., Basu, S., & Saluja, V. (2025). Artificial Intelligence for Development (AI4D) Usage, Learner Autonomy, Wellbeing and Digital Literacy in ODL. *Journal of Learning for Development*, *12*(2), 330–346. DOI: 10.56059/jl4d.v12i2.1580

Khasawneh, M. A. S., Aladini, A., Assi, S. A., & Ajanil, B. (2025). Portfolio assessment in AI-enhanced learning environments: A pathway to emotion regulation, mindfulness, and language learning attitudes. *Language Testing in Asia*, *15*(1), 5. Advance online publication. DOI: 10.1186/s40468-025-00345-0

Kim, K., & Kwon, K. (2025). From co-design to co-teaching: A comprehensive approach to an integrated AI curriculum in middle school STEM education. *Smart Learning Environments*, *12*(1), 57. Advance online publication. DOI: 10.1186/s40561-025-00413-1

Kim, S., Jung, J., You, T., & Cho, S. (2026). Fusing sequential recommender and ad-hoc planner for multi-faceted preference understanding in conversational recommendation. *Information Fusion*, *127*, 103735. Advance online publication. DOI: 10.1016/j.inffus.2025.103735

Lan, M. and Zhou, X. (2025) ‘A qualitative systematic review on AI empowered self-regulated learning in higher education’, *npj Science of Learning*, 10(1). Available at: .DOI: 10.1038/s41539-025-00319-0

Le, R. (2025). *Transformative AI tools for inclusive and holistic learning environments: Enhancing accessibility, equity, and emotional intelligence*., DOI: 10.4018/979-8-3373-5097-4.ch017

Lin, C., & Kuo, C.-F. (2025). Roles and potential of Large language models in healthcare: A comprehensive review. *Biomedical Journal*, *48*(5), 100868. Advance online publication. DOI: 10.1016/j.bj.2025.100868 PMID: 40311872

Lin, H.-C. (2026) ‘A Generative AI-Supported Flipped Classroom Model for Personalized Skill Training in Engineering Woodworking Education’, in *Lecture Notes in Computer Science*, pp. 366–376. Available at: DOI: 10.1007/978-3-031-98197-5_39

Lin, M. P.-C., ... (2026) ‘Mapping AI Tools in Education: A Topic Modeling Analysis of Cognitive, Metacognitive, and Affective Insights’, in *Lecture Notes in Computer Science*, pp. 88–101. Available at: DOI: 10.1007/978-3-031-98281-1_7

Mahmoud, M. I., & Surwanti, A. (2026). A bibliometric study on the role of artificial intelligence in enhancing investment decision-making processes. *Multidisciplinary Reviews*, *9*(2), 2026092. Advance online publication. DOI: 10.31893/multirev.2026092

Mahrishi, M., Abbas, A., Siddiqui, M. K., & Aladhadh, S. (2025). The genesis and prevalence of the HyFlex model: A systematic review and bibliometric analysis. *International Journal of Educational Research Open*, *8*, 100410. Advance online publication. DOI: 10.1016/j.ijedro.2024.100410

Mentzer, N., Mammadova, E., Koehler, A., Mohandas, L., & Farrington, S. (2025). Analyzing the impact of basic psychological needs on student academic performance: A comparison of post-pandemic interactive synchronous hyflex and pre-pandemic traditional face-to-face instruction. *Educational Technology Research and Development*, *73*(1), 91–114. DOI: 10.1007/s11423-024-10417-2

Mnguni, L. (2025). AI as a teaching augmentor: A review of the integration of AI in science education. *Multidisciplinary Reviews*, *8*(12), 2025390. Advance online publication. DOI: 10.31893/multirev.2025390

Namaziandost, E. (2025). Integrating flipped learning in AI-enhanced language learning: Mapping the effects on metacognitive awareness, writing development, and foreign language learning boredom. *Computers and Education: Artificial Intelligence*, *9*, 100446. Advance online publication. DOI: 10.1016/j.caeai.2025.100446

Neshaei, S. P., Mejia-Domenzain, P., Davis, R. L., & Käser, T. (2025). Metacognition meets AI: Empowering reflective writing with large language models. *British Journal of Educational Technology*, *56*(5), 1864–1896. DOI: 10.1111/bjet.13601

Olivier, C., & Weilbach, L. (2026) 'GenAI Chatbot Tutors as Agents of Inclusive Education: A Review Guided by Ethics of Care and Critical Pedagogy', in *Lecture Notes in Computer Science*, pp. 84–93. Available at: DOI: 10.1007/978-3-031-98185-2_10

Omirali, A., Kozhakhmet, K., & Zhumaliyeva, R. (2025). Digital Trust in Transition: Student Perceptions of AI-Enhanced Learning for Sustainable Educational Futures. *Sustainability (Basel)*, *17*(17), 7567. Advance online publication. DOI: 10.3390/su17177567

Reina-Parrado, M., Román-Graván, P., & Hervás-Gómez, C. (2026). PRISMA Review on the implementation of Machine Learning in education: Social challenges and opportunities in shaping the citizens of tomorrow. *European Public and Social Innovation Review*, *11*, 1–26. Advance online publication. DOI: 10.31637/epsir-2026-1620

Romero-Hall, E.. (2025). A decade of HyFlex learning: A systematic review in undergraduate education [Preprint]. *Educational Technology Research and Development*. Advance online publication. DOI: 10.1007/s11423-025-10544-4

Sagredo-Gallardo, M., González Campos, J., Alfaro Contreras, C., & Elias, M. (2026). Challenges and Opportunities of Artificial Intelligence in Collaborative Learning: Implications for Educational Innovation in Institutional Contexts. *European Public and Social Innovation Review*, *11*, 1–26. Advance online publication. DOI: 10.31637/epsir-2026-2211

Saini, B., Singh, D., Sharma, K. C., & Saini, D. K. (2025). AI-enhanced telemedicine: Transforming resource allocation and cost-efficiency analysis via advanced queueing model. *Scientific Reports*, *15*(1), 31551. Advance online publication. DOI: 10.1038/s41598-025-15664-8 PMID: 40866419

Sarchet, L. N., Love, K., Carson, C., & Rashid, M. M. (2025). Incorporating Universal Design for Learning in Hybrid-HyFlex College Courses to Enhance Student Belonging, Engagement, Equity, and Learning Outcomes [Preprint]. *College Teaching*, 1–5. Advance online publication. DOI: 10.1080/87567555.2025.2549331

Sheng, Q., Tang, W., Qin, H., Kong, Y., Dai, H., Zhong, Y., Wang, Y., Zou, J., & Yang, H. (2025). A review on an AI-driven face robot for human-robot expression interaction. *Science China. Technological Sciences*, *68*(10), 2010301. Advance online publication. DOI: 10.1007/s11431-025-3027-x

Vassileva, B., Stanimirov, E., & Miltenoff, P. (2026) 'Collaborating Across Roles: Shaping Strategic Directions for Institutional Implementation of AI Tools in Higher Education', in *Lecture Notes in Computer Science*, pp. 88–99. Available at: DOI: 10.1007/978-3-032-05607-8_10

Xiao, J., Yang, Y., & Li, M. (2025). 'Empirical study on the feasibility of hybrid-flexible training model for developing teachers' artificial intelligence competence'. *Education and Information Technologies*, *30*(12), 16835–16860. DOI: 10.1007/s10639-025-13460-5

Zhang, Z., & Qianjun, T. (2025). Integrating AI-generated content tools in higher education: A comparative analysis of interdisciplinary learning outcomes. *Scientific Reports*, *15*(1), 25802. Advance online publication. DOI: 10.1038/s41598-025-10941-y PMID: 40670544

Chapter 15
Student Perceptions of AI-Augmented HyFlex Learning:
A Mixed-Methods Study at a Malaysian University

Jens Thoemmes
http://orcid.org/0000-0001-8679-7425
Taylor's University, Malaysia

Li Liu
http://orcid.org/0000-0001-9935-4017
Taylor's University, Malaysia

Md Shamirul Islam
http://orcid.org/0000-0002-0098-3698
Taylor's University, Malaysia

ABSTRACT

This chapter examines student perceptions of an AI-augmented HyFlex learning model at a private university in Malaysia, using mixed-methods data from 1,168 undergraduates across 28 countries. Guided by the Technology Acceptance Model, Self-Determination Theory, and cultural dimensions theory, the findings show generally positive sentiment (60.7%), with technology effectiveness as the dominant theme. However, acceptance is polarized: while features such as recorded sessions and interactive tools are well received, AI avatar lectures face strong resistance (67.5% negative) due to their perceived lack of human presence. Although overall sentiment does not differ significantly by nationality or academic level, qualitative

DOI: 10.4018/979-8-3373-6182-6.ch015

insights reveal different emphases across groups. The study concludes that effective AI integration in HyFlex learning requires human–AI complementarity, supported by platform reliability and culturally responsive design.

1. INTRODUCTION AND ANALYTICAL CONTEXT

1.1 The HyFlex Model in Context

The Hybrid-Flexible (HyFlex) model of course design, first developed at San Francisco State University, offers students the ability to choose between face-to-face and online participation within the same course structure (Beatty, 2019). The foundational principle is that students in any modality should have comparable learning experiences, equivalent assessment opportunities, and meaningful access to course content (Abdelmalak & Parra, 2016). As higher education institutions have expanded their adoption of flexible delivery formats, a growing body of research has examined HyFlex outcomes, with studies reporting positive student satisfaction and reduced stress levels (Bockorny et al., 2024; Choi et al., 2024), though challenges remain, particularly around reduced peer interaction and uneven engagement across modalities (Howell et al., 2025).

Increasingly, higher education institutions worldwide have embraced HyFlex course designs and online delivery models in response to competitive market pressures, including cost efficiency, physical space constraints, quality enhancement, and the integration of emerging technologies (Yang et al., 2025). Within this evolving educational landscape, both faculty and students are required to adapt to hybrid learning environments that amalgamate digital and face-to-face modalities. Such transformations have not only reshaped teaching and learning practices but may also have reconfigured students' learning experiences and faculty members' professional identities (Islam et al., 2026).

The integration of artificial intelligence into HyFlex environments represents a more recent development, one that extends the model beyond its original design parameters (Liu et al., 2026). While the HyFlex literature has examined learner choice and equivalency (Xiao et al., 2025), the addition of AI-mediated instructional components raises questions about student acceptance, technology resistance, and the conditions under which AI tools support or complicate the learning experience. Large-scale implementations remain relatively rare, and evidence on how diverse student populations respond to AI-augmented HyFlex learning is still emerging (Yang et al., 2025).

1.2 AI-Enhanced HyFlex at Taylor's University

During the April to July 2025 semester, Taylor's University in Malaysia deployed an AI-augmented HyFlex learning model across 60 undergraduate modules spanning multiple faculties. Two AI-mediated features were introduced alongside the standard HyFlex infrastructure. First, AI avatar lecture videos were developed in which digital replicas of lecturers delivered pre-recorded content, allowing students to access lectures asynchronously. Second, the Noodle Factory AI learning assistant provided interactive quizzes, one-on-one tutoring, and personalised feedback intended to supplement in-class instruction.

A total of 1,168 students completed a structured survey capturing demographic information, self-reported AI interaction behaviours, perceptions of both AI features, and open-ended reflections on their HyFlex learning experience. The student body was internationally diverse, drawn from more than 28 countries, creating a setting in which cultural and linguistic backgrounds may shape how students engage with and evaluate technology-mediated instruction.

1.3 Conceptual Framework

This study draws on three established theoretical perspectives. The Technology Acceptance Model (TAM) posits that perceived usefulness and perceived ease of use are the primary determinants of technology adoption (Davis, 1989). Its extension, the Unified Theory of Acceptance and Use of Technology (UTAUT), incorporates social influence and facilitating conditions as additional predictors, recognising that technology acceptance operates within institutional and social contexts (Venkatesh et al., 2003). Both frameworks provide a lens for interpreting student evaluations of the specific AI-mediated features deployed at Taylor's University.

Self-Determination Theory (SDT) emphasises autonomy, competence, and relatedness as fundamental psychological needs that shape motivation and engagement (Ryan & Deci, 2000). The HyFlex model's emphasis on learner choice aligns with the autonomy component, while AI tutoring tools may support competence through personalised feedback. However, the replacement of human instructors with AI avatars may undermine relatedness, a tension that the data allow us to examine.

Finally, cultural dimensions theory provides a framework for understanding cross-national variation in technology reception. Hofstede's (2001) dimensions of collectivism, uncertainty avoidance, and power distance have been shown to influence educational technology acceptance (Straub et al., 1997; Teo & Huang, 2019), while Hall's (1976) distinction between high-context and low-context communication styles may shape how students from different cultural backgrounds articulate criticism and appreciation.

1.4 Research Questions

The study addresses four research questions:

RQ1: What are the dominant themes in student perceptions of AI-enhanced HyFlex learning, and what is the overall sentiment distribution?

RQ2: How do student perceptions vary across nationality groups (Malaysian, Chinese, Other)?

RQ3: How does academic progression shape the nature and sophistication of student feedback?

RQ4: What are the specific technology acceptance and resistance patterns for AI-mediated features?

2. METHODOLOGICAL FRAMEWORK AND ANALYTICAL APPROACH

2.1 Study Context and Research Design

This study examines student perceptions of an AI-augmented Hybrid-Flexible (HyFlex) learning model deployed at Taylor's University, Malaysia, during the April to July 2025 semester. The HyFlex approach, as defined by Beatty (2019), allows students to choose between face-to-face and online participation within the same course, with the aim of increasing accessibility and learner autonomy. At Taylor's University, this model was further augmented with two AI-mediated features: AI avatar lecture videos, in which digital replicas of lecturers delivered pre-recorded content, and the Noodle Factory AI learning assistant, which provided interactive quizzes, one-on-one tutoring, and personalised feedback.

The survey was administered across multiple faculties, drawing responses from 1,168 students enrolled in courses that had adopted the HyFlex model. The study adopted a convergent parallel mixed-methods design (Creswell & Plano Clark, 2018), collecting quantitative data through Likert-scale perception items and qualitative data through an open-ended response question within the same instrument. This design permits the simultaneous collection and subsequent integration of both data strands, allowing qualitative findings to contextualise and, where appropriate, complicate the quantitative patterns.

Four research questions guided the analysis. RQ1 asked what dominant themes characterise student perceptions and what the overall sentiment distribution is. RQ2 examined how perceptions vary across nationality groups. RQ3 investigated whether academic progression shapes the nature of student feedback. RQ4 focused on the specific technology acceptance and resistance patterns for AI-mediated features.

2.2 Survey Instrument and Data Collection

The survey instrument comprised 22 items organised into four sections. Section A collected demographic information through five items: Student ID, Nationality, Module Name, Faculty or School, and Semester of enrolment. Section B included eight items measuring students' self-reported AI interaction behaviours using a binary response format. Sample items include: "I use AI to get quick answers or direct explanations to academic problems" and "I learn complex topics by discussing them with AI."

Section C contained eight Likert-scale perception items, four addressing AI avatar videos and four addressing the Noodle Factory AI learning assistant. A sample avatar item reads: "The use of AI Avatars in videos supports my learning and helps me retain information better." A sample Noodle Factory item reads: "The quizzes provided by the Noodle Factory learning assistant effectively helped me check and confirm my understanding of the module's topics." The response scale used a four-point forced-choice format (Strongly Disagree = 1, Disagree = 2, Agree = 4, Strongly Agree = 5) with no neutral midpoint. This deliberate omission of a midpoint was a design decision intended to encourage definitive responses. The numeric coding preserves a gap at the scale centre (no value of 3) to maintain symmetry. Internal consistency for the 8-item perception scale was high (Cronbach's alpha = 0.933, n = 1,168).

Section D consisted of a single open-ended item: "Please share your experience with HyFlex Learning (Interactive Synchronous Learning) for this module throughout the semester. You may include what you found helpful or enjoyable, and suggest any improvements that could make the learning experience better for future semesters." The survey was administered via SurveyMonkey during the semester, with participation being voluntary and anonymous. Institutional ethical approval was obtained prior to data collection.

2.3 Sample Characteristics and Response Rate

A total of 1,168 students completed the survey. Open-ended responses were filtered to retain only meaningful contributions: empty responses, single-word answers, and responses of fewer than 10 characters were excluded. This yielded 476 responses suitable for analysis, representing a 40.8% response rate. Fifty-eight students appeared in multiple modules due to cross-enrolment; because each response pertained to a specific module experience, the analysis was conducted at the response level rather than the student level.

Students were grouped by nationality into three categories: Malaysia (n = 237, 49.8%), China (n = 134, 28.2%), and Other (n = 105, 22.1%), the latter comprising students from 28 countries. Academic progression was categorised as Early (Semesters 1 and 2, n = 232), Mid (Semesters 3 and 4, n = 166), and Advanced (Semester 5 and above, n = 78). Four module categories were identified: Education (n = 58), Hospitality (n = 35), Event/Tourism (n = 34), and Other (n = 349). Table 1 presents the full sample characteristics.

Table 1. Sample characteristics (N = 476)

Characteristic	n	%
Nationality group		
Malaysia	237	49.8
China	134	28.2
Other (28 countries)	105	22.1
Academic level		
Early (Semester 1-2)	232	48.7
Mid (Semester 3-4)	166	34.9
Advanced (Semester 5+)	78	16.4
Module category		
Education	58	12.2
Hospitality	35	7.4
Event/Tourism	34	7.1
Other	349	73.3

Note. Response-level analysis; 58 students appeared in more than one module.

2.4 Analytical Approach

2.4.1 Sentiment analysis

Sentiment analysis of the open-ended responses was conducted using the AFINN lexicon (Nielsen, 2011), implemented via the tidytext package in R. The AFINN lexicon assigns integer valence scores ranging from -5 (most negative) to +5 (most positive) to a curated list of 2,477 English words. For each response, sentiment-bearing words were identified and their scores averaged to produce a single mean sentiment value per response. This approach was chosen for its transparency and reproducibility, as each classification can be traced to specific lexical matches.

Responses were classified into three categories based on the mean AFINN score: Positive (mean > 0.5), Negative (mean < -0.5), and Neutral (otherwise). A sensitivity analysis was conducted at alternative thresholds (0.25, 0.75, and 1.00) to assess the stability of the classification. Cohen's d was computed as a one-sample effect size, comparing the mean sentiment score against a neutral baseline of zero (Cohen, 1988). It should be noted that lexicon-based methods do not capture negation, sarcasm, or contextual irony, and individual classifications should be interpreted with this limitation in mind.

2.4.2 Thematic analysis

Thematic analysis followed the six-phase reflexive approach outlined by Braun and Clarke (2006, 2021). The research team developed a codebook defining five themes grounded in the study's conceptual framework: Technology Effectiveness, Learning Quality, Social Interaction, Flexibility and Convenience, and Improvement Needs. Each theme was operationally defined with inclusion criteria, and sub-theme categories were specified for Flexibility (five sub-themes including Temporal Flexibility and Spatial Flexibility) and for technology feature evaluation (five features: AI Avatar, Interactive Tools, Recorded Sessions, Online Classes, and Platform Stability), each coded with a positive, neutral, or negative valence.

The coding was performed using a large language model (Claude, Anthropic) as a coding assistant, with the researchers providing the codebook definitions, reviewing outputs, and resolving ambiguous cases. This approach was adopted to process the full corpus of 476 responses systematically while maintaining fidelity to the predefined theme definitions. Each response could be assigned to multiple themes (mention-based coding) as well as a single primary theme (exclusive assignment). The use of AI-assisted coding represents a departure from traditional manual coding and its implications are addressed in the Limitations section.

2.4.3 Statistical testing

Group differences in sentiment were assessed using Pearson's chi-square test of independence (sentiment category by nationality group; sentiment category by academic level) and one-way analysis of variance (ANOVA) comparing mean sentiment scores across nationality groups. All tests were evaluated at an alpha level of .05. Effect sizes are reported where applicable.

2.4.4 Mixed-methods integration

Following the convergent design framework proposed by Creswell and Plano Clark (2018), quantitative and qualitative findings were integrated through a joint display table. The display juxtaposes quantitative results (sentiment distribution, statistical tests) with qualitative evidence (thematic patterns, representative student quotations) across each research question. Integration was assessed for convergence, complementarity, and divergence between the two data strands.

3. RESULTS

This section presents findings organised by the four research questions, followed by an integrated mixed-methods synthesis. All percentages for thematic prevalence are mention-based (a single response could address multiple themes) unless otherwise stated. Student quotations are presented verbatim with minor formatting adjustments for readability; each has been verified against the original survey data.

3.1 RQ1: What Are the Dominant Themes and the Overall Sentiment Distribution?

The overall sentiment distribution of the 476 analysed responses was predominantly positive. As shown in Table 2, 60.7% of responses (n = 289) were classified as positive, 31.1% (n = 148) as neutral, and 8.2% (n = 39) as negative. The mean AFINN score was 1.06 (SD = 1.26), yielding a Cohen's d of 0.84, which represents a large effect size by conventional benchmarks (Cohen, 1988). This suggests that student responses tended to carry positive sentiment, though the sizeable neutral category (31.1%) indicates that a substantial minority of students offered neither clearly positive nor negative evaluations.

A sensitivity analysis confirmed that the majority-positive pattern held across alternative classification thresholds: at a threshold of 0.25, 66.0% of responses were classified as positive; at 0.75, 57.8%; and at 1.00, 51.5%. Although the proportion varied with threshold stringency, a positive majority was observed at every tested level.

Table 2. Overall sentiment distribution (N = 476)

Sentiment Category	n	%
Positive	289	60.7
Neutral	148	31.1
Negative	39	8.2
Total	476	100.0

Note. AFINN lexicon (Nielsen, 2011). M = 1.06, SD = 1.26, Cohen's d = 0.84. Classification threshold: |mean| > 0.5.

Thematic analysis revealed five distinct themes. Technology Effectiveness was the most prevalent, mentioned in 37.6% of responses, followed by Learning Quality (20.4%), Social Interaction (20.0%), Flexibility and Convenience (18.7%), and Improvement Needs (10.7%). Table 3 presents the full distribution. The dominance of Technology Effectiveness as a theme indicates that students were primarily concerned with evaluating the specific technological tools they encountered, rather than broader pedagogical or logistical aspects of the HyFlex model.

Table 3. Theme prevalence (mention-based, N = 476)

Theme	n	% of Responses
Flexibility and Convenience	89	18.7
Technology Effectiveness	179	37.6
Learning Quality	97	20.4
Social Interaction	95	20.0
Improvement Needs	51	10.7

Note. Responses could mention multiple themes; percentages do not sum to 100%.

Student responses illustrate the thematic landscape. Technology-related evaluations ranged from appreciation for interactive features to frustration with platform issues:

"It is not like other AI tools that can directly summarize the courseware. When watching AI video teaching, I prefer AI to help me directly summarize the key points of the course, which is more convenient and faster. However, one thing Noodle Factory does well is the review and test part, which can help me quickly grasp the key points of the course." (Malaysia student, Other, Early (1-2), positive sentiment)

"I hope that lecture can be not in pre- recorded form cause is not helpful and the video did not explain in details just bring through the topic i would rather to have online lecture or face-to- face lecture this two is more helpful. thanks " (Malaysia student, Other, Mid (3-4), positive sentiment)

"I find that the hyflex lessons are less time consuming as I can be in the comfort of my own home and join class, but I do think face to face classes are more engaging. I would prefer hyflex learning over face to face though and I just hope there's a stricter rule for the completion so we don't feel like we're going to be okay even if we don't do it" (Other student, Education, Early (1-2), positive sentiment)

"I find Hyflex to be interesting, although it's very flexible and convenient, however I prefer physical learning instead. I feel like this is a good alternative to learn your modules but I feel like it's not enough. I still physically learning as I get

to convey my emotions and talk to a person. I highly value in person learning rather than online." (Malaysia student, Other, Mid (3-4), positive sentiment)

"I found HyFlex Learning flexible and convenient. It was helpful to attend both online and in-person depending on my situation. I enjoyed the real-time interaction during online classes and the recorded sessions for review. However, improving audio and video quality would make the experience better." (China student, Other, Mid (3-4), positive sentiment)

3.2 RQ2: How Do Student Perceptions Vary Across Nationality Groups?

No statistically significant association was found between nationality group and sentiment category, $\chi^2(4) = 6.53$, $p = .1628$, nor between nationality group and mean sentiment score, $F(2, 473) = 1.687$, $p = .186$. A descriptive trend was nonetheless observable: Chinese students appeared somewhat more positive (66.4%) than students from Other nationalities (60.0%) or Malaysia (57.8%). However, this pattern did not reach conventional levels of significance and should be interpreted with caution.

Negative sentiment rates varied descriptively across groups: China 3.7%, Malaysia 9.3%, and Other 11.4%. Chinese students expressed notably less negative sentiment, though again this difference was not statistically significant.

Table 4. Sentiment distribution by nationality group

Group	n	Positive %	Neutral %	Negative %	M	SD
China	134	66.4	29.9	3.7	1.22	1.1
Malaysia	237	57.8	32.9	9.3	1.02	1.34
Other	105	60.0	28.6	11.4	0.943	1.24

Note. $\chi^2(4) = 6.53$, $p = .1628$. $F(2, 473) = 1.687$, $p = .186$.

Table 5. Theme prevalence by nationality group (mention-based)

Theme	China (n = 133)	Malaysia (n = 237)	Other (n = 106)
Technology Effectiveness	30 (22.6%)	97 (40.9%)	52 (49.1%)
Learning Quality	36 (27.1%)	44 (18.6%)	17 (16.0%)
Social Interaction	8 (6.0%)	57 (24.1%)	30 (28.3%)
Flexibility and Convenience	36 (27.1%)	32 (13.5%)	21 (19.8%)
Improvement Needs	9 (6.8%)	30 (12.7%)	12 (11.3%)

Note. Percentages are within-group. Responses could mention multiple themes.

Qualitative differences in thematic emphasis were apparent despite the absence of significant quantitative differences. Chinese students placed relatively greater emphasis on Learning Quality (27.1%) and Flexibility (27.1%), while Malaysian students were most concerned with Technology Effectiveness (40.9%) and Social Interaction (24.1%). Students from Other nationalities showed the strongest focus on Technology Effectiveness (49.1%).

The qualitative data reveal how cultural and educational backgrounds may shape the focus of student feedback, even when overall sentiment levels appear comparable:

"I found the HyFlex Learning experience very helpful as it offered flexibility to attend classes both online and in person. The interactive synchronous format kept me engaged, especially during discussions and group work. One area for improvement could be better coordination between in-class and online students to ensure equal participation. Overall, it was a convenient and effective way to learn." (China student, Other, Early (1-2), positive sentiment)

"Was looking forward to the module, but the entire hyflex but just made it feel extremely unimportant. Despite my best efforts, answers input in the quizzes are marked incorrectly due to the inability of the ai to detect 'different' answers from those not structured as preprogrammed. I feel this hyflex limits this module and should only be used as a support system to a traditional lecture." (Malaysia student, Other, Early (1-2), neutral sentiment)

"It's helpful, but somehow it ends up making me confused about which one to open first, because there are just so many steps, both on MyTIMES and HyFlex. I think that's also why many students are still unsure how to access everything. Since our lectures are online, it depends on each student's situation. If the lectures were face-to-face, I believe students would be more focused and less confused.\" (Other student, Other, Early (1-2), neutral sentiment)

"i hate it. it just feels like ai slop to cut corners. the avatars are so painfully obviously ai. they're monotonous, their voices don't even match the lecturers, it's terrible. the quizzes are wrong sometimes. bring back the weekly quizzes on mytimes instead. and for q6, i don't use ai for any of this. i only use noodle factory for the compulsory weekly quizzes." (Malaysia student, Other, Early (1-2), negative sentiment)

3.3 RQ3: How Does Academic Progression Shape Student Feedback?

Academic level was not significantly associated with sentiment distribution, $\chi^2(4) = 1.22$, p = .8754. Positive sentiment rates were broadly similar across all three groups: Early (59.5%), Mid (60.2%), and Advanced (65.4%). Mean sentiment scores followed a slight upward trend from Early (M = 1.0) to Advanced (M = 1.14), but the differences were negligible.

Table 6. Sentiment and theme prevalence by academic level

Measure	Early (n = 232)	Mid (n = 166)	Advanced (n = 78)
Positive sentiment %	59.5	60.2	65.4
Neutral sentiment %	32.8	30.7	26.9
Negative sentiment %	7.8	9.0	7.7
Mean sentiment	1.0	1.1	1.14
Technology Effectiveness	88 (37.9%)	55 (33.1%)	36 (46.2%)
Learning Quality	44 (19.0%)	40 (24.1%)	13 (16.7%)
Social Interaction	57 (24.6%)	21 (12.7%)	17 (21.8%)
Flexibility and Convenience	41 (17.7%)	34 (20.5%)	14 (17.9%)
Improvement Needs	26 (11.2%)	14 (8.4%)	11 (14.1%)

Note. $\chi^2(4) = 1.22$, p = .8754. Sentiment from AFINN analysis; themes from mention-based coding.

While quantitative sentiment did not vary significantly, qualitative differences in thematic emphasis were apparent. Advanced students showed an elevated focus on Technology Effectiveness (46.2%) and Improvement Needs (14.1%), suggesting that academic progression may shape the specificity and constructiveness of feedback without necessarily altering its overall valence. Early-semester students, by contrast, were more likely to mention Social Interaction concerns (24.6%), possibly reflecting the adjustment challenges of newer students.

The following responses illustrate how feedback character may shift with academic experience:

"HyFlex learning was flexible and effective. I appreciated the recordings and live interaction. To improve, better online engagement and technical support are needed for a more balanced experience." (China student, Other, Early (1-2), positive sentiment)

"As a school with such prestige, it is saddening to see it begin to replace the lecturers and tutors with generative AI. As a student, it seems more of a way to lay off costs rather than for the benefit of students. Please reconsider the use of generative Ai as it sets a bad precedent to students and education as a whole. Question 6 doesn't even have an option to deny the use of ai." (Malaysia student, Other, Mid (3-4), neutral sentiment)

"The concept of Hyflex said that we can take our lecture anytime of the week but we are still required to attend an online night session that was at a very ineffective timing. I think this contradicts with the purpose and I think it's better

for real-time lectures to be optional. Apart from that, the AI video I find is really effective because lecturer will summarise the important knowledge into videos of 10 mins which saves a lot of time and is easier to understand" (Malaysia student, Other, Advanced (5+), positive sentiment)

3.4 RQ4: What Are the Technology Acceptance and Resistance Patterns?

A fine-grained analysis of technology-specific mentions reveals sharply differentiated acceptance patterns across the five AI-mediated features. Table 7 presents the evaluation of each feature by students who mentioned it.

Table 7. Technology feature evaluation by students who mentioned each feature

Feature	Mentions	Positive	Neutral	Negative
AI Avatar Videos	77	19 (24.7%)	6 (7.8%)	52 (67.5%)
Online Classes	36	14 (38.9%)	1 (2.8%)	21 (58.3%)
Interactive Tools (Noodle Factory)	77	49 (63.6%)	5 (6.5%)	23 (29.9%)
Recorded Sessions	31	29 (93.5%)	1 (3.2%)	1 (3.2%)
Platform Stability	23	0 (0.0%)	0 (0.0%)	23 (100.0%)

Note. Based on valence coding of technology feature mentions within coded responses.

AI avatar videos were the most contested feature. Of the 77 responses that mentioned avatars, 67.5% expressed negative evaluations, with only 24.7% positive. Student objections centred on the perceived artificiality of the AI-generated voice, the absence of real-time interaction, and a sense that avatar lectures represented a diminished learning experience compared with human-led instruction. This pattern of resistance may reflect perceived ease-of-use barriers as conceptualised in the Technology Acceptance Model (Davis, 1989).

The interactive tools (primarily Noodle Factory quizzes and tutoring) received a more favourable reception: 63.6% of the 77 mentions were positive, though 29.9% were negative, with complaints focusing on answer recognition and technical reliability. Recorded sessions were overwhelmingly well received, with 93.5% of 31 mentions being positive; students valued the ability to revisit content at their own pace. Online classes drew a majority-negative response (58.3% of 36 mentions), and platform stability was universally criticised (100.0% of 23 mentions reporting technical difficulties).

Acceptance patterns also varied across module categories, suggesting that implementation context may shape student reception. Table 8 presents the sentiment distribution by module type.

Table 8. Sentiment by module category

Module Category	n	Positive %	Mean Sentiment
Education	58	74.1	1.41
Event/Tourism	34	70.6	1.2
Other	349	59.6	1.03
Hospitality	35	40.0	0.582

Note. Module categories derived from curriculum classification.

Education modules showed the highest positive sentiment (74.1%, M = 1.41), while Hospitality modules had the lowest (40.0%, M = 0.582). This variation may reflect differences in how AI features were integrated into course delivery across disciplines, though further investigation would be needed to identify the specific pedagogical factors involved.

The following quotations illustrate the range of student responses to specific technological features:

"I don't like it, I would rather having lecturer to teach me instead. I don't feel like learning, the AI lecture video is horrible, the AI video always have the same sentence structure of xxx is not only, but also xxxx, and it is so annoying yet the content is not impactful and good. In short, I just don't like it, I don't feel like the experience reciprocates with the fees I have paid." (Malaysia student, Other, Advanced (5+), neutral sentiment)

"I feel like this concept is beneficial, especially for lectures. this is so lecturers can focus more on tutorial classes. this also makes sure that the lecturer doesn't miss out on any information. i also like it better as the voices are much clearer and i can go back and watch the AI videos again." (Malaysia student, Event/Tourism, Mid (3-4), positive sentiment)

"When using HyFlex learning, I found it helpful that the platform could provide instant feedback to improve my answers, especially in essay writing. However, I often experienced issues with the system not signing me in properly, and it took a long time to access the platform. This delay was frustrating and demotivating, especially during online classes when time and focus are important." (Malaysia student, Education, Early (1-2), positive sentiment)

"HyFlex offer us to have flexible schedules on when to watch lecture videos. We can watch whenever we are available. However, I still prefer physical lecture classes because it offers an environment where I needed to be focused on the module and impact me for having classes without blanking out" (Malaysia student, Other, Mid (3-4), positive sentiment)

"I appreciate using AI for my own reading and personalised reviews. However, I think it is not really beneficial as AI only covers minimal and surfaced content

of the class. I would prefer live sessions where I could learn and absorb information better. Moreover, my Noodle Factory gives me a lot of problem whenever I want to log in or use the application." (Malaysia student, Other, Early (1-2), positive sentiment)

"To be honest, I found the HyFlex learning experience this semester quite frustrating and ineffective. The idea of flexible learning is good in theory, but in practice, it didn't work well for this module. The interaction between online and in-person students felt very disconnected, and online participation was often sidelined or ignored." (Malaysia student, Other, Early (1-2), neutral sentiment)

3.5 Mixed-Methods Integration

Table 9 presents a joint display integrating quantitative and qualitative findings across the study's four research dimensions, following the convergent design framework of Creswell and Plano Clark (2018). The integration reveals patterns of convergence, complementarity, and divergence between the two data strands.

Table 9. Joint display: Integration of quantitative and qualitative evidence

Dimension	Quantitative Finding	Qualitative Evidence	Integration Assessment
Overall sentiment	60.7% positive; d = 0.84; 31.1% neutral	Technology Effectiveness dominant theme (37.6%); students focus on evaluating specific features	Convergent: positive majority aligns with appreciation for interactive tools and recordings; the 31.1% neutral share tempers the effect size
Cross-national	No significant difference (p = .1628)	Chinese students emphasise flexibility and learning quality; Malaysian students focus on technology and social interaction	Complementary: similar sentiment levels mask qualitative differences in what students attend to
Academic progression	No significant difference (p = .8754)	Advanced students show elevated Technology Effectiveness (46.2%) and Improvement Needs (14.1%)	Complementary: progression may shape feedback specificity without altering valence
AI features	AI Avatar 67.5% negative; Recorded Sessions 93.5% positive	Students object to avatar artificiality but value replay functionality	Convergent: human-like AI features face resistance; utility features gain acceptance
Module variation	Education 74.1% vs. Hospitality 40.0%	Implementation context shapes reception across disciplines	Divergent: discipline-level differences suggest context matters more than technology itself

Note. Following Creswell and Plano Clark (2018) convergent design integration.

The integration reveals three key patterns. First, quantitative and qualitative findings converge on the overall positive-but-nuanced character of student perceptions and on the polarised reception of AI avatar technology. Second, the qualitative data complement the null quantitative findings for cross-national and academic progression effects by revealing thematic differences that sentiment scores alone do not capture. Third, module-level variation suggests that the context of implementation, not merely the technology itself, shapes student reception, a finding that emerges most clearly from the qualitative data but is supported by the quantitative sentiment differences across module categories.

Two responses illustrate the convergence-divergence dynamic. The first exemplifies a case where quantitative and qualitative signals align:

> *"The HyFlex Learning experience for this module provided a flexible and inclusive approach. I found the live interaction, through Teams video conferencing, helpful in keeping me engaged and connected with both the lecturer and my peers. The ability to revisit recorded sessions was particularly useful for reviewing difficult topics. Overall, the HyFlex model supported my learning effectively." (Other student, Other, Advanced (5+), positive sentiment)*

The second illustrates a case of divergence, where the AFINN score classified the response as positive despite substantive criticism in the text:

> *"Don't like the hybrid teaching method of AI usage with online courses. Would prefer not to have this type of hybrid learning, not recommended. The AI alone is helpful, online classes are ok but the hybrid combination is a no-go. Please don't use this hybrid method again, would prefer face to face classes with usage of this AI, or more interactive online classes. Other than that, it's good" (Other student, Other, Early (1-2), positive sentiment)*

4. DISCUSSION

The findings reveal a nuanced picture of student engagement with AI-augmented HyFlex learning. While the overall sentiment was positive, the data pointed to important variations in what students attend to and how they evaluate specific technological features. This section interprets the results through the study's theoretical framework and considers their implications for practice.

4.1 Overall Reception and Technology Focus

The 60.7% positive sentiment rate, with a large effect size (Cohen's d = 0.84), aligns with broader findings in the HyFlex literature, where student satisfaction tends to be favourable when learner choice is preserved (Bockorny et al., 2024; Choi et al., 2024). From the perspective of the Technology Acceptance Model, this suggests that students perceived the HyFlex platform as broadly useful and accessible (Davis, 1989). However, the sizeable neutral category (31.1%) tempers this interpretation, indicating that a substantial share of students remained ambivalent.

A particularly notable finding is that Technology Effectiveness (37.6%) emerged as the dominant theme, rather than Flexibility and Convenience (18.7%). This suggests that students were primarily evaluating the specific technological tools they encountered, not the flexibility of the delivery format itself. The dominance of technology-related concerns is consistent with TAM's emphasis on perceived usefulness and ease of use as primary determinants of acceptance (Davis, 1989; Venkatesh et al., 2003). For practitioners, this implies that the success of HyFlex models may hinge less on the structural flexibility they offer than on the quality and perceived utility of the specific tools deployed.

The flexibility dimension, while not dominant, remains significant. At 18.7% of responses, it reflects an ongoing appreciation for learner autonomy that aligns with Self-Determination Theory (Ryan & Deci, 2000). The ability to choose when and where to engage with course materials appears to reduce perceived stress and support self-regulated learning strategies (Broadbent & Fuller-Tyszkiewicz, 2018), a finding consistent with the learner choice and equivalency principles central to the HyFlex design (Xiao et al., 2025).

4.2 Cross-National Patterns

The descriptive trend in sentiment across nationality groups (Chinese students 66.4% positive, Other 60.0%, Malaysian 57.8%) did not reach statistical significance, $\chi^2(4) = 6.53$, $p = .1628$; $F(2, 473) = 1.687$, $p = .186$. This finding cautions against drawing strong conclusions about nationality-based differences in overall satisfaction. However, the qualitative data reveal meaningful differences in thematic emphasis that the sentiment scores alone do not capture.

Chinese students placed relatively greater emphasis on Learning Quality (27.1%) and Flexibility (27.1%), while Malaysian students were most concerned with Technology Effectiveness (40.9%) and Social Interaction (24.1%). Students from other nationalities showed the strongest focus on Technology Effectiveness (49.1%). These patterns may reflect cultural orientations described by Hofstede (2001): students from collectivist cultural backgrounds may weight social and relational aspects differently, while uncertainty avoidance may shape expectations about technology reliability (Straub et al., 1997; Teo & Huang, 2019).

The qualitative data also suggest differences in communication style that are consistent with Hall's (1976) high-context/low-context distinction. Chinese students tended to embed criticism within overall positive framing, while Malaysian students adopted a more direct evaluative tone. Students from other nationalities often offered balanced assessments that weighed positive and negative aspects explicitly. These patterns, while qualitative and not generalisable, have implications for how feedback instruments are designed and interpreted in multicultural educational settings (Meyer, 2014).

4.3 Academic Maturation

Academic progression was not significantly associated with sentiment distribution, $\chi^2(4) = 1.22$, $p = .8754$. Positive sentiment rates were broadly similar across Early (59.5%), Mid (60.2%), and Advanced (65.4%) students. This indicates that favourable attitudes toward HyFlex learning are not contingent on academic experience, a finding that speaks to the model's appeal across different stages of undergraduate study.

Nonetheless, qualitative differences in thematic emphasis were apparent. Advanced students showed elevated attention to Technology Effectiveness (46.2%) and Improvement Needs (14.1%), suggesting that academic maturation may shape the specificity and constructiveness of feedback without altering its overall valence. This pattern is consistent with developmental models of critical thinking, which posit that students' progress from dualistic acceptance toward more contextualised and evaluative reasoning as they advance (King & Kitchener, 2004; Bloom, 2010). Early-semester students, by contrast, more frequently mentioned Social Interaction concerns (24.6%), possibly reflecting the adjustment challenges and relational needs of newer students (Yaban & Gaschler, 2025).

4.4 Technology Acceptance Polarisation

The most striking finding concerns the sharply differentiated reception of individual technology features. The AI avatar videos attracted the strongest resistance, with 67.5% of the 77 students who mentioned them expressing negative evaluations and only 24.7% positive. By contrast, recorded sessions were overwhelmingly well received (93.5% positive), and interactive tools (primarily Noodle Factory) received a favourable majority (63.6% positive). This pattern suggests that technology acceptance in HyFlex settings is highly feature-specific rather than blanket.

The avatar resistance may be interpreted through the lens of TAM and UTAUT. The perceived artificiality of the AI-generated voice and the absence of real-time interaction appear to have undermined both perceived usefulness and perceived ease of use (Davis, 1989). From an SDT perspective, the replacement of human instructors with digital replicas may have compromised the relatedness component of motivation, as students reported feeling disconnected from the learning experience (Ryan & Deci, 2000). This aligns with the broader finding that AI features are most readily accepted when they complement rather than replace human instruction (Abbass, 2019), a principle consistent with the human-in-the-loop frameworks advocated by the U.S. Office of Educational Technology (2023).

The acceptance of recorded sessions and interactive tools, by contrast, suggests that AI features offering clear utility (content replay, self-assessment) without displacing the human instructor face less resistance. The social influence component of UTAUT (Venkatesh et al., 2003) may also play a role: in collectivist educational cultures, the endorsement of specific tools by lecturers and peers may carry particular weight (Holden & Rada, 2011). Platform stability, universally criticised (100.0% negative across all 23 mentions), represents a facilitating condition failure that may independently undermine technology acceptance regardless of feature quality.

Module-level variation further complicates the picture. Education modules showed the highest positive sentiment (74.1%), while Hospitality modules had the lowest (40.0%). This suggests that implementation context, including how AI features are integrated into specific disciplinary pedagogies, shapes student reception in ways that aggregate statistics may obscure.

4.5 Implementation Implications

Three practical implications emerge from the findings. First, platform stability must be treated as a precondition for technology acceptance, not an afterthought. The universal criticism of technical infrastructure failures indicates that even well-designed AI features will be poorly received if the underlying platform is unreliable. Institutions adopting HyFlex models should invest in technical infrastructure testing and support before scaling AI-mediated features.

Second, the data support a principle of human-AI complementarity rather than substitution. The sharp contrast between the positive reception of interactive tools and recorded sessions, and the rejection of AI avatars, suggests that students accept AI when it supplements human instruction but resist it when it appears to replace the human instructor. This finding aligns with human-in-the-loop frameworks that position AI as a support tool for teaching rather than an autonomous delivery mechanism (Abbass, 2019; Office of Educational Technology, 2023). From the perspective of SDT, preserving the human element may be necessary to sustain the relatedness component of intrinsic motivation (Ryan & Deci, 2000).

Third, the qualitative differences across nationality groups, while not statistically significant at the aggregate level, suggest that culturally responsive design may improve technology acceptance across diverse student populations. The distinct communication styles observed, from indirect criticism embedded in positive framing to direct evaluative commentary, imply that feedback instruments and course design processes should accommodate a range of expressive norms (Hall, 1976; Herrera et al., 2012). Institutions serving internationally diverse student bodies may benefit from piloting AI features with students from different cultural backgrounds before full-scale deployment.

5. CONCLUSION

This study examined 476 student responses across 60 modules at Taylor's University to assess perceptions of an AI-augmented HyFlex learning model. The overall sentiment was positive (60.7%), but this aggregate figure conceals important variation. Students were primarily concerned with evaluating specific technological features (Technology Effectiveness, 37.6%), not with the flexibility of the delivery model itself.

Feature-specific acceptance patterns represent the study's most actionable finding. Recorded sessions were overwhelmingly well received (93.5% positive), while AI avatar videos were strongly resisted (67.5% negative). This polarisation suggests that the success of AI integration in HyFlex settings depends not on whether AI is used, but on how it is positioned relative to human instruction. Tools that supplement human teaching are accepted; tools perceived as replacing it face resistance.

Cross-national and academic-progression effects were not statistically significant at the quantitative level, though qualitative differences in thematic emphasis suggest that cultural background and academic experience shape the focus and specificity of student feedback. These findings point to the importance of culturally responsive implementation strategies and ongoing attention to platform stability as preconditions for technology acceptance.

The study contributes to the emerging literature on AI-augmented HyFlex learning by providing empirical evidence from a large, internationally diverse student sample in a Southeast Asian context. Its convergent mixed-methods design allows both the scale of student sentiment and the texture of individual experience to inform conclusions. Future research should examine longitudinal effects, compare pre- and post-implementation perceptions, and investigate whether targeted improvements to AI avatar design can shift the acceptance patterns observed here.

6. LIMITATIONS AND METHODOLOGICAL CONSIDERATIONS

Several limitations should be considered when interpreting these findings. First, the study was conducted at a single institution (Taylor's University, Malaysia), which limits the generalisability of the results to other HyFlex implementations, particularly those in different cultural and institutional contexts. The specific configuration of AI tools (AI avatars and Noodle Factory) is particular to this setting, and student responses may not transfer to different AI-mediated features.

Second, the open-ended responses were collected in English, which was not the first language for 50.2% of respondents (n = 239). This language constraint may have limited the depth and nuance of non-native speakers' feedback, potentially biasing sentiment scores toward shorter, less expressive responses. Future studies should consider collecting responses in students' preferred languages to address this limitation.

Third, sentiment analysis was conducted using the AFINN lexicon, a dictionary-based approach that does not capture negation, sarcasm, or contextual irony. A response containing positive words used ironically would be misclassified as positive. The sensitivity analysis at multiple thresholds provides some reassurance that the majority-positive finding is not an artefact of threshold choice, but individual classifications should be interpreted with caution.

Fourth, thematic coding was performed using a large language model (Claude, Anthropic) as a coding assistant. While this approach afforded consistency across all 476 responses and maintained fidelity to the predefined Braun and Clarke codebook, it represents a departure from traditional manual coding. LLM-based coding may introduce systematic biases that are not yet well understood, and the approach limits reproducibility to the extent that model outputs may vary across versions or configurations. The transparency of disclosing this method is intended to allow readers to assess its appropriateness.

Fifth, the survey used a four-point forced-choice Likert scale (1, 2, 4, 5) with no neutral midpoint. While this design decision was intended to encourage definitive responses, it may have pushed ambivalent students toward poles they did not strongly endorse. The perception data should be interpreted with this constraint in mind.

Sixth, 58 students appeared in multiple modules due to cross-enrolment, and the analysis was conducted at the response level. While each response pertained to a specific module experience, the non-independence of responses from the same student may inflate the effective sample size and should be considered a potential source of bias. The cross-sectional design also precludes any claims about change over time; a longitudinal design with pre- and post-implementation measures would be needed to assess whether student perceptions shift with extended exposure to AI-augmented HyFlex learning.

REFERENCES

Abbass, H. A. (2019). Social integration of artificial intelligence: Functions, automation allocation logic and human-autonomy trust. *Cognitive Computation, 11*(2), 159–171. DOI: 10.1007/s12559-018-9619-0

Abdelmalak, M. M. M., & Parra, J. L. (2016). Expanding learning opportunities for graduate students with HyFlex course design. *International Journal of Online Pedagogy and Course Design, 6*(4), 19–37. DOI: 10.4018/IJOPCD.2016100102

Beatty, B. J. (2019). Hybrid-flexible course design: Implementing student-directed hybrid classes. EdTech Books. https://edtechbooks.org/hyflex

Bloom, B. S. (2010). *A taxonomy for learning, teaching, and assessing: A revision of Bloom's taxonomy of educational objectives* (Anderson, L. W., & Krathwohl, D. R., Eds.). Longman.

Bockorny, K. M., Giannavola, T. M., Mathew, S., & Walters, H. D. (2024). Effective engagement strategies in HyFlex modality based on intrinsic motivation in students. *Active Learning in Higher Education, 25*(3), 455–472. DOI: 10.1177/14697874231161364

Braun, V., & Clarke, V. (2006). Using thematic analysis in psychology. *Qualitative Research in Psychology, 3*(2), 77–101. DOI: 10.1191/1478088706qp063oa

Braun, V., & Clarke, V. (2021). One size fits all? What counts as quality practice in (reflexive) thematic analysis? *Qualitative Research in Psychology, 18*(3), 328–352. DOI: 10.1080/14780887.2020.1769238

Broadbent, J., & Fuller-Tyszkiewicz, M. (2018). Profiles in self-regulated learning and their correlates for online and blended learning students. *Educational Technology Research and Development, 66*(6), 1435–1455. DOI: 10.1007/s11423-018-9595-9

Choi, S., Li, Z., Boonme, K., & Ren, H. (2024). Face-to-face, online or HyFlex instruction? The effects of self-directed learning on stress reduction and student satisfaction among emerging adults. *Journal of International Education in Business, 17*(3), 373–394. DOI: 10.1108/JIEB-09-2023-0064

Cohen, J. (1988). *Statistical power analysis for the behavioral sciences* (2nd ed.). Lawrence Erlbaum Associates.

Creswell, J. W., & Plano Clark, V. L. (2018). *Designing and conducting mixed methods research* (3rd ed.). SAGE.

Davis, F. D. (1989). Perceived usefulness, perceived ease of use, and user acceptance of information technology. *Management Information Systems Quarterly*, *13*(3), 319–340. DOI: 10.2307/249008

Hall, E. T. (1976). *Beyond culture*. Anchor.

Herrera, S. G., Holmes, M. A., & Kavimandan, S. K. (2012). Bringing theory to life: Strategies that make culturally responsive pedagogy a reality in diverse secondary classrooms. *International Journal of Multicultural Education*, *14*(3), 1–19. DOI: 10.18251/ijme.v14i3.608

Hofstede, G. (2001). *Culture's consequences: Comparing values, behaviors, institutions and organizations across nations* (2nd ed.). SAGE.

Holden, H., & Rada, R. (2011). Understanding the influence of perceived usability and technology self-efficacy on teachers' technology acceptance. *Journal of Research on Technology in Education*, *43*(4), 343–367. DOI: 10.1080/15391523.2011.10782576

Howell, E., Linder, S., Ryan, J., & Bridges, W. C. (2025). Examining higher education through HyFlex. *Open Learning*, *40*(3), 252–267. DOI: 10.1080/02680513.2024.2354245

Islam, M. S., Fujimoto, Y., Islam, S., & Haque, A. (2026). Teaching effectiveness in the Global South's digital shift: How work-family conflict and job insecurity shape faculty identity and performance. *Studies in Higher Education*, •••, 1–18. DOI: 10.1080/03075079.2026.2640099

King, P. M., & Kitchener, K. S. (2004). Reflective judgment: Theory and research on the development of epistemic assumptions through adulthood. *Educational Psychologist*, *39*(1), 5–18. DOI: 10.1207/s15326985ep3901_2

Liu, Y. L. E., Lee, T. P., & Huang, Y. M. (2026). Enhancing student engagement and higher-order thinking in human-centred design projects: The impact of generative AI-enhanced collaborative whiteboards. *Interactive Learning Environments*, *34*(1), 258–275. DOI: 10.1080/10494820.2025.2496973

Meyer, E. (2014). *The culture map: Breaking through the invisible boundaries of global business*. PublicAffairs.

Nielsen, F. A. (2011). A new ANEW: Evaluation of a word list for sentiment analysis in microblogs. In Proceedings of the ESWC2011 Workshop on 'Making Sense of Microposts' (pp. 93-98). CEUR Workshop Proceedings.

Office of Educational Technology. (2023). Artificial intelligence and the future of teaching and learning: Insights and recommendations. U.S. Department of Education. https://www.ed.gov/sites/ed/files/documents/ai-report/ai-report.pdf

Ryan, R. M., & Deci, E. L. (2000). Self-determination theory and the facilitation of intrinsic motivation, social development, and well-being. *The American Psychologist*, *55*(1), 68–78. DOI: 10.1037/0003-066X.55.1.68 PMID: 11392867

Straub, D., Keil, M., & Brenner, W. (1997). Testing the technology acceptance model across cultures: A three country study. *Information & Management*, *33*(1), 1–11. DOI: 10.1016/S0378-7206(97)00026-8

Teo, T., & Huang, F. (2019). Investigating the influence of individually espoused cultural values on teachers' intentions to use educational technologies in Chinese universities. *Interactive Learning Environments*, *27*(5-6), 813–829. DOI: 10.1080/10494820.2018.1489856

Venkatesh, V., Morris, M. G., Davis, G. B., & Davis, F. D. (2003). User acceptance of information technology: Toward a unified view. *Management Information Systems Quarterly*, *27*(3), 425–478. DOI: 10.2307/30036540

Xiao, J., Yang, Y., & Li, M. (2025). Empirical study on the feasibility of hybrid-flexible training model for developing teachers' artificial intelligence competence. *Education and Information Technologies*, *30*(12), 1–26. DOI: 10.1007/s10639-025-13460-5

Yaban, E. H., & Gaschler, R. (2025). Developmental regulation processes and age-related motivation of distance education students. *Higher Education*, *90*(1), 177–197. DOI: 10.1007/s10734-024-01316-9

Yang, H. H., Yin, Z., & Zhu, S. (2025). Examining students' acceptance of the large-scale HyFlex course: An empirical study. *British Journal of Educational Technology*, *56*(1), 42–60. DOI: 10.1111/bjet.13477

Chapter 16

Transforming Assessment With AI in a HyFlex Environment: From Automation to Authenticity

Motlokwe Calvin Thobejane
http://orcid.org/0009-0001-1347-0736
University of South Africa, South Africa

Eva G. Makwakwa
http://orcid.org/0000-0002-6565-3235
University of South Africa, South Africa

ABSTRACT

This chapter examines how assessment can be reimagined in HyFlex environments in response to the growing influence of artificial intelligence (AI). It argues that AI should not be positioned primarily as a tool for automation or surveillance, but as a carefully governed support for authentic, equitable, and pedagogically meaningful assessment. Drawing on TPACK and PESTEL as complementary analytical lenses, the chapter explores the challenges of multimodal assessment, including equivalency, workload, access, governance, and institutional readiness. It further proposes that authentic AI-supported assessment in HyFlex depends on the alignment of human academic judgement, equity-conscious design, and institutional capacity. In doing so, the chapter offers a practice-informed conceptual contribution with illustrative South African insights for institutions seeking to move from automation-centred assessment toward more transparent, responsive, and sustainable assessment practices..

DOI: 10.4018/979-8-3373-6182-6.ch016

1. INTRODUCTION: RATIONALIZING AI-POWERED ASSESSMENT FOR THE HYFLEX ERA

The contemporary higher education landscape is characterized by a triad of powerful, disruptive forces: a demographic and societal demand for unprecedented flexibility, a moral and legal imperative for genuine inclusivity, and the pressing need to prepare students for a rapidly evolving, technology-saturated world. The HyFlex (Hybrid-Flexible) model has emerged as a potent structural and pedagogical response to the first two demands, systematically dismantling temporal and spatial barriers to learning access. By empowering students to choose, on a session-by-session basis, whether to engage in person, synchronously online, or asynchronously, HyFlex promises to make high-quality education more responsive to the complex realities of modern life. However, this very strength reveals its core vulnerability, as detailed in Section 2: its foundational principles, namely student choice, equivalency, reusability, and accessibility generate a profound and complex assessment challenge (Guerreau-Jalabert, 2022). How can educators and institutions design and implement assessments that are demonstrably fair, academically valid, and authentically aligned with learning outcomes when a single cohort of students is dispersed across different temporal and modal planes? The traditional assessment arsenal, heavily reliant on high-stakes, time-bound, in-person examinations and standardized tasks, fractures under the weight of this multi-modal complexity. Concerns about academic integrity, unsustainable instructor workload, and the sheer logistical difficulty of providing truly equivalent learning experiences become paramount, threatening to undermine the entire HyFlex enterprise (Chen & Lai, 2024; Öz, 2024).

Simultaneously, the advent of sophisticated Artificial Intelligence (AI), particularly Generative AI and large language models (LLMs), presents a parallel disruption. It offers an existential threat to the integrity of traditional assessment while also holding the promise of its most significant transformation in a century. The ability of AI to generate coherent text, solve complex problems, and simulate human-like interaction challenges the validity of any assessment that can be easily outsourced to a machine (Kolade, Owoseni, & Egbetokun, 2024). Yet, this same capability provides the tools to solve the inherent assessment dilemmas of the HyFlex model. This chapter posits that the convergence of HyFlex and AI is not merely coincidental but is, in fact, *necessary and symbiotic*. AI provides the technological leverage to address the core pedagogical problems of HyFlex assessment, moving us beyond using technology simply to automate old, inefficient processes (such as automated multiple-choice grading or invasive remote proctoring) and towards a new paradigm of authentic assessment (Khlaif et al., 2024; Naseer et al., 2024). This new paradigm is designed to measure deeper learning, foster metacognition, provide personalized pathways, and, crucially, prepare students for the complexities of a modern workplace where human-AI collaboration will be the norm.

To navigate this complex transformation systematically and avoid the pitfalls of either technocentric hype or pedagogical conservatism, this chapter is framed through two complementary analytical lenses that operate at different scales of influence:

1. The TPACK Framework: This lens focuses on the *internal*, pedagogical, and context-specific integration of technology. It ensures that the adoption of AI into HyFlex assessment is not a mere technical add-on but a deeply considered, pedagogically sound, and discipline-aware practice. It asks the question: "What knowledge do educators need to integrate technology effectively?"
2. The PESTEL Framework: This lens focuses on the *external*, macro-environmental factors that enable, constrain, and shape this transformation. It situates the pedagogical work of the educator within the broader institutional, societal, economic, and political context. It asks the question: "What external forces influence whether this integration can succeed at scale?"

By weaving these two frameworks throughout our analysis—from the broad rationale to the specific case studies—we move from a simplistic "how-to" guide towards a strategic, holistic exploration of *why* this transformation is needed, *what* it entails at the level of practice, and *under what conditions* it can be sustainably and ethically implemented. The journey from automation to authenticity is, therefore, a journey towards sophisticated professional knowledge (TPACK) enabled by strategic institutional navigation of a complex external landscape (PESTEL).

1.1. Introducing the Analytical Lenses: TPACK and PESTEL

The TPACK Framework: Integrating Technology with Pedagogical Content Knowledge

The Technological Pedagogical Content Knowledge (TPACK) framework, developed by Mishra and Koehler (2006), provides a critical model for understanding the knowledge base required for effective technology integration. It argues that successful integration is not merely about adding technology to existing practice but requires an intricate, nuanced interplay of three primary forms of knowledge:

- Content Knowledge (CK): The educator's deep mastery of the actual subject matter to be taught and assessed. This is the knowledge of the field, whether it is History, Mechanical Engineering, Nursing, or Literary Theory. It encompasses knowledge of key facts, concepts, theories, procedures, and evidence frameworks.

- Pedagogical Knowledge (PK): The deep understanding of the processes and practices of teaching and learning. This is knowledge of how students learn, general classroom management techniques, lesson planning, instructional strategies, and, most critically for this chapter, assessment methods and theories. It is knowledge of how to teach, irrespective of the subject.
- Technological Knowledge (TK): Knowledge about how to use, apply, and understand digital tools and platforms. This includes standard technologies like learning management systems (LMS) and video conferencing, but in the current context, it centrally involves knowledge of AI tools—from generative AI and adaptive learning platforms to automated grading systems and analytics dashboards. Crucially, TK involves an understanding of how these tools work, their affordances, and their limitations.

The true power and complexity of the TPACK framework lie in the dynamic intersections of these three core components:

- Pedagogical Content Knowledge (PCK): This is the core of expert teaching. It is the knowledge of how to make specific content accessible and comprehensible to learners. It involves knowing the most effective analogies, examples, demonstrations, and assessment forms for teaching a particular topic (e.g., using a Socratic dialogue to explore philosophical concepts or a case-based approach to teach clinical reasoning in medicine).
- Technological Content Knowledge (TCK): An understanding of how technology and content influence and constrain one another. This involves knowing how AI can change the very nature of a discipline. For instance, in History, TCK involves understanding how AI-powered text analysis of vast archival databases can change the methods of historical inquiry, or in Biology, how AI-driven protein-folding models are revolutionizing the field. Assessment must evolve to reflect these changing disciplinary practices.
- Technological Pedagogical Knowledge (TPK): Knowledge of how various technologies can be used to change teaching and learning, regardless of the content. This involves understanding how different tools can support specific pedagogical strategies. For example, using a collaborative whiteboard (TK) to facilitate brainstorming (a pedagogical strategy), or using polling software (TK) to conduct formative assessment (PK).
- Technological Pedagogical Content Knowledge (TPACK): This is the ultimate goal, the integrative, context-dependent knowledge required to design and implement effective learning experiences using technology. It represents

a form of expertise where the educator can strategically select a tool (AI-powered simulation), deploy a pedagogical approach (problem-based learning), to teach a specific concept (clinical diagnosis) in a way that would be impossible without the technology. It is the sweet spot where technology, pedagogy, and content align seamlessly to address a specific learning challenge.

In this chapter, we use the TPACK framework as a critical lens to analyze how AI (TK) must be thoughtfully and intentionally woven into assessment design (PK) to validly measure and foster learning in specific disciplines (CK) within the unique and challenging context of a HyFlex learning environment. It forces us to move beyond the question of "What can this AI tool do?" to the more profound question of "How can this AI tool help me assess what my students truly need to know and be able to do in my specific subject, in this specific multimodal context?"

The PESTEL Framework: Scanning the Macro-Environment

While TPACK provides the internal map for effective integration, the PESTEL framework provides the compass for navigating the external environment. It is a strategic tool used to analyze the broad macro-environmental factors that can significantly impact an organization's plans and operations. For our purposes, the "organization" is the higher education institution seeking to implement AI-enhanced assessment in HyFlex programs. A PESTEL analysis examines six key domains:

- Political: This includes governmental policies, funding priorities, and regulatory pressures that influence higher education. Relevant factors include national strategies for AI adoption in education, government funding for digital infrastructure, political pressure to increase access and affordability, and the influence of accreditation bodies that set standards for assessment validity and institutional quality.
- Economic: This encompasses the financial realities facing institutions. Key factors are institutional budgets for technology procurement and support, the total cost of ownership of AI tools, the return on investment calculations for HyFlex classroom upgrades, evolving staffing models (e.g., the need for instructional designers or AI support specialists), and the pervasive issue of the digital divide that creates inequities in student access to required technology (Howell et al., 2024).
- Social: This refers to socio-cultural and demographic trends. It includes student and faculty readiness and attitudes towards technology, shifting societal expectations for flexible and lifelong education, public concerns about equity,

bias, and the ethical use of AI, and changing employer expectations about the skills graduates should possess.

- Technological: This involves the pace of technological change and the institutional capacity to keep up. It includes the availability, robustness, and interoperability of institutional IT infrastructure (networks, LMS, AV systems), the development and reliability of specific AI tools for assessment, issues of data security and systems integration, and the relentless pace of innovation that can quickly render specific tools or strategies obsolete (Chen & Lai, 2024;).
- Environmental: While often less prominent, this factor is increasingly relevant. It includes the sustainability benefits of HyFlex models (e.g., reduced student and staff commuting, lowering the carbon footprint of a campus) contrasted with the significant environmental cost of training and running large AI models, which consume vast amounts of energy and water for data center cooling.
- Legal: This is a critical domain, encompassing the laws and regulations that govern institutional action. It includes data privacy and protection regulations like GDPR (in Europe) and FERPA (in the U.S.), POPIA (in South Africa), intellectual property rights concerning AI-generated content and student data, emerging laws regarding algorithmic accountability and bias, and compliance with disability legislation that mandates accessibility for all learners (Shivshankar & Acharya, 2024).

By consistently employing the PESTEL framework, we ensure that our discussion of transforming assessment with AI in HyFlex is not an idealized, theoretical exercise. Instead, it is grounded in the real-world constraints, pressures, and opportunities that university leaders, administrators, and faculty must confront. A brilliant TPACK-based assessment design will fail if it is legally non-compliant, economically unsustainable, or socially unacceptable.

2. THE HYFLEX ENVIRONMENT AND THE ASSESSMENT CHALLENGE (THROUGH TPACK AND PESTEL)

The HyFlex model is far more than a simple technical setup of cameras and microphones; it is a fundamental re-imagining of course design where "each class session and learning activity can be experienced in person, synchronously online, or asynchronously" (Beatty, 2014). Originating from a need to provide genuine flexibility, it entitles students to "equivalent learning opportunities regardless of mode," allowing them to remain in a single cohort while exercising agency over their participation (Öz, 2024). This structure is underpinned by four core principles that directly shape its pedagogical and operational character: student choice, equivalency, reusability, and accessibility (Guerreau-Jalabert, 2022). The principle of equivalency is particularly paramount for assessment, as it demands that activities and assessments avoid creating a "learning deficit" in any mode. This is not about providing identical experiences, but rather ones that are different yet equitable in their rigor, engagement, and opportunity to demonstrate learning (Guerreau-Jalabert, 2022).

The implementation of HyFlex is not monolithic. Institutions adapt the model into workable patterns based on their resources and student needs, as summarized in Table 1. The Fully Synchronous Dual Delivery model prioritizes real-time parity but at a high cognitive and technical cost (Chen & Lai, 2024). The Asynchronous-Centred HyFlex model maximizes flexibility but requires exceptionally high-quality, self-contained asynchronous materials to maintain engagement (Öz, 2024). The Modified HyFlex for Large Classes scales the model but often at the expense of live interaction and a fully equivalent experience (Beatty, 2014). These implementation choices are not merely logistical; they are foundational to the assessment ecology that can be built within them.

Table 1. Common HyFlex implementation variants and trade-offs

Approach	What it offers	Typical requirements	Main trade-offs
Fully synchronous dual delivery	Real-time parity for in-room and remote students	Robust AV systems, reliable network, classroom mics/ cameras, live support staff (Chen & Lai, 2024)	High instructor cognitive load and tech cost; strong immediacy if implemented well (Chen & Lai, 2024)
Asynchronous-centred HyFlex	Maximum flexibility for learners who seldom attend synchronously	High-quality asynchronous materials, clear LMS organisation, explicit equivalency mapping (Öz, 2024)	Lower real-time interaction; requires well-designed asynchronous activities (Öz, 2024)
Modified HyFlex for large classes	Scales to large enrolments with choice to attend live or view later	Streaming platform, polling/ backchannel, recording workflows (Beatty, 2014)	Easier to scale; potential reduction in live engagement or parity of experience (Beatty, 2014)

Analyzing the HyFlex Challenge through TPACK

The assessment challenges inherent in the HyFlex model can be powerfully diagnosed through the TPACK lens. The core problem is a misalignment, or a deficient intersection, of the framework's components.

- The PK-CK Tension (Pedagogical Content Knowledge): Many traditional assessment methods, such as timed, in-person exams, are a deeply ingrained part of a discipline's PCK. They are "how we have always assessed" this content. However, in a HyFlex context, this PCK becomes problematic. The pedagogical approach (proctored exam) is no longer effective or equitable across the new learning modalities.
- The TK-PK Gap (Technological Pedagogical Knowledge): The initial response to HyFlex is often to use technology (TK) to replicate the old pedagogy (PK). This is the "bolt-on" approach. For example, using remote proctoring software (TK) to invigilate an online exam (an old PK). This demonstrates a basic TPK, but it is a negative one—using technology to enforce a pedagogical model that is ill-suited to the environment, often leading to student anxiety, privacy concerns, and a focus on integrity over learning.
- The Missing TPACK: The fundamental challenge is that HyFlex creates a new context that demands a new form of TPACK. Educators must develop the knowledge to design assessments (PK) that use technology (TK) to validly measure disciplinary learning (CK) across multiple modes. The problems of "equity of access," "fairness and validity," and "academic integrity" are, at their core, symptoms of a lack of appropriate TPACK (Chen & Lai, 2024; Lawrence-Slater, 2001). The solutions proposed in the literature such as using "authentic tasks," "shared rubrics," and "integrity by design" are all emergent strategies for building this new, context-specific TPACK (Gordon, 2016; Khlaif et al., 2024). For instance, the design pattern of creating reusable "concept capsules" is a TPACK-driven solution: it uses technology (TK) for capture and reuse to support a pedagogical goal of equivalency (PK) across different learning pathways for the same content (CK).

Analyzing the HyFlex Challenge through PESTEL

The implementation barriers and drivers for HyFlex are predominantly located in the external PESTEL environment.

- Political: Accreditation bodies (a political/regulatory force) require evidence of equivalent learning outcomes across modalities. A HyFlex program must be able to demonstrate to accreditors that a student who primarily participated asynchronously achieved the same standards as one who attended in person.
- Economic: The high cost of robust classroom AV systems, reliable networking, and support staff (Chen & Lai, 2024) is a significant Economic barrier. The "instructor workload" crisis is also an economic issue, relating to faculty

capacity and staffing models (Cumming et al., 2024). Conversely, the potential for HyFlex to aid student recruitment and provide continuity during disruptions is a powerful economic driver (Öz, 2024).

- Social: The primary driver for HyFlex is Social: the growing student demand for flexibility due to work, caregiving, and lifestyle preferences. However, social challenges include varying levels of digital literacy among both students and faculty and concerns about creating a two-tiered system where online students feel like second-class citizens.
- Technological: The entire model is dependent on Technological factors: "technical robustness, particularly classroom audio and reliable networks" (Chen & Lai, 2024). The lack of interoperable tools and standardized LMS features can be a major impediment.
- Legal: The principle of accessibility is not just a good practice; it is a Legal requirement under disability laws. HyFlex implementations must ensure that all content and assessments are accessible to students with disabilities, regardless of their chosen mode of participation (Guerreau-Jalabert, 2022).

In summary, the HyFlex environment creates a perfect storm of assessment challenges that are both pedagogical (requiring new TPACK) and systemic (shaped by PESTEL factors). The emergence of AI enters this storm not as a disruptive outsider, but as a potential force that can be harnessed to navigate it, provided it is guided by these same analytical frameworks.

3. AI IN ASSESSMENT: FROM AUTOMATION TO AUTHENTICITY (THROUGH TPACK AND PESTEL)

The application of AI in education has undergone a significant evolution, mirroring broader shifts in technological capability and pedagogical understanding. The initial, and still prevalent, wave has been characterized by a focus on automation and efficiency. This wave leveraged AI as a capacity multiplier, aiming to scale traditionally labor-intensive processes. The demonstrated benefits are clear: automated scoring of standardized responses and multiple-choice questions provides faster feedback to students and frees instructors from the drudgery of grading routine assignments. Plagiarism detection systems, an early form of AI, reduced manual investigation workloads. Learning analytics platforms used predictive algorithms to identify students at risk of failing, allowing for early intervention (Naseer et al., 2024).

However, the limitations of this automation-centric approach have become increasingly apparent. The rise of generative AI has fundamentally challenged the operational meaning of "originality," as models like ChatGPT can produce high-quality essays that easily bypass traditional plagiarism checks (Kolade et al., 2024). Furthermore, studies have shown that while LLMs can align with mean human grades, they often demonstrate risk-averse tendencies and lower inter-rater reliability on nuanced, discipline-specific criteria, making them unreliable as sole graders for complex work. The focus on automation, while efficient, often left deeper learning objectives unaddressed and did little to resolve the core assessment dilemmas of HyFlex; it simply automated them, sometimes with negative consequences (e.g., AI proctoring increasing student anxiety).

This has given rise to an emerging, more powerful perspective that argues for a shift from discrete outputs to authenticity and deeper learning. This second wave is predicated on two key anchors. First, a performance/process focus, which involves assessing "show how" and complex competencies through iterative work, rather than solely assessing "know what" through final products. Second, the design of tasks resistant to trivial automation such as complex collaborative projects, portfolios that document a learning journey, and messy, real-world problems—which preserves assessment validity in the age of AI (Kolade, Owoseni, & Egbetokun, 2024). In this paradigm, AI is reframed from a replacement for human judgement to an augmentation tool. It can provide scaffolding and adaptive feedback across extended performance tasks, power analytics that reveal learning trajectories, and act as a reflective partner for students, all while the crucial final judgements on complex, nuanced work remain with the instructor (Khlaif et al., 2024).

Table 2. Transition dimensions and operational strategies

Dimension	Key drivers	Operational strategies
Policy & governance	Institutional integrity pressures; regulatory expectations	Clear AI-use policies; updated academic-integrity rules; co-design with faculty and students (Shivshankar & Acharya, 2024)
Pedagogy & design	Need for authentic competency assessment; employer expectations	Redesign toward performance tasks, portfolios, collaborative projects; align rubrics to competencies (Naseer et al., 2024; Khlaif et al., 2024)
Technology & trust	Efficiency; formative feedback	Human-in-the-loop systems; explainable AI and transparent rubrics to support appeals (Naseer et al., 2024)
Capacity & equity	Instructor readiness; access disparities	Professional development; supported pilots; monitor equity impacts before scale (Khlaif et al., 2024)

Analyzing the AI Evolution through TPACK

The transition from automation to authenticity is, in essence, a journey from a lower-order to a higher-order application of TPACK.

- Automation as TCK and TPK: The first wave of AI in assessment primarily operated at the level of Technological Content Knowledge (TCK) and Technological Pedagogical Knowledge (TPK). Automated scoring uses AI (TK) to process student responses (CK). Proctoring software uses AI (TK) to monitor student behavior during an exam (a pedagogical context, PK). These are useful applications, but they leave the core pedagogy and content unchanged. They represent a "substitution" level on the SAMR model, not a transformation.
- Authenticity as TPACK: The shift to authenticity requires the full integration of TPACK. It involves rethinking the very nature of the assessment task (the Pedagogy) to make it authentic and AI-resilient. This new pedagogy is then enabled by AI tools (Technology) to manage the complexity that such tasks entail (e.g., providing continuous feedback on a process). Crucially, the task is designed to measure core disciplinary competencies (Content) in a way that reflects how knowledge is applied in the real world. The design pattern of converting a terminal essay into a staged portfolio with a reflective defence is a classic example of TPACK in action. It uses a new pedagogical process (PK), supported by AI for scaffolding and feedback (TK), to more authentically assess research and critical thinking skills (CK).

Analyzing the AI Evolution through PESTEL

This pedagogical evolution is being driven and constrained by powerful external forces.

- Social: The primary driver for authenticity is a Social one: the recognition that graduates need more than the ability to recall information; they need applied competence, creativity, and critical thinking—skills highly valued by employers. Furthermore, student and faculty concerns about the ethical use of AI are pushing institutions beyond simplistic detection and towards more thoughtful integration.
- Political and Legal: The "policy and governance" dimension of this transition is deeply rooted in Political and Legal factors. Institutions are under pressure to create clear AI-use policies, update academic integrity rules, and establish governance frameworks that comply with emerging regulations around AI and data privacy (Shivshankar & Acharya, 2024).
- Economic: The Economic implications are twofold. There is a cost associated with procuring advanced AI tools that support authentic assessment (e.g., simulation platforms). However, there is also a powerful economic driver:

the need to produce graduates who can thrive in a modern economy, thus enhancing the institution's reputation and attractiveness.

- Technological: The very possibility of this shift is enabled by Technological advancements. The capabilities of generative AI, natural language processing, and learning analytics platforms have reached a level of sophistication where they can now support complex, process-oriented assessment rather than just automate simple tasks.

The following sections will delve into the key dimensions of this transformation, consistently applying the TPACK and PESTEL lenses to provide a multi-faceted understanding of how AI can be harnessed to create a new, more authentic, and equitable assessment paradigm for the HyFlex world.

4. KEY DIMENSIONS OF TRANSFORMING ASSESSMENT WITH AI

The transformation of assessment through AI in a HyFlex environment is not a single change but a multi-dimensional shift. Here, we explore five critical dimensions, analyzing each through the dual lenses of TPACK and PESTEL to illuminate both the pedagogical mechanics and the broader contextual factors at play.

4.1 Personalization and Adaptivity: Tailoring the Learning Journey

The industrial-era model of education, with its standardized pace and content, is profoundly ill-suited for the diverse needs of a HyFlex classroom, where students enter with varying prior knowledge, learning preferences, and life circumstances. AI-powered personalization and adaptivity dismantle this one-size-fits-all model, creating a dynamic, responsive learning environment that treats each student as an individual (Owan et al., 2023). At its core, this dimension is about using AI to analyze student data and create a unique, optimized pathway for every learner, ensuring they are appropriately challenged and supported regardless of their chosen modality.

The mechanisms are sophisticated. AI systems continuously collect and interpret data from a student's interactions—time spent on resources, performance on formative quizzes, patterns in forum posts—and use machine learning to power features like personalized learning pathways (curating a non-linear journey through content), real-time formative feedback (acting as a 24/7 tutor), and adaptive testing (dynamically adjusting question difficulty to precisely measure ability). This adaptivity can be viewed at different scales: micro-adaptivity adjusts a single learning task in real-time, while macro-adaptivity reshapes a student's entire learning path over weeks or months, potentially even guiding them towards the HyFlex modality (synchronous vs. asynchronous) that best suits their current needs and performance.

TPACK Analysis of Personalization & Adaptivity:

This dimension represents a powerful synergy of all TPACK components. The AI system's ability to analyze student performance on tasks (Content Knowledge - CK) and provide tailored resources is a function of Technological Content Knowledge (TCK). Its capacity to sequence these resources and provide pedagogical scaffolding is Technological Pedagogical Knowledge (TPK). However, the *design* of effective personalized pathways is the essence of TPACK. An educator must possess deep PCK to know which concepts are foundational, which are complex, and what sequence and scaffolding are most effective for learning their specific subject. They then leverage the AI's adaptive capabilities (TK) to operationalize this PCK at scale. For example, in a programming course (CK), the instructor's knowledge that understanding for-loops is prerequisite to mastering while-loops (PCK) is encoded into an AI system (TK) that automatically provides remedial loop exercises (TPK) to a struggling student. This is a clear manifestation of context-dependent TPACK.

PESTEL Analysis of Personalization & Adaptivity:

- Economic: This is the most significant domain. The development and procurement of sophisticated adaptive learning platforms are costly (Economic). Furthermore, the digital divide is a critical Economic and social equity issue; personalized learning assumes all students have reliable, uninterrupted access to the technology, which is not a universal reality.
- Social: There is a growing Social expectation for services, including education, to be tailored to the individual. However, concerns about surveillance and data-tracking can create student and faculty resistance.
- Technological: This dimension is entirely dependent on robust Technological infrastructure, including data interoperability between the LMS, the adaptive platform, and student information systems.
- Legal: The extensive data collection required for personalization raises serious Legal questions regarding data privacy (GDPR, FERPA, POPIA). Institutions must have clear policies on data ownership, usage, and protection.

4.2 Authenticity and Real-World Tasks: Bridging the Gap Between Theory and Practice

The HyFlex model, by its very nature, breaks down the physical walls of the traditional classroom. Assessment must follow suit by breaking down the conceptual walls between academic exercises and real-world practice. Authentic assessment asks students to perform meaningful tasks that demonstrate application of essential knowledge and skills in contexts that mirror those faced by professionals in the field (Wiggins, 1990). AI is a powerful enabler for designing, managing, and evaluating these complex tasks, making them feasible even in large, distributed HyFlex cohorts.

The limitations of traditional assessment are starkly revealed in HyFlex. A high-stakes, proctored final exam is logistically challenging to administer equitably across modalities and often fails to capture the skills we claim to value: critical thinking, collaboration, creativity, and complex problem-solving. AI allows educators to replace these methods with assessments that are more valid and more resilient to academic dishonesty. This includes using AI to generate dynamic, branching scenarios and simulations tailored to individual students (e.g., a unique business case or a virtual patient simulation). It involves using AI to track and assess complex, process-oriented work like research projects or software development, analyzing version history and contribution logs to evaluate problem-solving strategies. Furthermore, Natural Language Processing (NLP) can be used for deeper analysis of open-ended responses, evaluating the coherence of an argument in a policy brief or a legal memo.

TPACK Analysis of Authenticity & Real-World Tasks:

This dimension is fundamentally about Pedagogical Content Knowledge (PCK). The very definition of an "authentic task" is discipline-specific. What constitutes authentic practice in History (e.g., analyzing primary sources to construct a historical narrative) is different from in Engineering (e.g., designing and testing a prototype under constraints). Therefore, the core of designing authentic assessment is a PCK challenge. AI (TK) then supercharges this PCK, enabling the creation of TPACK. For instance, an instructor's knowledge of authentic clinical practice (PCK in Nursing) can be operationalized through an AI-powered patient simulator (TK) that creates realistic, adaptive scenarios for students to diagnose and treat. The technology allows the pedagogy to achieve a new level of fidelity and scalability that was previously impossible. The assessment is no longer *about* the content; it is a performance *within* the content, facilitated by technology.

PESTEL Analysis of Authenticity & Real-World Tasks:

- Social: The primary driver is Social: employer demand for graduates with applied, practical skills and the ability to solve ill-structured problems. There is a growing social consensus that "knowing" is not enough; students must be able to "do."
- Economic: There are Economic costs associated with developing or licensing high-quality simulation software. However, the long-term Economic benefit is a more skilled and job-ready graduate, enhancing the institution's reputation.

- Technological: The feasibility of this dimension hinges on Technological advancements in AI, particularly in simulation fidelity, natural language understanding, and the processing power required for complex, interactive tasks.
- Political: Political pressure from governments and industry groups to align education with workforce needs can accelerate the adoption of authentic assessment models.

4.3 Feedback and Reflection: The Engine of Metacognitive Growth

Feedback is universally acknowledged as one of the most powerful influences on learning and achievement (Hattie & Timperley, 2007). Yet, in a large or distributed HyFlex class, providing timely, specific, and actionable feedback to every student is a Herculean task. AI transforms this dimension by automating the provision of immediate, formative feedback and by creating structures that foster critical self-reflection, the cornerstone of metacognition.

AI-driven feedback mechanisms include automated formative feedback on everything from code logic to essay structure, providing students with instant guidance they can act upon. Crucially, this can be personalized feedback at scale, where the AI tailors its responses based on a student's historical errors and challenges. Furthermore, AI can facilitate reflection through reflective journaling prompts and chatbots that act as Socratic partners, prompting students to explain their reasoning or identify their own knowledge gaps. AI-powered self-assessment tools can help students evaluate their work against rubrics and exemplars before submission, cultivating a growth mindset.

TPACK Analysis of Feedback & Reflection:

At its core, effective feedback is a Pedagogical Knowledge (PK) challenge. The principles of good feedback—that it should be timely, specific, and actionable—are general. AI's role in delivering this feedback is Technological Pedagogical Knowledge (TPK). However, the *content* of that feedback must be meaningful within the discipline, which requires TPACK. An AI tool might be excellent at identifying grammatical errors (a general TPK), but providing feedback on the strength of a sociological argument or the validity of a chemical engineering calculation requires the tool to be configured with an understanding of the disciplinary Content Knowledge (CK). The educator's TPACK is demonstrated in their ability to design feedback prompts and criteria (PK) that leverage the AI's capabilities (TK) to address common disciplinary misconceptions and advance discipline-specific ways of thinking (CK).

PESTEL Analysis of Feedback & Reflection:

- Economic: The Economic driver here is powerful: AI feedback can significantly reduce the time instructors spend on routine feedback, freeing them for higher-value interactions. The cost is the subscription or development cost of the feedback tools.
- Social: Students have a Social expectation for rapid feedback. Delayed feedback is often perceived as a lack of support, especially in asynchronous online settings.
- Legal: As with personalization, the data generated by student interactions with feedback tools is subject to Legal data privacy regulations.
- Technological: The accuracy and nuance of AI-powered feedback are Technological limitations. Over-reliance on imperfect systems can lead to the propagation of errors or superficial learning if not carefully managed.

4.4 Equity and Access: Designing for an Inclusive Future

The promise of HyFlex is to expand access to education for non-traditional students, those with caregiving responsibilities, individuals with disabilities, and those in remote locations. However, without deliberate design, technology can exacerbate existing inequities. The strategic use of AI in assessment presents a unique opportunity to advance equity, but it also carries significant risks that must be mitigated.

When designed with inclusivity as a core principle, AI can be a powerful tool for leveling the playing field. Personalized support ensures all students receive the scaffolding they need to succeed, directly addressing issues of varying prior preparation. AI can power built-in accessibility features like real-time captioning, text-to-speech, and language translation, removing barriers for students with disabilities and those who are non-native speakers. In a HyFlex setting, AI-driven engagement analytics can help instructors ensure that the contributions of asynchronous online students are valued equally with those of in-person students, preventing the formation of a two-tiered classroom.

However, the path to equitable AI is fraught with challenges. Algorithmic bias is a paramount concern; AI models trained on biased data can perpetuate and amplify societal biases, for example, by penalizing non-standard dialects of English or failing to recognize diverse facial features in proctoring software. The digital divide remains a stark Economic and social reality; requiring students to use sophisticated AI platforms without providing institutional resources will disadvantage lower-income students (Wong et al., 2023). The extensive data collection inherent in AI-powered assessment raises profound privacy and surveillance concerns.

TPACK Analysis of Equity & Access:

Equitable design is, first and foremost, a matter of Pedagogical Knowledge (PK). It is grounded in the principles of Universal Design for Learning (UDL) and a commitment to inclusive teaching. The integration of AI (TK) into this pedagogical framework is where TPACK becomes an ethical imperative. An educator with strong TPACK will not just use a tool because it is available; they will critically evaluate it for potential biases (e.g., "Does this NLP feedback tool work well for non-native English speakers?") and will design assessments and supports that use technology to *reduce* barriers rather than create them. For example, providing multiple means of action and expression (a UDL principle, PK) by allowing students to choose between a written report, an oral presentation (recorded for async), or a multimedia project, all assessed with a common rubric, is a TPACK-informed approach to equity.

PESTEL Analysis of Equity & Access:

- Social: Equity is a central Social justice issue. Public scrutiny of biased algorithms is increasing, and institutions have a social responsibility to ensure their technologies are fair.
- Legal: There are strong Legal imperatives for equity, primarily through disability legislation (e.g., the Americans with Disabilities Act). Using non-compliant tools can open institutions to lawsuits.
- Economic: Addressing the digital divide requires Economic investment in device loaner programs, campus technology hubs, and subsidized internet access (Howell et al., 2024).
- Political: Political movements and government policy can either fund initiatives to close equity gaps or, conversely, create environments where such concerns are overlooked.

4.5 Academic Integrity: Cultivating Trust in a Distributed Ecosystem

Academic integrity is often the foremost concern when assessing students in remote and online settings. The initial, and most common, application of AI has been as a policing tool—a digital monitor to deter and detect cheating. While this has a role, a transformative approach uses AI not just to police dishonesty but to create an environment where integrity is the natural outcome of well-designed learning and assessment.

AI as a policing tool includes AI-proctored exams that monitor students via webcam and plagiarism and contract-cheating detection systems that analyze writing style. However, a more powerful and educationally sound approach is to use AI to redesign assessments so that cheating becomes difficult and, more importantly, irrelevant. This involves the widespread adoption of authentic assessments (as in Section 4.2) that are inherently cheat-resistant. It also includes using AI to create personalized and adaptive assessments where every student receives a unique set of questions or problems, eliminating the possibility of answer-sharing. Furthermore, by promoting a culture of continuous feedback (Section 4.3), the grade pressure that often motivates cheating is reduced, reframing assessment as a part of the learning process.

TPACK Analysis of Academic Integrity:

A purely technological approach to integrity (e.g., relying solely on AI proctoring) demonstrates a limited Technological Knowledge (TK) applied to a Pedagogical Knowledge (PK) problem. It is a defensive, low-TPACK strategy. A high-TPACK approach to integrity integrates all three components. It involves designing assessment tasks (PK) that are so deeply connected to the core competencies of the discipline (CK) and so process-oriented that outsourcing them is either impossible or defeats the purpose of learning. The technology (TK) is then used to *support* this design—for example, by using AI to generate unique problem sets or to facilitate the peer review process for a collaborative project. The focus shifts from "catching cheaters" to "designing for honesty," which requires a sophisticated understanding of how pedagogy and content interact within a technological environment.

PESTEL Analysis of Academic Integrity:

- Social: The core of integrity is a Social and cultural issue. A "clicker" culture of mistrust, fostered by over-reliance on surveillance, can damage the learning community. Conversely, a culture of trust and academic honor is a social construct that must be nurtured.
- Legal: Legal factors are involved in the form of institutional academic integrity policies and the due process required when AI flags a student for misconduct.
- Political: The Political reputation of an institution is tied to the perceived rigor and integrity of its qualifications, making this a high-stakes issue for university leadership.
- Economic: There are Economic costs associated with both proctoring software and the faculty time required to investigate academic misconduct cases.

5. PRACTICAL STRATEGIES AND CASE EXAMPLES

The theoretical framework and dimensional analysis come to life through practical application. This section provides real-world examples of AI in HyFlex assessment, analyzed through the dual perspectives of instructors and students, and interpreted through our TPACK and PESTEL lenses. Understanding these contrasting viewpoints and contextual factors is essential for designing implementations that are technologically sound, pedagogically effective, and broadly accepted.

Case Example 1: The AI-Proctored High-Stakes Exam

- Context: A final exam in a large-enrollment, required course (e.g., Introduction to Psychology). Students can choose to take the exam in a lecture hall with human proctors or remotely from any location.
- AI Tool & Function: An automated proctoring system (e.g., Proctorio, Respondus Monitor) that uses facial recognition, behavioral analysis (eye movement, keystrokes), and room scans to flag potential academic misconduct for later review by the instructor.
- Connection to Key Dimensions: Primarily addresses Academic Integrity but heavily impacts Equity & Access (bias, privacy) and student anxiety, which can hinder Personalization.

Table 3. Case example 1: The AI-proctored high-stakes exam

Perspective	Practical Strategies	Concerns & Considerations
Instructor Perspective *Goal: Uphold Integrity at Scale*	1. Targeted Use: Employ AI proctoring only for significant, summative assessments where individual, unaided knowledge is essential. Explain the rationale. 2. Human-in-the-Loop: Use AI flags as a conversation starter, not proof. Assume good faith. 3. Provide Equitable Alternatives: Offer a physically proctored on-campus option.	- False Positives & Workload: Burden of reviewing flagged videos. - Erosion of Trust: Creates an adversarial classroom climate. - Technical & Equity Barriers: Assumes all students have a private space, reliable tech, and strong internet.
Student Perspective *Goal: A Fair and Unstressful Experience*	1. Environment Preparation: Create a dedicated test-taking space: clean desk, good lighting. 2. Practice Tests: Use a low-stakes practice exam to familiarize with the software. 3. Understand the "Rules": Be provided with a clear list of behaviors that trigger flags.	- Increased Anxiety: Being constantly monitored increases test anxiety. - Perceived Unfairness & Bias: Fear that the AI is biased against them (e.g., due to fidgeting or skin tone). - Privacy Invasion: The room scan feels deeply intrusive.

TPACK Analysis of Case Example 1:

This example demonstrates weak or negative TPACK. The instructor is using a sophisticated technology (TK) to enforce a traditional pedagogical assessment method (a high-stakes exam, PK) without rethinking the nature of the content being assessed (CK). The technology is in tension with the pedagogy and creates a negative student experience. It represents a "substitution" approach that does not leverage the potential of AI to transform assessment for the better.

PESTEL Analysis of Case Example 1:

- Legal: High Legal risks regarding data privacy and the potential for biased algorithms leading to discriminatory outcomes.
- Social: Creates significant Social friction through student anxiety and erosion of trust.
- Economic: Has Economic costs for software licenses and the instructor time required for review.
- Political: Could damage the institution's Political reputation if a high-profile case of false accusation occurs.

Case Example 2: AI-Powered Formative Feedback on a Writing Assignment

- Context: Providing feedback on the first draft of a major research paper in a Sociology course. The goal is to help students improve their writing before the final submission.
- AI Tool & Function: An NLP-powered writing assistant (e.g., Turnitin Feedback Studio, Grammarly for Education) integrated into the LMS. It provides automated, criterion-based feedback on grammar, clarity, conciseness, citation accuracy, and thesis strength.
- Connection to Key Dimensions: Directly enables Feedback & Reflection and supports Personalization. When used to improve a process-oriented task, it enhances Authenticity and reduces incentives to plagiarize (Academic Integrity).

Table 4. Case example 2: AI-powered formative feedback on a writing assignment

Perspective	Practical Strategies	Concerns & Considerations
Instructor Perspective *Goal: Improve Student Writing and Save Time*	1. Strategic Division of Labor: Configure AI to focus on "lower-order" concerns (mechanics, citations). Instructor focuses on "higher-order" feedback (argument, analysis). 2. Frame as Formative: Explicitly state that AI feedback is a "first draft"; final responsibility lies with the student. 3. Leverage Analytics: Use class-wide AI reports to identify common issues for just-in-time teaching.	- Superficial Learning: Students may "click accept" without understanding. - Contract Cheating Paradox: Students might use GPT to write the draft, then the AI to polish it. - Tool Access & Equity: Requires institutional licenses for all students.
Student Perspective *Goal: Get Faster, Actionable Help*	1. Iterative Revision: Use the AI tool on multiple drafts to see progress. 2. Ask Guided Questions: Use the tool proactively (e.g., "Is my thesis statement arguable?"). 3. Bridge to Instructor: Bring AI feedback to office hours for targeted help.	- Incorrect Feedback: AI may offer factually or stylistically wrong suggestions. - Lack of Nuance: AI cannot appreciate creative risks or subtle interdisciplinary connections. - Overwhelm: An avalanche of feedback on a first draft can be paralyzing.

TPACK Analysis of Case Example 2:

This example demonstrates stronger, more strategic TPACK. The instructor makes a conscious choice about the division of labor between human and machine, based on their pedagogical knowledge (PK) of what feedback is most valuable. They use the AI (TK) to handle routine, scalable tasks, freeing up their own capacity to provide high-value, discipline-specific feedback that requires deep Content Knowledge (CK). This is a "augmentation" approach that effectively blends TK and PK to enhance the learning of specific content.

PESTEL Analysis of Case Example 2:

- Economic: Strong Economic driver due to time savings for instructors. Requires investment in tool licenses.
- Social: Addresses the Social expectation for rapid feedback. The risk of superficial learning is a social-pedagogical challenge.
- Technological: Dependent on the accuracy and sophistication of the Technological NLP tools.

Case Example 3: AI-Driven Engagement & Participation Tracking

- Context: A seminar-style course where thoughtful participation is a key learning outcome. Students participate via in-class discussion, Zoom chat (synchronous online), and asynchronous discussion forums.

- AI Tool & Function: A learning analytics platform that uses AI to unify and quantify participation across all three modalities. It measures frequency, word count, and uses network analysis to map the influence and connectivity of student contributions.
- Connection to Key Dimensions: Aims to promote Equity & Access by valuing all participation modes fairly. Raises questions about the Authenticity of quantified engagement.

Table 5. Case example 3: AI-driven engagement & participation tracking

Perspective	Practical Strategies	Concerns & Considerations
Instructor Perspective *Goal: Fairly Value All Contributions*	1. Quality-Trumps-Quantity Rubric: Use AI data as one component. Grade primarily based on qualitative assessment of insightfulness. 2. Support Quiet Voices: Use analytics to identify disengaged students for proactive, supportive outreach. 3. Transparency & Co-creation: Share the dashboard/metrics with students; involve them in creating the participation rubric.	- Gaming the System: Students may post frequent, low-effort comments to inflate metrics. - Lack of Context: AI cannot discern if a comment is brilliant, wrong, or disruptive. - Technical Failures: Glitches may lead to inaccurate data.
Student Perspective *Goal: Be Recognized for My Efforts*	1. Mindful Participation: Use transparent metrics to ensure contributions are "counted" in their chosen modality. 2. Self-Advocacy: Feel empowered to inform the instructor if a contribution was not captured. 3. Focus on Learning: When the system is fair, can focus on using modalities to deepen understanding.	- Constant Surveillance: Feeling that every click and comment is graded creates pressure. - Performance Pressure: Forces performance of engagement over authentic engagement. - Unfair Weighting: May feel their preferred mode of participation is undervalued.

TPACK Analysis of Case Example 3:

This case shows the potential and pitfalls of TPK. The technology (TK) provides a novel way to gather data on a pedagogical construct—participation (PK). However, reducing the rich, qualitative nature of seminar discussion to quantitative metrics is a risky pedagogical choice. Strong TPACK here would involve using the AI data as a *diagnostic* tool to prompt human intervention and conversation, not as a *summative* grading tool. The educator's PK must guide the use of the TK to ensure it supports, rather than undermines, the authentic learning community (CK).

PESTEL Analysis of Case Example 3:

- Social: Touches on Social dynamics of the classroom and the pressure students feel to perform.
- Legal: Raises Legal questions about data privacy and the monitoring of student behavior.

- Technological: Highly dependent on the accuracy and nuance of the Technological analytics algorithms.

6. ETHICAL, PEDAGOGICAL, AND INSTITUTIONAL CONSIDERATIONS (THE SYNTHESIS OF TPACK AND PESTEL)

The practical implementation of AI-powered assessment in HyFlex environments ultimately converges on a set of overarching ethical, pedagogical, and institutional considerations. These considerations represent the synthesis of the internal TPACK challenges and the external PESTEL pressures.

Bias, Transparency, and Explainability

The multimodal data pipeline of a HyFlex course—LMS logs, video analytics, AI-generated feedback—concentrates familiar AI ethics concerns but in a more complex, distributed form.

- TPACK Synthesis: Addressing bias and ensuring transparency is not just a technical task (TK); it is a core responsibility of the educator's TPACK. An instructor must possess the knowledge to critically evaluate the outputs of AI tools for potential bias against certain student groups or disciplinary approaches. They must also be able to explain, in pedagogically meaningful terms, how an AI system arrived at a particular feedback score or recommendation to their students. This requires a blend of TK (understanding the tool's limitations), PK (communication and pedagogy), and CK (disciplinary standards of evidence and fairness).
- PESTEL Synthesis: This is a domain where Legal (data privacy, algorithmic accountability), Social (demands for fairness), and Political (reputational risk) factors intensely intersect. Institutions must implement "privacy by design" and maintain transparency catalogues, as suggested in the provided text, to meet these external pressures.

Pedagogical Balance: The Human-in-the-Loop

The central pedagogical challenge is to reconcile the scale and efficiency of AI with the nuanced professional judgment of the educator.

- TPACK Synthesis: The "pedagogical balance" is the ultimate expression of TPACK. It is the wisdom to know what to automate and what to humanize.

AI should be used for tasks where it excels: processing large datasets, providing immediate, routine feedback, and flagging patterns. Human judgment must be reserved for tasks requiring empathy, creativity, contextual understanding, and the appraisal of complex, discipline-specific reasoning. This balance will look different in a large introductory course versus an advanced graduate seminar, highlighting its context-dependent nature.

- PESTEL Synthesis: Maintaining this balance has Economic implications (workload models) and is influenced by Social norms about the role of the teacher.

Policy, Accreditation, and Institutional Readiness

Sustainable transformation cannot be driven by individual faculty champions alone. It requires a supportive institutional ecosystem.

- TPACK Synthesis: Institutional support is what allows TPACK to flourish. Faculty cannot develop sophisticated TPACK without professional development and time for course design. This is an institutional Economic and Political commitment.
- PESTEL Synthesis: This is the core PESTEL domain. Political alignment with accreditation standards is essential. Economic investment in technology and training is a prerequisite. Legal frameworks for data governance and AI use must be established. Social buy-in from faculty and students must be cultivated through clear communication and involvement. The "staged readiness plan" mentioned in the provided text is a direct response to this complex PESTEL environment, ensuring that technology, pedagogy, and policy mature in concert.

7. FUTURE DIRECTIONS: THE EVOLVING SYNERGY OF AI AND HYFLEX

The current integration of AI into HyFlex assessment, while transformative, represents only the initial phase of a longer evolution. Looking forward, the synergy between these two domains promises to reshape the fundamental nature of learning and evaluation. Three critical future directions—generative AI and co-creation, integrated ecosystems, and persistent research gaps—will define the next frontier, pushing the boundaries of what is possible from automation towards a deeply collaborative and authentic model of education.

Generative AI and Co-Created Assessments: The Student as Partner

The most profound shift on the horizon involves moving beyond using Generative AI (GenAI) as a tool for completing assigned tasks, towards leveraging it as a platform for co-creating the assessments themselves (Kolade, Owoseni, & Egbetokun, 2024). This represents the ultimate expression of authenticity, where the assessment process becomes a unique, personalized, and negotiated journey between the student, the instructor, and the AI.

In this model, students would not merely answer questions posed by an instructor or a static AI; they would use GenAI to *generate* potential research questions, design project proposals, or simulate complex scenarios based on their personal interests and the course's learning outcomes. The student's skill is then demonstrated not in their answer to a predefined problem, but in their ability to *formulate a meaningful and rigorous problem*, to use the AI as a "thought partner" to explore its dimensions, and to critically evaluate the solutions it proposes. For example, in a public policy course, a student could use GenAI to generate a portfolio of potential policy brief topics related to urban sustainability, select one, use the AI to simulate stakeholder responses and predict implementation hurdles, and then craft a final brief that synthesizes this co-created analysis with their own critical judgment. The assessment becomes a dynamic process of inquiry, design, and iteration, closely mirroring the unstructured problem-solving required in professional and research settings.

- TPACK Analysis: This direction demands an advanced form of TPACK. The educator's role shifts from being the sole source of assessment content (CK) to being a facilitator of a co-creative process (PK). This requires pedagogical knowledge of how to scaffold student-AI collaboration and assess the quality of the inquiry process itself. The technological knowledge (TK) extends to prompt engineering, critical AI literacy, and evaluating AI-generated content. The resulting TPACK is a dynamic, process-oriented expertise focused on cultivating student agency within a technologically rich learning environment.
- PESTEL Analysis: Co-creation raises significant Social and Legal questions. Who owns the intellectual property of an AI-co-created assessment? How do we ensure equitable access to the skills and resources required for such sophisticated AI use, mitigating a new form of Economic digital divide? Institutionally, this requires a Political and Legal shift in academic integrity policies, moving from prohibiting AI use to defining and rewarding its ethical and productive application (Shivshankar & Acharya, 2024).

The Integrated HyFlex-AI Ecosystem: Seamless, Predictive, and Responsive

Currently, AI tools often function as standalone applications—a proctoring system here, a feedback tool there. The future lies in the development of a fully integrated HyFlex-AI ecosystem. This ecosystem would be a unified platform that seamlessly connects the physical classroom, the virtual synchronous session, and the asynchronous learning environment, with AI as the intelligent core that orchestrates the experience.

In this ecosystem, AI would function as a central nervous system. It would analyze real-time data from all modalities—participation in the physical room, chat and audio from the Zoom session, engagement with asynchronous materials—to provide the instructor with a holistic "class pulse." This could manifest as a dashboard that alerts the instructor to a confusion spike among online students during a specific explanation, allowing for immediate clarification. It could automatically form small, mixed-modality breakout groups for a collaborative task, ensuring diversity of perspective. For students, the ecosystem would offer a truly personalized pathway, suggesting they switch from asynchronous to the next synchronous session to address a identified knowledge gap, or recommending peer collaborators based on complementary skills revealed through their work. This moves beyond personalizing content to personalizing the entire learning *context* and social fabric of the HyFlex course.

- TPACK Analysis: An integrated ecosystem elevates TPACK to a systems level. The educator's knowledge must encompass the interplay of multiple technologies (TK) and pedagogical strategies (PK) across different modalities simultaneously. The focus becomes designing learning experiences that leverage the ecosystem's intelligence to create a cohesive and responsive community, regardless of a student's physical location. It is TPACK for managing complex, adaptive learning environments.
- PESTEL Analysis: Such an ecosystem presents immense Technological challenges regarding data interoperability, security, and platform development (Chen & Lai, 2024). The Economic cost of building or licensing such a system is substantial. The Legal and ethical implications of pervasive, cross-modal data collection and analysis are profound, requiring robust governance frameworks to prevent misuse and protect student privacy (Shivshankar & Acharya, 2024). Institutionally, this demands a strategic (Political) commitment to a unified digital learning architecture.

Addressing Critical Research Gaps: The Path to Evidence-Informed Practice

For these future directions to be realized responsibly, significant research gaps must be addressed. The current evidence base is often anecdotal or focused on short-term, small-scale studies. A concerted research agenda is needed, focused on:

1. Longitudinal Impact Studies: We need research that tracks the long-term effects of AI-powered HyFlex assessment on student retention, deep learning, career readiness, and the development of metacognitive skills. Does the shift to authenticity translate into tangible, lasting benefits?
2. Equity and Bias Audits: Rigorous, independent studies are required to audit the performance of AI assessment tools across diverse student demographics. Research must move beyond technical accuracy to examine how these tools impact different racial, socioeconomic, and cultural groups within HyFlex contexts, informing more equitable design and implementation (Srivastava, 2022).
3. The Changing Role of the Educator: Empirical research is needed to document the evolving practices, competencies, and workload implications for instructors navigating this new landscape (Cumming et al., 2024). What does expert TPACK look like in this context, and how can professional development be most effectively structured to support it?
4. Scalability and Sustainability Models: Research should investigate the institutional costs, benefits, and effective governance models for scaling AI-HyFlex integration (Howell et al., 2024). This includes Economic models for sustainability and Political analyses of policy development.

Filling these gaps is not an academic exercise; it is a prerequisite for building a future that is not only technologically advanced but also pedagogically sound, equitable, and sustainable.

8. CONCLUSION: REALIZING THE PROMISE OF AUTHENTIC ASSESSMENT

This chapter has argued that the convergence of HyFlex learning and Artificial Intelligence is a necessary and pivotal development in higher education. We began by establishing that the inherent assessment challenges of the HyFlex model—ensuring equivalency, fairness, and integrity across multiple modalities—cannot be solved by simply transposing traditional methods into a digital space (Beatty, 2014; Chen &

Lai, 2024). The initial wave of AI, focused on automation, offered a partial solution, but one that often replicated existing inequities and failed to address the core goal of fostering deep, meaningful learning (Kolade et al., 2024).

Through the analytical lenses of TPACK and PESTEL, we have charted a more transformative path: the journey from automation to authenticity. The TPACK framework has illuminated that effective integration is not a technical feat but a deeply pedagogical one, requiring the thoughtful weaving of technology (TK) into assessment design (PK) to validly measure disciplinary competencies (CK). We have explored how this plays out across key dimensions: using AI for Personalization to meet individual learner needs (Owan et al., 2023), designing Authentic tasks that reflect real-world practice (Wiggins, 1990), leveraging AI for continuous Feedback & Reflection (Hattie & Timperley, 2007), advancing Equity & Access by design, and fostering Academic Integrity through pedagogical design rather than solely through surveillance.

Simultaneously, the PESTEL framework has grounded this pedagogical work in reality, demonstrating that success is contingent on navigating a complex macro-environment. The Political pressure of accreditation, the Economic realities of cost and the digital divide (Howell et al., 2024), the Social demands for flexibility and fairness, the Technological requirements of robust infrastructure (Chen & Lai, 2024), and the Legal imperatives of data privacy and accessibility (Shivshankar & Acharya, 2024) are not peripheral concerns; they are the very fabric within which transformation must occur.

The future directions of co-created assessments (Kolade, Owoseni, & Egbetokun, 2024) and integrated ecosystems point towards a more collaborative and responsive educational paradigm, while the identified research gaps underscore the need for a responsible, evidence-informed approach to this evolution.

In conclusion, the call to action is clear and directed at all stakeholders:

- For educators and instructional designers, the task is to actively develop your TPACK. Experiment, reflect, and share practices that use AI not to replace your expertise, but to amplify it, creating assessments that truly matter.
- For institutional leaders and policymakers, the mandate is to create the enabling PESTEL environment. Invest in professional development, infrastructure, and equitable access. Develop clear, forward-thinking policies and governance structures that encourage innovation while protecting ethical standards.
- For researchers, the challenge is to illuminate the path forward through rigorous inquiry into the long-term impacts, equity implications, and effective models of this transformation.

The ultimate goal is not merely to make assessment more efficient or more cheat-proof. It is to make it more human—more focused on the complex, creative, and critical capacities that define our unique potential. By harnessing AI within the flexible framework of HyFlex, guided by pedagogical wisdom and a commitment to equity, we can transform assessment from a terminal judgment of learning into a rich, authentic, and empowering part of the learning journey itself.

REFERENCES

Beatty, B. J. (2014). Hybrid courses with flexible participation: The HyFlex course design. In *Handbook of Research on Blended Learning: Technology and Practice* (pp. 153–177). IGI Global. DOI: 10.4018/978-1-4666-4912-5.ch011

Chen, G., & Lai, N. (2024). Enhancing interdisciplinary English learning: A systematic review of the HyFlex model's strategies, challenges, and implications. *Asian Journal of Education and Social Studies*. DOI: 10.9734/ajess/2024/v50i61388

Cumming, T. M., Gilanyi, L., & Han, C. (2024). Hyflex delivery mode in a postgraduate course: Instructor and student perspectives. *Discover Education*, *3*(1), 24. Advance online publication. DOI: 10.1007/s44217-024-00110-0

Guerreau-Jalabert, A. (2022). Space and time in hybrid teaching and learning environments: Two cases and design principles. In *Smart Innovation, Systems and Technologies* (pp. 29–46). Springer Nature Singapore. DOI: 10.1007/978-981-19-5240-1_3

Hattie, J., & Timperley, H. (2007). The power of feedback. *Review of Educational Research*, *77*(1), 81–112.

Howell, E., Linder, S., Ryan, J., & Bridges, W. C. (2024). Examining higher education through HyFlex. *Open Learning*. Advance online publication. DOI: 10.1080/02680513.2024.2354245

Khlaif, Z. N., (2024). The digital transformation of assessment: Moving beyond proctoring toward authenticity. *Educational Technology Research and Development*.

Kolade, O., Owoseni, A., & Egbetokun, A. A. (2024). Is AI changing learning and assessment as we know it? Evidence from a ChatGPT experiment and a conceptual framework. *Heliyon*, *10*(4), e25953. Advance online publication. DOI: 10.1016/j.heliyon.2024.e25953 PMID: 38379960

Mishra, P., & Koehler, M. J. (2006). Technological pedagogical content knowledge: A framework for teacher knowledge. *Teachers College Record*, *108*(6), 1017–1054.

Naseer, F., Khalid, M. U., Ayub, N., Rasool, A., Abbas, T., & Afzal, M. T. (2024). Automated assessment and feedback in higher education using generative AI. In *Transforming Education with Generative AI: Prompt Engineering and Synthetic Content Creation* (pp. 433–461). IGI Global. DOI: 10.4018/979-8-3693-1351-0.ch021

Öz, G. (2024). Hybrid flexible (HyFlex) teaching in foreign language education. In *Advances in Educational Technologies and Instructional Design* (pp. 235–259). IGI Global. DOI: 10.4018/979-8-3693-0353-5.ch011

Shivshankar, S., & Acharya, N. (2024). AI in assessment and feedback. In *Next-Generation AI Methodologies in Education* (pp. 119–146). IGI Global., DOI: 10.4018/979-8-3693-7220-3.ch006

Wong, B., Li, K. C., Chan, H. T., & Cheung, S. K. S. (2023). HyFlex learning research and practice: A longitudinal analysis. *Sustainability (Basel)*, *15*(12), 9699–9699. DOI: 10.3390/su15129699

About the Contributors

Lim Chee Leong is an Associate Professor and Senior Director of Learning Innovation and Development at the Centre for Future Learning, Taylor's University, Malaysia. He holds a Ph.D. in Educational Technology from University Putra Malaysia (UPM) and has over 25 years of experience in higher education, with a strong focus on technology-enhanced learning and pedagogical innovation. Dr. Lim is a nationally recognized educator, having received the prestigious National Academic Award (Anugerah Akademik Negara) in 2014, the highest honor for academic excellence in Malaysia. His scholarly contributions include authoring and editing three Scopus-indexed research books with IGI Global and publishing in numerous peer-reviewed journals in the areas of instructional design, blended learning, and self-regulated learning strategies. Dr. Lim has also served as guest editor for special issues in Scopus-indexed journals and has presented extensively at international conferences. He has led major university-wide initiatives in learning innovation and has served on national education committees and international judging panels, solidifying his role as a thought leader in the transformation of higher education. His work continues to influence educational policy and practice at both national and regional levels, positioning him as a thought leader in 21st-century learning innovation.

Gary Cheng is an Associate Professor in the Department of Mathematics and Information Technology and the Director of the Centre for Learning, Teaching, and Technology (LTTC) at The Education University of Hong Kong. He holds a doctoral degree and has over two decades of experience in higher education, with a strong focus on technology-enhanced teaching and learning. His research interests span Artificial Intelligence in Education, Learning Analytics, e-Assessment, and Technology-enhanced Second Language Learning. He has published extensively in leading journals such as Computers & Education: Artificial Intelligence, The Internet and Higher Education, and Educational Technology & Society. Dr. Cheng also serves as Associate Editor at the open-access journals called Australasian Journal of Educational Technology, Computers & Education: X Reality, and Artificial Intelligence in Language Education. Recognized among the world's top 2% most-cited scientists by Stanford University (2022, 2023, 2024), Dr. Cheng has led multiple funded research projects and received international awards for his innovative educational technologies. His academic leadership and editorial contributions position him as a key thought leader in the integration of AI and emerging technologies in education.

***

Sze Yuing Anrie Too has built a professional profile combining communication studies and performing arts, positioning herself at the intersection of arts education and pedagogy in Malaysia. Her work particularly addresses how drama and performance can act as educational tools for children, potentially opening pathways to more inclusive or egalitarian education through the arts.

Daniel Nesa Kumar C., MCA., M.Phil, Ph.D., is having 15+ years of teaching experience and currently working as Assistant Professor in the Department of Computer Applications(BCA) at Sri Ramakrishna College of Arts and Science, Coimbatore. He has completed his B.Sc Computer Science at CSI Bishop Appasamy College of Arts and Science, Coimbatore. His Masters in Computer Applications at Bishop Heber College, Trichy, M.Phil and Ph.D in Computer Science at Hindusthan College of Arts and Science – Bharathiar University, Coimbatore. His area of specialization is Networking, His research interest includes Digital Image Processing, Cloud Computing, Machine Learning etc. He has published several research papers in the field of Networking, Machine Learning, Image Processing in many reputed International Journals. Also presented his research work at various International and National conferences.

Tsz Cheung Chan, an Educational Development Officer at the Centre for Learning, Teaching and Technology, The Education University of Hong Kong. He contributes to the FITE and CRAC projects, with a particular emphasis on Metaverse applications and CAVE immersive initiatives designed to transform teaching and learning experiences. His research interests focus on leveraging emerging technologies, including multimedia content creation, game-based learning, and learning analytics, as scaffolds to enhance students' performance and engagement. He has been involved in several projects related to metaverse, CAVE, and immersive environments, as well as contributed to the development of innovative educational applications. He is proficient in designing and constructing multimedia resources and immersive learning environments, applying game-based strategies, and utilizing learning analytics tools. He also has practical experience in organising and delivering technology-enhanced teaching and learning activities.

Mike Choong has been in the education industry for 2 decades, having held academia and management positions from lecturing to business development and government liaison to Chief Operating Officer. He has extensive knowledge and experience in curriculum and pedagogy development for local, UK and Australian digital design and creative multimedia tertiary level programmes. He had also produced Pearsons BTEC programmes for a vocational training centre and e-learning programmes with one of the world's leading game development companies. Parallel to his academic career was his involvement with the creative content industry, where he has been a Creative Director, Managing Director, Business Development Consultant and a Grant Application Panel member. His passion is in cutting-edge 21st-century teaching and learning innovation, where technology plays the driving role in developing the next generation of creative innovators for the creative industry.

Mark Beau de Silva is a Malaysian playwright, director and theatre educator whose work centres on drama, identity and social themes. A Kuala Lumpur native, he has built his career within Malaysia's performing-arts scene — particularly through his affiliation with Kuala Lumpur Performing Arts Centre (KLPac) and other theatre platforms. He is currently a Senior Lecturer at Taylor's University, specializing in writing, directing and acting.

Jiaoyang Ding is currently an Educational Development Officer of the Centre for Learning, Teaching and Technology, the Education University of Hong Kong. His research interests focus on leveraging emerging technologies, including immersive learning environments, generative AI and robotics, as scaffolds to enhance students' performance and engagement. He has been involved in several projects related to metaverse, CAVE, LLMs, and robotics, as well as contributed to the development of innovative educational applications. He is proficient in implementing and deploying generative AI algorithms and applications, designing and constructing computer graphics and immersive learning environments, and applying robotics technology. He also has practical experience in organising and delivering AI & digital competency teaching and learning activities.

Yvonne M. Fromm is a postdoctoral researcher at the chair of Learning, Design & Technology at the University of Mannheim. Her research focuses on continuing education, self-regulated learning, adaptive learning, and learning analytics. She studied psychology at the Ludwig-Maximilians-Universität (LMU) in Munich and earned her doctoral degree at the University of Mannheim with a dissertation on adaptive learning environments and self-regulated learning in continuing education.

Joana Heil is a postdoctoral researcher at the Chair of Learning, Design and Technology at the University of Mannheim. She earned her Ph.D. with a dissertation on online assessment in higher education. Her primary research interests lie in adaptive assessments, AI-based learning applications, and learning analytics.

FuHong is the Associate Director of the Centre for Learning, Teaching and Technology and an Associate Professor in the Department of Mathematics and Information Technology at The Education University of Hong Kong. Her research primarily focuses on intelligent multimodal sensing algorithms and their applications in education, healthcare, and sports.

Dirk Ifenthaler is a Professor and Chair of Learning, Design and Technology at the University of Mannheim, Germany, and UNESCO Co-Chair on Data Science in Higher Education Learning and Teaching at Curtin University, Australia. Dirk's research focuses on the intersection of cognitive psychology, educational technology, data analytics, and organisational learning.

Mohammad Ishrat is currently working as an Associate Professor in the School of Computing Science and Engineering at VIT Bhopal University, Sehore-466114, Madhya Pradesh, India. Dr Ishrat has completed his PhD. (Computer Science and Engineering) in 2014. He has more than 23 years of teaching experience. His research interests are in the areas of Software Engineering and Requirements Engineering, AIML.

Md Shamirul Islam is a Senior Lecturer in Human Resource Management at Taylor's Business School, Taylor's University, Malaysia. His research interests lie in strategic human resource management, presenteeism, and employee well-being in organizational and higher education contexts.

Hanh Le is a passionate researcher and accomplished Full Stack Software Developer with deep expertise in software development, data analytics, data science, and cloud computing. She holds a Ph.D. in Information Technology and a Master's in Computer Science, bringing both academic rigor and a solution-driven mindset to her work. With extensive experience in front-end and back-end development, she specializes in scalable, database-driven applications that support evidence-based decision-making. Dr. Le has led transformative tech initiatives across healthcare, law enforcement, and retail, translating complex needs into high-performing systems. She values interdisciplinary collaboration, believing that impactful innovation often arises at the intersection of fields. Her blend of technical skill, research excellence, and collaborative spirit continues to drive progress in academia and industry alike.

Teoh Ming Li is an academic and researcher in Biomedical Science and Algae Biotechnology with over 12 years of experience at Taylor's University, Malaysia. She is dedicated to advancing biosciences education through innovative curriculum design and active pedagogical practices. Her research explores the impact of climate change and environmental contaminants on microalgae, as well as their applications in cosmeceuticals, integrating scientific inquiry with real-world impact. Dr. Teoh is also passionate about nurturing future-ready graduates and strengthening academia–industry collaborations to enhance the relevance and sustainability of life sciences education.

Li (Athena) Liu is a Senior Lecturer in Human Resource Management at Taylor's University and holds a PhD from University of Toulouse 1 Capitole. Her research focuses on context-specific HRM, the future of work, and employee well-being.

Eva G. Makwakwa is a Senior Lecturer in the Department of Mathematics Education at the University of South Africa (UNISA). She holds a BSc Honours in Statistics, an MSc, and a PhD in Statistics Education. Her research focuses on the teaching and learning of statistics, data handling, and probability, as well as emerging areas such as online learning, artificial intelligence, and academic integrity.

Indranil Mutsuddi holds a Ph.D. in Management from Amity University, Uttar Pradesh, India, and currently serves as Associate Professor and Head of the Department at JIS University, Kolkata. With over 24 years of academic experience, he has established himself as a distinguished educator and researcher specializing in Human Resources (HR) and Organizational Behavior. Dr. Mutsuddi is the author of three textbooks on Human Resource Management and has published more than 64 research papers in reputed national and international journals, including 31 indexed in Scopus. He has also contributed 36 book chapters to various edited volumes and presented 67 papers at national and international conferences and seminars. A frequent chair of technical sessions at prestigious management forums, Dr. Mutsuddi is a Double Gold Medalist from AIMA-CME and a recipient of the Prof. Narendra Mohan Basu Award from Presidency College, Kolkata, for academic excellence. He is a life member of several professional bodies, including the National HRD Network (NHRDN), the Indian Commerce Association, and the Presidency College Alumni Association. His primary research interests focus on employee retention and job skills, reflecting his commitment to advancing contemporary HR practices. Most recently, he served as the editor of a management research volume published by Bentham Books. Dr. Mutsuddi's enduring contributions to teaching and research continue to earn him widespread recognition and respect within academic and professional circles.

Sreelakshmi Sankara Narayanan is a lecturer in the School of Biosciences at Taylor's University in Malaysia. Her expertise lies in metabolomics, enzyme technology, and the screening and conversion of agricultural biomass into value-added products. She also conducts research on dietary marker exposure and biomarker discovery in non-communicable diseases. Dr. Sreelakshmi holds a PhD in Biotechnology from Anna University in India, along with a Master's degree in Biochemistry and a Bachelor of Science in Chemistry, Botany, and Biotechnology. At Taylor's University, she coordinates and teaches modules in Cell Biology, Epidemiology, Public Health & Biostatistics, Bioethics, and Nutraceuticals and Functional Foods. Her scholarly work includes investigations into dietary exposures, biomarker discovery using NMR metabolomics, and examining the impact of food advertising on children's health.

Artchie P. Padios was born on July 17, 1987, in Poblacion Kalamansig, Sultan Kudarat, to his parents Mr. Artemio Padios and Mrs. Teresita Padios. Growing up in a supportive and nurturing environment, he developed a strong commitment to education and personal growth early in life. He began his academic journey at Datu Guiabar Pilot School, where he completed his elementary education. Continuing with his pursuit of learning, he attended Notre Dame of Kalamansig for his secondary education, where he further honed his skills and strengthened his academic foundation. For higher education, Artchie enrolled at Sultan Kudarat State University – Kalamansig Campus, where he completed his tertiary studies and built the groundwork for his professional and intellectual development. His dedication to lifelong learning later led him to pursue graduate studies, earning his Master's Degree from Notre Dame of Marbel University.

Manju Priya. R, currently an Associate Professor at the School of Commerce, JAIN (Deemed-to-be) University in Bangalore, holds a M.Com., M.Phil, MBA, PGDCA, and Ph.D. She is a distinguished educator known for her ability to inspire, engage and guide students towards high academic achievement. With 20 years of teaching experience and 10 years of research expertise, she excels in maintaining students' interest and fostering a dynamic learning environment. She has guided numerous undergraduate, postgraduate and M.Phil students and is presently mentoring Ph.D candidates. Her academic interests are focused on Marketing and Human Resources(HR). She has served as a resource person for various colleges, sharing her insights with both students and faculty members. She has actively participated in over 50 National and International seminars and conferences, and has published more than 45 research papers in UGC care listed journals, Scopus, WOS, ABDC. Furthermore, she has authored 3 books and she has also contributed 10 book chapters to various academic publications.

Fahad Salendab is a scholar and leader in the field of higher education, holding a Ph.D. in Educational Administration. As a Licensed Professional Teacher and Associate Professor, he has dedicated his career to advancing the quality of education through research, teaching, and leadership. A multi-awarded faculty member, Dr. Salendab is recognized for his outstanding contributions to education, research, and institutional development. He is a registered author with the National Book Development Board (NBDB), where his works include the book chapter "Leadership in Higher Education," which explores innovative approaches to fostering resilience and excellence in academic institutions. His commitment to research is further reflected in his role as an Associate Member of the DOST-National Research Council of the Philippines, where he collaborates on initiatives that address critical issues in education and development. As an active participant in accreditation processes, Dr. Salendab ensures the continuous improvement of academic programs, demonstrating his dedication to quality assurance and institutional growth.

N Sathyanarayana has over 17 years of teaching experience at both undergraduate and postgraduate levels. He holds a Master of Business Administration degree from VTU and a Master of Commerce degree from Periyar University. He has completed his Ph.D. in Banking and Finance from Dayananda Sagar University. Currently, he serves as an Assistant Professor in the School of Commerce at Jain (Deemed-to-be University), Bangalore. He has published 24 research papers in international journals, including three indexed in Scopus, and seven papers in national journals. Additionally, he has presented 14 research papers at international conferences and 11 at national conferences. He has co-authored two books at the national level and contributed 24 Scopus-indexed book chapters.

Binastya Anggara Sekti has been a lecturer at the Faculty of Computer Science, Esa Unggul University, Jakarta, since 2016. He is actively involved in the Artificial Intelligence and Information Security Study Group. He holds a Bachelor's degree in Informatics Engineering from the Bandung Institute of Technology and a Master's degree in Information Systems Management from Trisakti University, Jakarta. Prior to entering academia, he accumulated over 25 years of professional experience as an IT practitioner in various companies across Jakarta. His work focused on developing data centers for internet service providers and delivering IT solutions for the manufacturing and oil & gas sectors. His research interests include artificial intelligence, cybersecurity, and the development of IT infrastructure.

Motlokwe Thobejane is an Executive Director: ICT Infrastructure and Systems within ICT portfolio at University of South Africa (UNISA). He holds a BSc in Computer Science and Statistics (UL), BSc Honours Information Systems (UNISA), an MPhil in Informatics (UP), and a PhD in Information Technology Management (UJ). His research focuses on the cloud computing, Artificial Intelligence, project management, cybersecurity and digital education.

Jens Thoemmes is research professor at CNRS, affiliated with the Centre d'Études et de Recherches Travail, Organisation, Pouvoir (CERTOP) and research chair for work, employment, and organization at Taylor's University in Kuala Lumpur, Malaysia.

Ahmad Maulana Ulumuddin is a researcher in the fields of artificial intelligence and online learning at Esa Unggul University, Jakarta, Indonesia. His research interests focus on intelligent learning systems, educational technology, machine learning, and the integration of AI in digital learning environments. He has been actively involved in academic research and applied projects aimed at enhancing the effectiveness of online education through data-driven approaches, adaptive learning technologies, and intelligent decision-support systems. His work reflects strong analytical thinking, interdisciplinary collaboration, and a commitment to innovation in digital education. Ahmad actively contributes to scientific publications and collaborative research initiatives that support the advancement of AI-driven learning systems and the development of modern educational technologies.

Lai Zee Wei is a dedicated educator, researcher, and innovator in teaching and learning at Taylor's University, Malaysia. She currently serves as a Senior Lecturer and Programme Director of the Bachelor of Biotechnology (Hons) programme. Passionate about transforming higher education, she has been a driving force in implementing the HyFlex (Hybrid-Flexible) learning model that integrates artificial intelligence (AI) tools to enhance student engagement, assessment, and personalized learning pathways. Her work emphasizes learner empowerment, inclusivity, and the integration of digital pedagogy in science education. Dr. Lai has successfully led several Global Classroom initiatives, fostering international collaboration between students and academics across Asia through project-based learning that aligns with the United Nations Sustainable Development Goals (SDGs). Her commitment to educational excellence has earned her multiple international awards in teaching and learning innovation, recognizing her efforts in advancing hybrid education, AI-assisted learning environments, and intercultural competency development.

Winnie Wong, Educational Development Manager with 20+ years of experience leading the eLearning and Digital Competency Team. Skilled in managing innovative educational projects, including leveraging Metaverse, VR, AR, and gamification to enhance learning outcomes. Supervised technical teams and spearheaded UGC-funded initiatives such as promoting technological social responsibility and academic integrity. Designed workshops for staff and students on cutting-edge tools like VR-CAVE, Metaverse, robotics, and Apple iOS platforms. Collaborated on inter-institutional projects to advance teacher training in virtual environments and supported Field Experience programs for aspiring educators.

Lee Khai Wooi is a Senior Lecturer at the School of Biosciences, Taylor's University, Malaysia. His teaching and research focus on digital pedagogy, HyFlex learning, and immersive technologies such as virtual reality and AI to enhance biotechnology education. He integrates research-informed teaching approaches that connect molecular virology, nanobiotechnology, and bioprocess research with innovative pedagogical design. Dr. Lee has led multiple award-winning educational projects recognized at IUCEL and INNOFEST. His work advances student-centered, technology-enhanced learning that fosters inquiry, creativity, and interdisciplinary engagement in STEM higher education.

Adeline Chia Yin is the Head of the School of Biosciences at Taylor's University, Malaysia. A passionate educator and curriculum innovator, she champions student-centred and research-informed teaching in the life sciences. She led curriculum reforms integrating hybrid-flexible learning, gamified pedagogy, and authentic assessments that bridge theory and real-world application. Recipient of the Anugerah Khas Menteri Pengajian Tinggi (2022) for curriculum innovation, Dr Chia continuously advances teaching excellence through mentorship, educational research, and cross-disciplinary collaborations that nurture future-ready graduates equipped with critical thinking, scientific literacy, and innovation skills for the global biosciences landscape.

Bo Zhang is an Assistant Professor at the Entrepreneurship and Enterprise Hub, XJTLU Entrepreneur College (Taicang). Dr. Bo Zhang is an interdisciplinary scholar and practitioner specializing in AI in Education, Augmented Reality, Metaverse, digital innovation, cross-cultural collaboration, and entrepreneurship ecosystem building. Her research integrates AIED, extended reality (XR), gamification, and educational evaluation frameworks, while her professional practice emphasizes international entrepreneurship competitions, cross-border incubation platforms, and high-level talent introduction projects. She is a strong supporter of XJTLU's Syntegrative Education model, aligning with the mission of promoting Syntegrative

Education, industry collaboration, and entrepreneurship practice. Her academic background and entrepreneurial practice provide a unique blend of innovation, governance insight, and risk-mitigation strategies, strengthening her ability to foster innovation, education and ecosystem development.

Index

A

B

C

D

E

G

H

I

L

M

N

O

P

S

T

U

Y

www.ingramcontent.com/pod-product-compliance
Lightning Source LLC
LaVergne TN
LVHW062340300926
849161LV00007B/1763
* 9 7 9 8 3 3 7 3 6 1 8 2 6 *